THEY ALL ...

IN

THE FIGHT FOR THE FOUR-GUN BATTERY

DURING

THE BATTLE OF RESACA
GEORGIA

MAY 15, 1864

Second Edition

BY
ROBERT G. MILLER

MAUVAISTERRE PUBLISHING

Cover: View from the Union Position from Hazen's position. Painted immediately after the Battle of Resaca on May 15, 1864 by James Walker, Oil on Canvas, 14 ½ x 36 ½ inches. Located at the Oneida County Historical Society, 1608 Genesee Street, Utica, New York 13502. Originally hung at the U.S. War Department. Art Inventories Catalog, Smithsonian American Art Museums, Control Number IAP 38330003. .1 This image is courtesy of Oneida County Historical Society. Digital color restoration of the painting was by Robert G. Miller. Pictured seated in center, General Howard, Commanding 4th Corps. On the right, pointing, General Hooker, Commanding 20th Corps, with General Sickles and Col. J. A. Reynolds, Chief of Artillery, according to a lithograph featuring the painting. The Red, White, and Blue Stars are of the 1st, 2nd, and 3rd Divisions of the 20th Corps of the Union Army.

The font is Warnock Pro.

THEY ALL WORE A STAR, Second Edition
Copyright 2018, 2020 by Robert G. Miller
www.TheyAllWoreAStar.com
www.MauvaisterrePublishing.com

ISBN   Hardcover   978-0-9994546-5-7
ISBN   Softcover   978-0-9994546-4-0
ISBN   epub   978-0-9994546-2-6

The book's website, www.TheyAllWoreAStar.com, has the maps and battle depictions in full format and detail.

Mauvaisterre Publishing

1 (Walker n.d.)

A Note On Illustrations

The original maps of the battle by George Blakeslee and Wilbur Kurtz are licensed from the Wilbur Kurtz Collection in the Kenan Research Center at the Atlanta History Center.

The Butterfield version of Blakeslee's map was provided by the Benjamin Harrison Home Museum.

Albert Castel's map of May 14 positions: Decision in the West: The Atlanta Campaign of 1864 by Albert Castel, published by the University Press of Kansas© 1992. www.kansaspress.ku.edu. Used by permission of the publisher.

Most other maps, including those by Blakeslee, are from the Library of Congress. Sources for the exceptions are noted.

Blakeslee's watercolor of Harrison's brigade storming of the fort is courtesy of the Benjamin Harrison Presidential Site.

Edwin Forbes' *"Coffee Coolers"* is from The Library of Congress.

J. F. E. Hillen's *"Rasaca on Coosa River"* is from Boston College.

Other Illustrations are mostly from Leslie's and Harper's weekly newspapers or from various sources, now in public domain, which are listed in the bibliography.

CONTENTS

DEDICATED

To inspiring us to keep the country ever

Aspiring to the ideals

Of the Revolution

By remembering what

Joseph Peters and all his comrades

Who fought in the Civil War

Endured and achieved

To preserve the Republic

And to extend freedom to all.

Between These Pages

From Trials and Triumphs,
the Record of the Fifty-Fifth Ohio Volunteer Infantry. 2

The leaves that green to summer branches clung,
Lit by the torch of autumn, flare and burn
In radiance more than summer's; then – they fall,
And leave the branches lone and tenantless.

The torch of Time with autumn splendor lights
Your summer memories, who here have told
Of battle-front and camp-fire comradery.
Viewed through the mist of years, you see your past
Aglow like autumn woods through autumn haze –
The glamour and the glory more than June's.
Too soon – O wearers of the sacred blue –
The frost that falls shall bare those golden boughs;
But as one lays away the autumn leaves
Between the pages of his book, so, here,
Forever safe from storms that dull and fade;
Forever safe from snow's oblivion;
Forever to your children's children's eyes
As bright and glory-hued as to your own,
These martial memories of your youth are kept.

—*Marian Warner Wildman.*

2 (Osborn 1904, 17)

We Remember

We remember the silent movement of the line through the woods, the ringing cheer for Indiana, the sweep across the field, the odor of resin as the canister burst above us, the sand thrown in our faces by the shot that struck before us, the rush through the thicket, the dash into the redoubt, the breastworks in rear deserted by the flying enemy, the agonizing cry to our men behind to stop firing on us, the determined feeling as we lay on the ground and clung to the captured lunette, while bullets from front and rear, from right and left pattered like hail on the leaves by our side. Ah, that might have been a glorious day had the Generals in command of the Second and Third divisions started all the columns at once, and instead of staying behind, gone with their inexperienced troops, as general Sheridan would have done; for then we would not merely have captured the battery, we would have driven the Confederates into the river. The narrative requires descriptions with increase of details and suppression of feeling.

—Merrill .3

The Soldier With No Personal Cause to Defend

The real literature of a war like the Great Civil War in America is not always written by the historian nor by the Generals who commanded in that war, but often by the private soldier. The historian depends on the writings of others and on his power of imagination to describe and give reality to events which he has not witnessed. The general will be tempted to sacrifice strict veracity in favor of his own reputation as a military genius. The soldier with no personal cause to defend will speak out of his own personal experience and more often give a just appraisement of affairs than those who write from a distance or had a greater degree of responsibility in the turn of events.

—Rev. Robert E. Bisbee (1851-1938) .4

3 (S. Merrill 1900).
4 (Ryder 1928, Forward)

They All Wore a Star

INTRODUCTION

If you are interested in what day-by-day life was like for soldiers in the Civil War, told in diaries and letters; details of a battle as they saw it and felt it; and how officers' abilities and ambitions influenced their decisions, hence the lives of the soldiers and the outcome of that battle—then you will be rewarded for the time you spend reading this.

This book is many telling their own parts in the whole story, which few of them could know when they lived it. It is a long read, a chronology in which each person knew only their part and what they did, saw, and felt. Their tales, put together here, tell their whole story. You will live the war, in its hardship, and misery, terror and tedium, fun and comradery. Summaries lose that.

Part One is the story of soldiers' lives before the big battle they've been working up to, starting with leaving home, for reasons they explain. Part Two is about that battle. You can skip Part One, but after reading Part Two you may wonder if you should have. The soldiers went through much which prepared them for what was to come; it helped them do well and earn their stars. Their officers demonstrated in other battles the traits that would determine the events and outcome in Resaca.

This story starts with one person, who left his family to go to war. His death in a battle is the beginning of this book and he is barely mentioned thereafter. In the rest of the book we learn of his experience, in a sense, through those who were comrades and others who affected their lives. We learn his story through their stories, which are much more varied and nuanced than his alone.

What you read here is not in history books except in gross summary; in some respects it is quite different too. It is what those who were there would tell you if they were in the room with you years later. It is what the war was like for them personally and about how a particular battle developed. Conflicts are many. Triumphs and tragedies abound, sometimes leavened with humor. In a sense you will be living history through them. None of it is fiction—it is real.

Why This Book

The letter was in the hands of a distant relative when I got a copy in 1980, and it sat some 30 years more until some genealogical research got me looking more closely at the Battle of Resaca and what might have happened to my great-great-grandfather, the only ancestor known to have been in the Civil War. Resaca was not a battle much discussed in history, and the land on which it was fought remained in private hands. The only site publicly accessible was a Confederate Cemetery. And the internet was unheard of. Since then, regimental histories, official records of the war, diaries, newspapers, letters, and a few more books have become readily available at the desk or armchair. Some have such intense descriptions by the participants and witnesses to the battle and to the particular part of it that claimed Joseph Peters, that a story in the words of those who were there began to appear which would have interest for the general public much beyond the few pages initially intended for family distribution. Soon the story became not only that of Joe Peters but that of the Scott County, Illinois companies, the regiment, the brigade, then division, and finally their whole Corps.

As stories turned up, questions loomed. Who was shooting into the backs of their comrades? Why did the generals press the assault on just the point of the angle instead of the whole line? Who really deserved credit for capturing the battery? These and many others, like climbing to the crest of a hill only to find still another to reach, lured me into more digging.

This book recounts and relives, in the words of their companions, their days to Resaca and the long afternoon that left many to be buried in a common grave. It was their first head-on battle, in the beginning of the campaign to take Atlanta, accomplished just in time to save the election for President Lincoln. Joe's was ultimately one life contributed to that end.

This book is the story of Joe Peters and his fellow soldiers from the time they left home through the battle that took Joe's life. It is pieced together in their own words taken from letters, diaries, and histories, as well as newspapers and official military records. Inside you will hear them tell of their struggles and their dedication. They will tell you of their hard experiences in the year and a half before the battle. You will also learn something of what shaped the decisions of their leaders in that battle. And you may agree with me that a military court of inquiry about the conduct of that battle would be justified. One officer in particular, I conclude, let his greed for glory disrupt the planned assault, causing many deaths and perhaps the failure of the plan to defeat the Confederate army on that day.

The Elephant

Florence Percy, in an exquisite little poem, represents Memory as a droll fellow dwelling in the upper story and having charge of all the facts and figures that are placed in his keeping. She calls this keeper of the psychological storehouse of past events "The Imp in the Attic." Some of the valuables placed in his charge are lost, and some are only found after long searching; and it is to be noted also that the controlling Imp of each attic has idiosyncrasies quite his own. Now that these events of the war have receded into the far past and can only be viewed from the beginning of another century, it will not surprise the reader that my Imp has tired of presenting the record in panoramic continuity, but sometimes prefers instead to give a series of views, each clear and distinct in itself, but not always sufficient for a continuous narrative. Thus many scenes and events are indelibly stamped upon my memory, undimmed by the passing of time, while others of equal or perhaps greater importance I am unable to recall in their proper order. Did not these memories touch here and there with persons and events of a later date I should sometimes doubt their reality and be disposed to think they belonged in some pre-existent state. –Charles E. Benton .5

The phrase "I've seen the elephant," in the time of the war, referred to something the seeker once sought with great effort and enthusiasm but wished to never see again, having been trampled. The ancient analogy of the blind men constructing, in their minds' eyes, wildly different objects by feeling different parts of the elephant, describes the wildly inconsistent memories and perceptions of battle. Both analogies are apt for the researching and building of this book, started as a short compilation of the travels and travails of Joe Peters and the Scott County boys, leading to the first battle of the Atlanta Campaign—their elephant. Soon the book itself became like an elephant in size and complexity—and far more fascinating than anticipated.

Think of a box full of jigsaw puzzle pieces, but in words on scraps of paper. Only part of the picture is known. The rest has to be put together from rarely more than what each writer knew of his own place, let alone of those nearby. Not just what they knew of place, but of time. Compound that with a view that is sometimes biased, seeing or even imagining what they wished.

It became progressively and painfully more obvious as things fit together that most commanders and observers, especially at the regimental and often brigade

---

5 (Benton 1902, 110) Elizabeth Akers Allen (Chase) wrote as Florence Percy. Author has not found the poem itself.

and even division level, were completely unaware of activities and positions of others in the heat of the battle. And they seemed to use different clocks. One might say 11 in the morning when another might say 1 in the afternoon. Sometimes that is due to the level of detail, saying, for example, they attacked at 10 am when others explained they gathered at 10 but their own movement did not start till 1 pm. One might say they all started simultaneously, but comparison of their stated alignment with other units to the reports of others reveals they started much later. And sometimes the writer does not even seem to know left from right, north from south, or a straight from roundabout distance. Sometimes "we" is interchanged, without mention, between a writer's various units, ranging from company to corps or whole army in one sentence, sometimes to the writer's advantage. Likewise, time. Writings immediately after the battle or many years later showed the same disconnected reflections, likely heightened by the intensity of events blocking awareness of anything beyond what took full attention.

The choice and arrangement of accounts of events are my interpretations, after careful comparison of details, so that each testament is placed in position with others according to time, place, and activity—allowing each their say without this author otherwise influencing their view. Only some that were entirely redundant, clearly secondhand, or so unquestionably wrong in the face of other reports that they would be useless, were omitted.

I spent much, much, time reviewing and cross-checking—matching reports of widely varying detail and accuracy from various commanders of regimental and higher level. These are tempered by diaries and letters of those who had less to invest in advancement and glory and more to tell of their experience, of which they had no control and little to crave from officialdom. But I tried not to be any more specific than the material states, thus leaving much to be desired, but still giving the reader enough to make sense of otherwise disjointed reports. Errors are mine.

How to Read This Book

In writing of heroic deeds, the truth, and nothing but the truth, may be told, and yet the reader remain in ignorance as to the actual facts; the whole truth not having been told, the fruitful imagination is left to supply the void with a beautiful conception. While a painting is more professional if deceptive art be practiced, and suggestions to the willing imagination be depended upon to supply conceptions beyond the truthful touch of the brush, the fact remains that the delight of the beholder is occasioned by fiction and at the expense of accuracy

...The writer fancies that he will not be accused of deceptive painting, his aim being to draw the lines true to nature. –Halstead .6

Halstead has only one story to tell, but it is a good one about a series of incidents involving one soldier, which we will cover as they occur in this chronicle. Meantime, the author will try to do as Halstead did and tell only what appears as facts, depending on you the reader to see in your imagination what Halstead describes. The author will supply and help guide from one tale to the other, explaining where they don't seem to have a real connection. But nothing is invented. No imagined events or characters will be seen here. They are far more real, though, than fiction that is based thinly on history. And they are far more moving, because they are stories by real people about their very real experiences and feelings.

This story is in small snippets from many yarns spun by the participants, pieced together by events and location to reveal the story each could not have told alone. Thus, the research has been like gathering yarns into a ball, so to speak, and then unraveling the snippets and matching them, long and short, into a coarse fabric. The thread of one person's narrative, interrupted and interspersed with the threads of others, weaves a fabric that, it is hoped, presents a more complete, and maybe more honest, picture—or less complete, as honesty requires.

Imagine yourself in a campfire circle of spirits of the veterans. Better, as moving from one campfire to another, as they take turns talking about events and their experiences. One fire bringing only memories of one part of the battle to light, another fire stirring different old memories. With you is another spirit, the author, helping to sort it out, introducing those around the fire, and explaining some of it. He has been attending these campfires, over and over, as ghosts and spirits tend to hang on, reliving what has become indelible in their recollections, and he is taking you from fire to fire as the stories relate to each other. Take your time, listen intently and reflect, but do not tarry so long that the campfires fade in your memory before the next starts roaring.

Words by me could not better, or more accurately, describe events than do the words of the witnesses. Though many were written days, months, even decades, after the events, these are their recollections and I choose not to second-guess them. Though some are plainly erroneous or self-serving, they still serve to document attitudes and difficulties in observation, as well as actual events and feelings. Efforts to explain or summarize tempt error as well. Yet, where

6 (Halstead n.d.)

discrepancies or misleading stories appear, the author tried to include others that balance the scale.

For the events in this story, only original sources are included, except for essential information with no other source available.

Original grammar, spelling, and punctuation are preserved except where the intent might not be conveyed as intended or the text is difficult to follow. Brackets or footnotes correct obvious errors, such as in date or place. Abbreviation and other forms have been left as written.

To follow who is talking, which unit they were with, and where they were at any time will take a bit of patience. Consult the list of yarn spinners. Each direct quote is labelled with that writer's name and unit, in uppercase. A full label shows the subordinate unit first, with brigade commander, brigade, division, and corps abbreviated, as in PETERS, PVT, CO F 129TH ILL WARD 1B 3D 20C. Rank is not always included. Unit designations are omitted if irrelevant in context or not known. This is particularly true in parts of the story before the Atlanta Campaign began. For those with no particular unit, the heading may show, for example, a newspaper name, but could include the unit from which the reporter viewed things.

The Orders of Battle lists in the appendix are only for the Atlanta Campaign. Units not relevant to the story are omitted.

The enlistees of 1862 worked long, hard days, with occasional relief, for a year and a half, missing major action, yet becoming experienced in relying on themselves in isolated, dangerous posts. Meantime, abilities, attitudes, and ambitions, which would eventually involve them, were becoming manifest in the conduct of battles elsewhere. So the tales progress with the paths of the 129th Illinois and the other regiments destined to become the 1st Brigade of the Blue Star Division, the 3rd, commanded by Daniel Butterfield, of the 20th Corps, under Joseph Hooker. Mingled with these are tales by other participants and observers of those far-off events which finally converged on a hillside at Resaca on May 15, 1864, the elephant for many of that brigade. This is that story.

And be a bit reverent. Imagine you are listening to the voices of those who fought and suffered. Though some suffered less and sought glory more, you are reading their stories.

We begin.

PART ONE
ENDURANCE
ON THE ROADS TO RESACA

Volunteers tell of their experiences chasing armies in Kentucky and guarding railroads in Tennessee while distant events reveal characteristics of leaders who will shape what will be their first battle, a year and half after their enlistment. Together they face destiny at the village of Resaca in Part Two. In this part we feel through their writing what a Civil War soldier lived through and how it shaped them. Not all will survive to Part Two. We also divert now and then to follow some who will be commanders in Part Two and who will directly affect these soldiers' destinies. The abilities and weaknesses of these officers as shown by their performance in these earlier battles will directly influence the outcome in Part Two.

Both parts revolve in particular around one brigade. For two reasons. The author's great-great-grandfather was in that brigade, along with future President Benjamin Harrison. And that brigade spearheaded an assault lead by Harrison to break through the Confederate fortress at Resaca. The author's great-great-grandfather died in that assault.

In particular, Part One has telling glimpses of a particular general, Joseph Hooker. It is him and those under him who determined the conduct and outcome of the battle in Part Two.

The Letter

She often told my Mother the story of how she rode horseback to Exeter to get this, knowing the minute she saw it what it was. She rode part way home and then dismounted and sat under a shade tree to read this. She was a mere slip of a girl with 2 babies at home -Louise May, great granddaughter of Joseph and Nancy Peters.

Cassville Georgia, May 22nd 1864

Mrs Nancy Peters

I take the obligation on myself of writing you a few lines this evening to inform you of the Death of <u>your beloved husband</u> It is painful for me to write such sorrowful news but these are the horrors of war and we must submit he was killed in the battle of May 15th near Resaca while charging a Fort our Brigade was ordered to charge a fort and Rifle Pitts which we done capturing the fort and 4 pieces of Canon and driving the enemy before us but our ranks were thined while I write I shudder at the thought of that Sunday evening and wonder how any could escape among the torrents of grape and canister and musketry Joseph and James Clark fell side by side near the Fort they were brave and noble boys niver was there any better slain on the battlefield but they are gone and we sincerely mourn there loss Joseph was like a brother to me many of the days we have passed together both as school boys and out of school but he is gone and I am left maybe soon to follow as we expect to meet the enemy at any moment I gathered them up with the assistance of the ballance of the boys of the company and we buried them as nice as we could Joseph was shot through the head killing him instantly the ball passing through the back part of his head he looked very natural when we buried him we buried all that was killed in the Brigade making 52 in number all side by side we wrapt them nicely in there blankets and covered them good with cedar before covering them with dirt and put a board to each of their heads with the name and Co and Regt on them I cannot forbear shedding tears as I write we miss them so much it seems as though I cannot give them up but they are at rest There names will never be forgotten on the pages of history may heaven protect you in your distress and comfort you in this life and may we all meet in that land where war has ceased to be The captain and I take this as an opportunity of expressing our simpathys to you in your bereavement we will write again and let you know all about his effects so as you can get what is due to him.

There was 9 killed and 38 wounded out of our Regt the wounded in our Company was Patrick McCart and Francis Dunham and Lieut Scott Lieut Scott was wounded slightly in the hip and both the other boys was wounded in the arm Pat McCart had to have his arm amputated above Elbow it was his right arm.

But I must close anything that you want to know that I have failed to mention write to me and I will freely do it

Yours truly, Lieut Wm Smith

And Capt Geo W Horton

Why?

Many of our friends and acquaintances had set a good example and gone to the field of battle before us and many had already shed their blood in the defence of the country, while others were lying ill in the hospitals. -Grunert

Nancy's road from Exeter back to the farm was used three years earlier .7 by Colonel Ulysses S. Grant to march his first command of the war, the 21st Illinois Infantry, from Springfield, right past the farm, to water and rest at Exeter, on Mauvaisterre Creek, then to Naples, on the Illinois River. Crowds had gathered to watch the soldiers go by and then thronged to Naples where the soldiers waited for orders. .8 Nancy was carrying their second child then. Neither Joe nor his older brothers, Oliver and Henry, all with wives and children, would have thought to leave their farms to go off to war. Yet, a year later they did. Why?

The war that took Joe was rooted in a great conflict between those who abhorred slavery and those who depended on it.

Northern states were rankled because the slaveholding states often got their way in Federal government. They had extra power in the House of Representatives, the result of a compromise to get them to form the original Union: they were allowed to count 3/5 of a slave in determining population—thus voting power— for the *white* population. The north originally accepted this out of necessity. Without the Union, the newly independent states would have been unable to defend themselves as a nation. Georgia's population was now more slave than free, giving the white population alone quite some power in getting favorable laws. While the north resented the violation, in slavery, of the principles of the Declaration of Independence, the south tolerated no such sentiment, though many there quietly disapproved. The north seethed with resentment that the south, having been forgiven their share of Revolutionary War debt, now whined

7 Three years before Joe's death, one year before the call for enlistments.
8 (Moore 1912)

over perceived impositions, while using the slave vote to make impositions for themselves on the northern folks.

Now the north was forced into complicity in slavery! The Fugitive Slave Act required northerners to return slaves found in their territory. And the Supreme Court had ruled that a slave taken north with its master to a state that prohibited slavery could not claim freedom and must be returned, even forcing local law enforcement of that state to do it for the slave owner or face jail themselves. This, while Jacksonville, 10 miles east of Exeter, though divided by opposing attitudes of some who came from the south and some from the north, was a station on the underground railroad and home to many abolitionists. Slavers were even coming north to claim free negroes as escaped slaves, who depended on local citizens for help or had to escape to Canada if they could.

So by the time Joe and Nancy married in 1858, the year of the Lincoln-Douglas Debates, the unresolved slavery conflict was being fought in Kansas and Nebraska, fed by southerners trying to get slavery allowed in those states' consitutions. That was already war, right next door!

Abraham Lincoln realized, perhaps more than most, that the slaveholding states and those remaining in the Union must inevitably battle over the issues that divided them and that fight would then be over new territory, especially for the expanding slave trade; over commerce with Europe; and for control of things they had shared, such as free access to the Gulf of Mexico via the Mississippi River, of which the navigable Illinois River was a tributary. Lincoln had taken flatboats of agricultural product down the Illinois to New Orleans. Exeter, with plenty of rich farmland producing good grain, supplied whiskey sold in New Orleans. Many families emigrating from Europe had entered at New Orleans and come up the Mississippi.

Railroads were already important for travel, settlement, and trade, especially between the east and the expanding west, and Lincoln was involved in efforts to control whether east-west railroad routes would cross the northern reaches of the Mississippi or the southern. The local war over whether Kansas would be admitted to the Union as slave or free resulted from political maneuvering over whether a railroad route to the west would be from Chicago or New Orleans. Stephen A. Douglas had proposed allowing Kansans themselves to decide whether to be slave or free—as a sop to the south to gain the railroad in the north. Bitterness from this earlier war helped precipitate the wider war after Lincoln was elected and southern states began to secede. .9

9 (McPherson n.d., 125)

The hope to stop the spread of slavery and let it die out was extinguished.

Let us first hear in their own words from two who were leading their respective sides as the conflict boiled. First, the claim of justification and of destiny for the south. Then Lincoln explains the dilemma of the Union.

Alexander Stephens, Confederate Vice President

We ... will become the controlling power on this continent. -Stephens

March 21, 1861

Our new government ... was founded on slavery. Its foundations are laid, its cornerstone rests upon the great truth that the Negro is not equal to the white man; that slavery, submission to the superior race, is his natural and normal condition.

Our growth, by accessions from other States, will depend greatly upon whether we present to the world, as I trust we shall, a better government than that to which neighboring States belong. If we do this, North Carolina, Tennessee, and Arkansas cannot hesitate long; neither can Virginia, Kentucky, and Missouri ... The process of disintegration in the old Union may be expected to go on with almost absolute certainty if we pursue the right course. We are now the nucleus of a growing power which, if we are true to ourselves, our destiny, and high mission, will become the controlling power on this continent. .10

Abraham Lincoln, Inaugural Address

We cannot remove our respective sections from each other, nor build an impassable wall between them. -Lincoln

March 4, 1861

One section of our country believes slavery is right, and ought to be extended, while the other believes it is wrong, and ought not to be extended. This is the only substantial dispute. The fugitive slave clause of the Constitution, and the law for the suppression of the foreign slave trade, are each as well enforced, perhaps, as any law can ever be in a community where the moral sense of the people imperfectly supports the law itself. The great body of the people abide by the dry legal obligation in both cases, and a few

10 (Stephens 1861)

break over in each. This, I think, cannot be perfectly cured; and it would be worse in both cases after the separation of the sections, than before. The foreign slave trade, now imperfectly suppressed, would be ultimately revived without restriction, in one section; while fugitive slaves, now only partially surrendered, would not be surrendered at all, by the other. ...

Physically speaking, we cannot separate. We cannot remove our respective sections from each other, nor build an impassable wall between them. A husband and wife may be divorced, and go out of the presence, and beyond the reach of each other; but the different parts of our country cannot do this. They cannot but remain face to face; and intercourse, either amicable or hostile, must continue between them. Is it possible then to make that intercourse more advantageous, or more satisfactory, after separation than before? Can aliens make treaties easier than friends can make laws? Can treaties be more faithfully enforced between aliens, than laws can among friends? Suppose you go to war, you cannot fight always; and when, after much loss on both sides, and no gain on either, you cease fighting, the identical old questions, as to terms of intercourse, are again upon you ... In your hands, my dissatisfied fellow countrymen, and not in mine, is the momentous issue of civil war. The government will not assail you. You can have no conflict, without being yourselves the aggressors. You have no oath registered in Heaven to destroy the government, while I shall have the most solemn one to preserve, protect and defend it.

I believe this government cannot endure permanently half slave and half free ... It will become all one thing, or all the other. .11

Debate stops when shooting starts. The fight becomes for home, not over the issues. One death of a friend or neighbor is enough to make enemies. Few agonize over loyalties then. It is said that Robert E. Lee agonized but could not fight against home, family, and friends. Another Virginian, from a slave-holding family, General George Henry Thomas, fought for the Union and was forever disowned by family. For southern soldiers, if they had any choice about fighting, it was simply home and the people in their lives—us or them.

Indiana's Anger

Attempts to legally "steal" free negro citizens had more effect on attitudes in Indiana than did efforts to retrieve actual slaves. Leaders in that state were now the first generation of the original settlers and they sympathized with effort

11 (Lincoln, Inaugural Address 1861)

under adversity. Several attempts by whites to claim free negroes as slaves under the Fugitive Slave Act aroused lawyers to the defense of those whom they had come to know as fellow citizens. These cases played out in the newspapers and did much to arouse Indiana against secession. (See Lincoln's speech above.) .12 .13

John Coburn, John Ketcham, and other lawyers put much effort into travel and research to prove in court that their clients were not who the claimants said they were. They did not hesitate to pitch in when the war broke out. Coburn eventually commanded a brigade. Benjamin Harrison, grandson of a President, commanded a regiment he recruited, and often took charge of his own brigade when its commander was absent. Ketcham's son was married to a sister of Samuel Merrill, Harrison's second in command, and their son was Sergeant Major. The Battle of Resaca will test them.

Wes Connor and the Wrights

Three brothers Wright of Georgia opposed secession. Edwin Wright had taken in his wife's eight-year old brother, Wesley Connor, after their father's death. Wes became a teacher of the deaf and in later years was principal of the school and an ardent student of nature. Relations notwithstanding, when the war broke out, Connor enlisted in Belgian Max Van Den Corput's "Cherokee" Artillery. In his diary he refers to his brother in-law as "Mr. Wright." Augustus Wright served in the Georgia Legislature and argued against secession at first and later for making peace, at his peril. He worked with Sherman to try to broker a peace. Moses Wright fled to Louisville rather than fight for the Confederacy. Edwin, "Mr. Wright," went further: he aided the Union cavalry after it reached his home south of Resaca and then disappeared, having joined a Union regular army regiment in Ohio, absent thereafter from family records, and leaving his wife bereft even of a pension. Among Wes Connor's admirable traits was loyalty to his comrades and his cause — as he saw it. .14 Wes wrote in his diary after Vicksburg:

> Connor, Corput's Battery: Though most southerners were not slaveholders, many fought for their country regardless. Heard a Yankee tell one of this class, he fought because he was north and believed he was right, and if he had been south he might have been on the other side. You are South, your

12 (Bates 2018)
13 (Money, The Fugitive Slave Law of 1850 in Indiana 1921)
14 (Dixon 2013)

home is south, and I say damn a man that wont fight for his country and his home. It did me good all over. .15

He seems to have no particular attitude toward negros, but he never lost that commitment, even after the war. Wes's diary and later correspondence with an opposing Union comrade-in-arms give us another first-hand account of one side of the war.

August 1862 -Answering the Call

He enlisted in the army. They were drafting men then and Grandma said he did not want to get drafted. .16 – Bess Peters Vondras, granddaughter of Nancy Peters, in a letter to a niece.

The War to July of 1862

PARTRIDGE, 96TH ILL: The early engagements of the war were rather disastrous than otherwise. Bull Run was a crushing defeat, the Union troops falling back upon the National Capital in sore discomfiture. At Wilson's Creek, Mo, the army was obliged to retreat, after the loss of their gallant leader, General Lyon, and many men. The advantages gained at points in Missouri and in West Virginia were not decisive. The battle of Belmont, Mo. fought in November, 1861, served to give the Western troops confidence in themselves, although the results achieved were not of great magnitude. The late Winter and the early Spring witnessed some striking victories in the West, and were greatly encouraging. At Mill Springs, Ky, the Union forces achieved a handsome victory, the rebels being driven southward with the loss of their commander, Gen. Zollicoffer, and many men. They were also driven from Missouri and defeated at Pea Ridge, Ark. Fort Donelson was captured with 15,000 prisoners and an immense number of cannon. Pittsburg Landing, fought in April, 1862, was a pronounced victory, though dearly won, and Corinth was occupied by the National forces in the early summer. Missouri, Kentucky and Tennessee were now reclaimed. New Orleans had been occupied by the National forces. On the Atlantic coast important points had been captured. But with the Summer of 1862 came

---

15 (W. O. Connor, Wesley Olin Connor Diary 1867) July 7, 1863 after surrendering at Vicksburg.

16 Enlistment meant serving in a company with friends and neighbors, where trust and support, with officers who knew you, and common bonds between families, were more assured. Draftees had no options.

reverses. The Western armies, decimated by frequent and severe engagements, weakened by the enervating influences of climatic and other diseases, and the severe strain in maintaining their long lines of communication, were barely holding their own. The Eastern armies, which had been expected to capture the Confederate Capital, had come to a halt, and were being rapidly thinned by disease in the Chickahominy swamps. Their gallantly fought battles had been but half victories at best, and it became apparent that retreat was possible, if not probable. Evidently a crisis had been reached, and it was a question whether the Union armies were not to be forced backward, the scenes of strife transferred to the States north of the Potomac and Ohio rivers, and free soil watered with the blood of the heroes who should fall in battle. .17

MERRILL, 70TH IND: The failure of General McClellan to take Richmond during the last days of June, 1862, and the great losses of the Union army in the battles near that city, made apparent the necessity for more soldiers. On July first President Lincoln accepted the proposition of the Governors of the

---

Jacksonville Sentinel
Friday, August 22, 1862.
Jacksonville, Illinois.

THE DRAFT. WAR DEPARTMENT.

Washington D.C., Aug. 9th, 1862

Regulations for the enrollment and draft of 300,000 militia.

In pursuance of an order by the president of the United States, bearing date of August 4th, 1862, whereby it is provided that a draft of three hundred thousand militia be immediately called into the service of the United States, to serve for nine months, unless sooner discharged, and that the secretary of war shall assign the quotas of the several states, and establish regulations for the draft; also, that if any state shall not by the 15th of August furnish its quota for the additional three hundred thousand volunteers authorized by law, the deficiency of volunteers in that state will also be made up by special draft. from the militia; and that the secretary of war shall establish regulations for this purpose—it is ordered: ...

---

17 (Partridge 1887, 23)

loyal States to raise more troops, and decided to call into the service an additional force of three hundred thousand men. .18

GRUNERT, CO D 129TH ILL: President Lincoln had scarcely issued his call for three hundred thousand volunteers in the year 1861 [1862], when the loyal hearts of the inhabitants of Scott County, Illinois, were moved and filled with enthusiasm. Every one that could leave his loved ones hastened to be mustered in, thinking that his country needed his services in the pending danger more than father, mother, wife or children. The love of country caused the farmer to leave his plow, the mechanic to change his implements of peace with implements of war, to take part in the great work of suppressing the rebellion. Many of our friends and acquaintances had set a good example and gone to the field of battle before us and many had already shed their blood in the defence of the country, while others were lying ill in the hospitals. It was the duty of every loyal, upright man to assist in saving the country from ruin, and in consequence of the call of the President for volunteers, a company was raised and organized under the care of the later Col. Henry Case, in Winchester, Scott Co, Ill, in July, 1862. .19

How Can I Refuse to Give My Son?

MERRILL, 70TH IND:While many of the men composing this body of troops were from Indianapolis, and from the towns and villages of the neighboring counties, the majority were from the country, farmers and sons of farmers. A large number who enlisted were men profoundly convinced that all was lost, unless they made the sacrifice of leaving their wives, their children and their business until the Government should be re-established.

Many incidents in connection with enlistments for this regiment throw a light on the heroism of the national character. One mother exclaimed, "I could not have felt he was my son had he hesitated." Another, "My son, you will be faithful. It is a noble duty." A boy, an only child, who wished to enlist, asked the recruiting officer to see his mother and gain her consent. There was an indescribable radiance on her beautiful face as she replied, "Yes, he may go. How can I refuse to give my son to the country when I remember that my Heavenly Father gave His only son to save the world?"

To the fathers and mothers the enlistment of their sons was a terribly serious thing, and to the man who was leaving wife and children it was inexpressible

18 (S. Merrill 1900) Lincoln made another call in August.
19 (Grunert 1866, 3) Grunert was with Company D, of Scott County.

anguish; but to the boy, who had been longing for the time when he should be old enough or large enough to be acceptable, the only distress was the fear that the mustering officer would fail to receive him.

U. H. Farr of Company D, who had not yet seen his sixteenth birthday, says: "The fife was playing, the drums were beating, and the new soldiers fell into line. When I saw among them boys no larger than myself I suddenly resolved to see if they would take me, and stepped into the ranks with the others. I kept the step till the war was over." .20

And they were supported by song, sung over many a patriotic gathering.

Three Hundred Thousand More

We are coming, Father Abraham, three hundred thousand more,
From Mississippi's winding stream, and from New England's shore;
We leave our ploughs and workshops, our wives and children dear,
With hearts too full for utterance, with but a silent tear;
We dare not look behind us, but steadfastly before:
We are coming, Father Abraham, three hundred thousand more!

If you look across the hill tops that meet the Northern sky,
Long moving lines of rising dust your vision may descry;
And now the wind, an instant, tears the cloudy vail aside,
And floats aloft our spangled flag, in glory and in pride,
And bayonets in the sunlight gleam, and bands brave music pour:
We are coming Father Abraham, three hundred thousand more!

If you look all up your valleys, where the growing harvests shine,
You may see our sturdy farmer boys, fast forming into line;
And children from their mothers' knees, are pulling at the weeds,
And learning how to reap and sow against their country's needs;
And a farewell group stands weeping at every cottage door:
We are coming, Father Abraham, three hundred thousand more!

You have called us, and we're coming, by Richmond's bloody tide
To lay us down, for freedom's sake, our brother's bones beside;
Or from foul treason's savage group to wrench the murderous blade,
And in the face of foreign foes its fragments to parade;

20 (S. Merrill 1900, 2)

Six hundred thousand loyal men and true have gone before:
We are coming, Father Abraham, three hundred thousand more! 21

—James Sloan Gibbons

GRUNERT, CO D 129TH ILL: In a few days the company was full nevertheless more volunteers came and offered their services. During the same month a second company was raised by Captain (later Lieut. Colonel) Thomas H. Flynn. On the 5th day of August, 1862, we left our homes and friends and dear ones, for how long a period no one could tell, to command a halt to the enemy that grew bolder and more daring every day. Early in the morning of the above day we entered the wagons of our friends who wished to do this last act of kindness and bring us to the next railroad station. It is almost needless to say, that tears glistened in many eyes when the parting farewell was said! At noon, on the 5th of August, we reached Jacksonville, and after the last friends had bid us adieu and wished us a speedy and safe return, cheers were given, hats waved and the locomotive steamed with us towards the State Capital, Springfield. There we remained until 9 o'clock, P.M, when we again entered a train of open cars, while a heavy drenching rain saturated every thread of our clothing, and a few hours before daybreak on the 6th of August we reached Pontiac, Ill. where we went into camp. The next day was also a rainy one, and our barracks offered us but very poor shelter. As a matter of course, this new mode of life did not suit us exactly, until we became more accustomed to it. Bad as our barracks were, we began to be satisfied with them, after we had stood guard for several hours, and wind and rain made this part of the service rather unpleasant. When not on guard, we went to town, after procuring a pass, where we were well received and kindly treated by the citizens. A company of volunteers was also being organized here, which afterwards became the first company of our regiment. Three weeks passed quickly, during which time we did guard duty with clubs. By this time the requisite number of ten companies for the regiment were full and had arrived, and now we received uniforms and muskets and the drilling was done with more exactness. On the 8th of September we were sworn in for three years, unless sooner discharged, and

---

21 James Sloan Gibbons, New York Evening Post, July 1862. (James Sloan Gibbons was an abolitionist, Quaker, and cousin to Horace Greeley. Married to fellow Quaker, abolitionist, and founder of the Women's Prison Association, Abigail Hopper, their home in New York is recognized as a Manhattan station on the Underground Railroad. (www.poetryfoundation.org)

received two months' pay in advance and twenty-five dollars bounty; after which we moved nearer to the enemy's country. [22] [23]

COX, WILLIAM, CO F 129TH ILL: September 14. We have erected comfortable quarters here ... Oliver Peters and his brothers are well and in good spirits. They occupy the bunks on the right. On the left are James Clark ... We are a jolly romping set as ever was in any camp. We have our Exeter string band of music to cheer us. [24]

The Confederacy, having been pushed out of Kentucky and most of Tennessee, was pushing back. General Braxton Bragg crossed the Cumberland River on August 27, headed north, aiming for Louisville and Cincinnati. Bragg was aided by Confederate cavalry under General Morgan. Our western volunteers were rushed to Louisville.

The Union army retreated to Washington on August 30 after Stonewall Jackson and James Longstreet routed them at the Second Battle of Bull Run, also known as Manassas. Lincoln put McClellan back in command as Lee took 40,000 Confederates to Harpers Ferry. They met at Antietam September 7 and Lee retreated, leaving 26,000 dead on both sides. This was Lincoln's long-awaited chance: he issued the Emancipation Proclamation on September 22, 1862.

September - Louisville [25]

Moving to Louisville, on September 22, the 129th joined the 38th Brigade, 12th Division, Army of the Ohio.

22 (Grunert 1866, 4)
23 Grunert was with Company D, of Scott County. Many of the recollections in his history are of activities of that company but are relevant for the entire regiment.
24 (W. J. Cox n.d.)
25 George Blakeslee's maps, though made long after the war, give us a good idea of places and distances covered in his brigade's travels in Kentucky and Tennessee.

PEAK, CO F 129TH ILL: They again mounted the iron horse that took them to Jeffersonville, Indiana ... A short time after the regiment arrived at Jeffersonville, they crossed the river to Louisville, Ky. .26 .27

FLEHARTY, 102ND ILL: At Louisville the regiment was brigaded with the 79th Ohio and 105th Illinois regiments, under the command of Brig. Gen. W. T. Ward. Subsequently the 70th Ind. and 129th Ill. regiments were attached to the brigade, and thenceforward until the close of the war the brigade retained the same organization. Never were regiments more harmoniously associated. .28 .29

PEAK, CO F 129TH ILL: Braggs was threatening Louisville at that time, being only a few miles away from the city. Reinforcements came in so rapidly that Braggs decided to abandon the attack, and withdrew his troops from the city. The 129th regiment was then stationed near Louisville, Ky. where they begin to experience something of what it was to be a soldier, drilling, dress parade and doing picket duty was the order of the day for two weeks. They were then told to be ready to march at a moment's notice. The men began to pack their knapsacks to be sure nothing was left at the old camp ground, and to the dismay of the men, were not able to get all of their belongings in their knapsacks. They packed and repacked with all of their packing the knapsacks failed to give room for all they wished to take with them. They were raw troops coming from most every walk in life, and they had many things to learn about soldier's life, however, they were soon to play the real soldier.

New regiments were being pushed to Louisville to hold off Bragg. General Thomas was hastening his own regiments to Louisville at the same time.

GRUNERT, CO D 129TH ILL: When one day some cannon shots were heard, we supposed the enemy was making an attack, our camp was alarmed and the regiment posted into line—but no enemy appeared. We had been in camp near Louisville two weeks, done guard duty and improved in drilling, when one morning at 3 o'clock we were ordered to "fall in" line of battle. We were told to be ready at a moment's notice, though the day of our march had not been fixed. We were of course all very anxious to know the time and direction of our march or "tramp," but could get no positive information. So we packed up our knapsacks every day anew, in order to leave nothing behind, until finally some had such a heavy load that it was an impossibility for them to march, much less run after the flying rebels.

COX, WILLIAM, CO F 129TH ILL: Dear Daughter, We are both well and in good spirits. We are now in the midst of our enemies. There will be a terrible clash of the armies here in a few days … I have just been chosen fife major … we have one boy of 12 years of age in our band, an orphan boy at that, who is undoubtedly the best performer in the fife except myself. .30

Many Things to Learn

Bullets, bayonets, and cannon might be dodged but not the marches, where they had to endure cold and wet, hot and dry, thirst, hunger, disease, homesickness, sleep loss — things that kill more than actual battle. To avoid conquer, a soldier must first overcome these, if he can, before the bullets come. Our brigade will have time for the tough lessons coming.

BOYLE, ADJUTANT, 111TH PA: The seasoning process which transforms recruits into soldiers is almost as radical as that which transmutes hides into leather, and a first campaign is always a severe test of physical stamina. Field service takes the romance from the soldier's life as quickly as it removes the polish from his buttons. It is discipline of the severest possible sort, and means business every hour. The infantryman is loaded with from forty to sixty pounds of arms, accouterments, rations, and clothing. His toilet articles consist of a small comb, a towel, a piece of soap, a folding tin lookingglass, and possibly a toothbrush and hairbrush. He must conquer homesickness, a malady from which some die. He must become inured to heat, cold, and storm in the open weather. He is expected to be able to march on wet or dusty roads from fifteen to thirty miles per day, and to live on the field ration of hard bread, coffee, sugar, and salt pork or beef, which he cooks as he can for himself or consumes it as it is issued. He must learn to endure hunger and thirst without complaint. He must march with blistered and raw feet until these important extremities attain a hornlike hardness. He must learn to have his rest broken at night by picket duty, and by intrenching and marching, and to make up his lost repose when and how he can by day. He

30 (W. J. Cox n.d.)

must endure certain forms of disease without leaving the ranks that would put him to bed in civil life. And after and beyond all else he must be ready anywhere and at any moment to do the one thing for which he has entered the field, that is, to fight battles. He never knows, when he is called to arms, where he is going or what he is to do. His time, his energy, his life are in his commander's hands. It is the severest physical training that men can undergo, and its hardships and its heroism cannot be described. Men of the lymphatic temperament rarely endure it; those having tendencies to vital organic weakness quickly retire from it or die; and a full year's time is required even for the strong and vigorous to become toughened and fit for the rough and exhausting life. But the men who do not break down become athletes. Their faces are bronzed and hard, their muscles are like steel, and their nerve is indomitable. Their spirits are gay, and they sing their songs and crack their jokes under the most disheartening and grewsome circumstances. The elements seem to have no effect upon their health. They march or camp in scorching heat or soaking rain or freezing sleet with the same grim strength. Wounds themselves lose much of their effect, and it is a fact that in the later years of the war hundreds of men recovered easily from injuries that would, in their unseasoned period, have been mortal, while lighter injuries, that once would have been thought serious, were scarcely noticed, and sometimes were not even reported. Every soldier that remained in the field learned to bear the strain with the minimum of food and care. He became, of necessity, not only an expert soldier, but in some degree a cook, a cobbler, a launderer, and a tailor. _31_

Reid, Co A, 22nd Wis: And here I wish to correct a false idea, generally prevalent among civilians ... A man can walk thirty or forty miles a day when alone, without injury or fatigue, and he listens with contempt when soldiers speak of 15 to 20 miles being a hard march, but let him enter the ranks and be obliged to conform his movements to that of a thousand others—let him put on heavy clothing, tightly buttoned, and then confined by a belt and shoulder straps—let him hang heavy weights on each shoulder by mere strings and then add the unequal arm wearying load of a gun to be shifted from shoulder to shoulder—let him stop to rest, not when he gets tired and sit until he is rested, but when the order comes from the front, and start again when ordered, after you are not sufficiently rested or have sat long enough to become stiffened almost to rigidity—and then he will know the difference between a soldier's march and a civilian's walk, and will understand one reason why the armies "don't move faster." The general rate

31 (Boyle 1903, 38)

of heavy marching is two miles an hour, and rest 10 minutes every hour, and this is least fatiguing to the soldier. .32

These men have not yet been seasoned by grueling tests of their stamina and strain on their bodies. But they are about to be, suddenly, with little preparation. Many will not survive the transformation.

The short time they had for training and drill barely got them started. Later, they would need all the practice they could get to learn to adapt to circumstances and still be effective as a group. In the Civil War, infantry firepower comes from many working in close coordination and control.

> MERRILL, 70TH IND: At the beginning, ignorance prevailed among officers as well as among men. Stories were rife of officers falling flat as they marched backward in front of their companies, of their helplessly rushing men into obstacles, of their expecting wheeling to be done when they gave the order "swing around like a barn door," of their giving command exactly as laid down in the tactics, that is, without omitting "to the right or left as the case may be," of their commanding "Arms eport," of orders as impossible of execution as going east and west at the same time. However, the men in line had quite as much difficulty in executing properly given orders as those not according to Hardee. Ignorance gradually gave way to intelligent command and proper execution. .33

Harrison, from July to September and beyond, studied as many tactics manuals as he could obtain. This would be of great benefit to the brigade when the time came.

The 70th was immediately sent to protect railroads near Franklin, south of Bowling Green, Kentucky. There is no room to cover their escapades here, but this one sheds light on their abilities and willingness to use them:

> MERRILL, 70TH IND (J.M. WILLIS): At nine o clock A. M., September thirtieth, five hundred men of the Seventieth Indiana and about one hundred from the Eighth Kentucky cavalry and from Company K, Sixtieth Indiana, all under the command of Colonel Harrison, took stock cars for Russellville, where a report said a Confederate regiment was being recruited. As the train approached Auburn it was found that the enemy had burned the bridge over

32 (Reid 1965, 21)
33 (S. Merrill 1900) The 70th had left Indianapolis on the 12th of August, was the first Yankee regiment to enter Louisville, on the 13th, and then was carried by rail to Gallatin on the 15th to start guarding against Morgan's raiders.

Black Lick, but the enthusiastic work of the men under the intelligent supervision of Captain Fisher, an old railroad contractor, ably assisted by Captain Carson, made an entire change in the condition of affairs. The woods furnished heavy timbers for piers and stringers to span the forty feet of space where fire had wrought destruction. This material was cut, carried and placed in position by the men. Crossties and spikes were picked up, crooked iron rails were straightened, and in less than three hours the ravine was passable. .34

Not to mention their trust in Captain Fisher! A three-hour reconstruction, strong enough to support a moving locomotive!

October - Hard Marching in Kentucky

Falling by the Wayside

GRUNERT, CO D 129TH ILL: On the first day of marching, blankets, overcoats, socks, &c. &c. were thrown away in all directions and the knapsacks lightened. The day for our departure had come at last. On the 3d of October, 1862, we turned our backs to the city of Louisville, after having received sixty cartridges, and after many a "parting bumper" had been taken. The sun was tremendously hot, and as the water in our canteens gave out, no springs or creeks on our way, the knapsacks overloaded and heavy, it may be imagined that this our first day's "tramp" was anything but pleasant. The sun had long departed and it was dark, and yet we were on our march toward Shelbyville, Ky. Every one that was with us this night, will never forget the scene when by the light of the moon a small spring, half dry, was discovered close by the road. The confusion that followed this discovery is indescribable. Everybody rushed to the water, quenched his thirst and returned to his former place—no company there—the different companies were completely intermingled—from all sides the cry: "Where is my company?" was heard—the officers sought their men and the men their officers. The officers strove in vain to bring some order in this confused mass of human beings, until some of the men, tired and worn out, threw themselves down on the ground to rest and sleep, despite the entreaties and commands of the company officers. The part of the regiment not so tired followed the officers, and when we halted at two o'clock, near a small creek, I counted not more than eight of my company. Although we were hungry,

34 (S. Merrill 1900, 25)

we were too tired and worn out to cook anything, but stretched ourselves on the ground and were soon asleep. .35

PEAK, CO F 129TH ILL: Many suffered for water, and to make it more painful, the dust from the pike road which was built of limestone rocks, settled on the lips of the soldiers, and many soldiers had sore lips. By the middle of the afternoon overloaded knapsacks were being unloaded, overcoats, blankets and extra shirts and pants were strewn along the roadside

FLEHARTY, 102ND ILL: For a time the men kept their places very well, but at length they commenced dropping out, one by one, then in quads, until finally the roadside was lined with exhausted soldiers. Water was extremely scarce. Relentlessly our commanders kept on their way. Why, no one could tell; no one could detect the wisdom of a movement which if continued would precipitate a disordered column of worn out and exhausted men upon the enemy. Far into the night the march was continued. At midnight probably three-fourths of the regiment had turned in by the wayside, to rest at will until morning. A few continued on, scarcely enough to keep up the organization of the regiment. Scattered like flocks of quails, they would call to each other in the darkness, thus; "Here's the 102d." "Co. D," "Co. B." "Right this way to Co. K." .36

GRUNERT, CO D 129TH ILL: October 4th, 1862. Before sunrise a good many of the sleepers left behind had rejoined us. Some of my comrades, hungry as they were, shot a hog in a corn field close by, cut a few slices off and roasted them over the camp-fires on bayonets or sticks of wood. We missed the necessary salt very much. Many had just arisen from their sleep, when the signal was given to fall in, and many had to march the second day also with an empty stomach. This day's march was, nevertheless, not as severe on the men as the day before, and there were less sore feet. We had to march only thirteen miles this day, and reached Shelbyville, Ky. long before sunset, where we went into camp and remained until the seventh of October.

Frankfort, 22 Miles

PEAK, CO F 129TH ILL: The bugle called them up rather early and they were told that 22 miles would be their day's march. After two days' rest most of the soldiers were feeling fine, and the tramp was not so hard. Evening came

35 (Grunert 1866, 5) From here on, Grunert's quotes are not footnoted, being so numerous and scattered, since they are dated and easily found in the original source.
36 (Fleharty, Our Regiment. A History of the 102d Illinois Infantry Volunteers 1865, 14)

and there was no prospect of going into camp. Later an orderly from the brigadier general told the colonel they would have to make Frankfort, Ky. before morning. The whole column moved along silently, not a word spoken by officers or men, until they came to a small creek where the men could get water. Here they rested two hours, but those hours seemed only a few seconds. Scarcely had the men closed their eyes when the command was to fall in, that tore them from their slumber. No march had been so hard on the men of the 129th regiment as this one; many of the men left the columns, and in one or two instances whole companies fell out, seemingly completely worn out, and not able to march any further without a little rest. Before day break the morning of the 8th, the shattered regiment reached Frankfort, Ky. the capital of the state, but too late, to accomplish what they had planned on doing, capture a part of Bragg's army that was at Frankfort. The rebels had left the city on the approach of the Yankee boys as they were called in the Southern country, however the Union cavalry had a skirmish with the rebels at the Kentucky river, two or three rebels being killed and several wounded; the unions' loss was two men wounded. By this time the 129th regiment began to know something of what it was to be a soldier, and when the bugle sounded to fall in line it was difficult to get some of the men to even move, they were so completely worn out, their feet were sore and limbs ached so it seemed to be a punishment to make them move. They were assured they would go into camp a short distance from the city, and would remain in camp for several days. On this promise they took their places and marched one mile out of town and went into camp on a high piece of ground to guard some guns that were on this elevated spot of ground. After being settled in camp for a few days most of the men went to the river to bathe their aching limbs, and cool off. So great was the effect of this bathing, that the next day most of the men were ready for another tramp. They remained in camp three days, and on the 11th they were called on to tramp again, however nothing of importance happened until the 13th.

GRUNERT, CO D 129TH ILL:October 8th. Before day-break we had reached Frankfort, the Capital of Kentucky, but too late nevertheless, as the enemy had fled. Our advance guard of cavalry had a skirmish with the enemy at the bridge over the Kentucky river, while the latter were endeavoring to demolish the bridge. The enemy had to flee with the loss of several wounded and killed. Blood-spots were to be seen on the walls of a house up to nearly eight feet from the ground, where some wounded rebel had laid his bleeding hands. The enemy had been successful in destroying part of the bridge, and we had to remain on the other side of the river until the repairs could be made. This was done a few hours after sunrise, and, marching over the bridge, we saw three of our killed cavalrymen lying there; several wounded had been brought to the hospital. We remained upon our arrival in the city on the streets, while part of the men laid down on the hard pavement, another part prepared breakfast, and a third went to the citizens for something to eat. The sun was scorchingly hot, and it was with the greatest difficulty that some of the men, when the bugler blew forward, could be brought to move, and kept in line. We did not march but a mile south of town, where we were stationed as guard on a high hill to protect some guns stationed there. After we had rid ourselves of our knapsacks and muskets, most of the men went to the river to bathe and cool and refresh the aching and worn out limbs. We were enjoying ourselves finely, when the report of a cannon and the buglers called us under arms again. We were posted in line of battle and were expecting an attack from the enemy; but in vain, no enemy appeared.

The 129th, then in Gilbert's 12th Corps, was among those who marched hither and yon in the game against Bragg yet were not there for the Battle of Perryville. Buell had intended to attack Bragg on the 8th but decided to wait till the 9th, when Gilbert should arrive. So Bragg attacked Buell and won—but left the field to Buell, to not be outnumbered and trapped by arriving troops.

The Battle of Perryville - Missed

W. F. CODDINGTON, 19TH IND. BATTERY: Some eight or nine years ago I read an article by J. M. Wright, who was on Buell's staff. He said that Buell had ordered his corps commanders (McCook, Crittenden and Gilbert) to be ready to attack Bragg on the 8th. But one corps (Gilbert's) did not get on the ground in time; consequently the time of the attack was delayed until the morning of the 9th. McCook was in line and ready when Buell ordered him to hold his ground, but not to bring on a general engagement that day. Bragg was smart seeing that Buell had but one corps in line, while his own army was ready, he ordered two corps to attack McCook. McCook had one or two things to do fight or run, and whoever heard of a McCook running? When Gen. McCook saw that the fighting was severe all along his line, he sent to Buell for help. Buell said no; that McCook had brought on the battle, and he must fight it out himself. How true this is I don't know, but I do know that reinforcements did not come. Wright said that Buell was very much surprised when he learned that Bragg had attacked McCook, as he did not expect it Buell ordered an attack on the morning of the 9th. But as Bragg withdrew in the night, there was nothing to do but bury the dead. .37

The 129th was still more than a day away, according to Grunert's diary.

Tramp to Near Rough and Ready

GRUNERT, CO D 129TH ILL: Near Frankfort we remained for three days, but on October 11th, the tramp commenced again; nothing of importance, however, appeared until October 13th. October 13th. It was some time after sunset, when we arrived near the small town of Rough and Ready, with a large force of rebels but a short distance from our front. As we were unacquainted with the country and the night a very dark one, it was impossible for us to move on, and we remained in front of the town on the road, where every one made himself as comfortable a resting place as the road would permit.

Early on October 14th, we were awakened and commanded to get ready for a move; what this new move was to be no one knew or could find out just then. We soon found out that we were reconnoitering and were marching with great caution several miles east of the town, when the command to load was given, after which we again moved forward very quietly and with great caution. Finally we found tracks of the rebels, who appeared to have been a whole brigade of cavalry, as in every fence corner the leavings of the horse fodder were seen. The rebels had fled on hearing of our approach. We advanced about five miles from Rough and Ready, when the pursuit was given up. After having partaken of a scanty breakfast, consisting of coffee, pork and crackers, we returned to the city, where we remained during the day.

55 Miles to Crab Orchard

October 15th. We were aroused at four o'clock in the morning, and after marching 10 miles reached Lawrenceburg, where we encamped.
October 16. After another march of ten miles we reached Harrodsburg and camped.
October 17. We reached Danville, after having marched twenty miles, where

37 http://chroniclingamerica.loc.gov/lccn/sn82016187/1894-06-07/ed-1/seq-3/

we pitched our tents.

October 18. A march of fifteen miles brought us to the town of Harrisport, where we remained over night.

ALBERTUS DUNHAM, CO C 129TH ILL: October 17. They have poped us through ever since we left L. at a 2.40 gate. .38 If a person wants to try to see what they can endure let them try soldering, for it will kill or cure.

ALBERTUS DUNHAM, CO C 129TH ILL: October 18. We had a prayer meeting here last evening. I would like to have you a few minutes some evening to see the different things that are going on. Some swearing at the praying and singing. Others making a mock of it, some writing letters, others talking about taking Bragg and his army, and every thing else you can think of good or bad all talking at once, just think about a thousand men all talking at once. .39

GRUNERT, CO D 129TH ILL: OCTOBER 19. We struck tents at eight o'clock A.M. and reached Crab Orchard after having marched twenty miles. The place assigned us for camp ground was so covered with briars and brush, that we had to cut these before we could commence to pitch tents. We took some corn stalks from a cornfield close by, belonging to an arch rebel, for which crime (thanks to our contemptible General) we had to drill for two hours with knapsacks.

PEAK, CO F 129TH ILL: The more they talked about it the more they felt like they must have revenge, and believe me they were not long in getting rid of the contemptible general.

According to the Illinois Adjutant General records, "On October 3, marched in pursuit of Bragg, via Frankfort and Danville, to Crab Orchard. On 17th, the Brigade was transferred to Tenth Division, Brigadier General R. S. Granger commanding. Commenced the return march October 20." .40 A logical inference is that Granger commanded after they reached Crab Orchard and was not that "contemptible" general.

Too late. William Cox, who started with such good spirits, was down and close to out already.

38 (Popped through, marching at a gait of 2 miles in 40 minutes ever since they left Louisville.)
39 (DeRosier 1969, 27)
40 (Illinois Adjutant General 1901)

COX, WILLIAM, CO F 129TH ILL: October 20th. Dear wife; I am glad that I am able to sit up and write you a few lines' I have been sick ever since we began our Dreadful march out of Louisville; a great portion of the time I did not know where I was or what I was doing; I have not seen John Thomas for 2 or 3 weeks; he was well and soldier like marching away to the field of battle since our army left us the sick. They have had some experience in the art of fighting. .41

ALBERTUS DUNHAM, CO C 129TH ILL: Whareever the army goes they strip evry thing. I have seen a mile of fence laid flat in 15 min. and on fire. Where we camped at Crab Orchard thare was a farm of 900 acres well fenced and before we left thare was not a rail fence left on the farm and corn and other things in proportion. .42

GRUNERT, CO D 129TH ILL: Here we remained for eight days, when we received marching orders for Lebanon.

March to Lebanon - Seeing Devastation

GRUNERT, CO D 129TH ILL: As I cared but little for keeping a diary from here, I cannot give the exact date of our departure from Crab Orchard. Our march to Lebanon brought us again to Danville, thence to Harrodsburg, where we camped. When the sun arose the next morning, we were already on the march which we continued until we had reached Danville and the sun disappeared. As there was not water enough for the horses and men, we were compelled to march five miles further to a creek. Hundreds of the men did not reach the creek on account of being too tired and having sore feet. The road from Danville to the creek was covered with stragglers and sick soldiers, while in every fence corner one or more sleepers could be seen. Myself and my comrades H. D. and H. F. belonged to the worn-out men, and without thinking of supper, stretched ourselves in the cool grass of a meadow to sleep, and let the others who chose to endeavor to follow their officers in order to get to the creek.

The next morning, after taking coffee, pork and crackers, we packed our "things," and went towards the creek in search of our regiment. The regiment, however, had left, and we were compelled to continue the march alone. We reached the regiment just after the dinner was over, and had scarcely taken our places, when the order to move on was given. We reached

41 (W. J. Cox n.d.)
42 (DeRosier 1969, 31)

Perryville after a march of eight miles at five o'clock P.M. and went into camp. But a few days had passed after the battle between Bragg's and Buell's command, and this was the first battle-field we had ever seen. The houses were riddled by bullets and inhabited or rather filled with the wounded of both armies. The inhabitants were gone, either to the rebel or to the Union army. The dead had been interred but lightly, and here and there a leg or hand was protruding out the ground, or lying unburied. The devastating effects of war were but too plainly to be seen. Here we remained but one night, and continued our march early the next morning. Despite the stony and sandy road, that frequently led through the bottom of a creek, we made twenty-four miles that day, and camped only a few miles from Lebanon. As our place of destination was Lebanon, we commenced our march the next day later than usual and reached Lebanon about noon. I had kept my diary very accurately till now, but lost all pleasure in its continuation in consequence of the hardships we passed through. The wish to continue the diary, arose again on Christmas, 1863, and from there I did not stop with it until my safe return home. If I remember right, we remained at Lebanon but one or two days, when we were ordered to Bowling Green, Ky.

ALBERTUS DUNHAM, CO C 129TH ILL: I suppose you heard of the Perryville fight. We was on the battlefield a few days after the fight, it was a horrible site. Our men were well buried but some secesh were covered with straw some with brush and some pretending to be buried but thare hands and feat were sticking out. The town was pretty well riddled, one house I counted 18 cannon balls through it. .43

Does the sight and smell of death and destruction, the dread of facing pain and mortality far from home, worry the mind of inexperienced soldiers, who have not yet faced battle? More such sights would come before their own turn.

Coffee

Complain about hard tack and pork, a soldier might, but he could not go without coffee.

There is a good deal of complaint, in our company at least, about the coffee we get. It seems not quite so good as that we have had, and I suspect it has been adulterated by somebody who is willing to get rich at the expense of the poor soldier, whose curses will be heaped strong and heavy on anybody who deteriorates any of his rations, and particularly his coffee. The only

43 (DeRosier 1969, 31)

time a soldier cannot drink his coffee is when the use of that ration is suspended. In fact, there is nothing so refreshing as a cup of hot coffee, and no sooner has a marching column halted, than out from each haversack comes a little paper sack of ground coffee, and a tin cup or tin can, with a wire bale, to be filled from the canteen and set upon a fire to boil. The coffee should not be put in the water before it boils. At first I was green enough to do so, but soon learned better, being compelled to march before the water boiled, and consequently lost my coffee. I lost both the water and the coffee.

It takes but about five minutes to boil a cup of water, and then if you have to march you can put your coffee in and carry it till it is cool enough to sip as you go. Even if we halt a dozen times a day, that many times will a soldier make and drink his coffee, for when the commissary is full and plenty, we may drink coffee and nibble crackers from morning till night. The aroma of the first cup of coffee soon sets the whole army to boiling; and the best vessel in which to boil coffee for a soldier is a common cove oyster can, with a bit of bent wire for a bale, by which you can hold it on a stick over the fire, and thus avoid its tipping over by the burning away of its supports. 44

44 (Oldroyd 1885, 60) Oldroyd was discussing his own company's coffee at the time.

Bowling Green, a Whole Month

Buell had not pursued Bragg after the Battle of Perryville and was replaced by William Rosecrans on October 24. General Thomas had been offered command but deferred to Rosecrans, who Washington then expected to drive Bragg out of Tennessee. The 14th Corps was renamed the Army of the Cumberland.

> GRUNERT, CO D 129TH ILL: Here we were for some time, and at one time Gen. Rosecran's held review. Our time was spent in drilling and doing guard duty.

> ALBERTUS DUNHAM, CO C 129TH ILL: November 4-5 Since we left Louisville, we have marched 250 miles. Have not slept under shelter but two nights since we left Louisville. Slept on the ground with nothing but our blankets over us, the earth for a bed. A week ago last Sabbath-morning, woke up and found four inches of snow on top of our blankets. We have had a very hard time so far, but I gues we will fair better now. We lived on crackers so hard that if we loaded our guns with them we could of killed seceshs in a hurry. Day before yesterday we received our tents, and since we camped have had bakers bread and fresh beaf which is quite a treat. .45

With the brigade not wandering, the sick were taken to camp with their units. William Cox has not recovered.

> COX, JOHN THOMAS, CO F 129TH ILL: November 8. Dear brother ... I am well at present ... I am out on picket guard and we expect to have a good time. We are about one mile from camp and about two miles from Bowling Green. Father came up from camp yesterday. He is able to eat a little but he is very weak yet and looks worse than I ever saw him. He has had a very hard time and I am going to do my best to get him a discharge so he can go home. .46

The brigade moved to Mitchellsville, Kentucky November 21 and in December was guarding the railroad from Bowling Green to Gallatin.

Rosecrans remained in Nashville, and Bragg went into winter quarters at Murphreesboro while Morgan spent the winter disrupting the Union Army wherever he could.

45 (DeRosier 1969, 33)
46 (W. J. Cox n.d.)

November - Guerillas in Tennessee

Mitchellsville

GRUNERT, CO D 129TH ILL: We were then ordered to Mitchellsville, Tennessee, where we also remained a longer period, until part of the regiment was ordered to Buck's Lodge, a station on the Louisville-Nashville Railroad. Our chief duty now was to keep the rebels and guerrillas from the road between Gallatin and Mitchellsville, which we did with a good will. The hiding places of the guerillas were soon known to us, and no accidents happened on that part of the road under our control, as long as we remained there. The guerrillas were completely powerless. We did not see anything of them until Christmas 1863.

Sunday Dinner

Some soldiers became almost local citizens, as did scout Blakeslee.

BLAKESLEE TO PEDDICORD: Buck Lodge Station is about 3 miles south of Fountain Head just beyon Sanders Tan yard. Old man Ashford lived close by – Our camp there was at the water tanks at Staggs – across the creek lived Robert McCloud—and we called our camp—"Camp Mccloud" further on toward S Tunnel lived – & still lives Sam King—there was two bridges R.R. west of his house—we knew them as Kings Bridges we had a stockade there in charge of this post one dark & stormy night some of You'ns tried to stamped We'uns – but no one was hurt but our fusilade brought reinforcements of 10 men from the Camp on the run #

Old Father Ashford at B. Lodge then an old man, always expected me to Sunday dinner in 62 ... Widdow Clendening—"Mother Clen" our boys used to call her—we had more men captured at her house an several Killed from ambush there # until Col Smith had orders to burn her house. .47

PEAK, CO F 129TH ILL: Just the month we were stationed at Mitchellsville, I don't remember, as I had lost all interest in keeping account of what had taken place, and seldom knew the day of the month. While we were stationed here several of our men died with the measles. Three of Co. F. died, some of Co. I. and quite a number of Co. E. The weather was cold and damp, and when one took the measles, it meant almost every case, sure death. A man by the name of Green, who belonged to Co. I, said to me one

---

47 (G. H. Blakeslee, Correspondence with K. F. Peddicord n.d.)

day when I visited the hospital, to see some of the boys that were sick, that he expected to take his last ride from this place if he took the measles. The next day it was reported he had taken the measles, and the third day he had taken his last ride. So fatal was the measles that the men who had never had them became frightened at the number of deaths, and the officers asked to be assigned some other post of duty, which they were granted. We were sent to Bugs Logg, some 10 or 12 miles south of Mitchellsville. The regiment seemed to have run away from the measles as none of the men took it at Buck Logg.

Thomas White died at Bucks Logg, with some kind of camp fever, and some of the boys had the malaria fever, while we were camped in the valley, close to the creek. Our camp was moved to the west side of the railroad, on a high piece of ground, where all seemed to enjoy the best of health, so long as we remained camped at Buck Logg. 48

Potatoes and Peddicord

PEAK, CO F 129TH ILL: When our regiment was stationed at Bucks Lodge, Tennessee, a company of ours went foraging one day with Lieutenant Smith, to get hay and corn for the mules. The hay was stacked in the meadow west of the farm house. Soon the last forkfull was on the wagons, and the boys began to make a search for something that possibly had been buried under the stacks and to our surprise we soon found a lot of potatoes buried under one of the stacks. Lieutenant Smith informed us we were sent after corn and hay, and corn and hay was all that he would allow to go to camp. We were to return to the field that night with sacks and carry away as many potatoes as we could. This was rather a hazardly undertaking, for there was two companies of rebel cavalry scouring that section of the country of nights, but that did not appease our appetite for potatoes. We were soon at the place where the potatoes were buried, and had our sacks filled with as many potatoes as we could carry, and was about ready to start on our return trip, when a company of rebel cavalry came dashing up to the farm house from the east. The moon was shining bright at that time, and I gave the order to lie down, so it would be difficult for the rebels to see us, but we could see them. They halted at the house and a number of them dismounted, leaving some to hold their horses. When the rebels saw us running for the timber, as many of them as were in a position to do so made a dash to head us off, but we beat them to it. I think I can almost hear you say they were dear potatoes, and they would be if the value of the potatoes were all. It was the

48 (Peak 1931)

key to open the way for a raiding party to be organized and sent out to their farmhouse, only two nights later, when they were successful in capturing the notorious Petecord, a bush whacker, who had captured several of our boys.

This was not all that little foraging party brought to light. An old rebel by the name of Captain Curby Smith, purporting to be a Union man, made daily visits to our camp, and would make speeches to the boys. He was taken and put in military prison at Nashville, Tenn.

We decided to bury them for a while, and when everything was quiet we were enjoying our baked potatoes. Uncle Ned came in for a good share of them, for baking them for us.

After Petecord and Captain Curby Smith's capture, the camp soon became very quiet. We had no fear of eating our potatoes, which seemed to have the best taste of any potatoes I ever ate. .49

Now Father and Son Cox are both sick from exhaustion and bad airs.

COX, WILLIAM, CO F 129TH ILL: Mitchellsville, December the 4th. Dear wife and family. I take my pen in hand to inform you that I am now in the tent with John Thomas and have been for 3 days and nights. I have just left the hospital where I have been since the 4th day of October. I am yet very poorly. Just now some of the boys of our regiment is a getting my discharge and God being my helper I will be with you in 15 or 30 days ... John Thomas is not very well. He is very restive and has no appetite to eat and is beginning to look very pale. I hope he will not have to go to the hospital for it is a bad place. .50

On December 6, Confederate General Morgan led his cavalry from Lebanon to capture an entire brigade of Yankee soldiers, both infantry and cavalry, near Hartsville. This raid helped establish Morgan's reputation and caused much consternation in Union command. .51

49 Uncle Ned started staying with the company much later, at a different location, in Peak's memoir. Allowing Peak some leeway for memory in his 90s of events many years ago, Uncle Ned remains in the story of the potatoes.
50 (W. J. Cox n.d.)
51 (Logan 1908, 50-60)

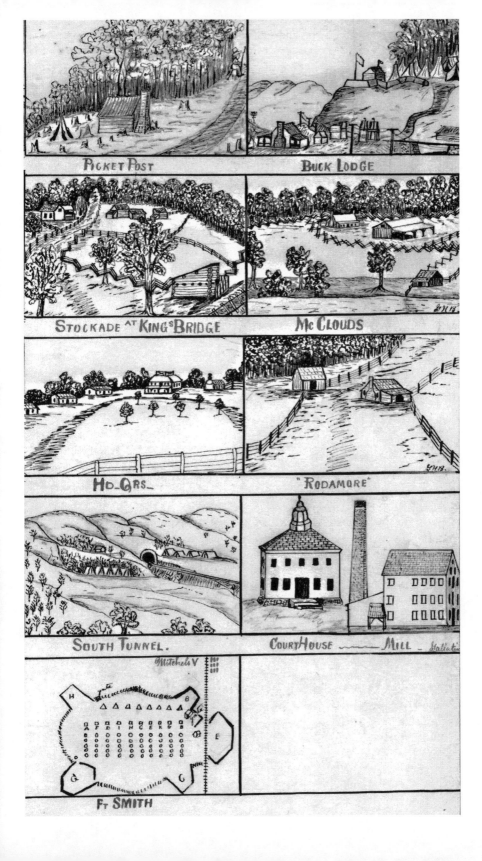

PICKET POST

BUCK LODGE

STOCKADE AT KING'S BRIDGE

McCLOUDS

HD. QRS.

"RODAMORE"

SOUTH TUNNEL.

COURT HOUSE ——— MILL — Gallatin

FT. SMITH

Let the Dead Bury Their Dead

MERRILL, 70TH IND: It was naturally hard for Kentucky Union officers to keep from grieving for the devastation that necessarily swept over their State, in having it made the seat of war. The commander of the post, Colonel S. D. Bruce, a very pleasant gentleman, was a Kentuckian, as one might gather from his instructions to a Captain who had charge of a scouting expedition: "Tell your men to beware of entering orchards, or cornfields." "Any other instructions, Sir?" "No! Well, yes. You may also tell them to be on the alert for Morgan." We cannot wonder at the bitter words in a letter of the officer so instructed: "It is more important to keep the men from surprising a corn field, or a turnip patch, than to keep Morgan from surprising the men. And this, too, while poor fellows from want of fresh food are sickening daily unto death."

The hot days and cold nights of September, the water, the half-cooked beans, the pancakes soaked with grease, the want of variety, resulted in numerous cases of sickness. At first the men from the farms suffered most, as they had been unaccustomed to irregularities in sleep and had not been exposed to contagious diseases, such as the measles, mumps, and whooping cough, but it was not long until almost every one paid the penalty to the radical changes in the method of living.

In spite of all precautions many went to the comfortless hospital, where millions of flies and insects more disgusting rioted, and there remained till their comrades bore them out for burial. Company after company formed with reversed arms and followed the wailing fife and muffled drum, as the wild melody of Pleyel's Hymn, or other equally solemn tune, quivered on the air. When the order came, no more funeral dirges, no more volleys over the sleeping dust, because of the depressing effect on those who tremblingly trod the border line of life and death, all began to learn the stern nature of war. No place for the delicate attentions of affection, no place for tokens of regard for the departed, no place for sighs, no place for tears. "Let the dead bury their dead."

In a letter an officer says: "My company seems to be fated. After I had come to the conclusion that so many had died, surely no more would be taken, four died in less than a week. Strange that life in the open air, with really but little exposure for we have not seen hard service should result so unfortunately. I am weary of being Captain. It is so terrible to see men die whom one has persuaded from their homes." 52

Officers' families often came to help in nursing the sick and wounded.

JANE KETCHAM, 70TH IND: While the Seventieth was at Bowling Green I worked in the kitchen at home, putting up quantities of jelly, marmalade, pickles of every variety, anything that would be a relish with their bacon, beans, hard tack and rice. I even tried to make concentrated milk, which the boys thought too good to dissolve in coffee and ate as candy. As a relief to this kind of work I visited the hospitals in the city, and in the evening sat in my corner knitting. One Sunday evening some of the family happened to look at me, and exclaimed at my knitting, just as on week days. I had heard how the soldiers suffered for want of socks, and I could not sit still and think of their cold, bare feet.

"When Dr. Bullard returned from Gallatin and told his story of the suffering, he asked, Are there no two women who will go? Miss Bates responded at once. I pondered over it. Leave such a family? But how many husbands had left their wives and children; how many sons their homes. Yes, I could go. I could surely trust the children to those around and to Providence. I might knit on forever, make all the good things I could and send boxes, but in a few weeks nursing perhaps I could save life. At any rate I could do far more than I was doing. So Miss Bates and I were made ready and were off with speed toward our field of labor. 53

Miss Bates was aunt of Major Vance. Jane Merrill Ketcham was Lt. Colonel Merrill's sister and mother of Sergeant Major John Lewis Ketcham Jr. Wish this book had room for her and others' stories of the sick and wounded.

MERRILL, 70TH IND: (Late December) While we were at Edgefield Junction Sergeant Wm. Griggs 54 died. He was a fine soldier, a noble young man, and greatly beloved by all his comrades. A messenger was sent to headquarters with the request that the Chaplain come and conduct the funeral services, but we were informed that he had gone to Indianapolis on leave. Then we concluded to bury our dead comrade with such services as we could improvise. The Captain read a chapter from the Bible, spoke a few

---

52 (S. Merrill 1900, 16)
53 (S. Merrill 1900, 16)
54 Died Dec. 21, 70th Indiana Roster Company E
https://civilwarindex.com/armyin/soldiers/70th_in_infantry_soldiers.pdf

words, and others made remarks. An appropriate hymn was sung, and we were about to lower the coffin into the grave, when one of the soldiers, looking up, saw our Colonel riding over the hill behind us. He had come down to supply the place of the Chaplain. He dismounted, uncovered, walked to the edge of the grave, extended his hands over the coffin, and offered one of the most feeling and eloquent prayers to which we had ever listened. Then the remains were lowered into the grave, the earth thrown in, the salute fired, and the sad rite was finished. It was a touching scene, the funeral of that soldier on the hillside in Tennessee, away from his young wife, his parents, and his many dear friends at home. .55

COX, WILLIAM, CO F 129TH ILL: December 22. Dear wife and family, It is with sadness that I sit down and write you these few lines and that I am compelled to tell you that we have lost a dutiful and affectionate son and that the family have lost a brother. John Thomas is no more. He died yesterday after several weeks sickness. The doctors said he had the lung fever. We shall all miss him greatly but I think he is where sickness and sorrow pain and death is felt and feared no more. .56

John Thomas left a widow. William Cox died December 23, two days after his son. Back home, his widow and eight other children faced the future without him.

The Battle of Stones River

On December 22, Morgan began another raid, crossing the Cumberland at Carthage, and reaching well toward Louisville, returning at the end of the year, having helped Bragg's effort at Murphreesboro in the Battle of Stones River. .57

Rosecrans and Bragg slugged it out at Stones River starting December 31, but Bragg retreated in the face of continuing Union reinforcements.

55 (S. Merrill 1900, 50) The 70th Indiana was stationed 40 miles from Stones River at the time and could hear the sound of the cannon in the battle.
56 (W. J. Cox n.d.)
57 (Logan 1908, 63-81)

GRUNERT, CO D 129TH ILL: This was at the time when the two great armies under Rosecrans and Bragg were confronting each other at Murfreesboro, Tenn. and fighting the battle on Stone River. In times when the great armies

BATTLE OF STONE RIVER, TENN.—DECISIVE CHARGE AND CAPTURE OF BYRNES CONFEDERATE BATTERY BY THE SEVENTY-EIGHTH PENNSYLVANIA AND TWENTY-FIRST OHIO VOLUNTEERS.

were lying idle, the bushwhackers generally remained quiet, but were very troublesome when these were making some move or fighting, in order to prevent the transportation of provisions, ammunition, etc. But all their efforts were of no avail. As mentioned above, the 129th Ills. regt. was stationed at Buck's Lodge, six miles above Gallatin, at a water tank of the Louisville-Nashville Railroad, when we heard of the approach of a strong band of guerrillas, whose object seemed to be to steal on us, attack us suddenly and then destroy the road, bridges, water tanks, etc. But our officers and men were on the alert. Christmas night, when the news came that the neighborhood was full of rebels, we were under arms. The guards were reinforced and instructed to keep quiet, strong patrols went up and down the road, while the balance of the regiment was under arms in camp. From 2 o'clock until sunrise we waited and watched patiently, a grave-like silence reigned, but no enemy appeared. As the danger seemed past, we stacked arms to satisfy the cravings of our stomachs by a hearty breakfast. Great prudence was nevertheless necessary, and the men were allowed to leave the camp only in large numbers. Several companies were now sent to Fountain Head, several miles north of us, where they did guard duty for some time, while we spent our time in drilling and trench work. Sometimes we would scour the neighborhood in search of guerrillas and forage "for man and beast."

The bi-monthly muster and review took place on the December 31, 1862.

After the battle, Rosecrans moved headquarters to Murphreesboro. Bragg was not far away, in Shelbyville. Then began a period of harassment of Federal troops, and ambushes of the railroad, where the 129th and others of the brigade were stationed. Morgan was headquartered at McMinnville.

Picket Duty and Other Pleasantries

Let's pause here to get an idea of what picket duty amounted to on a winter night, compliments of Brown, of the 27th Indiana:

> BROWN, CO C 27TH INDIANA: One night during the winter there was an unusually heavy, wet snow; it accumulated upon the trees until it broke down and uprooted a great many, and stripped the limbs off of a still larger number. All night long, there was a continuous snapping and roaring in the forests, followed by the crash of the falling timber, until one might have supposed there was a battle in progress. When relieved the next morning the men on picket could scarcely get to camp, as those who relieved them could scarcely get out from camp.

> Another night a picket awoke the echoes, in the stillness of the dark jungle, and had the reserve rush to his aid at break-neck speed, through the tangled undergrowth and over the rough ground, by firing his musket at an old horse, that was grazing outside. Nobody believed him when he said he had mistaken the old horse for a mounted rebel scout. They all knew he was only tired of standing out there alone.

> Many nights were so inky dark that no one could see anything. Even those objects near at hand could be discerned quite as well with the eyes closed as open. For the relief to cross the various foot-logs, and get around to the different posts, was a great undertaking. At every foot-log one or more of the men fell into the creek, which at the time was a roaring torrent.

> Several nights the pole-cats almost stampeded the entire Third Brigade picket line. They were really expected to assail the line every night. The rocky ledges along the creek furnished them a natural place of rendezvous,

and, sallying out in platoons and battalions, they were formidable foes. Their military pomp may not have been quite equal to ours, but their equipment for effective, aggressive warfare was hard to withstand. A peculiar advantage they possessed over us was that, if any difference, they were more to be dreaded dead than alive. The old, old maxim is certainly true in a war with pole-cats, if nowhere else, namely, "Discretion is the better part of valor." One of our American humorists says, "He is called a pole-cat, because it is always best to handle him with a pole, and the longer the pole the better."

There was more snow this winter than the winter before, several very deep ones. One at least, was sixteen inches on the level. There was also the endless amount of rain, peculiar to the South in war-time. One might conclude on noting how all the data of that period are burdened with references to rain and snow, that there was no fair weather whatever. Yet there was. There were very many clear, sunny days this winter, delightfully mild and cheerful. On such days all the camps were full of life. With those off duty, or in the intervals of drill and other responsibilities, numberless pastimes, games, trials of strength and of speed, visits to other camps, shopping errands to different suttlers, etc., etc., were the order. The hardship and drudgery of picket duty were largely mitigated this winter by the sociability and good fellowship of those detailed for it. No better instance could be cited showing how elastic the spirits of young soldiers were, and how completely they adjusted themselves to all conditions. Fidelity to duty was balanced with relaxation and amusement the extent that many will remember pleasantly. Around blazing log heaps the men of the reserve played games, spun yarns, related former experiences and achievements (never the least bit colored, of course) cracked jokes (never stale ones) and discussed all kinds of questions, the livelong night. This was not only a pastime, but greatly promoted mutual acquaintance, especially between men of different companies, who saw little of each other at other times. Friendships were then formed that have continued to the present. Despite the uncanny locality, and some as foul weather as only Southern weather could be, in war time, we came off duty in a cheerful state of mind, and not dreading to have our turn come again.

Another feature of picket duty here (and camp guard as well) that the boys will not forget, was the many clear, far sounding bugle calls, that were usually the first harbingers of the approaching day. A number of artillery and cavalry commands were encamped in the vicinity, and some of them must have been upon higher ground than most of the surrounding region.

The buglers, too, must have been unusually proficient. They could sound a bugle equal to Gabriel himself. Almost the first intimation that the lonely sentinel, pacing his beat in the darkness, would have that light was about to dawn, would be the loud and distinct, but really sweet and beautiful, notes of one of these bugles, sounding the reveille. How that bugler would wake the echoes in every valley and glen and in every nook and jungle! With what a prolonged, stirring crescendo he would sound the last notes. Immediately other buglers would take up the same call and. one after another, the fife and drum corps would join in, with their squeak and clatter, until the whole region to our rear would be in a pleasing uproar. .58

Guarding Railroad - Bowling Green to Gallatin

I expect to hear that the rebels fell off their horses and broke their necks. —Paine

From January to June, the 129th Illinois was spread out from Bowling Green to Gallatin.

Here the brigade was in the service of a notorious general who General Grant, from experiences earlier, in Cairo, Illinois and Paducah, Kentucky, had declared "unfit to command any post." Still, connections with politicians kept him in command of garrisons. General Paine dealt with guerillas harshly—and not just the guerillas themselves. The population was guilty until shown to be otherwise..59

The Reign of Terror in Tennessee

TROUSDALE: In November, 1862, by order of General Rosecrans, E. A. Paine, a brigadier-general of volunteers, United States Army, established his headquarters at Gallatin, and remained in command there until May 8, 1864. He commanded the military district embraced between the southern boundary line of Kentucky and the north bank of the Cumberland River in Tennessee, as well as the post at Gallatin.

As military governor of a conquered district, he revealed the true inwardness of his unenviable nature, in which were discovered a painful absence of all that was noble and philanthropic, and traits unspeakably inhuman, malicious, and degrading. He looked upon those under his sway as criminals until their innocence was established, and regarded their rights

58 (E. R. Brown 1899, 294)
59 (Logan 1908, 63)

of life, liberty, and property as forfeited, and only to be enjoyed subject to his will. His tribunal was his own self-sufficient person, acting as judge and jury, though not always directly as executioner.

As to how many men were thus executed and are clearly chargeable to the same crimson accounts, the statements of the witnesses in the records referred to vary widely. General Paine's depositions were taken in these cases, and we quote his language on this point: "I only recollect of ordering two to be shot, and they were shot without trial." Another witness says of it: "I think he killed about twenty or thirty men in Sumner County while in command at Gallatin." And another, who resided in Gallatin throughout this eventful and trying period, a man of mature age, intelligence, professional reputation, and promise, states: "Upon one occasion, the day I think that Reese was taken out and shot, I heard Paine say (if my recollection serves me right,) as to the number, that he (Reese) made the one hundred and sixth man that he had killed."

I heard General Paine repeatedly say that he had ordered his officers in charge of scouting parties, to bring in no prisoners, but to shoot the scoundrels down whenever they caught them, I am not positive that I heard him say how many he had caused to be shot; but to the best of my recollection he said he had shot, or caused to be shot, one on every road leading into Gallatin. I never knew him to have any man tried while he was in command here. There are a great many roads leading into Gallatin. 60

Emancipation, Guerillas, Work, Wet

Lincoln's Emancipation Proclamation was made official January 1. Tennessee was unaffected because it was not in rebellion.

GRUNERT, CO D 129TH ILL: JANUARY 1, 1863. The day was beautiful. We were busy digging trenches. The trains had come very irregular and for several days no mail had arrived. Nothing of importance happened until the 3d of January, when two trains ran into each other near our camp. Both trains came from Louisville, and the first had been delayed. The locomotive of the last train was totally destroyed, several cars were smashed to pieces and two persons badly wounded.

January 5th. I was on picket duty; the day was very pleasant. We received good news from the army of the Potomac. The next day passed without anything of importance.

60 (Trousdale 1885) This is an extract from a much longer indictment.

January 7th. The day was clear and pleasantly cold. Myself and several comrades went several miles from camp, where we found a German family, the first in the neighborhood. We were well received and kindly treated. In the afternoon we worked on the trenches.

January 8th. I was again on picket duty on this cold and rainy day. My place was in a deep hollow near the railroad. The night was dark, and rain and snow coming down in an unpleasant way.

January 9th. Two members of our company, Jordan H. Whitehurst and John died to-day. Three trains with rebel prisoners passed north. A rebel captain was brought in a prisoner by our scouts. The night was very rainy.

January 10, 1863. The whole day was rainy and cold.

LAFOREST DUNHAM, CO C 129TH ILL: I take my pen in hand to write you the painful news of the death of dear Albertus. He died Jan. the 7 about 4 o'clock in the afternoon. He was out of his head most of the time during his sickness. When he was in his write mind he wanted me to read the Bible to him ... The boys in the company got a nice hed board and set out to nice cedar treas, one at the head and one at the foot, and Delos Robinson and myself made a fence around it. .61

GRUNERT, CO D 129TH ILL: January 11, 1863. The day was very cold and I had the pleasure of doing picket duty.

January 12, 1863. Another cold day—everything was very quiet. We received a very large mail.

January 13, 1863. A negro that had been shot by his master, but not fatally wounded, came to us and offered his services, "to live and die with us," he said. Several companies had to go to Buck's Lodge to reinforce the part of the regiment stationed there.

January 14, 1863. I was again doing picket duty. The morning was very rainy, and turned afterwards to snowing and became so cold that I could hardly move a limb.

January 15, 1863. A snow of five inches, accompanied by great cold fell. On arising we found our blankets frozen tight to the ground and covered with sleet. It is hardly necessary to say that we froze very much.

January 16, 1863. Despite the chilling blast and snow I had to stand guard, but as permission had been given to kindle a fire, I liked the day better than the day before in camp. A number of volunteers were demanded to-day to go in search of a gang of guerrillas. They left the camp in the evening.

January 17. The cold weather continued. The road was out of order and no trains passed. A company was ordered to go in search of the volunteers that

61 (DeRosier 1969, 51)

went on a guerrilla hunt. We had heard nothing from them since they left. Both detachments soon returned, without having seen a trace of the enemy.

January 18. A strong detail was sent out foraging with wagons and returned well loaded before nightfall.

January 19. The unpleasant duty of standing guard in a very heavy rain was my lot to-day, and wet to the skin I returned to camp the next morning.

January 20. Another cold day; all quiet in camp.

January 21. Since standing guard the last time I felt sick and broken down in consequence of getting wet. A friend thought I would have to go to the hospital.

January 22. I felt decidedly better to-day, well enough to go along with a foraging party. The negro mentioned above, shot by his master, was our guide, and led us immediately to the house of his (former) master, where we confiscated everything that we could use. The negro took a couple of blankets along, and under his lead we returned with our well loaded wagons towards evening into camp.

January 23. Although not entirely well, I went on picket duty again. Three men of Morgan's command surrendered to-day. Fifteen men on horseback, under command of our (then) Colonel Smith scoured the country in order to confiscate all serviceable horses of the rebels. Part of our regiment was to be mounted to clear the surrounding country of rebels.

January 24. We received another mail to-day and the trains are running regular again. We had much fun to-day and spent the time with music and singing until we went to bed.

January 25. The day was rainy; nevertheless we were inspected by a staff officer of Gen. Ward, and our drill and general looks were perfectly satisfactory to Col. Smith, as well as to the inspecting officer. This satisfaction was a hint that we were sufficiently posted in tactics and rules of warfare to be sent to the front.

Hooker's Promotion

Lincoln placed "Fighting Joe" Hooker as Commander of the Army of the Potomac, his first command above corps level, on January 25, despite misgivings:

I have placed you at the head of the Army of the Potomac. Of course I have done this upon what appear to me to be sufficient reasons. And yet I think it best for you to know that there are some things in regard to which, I am not quite satisfied with you. I believe you to be a brave and a skilful soldier, which, of course, I like. I also believe you do not mix politics with your profession, in which you are right. You have confidence in yourself, which is a valuable, if not an indispensable quality. You are ambitious, which, within

51

reasonable bounds, does good rather than harm. But I think that during Gen. Burnside's command of the Army, you have taken counsel of your ambition, and thwarted him as much as you could, in which you did a great wrong to the country, and to a most meritorious and honorable brother officer. I have heard, in such way as to believe it, of your recently saying that both the Army and the Government needed a Dictator. Of course it was not for this, but in spite of it, that I have given you the command. Only those generals who gain successes, can set up dictators. What I now ask of you is military success, and I will risk the dictatorship. The government will support you to the utmost of it's ability, which is neither more nor less than it has done and will do for all commanders. I much fear that the spirit which you have aided to infuse into the Army, of criticising their Commander, and withholding confidence from him, will now turn upon you. I shall assist you as far as I can, to put it down. Neither you, nor Napoleon, if he were alive again, could get any good out of an army, while such a spirit prevails in it.

And now, beware of rashness. Beware of rashness, but with energy, and sleepless vigilance, go forward, and give us victories. .62

Hooker was moved:

That is just such a letter as a father might write to his son. It is a beautiful letter, and, although I think he was harder on me than I deserved, I will say that I love the man who wrote it.

Hooker's career is now on the line. Lincoln and the country depend on him. While Hooker looks for how and where to defeat Lee, our brigade goes about their business. Their roads will meet at Resaca.

GRUNERT, CO D 129TH ILL: January 26. In the forenoon we received firewood for a couple of days. In the afternoon I was detailed with several others to guard some female prisoners, among them the wife of the noted and feared guerrilla chief Petticord, in a neighboring house. It rained hard the whole day.

January 27. News was received that a large quantity of salt was to be smuggled by the rebels close by, and a number of men, among which myself, under command of Capt. Flynn and Lieutenant Haldeman were ordered to capture it. All mounted, and with a faithful guide, we left camp immediately after breakfast, and rode in full gallop to our place of destination. Evening

62   (Lincoln, The Collected Works of Abraham Lincoln 1809-1865 n.d.) https://www.abrahamlincolnonline.org/lincoln/speeches/hooker.htm

came, and we were yet without any positive information of the whereabouts of the smuggler. As night came on and we were unacquainted with the country, we resolved to go to a neighboring mill for information and then seek a shelter for the night. The mill was not far from Franklin, Ky. and soon reached. But unfortunately we were separated from it by a creek very high in consequence of the heavy rains and over which no bridge could lead us to the mill. To swim through seemed impossible and too hazardous. The miller was called, and asked about the narrowest and shoalest place of the creek. The place was shown us, but the miller thought that the current would be too strong for us to cross. The feeling of finding our reward in the mill, however, overpowered every other consideration. Lieutenant Haldeman kneeled on his horse, led it to the water, and although only after great exertions and danger, the horse reached the other side of the creek. We followed the example, fastened our muskets and cartridge-boxes around our necks as well as we could, so they could not get wet, and in a few minutes joined our lieutenant on the other side of the creek. The mill and neighboring houses were thoroughly searched, but all labor was in vain; our swim through the creek had been for nought and we were obliged to swim the creek another time, in order to find a shelter for the night and to attend to our jaded horses. The sun had long disappeared, darkness reigned everywhere, and the cold had given the ground a hard surface. As we all got more or less wet, it may be imagined that our situation on horseback was not a very enviable one. We would rather have camped in the bushes close by, but our commander, Capt. Flynn, would not listen to such a proposition, until about ten o'clock we reached a well filled corn crib and a large farm-house. The inhabitants were at first very much frightened at this armed visit at night, but were soon pacified on being told whence we came and what our object was. A couple of negroes took charge of our horses, after which we went to the house, where shortly after we were invited to a substantial supper. After supper beds were prepared and guards posted, the beds we refused, because our clothes were too wet, and because it was not advisable to "strip." We laid down around a roaring chimney fire on the floor of a room, where we slept soundly the next morning, better than in a feather bed.

January 28. Before daybreak we were up again, and after having taken a substantial breakfast and our horses a sufficient quantity of corn and hay, we intended to confiscate horses in the neighborhood, doubting the successful accomplishment of the object of our expedition, the capture of the salt smugglers. The horses were completely worn out, and the horses of the neighboring farmers were not much better, the good ones having been confiscated already. We determined to send three men back to the camp, over twenty miles distant, and fetch fresh horses. At this moment we heard the noise of galloping horses and our guards cry "halt." Our frightened commander gathered his small and scattered force as quickly as possible, when several "blue jackets" hastily rode up and made ready for firing. The officer of the party now demanded of us who we were and what we were after. Satisfactory answers having been given, we learned that we had been pursued by Union troops. The miller, to whom we had paid a visit the night before, had immediately after our departure sent word to the commanding officer of the Union troops at Franklin, that what he supposed to be a fact, "guerrillas in Union uniforms had been at his mill." This officer immediately sent half a regiment of cavalry in our pursuit. This mutual explanation caused a good deal of merriment, and the cavalry returned to Franklin, while three of our men returned to the camp. The others scoured the country for horses, and succeeded in finding and bringing away eleven very fine horses.

On January 29, General Grant was given command of the west, with orders to capture Vicksburg, the Confederate stranglehold on the Mississippi.

GRUNERT, CO D 129TH ILL: JANUARY 29. A detail was sent to Gallatin, Tenn. as escort of a train for provisions. The guerrilla chief Petticord sent a flag of truce which was admitted into camp, with the following propositions:

1. The return of all property confiscated by our men, to its rightful owner; 2. this done, to surrender; 3. in case of refusal of these propositions to prepare to smell powder. The last proposition we were willing to accept. The flag of truce, however, was not allowed to leave the camp again. We received additional ammunition, and towards evening one hundred men on foot and twenty mounted men were sent out to see if there really was danger, while the remainder of the regiment staid in camp under arms. The night passed as peaceably as the former.

January 30. Our detail returned without having found a trace of the enemy.

January 31. A number of rebel prisoners were sent to Gallatin, Tenn. among them the bearer of Petticord's flag of truce.

PAINE, BRIG. GEN: 1863 Feb 1, At dusk last evening an outlaw by the name of Peddicord, with 40 men, tore up four or five rails in the Richland Woods, about 14 miles from here. They were attempting to burn a cattle guard on the road, when 15 men of the One hundred and twenty-ninth Illinois approached. The rebels ran. They were dressed in our overcoats. I have 350 men after them, and I expect to hear that the rebels fell off their horses and broke their necks. Fifty or more citizens collected at the place with the rebels, to look on, aid, and assist. I propose to make an example of some of them. The trains are running. .63

GRUNERT, CO D 129TH ILL: February 1. The day was rainy, and nothing of importance happened. The general subject of conversation was our pending move, as we had received marching orders the day before.

The "Kentucky Policy"

Kentucky, not having seceded, was not subject to the Emancipation Proclamation. So slaves there were not yet free and some sought shelter in Union camps. As noted earlier, Colonel John Coburn, commanding the brigade that included the 22nd Wisconsin, had before the war defended free negroes in Indiana from those who attempted to claim them as slaves and take them south. During their stay in Kentucky, Coburn's brigade was harassed by slave owners coming into camp and taking slaves who had sought shelter. The general in charge at the time, Gilmore, allowed it. General Thomas, a Virginian, was not particular about it if the claimant said he was "a Union Man." A Kentucky supreme court judge was persistent in attempts to take away one small slave who he had treated miserably. Colonel Utley, of the 22nd Wisconsin, in Coburn's brigade, resisted strenuously. His whole regiment was behind Utley in the matter. They left Danville, Kentucky on their way to Louisville, the slave with them, by marching down the street with fixed bayonets. When they left Louisville in February, the judge tried again.

DICKINSON, CO E 22ND WIS COBURN 2B 3D 20C: The 22nd Wis. Staid in camp at Louisville until 10am Feb. 1st. The rest of the brigade went on board the transports, the day before, and we were left behind, alone, and there came near being a riot in the city when we marched down the street, to the river, to go on board the steamer.

Here happened our second meeting with Judge Robertson. The first was in Georgetown, and he, failing to get his slave at that time, declared he would have him now; that no slave up to that date, had left the state with the northern soldiers, and should not, now.

63 (OR, Series I Vol 23 Part 2 Serial 35: Reports n.d., 33)

The citizens were lined up along the sidewalk, the whole length of the regiment and the slave was marching to the rear of Co. H. and the right of Co. E. and when the column halted, the judge was on the walk opposite the boy, he rushed onto the ranks, seized him by the shoulder, and tried to drag him out; but the first file of Co. E. composed of the four tallest men in the regiment, closed around them, and with their bayonets commenced prodding him, so he was glad to beat a retreat.

Judge Robertson, while ahold of that slave boy, had the narrowest escape of his life. For one of the men of Co. H. had furnished the boy with a single barreled Derringer pistol; and it was loaded and capped for business, and when the judge seized him, and tried to drag him out, he reached up and snapped it in his face; and fortunately for the judge, it missed fire, and just then Col. Coburn, our brigade commander, came riding down the line, and gave the order, so everyone could hear him, men, shoot the first damned man, that tries to break into your ranks.

That was what the men wanted to hear, and the butts of their guns came down onto the pavement, and I'll guarantee, they were loaded, capped, and bayonets fixed, quicker than they were ever loaded before. But quick as it had been done, the citizens were all out of sight, or if any were left, they were running for dear life. Then the order was given to march, and the column moved down to the wharf, and onto the steamer.

Then the man that owned that Derringer pistol, took it from the slave, examined it, pointed it off onto the river, snapped it, and it went off, he said that's the first time I ever knew it to miss fire.

We didn't get the baggage all on board, until the next forenoon, the Col. Instructed the Captain of the boat (who was a Southerner) to order the engineer to get up steam, and be ready to start. He said no such order would be given by him, until that slave was put on shore. The Col. gave him just five minutes to give the order, and if not given, he would have him put in irons, and would appoint a captain from his own men. It is needless to say, the order was given, and in a short time we were steaming down the beautiful Ohio. And here let me state; that slave boy, staid with the regiment, until the close of the war, then came with them to Wisconsin. .64 .65 .66 .67

Colonel Coburn's wife, Caroline, known to the boys in the brigade as "Mother Coburn," was energetic in getting those she could hidden aboard the steamer before it left. She also was busy encouraging and helping soldiers in camp during the time when most of the regiment were prisoners, captured by Forest.

GRUNERT, CO D 129TH ILL: February 2. On arising we received orders to be ready for marching immediately. At 7 o'clock we left the camp at Fountain Head and repaired to the South Tunnel, two miles north of Gallatin, where we arrived at 12 o'clock and went into camp. During the whole day it was very cold.

February 3. A better and more suitable place for camping was selected, tents erected, &c. It was very cold.

February 4. The day was spent in making the tents more comfortable. I had the honor of standing in the cold on guard. A deep snow fell.

February 5. A very cold and snowy day. A messenger from Mitchellsville brought the news that a train with clothes had been attacked by guerrillas, and fifty men were detached to assist the garrison there. The detail were met on the way by a second messenger, who reported that the guerrillas had been compelled to retreat, whereupon our men returned to camp, as it was very cold.

February 6 and 7. Everybody that could made the camp and tent more commodious and pleasant.

February 8. The whole regiment was busy to-day digging ditches around our camp.

February 9. The whole day rain; was on guard.

February 11. A beautiful warm day. Two soldiers that were buried near our camp, were disinterred and sent north to their friends. Both corpses were in an advanced stage of putrefaction.

February 12. Was sick.

February 13. Half sick I went on guard, and reported myself at the doctor sick, when I got worse.

February 14. Was sick a-bed until February 23.

February 23. Went to do guard duty again for the first time. The corpse of another soldier that had lain two months, was disinterred.

64 (Dickinson n.d.)

65 (McBride 1900, 71)

66 (Reid 1965, 21)

67 (Bradley 1865, 63) Article title "The Kentucky Policy."

February 25. Early in the morning at three o'clock the camp was alarmed, as our pickets had been fired upon. In ten minutes the regiment stood in line of battle, awaiting an attack. It was found out afterwards that a certain captain of our regiment had only tried us, and wishing the disturber of our night's rest all ill, we retired to sleep again. The afternoon brought us a heavy rain, nevertheless we had an inspection of arms.

February 27. Was on guard again; in camp the inspection was continued.

February 28. The bi-monthly muster took place to-day; in the afternoon we had rain again.

March 1. The day was a very beautiful one, nothing of any importance happened.

Busy with Guerillas

GRUNERT, CO D 129TH ILL: March 2. A company of mounted men were sent off, as we had received news of the notorious guerrilla chief Petticord. March 3. During the night the long sought for guerrilla chief Petticord was captured and placed under guard. When caught he was at a house in the neighborhood, taking his supper. At the sight of our "boys in blue," he endeavored to escape, and ran through a back door, away from our men. When a few shot "blue beans" were sent whistling about his ears, however, he surrendered and begged for life. On his arrival in camp, he became very insolent, but trusty men were placed to guard and soon quieted him.

INDIA P. LOGAN (PEDDICORD): Columbus A. Peddicord Capt. Independent Scouts. Morgan's Cavalry: After The first Year of service in the "Silver Grays," a company of Gallatin, Tennessee, in Colonel Bates' regiment, Second Infantry, Company K. he was with H. Morgan, and was often sent on detached service. He was taken prisoner in 1863, and spent nineteen months starving and freezing at Johnson's Island. Exchanged in November, 1864, he returned to find his wife in a Federal prison at Gallatin, Tennessee—a ruse to catch him. His father succeeded in getting her freed by going to Nashville to General Rosecrans, who banished her from Tennessee, where she owned one hundred and sixty acres of land, which was sold for taxes during reconstruction days. My brother Columbus was furious at his wife's treatment, and he and his men were conspicuous for their daring until the close of the war. .68

68 (Logan 1908) Nineteen months in prison till November puts his capture at seven months before the previous November, or about April, close enough to March, allowing for delay in sending him to prison and so on.

On March 4-5, two hundred men of the 22nd Wisconsin, of Coburn's brigade, were captured at Thompson's Station in Tennessee by Bragg's cavalry under Van Dorn.

GRUNERT, CO D 129TH ILL: March 5. It was very cold, accompanied by a March 6. A rainy day; nevertheless several companies were sent out foraging. This was a rather difficult task to be accomplished in the neighborhood of our camp, and the party had to go about twenty miles with the wagons before they succeeded in getting corn. We got the corn at a large plantation that was well stored and stocked with corn, cattle, &c. and as night was near it was impossible for us to return to camp, but we remained on the plantation. The inhabitants of the house treated us kindly and gave us a hearty supper. The night passed quietly.

March 7. Early we went to work to load our wagons, which caused the smiling face of our landlord to change to a very sour and angry one, because we were not satisfied with supper and lodging. The family no doubt considered us very impudent, but such is war; and we did not provoke it. After we had filled about half a dozen wagons with oats and corn, perhaps compelled a hog or chicken to go with us, we started on our return. The day was very rainy and the roads worse than bottomless, and the drivers could with the greatest difficulty only compel the animals to pull. The camp was reached at last about eight o'clock. During the night one of our pickets shot a horse, that did not understand the meaning of the command: "halt," and the picket not being able to see whether the horse was riderless or not.

March 10. The day was very rainy.

March 12. Myself with several comrades were in the country to get some fresh meat. Our cavalry captured twenty-six prisoners to-day. We were ordered to sleep on our arms, because it was feared that the friends of Petticord intended to pay us a visit. The night passed quietly however.

March 13. The prisoners were taken to Gallatin by a guard of honor.

March 14. I was on guard; the day was fine.

March 15. All our "duds" were inspected minutely and to the satisfaction of the officers.

March 16. At the usual battallion drill, during the pause, we laid our arms on the ground, when one gun that was left loaded imprudently, went off and the ball entered the right foot of a sergeant of co. I. The wounded man was taken to the hospital, where the surgeon removed some bone splinters from the wound. The sergeant became forever unfit for duty.

March 17. On guard to-day; nothing new happened.

Blakeslee, Co. K 129th Ill: To K. F. Peddicord: Co. K 129 was posted at Richland (now Portland) 3 companies including my own at Buck Lodge – 3 companies at South Tunnel the ballance Regt. with Hd Qrs at Fountain Head #. I was on scout duty when taken in by Jones + C. J. My recolection is that your boys at least most of them rode their horses on their retreat – The train was Captured 1 ½ miles south of Mitchelsville Tenn in a Maple swamp # It must have been near your old home where Jones left one of his men mortaly wounded – and who, on my guiding a party there the next day we found him dead – we gave him a soldiers burial in an apple orchard back of the house = There was but two lone women at the house = No equipments were there excepting his saddle = Those women would not tell anything – and I have never been able to learn any thing of this soldier – I have personaly questioned the residents of that neighborhood but all are reticent as to the man. .69 .70

GRUNERT, CO D 129TH ILL: March 20. The passenger train from Nashville was this evening attacked by a band of guerrillas near Richland station, Tenn. where companies A. and K. of our regiment were stationed. The train was stopped by tearing up the track, while the guerrillas were in bushes near by, and a briggadier general, several colonels, the mail and all goods on the train captured by the enemy. Companies A. and K. however, always on the look out, attacked the rebels, a small skirmish took place, and the guerrillas lost one dead, several wounded, horses and guns, and also the prisoners, mail and provisions. The train was soon put back on the track, and went on. We received orders to be on our guard, and ten men, reinforcements, were sent to the two companies. They returned, however, on hearing on the way that all danger was past. The night passed quietly. .71

March 20. Was on picket duty during a heavy thunder storm, accompanied by incessant rain the whole day. The prisoners taken yesterday were to day brought in.

March 21. The day was cloudy and cool.

March 22. It was Sunday, and we had inspection of arms and dress, and in the evening, dress parade. The day was cloudy and rainy.

69 (G. H. Blakeslee, Correspondence with K. F. Peddicord n.d.) Date not clear. Blakeslee said Jones captured him. K. F. Peddicord wrote the name C. J. Peddicord in place of Jones. C. J. may have used an alias. Written June 15, 1902. Date of event not stated. Blakeslee's punctuation is not explained. Periods added by editor.
70 Blakeslee wrote another account giving the date only as in March.
71 Reports are in (OR, Series I Vol 23 Part 1 Serial 34: Reports n.d., 147-149)

March 23. Incessant rain; a foraging expedition was sent out to-day.

March 24. Was on guard; it rained again day and night.

On March 25, the rest of the 22nd Wisconsin was captured by Forrest at Brentwood, Tennessee. Much dissension in the regiment over this and the earlier capture divided the regiment between its Colonel, Utley, and Lt. Colonel, Bloodgood. They were eventually paroled and returned to service in Coburn's brigade and would participate at Resaca. A pending promotion for Coburn did not happen, though all accounts point to his commander having sent the brigade to its doom. See the appendix for where to get full accounts.

GRUNERT, CO D 129TH ILL: March 25. The weather was cold and cloudy, sometimes an occasional fall of snow. We had to keep our arms loaded and ready on hand, as the neighborhood had become unsafe.

March 26. The day was beautiful, and a number of men were sent foraging; five men from each company were detailed to act as escort.

March 27. Companies A. and B. were again troubled by guerrillas and had to be on their guard.

March 28. I was on picket; a heavy thunder storm, accompanied by torrents of rain fell upon us during the night, and everybody got wet to the skin. Three of Morgan's men were captured by our cavalry to-day. They were well armed and fired four times on our men, before they surrendered. It was reported that the passenger train had run off the track, and six men been killed. The report was afterwards corrected, that a freight train had been demolished at a bridge below Gallatin, while in motion. Three soldiers were killed and several others crippled; seventy head of cattle were burnt with the fragments of the cattle cars.

March 29. Inspection took place to-day. The cavalry at Gallatin were driven back to-day by 400 rebels.

March 30. Our camp was moved to a high mountain, and consequently our line of pickets could be reduced.

March 31. I was on guard to-day; the day was fine, in the night a deep snow fell, accompanied by a heavy wind.

LAFOREST DUNHAM, CO C 129TH ILL: I should have writen last Sunday but I had not more than got cleand up as I was to do at home, all except poting on my Sunday go to meeting close, than the news came in that thare was some five rebels ·within about 15 or 20 miles from heare, so we had to strike out. We rode 15 miles in just about an hour. We got in yesterday afternoon.

It snowed quite hard heare last nite and froze considerable. It is quite cold to day all though the sun shines. .72

GRUNERT, CO D 129TH ILL: April 1. We made improvements in our camp; had battalion drill in the afternoon.

April 2. The trains came very irregular; our picket line was reinforced during the night; had company drill in the afternoon.

April 3. The day was clear and cold; drilled in the fore and afternoon.

April 5. Had inspection and in the afternoon a visit from Gen. Paine, staff and daughters, who were well satisfied with our discipline and state of health. Towards evening dress parade. The day was cloudy.

April 6 and 7. We drilled the principal part of both days.

April 8. Two men were shot to-day through the carelessness of another, who was cleaning his loaded gun. The bullet went through the breast of one and the head of the other. As we intended to remain at South Tunnel for some time yet, we commenced the erection of small buildings, in order to live more comfortable.

April 9. We made several improvements in our camp; a detachment of cavalry captured two of Morgan's guerrillas.

April 10. We had general inspection, and the inspecting officers were well satisfied.

April 11. It was Sunday, and the inspection of our "duds" was continued. A larger portion of the regiment was sick to-day than usual. The weather was dark and cold.

LAFOREST DUNHAM, CO C 129TH ILL: April 12. Morgans men got another good thrashing the other day. Our men took to prisoners and day before yesterday thare was too came and gave themselves up at the tunnel. Our cavalry squad came heare the first of last weak I dont know how long we will stay heare. Co. A H & F are stationed heare; it is about nine miles from the tunnel. we came heare on the account of saving traveling so far. we wer neaded heare the most. It is splendid wether. The farmers are planting corn. Thare was too boys kild in Co. G. the other day by an accident. One was cleaning his gun and some how his gun went off and shot one through the hart and one through the head, one lived about a minute. .73

GRUNERT, CO D 129TH ILL: April 13. A negress that had been maltreated by her mistress, came into camp crying and begging for admission into camp and protection. It was granted, and she was set to work in the hospital.

72 (DeRosier 1969, 63)
73 (DeRosier 1969, 63)

April 14. A dispatch from Franklin, Ky. reported that a large band of guerrillas had shown itself near there with the intention of destroying the railroad. A strong detachment of our regiment was sent off to Franklin, but before the men reached their destination they learned that the guerrillas had withdrawn without accomplishing their object, and our men returned to camp.

LAFOREST DUNHAM, CO C 129TH ILL: April 15. Thar is some 60 mounted men piked out of the Regiment on for scouting. I hapened to be one of them. We are out some times a weak at a time; we go nite and day. I like it much better than staying in camp all though we run a good deal of risk. We hardly ever go out with out caching a number of prisoners or spying out something new. Day befor yester thare was 57 rebels came with about 12 miles of heare to make a raid on the railroad but we was to sharp for them. We new all about thare moves. They ran in contact with some of our cavelry that are stationed at Franklin, Ky. and they fed them some of uncle sams pils, kild a number of the rebs and took several prisinars. None of our boys wer hurt. we run our horses to about 5 miles to cut off thare retreat but they went another road. We rode all nite after them but did not get any of them. We are haveing splendid wether heare. Thare is a going to be a great deal of fruit heare this seson, peach treas are loded down. That is all this country is fit for just to rais fruit. Know Wonder that this state rebeld. You cant find one in 20 and be safe in saying so thay can read or write. The country is all rocks and mountains.The union ladies of this state and along the line of Ky. gave ous a picknick the other day. we had a fine time, it seamed a good deal like home. I think if nothing happens I will get a furlow to come home about August. I think we will stay heare all summer. General Pain sais that this Regiment has done more good along this road than a briggade had done before. Since we have ben out we have taken some 900 prisinors. .74

GRUNERT, CO D, 129TH ILL: April 15. A detail of men was sent to Gallatin to escort the paymaster to us; after having received our money we made preparations to send it home. The day was rainy.
April 17. A foraging party was sent out to-day.
April 19. Inspection of arms was ordered, but the rain prevented it. A member of company I deserted last night, and cavalry was sent after him, but in vain. At night dress parade.

A. J. CROPSEY, MAJOR, CMD 129TH ILL: Richland, April 27. I have to report to the general commanding that a band of thirteen guerrillas, on the evening

74 (DeRosier 1969, 64)

of the 23rd instant, attacked a Union man named Thomas Nowil, at his residence, some four miles from our camp. After severely wounding him, they succeeded in capturing; took him his family without hat or coat; took him off some fifteen miles and there murdered him, literally hewing him to pieces. With them were some at least of what Captain Peddicord used to call his "command"—Ellis Harper,—Berryman, and, some say, Peter Blane. As we could not take the murderers, I sent down yesterday the fathers of Harper and Berryman. .75 Last night, some 2 a.m. I received pretty reliable information that a band of some seventy-five rebels were moving toward Franklin, on La Fayette road. My mounted men were then out and did not return until about daylight, and then so jaded were their horses that I have not been able to ascertain any further news. Almost nightly robberies are committed in the country out from five to fifteen miles from this station. If we are expected to stop this a much larger mounted force will be indispensable; though if there were one of the companies from the tunnel sent here, so that I could send 75 or 100 into the country to watch roads, fords, and houses at night, we might possibly effect something more. If four companies at the tunnel would build some little stockades they would be quite as safe as the five now are. Should the general see fit to move any company from the tunnel here, Captain Baird, of Company E, has asked me to get his company moved here, if be in accordance with the best interests of the service. He would be a very efficient officer in that kind of service. .76

GRUNERT, CO D 129TH ILL: April 27. When the drum beat for roll-call this morning, and the men were taking their places, the gun of a member of company C went off and the bullet wounded him on the right hand. His wife, who was with him at the time, became very excited, but was soon pacified. April 28 and 29. Had battalion drill this as well as the next day. April 30. The bi-monthly muster took place to-day; there was much talk about marching orders.

Trading Coffee

STRONG, 105TH ILL: Our coffee was generally parched. As we had no coffee mills or grinders, we would put the parched beans in our tin cups and pound

---

75 Does not say what was done with the fathers of Harper and Berryman in Gallatin. Harper had his own company under General Morgan, harassing the Union, like the Peddicords. Blaine was also a member of the company.

76 (OR, Series I, Vol 52, Serial 109 n.d., 355) Reporting to Captain Phelps Paine, Assistant Adjutant-General, son of General Paine.

them with our bayonets, then boil them right in the cup. Sometimes we would not pound our coffee, but would boil it whole, save the berries, dry them, then put them neatly in a little sack and trade the "fresh coffee" to the natives for cornbread, milk, or butter. Even though once used, the beans still made very good coffee. Anyhow, it was a fair exchange for the pies and cakes that we sometimes got in return. No one but a soldier or an ostrich could digest their pies and cakes. .77

Chancellorsville

God Almighty cannot stop me.—Hooker

I just lost confidence in Joe Hooker.—Hooker

In the east, Lee was destroying careers of Union generals. Lincoln was desperate for a fighter and had taken a chance on a genuine fighter who also was a bit vain and swashbuckling, given to criticizing the others, but an effective corps commander. Hooker managed to bait Lee to Chancellorsville. Lee sent Stonewall Jackson with most of his command on a long, overnight march to flank Hooker's right, while some of Hooker's support was stalled crossing a river.

> WILLIAMS, 1ST DIVISION, 12TH CORPS, ARMY OF THE POTOMAC: April 30th: It was a pleasant, moonlight night. Chancellorsville house became the center of hundreds of officers (generals and staff). It was a gay and cheerful scene. We had successfully accomplished what we all supposed would be the great work of the campaign. Everybody prophesied a great success, an overwhelming victory. Everybody was full of enthusiastic congratulations. Gen. Hooker came over during the evening and issued a flaming order complimenting the splendid operations of the 5th, 11th and 12th corps. We began to think we had done something heroic, we didn't exactly see what, except we had put three of the smallest corps on the flank of the Rebel stronghold. But it was rumored that others were coming to help us, and that others had crossed and driven the enemy from his entrenchments at Fredericksburg. All was *couleur de rose*! How many joyous hearts and bright cheerful faces beat and smiled happily for the last time on that delightful moonlight night at Chancellorsville! .78

77 (Strong 1961, 104)
78 (Williams 1963, 242) Hooker had crossed the Rappahannock and managed to get his forces into position to squeeze Lee, front and back, like a sandwich.

GRUNERT, CO D 129TH ILL: May 1, 1863. Company D left South Tunnel and went to a station fifteen miles further North, called Richland, where three companies were stationed already.

WILLIAMS, 1ST DIVISION, 12TH CORPS, ARMY OF THE POTOMAC: May 1st The morning was foggy but soon cleared up before a strong sun. I went early to Chancellorsville house, where the headquarters of the army and several corps commanders were concentrated. Hundreds of horses held by orderlies filled the broad space in front, and the piazza and rooms were filled with general staff officers. Everybody supposed it was the beginning of a day big with the fate of the nation. Meade, Sickles, Couch, Howard, [besides] corps commanders and dozens of division commanders were floating around talking anxiously but still confidently. It was known that Hooker had boastingly declared the night before that "God Almighty could not prevent his destroying the Rebel army." The blasphemy did not please the most irreligious as appropriate to any, and least of all to an occasion so momentous, but allowance was made for excitement. Still, there was an uneasiness in the best military minds. There was too much boasting and too little planning; Swagger without preparation. .79

Much has been written about what went wrong. General O. O. Howard was responsible for the right and, though warned (but insufficiently reinforced), was not prepared for the massive flank attack by Stonewall Jackson. The following day, Hooker, though caught between two Confederate armies, had two corps ready to flank Lee. But Hooker, unable to concentrate and command effectively after a Confederate shell knocked him out for almost an hour and left him mentally ajar, did not turn over command and instead ordered a retreat even though those around him were ready and anxious to carry out his plan. .80

But perhaps more telling of overall conduct was criticism by more than one general: inability to grasp in his mind what he could not see with his eyes.

79 (Williams 1963, 242) Lee had split his army, sending Stonewall Jackson far left to attack Hooker's weak right, O. O. Howard's corps, to squeeze Hooker. Hooker was aware of Jackson and had warned Howard and sent Sickles, with part of Howard's reserves, to stop Jackson. Howard perhaps thought that relieved him. But Sickles was unable to pursue Jackson, who had simply shifted to another road. The forces from Fredericksburg never got there.
80 (Doubleday 1882)

A Daily Allowance

Boyle told us what made a soldier so tough, if he lasted long enough. Often he survived on little food and water. What was sufficient sustenance, plain but nourishing?

> MERRILL, 70TH IND: A ration or daily allowance of food for each man was composed of twelve ounces of bacon, or one pound four ounces of beef, one pound six ounces of soft bread or flour, or one pound of hard bread; and to every one hundred men were issued fifteen pounds of beans, eight pounds of coffee, fifteen pounds of sugar, four quarts of vinegar, one pound four ounces of candles, four pounds of soap, and three pounds twelve ounces of salt. Rice, potatoes, meal and molasses were seldom issued, but desiccated, compressed, mixed vegetables were sometimes substituted.
>
> When bread gave out the preparation of food from flour was perplexing. The customary method was to make the flour into a batter with water, and boil it in grease, as the boys had seen their mothers cook doughnuts. These slapjacks came dripping from the unctuous fluid, and though not garnished with honey or treacle, were voraciously and imprudently devoured by the self-satisfied cooks. When frying was preferred to boiling, the culinary artists were skillful in throwing the cakes from the frying pans high in the air, turning them in the descent.
>
> The hardtack or sea-biscuit, though by all odds the most wholesome article of food the soldier received, was not always appreciated. "A good-natured lad," to quote from an officer' letter, "who is toasting a cracker, exclaims, 'Gosh, boys, this here's more n splendid,' while another who has been pampered at home retorts, 'By jingo, I could cut a nice chunk from a hickory log and make a decenter breakfast of it." .81

Richland Station

> GRUNERT, CO D 129TH ILL: May 2. We reached Richland station and erected our tents and camp according to order. We chopped wood for houses, which we finished on the third and fourth day of the month.
> May 6. It rained the whole day. In the evening one of our pickets shot at a person stealing on him; the person escaped, but was captured half an hour later by our cavalry returning from a scout. The prisoner was placed in the

---

81 (S. Merrill 1900, 13)

guard-house under a strong guard, where several of his captive friends were enjoying themselves.

May 7. The day was very rainy, and many of our men went home on a furlough.

May 9. We dug ditches near our quarters; the war news received to-day was not very pleasing.

May 10. Five men were detached from each company to go to Gallatin, and assist Gen. Paine in arresting several disloyal persons that had acted the traitor to the Union cause. A number of them were sent beyond our lines. In the evening dress parade.

May 11. Twenty-five men infantry and a detachment of cavalry went off on a scout to-night.

May 12. To-day a dinner was brought us by a neighboring Union family. After dinner dancing took place, and speeches were made by Col. Case, and other officers, which were well received by the Union family and by our men. The report that Richmond had been taken, reached our camp the third time.

May 13. The report came in that sixty guerrillas, in Federal uniforms, had shown themselves at Woodburn station, near Franklin, Ky. and were destroying the road property. A detachment of infantry and cavalry was sent from here, but came too late, and returned without accomplishing anything.

May 14. Our whole camp was fortified and the trees around it cut down. Part of our cavalry went after guerrillas. In the afternoon drill.

Captain Gillham of Company F resigned May 14, 1863.

May 15. A party went foraging, but were in great danger on account of bushwhackers that had been reinforced and were becoming bolder.

May 16. To-night a number of bushwhackers fired on one of our pickets, but, as the man was standing right behind a tree, not harmed. The guerrillas were kept back by our pickets and retreated. We were in line of battle from 12 o'clock until daybreak, but nothing occurred. One rebel was taken prisoner.

May 17. Had inspection of arms and towards evening dress parade.

May 18. Several shots were fired during the night, but the camp was not alarmed. One of the pickets had in the darkness shot a calf for a rebel.

May 20. Inspection of arms, cartridge boxes, and ammunition; in the afternoon drill. The necessary water began to get scarce and we commenced digging a well.

May 22. The digging of the well was continued incessantly.

May 23. The report was received that one thousand rebels had crossed the Cumberland river and driven in part of our cavalry that was out on a scout.

The report was not believed by many.

May 25. Several of our officers had arranged a ball, but during the dancing some jovial fellows fired a couple of shots, and the enjoyment of the officers had an end.

May 26. All wagons and twenty mounted men went out foraging, who, in order to get forage faster, divided off into small parties, and intended to return as soon as possible. One party arrived at a plantation, where corn, &c. was in the field, and as they needed an axe one man went to the house to get it. When near the house this messenger saw several armed men there, and immediately made a retrograde movement; but too late, the armed men had seen him, and went in pursuit. A race took place and five shots fired at the fleeing man, until the supposed rebels reached the wagons, where it was found that our own party had pursued our messenger, which caused a good deal of merriment.

May 27. A regiment of cavalry passed by here to-day en route for Murfreesboro. Many of our men off on a furlough, returned to-day. Received the report as a fact that Vicksburg had been taken.

Grant had put Vicksburg under siege, making them prisoners without help or supplies.

May 28. It rained the whole day; nothing of importance happened.

May 29. The day was dark and sultry. There was a good deal of talk about marching orders having been received.

Gallatin

The 129th Illinois was garrisoned at Gallatin, Tennessee at the beginning of June, replacing the 70th Indiana.

June 1. It was announced that an inspection of arms would take place, but afterwards we were ordered to be ready for marching. It turned out finally, that companies F and C had marching orders, and that companies D and K would remain. .82

June 3. Company K received marching orders, and left for Gallatin on the 8 o'clock train.

June 4. In the forenoon we had target shooting, and were served a substantial dinner in the afternoon, for the second time, by a Union lady living near. Lieut. Haldeman and Corporal Clark, both of company D, went

---

82 Company F, including Peak and Peters, were going to Gallatin. Company D, Grunert's, remained in Bucks Lodge.

about twilight to the house of a widow lady near, where they were by treachery surprised by guerrillas. Clark escaped, but Haldeman, according to Clark's testimony, taken prisoner and shot. During the night a scout of mounted men was sent out to learn something definite of the fate of Lieut. Haldeman, and, if possible, rescue him. As the scout remained absent so long, another detachment was sent out after the first, and, as we supposed, captured one.

June 5. Ten more men were sent out after the two detachments sent out before, of whom no news had as yet been received. There were now but few men left in camp, and as the bushwhackers were aware of this, they showed themselves openly and often, but did not venture an attack, knowing that we were well fortified and always prepared for them. About 7 o'clock in the evening the long expected men returned from their troublesome and dangerous ride. They had made inquiries about Lieut. Haldeman, giving his description to several citizens and received the answer that they had seen a wounded Federal officer on a mule between some Confederate soldiers, and had given our men the direction the party went. But all was in vain, and being convinced that Lieut. Haldeman was in the enemy's hands, they returned to camp, after a ride of more than fifty miles. This evening, sufficient proof having been given that Haldeman had been captured through the treachery of the widow lady, her house was set on fire by Colonel Case and several men, and the woman ordered beyond our lines.

June 6. The whole company was again on duty, The guerrillas had heard that Gen. Paine was going on a furlough, we had to patrol the road and prevent its destruction. In the afternoon we were reinforced by two companies of the 106th Ohio regiment. Towards evening nine men of Capt. Flynn's company, under command of a corporal, were posted at a place where a road crosses the track, which road was much used by the bushwhackers. The men were well posted behind trees and very quiet. About 10 o'clock they heard the clatter of horses' feet, and soon two riders came in sight. When near enough the command to halt was given, but scarcely was this uttered, when the two horsemen turned their horses to flee. Faster than I can write this the reports of nine guns were heard, but alas! but one bullet hit the aim. One of the horsemen staggered in the saddle, but as he had strength enough to hold himself, both horsemen escaped. As the shots were fired, the whole camp was alarmed, and all men were under arms until they learned that there was no danger of an attack.

June 7. A foraging party, sent out to-day, found the hat of the guerrilla shot last night on the road. The guerrilla was found dead in a house in Mitchellsville, and was buried by our men in the later part of the day.

June 8. When we returned from our foraging tour, we found the whole camp deserted, excepting by the men that had been on guard the night before. The guerrillas were very troublesome, and attacked the trains very frequently; our "garrison" had to guard a train to Bowling Green, Ky. and did not return till late in the afternoon.

June 9. Our company D received marching orders and went to Gallatin on a train at night, where the whole regiment was once more united—the first time for a long while. A member of company A drowned in the Cumberland river while bathing.

June 10. We received two months' pay to-day. A young lady, dressed in men's clothes, was taken prisoner and put under guard. A great excitement was in camp to-night in consequence of the report, that a large force of rebels were approaching town. All our cavalry, not otherwise on duty, were sent out on the main roads, and stationed at the entrance of the roads into the city, wagons were placed as barricades, and all the regiments of infantry posted in line of battle. The night passed without any attack, and it was doubted very much the next day, whether there really had been any danger.

June 11. A rainy day; nothing of importance happened.

June 12. We had to drill in the forenoon.

June 13. News had come in from Lieut. Haldeman's place of captivity and a detail ordered to rescue him. On arriving at the house described, it was found that he had been removed by the guerrillas. A freight train was burnt by guerrillas near Elizabethtown, Ky. From now until the 20th everything remained quiet in camp and neighborhood, the service however became more arduous on account of having to patrol the principal roads, outside our picket lines, every night.

June 20. A tremendous excitement existed last night, as it was generally believed that an attack would be made by the enemy. Reports had come in continually that the rebels were gathering around us, of which smaller or larger squads had been seen by our scouts, and our cavalry had to patrol all roads leading to the city, as on a former occasion; the regiments of infantry were posted in line of battle to await the attack of the enemy. But again we were unnecessarily robbed of our sleep, and the morning dawned without an enemy having appeared in sight.

June 21. It was generally reported that the rebel Gen. Morgan, with eight thousand men, was moving against us to attack Gallatin. No man was permitted to leave camp without permit, from which we drew the conclusion that the report was believed at headquarters. We received marching orders to-day. Morgan, who had the night before attacked Alexandria, had been beaten back by the Union troops.

June 22. Another dreadful night. Nobody doubted an attack of the enemy that had the day before been seen in numerous large squads by our scouts, and we knew that Morgan was close on hand with a large force. All our tents, whose erection and commodious arrangement had caused us so much trouble, had to be struck, so that the enemy should not see our exact strength and position from a distance. The whole 129th regiment marched to Fort Thomas, near the camp, as we could defy the enemy better there. After all preparations had been made, the necessary caution taken, plenty of ammunition given out, and the silence of the grave reigned everywhere, we swore "never to surrender Fort Thomas as long as a cartridge was left us." In vain we listened, but no report of a single shot was heard from our picket line, and when morning came, and no enemy had appeared yet, we left our guns, went to the camp, and commenced erecting our tents again.

Uncle Ned

PEAK, CO F 129TH ILL: Southeast of Galiton, about six miles, was a river where at one time there had been a packing house, called the porkery. Our company was sent there to guard this river to prevent the rebel cavalry's crossing the river, and attacking Galiton from the south.

An old colored man came to camp that evening and said he wanted to stay with us. We assured him he could stay as long as he behaved himself, to which he replied he would sure behave, and do whatever we told him to do, if he could. Some of the boys asked him what his name was, and he said, "They always called me Uncle Ned." The boys told him not to worry, he wouldn't be molested, and should have all he could eat as long as he remained with us, and done the right thing.

That evening, when the boys went down to the river to fill their canteens as usual, one of them wanted to drink from the river, getting down on all fours to drink. When his ears came close to the water, he could hear a sound, like horses crossing a bridge. What could it be, was it a decoy to draw some of his men from camp, so they could capture the camp? Finally one of the boys said he had went up the river about two miles fishing, and he thought he could see cavalrymen coming down the hill on the south side of the river, about one mile east of him. He was sure he had seen men on horseback, and thought he could see the sabers glisten. What was we to do if Morgan and his band came down the river on us, we would not be a shot a piece for them.

We went to see Ned and he had disappeared. Was he a spy and a traitor, was the thoughts that ran through most of the boys' minds, but the search was kept up and at last he was found, in one of the wagons covered with the hay and fast asleep. "Do you know where Morgan and his men are?" He said that he didn't know Morgan, "but I know there is a lot of men on horseback south of the river, and about six miles east of here. They had two big guns on wheels and two wagons with boxes on them, full of guns, four big covered wagons, loaded with something, two wagons that looked like my mosey's carriage that he went to church in."

...

When we were about half way back to Galiton, a courier met us and told us that Morgan had struck the railroad about four miles north of Galiton, captured a trainload of provisions and torn up the track for a mile or more.

Ned was still with us and when he seen the full regiment he said, "Mosey, where did all the folks come from." We told him they were yanks who came from the north and that they were only a handful to what was coming and he replied, "Mosey, you will lick them sure, when all your people get here." .83

Not all Union soldiers thought well of the negro, so it is gratifying to learn that these from Scott County accepted Uncle Ned, of whom we learn more later.

BLAKESLEE, Co K 129TH ILL INF: When in spring of 63 the second company of mounted scouts was formed at Gallatin, I volunteered in that duty & rode 3 months = up to or about the time Morgan started from Alexander on his Ohio Raid – At Gallatin we got word that Morgan was moving towards G – we went out with both companies & a section of 13 Ind battery to dispute the crossing of Cumbrland at the Lebanon pike ferry – hearing nothing we (20 men) was set across & to scout on south side of River – going up the bluff from river we were fired upon from the brush, which stampeded all our horses (it being then about 10 at night) and dark) and away we went into the river – in swimming over my horse was Killed & I put my Carbine to soak in the river & 40 rounds with it & was glad to reach shore in safety +

Returning to G – getting another horse & arms we started up the river to some point. I forget the place – but found Morgan had crossed and gone – about 2 hours before we got there – (for which I have ever since been thankful # returning to G – we run into the 5th Tenn Cav. Col Stokes – and each thinking the other was Johnnies came near having a little fuss on the side #

83 Extracted from a much longer tale by Peak about his midnight ride to get help.

My second horse proved a stumbler & he falling with me 3 times & being run over as I rode at head of collumn = taken with an 80 mile ride that night – it used me up & I quit & went back to old "Co G" = .84

Ordered to raid Kentucky to draw Rosecrans' resources from the Battle of Tullahoma, Morgan carried the raid into Ohio, against orders, and was captured, spending some time in prison before escaping.

June 23, 1863

Rosecrans started pressing Bragg at Shelbyville, Tennessee. Thomas had the larger corps against General Hardee.

GRUNERT, CO D 129TH ILL: June 23. Many of our men went on a furlough; we had inspection of arms.

June 24. Twenty-five men were sent to a plantation eight miles from Gallatin, confiscated by the Government, with a number of negroes, to protect them in harvesting the wheat on the field against an attack of the guerrillas. Rain set in and prevented the work to-day, and the men were compelled to remain on the plantation over night.

June 25. It rained the whole day.

June 26. Thunderstorm and rain the whole day.

June 27. Another day of rain; a foraging party was sent out after the most necessary things.

June 28. Rain the whole day.

June 29. Storm and rain during the day; a detachment of cavalry met twenty rebels, several shots were fired but nobody hurt; the rebels escaped.

June 30. It rained again. The bi-monthly muster took place to-day. The 106th Ohio regiment that took our place at Richland station, was attacked by eighty rebels. Fifteen of the "rebs" were taken prisoners and several killed; no loss on our side.

On June 30, Rosecrans and Thomas had Bragg in such poor position at Tullahoma that he departed for Chattanooga, leaving Rosecrans to follow.

July 1. This was the first clear day since the 23d of June.

July 2. Another party was sent to a confiscated plantation, to protect the

84 (G. H. Blakeslee, Correspondence with K. F. Peddicord n.d.) Morgan crossed the Cumberland later, much further northeast in Kentucky.

negroes working there against an attack of guerrillas. The party returned on the 3d of July.

July 1-3 Gettysburg

The whole fight was under my control, no one to interfere.—Geary

Two brigades of Geary's division ... did not arrive at the scene of action, owing to having mistaken the road.—Meade

Save me from my friends.—Williams

Nothing, not even a pie, is so dear to the heart of the American soldier as a speech. — Merrill

Joe Hooker gets credit for anticipating Lee's path into Pennsylvania and a probable battle at Gettysburg. But Washington had lost faith in Joe Hooker. One thing held against him in Washington was his bravado the night before the disaster of Chancellorsville began. General Halleck, the commander of all the armies, made it hard for Hooker to be effective, so Hooker resigned while the army was shadowing Lee. Meade was placed in command.

The Battle of Gettysburg began July 1. On the second night, General Williams' division was called away to rescue a battery and then returned to its position north of Cemetery Hill:

WILLIAMS, 12TH CORPS: to daughters: I returned toward my entrenchments after dark and was met with the astounding intelligence that they were taken possession of by Rebels in my absence! Gen. Geary (whom I had left to guard them) had been ordered out after I left by Gen. Slocum and though he did not reach the front, by mistaking his way, he was gone long enough for the Rebs to seize upon two-thirds of our line, which had been prepared with so much care. .85

GEARY, 2ND DIV, 12TH CORPS: July 4th, 1863. Yesterday I had the honor to defeat Gen Ewell's Corps (formerly Jackson's). They attacked my command at 3 oclock a.m. and we fought until ½ past 11. The result was I repulsed his command with a loss of about 1000 killed and 3000 wounded. We took also

85 (Williams 1963, 302) Williams had gone to help rescue a battery.

500 prisoners, about 5000 stand of arms. My loss is 110 killed, 584 wounded. The whole fight was under my control, no one to interfere. .86

WILLIAMS, 12TH CORPS: to daughter, Nov 20, 1863: We are all just now terribly disgusted after reading Meade's report. He not only ignores me as corps commander, but don't even allude to the 1st Division, which lost more men on the morning of July 3rd than the 2nd Division to which he gives the whole credit of the contest on that part of the field. ... but ignores me and my report, too, who commanded a corps the (entire) three days at Gettysburg. To make the matter worse, another Pennsylvanian, Gen. Geary, gets all the credit of the operations on the right during the morning of July 3rd, and myself, who spent a sleepless night in planning the attack, and my old division commanded by Gen. Ruger, which drove the Rebs, from their double line of entrenchments, are not alluded to. Save me from my friends! I am pretty mad, but I think Gen. Slocum is a mile or so ahead of me in indignation. I do not remember to have passed forty-eight hours in a more vexed and annoyed state. .87

WILLIAMS, 12TH CORPS: [after Gettysburg] I was passing a column of our soldiers and endeavored to take the side of the road, passing along a deep roadside or ditch on a narrow strip between a stone wall on one side and the deep ditch on the other. I finally came to the end of the wall where a rail fence had been partly thrown down. Here I tried to jump my horse over, but in turning him on the narrow ledge he slipped and tumbling down the bank landed flat on his back in the bottom of the ditch. Fortunately, as he slipped I jumped from the saddle and landed safely on the bank. Old Plug Ugly must have fallen eight or ten feet and as he groaned hugely I supposed he was finished at last, after passing through diverse battles and one heavy fall into the pontoon boats. The men got his saddle off while he lay as quiet as a lamb and turning him round, with a big grunt he got to his feet and was led to the upper end of the ditch to terra firma, apparently as sound as ever. My saddle, which I supposed was crushed beyond repair, came out scarcely injured, saved I supposed by the overcoats and blankets strapped before and behind. Altogether, it was a lucky escape for man, beast, and saddle. Old Plug was somewhat stiff the next day, but I rode him every day. He is a regular old soldier, however, and takes great advantage of my indulgence and his long service and five or six wounds. As we march along he grabs at every knot of grass, corn, shrub, or any vegetable substance that presents itself on his way.

86 (Blair n.d., 98) Fighting north of Cemetery Hill the night of the 3rd.
87 (Williams 1963, 352) Meade sent an official correction after Slocum complained and explained (Kindle March 5, 1863).

No amount of spurring or whipping can break him of this habit of laying in a supply against short rations. He is an odd, lazy old fellow, sometimes pretending to be very scary, especially after every battle, at other times apparently afraid of nothing. For a year and a half we have been daily companions. We get up a great love for even brutes under such circumstances. I should grieve to part with old Plug Ugly, with all his faults. .88

July 4, 1863 Vicksburg Surrender

After a long siege following several relentless attempts by Grant to capture the last point controlling Mississippi River travel, Vicksburg surrendered on July 4. The Father of Waters was now fully in Union hands, and Grant was freed for further pursuit of the original Anaconda Plan to squeeze the south between rivers and coasts. Many of the regiments at Vicksburg, including the 101st Illinois, would soon be at work further east.

GRUNERT, CO D 129TH ILL: July 4. The day was foggy; everything was quiet until noon, when thirty-two guns were fired in Fort Thomas in honor of the day. The locomotives that passed here were completely covered by the stars and stripes. In the afternoon speeches were made by Col. Case, Lieut. Col. Cropsey, and others. The rebel Gen. Morgan was fighting in Kentucky. The telegraph wires were in disorder.

AYERS, CO E, 129TH ILL: At Gallatin Tenn July 4th 63. Being sent for into Camp of 129th ills Reg, I went in Town and made A Small and Spicy speech to Collered men and Mustered them to the No. of 60 in Ranks. .89

MERRILL, 70TH IND: On June thirtieth the regiment marched under the broiling sun and encamped on the Murfreesboro battle field in a pouring rain. Here in a few days came news of the Gettysburg victory and the capture of Vicksburg. Nothing, not even a pie, is so dear to the heart of the American soldier as a speech, and on this day of rejoicing Colonel Harrison and officers of other regiments in the brigade complied with solicitations and

88 (Williams 1963) At Chancellorsville, a shell had exploded in the mud directly under Old Plug, Williams astride, leaving Plug bleeding but not seriously wounded.
89 (Ayers 1947, 106) Saturday. Ayers was a Methodist preacher, later to be detached to recruit colored soldiers. Here, he is doing that already, while still with the 129th.

made speeches that refreshed and exhilarated the souls of their audience. .90

The war was not over; out of Vicksburg marched Stevenson's Division of Confederates, paroled and set loose to find their way home. One of those was Captain Maxmillian Van Den Corput, of Rome, Georgia, and his battery—minus cannon but keeping their flag.

> WESLEY CONNOR, PRIVATE, CHEROKEE ARTILLERY, CSA: "Capt. Corput sewed it up in his saddle blanket and brought it out of Vicksburg." .91

> GRUNERT, COMPANY D, 129TH ILL: July 5. Another fight in Kentucky; we could plainly hear the roar of the cannons. No trains to-day. A heavy rain set in towards night.
> July 6. Another hard rain. A train was taken by guerrillas between here and the border of Kentucky. The guard of the train was paroled, mail and other valuables taken, passengers, etc. taken off the train and the train set in motion again.
> July 7. More rain. The track had been destroyed somewhere, as the trains did not run. We got new uniforms to-day.

> AYERS, CO E, 129TH ILL: On Tuesday 7th spoke Again and Recvd Authority from Gov Johnson and General Paine and formed Co. inroled some 80 men. Have mustered Every day since save Sabbath and now have inroled 120 men. .92

> GRUNERT, CO D 129TH ILL: July 8. Received the news that Vicksburg had surrendered on the Fourth. A negro regiment was organized here and many of our men applied for officers' posts in the same. No train to-day—more rain.
> July 9. Received the news that Morgan had gone to Indiana with his gang, and that preparations were made there to capture him. A train was expected.
> July 10. Beautiful and very warm weather.
> July 11. One hundred and twenty men infantry and some cavalry were ordered to be ready for a scout, under command of Lieut. Col. Cropsey and Maj. Flynn. According to the testimony of some loyal citizens there were

90 (S. Merrill 1900, 60)
91 (W. O. Connor, War Stained Banner 1866) Wes Connor, Letter to Comrade, Feb.1, 1896 (Hollingsworth, scrapbook)
92 (Ayers 1947, 106) Governor Andrew Johnson, later to be Lincoln's second term Vice President.

about two hundred rebels near a place called Cottontown, situated near Gallatin, which robbed and plundered and threatened the Union men. At half past 11 o'clock the expedition was ready, and started. We soon reached the Red River Pike, leading to the place named, our cavalry taking the lead, and about the dawn of day we arrived at Cottontown, where we halted. The infantry was brought in position, while the cavalry, led by a trusty guide, approached the camping ground of the rebels. A citizen of the town, however, had acted the spy and reported to the rebels the fact of our arrival and our strength, whereupon the rebs fled. The spy did not escape, was taken prisoner and his property burnt.

AYERS, CO E, 129TH ILL: Have our head quarters South West corner Publick Square at Gallatin in Big Brick Building this Saturday afternoon July 11th 63. Still in same building and have 149 men this Saturday eve. .93

GRUNERT, CO D 129TH ILL: July 12. As we had missed the object of our yesterday's expedition in consequence of treason, it was resolved to search the neighborhood further and more thoroughly. We started again, but the country, a continuous changing of high mountains and deep valleys, with roads almost bottomless in consequence of the heavy rain, presented such obstacles that we could advance only with great trouble and very slowly. We were about twenty-five miles from camp, in a country, offering every facility to guerrilla warfare, and frequently we saw the traces of these gangs of rebels. Our men were divided now, all by-roads and houses searched, and frequently men captured, who were afraid of Yankees, but in their hearts good Union men. The more we advanced, the more impassable the country became, and as our small stock of provisions was giving out we were compelled to return to camp, which we reached about dusk, after having been thoroughly drenched by a heavy shower of rain.

July 13. Col. Henry Case received the first authentic news about the whereabouts of Lieut. Haldeman in a letter from his mother. She stated that he was in Richmond, Va. in prison, and that he had been wounded when captured, because he refused to surrender, when demanded to do so.

July 14. The pay rolls were signed and some time afterwards we received two months' pay. It rained heavily the whole day.

July 18. Several Union families were admitted in our lines, because their lives had been threatened by guerrillas. This afternoon a dress parade took place.

July 19. Several of our men were punished very severely to-day, by

93 (Ayers 1947, 106)

deductions being made from their pay, and the men themselves put under arrest for months.

COX, CHARLES H. CO E 70TH IND: July 22. Col Harrison assumed temporary command of our Brigade this morning. Genl Ward has gone to Nashville and will probably go home on a furlough (if he can get one) which I hope he can and will go home and stay, it would be for the "good of the service" if he should. He is the ranking Brigadier in this Dept, but by his incompetency, has been continually kept in the rear, and never assigned a responsible command. I wish the 70th was in another brigade, for we will never see a fight while under him ... Confound such a General as Ward! .94

GRUNERT, CO D 129TH ILL: July 23. Inspection of our arms, uniforms, tents and kitchens took place to-day.
July 24. We received new tents to-day and the camp was moved to a higher piece of ground.
July 25. The day was rainy and the men busy in making the camp commodious.
July 26. Part of our cavalry, that was always on a scout, came across a gang of rebels that as usually fled on the approach of the Union troops. Several rebels were wounded by our boys.
July 27. The work on the camp continued, although there was a good deal of talk about marching orders, and many stopped working in consequence.
July 28. Drill in the forenoon and afternoon.
July 31. One of the Union men, admitted into camp a few days ago, asked for an escort to his farm, where he had some harvesting to do. His wish was granted, and, although the party had to suffer much from the enemy, they returned to camp in safety.
August 1. The day was very hot, and during inspection and review many men left their places, others drilled until they fell down. Generally speaking the drill was satisfactory.
August 2. The train that left Gallatin at 9 o'clock P.M. was attacked by guerrillas between this place and Bowling Green, Ky. As the train was not off the track and the conductor supposed the track to be torn up, the train returned to Gallatin. The behavior of every soldier in camp and on duty was put down in writing every day, and the whole report read at the end of every week on dress parade in front of the whole regiment. A scout of 150 men infantry was sent out to-day.
August 3. The scout sent out yesterday, returned. They had killed one

94 (Wyatt 1972)

guerrilla and taken several others prisoners.

August 4. The day was very hot.

August 5. Thunder storm and rain, the lightning felled one man of company A in camp to the ground, without injuring him otherwise much.

August 8. Inspection of arms to-day.

August 9. Many of our boys went off on a furlough; inspection of arms and dress took place again.

August 10. A number of horses were taken to Nashville by our cavalry.

August 11. A rebel deserter came in our lines; the day was made interesting by thunder storms and rain.

August 12. Company D received a new recruit.

August 13. To-day a year ago we left Pontiac, Ill. for the three years' service. In the afternoon drill.

August 14. Drill.

August 15. Inspection.

August 16. Tremendous heat and rain.

August 17. The second Lieutenant of our company, Burch, received his commission as Captain. In the afternoon dress parade.

August 18. One hundred men infantry were sent off again on a scout.

August 19. Inspection; the scout returned with several rebel prisoners.

August 20. We received marching orders.

August 21 - Nashville

Ward's brigade moved to Nashville. Their duties became lighter, except for guarding railroad travel to the Tennessee River.

GRUNERT, CO D 129TH ILL: August 21. We packed up and at 4 o'clock P.M. turned our backs upon Gallatin. Five miles west of the city, on the Nashville Pike, we halted and camped for the night.

August 22. Left camp at 5 o'clock A.M., and as the sun was very hot we did

not continue our march longer than 9 o'clock, when we rested near a creek. At 5 o'clock we resumed our march and camped 5 miles from Nashville for the night.

August 23. We struck our tents at 4 ½ o'clock and reached the Cumberland River at 8 o'clock; we rested some time before we crossed. At 12 o'clock we were on the ground assigned us for camping, between Fort Negley and the Murfreesboro Pike, near the eastern part of the city.

August 24. The ground assigned us for camp, was so covered with stones, wood, etc. that but a small part of the regiment had been able to erect tents the evening before, and it required the hardest work of every man to get everything fixed and right.

August 25. Worked on our tents again. One man of the regiment was tied to a tree for bad behavior; he broke loose, however, and escaped, but was afterwards recaptured and tied again. We delivered up our old Springfield muskets and received Enfield rifles in their stead. Got another new recruit in company D.

August 29. Had brigade drill for the first time under command of Gen. Ward.

August 30. Inspection of arms and dress.

August 31. Gen. Ward's brigade had parade before Gen. R. S. Granger .95; the bi-monthly muster took place.

September 1. Brigade drill in the forenoon and company drill in the afternoon.

Sept. 2. Part of the 129th went as escort on the trains to Stevenson, Ala.; brigade drill in the afternoon.

Sept. 3. Another escort went with the trains to Stevenson, 113 miles from here.

Sept. 5. Company drill and dress parade.

Sept. 6. Another escort went to Stevenson, Ala.

Sept. 7. On our return from Stevenson, when near Nashville, one of our men jumped out the car, while the car was in motion and crossing a bridge, which the man could not see in consequence of the darkness. The poor fellow was badly hurt and carried to camp.

Sept. 10. On the 9th we went to Stevenson again. On our return on the 10th, the locomotive of our train ran off the track near Andersonville station in the Cumberland Mountains, and as the engine could not be brought on the track again, we had to remain over night on a switch close by.

Also on the 9th, just up the Tennessee River from Andersonville, Generals Rosecrans and Thomas drove Bragg's Rebels out of Chattanooga. They began to plan a campaign in the mountains to the south.

Sept. 11. About twenty miles from the place where the locomotive had run off the track, another like mishap befell us, and all endeavors to bring the locomotive on the track again were fruitless. As our cars were on a switch, other trains were not stopped by our disaster. Afterwards we took another train, as we were beginning to feel hungry, and the country being hardly able to feed the bushwhackers, much less us half-starved Yankees.

Sept. 13. Our orderly sergeant, William Lemon, died to-day in the hospital with the flux. The whole regiment mourned the loss of this much-liked, brave soldier, but all mourning could not recall him to life. A few hours after his death he was buried with the usual military honors, the customary salutes fired over the body of the brave man now resting in the cool sod, and slowly and mournfully the regiment returned to camp.

Sept. 14. Inspection of arms, equipments, etc. was announced, and everything prepared for it.

Sept. 15. In consequence of the rain no inspection was held.

Sept. 16. Rain and heavy storms.

95 Not the General Gordon Granger of the Atlanta Campaign.

Sept 17. The inspection announced for the 14th, took place to-day.
Sept. 19. The paymaster arrived here, and we received pay for two months.

McGuffey Versus Webster

MERRILL, 70TH IND:The negroes who attached themselves to the regiment were very anxious to learn, but when McGuffey's Spellers were given them could not believe they could "larn to read in them thar kind of books." Their happiness and diligence were indescribable when a new supply was ordered, and they received the blue back Webster's Elementary Speller they had seen their young masters formerly use. One old fellow, after vainly wrestling with the alphabet for months, sold his book to a younger man for five dollars. As the speller had cost him nothing, his disappointment was attended with at least one consoling feature, that though not a man of learning, he certainly was a man of business. .96

Webster's was a better starting point. McGuffey's required a teacher or at least some earlier learning.

Luck and Audacity

While Ward's brigade had lighter duty at Nashville, they sometimes guarded trains carrying supplies to Alabama for the armies, which had first driven the Rebels out but then were surrounded and trapped at Chattanooga, to be rescued by Grant, Sherman, Hooker, and others, brought from east and west. The culmination was a series of battles to drive the Rebels out. Stories from those battles illustrate for us some significant attitudes and talents among the generals that will show, at Resaca, how little a hill is like a mountain. How large that difference will be left for the reader to notice. Readers will also notice differences that luck makes. There are stories of opportunities and unintended consequences, seeking and hogging glory, and shifting of blame. But through it all honest perseverance overcoming many obstacles.

---

96 (S. Merrill 1900, 61) Who provided the spellers? Perhaps the same benevolent societies that were supporting Ayers' recruiting efforts.

Chattanooga

A Small Mistake - a Disastrous Defeat

Rosecrans and Thomas prepared to drive the Rebels out of Tennessee and beyond, facing a maze of hills and ravines, traps for the unwary, where one side or the other could hide from their foe or surprise them.

Though not an original source, Draper gives a good explanation of how Chickamauga arose:

> DRAPER: The Richmond government, perceiving the imminent peril in which the Atlantic States were about to be placed by the falling back of Bragg and the unresisted advance of Rosecrans, used every exertion to reenforce their army under the former general, sending to him Buckner from East Tennessee, Longstreet from Virginia, and Polk from Alabama. Bragg was enjoined to turn forthwith fiercely on Rosecrans, and stop his advance. .97

> BUTTERFIELD: The lack of organized and serviceable information on the part of our Government and Commanders in the East, with the skill and ability of our opponents, permitted Longstreet's corps to be detached from the Army of Northern Virginia under Lee, in the presence of the Army of the Potomac under Meade, and fall upon the Army of the Cumberland with superior forces, while its Commander, General Rosecrans, had been assured that no troops had been so detached. .98 .99 .100D

Longstreet's army was thought to still be in Virginia, not lurking in these hills.

Rosecrans had driven the Confederates out of Chattanooga but met disaster on September 20 at Chickamauga after Bragg turned back on him and Thomas with new troops. A mistake in orders created a gap in the line. Longstreet poured through. Rosecrans' part of the army left in panic, leaving Thomas holding fast like a rock till Bragg wore out, allowing Thomas to cover a night retreat to Chattanooga, where he remained, trapped under siege. Lincoln immediately sent

---

97 (Draper, History of the American Civil War Vol 3 1870, 63) Not an original source nut consistent with later research.
98 A footnote says "See correspondence with General Sharpe in addenda" but addenda was not included in book.
99 (D. Butterfield, "Major General Joseph Hooker; Battlefield Dedication at Chattanooga" 1896, 4)
100 Blaming Meade?

Generals Hooker and Slocum, which included Williams and Geary, from Virginia, to the rescue. Grant was brought from Vicksburg to take overall command and he later brought Sherman.

Prisoners

DRAPER: Bragg had now occupied the passes of Lookout Mountain; he had broken the line of communication along the south bank of the Tennessee with Bridgeport. The destruction of the bridge at that place had severed the railroad communication with Nashville, the base of supplies; this compelled the wagon-trains which fed Rosecrans' army to move by a circuitous route along the bottom-land of the Tennessee and Sequatchie Valleys for some distance, and then to ascend and descend the Waldron Ridge by very steep, narrow, and rough roads. Bragg, therefore, not only commanded the railroads connecting Chattanooga with the North and West, but also the navigation of the Tennessee River, and the roads upon its banks.

Rain commenced early in October. The roads became almost impassable. The Confederate cavalry, crossing the Tennessee above Chattanooga, fell upon the trains entangled in the mud of the Sequatchie Valley and on the rocky western ascent of Waldron's Ridge. In one day they destroyed about 300 wagons, and killed or captured 1800 mules. Distress began to reign in the camps: the animals of the trains starved to death—the roadsides were lined with their bodies; the artillery-horses died at their picket-ropes.

It was doubtful whether the national army could hold Chattanooga much longer. Starvation had so destroyed the animals that there were not artillery horses enough to take a battery into action. The number of mules that perished was graphically indicated by one of the soldiers of the Army of the Tennessee, "The mud was so deep that we could not travel by the road, but we got along pretty well by stepping from mule to mule as they lay dead by the way." 101

Our brigade tended things in Nashville, while the rescue of Thomas and Chattanooga got underway. Here is a timeline to help keep dates and events straight:

Sep 9 Rosecrans Captures Chattanooga
Sep 20 Rosecrans Defeated at Chickamauga

101 (Draper, History of the American Civil War Vol 3 1870, 75) Draper published in 1870 without references.

Oct 5 Help Begins Arriving
Oct 20 Grant Arrives in Nashville
Oct 23-26 Williams' First Cumberland Excursion
Oct 27 Brown's Ferry Captured
Oct 28 Battle of Wauhatchie
Nov 6 Longstreet Leaves Chattanooga
Nov 23 Orchard Knob Captured
Nov 23? Williams' Second Cumberland Excursion
Nov 24 Battle of Lookout Mountain
Nov 25 Battle of Missionary Ridge

GRUNERT, CO D 129TH ILL: Sept 20. A detail of our men were ordered to guard the negroes working for the Government near the city on the Cumberland river.
Sept 21. The unpaid part of the regiment was paid off to-day. The guard sent out yesterday, returned.
Sept 22. Company and battalion drill.
Sept 23. Inspection took place again; fire-wood was received; in the afternoon battallion drill.
Sept 24. Four hundred Wounded from Rosecran's army were brought to Nashville.
Sept 25. Many Eastern regiments passed through here for Rosecran's army; in the afternoon brigade drill.

Help Coming

Help is on the way, but already Hooker's previous problems with other generals gets in the way. It will rob Thomas and Sherman of Slocum's services.

SLOCUM: to Lincoln, September 25th: I have just been informed that I have been placed under command of Major General Joseph Hooker. My opinion of General Hooker both as an officer and a gentleman is too well known to make it necessary for me to refer to it in this communication. The public service cannot be promoted by placing under his command an officer who has so little confidence in his ability as I have. Our relations are such that it would be degrading if made to accept any position under him. I have therefore to respectfully tender the resignation of my commission as major-general of volunteers. _102

102 (OR, Series I Vol 29 Part 1 Serial 48: Reports n.d., 156)

GRUNERT, CO D 129TH ILL: Sept 26. In the fore and afternoon company drill.
Sept. 27. Had company drill twice.
Sept. 28. Brigade drill in the afternoon.
Sept. 29. Part of Zollikoffer's large building in the city, which served as a prison for rebel soldiers, caved in, over two hundred prisoners were crippled and six killed.
Sept. 30. A rainy day; inspection was announced, but did not take place.
October 2. Inspection took place today, and in the afternoon brigade drill. Sergeant Howard of company H died in the hospital.

AYERS, CO E, 129TH ILL: Oct, 2nd A D. 1863. Nashville. This day is fine after Raining all day yesterday. Soldiers have been pasing two days past on Trains by thousands from the East to Reinforce Rosecrance Generals Hooker and Seigle is now her at the St. Cloud Hotell on there way to Roscy with there Corpse [Corps]. God give them good speed. _103

GRUNERT, CO D 129TH ILL: Oct. 3. Company drill in the forenoon and dress parade in the afternoon.
Oct. 4. Inspection and dress parade.

GEN. ALPHEUS WILLIAMS: at Nashville, October 5: I am stopped here by a guerilla raid, which has broken up the track below ... I left [Washington] Monday morning on the express train upon which I found ... Gen.Hooker, who took me into his private car and discussed by the hour ... his military matters. He had been ordered to command the 11th and 12th corps but Gen. Slocum demurred and sent in his resignation, but the President, I believe, decided to relieve one corps from Hooker's command. I expect that Gen. Slocum talked pretty plain to the President, but of that I can talk to you, not write. At any rate, Gen. Hooker and myself talked on the same subject. I believe you know what I think of Gen. Hooker, a gallant and chivalrous soldier and most agreeable gentleman, but as an army commander his signal failure at Chancellorsville under such advantages as no general officer has a second time will ever prevent any confidence in him as a great commander. _104

GRUNERT, CO D 129TH ILL: OCT. 5. The regiment received marching orders. The rebels burned a bridge near Murfreesboro, Tenn. All the camps had

103 (Ayers 1947, 107)
104 (Williams 1963, 335) To a daughter. The 11th and 12th Corps had been ordered from the Rapidan in Virginia to the west after the defeat at Chickamauga.

been alarmed, and all regiments near Nashville, had hereafter to be in line of battle from 3 o'clock A.M. to daybreak.

REID, CO A 22ND WIS: October 6 letter from Fort Rosecrans, Murphreesboro: We had been notified early in the morning from Nashville that a train had left there loaded with Potomac troops and that they would stop here if needed. About 11 o'clock the whistle of the approaching train was heard, and I got permission to go back to camp after some dinner, and so had an opportunity of seeing them when they arrived. The train contained three regiments of the 12th or General Slocum's Corps—the 98th and 149th New York and 5th Ohio. As they could proceed no further at any rate, these regiments disembarked and were also assigned positions in the Lunettes.

Among the passengers upon the train was Brigadier General Ward of Kentucky who had been ordered by General Granger to take command here ... The 11th and 12th Corps were being sent from the Army of the Potomac in Virginia to reinforce Rosecrans ...This General Ward deserves more than a passing notice. He is the roughest looking old fellow I ever saw. When he came off the train and during the entire day he wore a blue private's over coat, dirty and almost ragged, a black hat that looked as if its owner had been in a "free fight" and had received several punches in the head—a common black scabbard sword with gilt belt that had seen so much service that the leather was red in places, and his face and figure corresponded with his attire. In person he was short, stocky, almost corpulent. From beneath his battered hat, long, iron-gray, uncombed locks depended nearly to his chin on one side, while the other side was cut so short as to be scarcely visible under the hat—a string of iron-gray whiskers ran under his chin, seemingly designed to tie his face and hair together, and the face bronzed almost to Indian darkness gave him the appearance of an old Western trapper or California gold digger. _105

GRUNERT, CO D 129TH ILL: Oct 7. To-night at 10 o'clock the camp was alarmed again. The order came to our regiment to draw rations for two days and be ready for marching. The order was promptly obeyed, everything packed up, and shortly after we marched to the Chattanooga depot, where a train was awaiting us to take us to Franklin, Tenn. which place was threatened by the enemy and contained but a small Union garrison.

---

105 (Reid 1965, 96) The brigade of the 22nd Wisconsin was to join Butterfield's division. Reid was company clerk, responsible for gathering and distributing rations, and performed a variety of errands.

Oct 9. A sergeant of the regiment, on guard at the time of the departure to Franklin, got into a difficulty while in company this evening, and was wounded slightly on the hand by a pistol ball.

Oct. 10. The regiment returned from Franklin, without the loss of a man; the enemy had kept away from the place.

Oct. 12. The day was very cold. One hundred rebels came to Nashville with horses, accoutrements and arms, and surrendered.

Lincoln solved Slocum's problem by removing the 11th Corps from Hooker's command. They then were to guard the railroad while Hooker's 12th Corps went to help relieve Chattanooga.

WILLIAMS: My command extends from Tullahoma south, half way between Cowan and Tantalon, so as to embrace the railroad tunnel which runs through the mountains six miles below this, a distance of twenty-two miles! Of course we can guard only the bridges, tunnels, culverts, water-tanks, etc. Gen. Ruger's brigade is from Tullahoma to Elk River, his headquarters at Tullahoma. Gen. Knipe's brigade extends the rest of the way to Cowan. His headquarters are here. The country about this is not well cultivated and the people who are left look shabby and forlorn. But there is a fine town two or three miles off (Winchester) and the country about it is said to be fertile and well cultivated. It has been pretty well stripped, for Bragg's and Rosecrans' armies have both encamped here. It was near Murfreesboro that the three-days' battle of Stone River or Murfreesboro took place.

My horses arrived yesterday. Old Plug Ugly has lost pretty much all his tail. His length is so great that he rubbed at both ends of the car and has bared the bones of his head and his tail, besides having had his neck badly bitten by some indignant horse. He looks worse than after the shell exploded under him at Chancellorsville. He looked at me with most sorrowful eyes on our first meeting. The stallion looks better, though he is badly rubbed on both hips by his two weeks railroad voyage. None of the horses are badly injured, however. _106 _107

106 (Williams 1963, 274) Williams had been left to guard the worst part of the rail lifeline while the rest of Hooker's command went on to relieve Chattanooga. (Williams was relieved later by General Paine, of Gallatin notoriety, who was despised as much at Tullahoma.)

107 Old Plug finally wore out, after Savannah, and had to be sold. He died soon after. (General Williams had other horses—but not like Old Plug.)

GRUNERT, CO D 129TH ILL: Oct. 16. A rainy day.

Oct. 19. Company and battalion drill in the forenoon, and brigade drill in the afternoon.

Oct 20. Spent the day with drilling, as yesterday.

First, save Thomas' army. And perhaps some horses and mules.

HALLECK, GENERAL-IN-CHIEF: October 20: Thomas says if the supply wagons now on the road arrive safety they will be all right till November 1, at least. General Grant ordered him to hold Chattanooga at all hazards. He replied: "I will hold the town till we starve." _108

Also coming to the west after service with the Army of the Potomac, including the Battle of Gettysburg, was an Indiana regiment, having passed through home on their way to Tullahoma. Veterans of Gettysburg get their first look at the hero of Vicksburg.

GRUNERT, CO D 129TH ILL: Oct. 21. Companies A and D had to do picket duty. Gen. Grant came through Nashville to take command of Gen. Rosecrans' army; Gen. Rosecrans was called to Washington.

BROWN, CO C 27TH INDIANA RUGER 2B 1D 20C: Just at this time an army incident transpired that carried us all entirely away. A number of officers and soldiers assembled at the station one day with the band, to see and greet one whom they had learned incidentally was to pass through on the cars. We had all known of him, but no one of us had ever seen him. When the train arrived he stepped out on the rear platform. He was then a major-general and held the highest command of any one in the United States army—the reward of his previous successes. Yet he wore a faded coat, the buttons of which indicated the rank of brigadier-general, and in his demeanor he was as bashful and modest as a school boy. What he said could not be heard a rod away. No need to say that this was General Grant.

The sight of this plain, unassuming Western man, with his Western ways, brought our hearts right up into our throats. We cheered with a wild abandon, Bless God! the days of our serfdom were over. At last we were under men who could think of something besides brass buttons, tinsel and gilt lace. There were to be other standards of excellence than parades and reviews. _109

---

108 (OR, Series I, Volume 31. Serial 54 n.d., 0666)
109 (E. R. Brown 1899, 448)

GRUNERT, CO D 129TH ILL: Oct. 22. Company and battalion drill in the forenoon, and brigade drill in the afternoon.

AYERS, CO E, 129TH ILL: Oct 22, 63 at Nashville Tenn. Fine Beautiful day. We have been here 2 months this day. No cases in Hospital that are dangerous and but few are there. Boys all well. General Grant was in the Citty and Left yesterday for Chatanooga and Rosey Left for Cincinnatia. We will have fun now soon. .110

Grant had been sending orders but has just now arrived. General Howard and Hooker greet Grant. Recalling Chancellorsville, this seems ironic.

HOWARD One day I was at Stevenson and, while at the railroad station, the Nashville train brought Grant, Rawlins, and one or two more of his staff. On his car I was introduced to him. He gave me his hand and said pleasantly: "I am glad to see you, General." Then I had to do the talking. In a few minutes a staff officer from Hooker came in and offered Grant a carriage to take him to Hooker's headquarters, a quarter of a mile distant—extending also an invitation to the general to stay and partake of Hooker's hospitality. Grant replied: "If General Hooker wishes to see me he will find *me* on this train! "The answer and the manner of it surprised me; but it was Grant's way of maintaining his ascendency where a subordinate was likely to question it. Hooker soon entered the car and paid his respects in person. .111

That may not have been significant. But, in light of later events, perhaps it was.

GRUNERT, CO D 129TH ILL: Oct. 23. A cold and rainy day, in consequence of which no drill took place.
Oct. 25. Received the news that the escort of the train, sent off a few days ago, had been taken prisoners and the train burned. The report was not believed. In the evening inspection of the regiment took place. Another party was detailed as train guard, but as no trains were running, the men returned to camp.
Oct. 26. A member of company H was buried with military honors. The detail again went to the depot, but returned again, as no trains were running.
Oct. 28. Battalion drill in the forenoon and brigade drill in the afternoon.
Oct. 29. Battalion drill in the afternoon.

110 (Ayers 1947, 107)
111 (Howard 1907, 460)

Cumberland Excursion, the First

Between Nashville and Chattanooga was a major obstacle, the Cumberland Mountains, confounding efforts to move troops and material. Here is the first.

BROWN, CO C 27TH INDIANA RUGER 2B 1D 20C: A little later the following entries were made in the diary of a Twenty-seventh soldier: October 23, to Dechard; October 24, to Anderson; October 25, to Dechard; October 26, to Tullahoma. Brief, but true. With more detail, these entries mean that under orders, which had every appearance of being serious, we started to the front. We carried ten days' rations of bread, five of meat and an extra supply of ammunition. The first day we marched to Dechard, over a good road and through a level country—an easy march of Fifteen miles. The next day we toiled up the rocky side of the main chain of the Cumberland Mountains and descended again on the opposite side. We went over the mountain exactly where the railroad goes partly under it. There had been little or no road there before. The only time it had ever been used, we were told, was while the railroad was being built. With infinite labor we pulled the artillery and baggage wagons up by hand on one side and eased them down again on the other. In places ledges of rock rose from one to three feet, almost perpendicular, and in others the wheels cut down in the soft, black soil squarely to the hubs. That night we camped at Anderson's depot After crossing the mountain the road follows down the Crow Creek Valley, a very wild and picturesque locality, hemmed in by high mountains. Near where we camped was a spring large enough to run a mill. It issued from a cavern in the side of the mountain into which a man could walk almost upright. Beech nuts were again plentiful.

Next morning there was a delay in starting. When the start was made we took the backtrack; and the march that day and the following one were the exact counterparts of the two previous days, except that the direction was reversed. The fourth night found us back at Tullahoma, upon the precise spot from which we had started. Several thousand men had just had a nice promenade, of some seventy miles, for their health.

The explanation of this transaction, current at the time, was to the effect that an order was issued for our division to go to the front and the Second Division to remain in the rear. But General Geary, the commander of the Second Division, objected. He was a large man, with a rugged, if not violent, disposition. When he learned of the arrangement he went to the higher authorities and made a disturbance. He complained that the First Division had too often been preferred over his. It had been given all chances to distinguish itself, while his division had been kept in the back-ground. Whether this report was true or not. our division was ordered back and the other division went forward. Williams' division guarded the railroad and Geary's division participated in " the Battle Above the Clouds." In the absence of any other, this explanation is given for what it is worth. _112

Indeed, it was tragically true for the instigator of this disturbance, the seeker of opportunity.

Battle of Wauhatchie

Grant, taking charge, with the corps of Hooker and Howard from the eastern theater, and Thomas and Sherman from the west, proceeded methodically to relieve Chattanooga and then Knoxville.

> POWELL, 66TH OHIO CANDY 1B 2D 12C: After the defeat of the Union army at Chickamauga it fell back and took shelter behind the defenses of Chattanooga. Bragg followed and took up a position in front on Missionary Ridge and also upon the flank of the Union army upon the greater heights of Lookout Mountain. From these respective heights the Confederate commander looked down upon the Union army. To some visitors who called upon him at his headquarters on Missionary Ridge he said that he held over there pointing to the Union army some 40000 prisoners but as he had not the provisions on hand to feed them he had deferred taking formal possession of them and preferred for the time being that they should feed themselves as best they could. Had he taken possession of them it is probable that the rations that he would have issued to them would not have been less than was the pittance that the Union commander was able to dole out to his own soldiers. _113

> POWELL, 66TH OHIO CANDY 1B 2D 12C: This situation and the danger of the capture of the Union army put Hookers forces the Eleventh and Twelfth Corps of the Army of the Potomac and Sherman's Army of the Mississippi in motion for the relief of Braggs so called prisoners cooped up about Chattanooga and whom Bragg had declined to gather in. At the same time Grant started to take personal command of all the Union forces that should be concentrated at Chattanooga. Hooker's movement was by rail and was a most remarkable one for the speed with which it came as his troops did not

112 (E. R. Brown 1899, 448)

113 (Powell 1901)

disembark from the cars from the time they entered the same until they reached their several destinations on the Nashville Chattanooga Railroad in the vicinity of Bridgeport, Alabama. The arrival of Grant and of Hookers forces upon the field of their new operations was simultaneous. Grant's first move was to furnish provisions or open up the Cracker line as it was called for the relief of the Union army then under command of Thomas. To accomplish, this Hooker crossed the Tennessee River near Bridgeport and moved down the Wauhatchie Valley with such troops as he could spare from

Battle of Wauhatchie, Tenn., October 29, 1863. Death of Major Boyle

the defense of the railroad line and struck the Tennessee River again at Browns Ferry, uniting there with troops sent from Chattanooga in effecting which Hookers forces were assaulted in the night near Wauhatchie Station by Confederate forces from off Lookout Mountain from which heights they could look down upon every movement of Hooker and could perfect their plans accordingly. The result of that night battle was that Hooker drove whatever Confederates there were within that district back upon Lookout Mountain thus establishing connection upon a direct line between Bridgeport and Chattanooga. That line thus established was never broken or interrupted by the Confederates and was ample to furnish the Union army with all the supplies and reinforcements needed so that eventually it won the great battle of Chattanooga. .114

General Geary's division took the brunt of the attack, on the night of October 28, losing many men.

COLLINS, 149TH NY IRELAND 3B 2D 20C: When the rays of the rising sun came over Lookout Mountain they fell with a mellow light upon the tall and portly form of Gen. Geary, standing with bowed head on the summit of the knoll ... while before him lay the lifeless form of a lieutenant of artillery. Scattered about were cannon, battered and bullet marked caissons and limbers, and many teams of horses dead in harness. And there were many other dead, but none attracted his attention save this one, for he was his son. The men respecting his sorrow stood at a distance in silence while he communed with his grief. At a moment like this hollow seems the glory of military honors and how priceless the privileges of a free and united country, which cost so much to attain! .115

WILLIAMS: to daughter, November 11. In my first trip down with my division when I expected to have been a part of Hooker's advance, I had as companions Capt. Atwell and Lt. Geary of Knapp's Pennsylvania Battery, and I relieved at Anderson a lieutenant colonel of the 111th Pennsylvania Infantry, all of whom were killed in the recent night attack upon Hooker's command. They were all attached to the 2nd Division of our corps. It is hard to realize these sudden removals of one's friends, with whom but a few hours before one has talked in health and cheerfulness. But what a long list I can recall in this war! .116

The irony! Williams struggled down to Bridgeport only to go back after Geary was sent to the front instead—and dined with Geary's son, who went to his death while Williams struggled back up the mountain.

114 (Powell 1901) Grant had accepted Thomas' plan to float the river at night and was blessed by a fog that kept them out of sight.
115 (Collins 1891, 198) Geary's division defended Wauhatchie. and his son was with their artillery.
116 Williams, Nov 11. To daughter. Referring to the excursion of October 27, prior to the Battle of Wauhatchie.

Williams' Tough Job

Slocum, being separated from Hooker, has Williams in the middle. Williams reflects on an excursion on the Cumberland and the result for General Geary.

WILLIAMS: to daughter: I have hardly been quiet since I returned, for I am obliged to have a guard at every bridge, culvert, tank, and trestle on the railroad for over ninety miles. So I am kept going up and down to see how they are placed, what defense works, whether patrols are kept up, and generally if the railroad is as well guarded as possible. If important bridges are lost the whole army goes up, as they are just able to live now. You see the responsibility is immense, without any possible credit. On this long road, bridged over mountain streams and trestled across mountain valleys and ravines for two or three hundred miles, the whole Army of the Cumberland now in and about Chattanooga must get its supplies for man and beast. The country is full of guerrilla parties and the Rebel cavalry are always menacing right and left to pounce in upon a weak point. I got back only yesterday from my last trip of four or five days, going with Gen. Slocum to Bridgeport. At this point the railroad stops by reason of a destroyed bridge where it crosses the Tennessee.

Until within a few days the whole supply of the army at Chattanooga has been carted over the most infamous mountain roads from this point, nearly sixty miles. The recent rains have raised the river so that the boats can now go part way up, to within eight or ten miles of Chattanooga. Gen. Hooker, with the 11th Corps and one division of the 12th Corps, has cleared the intermediate valley. They had quite a smart "skrimage" on the way, a night attack by part of Longstreet's men. Gen. Greene was badly wounded in the face and Capt. Atwell of the Pennsylvania Independent Battery mortally wounded. Lt. Geary, son of Gen. Geary, was shot dead. Both of these officers sat with me during the night I was trying to get over the mountain, as I have mentioned above. Geary's troops were on railroad trains and mine marching. For this reason, and perhaps a little partiality of Gen. Slocum for my division, was the reason mine was sent back to meet, as was supposed, a great cavalry raid. Geary gets the glory, but he suffers, as mine would, in loss of officers. It is singular, but after all and with these hazards, officers complain of being sent to inactive life and Losing their chances!

We have very beautiful moonlights just now and an immensity of whippoorwills, and there are two mocking birds which begin their imitations every night in apple trees close to my tent. They mock everything from a frog to a crow. Some of their notes are beautifully sweet. The boys have tried to capture them but without success so far. .117

Our brigade helped. The 129th Illinois guarded supplies, up and down that mountain.

> GRUNERT, CO D 129TH ILL: Oct 30. Company D was detailed as train guard, and left camp at 6 o'clock P.M. had to remain at the depot the whole night, and did not leave Nashville until the next morning.
> November 1. Nothing particularly unpleasant happened on our trip to Stevenson, excepting that we had to wait several times rather long for trains bound North. We did not reach Stevenson until 10 o'clock at night.
> Nov 2. Company D had to remain in Stevenson, because the next train would not leave before tomorrow.
> Nov 3. At five o'clock A.M. the train with company D and a number of disabled horses left Stevenson; between Smyrna station and Nashville two cars with horses were thrown off the track and several horses slightly hurt. Reached Nashville at 8 o'clock.
> Nov. 4. In the afternoon company drill.
> Nov. 5. Rainy and cold weather; no drill took place.

An unhindered personal inspection of the Rebel line.

> GRANT: November 1863. After we had secured the opening of a line over which to bring our supplies to the army, I made a personal inspection to see the situation of the pickets of the two armies. As I have stated, Chattanooga Creek comes down the centre of the valley to within a mile or such a matter of the town of Chattanooga, then bears off westerly, then north-westerly, and enters the Tennessee River at the foot of Lookout Mountain. This creek, from its mouth up to where it bears off west, lay between the two lines of pickets, and the guards of both armies drew their water from the same stream. As I would be under short-range fire and in an open country, I took nobody with me, except, I believe, a bugler, who stayed some distance to the rear. I rode from our right around to our left. When I came to the camp of the picket guard of our side, I heard the call, "Turn out the guard for the commanding general." I replied, "Never mind the guard," and they were dismissed and went back to their tents. Just back of these, and about equally distant from the creek, were the guards of the Confederate pickets. The sentinel on their post called out in like manner, "Turn out the guard for the commanding general," and, I believe, added, "General Grant." Their line in a

117 (Williams 1963, November 20, 1863)

moment front-faced to the north, facing me, and gave a salute, which I returned.

The most friendly relations seemed to exist between the pickets of the two armies. At one place there was a tree which had fallen across the stream, and which was used by the soldiers of both armies in drawing water for their camps. General Longstreet's corps was stationed there at the time, and wore blue of a little different shade from our uniform. Seeing a soldier in blue on this log, I rode up to him, commenced conversing with him, and asked whose corps he belonged to. He was very polite, and, touching his hat to me, said he belonged to General Longstreet's corps. I asked him a few questions—but not with a view of gaining any particular information—all of which he answered, and I rode off. 118

Friendly relations indeed. General Longstreet was Grant's friend at West Point, and was best man when Grant married his cousin.

On November 6, General James Longstreet reluctantly took several thousand soldiers away from Chattanooga, after being ordered to take Knoxville from Burnside at the insistence of the Confederate President. Grant constantly labored to take control of the Chattanooga area so they could send soldiers to relieve Burnside. Longstreet's absence helped.

> GRUNERT, CO D 129TH ILL: Nov. 7. A foraging party was sent 18 miles from the city after hay.
> Nov. 8. Inspection and dress parade.
> Nov. 9. Cold weather; brigade drill in the afternoon.
> Nov. 10. Battalion drill in the forenoon and dress parade towards evening. Company D was again detailed as train guard.
> Nov. 11. The report was current that we would be paid off to-day.
> Nov. 12. Company D returned from Stevenson.
> Nov. 13. Company drill in the forenoon; brigade drill and practice in firing in the afternoon.
> Nov. 14 Were paid off for two months.
> Nov 16. Between the hours of 3 and 4 o'clock, a fire broke out in the city; but one building burned down.

Longstreet, after a difficult journey, with 10,000 infantry, began the siege of Knoxville.

118 (Grant 1886, 42)

GRUNERT, CO D 129TH ILL: Nov. 17. General inspection and dress parade. A corporal of company C was stabbed by an Irish storekeeper, and died afterwards in the hospital; the Irishman escaped.

Nov. 18. Battalion drill in the afternoon.

Nov. 19. A number of men were arrested for firing their guns in the camp which had been prohibited; they were, however, not severely punished. In the afternoon the following regiments had brigade parade before Gen's. Ward and Granger; the 129th, 105th, 102d Illinois, 79th Ohio, 13th Wisconsin and 70th IND; also, a regiment of cavalry. The parade was the finest we ever had, and both Generals were well satisfied. The day was sultry and dark.

Nov. 20. A foraging party was sent out again, but as a heavy rain set in, the party was compelled to return to camp, without having accomplished their object. A large part of the regiment went as train guards to Stevenson and Chattanooga.

Nov 23. The men returned from Stevenson; a good many of the boys got furlough.

Champagne with Starvation

WILLIAMS: In returning from Bridgeport we were obliged to stop a day at Stevenson where the officers of the 4th Artillery battery gave us an extensive supper. We had oysters and champagne! Just think of that, away down in northern Alabama and over these hard roads! The explanation is, that about fifty purveyors had been ordered away from the front and were all congregated at Stevenson with their unsold goods, and with some they had not been able to get farther toward the main army. It seemed strange, when our soldiers and officers, too, all along the railroad and in front were living on half and one-quarter rations, that oysters and champagne should be abundant at Stevenson. But by bribery and other tricks these sutlers contrive to get transportation often when men are starving for necessary supplies. What an immensity of rascality this war produces or develops! It makes me sick, sometimes, to hear of the frauds and rascality that are practiced in all departments, often to the suffering and misery' of those exposed in the field. These things are found, from the miserable pasted shoes that men pay high prices for to the food they eat. In everything there is proof of contractors' and government agents' fraud and cheating. I think it was Wellington who said that these things could be stopped only by hanging a contractor and inspector every Saturday night! I wish often it could be tried. .119

Grant's Plan for Chattanooga

Sherman was to cross the river above Chattanooga and assault the north end of Missionary Ridge while Hooker assaulted from the east, with Thomas and Howard pressed along its length. There were, as always, several problems.

WOOD, 3D 4C: During the week commencing on the 15th and terminating on the 22nd of November, 1863 it was decided to operate simultaneously on both flanks of the Confederate army for the purpose of dislodging it from its very formidable position. The flank attack, on which the chief reliance was placed to produce this desideratum, was to be made by General Sherman, with his own command, supplemented with troops drawn from the Army of the Cumberland. General Sherman was to cross the Tennessee River, with his command, at the mouth of North Chickamauga Creek, ascend the northeastern flank of Missionary Ridge (which here juts against the river), sweep the ridge, and take the enemy's intrenchments.

Two divisions of the Fourth Corps, General Sheridan's and my own, were to cross Citico Creek near its mouth, just above Chattanooga, move up the peninsula enclosed between the creek and the Tennessee River, form a junction with the right flank of General Sherman's force (after he had made a lodgment on the north-eastern extremity of the crest of Missionary Ridge), and, after making the junction, swing to the right, and sweep along the lower slope and base of the Ridge ... The force in Lookout Valley, General Hooker's, was to demonstrate against Lookout Mountain; and, if the opportunity seemed propitious, to assault, and, if possible, to occupy the summit of Lookout Mountain ... But a heavy fall of rain, Friday P.M. with other causes of delay, prevented General Sherman's command from reaching in time the point at which it was to cross the Tennessee River. .120

GRANT: Hooker ... was to get from Lookout Valley to Chattanooga Valley in the most expeditious way possible; cross the latter valley rapidly to Rossville, south of Bragg's line on Missionary Ridge, form line there across the ridge facing north, with his right flank extended to Chickamauga Valley east of the ridge, thus threatening the enemy's rear on that flank and compelling him to reinforce this also. Thomas, with the Army of the Cumberland,

119 (Williams 1963, October 12, 1863)
120 (Wood 1896, 24)

occupied the centre, and was to assault while the enemy was engaged with most of his forces on his two flanks . . . By crossing the north face of Lookout the troops would come into Chattanooga Valley in rear of the line held by the enemy across the valley, and would necessarily force its evacuation. Orders were accordingly given to march by this route. .121

Notice that Grant said to go around Lookout, which did not mean to get across, which would entail another battle, not seen by Grant as necessary.

But first, they needed get closer to Missionary Ridge for Thomas to press it in the planned battle.

Orchard Knob

WOOD, 3D 4C: During the entire day of Sunday, the 22d, much movement, some of it singular and mysterious, was observed in the Confederate army. This led to the issuing of the following orders . . . throw one division of the Fourth Corps forward, in the direction of Orchard Knob (and hold a second division in supporting distance), to discern the position of the enemy, and determine if he still remains in the vicinity of his old camp . . . These orders directed a reconnaissance in force—nothing more. It was not expected there would be a collision with the enemy ... Furthermore, the verbal instructions from General Thomas and General Granger directed the return of my division to its position within the fortifications of Chattanooga, when the reconnaissance was completed. Orchard Knob, given in the orders as the directing point of the reconnaissance, is a bold and rocky eminence, arising some hundred feet above the general level of the plain of Chattanooga.

At the signal to advance the grand array moved forward rapidly, crossed the open space, and, pressing rapidly onward, the two deployed brigades found themselves in close proximity to the Confederate intrenchments; indeed, not more than a stone's throw from them. .122

SHELLENBERGER, CO K 64TH OHIO 3B 1D 21C: It was shortly after noon of November 23, 1863, when Sheridan's division marched out of its camps behind the intrenched line at Chattanooga, leaving the tents standing, and formed in battle array across the hill now occupied by the National Cemetery. From the western side of the hill, where the Sixty-fourth Ohio

---

121 (Grant 1886, 55) Grant considered having Hooker cross and then recross the river from Lookout Valley to get around the mountain, but the water was too high.
122 (Wood 1896, 25)

stood, looking off to the right front across some open fields, we could plainly see the Confederate picket line only a few hundred yards away. The pickets in gray were sitting on top of the little mounds of earth that marked their picket posts like ground-hogs in front of their burrows, apparently taking much interest in our movements without having any suspicion that we were preparing to attack their line. Some of the prisoners afterword stated that they thought we were coming out for an inspection or a review. A few days after the battle of Chickamauga an agreement had been made by the rank and file of the opposing armies that they would not fire at each other on the picket line except in resistance of an aggressive movement. This agreement had been faithfully carried out, and while the batteries on Lookout Mountain and Moccasin Point were pounding away at each other perfect peace prevailed along the picket line across the Chattanooga Valley.

On this 23d day of November, our pickets, who were to act as our skirmish line, had been carefully instructed, and when the bugles suddenly sounded the charge, they sprang forward with such a dash that they actually ran over some of the Confederate pickets before the latter had recovered from their astonishment. Their intrenched picket line was carried with a surprisingly small amount of resistance and with a correspondingly small loss to our side. .123

WOOD, 3D 4C: When two hostile bodies of troops find themselves in such close proximity, the alternative is a fight or a foot race. As neither of the belligerents, on that occasion, seemed disposed to accept the role of runner, the alternative was to fight. Fortunately the officers and the rank and file, spontaneously and instantaneously, discerned the exigencies of the situation, dashed forward, at the double-quick, and, by a "bold burst," carried the Confederate line to the extent of two brigade fronts ... I signaled from Orchard Knob to General Thomas, who was standing on the parapet of Fort Wood, "I have carried the first line of the enemy's intrenchments." He promptly replied, by signal, "Hold on; don't come back; you have got too much; intrench your position." .124

SHELLENBERGER, CO K 64TH OHIO 3B 1D 21C: A little later, after the Confederates had recovered their self-possession, and the two skirmish lines were spitefully pecking away at each other, one of the Confederates called over:

123 (Shellenberger 1896, 52)
124 (Wood 1896, 28)

"Hello, Yanks, what's got the matter with you all over there?"

One of our men called back: "We're out of wood." This was literally true; for not only all the timber inside our picket line had been cut off, but the stumps and the roots of the trees had been dug out of the ground in the growing scarcity of fuel. The Confederate called back:

"If you wanted wood why didn't you. Say so? We have more than we need out here, and if you had only asked us you might have sent out your teams and got all the wood you wanted without kicking up such h— of a fuss about it." _125

WOOD, 3D 4C: The consequences of this success were far-reaching.

1st. A strong salient, thrust far out against the enemy's center, equally important for offense or defense, and for observation, had been gained.

2d. But for this initial success, the movement which culminated in dealing the final and decisive blow to the enemy could never have been made.

3d. The first immediate and important consequence of the success so unexpectedly gained was the withdrawal of Bate's division of the Confederate army from Lookout Mountain, to further strengthen the Confederate center on Missionary Ridge. The withdrawal of Bate's division from Lookout Mountain assured the success of General Hooker's attack on that position.

4th. The menace of this strong salient, so far advanced, compelled the Confederates to hold the preponderating part of their force on the crest of Missionary Ridge to secure the safety of their center. _126

GRUNERT, CO D 129TH ILL: Nov. 24. The boys went off on a furlough.

November 24 - Battle of Lookout Mountain

I have been the instrument of Almighty God ... This feat will be celebrated until time shall be no more. —Geary

POWELL, 66TH OHIO CANDY 1B 2D 12C: After the battle of Wauhatchie Hooker's forces took a permanent position near the battlefield his picket line being along Lookout Creek. From the point where that stream enters

125 (Shellenberger 1896, 53)
126 (Wood 1896, 30)

the Tennessee River thence for several miles up that stream the course of that creek was parallel with the mountains. The Confederates occupying the mountain established their picket line at the bank of the creek near the foot of the mountain so that small stream separated the two armies. At several points across that small stream these pickets at times had talks and exchanged many articles from their respective stores. I believe the truce thus established by these soldiers was never broken by a hostile shot as on both sides those pickets walked their beats openly and in plain sight of one another. _127

While at my tent I was awakened by the rapid riding of an Orderly approaching who, upon being halted by the sentinel at my tent, sang out "I have orders for Col. Powell." . . . [after Powell reported to Geary] "Colonel I have sent for you I have orders to make a demonstration upon Lookout Mountain. I wish to know where and how I am to cross that creek with my command."

It is not probable that Gen Geary in the presence of the staff officers who had brought him his orders would have mentioned to me his having orders to make a demonstration on Lookout Mountain if those orders were that he should assault and capture it but Gen Geary then added to what he had already said as to what his orders were that he intended to show the world what his ideas of a demonstration meant. ... So I think that Gen Geary then upon his own responsibility resolved that he would make the most of his orders and push a demonstration to the utmost limits that a construction of that phrase would admit of showing that in his own mind he had already turned a demonstration into an assault and was going to make a reality of it. That resolve of Gen. Geary and the subsequent success of the reserve pickets in building a footbridge across that creek were very important factors in one of the most successful and brilliant assaults upon what was regarded as an impregnable position that the annals of war make mention of ... This bridge was made without hammer nails, or saw, simply by lashing the timbers to the knees, and as the boards had been torn off the dam the water passed under the foot bridge without any resistance from it. Much to our surprise not a shot had been fired by the enemy ... Gen. Geary then returned to his division and in a few moments around upon the path from the hill the column came crossed the foot bridge and went climbing up the mountain side as he had directed where we joined them and at once moved forward far above the heads of the Confederate pickets who yet remained in ignorance of our movements along the line of Lookout Creek watching our

127 (Powell 1901)

pickets upon the opposite side. Our rapidly advancing troops drove in the outlying posts of the enemy and this enabled Geary to come almost upon their main camps which were situated near the foot of the palisades, at the point of the mountain fronting Chattanooga, before the army had full knowledge that he had crossed the creek, virtually making a surprise of it and enabling him to get the better of the battle upon the elevated plateau, the progress of which was being eagerly watched by the Army of the Cumberland, who could be seen through the floating mists the incessant flashes of the opposing guns and the movements of the hostile troops as they struggled for the mastery far up on those dizzy hights making a living picture seldom witnessed and one that may never be repeated with any hope of success. ... the night following the enemy began to evacuate the mountain and easily in the morning some brave soldiers of Whittakers Brigade climbed up the palisades and planted the Stars and Stripes upon the highest point on Lookout Mountain and as the uprising sun dispelled the mist and presented that scene to view the sight our flag living there in all of its glory sent a thrill of enthusiasm throughout the Army of the Cumberland and inspired those soldiers for their brilliant assault upon Bragg's center on Missionary Ridge. _128

GEARY, 2D 20C: Had we not succeeded, in opening the navigation it is easy to see, that our army must evacuate Chattanooga from necessity. The calamities which would undoubtedly have followed, it is impossible to describe ... The successful battle of Wauhatchie solved the question. And has been pregnant with results, viz: The navigation opened. The army fed and impending danger removed. But alas! A portion of the price paid for these essential benefits, was the precious life of our own inestimable Eddie, brave spirit, it rests in the bosom of his Saviour and his God. I am bereaved and transformed. Like the tiger robbed of his whelps, I have been like a destroying angel ever since, no height has been too bold, no valley too deep, no fastness too stormy, that I did not solicit to be permitted to storm. Permission was granted, and with the assistance of bold hearts and willing hands, I have been the instrument of Almighty God, of carrying terror and terrible destruction wherever it has pleased God to direct my footsteps. Under such impulses I stormed, what was considered the impassible and inaccessible heights of Lookout Mountain, I captured it, turned the right flank of Bragg's army and drove him from his position. This feat will be celebrated until time shall be no more. _129

---

128 (Powell 1901)
129 (Blair n.d., 143) Whitaker and others stormed the heights.

POWELL, 66TH OHIO CANDY 1B 2D 12C: After the battle of Chattanooga had been won a Confederate picket party, some 20 in number, came in at the foot bridge from off Lookout Mountain and gave themselves up as prisoners stating that they saw the force building the bridge but as that force was small they decided it was merely a scouting party and they would let us come over. Then they would charge us and cut us off from the bridge and capture our entire party so they decided not to fire on or molest us, but when the bridge was completed what was their surprise at seeing not the balance of our pickets coming over but instead Geary's Division and on the run. Then they saw it was too late to fire or retreat so they hid themselves in the bushes being cut off from regaining their own camps or giving the alarm by Geary's rapid movement and as the battle went against them they decided that they would in come in and surrender which they did, crossing upon the foot bridge which they had allowed to be built. Had that picket line done its duty and as soon as they saw that we were endeavoring to cross the creek begun firing upon, us no bridge would have been built at least not in the way or in the time that we built it and the battle above the clouds might have resolved itself into what was intended, a demonstration on Lookout Mountain ... Thus by the success of those pickets in building a bridge across Lookout Creek, at the foot of the mountain, Geary was able to turn a demonstration into the famous battle above the clouds and the sight that followed of the Stars and Stripes floating in triumph from that lofty peak helped to inspire the Army of the Cumberland then standing upon the lowlands about Chattanooga for their brilliant dash upon Missionary Ridge and in that rush they broke Braggs line of battle into fragments and took more guns and prisoners from his army than he had captured at Chickamauga. 130

Missionary Ridge

Another reinforcement was turned loose to face Sherman. It had been paroled at Vicksburg. Now it would assist in defeating Sherman's repeated attempts at the north of the ridge.

WESLEY CONNOR, PRIVATE, CHEROKEE ARTILLERY, CSA: During this fight ... Corput's Battery occupied a position near the extremity of Lookout Pt. ... It was a privilege of a lifetime. ... We brought our guns off after dark, and as we came down the Mountain road, to our left we could hear the Infantry fire and see the flashes of their guns through the trees, that looked like myriads of fireflies. Passing through Ross' Gap and around behind Mission Ridge, we were run up to the top of the Ridge the next afternoon, in a

130 (Powell 1901)

position almost over the tunnel on the Southern Railway, just in time to assist in the repulsing of Thomas' [Sherman's]charging columns. .131

WESLEY CONNOR, PRIVATE, CHEROKEE ARTILLERY, CSA: Came into position with the first section immediately to the left of the tunnel on the Cleveland and Chattanooga Railroad, just as Stevenson's Division had driven back a column of Yankees, which had been holding a position a few hundred yards in front of our line for several hours. Our guns with six others turned loose upon the broken and scattered Yankees, which had the effect to considerably increase their speed and disorder. This was about 4 o'clock P.M. .132

GRUNERT, CO D 129TH ILL: Nov. 25. Kitchens were erected by the regiment, brigade drill the afternoon. There was an alarm of fire in the city.

SHELLENBERGER, CO K 64TH OHIO 3B 1D 21C: During the night of the 24th, General Bragg had called in all his forces from Lookout Mountain and from Chattanooga Valley, and it was the troops let loose by this shortening of his left that he was concentrating in front of Sherman. They all came from the direction of Rossville, marching in plain sight along the crest of the Ridge and across our front. I gave close attention to these movements, having nothing else to do, and I sat on our breastworks watching them with a good field-glass. I could see the marching troops so plainly that I could easily count the files, and I am confident not a man nor a gun was taken from the line that confronted us. .133

WOOD, 3D 4C: According to the plan of battle, General Hooker's command, if successful in carrying Lookout Mountain, was to descend the eastern slope of the mountain, cross Chattanooga Creek, ascend the western flank of Missionary Ridge, and attack the left flank and rear of the Confederate position on the Ridge. It was supposed that General Hooker's command would make its appearance on the left flank of the Confederates on Missionary Ridge by twelve M. on the 25th. But our Confederate brethren were too experienced soldiers not to block that very well arranged little game. After crossing Chattanooga Creek, which flows through the valley between Lookout Mountain and Missionary Ridge, the Confederate force destroyed the bridge over the creek. The necessity of repairing this bridge

131 (Connor, Wesley O.; Blakeslee, George H. 1899)
132 (Connor, Wesley O.; Blakeslee, George H. 1899)
133 (Shellenberger 1896, 56)

so delayed General Hooker's movement that his command did not appear on the battlefield of Missionary Ridge proper at all. .134

So, after that "demonstration" on Lookout, Grant's forces, facing Missionary Ridge, faced more than expected. First, infantry and artillery released from Lookout now faced Sherman on the east, right where Grant intended to force Hood's forces back. These added to the forces moved there after Orchard Knob was taken. And second, Hooker, who was intended to attack from the other end, could not even get across a creek to attack the east end.

CLEBURNE'S REPULSE OF SHERMAN AT MISSIONARY RIDGE.

WOOD, 3D 4C: During Wednesday, the ever-memorable 25th of November, 1863, the Confederate army, commanded by General Bragg, of "a little more grape" fame, occupied the crest of Missionary Ridge. My division, nearer to the base of the Ridge than any other of the national troops, was in the position occupied Monday, P.M. General Sheridan's division was in echelon to the right of my division, with General Johnson's division in echelon still

134 (Wood 1896, 32)

further to the right. General Baird's division was in echelon to the left of my division.

My headquarters had been on Orchard Knob since the afternoon of the 23d. Quite early in the forenoon of the 25th, General Grant, General Thomas, and General Granger commanding the Fourth Corps, with their staff officers, took position on Orchard Knob.

About the middle of the forenoon, or perhaps somewhat earlier, General Sherman's command began the ascent of the north-eastern flank of Missionary Ridge. The progress was steadily onward and upward, with heavy opposition, however, till the head of the assaulting column had advanced up the slope about two-thirds or three-fourths of its extent, when a polite gentleman was met, who said: "Thus far, Mr. Yanks, but no farther." In other words, the advance of General Sherman's command had butted its head against a heavy line of intrenchments, held by Cleburne's division of the Confederate army. _135

FIFTY-FIFTH ILLINOIS: The general plan of battle proposed for Wednesday, the twenty-fifth, was for General Hooker to cross the Chattanooga valley as rapidly as possible to Rossville, and facing north to envelope the left flank, while Sherman, facing south, vigorously assailed the right flank of the Confederate army; and when Bragg should have weakened his centre in his efforts to resist these flank attacks, Thomas was to assault with his whole line. Shortly after sunrise the Fifteenth Corps began its advance, and General Corse's brigade was soon hotly engaged with the Arkansas and Texas brigades on the fortified hill. We were five miles from Chattanooga, strongly entrenched across the northern end of Missionary Ridge within musket shot of the tunnel, our left flank protected by the Chickamauga River, our right within support of the left of the Army of the Cumberland.
...

The contest continued for hours upon the same ground with varying success. Where we had hoped to find the enemy the weakest and least prepared, they were evidently in great force and amply fortified. General Bragg had sent regiment after regiment from his left to mass against us at the wooded gorge at the tunnel. ...

In pursuance of the plan of battle the general assault was expected to be made before noon, but as is usual in complex tactics over large areas,

135 (Wood 1896, 33)

unforeseen delays had arisen. General Hooker had no considerable force opposing him, for the troops that had garrisoned Lookout Mountain and the Chattanooga valley had marched to confront Sherman. But the distance to Rossville was about five miles, and the bridge over Chattanooga Creek was found destroyed, causing four hours' detention. _136

WOOD, 3D 4C: Every eye on Orchard Knob was turned on General Sherman's operations, keenly watching his movements, and, in profoundest sympathy, ardently desiring success to crown his sturdy efforts. But all in vain! Assault after assault was repulsed. About half past two P.M. it was plainly and painfully evident to every beholder on Orchard Knob that General Sherman's attack, which, according to the plan of battle, was to be the dominant coup of the battle, had been hopelessly defeated, and was an irretrievable failure. It was evident that his further progress toward the crest of the Ridge was peremptorily stopped.

It chanced that at the moment of the repulse of General Sherman's last assault, General Grant was standing near me. He approached me and said "General Sherman seems to be having a hard time."

I replied, "He does seem to be meeting with rough usage."

To this General Grant said, "I think we ought to try to do something to help him."

I said, "I think so, too, General, and whatever you order we will try to do."

General Grant continued, "I think if you and Sheridan were to advance your divisions and carry the rifle pits at the base of the Ridge, it would so threaten Bragg's center that he would draw enough troops from the right, to secure his center, to insure the success of General Sherman's attack."

I replied, "Perhaps it might work in that way; and if you order it, we will try it, and I think we can carry the intrenchments at the base of the Ridge."

General Grant walked immediately from me to General Thomas, distant about ten paces. I did not accompany him, though there would have been no impropriety in my doing so. Generals Grant and Thomas were in conversation a very short time, perhaps two or three minutes, when General Thomas called General Granger, who stood near to him. After perhaps two

136 (F.-f. Illinois 1887, 285)

minutes conversation between Generals Thomas and Granger, the latter came to me and said:

"You and Sheridan are to advance your divisions, carry the intrenchments at the base of the Ridge, if you can, and, if you succeed, to halt there."

He further said, "The movement is to be made at once, so give your orders to your brigade commanders immediately, and the signal to advance will be the rapid, successive discharge of the six guns of this battery." .137

SHELLENBERGER, CO K 64TH OHIO 3B 1D 21C: It was shortly after three o'clock when we began to move out from our breastworks to form for the assault ... Nothing was said as to what it was expected we were to accomplish ... When all was ready, a battery stationed at Orchard Knob fired its six guns in rapid succession as a signal for the charge. Before the signal was fired, the quiet of expectancy had prevailed along our line, but, when it sounded, a scene of intense animation at once ensued. Far and near could be heard the bugle notes and the voices of the officers calling the men to attention, and as they sprang to their feet there was a great rustling of dead leaves and a snapping of dried twigs. I cast a hurried look to the right and the left, and on either hand, as far as I could see, stood two lines of blue coats with beautiful flags waving and bright arms gleaming in the pleasant afternoon sunshine. It was a splendid sight that sent the blood tingling to the finger tips. The moral effect which it produced upon the enemy must have contributed greatly to our success. We were standing in a stretch of open timber, but the leaves were all off the trees, and we were in plain sight. As we advanced, every Confederate soldier along the crest of the Ridge in our front could take in our entire array with one sweeping glance, while looking to the right or left along their own line, on account of the inequalities of the Ridge and other obstructions, he could see but a small number of his own comrades. He would naturally get the impression that they were being attacked by overwhelming numbers. Some of the prisoners afterward said it looked like all creation was charging on a few hundred of them.

We had approached near enough to see that there were no head-logs, and I was wondering why I could see no heads showing above the works, when I remembered what I had read of the orders given by General Putnam to his

---

137 (Wood 1896, 33)

men at Bunker Hill, and almost with a groan I mentally exclaimed: "They are waiting till they can see the whites of our eyes."

It was a tremendous relief to discover that the breastworks were not occupied. There had been a skirmish line behind them when we started, but the skirmishers had promptly run away when they first saw us coming, except those who lay still and surrendered when we came up.

When it was manifest that the breastworks would not be defended, I raised my eyes toward the crest of the Ridge, and then saw the skirmishers falling back through the timber near the top. In our charge across the plain, I did not see a single musket shot fired from the breastworks at the foot of the Ridge, nor did I see a single man hit by the fire coming from the artillery posted along the crest above. General Bragg certainly made a great mistake when he withdrew from the lower line. If the plunging fire which we encountered in going up the steep ascent, and which mostly overshot us, had been delivered from the breastworks below while we were crossing that level, open plain, it must inevitably have cut us to pieces. The conditions would have been similar to those which confronted Burnside's army when it charged Lee's lines at Fredericksburg, and there is every reason to believe that the result would have been the same.

All the dirt used in building the breastworks had been thrown from a ditch on the inside, in which the defenders would stand, and therefore the parapet on the outside was so low that we could run up over it without difficulty. As I leaped down into the ditch, I paused there just long enough to take a look to the left. The line in that direction, having a little shorter distance to traverse, had already passed beyond the breastworks and was sweeping onward without halting. I then jumped out of the ditch, and calling "Forward!" to my company, pushed on up the hill.

It is now well known that the orders under which we were acting contemplated carrying the line at the foot of the Ridge, which it was supposed the enemy would defend, and there stopping. But when we arrived at these breastworks, we had not come in contact with a battle line of the enemy, nor had we fired a single shot. The men, having listened for nearly two days to the sounds of the fighting which had been going on to the right and the left of them, naturally supposed that they had now been sent forward to take a hand, and not meeting with the expected opposition at the breastworks, they went on of their own accord, and without orders, to engage the line so plainly visible on the crest above.

It would be interesting to know what the actual thoughts of General Grant were, as he stood on Orchard Knob and watched the soldiers whom he had characterized to General Sherman only a few days before, as so badly demoralized by the battle of Chickamauga that he feared he could not get them out of the trenches to fight, now assaulting of their own volition a position which the leading generals, Federal and Confederate, believed to be too strong to be carried by a direct attack. 138

WOOD, 3D 4C: As soon as the troops were in motion the enemy opened on them a terrific fire from his batteries on the crest of Missionary Ridge. These batteries were so posted as to give a direct and cross fire on the assaulting troops. It would not, perhaps, be an exaggeration to say the enemy had fifty pieces of artillery disposed along the crest of the Ridge.

But the rapid firing of this artillery could not stay the onward movement of our troops. They pressed forward with dauntless ardor, and carried the line of intrenchments at the base of the Ridge. Having a shorter distance to pass over, the troops of my division were the first to arrive at the base of the Ridge. When the intrenchments were carried, the goal for which we had started was won. The orders carried us no further. We had been instructed to carry the line of intrenchments at the base of the Ridge, and then halt.

But the enthusiasm and impetuosity of the troops were such that those who first reached the intrenchments at the base of the Ridge bounded over them, and pressed on up the ascent after the flying enemy, without orders from any commander. The rank and file took in the exigencies of the situation, and quickly adopted the only way out of the danger with which they were environed, namely, to assault and carry the crest of the Ridge. The barricades at the base of the Ridge were no protection against the artillery on the summit. To remain at the base would be destruction; to retire would be both expensive of life and disgraceful. Officers and men all seemed impressed with this truth. In addition, the example of those who first bounded over the intrenchments and began the ascent was contagious. Without waiting for orders, the vast mass pressed onward up the rugged ascent, in the race for glory, each man apparently eager to be the first on the summit. 139

SHELLENBERGER, CO K 64TH OHIO 3B 1D 21C: While lying there recovering our wind, Colonel McIlvain came walking along our line from the right,

138 (Shellenberger 1896, 56)
139 (Wood 1896, 36)

and as he came I saw the men rising up and running back in a straggling manner to the rear. When he reached me, he said: "Lieutenant, you must take your company and go back to the breastworks." The order was so manifestly a blunder, and my social relations with the colonel were of such a character, that ventured to violate the military proprieties by remonstrating against it. I pointed out how the enemy were overshooting us, and declared my decided conviction that we could inflict far more damage upon them, and with much greater security to ourselves, by remaining where we were; to which he replied, somewhat impatiently: "I know all that very well, but the orders are to go back to the breastworks, and we must obey orders."

When I got back to the breastworks, I found them packed on the outside with our second line, which had stopped there, and with the men of the first line who had run back, all of them hugging the ground as closely as possible.

When the front line fell back, all aggressive action on the part of Sheridan's division came to a standstill, and I have never doubted that at this time it was Sheridan's intention to comply strictly with the orders and stop at the breastworks, at least until he should receive orders from the rear to go on. But it was soon evident that it would be intolerable to lie there doing nothing under the plunging fire of the enemy, and as Wood's division on our left could be plainly seen slowly but steadily pushing its way up the hill, Sheridan quickly decided to follow Wood's lead; for he came riding along the line, calling out: "As soon as you get your wind, men, we will go straight to the top of that hill." The time was not altogether lost while we were lying there, for after the men had rested they were able to go forward so much more rapidly than could Wood's tired men, who had not halted, that it is a hotly disputed question to this day which division first broke over the top of the Ridge. The mistake was in ordering back the first line from the advantageous position which it had secured. It was a much safer place at the timber line to regain our wind than it was at the breastworks, to say nothing of the many brave men who were unnecessarily sacrificed in falling back and in advancing a second time over that dangerous belt of ground between the breastworks and the timber line, which was so thoroughly combed by that terrible canister fire, and where we met with our heaviest losses. ₋140

WOOD, 3D 4C: I was conscious from the moment the skirmishers of my division commenced the ascent of the steep acclivity, that the movement was in direct contravention of positive orders, and that nothing but success

140 (Shellenberger 1896, 63)

could excuse this palpable disobedience of orders. I did not need to be reminded, by message of inquiry, sent by General Grant, through General Fullerton, asking whether I had ordered the assault, that I had gone beyond the pale of his orders, and that possibly dire consequences might flow from this disobedience. But the possible consequences, personal to myself, did not much trouble me in that perilous ascent. It was the result that I clearly saw would fall on my noble division, if the assault should be repulsed, that put the heavy strain on me . . . Speaking for myself, individually, I frankly confess I was simply one of the boys on that occasion. I was infected with the contagion of the prevailing enthusiasm. The enemy's artillery and musketry could not check the impetuous assault. The troops did not halt to fire; to have done so, would have been ruinous. Little more was left to the immediate commanders of the troops than to cheer on the foremost, to encourage the weaker of limb, and to sustain the very few who seemed to be faint-hearted. To the eternal honor of the troops, it should be recorded that the laggards were, indeed, few in number. Upward, upward, steadily went the standard of the nation, borne onward by strong arms, upheld by brave hearts, and soon it was seen flying on the crest of Missionary Ridge! . . . The enemy, whom we had seen during the two lonely months of the investment occupying this dominating position, was in full retreat!! .

Pollard, the historian of "The Lost Cause," explains why the Confederates did not assume the offensive when the national advance had nearly reached the crest of the Ridge. He says, old, veteran, and disciplined soldiers as they were, the Confederates were simply dazed, dumfounded, by the very audacity of the assault. And I may add, the successful assault of Missionary Ridge is a most pertinent illustration of the soundness of the old French military maxim-*l'audace, toujours l'audace.* _141 _142

FIFTY-FIFTH ILLINOIS: Chickamauga was avenged. General Hooker came up in good time from Rossville on the right. The battle was won, and Bragg's left wing, a disorganized mob, was madly for the mountain fastnesses of Georgia. _143

BUTTERFIELD, QUOTING HOOKER: "November 24, attacked the enemy and drove him from Lookout Mountain. Followed in pursuit and fought him

---

141 (Wood 1896, 36)
142 Audacity. Always audacity.
143 (F.-f. Illinois 1887, 288)

again at Missionary Ridge on the 25th, and at Ringgold Ga. on the 27th. We were victorious in every encounter." _144

Readers may be incredulous about Hooker's "we" claim to victory. We take "we" to mean the "Union"

Readers may wonder what the Battle of Missionary Ridge has to do with the 129th Illinois and the rest of their brigade, back in Nashville. The earlier battles of Wauhatchie and Lookout Mountain primarily reveal more of the character and overriding ambition of General Geary, which will be manifest at Resaca. Missionary Ridge illustrates that luck always has a variety of unforeseen consequences in the best of plans. Generals must recognize that, even when celebrating their successes. Luck was beneficial at Lookout and Missionary Ridge. Will the Generals plan for it at Resaca? Will it be beneficial or adverse?

Man in the Middle

Slocum was not entirely separated from Hooker. Williams tells his daughter of being caught in the middle during the Battle of Chattanooga.

WILLIAMS: November 31: My Dear Daughter: It is a cold, leaden, cloudy, snow-feeling day. My fingers are so stiff that I can hardly guide a pen; and yet I am away down in the sunny south, close to the Alabama line. Indeed, I have just come from Alabama. I don't see that the skies are more genial or the temperature much milder than in northern Michigan at this season. Indeed, the whole month of October has been mainly rainy and disagreeable, not half as pleasant as those misty, smoky, warm days we generally have up north . . . You see I have changed my locality and I must first tell you how. About a week ago I got orders by telegraph to put my division in march for Bridgeport, the place where the Chattanooga Railroad crosses the Tennessee River. They were in motion at daylight in the morning along my whole line. Between Decherd and Tantalon is the first high range of the Cumberland Mountains, and the road over it is nothing but a bed of high rocks and deep mud-holes. The ascent of the mountain begins just beyond Cowan. Having crossed this mountain the road runs down the deep valley of Crow Creek to Stevenson and then turns east toward Chattanooga. The railroad follows pretty much the same line, except that it pierces the mountain crest by a tunnel, three-fourths of a mile long.

144 (D. Butterfield, "Major General Joseph Hooker; Battlefield Dedication at Chattanooga" 1896, 20)

I waited for my rearmost brigade to come up and then [went] to the cars, expecting to reach Bridgeport before the advance, but I found that such railroads run in such a way as this one is are not exactly to be relied on. The grades are tremendous, and the locomotives old, worn-out affairs. To this add the fact that no fuel is provided on the road. I started from Decherd in the afternoon and reached Cowan (four miles) without much trouble. But here began the heavy mountain grades and the tug of war. They keep at this point a locomotive called a "pusher" which pushes behind each train. The ascent to the mountain tunnel is about two miles. All night the locomotives tugged and pushed and screeched out signals and blew whistles, but it was "no go." We were obliged to go back to Cowan, where conductors and engineers and firemen all went to sleep. I didn't much blame them, for they had been out several nights without sleep. I rather envied them, as my seat was a board close to a broken window.

The night was very cold and (what is strange with me) I could not sleep. I had received a telegram that Wheeler, Roddey, Lee and other Reb. cavalry commands had crossed the Tennessee to make another raid, and I was ordered to halt my command to meet them. Here I was, unable by rail to reach my command not ten miles ahead of me. I fumed and, I fear, swore, and walked the sidetrack for hours to keep warm and to keep down my indignant spirit. At length day-light broke on Cowan's Cove (a cove here is a tract of bottom ground in the mountain valleys) and I stirred up engineers, conductors, and stokers with a vengeance and insisted upon another trial. Wood was collected and we started up the grades, luckily made a successful effort, got through the tunnel, and went tumbling fiercely down the slopes into the Crow Creek valleys, where I found three regiments of Knipe's and all of Ruger's brigades. Part of the artillery, after three days' labor, had got over the mountain by the aid of a regiment to each battery. Ten gun-carriage wheels were reported broken and the horses used up.

I was obliged to go on to Anderson to find a telegraph station. Here I began a library of telegrams to Hooker on one side (Stevenson) and Slocum on the other (Wartrace) both sending conflicting orders, Slocum ordering me to move on to Bridgeport, Hooker (through his Chief of Staff, Butterfield) ordering me to relieve certain posts along the railroad. In the meantime, the telegraph wire was so constantly employed by headquarters of the department that it was only now and then I could get in a word. All my baggage, bedding, mess, etc. was left at Cowan. Anderson has a depot building and one or two shanties. Luckily the telegraph operator was from

Grand Rapids (a Mr. Atwater) and he saved me from a fast of forty-eight hours, besides exerting himself professionally.

After much tribulation and after collecting my whole division within fourteen miles of Bridgeport, I got an order to retrace my steps, or rather to distribute my division from Bridgeport to Murfreesboro to guard the railroad bridges, tanks, culverts, etc. But the trouble was not over. Butterfield ordered the batteries at Tantalon to be shipped to Bridgeport. So I sent across the horses and put the guns on cars, when I was notified that my guns were not wanted. The messenger, with instructions from Gen. Slocum, was detained by a torpedo-blowing-up of track near the tunnel. I waited another night in the windowless depot, trying to get orders. Near morning a locomotive came along and I hitched on my train of guns and repeated the struggle to get up the grades and through the tunnel to Cowan, which, after many hours, was accomplished; to find, however, at Cowan written orders to leave the batteries at Stevenson and Bridgeport,

These orders could have reached me hours before and saved an immensity of trouble and annoyance if the staff officer of Gen. Slocum had done as he was ordered. My guns were brought on to Decherd and there they stand on the railroad "flats" waiting to be drawn back. My troops were marched back, and now occupy in small posts (just large enough to be gobbled) the railroad from Murfreesboro to Bridgeport, ninety-one miles. I changed my headquarters to this place as being more central, and because the buildings used at Decherd for my offices were occupied in my absence by cavalry officers.

How long this arrangement will last I can't guess. The 2nd Division of our corps has gone to the front and probably crossed the river at Bridgeport with the 11th Corps. They went down by rail, but as I was nearer Bridgeport than they were, with my whole command, I was somewhat annoyed at being countermarched. I went to Wartrace to see Gen. Slocum, and the only satisfaction I got was that he preferred to trust my division with the responsible duty of guarding the long channel of supplies for the whole Army of the Cumberland. Very complimentary, but I dislike this railroad guarding in small posts. The whole country is full of small guerrilla parties who can get to the track and tear it up in spite of anything that infantry can do, over a line ninety miles long. Besides, the posts at important bridges are too small to defend themselves against any serious attack. I prefer the field with my whole division to this kind of duty, and hope I shall get away soon, if I carry nothing but pork and hardtack on my saddle.

This town of Tullahoma, which you have seen in the papers as the headquarters of Bragg and of times of Rosecrans, consists of a hundred straggling houses of faded paint and retrograding look. Indeed, it reminds me strongly of some Michigan towns after the speculating fever of 1836 had subsided, a great town-plat with here and there a pretentious frame house of thin boards, half-finished and destined to remain so for years. Judge Catron of the Supreme Court has a neat summer cottage in the suburbs, but it is badly soiled by the occupation of soldiers.

All the towns along this railroad excepting Murfreesboro are the veriest pretenses, most of them sounding names and nothing else, and the people—the "poor white trash"—are disgusting: the mere scum of humanity, poor, half starved, ignorant, stupid, and treacherous. The women all "dip" snuff; that is, rub their teeth and gums with a pointed stick dipped in Scotch snuff! If anybody doubts the damning effects of slave labor upon the poor whites, let him come into Kentucky and Tennessee and see the poorer classes of whites. Of course, there is a rich and educated class, but they are mostly gone and the poor now stand out in bold relief, with not even a bright background. Travel through this country by rail and you will never see this poor class; none but the rich planters and traders. You must stay here and move through the country to see how many there are vastly inferior to the Negro in common sense, shrewdness, and observation, and in the comforts of life. Let us not grieve for the Southern Negro as much as for the poor Southern white man—covered with vermin and rags, and disgusting with the evidences of a cureless "Scotch fiddle," which they dig at continuously.

I must close my long letter as the carrier has just called. I am afraid I can't get leave, as we are expecting to do or suffer great things this fall. If we don't go ahead, and we can't in the present state of supplies, I think Bragg will come ahead on us. It will be an awful country to concentrate troops in, so full of pathless mountains and roadless valleys. How they ever got into Chattanooga is a marvel, and how they will ever get out now the mud roads have begun is a greater wonder. I hope we shan't get out, but things look squally for supplying an army down through this winter. 145

GRUNERT, CO D 129TH ILL: Nov. 26. In the evening dress parade.
Nov. 27. In the afternoon brigade drill.
Nov. 28. It was cold and rainy, and no drill took place.
Nov. 29. A large part of the regiment was again detailed as train guard for to-morrow's trains. Dress parade in the evening.

145 (Williams 1963, November 30, 1863)

Nov. 30. The train guards left the camp at 3 o'clock A.M. but did not reach Stevenson until December 1.

Totton Off Duty

After Chattanooga was secured, Sherman took a large force on a hard march to relieve Burnside at Knoxville. We now get our first glimpse of one who would become known as the Hero of Resaca, and of Averasborough as well. One company of the 79th Ohio was detailed as Burnsides' bodyguard. There began Private Totton's renown.

HALSTEAD, BENTON CO F 79TH OHIO: In piacing upon the mental canvas the heroic deeds of George W. Totton, of Company F. Seventy-ninth Ohio Volunteer Infantry, the writer fancies that he will not be accused of deceptive painting, his aim being to draw the lines true to nature.

George was a locomotive builder and physically perfect at enlistment. On the march his trousers were drawn tightly about the ankle and his stocking legs pulled up upon the outside, showing to advantage his symmetrical calves. His hair was black, and a bald patch at the crown rendered him conspicuous when in advance on a charge.

To "storm their works" during the war was not an advance upon the enemy on the double quick with measured step and bayonets at a charge, but a grand race for the enemy with bayonets fixed and arms at a right shoulder shift. Not to yell whilst on a charge would have been an eccentricity. To get there soon was the object, the bayonet to be used in case of hand-to-hand encounter, which was not unusual, but always brief.

At Knoxville, Tenn. during the siege in 1863, when the bullets were chirping in the air, George was discovered seated in a secure place, with his back against a stone wall, smoking his pipe. A report was at once made to his Captain that Private Totton had shown and was now showing the white feather. The Captain examined the situation, but did nothing further, as George was off duty at the time, and it was only prudent for him to select a safe and secure place to smoke and meditate. But from this time forward on the long, weary marches to Chattanooga and to Nashville, and back to Lookout Mountain and on to Resaca, Ga. although Private Totton had stood up to the work in several hot places, the majority of his comrades insisted upon it that George "wouldn't do." One would remark: "He's a fine thing to look at, but that's about all." "We all know him!" Another would chime in, "He's good enough for guard mount, or mount your horse, or Look Out

Mount, or Mount Wild Cat!" "Say, Stiney, do you recollect when he said he struck Wild Cat?"

Private Totton having once been detailed on special service that required him to ride a horse, occasioned frequent reference to that event. They called this kind of talk "running him." He took it all good naturedly, and would laugh with the rest of them at his own expense, but it was generally believed that he took to heart the insinuations against his soldierly qualities. _146

A fighting rooster with a white tail was thought cowardly and a poor bet, however fancy. More so in the battle line. In due course, Totton will display his real colors.

Winter Refuge

Pursued past Ringgold, Bragg took his army into winter refuge at Dalton, behind Rocky Face Ridge.

> GRUNERT, CO D 129TH ILL: December 2. One hundred and eighty rebel officers were escorted by the train guard from Stevenson to Nashville; among them was a son of the rebel Gen. Breckinridge.
> Dec. 3. Drill in the forenoon and afternoon; no passes to the city were issued, on account of the small-pox raging there.
> Dec 4. Battalion drill in the afternoon

On December 4. Longstreet's siege of Burnside at Knoxville ended with Sherman on the way from Chattanooga to break the siege. Shortly, Longstreet would be out of the way and the Union finally in control of most of Tennessee.

> GRUNERT, CO D 129TH ILL: Dec 5. Dress parade in the afternoon.
> Dec 7. All regiments of infantry, some cavalry and artillery were reviewed by Gen's. Rosseau, Ward, Granger and Paine. The day was cool and suited for the occasion.
> Dec. 9. The small-pox broke out in the regiment. There was talk about marching orders to Gallatin. General inspection was announced.
> Dec. 10. The regiment was inspected and passed review before Gen. Hunter.
> Dec. 14. In honor of the victories won by the armies of the Cumberland, large bonfires were kindled; Generals Hunter, Granger and Ward were

---

146 (Halstead n.d.) Company F was detached as bodyguard for General Burnsides while the rest of the 79th Ohio was guarding railroad in Tennessee and rejoined the regiment in early 1864. Knoxville was under siege by the Confederates until relieved after the Battle for Chattanooga.

present.

Dec 15. Firewood was received by the regiment. A member of company B shot at the captain of his company this evening, but missed him; he was put under guard.

Dec 16. The day was rainy and cold. A number of men were sent out to catch negroes, who were to unload the steamboats.

Dec 17. A strong detail was sent out to guard a number of wagons dispatched after some timber for a new powder magazine.

Dec. 18. Brigade drill in the afternoon; the day was very cold.

Dec 19. Dress parade towards evening. A member of company D who had imbibed too much, was robbed of his watch when returning to camp.

Dec. 20. Company inspection in the forenoon, and in the evening dress parade.

Dec 21. It was the general talk that we were ordered back to Gallatin. Brigade drill in the afternoon. The provost guard shot a soldier through the head, who refused to stop when ordered to do so.

Dec. 23. Brigade drill in the afternoon.

Dec. 24. Christmas eve shots were fired in every direction.

Dec. 25. A beautiful day. The officers of the regiment took their men to a neighboring brewery, and treated them to several barrels of beer.

MERRILL, 70TH IND: The following letter from Lieutenant Grubbs will give an idea of how pleasantly Christmas eve was spent at Nashville: "Dress parade was over and all retired to their quarters. Here, there, and all over the regiment you could see the boys gathering in knots and busily engaged in discussing some apparently important project. The crowd gradually increased, and the talk grew more animated, until company streets became full. It was easy to see that something was meditated, and yet that the boys were hesitating somewhat. The officers noticed that something unusual was up, but could not imagine what it was. I had gone to supper at Captain Fisher's, and we were quietly eating, when we heard a wonderful yelling up on the right. Company E is at something, says Captain Fisher, and a look convinced us of the truth of the remark. Coming down the street was a noisy crowd of perhaps thirty men, and elevated over their heads was Captain Meredith. They rushed him to the sutler and demanded a treat. Of course he complied, and soon every man was puffing away at a cigar. Another crowd now came rushing down amid shouts and laughter, and this time it was Company G, and on their shoulders they bore Captain Carson, one of steadiest old men in the regiment. The Captain seemed a little perplexed, but took it all good humoredly. Officers stood around laughing uproariously at the unlucky wights whom the boys had seized, and not until ominous crowds had gathered around them and rough hands were laid upon them did they realize that their time had come. I had just stepped out of the tent, and was watching Company C hurrying their Captain, a spruce old widower, up to the sutler's, and was laughing at his vigorous struggles to get away, when I heard a shout, 'There he is, there he is,' and turning around I saw Company F coming toward me on the run. I started to run, too, but was caught, mounted upon a dozen shoulders, and taken double quick to the sutler's. I called for a box of cigars, handed them to the boys, and was free. Then I could laugh at the others. Not an officer escaped. Even Captain Fisher was taken from the table and subjected to the same ordeal. Colonel Harrison and Major Merrill were each with their wives out of camp. But the boys were not to be disappointed. They found a Government wagon, fifty strong arms seized hold of it, and away they went after them. They drew the wagon up in front of the house where the Colonel and Major were boarding; half a dozen waited on and informed them of their business. Only giving them time to get their hats, they bore them to the wagon and started with headlong speed for the camp. There the regiment joined the wagon pullers, and a long, loud shout went up from five hundred voices. After the treat a speech was called for, and the Colonel made us one of his happiest little speeches. Then with three times three cheers the crowd dispersed and that part of the performance was over. As the beautiful moonlight evening came on, crowds to gather in the broad street, violins were brought forth, sets were formed, and the awkward but entertaining dance of the soldier began. Music and dancing was the order until taps, when everything grew quiet and the sports of Christmas eve were over." _147

During festivities, one of the 129th was being detailed to recruit those who had been called contrabands for Federal service.

AYERS, CO E, 129TH ILL: Recvd my Appointment Fri. Dec 25th, 63 at Nashville to report immediately to Wm F Wheler General Agent for Col. Recruits. _148

The New Year did not begin well at all. More death by exposure.

MERRILL, 70TH IND: As the last night of the year approached, a cold wave from the North drove the mercury many degrees below zero, and produced indescribable suffering. The exposure on the picket posts was very great, but the distress of the sentinel who could be relieved and could approach

---

147 (S. Merrill 1900, 66)
148 (Ayers 1947, 1) He was then detached and arrived in Stevenson on the 28th.

the log heap fire once in two hours was mild compared with the agony of the train guard, who rode on top of the box cars to and from Stevenson, Alabama. Some were frozen to death, and many contracted diseases that terminated fatally, or crippled the unfortunates for life. .149

GRUNERT, CO D 129TH ILL: Dec. 26. A rainy day; except guard duty we had nothing to do.

Dec. 27. It rained day and night.

Dec. 28. Company and regiment inspection.

Dec. 29. We drilled twice to-day. During the night heavy rain.

Dec. 30. Brigade drill in the afternoon.

Dec. 31. Muster for pay; rain and snow fell.

January 1, 1864. New Year's day; very cold and frosty; snow fell more abundantly.

New command and new tents.

MERRILL, 70TH IND: On January second, 1864, the Seventieth Indiana was transferred to the First Brigade, First Division, Eleventh Army Corps, commanded by General Howard. General Ward was placed in command of the division and Colonel Harrison of the brigade. The shelter or dog tent, as it was nicknamed, was issued on the thirtieth of this month. A piece of light canvas about six feet square, with a row of buttons or buttonholes on three sides, was given to each man. The soldiers usually united two or four of these pieces, then stretching them over a horizontal pole, raised on forks about three feet high, fastened the short ropes attached to the corners to stakes in the ground. The patriots entered this dwelling on all fours. The single piece of muslin and a small oilcloth was carried by each man, and by them he was protected at night from the dampness of the ground and the pelting of the tempest. .150

GRUNERT, CO D 129TH ILL: Jan. 2. It snowed the whole day and turned very cold, so that those out with passes returned.

Jan 4. The report came that our Doctor Johns who went along with a boat guard several hundred miles up the Cumberland river, had been shot by guerrillas. The guard returned and reported that the Doctor had been shot through his coat tail; otherwise "nobody hurt" nor killed. .151

Jan. 6. Very cold weather.

149 (S. Merrill 1900, 67)
150 (S. Merrill 1900, 70)
151 Creelsbore built boats, far up the Cumberland from Nashville.

Jan. 9. Company K was called to the city on duty. Col. Harrison, of the 70th Indiana regiment, took command of our brigade provisionally, our former commander, Gen. Ward, having assumed command of the first division of the eleventh army corps.

Jan 10. Company inspection; the day was very cold.

An affair of blame, redemption, and loss.

On January 10, General Carl Schurz read General Hooker's report on the Battle of Wauhatchie in a New York paper and, along with General Hecker, another veteran of the German Revolution of 1848, became so incensed at Hooker's public "regret" that they had failed to perform their duty in that battle that Schurz immediately requested a court of inquiry. After testimony, the court completely exonerated the Germans—those Germans who had been blamed by Hooker and others for the loss at Chancellorsville, the loss despite the efforts of Schurz to get units to the flank when General Howard did not think it necessary. One who stood up for Schurz after Chancellorsville had been General Howard himself. But now, with relations between Hooker and Schurz beyond repair, Schurz was sent to Nashville, no longer available to Sherman for the coming campaign. ₋152

> GRUNERT, CO D 129TH ILL: Jan. 11. As the inspecting officer was not satisfied yesterday, another inspection took place to-day.
>
> Jan 13. It commenced thawing. Several citizens from Scott County. Ill. in order (perhaps) to escape the draft at home, came to Nashville to offer their services to the Government.
>
> Jan. 15. It was reported that certain parties tried to persuade the whole brigade to re-enlist, in case the Government would permit.
>
> Jan. 16. Inspection of the regiment in the afternoon.
>
> Jan. 17. A heavy rain night and day.
>
> Jan. 18. Snow, rain and frost.
>
> Jan. 21. Gen. Rosseau received orders to hold all troops in Nashville ready for marching at any moment.
>
> Jan. 22. A warm and clear day.
>
> Jan. 23. Inspection of the regiment in the afternoon.
>
> Jan 24. A beautiful and pleasant day. Dress parade in the evening.
>
> Jan. 25. Got the news that the guerrilla chief John Morgan had escaped from prison; everybody was angry about the prison-keeper of Morgan's place of confinement.
>
> Jan. 26. The day was hot; drilled in the afternoon.
>
> Jan. 27. Company drill in the forenoon; received marching orders.

152 (Schurz 1908, 85) And other readings, not all original.

Jan. 28. All necessaries were packed up, and all unnecessaries boxed up to be left here.

Jan. 29. Had brigade drill; the time fixed for our departure was Sunday morning at 6 o'clock.

Jan. 30. A rainy day; we got shelter tents.

Jan. 31. Delivered up our old tents; had general inspection in the afternoon.

February 1. Guards were again sent out as usual, and the talk was that we would remain until further orders.

Feb. 2. A number of men went off on a furlough; the order came that we would remain but three days longer. In the night all pickets were drawn in, and yet the report was that we would not move.

Feb. 3. The tents were again erected and the camp made as commodious as possible.

Feb. 4. Firewood was received, and many of the men commenced erecting houses, and worked generally as though we would spend the balance of our time of enlistment in Nashville.

Feb. 5. The pay rolls were signed as we were to be paid off the next day.

Feb. 6. The weather was very cold to-day; to-morrow was fixed for pay day.

Feb. 7. Received two months pay.

Feb. 9. Inspection was afterwards countermanded; had brigade drill instead.

Feb. 10. Battalion drill in the afternoon.

Feb. 11. Company drill in the forenoon and afternoon.

February - We Will Have Fun Now

Chattanooga regained, the Union plans to squeeze the South hard. Our brigade gets in the game.

Time to Go

No one knew whether he would return alive or as a cripple. –Grunert

Let Us Eat and Drink for To-Morrow We Die

MERRILL, 70TH IND: A strong effort was made by the authorities at Nashville to keep the brigade from moving southward, but the desire on the part of most of the men, who had been so long in what was called the rear to be on the front line, had grown more intense as the months passed. The officers were even more anxious to get away from the city, with its temptations, than the soldiers they had to restrain. One in rather a sweeping way writes, January twenty-first, 1864: "I have a hard company to manage. The men will get drunk whenever they can get whisky, and soldiers can adopt many expedients to get that article. It is the curse of the army, from general down to private. If I had never been for temperance in principle and practice before, my experience and observation in the army would make me uncompromising and unyielding upon that subject." There were men and women in the city, who in their dens of pollution preached from the text, "Let us eat and drink for to-morrow we die," and as there were hundreds in the regiment who were not yet of age, what wonder that some, out from the restraints of home, listened to the damnable doctrine. 153

Granted

BUTTERFIELD, MAJ. GEN. CHIEF OF STAFF, ELEVENTH AND TWELFTH CORPS: Lookout Valley, Tenn. February 12, 1864. Maj. Gen. Hooker: General I would respectfully report that in compliance with your order, I visited Nashville. My opinion in the premises is that the interests of the service would be best promoted by moving General Ward's brigade, if not his division, to the front. Their present condition near Nashville, with its

153 (S. Merrill 1900, 72)

temptation to soldiers, will not be improved. The command is represented to be in a very high state of discipline and perfection in drill. .154

So, now after a year and a half of invaluable experience:

MERRILL: Yet the Seventieth Indiana as a whole, was the better for its varied experience. This experience had been of a nature that but few, if any other regiments had enjoyed. Many troops entering the service about the same time were hurried into battle without preparation, and were sacrificed in the vain struggle to stop the advance of General Bragg's veterans. Our regiment while cut off from home and from the rest of the army, and for a long period outnumbered by large bodies of the enemy on every side, was taught there was nothing to depend upon but constant watchfulness, and confirmed in the determination never to be captured, a fate known to be worse than death. Night after night it was called out and formed in line of battle, and day after day the monotony of drill was relieved by expeditions against and skirmishes with marauders. Discipline was severe, for the commander, Colonel Benjamin Harrison, knew that without discipline a thousand men are no better than a mob. He proposed to form a battalion that in the day of battle would move as if animated by one soul. He had the intellect and the will, and he accomplished the work. If vigilance and labor could keep the men supplied with food and clothing, nothing was wanting. Such was the care for the health that no other Indiana regiment in the service for three years, lost as few by sickness, except the Thirty-second, which was composed for the most part of veterans who had seen service in Germany and were inured to hardships of war. The regiment was fortunate in having for the first eight months of its history, a superior drill master in the person of Maj. S. C. Vance. Under his able supervision the battalion moved with clock-like regularity. Now after a year and a half of invaluable experience in discipline, drill, skirmishing, scouting, bridge guarding, railway and train guarding, provost duty in village and city, picket duty, regimental, brigade and division evolutions in the field, it was ready to take a place at the front, and enter upon a campaign, which was not to end until the surrender of all the Confederate armies in North Carolina, and upon a march which was not to cease until it passed through Atlanta, Savannah, Raleigh and Richmond, and entered in triumph the national capital, Washington. .155

154 (S. Merrill 1900, 72)
155 (S. Merrill 1900, 70)

Thus, from the rear to the front, to dangers they would face with resolution.

Going to Wauhatchie

GRUNERT, CO D 129TH ILL: Feb. 12. Brigade drill in the afternoon; the weather was cool; many soldiers got permission to go to the theater to-night.
Feb. 13. General inspection in the afternoon.
Feb. 14. Our regiment had to guard the gun powder magazine. A sergeant of the 105th Ill. regt. was murdered to-day near our camp; his skull had been split and the body thrown across the track where it was found the next morning.
Feb. 15. Furloughs were granted again.
Feb. 16. Our regiment had many sick members who were brought to the hospitals; the weather was cold; brigade drill in the afternoon.
Feb. 17. Battalion drill in the afternoon.
Feb. 18. Intensely cold weather to-day.
Feb. 19. Half the regiment was on duty; as laborers were wanting the soldiers had to help; the other half of the regiment was free from duty.
Feb. 20. The other half of the regiment had to assist in unloading the boats.
Feb. 21. A number of men, anxious to make a little, went to the landing to assist in unloading the boats. The day was beautiful. In the evening dress parade. At 12 o'clock at night the regiment again received marching orders.
Feb. 22. Our things were unpacked for the second time, and things drawn when the last marching orders came, were offered to the citizens for sale for almost nothing. We were not allowed to take them along, and could not send them home. We were permitted to have in our knapsacks 1 shirt, 1 pair of drawers, 1 pair of socks, a woollen blanket and an oil cloth.
Feb. 23. The time for our departure had been fixed at to-morrow morning 5 o'clock and to-day was the last day that we were here. No one had any idea that the whole company, regiment or brigade would ever return. The men, therefore, amused themselves highly, because they know that with them garrison duty had an end now, and that hereafter fighting had to be done,— and also because no one knew whether he would return alive or as a cripple, that had to live off the small starving penny, called pension, the balance of his days.

Boys All Gon I Left Behind

Mr. Ayers, off on recruiting, came back to find his regiment had left an for uncertain future.

They All Wore a Star

A song Composed on the occasion of A Ramble over the incampment of the 129th Reg ills Vol, after they had Left at Nashville Tenn. By J. T. Ayers one of its members, Huntsville Ala Feb 27th 64

1st Oh how fleeting and uncertain
Is the things of time and since
Past Events are now before me
All is Drear and in suspence

2nd Walking ore the oald incampment
Of the hundred Twenty nine
How forlorn things seem to whisper
Boys all gon I left behind.

3rd What strange stillness seems to whisper
Round the oald incampment here
Something whispers mid the silence
Why should I be in the Rear

4th What Events Await the Regiment
Time Can only that Reveall
(Here I am I A pore oald bachelor)
Here amid A Land of traitors
Oh how sad Alone I feel.

5th Shall I meet those boys Again
While we Linger on this shore
Or will war and deadly Combat
Seperate us Evermore.

6th Yes we may A while be parted
Amid the carnage we may fall
But I hope in Gods good mercy
Once again to meet them all.

7th God of mercy grant they blessing
Send it down upon us all

Spare us Lord from Rebel bullets
Spare us Lord for this I call. .156

"O God, boys!"

"Twelve miles beyond Hell"

GRUNERT, CO D 129TH ILL: Feb. 24. We were awakened at 5 o'clock, and everything packed up, while our cooks were preparing the breakfast of coffee, crackers and meat for the last time in our kitchens. After breakfast we "fell into line" immediately, and at 8 o'clock the whole brigade, consisting of the 79th Ohio, 70th Indiana, 102d, 129th and 105th Illinois regiments, was assembled on the Murfreesboro Pike. Many of the citizens, with whom we had become intimately acquainted during our six months' stay in Nashville, accompanied us to the suburbs of the city, until the command "forward" was given, and the band of the 79th Ohio played a beautiful march, we turned our backs to Nashville, the friends we had won there, and our own sick in the hospitals. The day was pleasant for marching, but soon in the afternoon the brigade camped near Lavergne, a station on the Nashville and Chattanooga rail road, about 10 miles from the former place. The camp was in the field of a rebel, and in order to have a good remembrance we burned a considerable number of fence rails in the camp fires, which kept us warm.

Feb. 25. We left camp at 6 o'clock and reached Lavergne at 8. The weather was very hot, the road dusty, and in consequence of this we camped at 12 o'clock M. already.

Feb. 26. Broke camp before sunrise and reached the battlefield of Murfreesboro about 10 o'clock. Here we rested and visited the graves of the brave Union defenders, quietly sleeping beneath the sod. Here and there bones were bleaching in the sun. The trees near the battlefield were nearly all withered, others shot down or at least robbed of their crowns and branches by bullets and balls. Shells, canister shot and rifle balls were scattered about, in pieces or entire, in every direction. We were yet looking on these to us unwonted things, when the bugle called us to return. We had several miles to march to the city, and at 12 o'clock we were treading the streets of Murfreesboro, delighted by the music of the 79th Ohio. We camped on the south side of the place, near the Shelbyville road.

Feb. 27. We left Murfreesboro early in the morning. The march was more fatiguing than the day before. Had to cross several creeks without bridges,

---

156 (Ayers 1947, 109) A 57-year-old regimental mail messenger, missing his boys.

which caused much loss of time. The road was either covered with several inches of dust, or led through a rocky, hilly country, and as we had rations for several days, sixty cartridges and a full knapsack to carry, many a drop of sweat was squeezed out of us. We marched 13 miles and camped in a fenced field of a rebel; the fence rails of which were of course confiscated and used.

Feb. 28. We commenced our march early, and reached Shelbyville at 12 o'clock M. After passing through the city we crossed to the south side of Dog river, and stopped near by half an hour, for dinner. The afternoon was rainy, and we continued three miles, when we camped, after a march of 15 miles.

Feb. 29. As usual we left our camp early. It had rained during the whole night before and rained to-day, the weather was disagreeably cold, nevertheless we marched to Tullahoma, 15 miles distant. Some of our baggage wagons reached camp to-day, while others, after sticking in the mud every now and then, did not reach us until morning. Our camping ground became a regular sea during the night, and only those who were fortunate enough to be encamped upon high ground found rest; the others could choose between a drenching in the shelter tents, or have the rain outside from the first hand, and freeze too.

MERRILL, 70TH IND: It began raining at night and continued for thirty-six hours, changing at last into a sleet. I can't tell how many times I heard remarks similar to these: "Wouldn't my mother think her boy was gone up if she could see this?" "What would your wife say if she could see you now?" Twenty-five of our mules died in the harness, but the men bore up wonderfully; indeed it would have made you cry to hear them cheering each other. Now and then some poor fellow stumbling, would sink down under his gun and knapsack, and groan in a semi-ludicrous manner, "O God, boys, I'm ready for peace on any terms." When after wading through knee deep mortar the troops were encamped at night in a swamp near Tullahoma, it was thought wise to issue a ration of whisky to each man. Many refused to accept, but passed it on to those who felt the need of a double or triple dose, and as a result, not a few became howling drunk.

MERRILL, 70TH IND: J. H. KELLY: "The regiment marched in rear of the brigade, and Companies I and K, in charge of the wagons, behind everything. The rain and the tramping in front soon put the dirt road in a fearful condition, so that we struggled and floundered along all day in the red, sticky Tennessee mud. When night came we found ourselves left alone, with the train stuck fast. It was so intensely dark we could see nothing, but found some rotten logs by feeling around with our feet, and breaking them up, placed them side by side as a platform, with top above the surrounding water. On this we kindled our fire with bark stripped from the side of a tree that was least soaked. Fuel was so scarce and poor that it kept one or two busy hunting it up to replenish our fire. There was no place to lie down or even sit, except on a water-soaked log or chunk. Men would go to sleep leaning against a tree, slip and fall into the water. At intervals through the night could be heard above the pattering rain and the dashing sleet the struggle of a mule as he fell, having succumbed to fatigue and exposure, and sacrificed his life for his country."

An officer writes: "I gave my tent and blankets to Captain Fisher, for he is an old man and not very well. There was little or no self denial in this, for I was so wet that it seemed safer to sit through the night by a smouldering log heap than to fall asleep in damp clothes." 157

CRAM, CO F 105TH ILL: We started for Tullahoma in the midst of a driving rain which did not cease for forty hours. We reached T— at dusk, built up large fires and pitched our tents but twas no use to try to sleep for the waters ran under us and soaked us through. By keeping close to the fires however, we managed to keep from freezing and at noon next day it ceased and we were enabled to dry our clothes and blankets. I tell you if ever I was thankful to see the blessed sunlight it was then. It would [have] amused you to see us reading the letters which we got that morning, while the cold rain was pouring down on us. 158

GRUNERT, CO D 129TH ILL: March 1, 1864. The rain continued, the roads had become bottomless, and in consequence we were unable to advance.

MERRILL, 70TH IND: J. E. Cleland, dating his letter two days later, "Twelve miles beyond Hell," writes: "It took six gallons of commissary to drag Companies I and K through the mud, ice and water into camp." J. M. Brown: "It was the coldest rain I ever saw. I lay in the water about three inches deep all night, so you may know how I slept." The following day many were engaged in extricating the wagons from the mire, many of the whisky drinkers were on the stool of repentance, while the commanders of the regiments made the monthly muster. 159

157 (S. Merrill 1900, 73)
158 (Cram 2001, 80)
159 (S. Merrill 1900, 75)

HARRISON, 70TH IND: I thought I had seen things a little rough, but . . . yesterday's march and yesterday in camp at Tullahoma surpassed anything I had ever dreamed of. It rained . . . and the holes in the road were up to the axles of the wagons. Some of the wagons did not get in until noon the next day and the rear guard were forced to stand all night in a swamp and without fire to do any good. I went out four miles the next day to help them and took a ration of whiskey to them. Last night when we and all our bed clothes were wet it turned cold and froze quite hard and this morning we got up stiff all over. _160

GRUNERT, CO D 129TH ILL: March 2. The sky had cleared off, and although the roads had by no means improved, we broke camp and left Tullahoma. The sappers had to place wood and fence rails for miles on the road, in order to get the wagons along. Early in the afternoon we reached Elk river, which we crossed, and camped after a march of 10 miles.
March 3. The weather was beautiful, the roads had dried off remarkably and the marching went in a fine style. At noon we reached Orchard Station and soon after Cowan station, when we camped at the foot of the Cumberland mountains, after a march of 10 miles.

Tullahoma was behind them and the sun was shining. The mountains ahead must have looked nice from their camp.

"Harrison's Pass"

They went not-so-parallel to the railroad. From Cowan to the tunnel at the very top is steep. From there down to Tantalon is steep and narrow—too narrow. Grunert, with Company D, was to help get the wagons over.

GRUNERT, CO D 129TH ILL: March 4. Soon we were up, climbing the mountains. Our regiment was detailed to-day to guard the train of wagons against an attack of guerrillas and to help them along through the mountains,—three or four men to each wagon. We got along slowly during the day, and as the last wagons were several miles behind the brigade, (which had marched on), the situation became critical. The darkness was impenetrable, many wagons ran against trees, stumps and rocks, and had to remain in that position until daylight; the others were drawn together on an open place, where they remained.

160 (Sievers 1952, 237) Letter to wife, March 5, 1864

CRAM, CO F 105TH ILL: We began ascending the mountains and after traveling about five miles our drunken old Genl. found he was on the wrong road, so after retreating about a mile we left the path and struck right across the unbroken mountains. _161 We traveled this way about an hour over huge rocks, down steep hills, across ravines, amid all sorts of laughable casualties. When we came to the right road and began to file into it, the companies and even regiment were so mixed up that we could scarcely find our places. Here I was much amused at one fellow who after looking in vain for his company, stepped up to a soldier just ahead of me and said he, "Soldier, can you tell me what my name is?" Such little incidents occur often and tend much to break the monotony of the march. _162

STRONG, 105TH ILL: At this point, we were still back in Tennessee, not far from Chattanooga. The road we were on was cut up by Ewell's and Bragg's armies until just about impassable. Harrison found a guide who said he could take us through the mountains by a nearer and better road. So we marched off on a side road running nearly parallel to the big road, but more to the left. As we went on, the road became dimmer and dimmer, and finally became impossible for our wagons and artillery. So Harrison sent them back all the way to the forks of the big road with a strong guard. He sent all the horses back. Then he put the guide under arrest. The guide was undoubtedly leading us in to ambush. _163

Strong seems to blame Harrison. After all, Harrison was leading them. Ward had left them behind.

STRONG, 105TH ILL: After all that, we left the road, such as it was and plunged in to the woods on our right in an attempt to cut across country and find the main road. Oh, my country men, what a journey that was! There was not even a sign of a path. Our way was impeded by rocks and fallen trees. In places we had to climb or jump as much as eight feet. In the steeper and longer places, one of us would help another down. Our clothes were torn and so were our hands. It was about three miles from the foot of the mountains to the main road, and it took us four hours to make the journey. We called our trail "Harrison's Pass." _164

161 Referring to Harrison or Ward?
162 (Cram 2001, 81)
163 (Strong 1961, 88)
164 (Strong 1961, 88)

MERRILL, 70TH IND: On March fourth the wrong road was taken, and the troops tramped many miles over the mountains unnecessarily. Instead of retracing their steps, they wisely made their tiresome way through woods and over rocks till they arrived at the point they should have reached hours before. .165

HARRISON, 70TH IND: I worked like a Turk correcting his [Ward's] errors and finally got the troops and the train on the right road. The Gen. got a good deal of cussing I hear, for the blunder, and right well did he deserve it. . . . I marched the troops right across the mountain from one road to another where I venture no horseman ever rode before. .166

One wonders how much blame Harrison got for other blunders by Ward.

CULVER, CO A 129TH ILL: March 5th. We left Tantalon at one o'clock this afternoon. We are now in camp about 5 miles south of Tantalon and 4 miles north of Anderson. We expect to reach Stevenson, Alabama, to-morrow. The [wagon] train just got up as we Started. All right. We are still among the mountains. Our Head Qurs. to-night are upon a little island, about 50 feet wide & perhaps two hundred long. It is "a sweet little nook by the babbling brook." The moss is growing all around us, & we found some very beautiful flowers, one which contains the colors beautifully blended, red, white and blue. My health never was better. We have not lost a man crossing the mountains. The valley [of Big Crow Creek] through which we are passing is very narrow. The troops marched all the way upon the Rail Road track. We will break camp at 6 o'clock to-morrow morning. Reveille sounds at 4-1/2 o'clock. It is 14 miles to Stevenson. .167 .168

GRUNERT, CO D 129TH ILL: March 5. We were under way soon, and as the roads were in better condition, we soon reached the brigade camp, but the brigade had gone on. We went into camp early, after having made a march of 12 miles in the last two days.

And one wonders how much Company D would have said had they read Culver's letter.

165 (S. Merrill 1900, 75)
166 (Sievers 1952, 237) Letter to wife, March 5, 1864
167 (Culver, Your Affectionate Husband, J.F. Culver n.d., 235)
168 Culver said nothing to his wife about the wrong road and having to drag the wagons, except: "We have lost not a man crossing the mountains."

GRUNERT, CO D 129TH ILL: March 6. We reached Andrew station, and camped 2 miles north of Stevenson, Ala.

March 7. Passed through Stevenson, and stopped, after a march of 12 miles, at Bridgeport, Tenn.

March 8. Remained in camp and spent the day washing our clothes.

Coburn's brigade came later, in the spring, but by another steep road, from Cowan to University and then down the mountain.

From other things reported in his letters, one gets the idea that Harrison was able to manage the brigade well enough during Ward's absences but had to work much harder when Ward was back in "command."

HARRISON, 70TH IND: Gen. Ward rides on ahead and buys up all of the chickens. I think he and his staff must have been tracking a chicken when they lost the road yesterday. If we had not stumbled on a house in the hills, we would have been going yet on the Battle Creek Road. .169

Friend of Man

STRONG, CO B 105TH ILL: As a consequence of having no washing done, that particular "friend of man" who stuck closer than a brother, caused us much annoyance. They would get into the seams of our shirts and pants and drawers, and when not engaged in laying eggs, would sally out and forage off our defenseless bodies. Next, he, his children and his children's children, with their brothers and sisters, would hold squad drill on our backs. At every leisure moment, the boys would pull off their shirts and such a cracking of thumbnails never took place anywhere but in the army. At every opportunity, we would strip ourselves and boil our clothes, and for a few days we would have peace. As none of us had but one suit of clothes by now, the spectacle we made at such times was somewhat ludicrous. While our clothes were boiling, some of the boys would put on a woolen blanket, some a rubber blanket, some nothing. Next to fighting and eating and sleeping, and perhaps praying and gambling, came washing. After being in a hard battle all day, we were always dirty. What with sweat and dust or burnt gunpowder, our own mothers would not have known us. During this time, we became so used to noise, the firing of guns and cannon, the yelling and cursing of teamsters and artillerymen and the blaring of the bugles, that we would, when tired and permitted to do so, lay down and sleep amid it all. Only our brigade bugle call would rouse us. It was queer, but while sleeping

169 (Sievers 1952, 237) Letter to wife, March 7, 1864

in all this noise, let our bugle play out the first bar of "Hail Columbia," then every man would hear it. The brigade call was the first bar of the song, no more, but it was enough. After playing it, the brigade bugler would follow it up by whatever call he was ordered to make, and he was followed by the regimental buglers who took it up. In the morning it was reveille, or call to get up. After the buglers were all through, the regimental bands would take it up. Our regiment had also a drum corps, consisting of a bass drum, two or more snare drums, and several fifes. Our musicians were a kind-hearted, jolly set of boys, who during a battle wore a yellow ribbon on their arms to show they were noncombatants engaged only in carrying the wounded off the field. At reveille the musicians would march up and down in front of the regiment playing as if their lives depended on it. Then out the boys would tumble, or rather, jump. We had three minutes to dress, if that was necessary, and to get in line for rollcall and doctor's call. Then to strike tents and march to breakfast. Then "attention" and doctor's call for those who reported sick at rollcall. After that, we fell into line with accoutrements on, ready for the day's work. _170

Last Leg to Wauchatchie

On March 9, 1864, Lincoln appointed Grant to command all the armies of the United States. Sherman became commander in the west.

Our heroes carry on just the same. Amid the beauty, the "remains" of war.

GRUNERT, CO D 129TH ILL: March 9. Left Bridgeport, crossed the Tennessee river twice on pontoons, and had dinner at Bellefont station, where we visited a large cave. We went further until we reached a valley, entirely surrounded by high mountains, where we camped during the following, very rainy night.

MERRILL, 70TH IND: March ninth found the regiment on its way across the Tennessee pontoon bridge, into the region of dead mules. The road was lined with decomposing carcasses, forty or fifty lying within a few rods in some places, so that from Bridgeport to Wauhatchie it was impossible to draw a pure breath. _171 _172

---

170 (Strong 1961, 24)
171 (S. Merrill 1900, 75)
172 (Partridge 1887, 252) "It is calculated that ten thousand mules died of starvation on the terrible roads during the siege of Chattanooga."

GRUNERT, CO D 129TH ILL: March 10. We had to wait for the wagons that lagged behind, and did not resume our march until 9 o'clock. The country was mountainous. At noon we reached Whiteside station and about sunset the Lookout Valley, after passing through immense hollows and passes. This last day and the bad roads had cost us many mules. During the night it rained heavily, accompanied by thunder and lightning.

HARRISON, 70TH IND: We had a terrible day's march from Bridgeport here. The road was lined with dead mules and horses and the stench was sickening. Dr. Reagan got to vomiting and I had hard work to keep my stomach quiet. We got our water for coffee out of a creek in the morning; and when we started to march up it, found dead mules in and along the creek at the rate of a hundred to a mile. We joked it off, however, as only soldiers can, and suffered no detriment from our cups of mule tea..173

MERRILL, 70TH IND: The tenth of March, after a dozen miles of trudging, brought the regiment to the Wauhatchie encampment on a picturesque hillside, under the frowning heights of Lookout Mountain. Major General Howard, the Corps commander, met it on its arrival, and inspected it minutely. The men were exhausted by the last days march through the hot sun and the polluted atmosphere, and some fainted as they stood in the ranks, while General Howard was riding along the lines. .174

LAFOREST DUNHAM, CO C 129TH ILL: Let people talk about the balm of a thousand flowers but we can beat that heare, we have the balm of a thousand mules. The roads are strewn with dead mules. It beats any thing that I ever hurd tell of. If I could see you I could tell you of my great sights but it would take me a month of Sundays to wright it. .175

Coffee

OLDROYD: In the afternoon we stopped awhile, and taking advantage of the halt made coffee, which is generally done, whether it is noon or not. There is a wonderful stimulant in a cup of coffee, and as we require a great nerve tonic, coffee is eagerly sought after.

Orders this morning to draw two days' rations, pack up and be ready to move at a moment's warning. We drew hard-tack, coffee, bacon, salt and

---

173 (Sievers 1952, 238) Letter to wife March 11, 1864
174 (S. Merrill 1900, 75)
175 (DeRosier 1969, 108) Letter of March 13.

sugar, and stored them in our haversacks. Some take great care so to pack the hard-tack that it will not dig into the side while marching, for if a corner sticks out too much anywhere, it is only too apt to leave its mark on the soldier. Bacon, too, must be so placed as not to grease the blouse or pants. I see many a bacon badge about me—generally in the region of the left hip. In filling canteens, if the covers get wet the moisture soaks through and scalds the skin. The tin cup or coffee-can is generally tied to the canteen or else to the blanket or haversack, and it rattles along the road, reminding one of the sound of the old cow coming home. All trifling troubles like these on the march may be easily forestalled by a little care, but care is something a soldier is not apt to take, and he too often packs his "grub" as hurriedly as he "bolts" it. 176

March - Much to Do

Drill, Parade, and Mock Battles

GRUNERT, CO D 129TH ILL: March 11. A camping ground was found at last for the brigade. The weather was fine.

March 12. Inspection was ordered, but did not take place. We chopped wood for houses and preparations made to draw clothes.

March 13 Inspection of the company took place. Major General Hooker was introduced to-day. It was currently reported that the 11th army corps would be ordered to Virginia.

March 14. The regiment was on picket, for the first time, since our arrival, and for 48 hours at that.

March 18. A grand parade took place; the whole brigade was inspected by its commander, Gen. Harrison. We got new clothes.

March 19. The parade announced took place to-day. At 8 o'clock the brigade assembled and marched to the parade ground two miles distant, where the regiments were posted according to their number, and had to await the arrival of the commanding General. At the appointed hour some cannon shots announced the arrival of Major Generals Hooker and Howard, who, after having passed along the front and rear of the column, took their places, and the column moved forward, delighted by the excellent music of the 33d

176 (Oldroyd 1885, 11)

Massachusetts regiment. The parade went off fine, and both Generals seemed well pleased with the maneuvers of the brigade. The day was very cold. A member of the 79th Ohio fell from the top of the Lookout, 100 feet, and was killed.

March 20. Company inspection and muster for pay took place; in the evening, dress parade.

March 21. It was very cold; fire-places were built by the whole regiment. Major Flynn was appointed lieutenant colonel.

March 22. We remained in our bunks under the blanket nearly the whole day, in order to keep warm.

WAUHATCHIE   TENN

The Rebel camp at Dalton, after a period of despondency and desertions, was becoming more hopeful. Johnston having taken command, rumors of a Spring offensive and of possible foreign support were circulating. So they were making the best of the weather, staging another kind of mock battle.

WESLEY CONNOR, PRIVATE, CHEROKEE ARTILLERY, CSA: Quite a lively time among the troops, fighting battles with snowballs. Hoxton's Battalion charged our camp this morning. Our boys fought gallantly for a short time, but having no intimation of the attack, were soon compelled to give up. Hoxton's Battalion and ours Palmer's) then united to repel an attack from Hodgkiss' Battalion and a regiment of infantry. We advanced some distance beyond our camp, when the skirmishers became engaged. Soon after, the whole force on each side were engaged in a hand to hand contest – both parties stubbornly maintaining their ground, but we, out numbering them, began to push back their columns. Then the bugle would sound the rally, and they would unite and come again. Finally we made a desperate charge upon their center, which broke and fled. Then ensued a stampede, but they soon rallied, and began to retreat in order. We pursued them to their camp, near which they made a final stand, but being considerably demoralized, they offered but feeble resistance. Their camp, horses and artillery fell into our hands. Having accomplished camps. 'Twas the most exciting scene I ever witnessed. Leaving out the musketry and cannonading, it came nearer up to my schoolboy ideas of a battle than any real battle in which I have participated since the beginning of this war. .177

The Yanks' expectations of battle were by now not like those of yore, though parade and practice might have been. Our brigade had seen enough "remains" of battle to temper their expectations.

GRUNERT, CO D 129TH ILL: March 23. The day was milder, and in order not to be compelled to remain a-bed again during the day, the fire-places were completed.
March 24. The whole camp was cleaned; a heavy snow fell in the night.
March 25. It rained the whole day.
March 26. A brigade hospital was erected.
March 27. In consequence of the continuous change of weather, there were many men on the sick report.
March 28. Company and battallion drill; in the afternoon heavy rain.
March 29. We got the first bread from our newly erected brigade bakery; trees were dug out in camp.
March 30. Company and battalion drill in the forenoon; brigade drill in the afternoon. The weather was fine, and the camp was decorated by planting budding trees therein.
March 31. Company and battalion drill in the forenoon, and brigade drill in the afternoon; inspection was announced for to-morrow.

Nancy Peters observed her 24th birthday on March 31, with her husband away.

177 (W. O. Connor, Wesley Olin Connor Diary 1867).

What Ails You?

COX, CHARLES H. COMPANY E, 70TH IND: Cousin (Dr) Fitzgerald is the only Surgeon now with the Regt and I could myself do all the service he has to do or rather does. A soldier is hardly better than a dog in a Surgeons point of view and no matter what his complaint is, dover powders or quinine pills are administered. Sick Call is sounded at 7 A.M. when the 1st Sergt of each Co collects the sick, blind and halt of his company and marches them to the Surg quarters, where the Surg has a stool and each man takes his turn to be attended to. The first man takes a seat on the stool, the Dr says, "what ails you?" "Pain in my side," he answers and a prescription is given him for quinine, when the man has to go to the Regm'l "shoticary pop" show his prescription and is issued his valuable medicine, the next man takes the stool,—"Well, what ails you?" "Sore foot" he says, another prescription for quinine and off he goes. The third man takes his turn, says "Have the sore eyes" the Dr will look at his tongue, feel his pulse and prescribe quinine or dover powders, probably 50 men will attend Sick call and the Dr will look at every mans tongue feel his pulse and prescribe dover or quinine no matter what his complaint. No matter how sick a man is if he dont attend sick call in morning he cannot get any medicine untill the next morning. Quinine pills and dover powders have become such a common thing amongst the boys that every time the bugle sounds the sick call, half the regt will sing out "come get your quinine" until the bugle has ceased, keeping the words in chord with tune of the call. .178

This is My Last Ride in Tennessee

PEAK, CO F 129TH ILL About the first of April, 1864, I was detailed Forage master on the Nashville and Chattanooga railroad. One man from each company of the 129th regiment was detailed, being the non-commissioned officer of the detail and was placed in command of the squad. We were to load cars with grain and hay at Nashville and when loaded was to go with the train to Stevenson, Tenn. as guards. This seems like an easy job and one to be coveted, but it was far from it. One never knew when they would get a bite to eat or when they would get any sleep. Sometimes we would get a good night's sleep at Nashville and one at Stevenson and possibly a square meal or two, but this was not to be counted on for sure. The Nashville and

178 (Wyatt 1972)

Chattanooga railroad ran through Murphysboro over the Cumberland mountains to Stevenson. Down the mountains was a seven mile grade, the grade being so steep that trains running from Stevenson to Nashville ran by the way of Columbia to Nashville, forty miles longer route than to go by the way of Murphysboro. We had made six trips down this mountain road, some of the trips were in daytime and some at night and we had a chance to see

THE TOWN OF STEVENSON, ALABAMA, HELD BY THE UNION FORCES.—Sketched by Mr. H. Mosler.—[See Page 148.]

the road from the top of the mountain to Stevenson. There were hundreds of box cars strewn from the top of the mountain to Stevenson. Some were smashed to pieces, some were standing on and leaning against big trees that prevented them from turning over. To look at the wreckage along the side of the mountain was enough to make one feel a little leary in going down it. On our seventh trip it was night when we came to the top of the mountain, and raining. Dawson and I had crawled into a box car to be in the dry. The cars were loaded with sacks of thrashed oats. We had not been in the car long when we both were sound asleep, having lost so much sleep and not having a nice warm place to rest. We were soon lost to the world and danger that was around us. When the train reached the grade the train men set all the brakes to try and hold the train from gaining too much speed, but on it went slipping on the track. Apparently, the brakes had no affect on checking the speed of the train. The engine was reversed but that seemed to do no better and finally the train began to bounce and jump and make such a racket it woke us up. I went to the door of the car and never before had I seen such a sight. Fire was streaming from under every where on the train. I never will forget what Dawson said when he came to the door of the car, "this is my last ride in Tennessee." We finally reached the foot of the mountain safely and it seemed a miracle that the train was not wrecked. I said to Dawson, "what you said last night is going to be true, as soon as we get this train unloaded, I am going to ask to be relieved of this job and I know all the boys will sanction it." My request was granted and all the boys were returned to their companies.

Last Month in Tennessee

GRUNERT, CO D 129TH ILL: April 1. Inspection of the regiment in the afternoon; the day was rainy.

April 2. A rainy day; a number of men went fishing; company drill in the afternoon.

April 3. Inspection and dress parade; the day was fine, but in the night, thunderstorm and rain.

April 4. As it rained the whole day, no other than guard duty was performed. Grant assigned Slocum to command Vicksburg. The 11th and 12th Corps were to be combined as the 20th Corps under Hooker.

April 5. The camp was cleaned and inspected by our brigade commander, Harrison, in the afternoon.

April 6. Company and battalion drill in the forenoon and brigade drill in the afternoon. Some more decorations were added to the camp of company D, but not so generally as would have been the case, if the report had not been current that we had marching orders again.

April 8. Gen. Hooker was expected in camp, but the rain in the latter part of the day prevented his coming.

April 9. A beautiful day; no duty to do.

April 10. Inspection of the regiment took place in the forenoon and dress parade toward evening; the day was rainy.

April 11. A great many troops went to the front, and the report of an advance on our part, was current again.

April 12. Rain the whole day.

April 13. The day was beautiful. Gen. Hooker arrived, and a parade before Gen. Thomas was announced.

April 14. The parade announced yesterday took place to-day. At 8 o'clock the brigade marched toward the parade ground, and soon after Gen. Thomas appeared. Gens. Hooker, Ward, Butterfield, &c. were present. The parade was one of the finest we had ever witnessed.

April 15. Gen. Butterfield was expected in the camp, but did not come; in the morning we had company and battallion drill, in the afternoon brigade drill.

April 16. Inspection was announced for to-morrow; company drill in the afternoon. Large portals were erected at the entrance of every company's street, and our camp was one of the finest now of all the camps around, and presented a handsome and pleasing appearance.

April 17. Inspection of the regiment in the afternoon. As it was Sunday, there being no duty to do, many of the men went to the top of Lookout and to Sommerville, near there, whence Chattanooga and the whole surrounding country with its camps and soldiers could be seen distinctly. In the evening dress parade. Gen. Ward again assumed command of the brigade, and his provisional successor, Col. Harrison, again assumed command of his, the 70th Indiana regiment. Gen. Butterfield assumed command of the division. The 4th and 12th army corps were consolidated and called the 20th. Our division, formerly the first in the 11th army corps, became the 3d in the 20th. Many of our men were sent fishing every day, and the fish divided among the regiment.

April 18. More decorations were fixed through the camp. Brigade drill took place in the afternoon in the presence of Gen. Thomas and other strange officers. Gen. Thomas inspected our camp after the drill. The day was rainy and cool.

While Ward's brigade was resting and drilling, regiments of Coburn's brigade were trudging to Wauhatchie, crossing the Cumberland over a slightly different route. They would arrive just in time to start again for another long march, with no rest and without benefit of drill or sham battles. [179]

REID, CO A 22ND WIS: April 18. Pursuant to the order we started again at two o'clock P.M. The foot of the mountains was reached in about a mile's walk and then it was a zig-zag road up, up, as steep as your bluffs at Sabula [Iowa], five times higher, and a road that no description can enable you to appreciate. It was a good deal like attempting to drive a wagon upstairs, for the rocks formed steps unlike only because irregular. The edge of the projecting rock is always rounded however and sometimes a small spring would keep them constantly wet and slippery, so that the animals could gain no foothold. Here is where the superiority of mules over horses is shown. The little animals would sometimes slip down half a dozen times in going two rods, but would spring to their feet again in a second and keep scratching away till the bad spot is surmounted. After gaining the top of the mountain we followed the summit of the ridge, finding a comparatively level road, but was cut at short intervals by streams of water, making in the half clay, half quick-sand soil almost impassable mud-hole. We traveled probably five miles along this ridge, and then camped in the woods near the rail road,

179 Readers are referred to Anderson and Groves, in the bibliography, about troubles of the 19th Michigan and 22nd Wisconsin before arriving at Wauhatchie.

where there seemed to have once been extensive camps of troops—and that is all I know of University [Sewanee]. .180

GRUNERT, CO D 129TH ILL: April 19. Company and battalion drill in the forenoon; brigade drill in the afternoon.

Capture of Fort Pillow by the Rebels

Scene of Cold Blooded Butchery
400 Out of 600 Troops Killed, Mostly After the Surrender. –Headline

CAIRO, April 14.—As stated in a dispatch yesterday, the rebels attacked Fort Pillow with some six thousand men on the morning of Tuesday, the 12th. Forrest, soon after the attack began, sent in a flag of truce, demanding the surrender of the fort and garrison, and in the meantime disposed his troops so that he gained a decided advantage. Major Booth, of the 13th Tennessee cavalry, was in command of the fort, having under him about 400 of that regiment, and 200 of the 1st battalion of the 6th United States heavy artillery, formerly the 1st Alabama colored cavalry. The flag of truce was refused, and returned to the rebel headquarters, and the fighting was resumed. Afterwards a second flag of truce came in, and this also was refused. Both flags gave the rebels an advantage in gaining new positions. The battle was kept up until about 3 o'clock in the afternoon, when Major Booth being killed, Major Bradford took command. The rebels followed up their last flag of truce in swarms, overpowering our forces and compelling them to surrender. Immediately upon the surrender ensued a scene which baffles description. Up to that time comparatively few of our men were killed, but insatiate as fiends and blood-thirsty as devils incarnate, the Confederates commenced an indiscriminate butchery of whites and blacks, and even those of both colors who had been previously wounded. The black soldiers became demoralized and rushed to the rear of their white officers, having thrown down their arms and become defenseless. Both white and colored were either bayoneted or sabered; even the dead bodies were horribly mutilated. Children of seven or eight years and several negro women were killed in cold blood. This all occurred after the surrender. Soldiers, unable to speak from wounds, threw up their arms and were shot dead, and their bodies in many cases were rolled remorselessly down the

---

180 (Reid 1965, 130) University of the South, on land donated by the railroad. Founded by General Polk, who was a Bishop at the time. The railroad took empty cars up a 10% grade from Cowan to University—and carried coal down.

high bank into the river. Dead and wounded negroes were piled up in huts and burned, and several citizens who had joined our forces for protection were killed or wounded. When it came to collecting the living men, it was ascertained that all out of six hundred that could be found was about two hundred.—The most of these were killed after the surrender. Among our dead commissioned officers are Capt. Bradford, of the 13th Tennessee cavalry; Lieut. Barr, Lieut. J. C. Akerson, Lieut. Wilson, Lieut. Revel and Major Booth, of the same command; Lieut. N. D. Logan, of the 13th Tennessee cavalry; Capt. John C. Young, 24th Missouri, acting as Provost Marshal, and Capt. J. H. Poston, 13th Tennessee cavalry, were taken prisoners. Major Bradford was also captured, but is said to have made his escape. It is feared, however, that he has been killed. The steamer Platte Valley came up at about half-past three, and was hailed by the rebels under a flag of truce, and men were sent ashore to bury the dead and bring on board such wounded as the rebels had allowed to live. Fifty-seven were taken on in all, including seven or eight colored men. Eight died on the passage up. The steamer arrived here late this afternoon, and was immediately sent to Mound City hospital to discharge her suffering cargo. Of the number known to be wounded in the 6th regular heavy artillery are

Lieut. Libberts, company A, Capt. John A. Porter and Adjutant Lenning.
˷181

News of Fort Pillow

GRUNERT, CO D 129TH ILL: April 20. Company and battalion drill again in the forenoon; inspection was announced for the afternoon, but did not take place, but brigade drill took place in its stead. We received the news of the surrender of fort Pillow, and the barbarous treatment of the union soldiers after the surrender on the part of the rebels under Forest.

THE MASSACRE AT FORT PILLOW.—[SEE PAGE 253.]

That news will be on their minds in battle to come shortly.

April 21. The parade ground was made more level and cleared of the shrubs and rocks. The men not at work had to drill in the afternoon. General Butterfield drilled his division for the first time to-day. Below Chattanooga, in the neighborhood of Ringgold, our pickets met the enemy, and a considerable skirmish took place. Everything quiet in the front. The enemy, under Gen. Johnson, lay behind his entrenchments near Dalton and

181 (Capture of Fort Pillow by Rebels Illinois)

Buzzard Roost. A bloody spring campaign was expected, and from all signs and orders we could begin to believe that the "dance of war" would soon begin. The troops, now under the command of Gens. Sherman and Thomas, were "full of fight" and in the best condition.

April 22. Company drill and skirmish drill by signals; brigade drill in the afternoon. The band of music of the 33d Massachusetts, which regiment belonged to the 3d brigade of our division, serenaded our brigade commander and all the regiments to-night. The evening was spent joyfully and merrily. It was reported for certain that we would have to leave our beautiful camp in a few days, the erection of which had cost us so much labor, and to commence the campaign against the enemy. As yet we had no marching orders, and all these reports were to be believed but half.

April 23. We had no marching orders yet, nevertheless the report of our advance became more positive.

CRAM, CO F 105TH ILL WARD 1B 3D 20C: Dear Mother, I rec'd a letter from you a few days since, by Sergt. Grant and in addition to them, I had quite a good visit with him. It is always a great privilege to see anyone just from our home and feel that a few hours previously, they conversed with our friends. Always when such a one makes his appearance in camp, you will see him immediately, surrounded by an eager, interested group, all intensely anxious to know if anybody said anything about them or if they sent a letter, a line, or a word. And then a little token he brings from home, how they talk about it and show it to all the others and rejoice to see that they are not forgotten. If there is anything that makes a soldier discouraged and in fact homesick, it is to feel as though he was unthought of. And such is frequently the case too, with our soldiers. The good people at home are too much engrossed in every day matters to care sufficiently for their friends so far away. I write this not for you but for you to read or tell to some of those Mothers and sisters there who have sons and brothers here exposed to dangers and all the hardships of war besides the thousand and one vices of camp life, with far too few cheerful letters from home containing good wholesome advice and words of affection. _182

Momentous change. Our brigade is now under Hooker, with the 11th and 12th Corps combined into the 20th Corps, in Thomas' Army of the Cumberland. Under Hooker, they are in the 3rd Division commanded by Daniel Butterfield. He had been Chief of Staff under Hooker and was known for being meticulous.

182 (Cram 2001, 88)

Ward and Harrison revert to their previous responsibilities. Drill and mock battles intensify.

CRAM, CO F 105TH ILL WARD 1B 3D 20C: Our corps has been consolidated with the 12th and we form what is called the 20th army corps commanded by Hooker. We are the 1st brigade, 3rd division, 20th army corps. The brigade is commanded by Brig. Genl. Ward, a regular old Falstaff whose sheer delight is to swill whiskey, etc. No one respects him and all unite in hoping that he will soon be removed. The division is under the guidance of Maj. Genl Butterfield. He has the appearance of a thorough going man and his previous military career warrants us in respecting him. With regard to Hooker, everybody loves him and to see him as he rides along our lines is only to like him more each time. The corps is about thirty thousand strong, and will no doubt have an important position in the grand army. We have received orders to have constantly on hand 150 rounds of cartridges to each man. Some of the officers think the rebels are going to make the attack but I do not believe such will be the case, and do not think a battle will be fought yet for some weeks. ... The health of the regiment at present is better than ever before. I do not think there are five in the regt. Too sick to be able to march. The weather is still cold but bids fair to become more pleasant now and the mud is fast drying up. If this continues the roads will be in good condition in a week. Troops are marching by every day in great numbers. I have no doubt there are a hundred thousand men here to take part in the coming battle. 183

CRAM, CO F 105TH ILL WARD 1B 3D 20C: April 29. Yesterday afternoon we had one of the grandest performances that our regiment ever took part in, namely, a division drill and sham fight. The men all went out with thirty rounds of blank cartridges and aiming at the grounds selected for the battle, they were drawn up as follows. The 105th were thrown forward as skirmishers and formed into a double line. At proper intervals behind was the first line of battle consisting of three regiments deployed, extending the line a little over a mile. Behind this line was the second. This was drawn up in column by division, consisting of four regiments. And still behind this line were two regiments at either flank in close column. The artillery were posted on the flanks, taking positions on two small hills, covering our grand advance. First the skirmishing commenced by our regiment and continued till we had advanced about three miles and taken possession of every point. Then the enemy were supposed to be found in force, and our regiment were withdrawn and formed in line with the first line of battle. Now the fight

183 (Cram 2001, 88)

commenced in earnest, and the quick rapid discharge of musketry soon filled the valley with dense smoke. The artillery firing too was executed beautifully and the booming of the cannon echoed from hill to hill and thence to the grim wall of Lookout. Of course, we drove the enemy and took any amount of prisoners, without any loss whatever on our side. Genls. Thomas, Hooker, Butterfield, Brannan and Whipple were there to witness our movements. Butterfield conducted them. .184

GRUNERT, CO D 129TH ILL: April 24. Inspection of company and dress parade in the afternoon; the weather was rainy.

AUSTIN, 19TH MICH COBURN 2B 3D 20C: Cowen Station Tenn April 25th ...I suppose if I was at home & no lady to bring water to wash my hands with you would let me go without my dinner. Well I would not go without it long for I would be the best boy you ever see if I only was at home & could have you to cook my dinner again, but we must not talk about this now. I am here & have got to stay till thare is different times with rebble affairs. I hope it wont be long before that time comes. John thinks they can do something at the ballot box to help put down the rebellion. I think the most any one can do thare to help stop the war is to vote for good men that are true to their country & are bound to see the end of this affair & see it come out just as it has been calculated on & not give the rebs a thing but whip them till they are glad to ask for quarters instead of demanding them as they always have done so far. Who would cast their vote to have things put back in the same shape they were 3 years or more ago with so many thousand of our boys whose bones are left in the southern states never more to return to their homes & those that they loved. Who can think of such a thing after such a sacriface of life as has been going on for the last 3 years. I say do all you can to support our soldiers & get as many into the army as as are wanted to to fight these wicked rebs & when they are whiped let us give them what belongs to them & if we are whiped we will take up with what we can get. I dont know but I have writen enough of this so I will close before I make some one mad or the next thing to it. .185

184 (Cram 2001, 90)

185 (Austin 1864) Many soldiers complained of Copperheads at home trying to defeat Lincoln in the election and end the war. The 2nd Brigade had paused a couple of days before starting down the mountain after marching from McMinnville and would arrive at Wauhatchie just in time to start the campaign with no rest and without the benefit of the drill and sham battles.

From newspapers and letters, soldiers knew of efforts of northern Copperheads to end the war without an end to the cause of it. While practicing to fight the war to Georgia, reflecting on so many comrades and neighbors who had given their last and of the sacrifices of those left at home, these words of Lincoln's remarks at Gettysburg must have echoed in these soldiers minds: "from these honored dead we take increased devotion to that cause for which they gave the last full measure of devotion that we here highly resolve that these dead shall not have died in vain." They hated Copperheads. They would finish the fight.

GRUNERT, CO D 129TH ILL: April 25. Company and Battalion drill in the forenoon and brigade drill in the afternoon.
April 26. Brigade drill in the afternoon; weather warm.
April 27. Company drill in the forenoon and Battalion drill in the afternoon.
April 28. Division drill and practice in firing in the afternoon. Two members of company I, of our regiment deserted to-night, after having borrowed revolvers and watches from several men. Preparations to capture them were made, but not a word was heard of the successful accomplishment of this object.

MERRILL, 70TH IND WARD 1B 3D 20C: The following extract from a letter by Lieutenant Grubbs, dated April twenty-ninth, should be inserted to show how well the Third Division of the Twentieth Army Corps could move at the command of one of the greatest men the war produced, Gen. George H. Thomas; how thoroughly it was prepared for the great movement in which it was about to engage, and above all, how little a sham battle is like a real one.

"Yesterday we held a division drill and went gallantly through all the maneuvers of a sham battle. We moved from camp at ten o'clock and marched four miles to the drill ground. There we rested while the other brigades came on the field. A half hour later General Butterfield and staff rode up and the long line was formed. We stood at attention while Generals Thomas, Hooker, Brannan, Whipple and others rode through the lines and took their station on an eminence that overlooked the entire field. In the center were the dense columns of troops, on the right and left batteries, in the rear ambulances.

We maneuvered for an hour, now advancing, now retreating, now forming heavy columns, then breaking into line of battle, moving first in quick, then in double quick time; then there was a rest for a few moments, then the work commenced. To repel a charge of cavalry we were first thrown on the double quick into squares. Sections of artillery were formed in the angles, and a heavy fire was opened on the imaginary enemy. Then we were moved eastward a short distance, and the four miles of the valley lay before us. We had provided ourselves with forty rounds of blank cartridges and were anxious to use them. One regiment was thrown forward as skirmishers, and extended its lines clear across the valley and up the hills on either side. Two long lines of battle two hundred yards apart were formed across the valley, while our regiment and the Thirty-third Massachusetts were held in column in reserve. Our two right companies were sent to the extreme right to cover and support the battery which had commenced to play from a little hill that looked out upon the valley.

The call sounded and the entire division moved forward. We were advancing upon the enemy and it was our first even sham battle. Soon the sharp crack of guns in front proclaimed that the skirmishers were engaged. We had been advancing about five hundred yards, and the firing was rapid and continuous in front, when we came upon a small ridge that ran directly across the valley, and the whole field opened like a map before us. A quarter of a mile beyond was the beautiful line of skirmishers, swaying from hillside to hillside as the men alternately halted to load and fire, and then advanced, the white puff of smoke springing from the guns and curling above their heads as each one shot. In rear of them and a hundred yards apart were two long lines of battle, each three thousand strong, moving steadily forward and keeping pace with the skirmishers. Imagine now a fight; the skirmishers drawn in, the troops that were yet in column thrown into line on the double quick, we hastening a mile around to the left; the roll of musketry, the thunder of cannon." _186

GRUNERT, CO D 129TH ILL WARD 1B 3D 20C: April 29. The weather was excessively warm; brigade drill in the presence of Gen. Butterfield; a heavy rain fell during the night.
April 30. Inspection and muster for pay in the forenoon; the weather was very hot.

Things will now indeed get hot. The time had arrived. They were prepared. But not all were to leave camp and pleasant days because they had neither to leave; John Coburn's brigade, now Butterfield's 2nd, has just arrived after long marches from Tennessee, only to start again, for battle, without rest and without benefit of the constant drilling and sham battles. Williams' division also had to march to start the campaign with no rest. At least they did have battlefield experience.

---

186 (S. Merrill 1900, 77)

Sergeant Morhous of Company C of the 123rd New York in Knipe's 1st Brigade, had been guarding railroads.

> MORHOUS, CO C 123RD NY KNIPE 1B 1D 20C: The next day, April 30th, they reached old Bridgeport, which was almost like getting home again to the boys, so familiar were they with everything in and around the place. They bivouacked on the island. The island is perhaps four miles long, and from one-fourth to one-half a mile wide, covered with wood, and has a rich alluvial soil. May 1st they crossed the other branch of the Tennessee river on a pontoon bridge, and reached Shellmound in a few hours, where they camped for the night. The Regiment pushed on again next morning, passing around the point of Lookout Mountain, and on the 3d camped near Chattanooga. _187

> GRUNERT, CO D 129TH ILL WARD 1B 3D 20C: May 1. This morning at last we received the long expected marching orders, to be ready for the tramp to-morrow morning early. Rations for three days were drawn, and all things more than the prescribed baggage, which had been taken along from Nashville, were put in chests and left. The officers had to leave their writing desks, paper, ink, &c. Hereafter we were to be loaded down by provisions, cooking utensils, ammunition, etc. The last dress parade took place towards evening, in Lookout valley, by the 1st brigade of the 3d division of the 20th army corps. In order to be ready early in the morning, we slept early and soundly for the last time at the foot of the grand Lookout, whose peak towers high toward heaven.

> PEAK, CO F 129TH ILL WARD 1B 3D 20C: About May 1, 1864, the long looked for order came to be ready to march early in the morning with 100 rounds of cartridge box and three days' ration in haversacks. While most of the men knew sooner or later the regiment would be ordered to the front, they were a bit sorry to leave the good camp where they had spent so many pleasant days. Many of the boys, when the regiment marched out of camp would say, "goodbye old shack, I'm going to leave you for the bats and mice to live in, and I will sleep on the cold damp ground from this on, under my puppy tent." The change from a bunk to the cold damp ground was so sudden that most the regiment took cold and for several days seemed to be lifeless. After several days of marching and skirmishing the men seemed to return to their vigor.

187 (Morhous 1879, 85)

Later, the "elderly" James Ayers recounted the tribulations they are to encounter and their resentment of some for attitudes of a noisy few back home who revolted against the war others were fighting.

1 Fellow soldiers of the Cumberland Loyal brave and true
Who have Left your Northern firesides Southern traitors to subdue
Lets send home for A Copperhead A Regular blatant cuss
And the beauties of A soldiers Life make him share with us.

2 Well put him in A puptent with coald ground for his bed
With no Rubber blanker under neath no Goverment overhead.
Let him Shiver thare till morning sleepless and in pain
And Each succeeding night should the same thing do again.

3 At breakfast time no dainty dish his appetite would tempt.
Far from such Dainty Luxurys most soldiers are Exempt
Sowbelly should he breakfast on, Rusty pore and Black,
Accompanyd by coffee weak and miserable hard tack.

4 Then preparation quickly make get everything in trim
March him oft on Picket and may A secesh pick at him
May every bush A Rebel seem strange sounds salute his cars
And all he sees and all he hears but serve to wake his fears.

5 Let him slosh Round shoeless, in the mud into puddles fall
And always Late to dinner be also at bugle call
While shivering Round the campfire may he burn his boots and close
May the smoke blow always in his eyes and curl stinging up his nose

6 May he six months without money be and no trusting sutter bout
And should he get his Canteen filld may it somehow all Leak out
May he never have A postage Stamp and for his Aching Jaw
Of tobacco not quiet half Enoughf for even half A chaw.

7 Forced marches may he have to make in Rain and snow and mud
The driving Rain his clothing soak the chill winds freese his blood
And that the beauties of a march he might the better see
Rheumatic twinges all day have and the Chronick dierhea.

8 From Nashville down to Huntsville the Comeing summer days
Lct him hoof it on the dusty Pike beneath the suns hot Rays

157

They All Wore a Star

His face with blisters covered his Lims all weak and Lame
And I guess hell think a soldiers Life is Anything but tame.

9 Infested may his clothing be with all the Little fry
That the soil of Allabamma can so Abundantly supply
Have all his dirty shirts to wash in water scant and black
Shiftless and Lousy weeks to go no Clean Rags for his back.

10 And when the Conflict Rages fierce keep him always in the front
Let him feel beside Exposure the battles fiercest brunt
Let minies whistle Round his head shricking sheel burst near
Let him keenly feel the agonies which Alone the gilty fear

11 And finally in A Hospital minas A leg or so
Somewhat ematiated and most dredfully low
Well Lay whats Left of Copperhead upon A dirty bunk
To Regain his waisted energies on weak tea and tough junk.

12 To the Call of uncle Abraham we Cherfully all flew
Severed the tyes which bound our Harts bade cherished ones adieu
And we will not brook the insults which are heaped upon our heads
By the traitorous northern Cowards the Slimy Copperheads. .188
                                                                –Ayers

188 (Ayers 1947, 119)

MAPS AND DEPICTIONS

For full size copies views see the book's website, www.TheyAllWoreAStar.com.

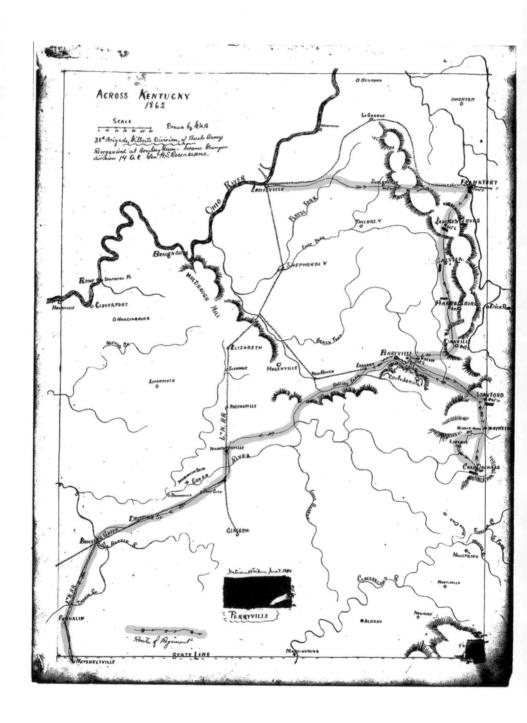

Middle Tennessee

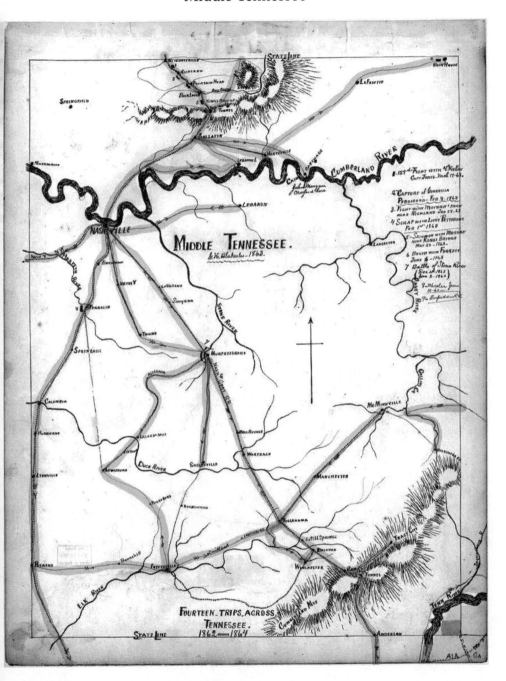

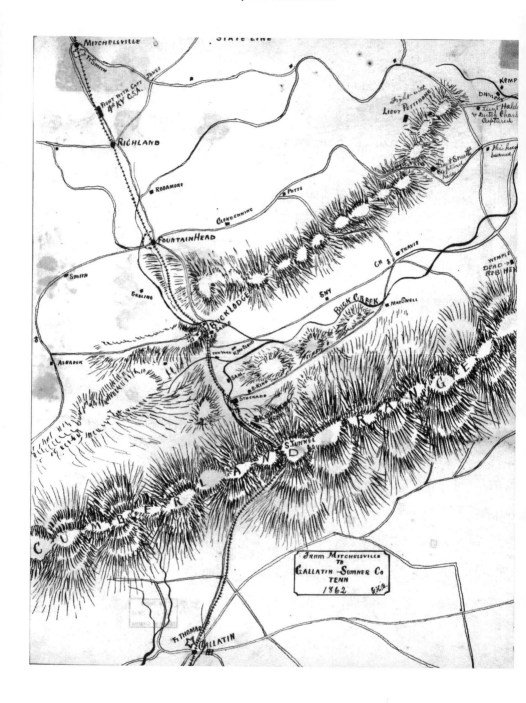

Rosecrans' Map of Tennessee and Georgia

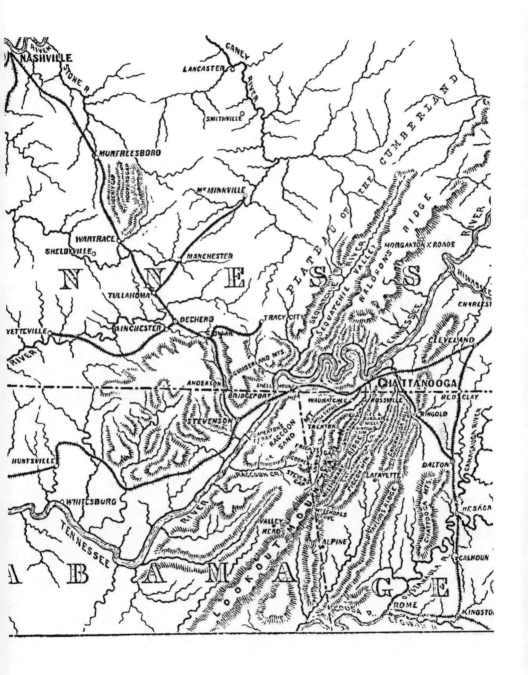

Draper's Map of Chattanooga

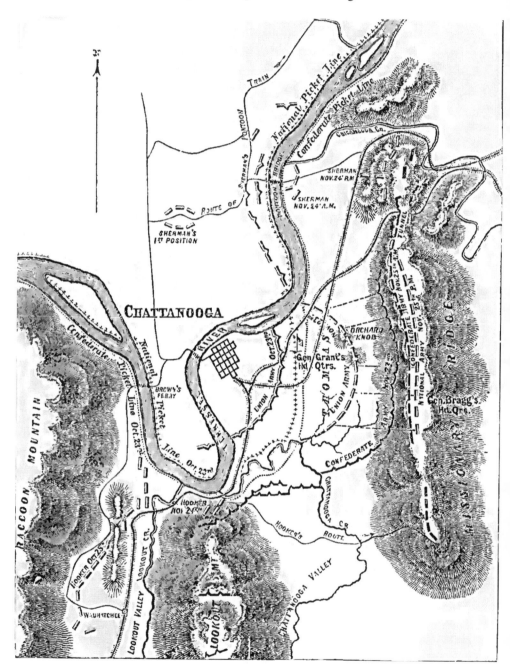

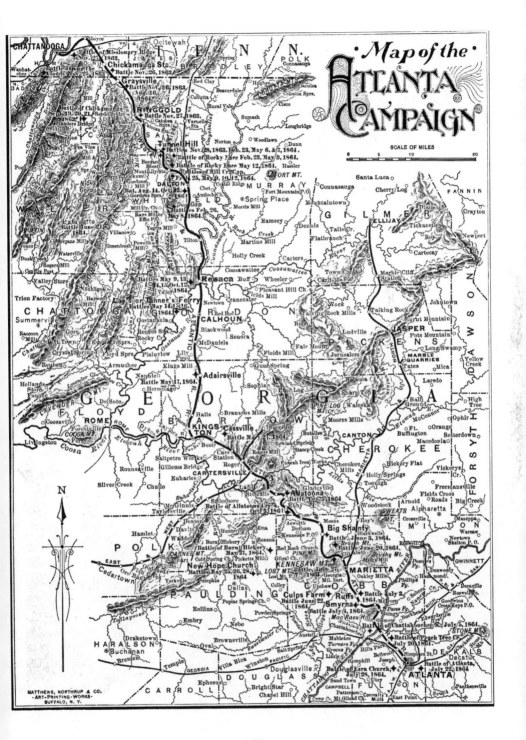

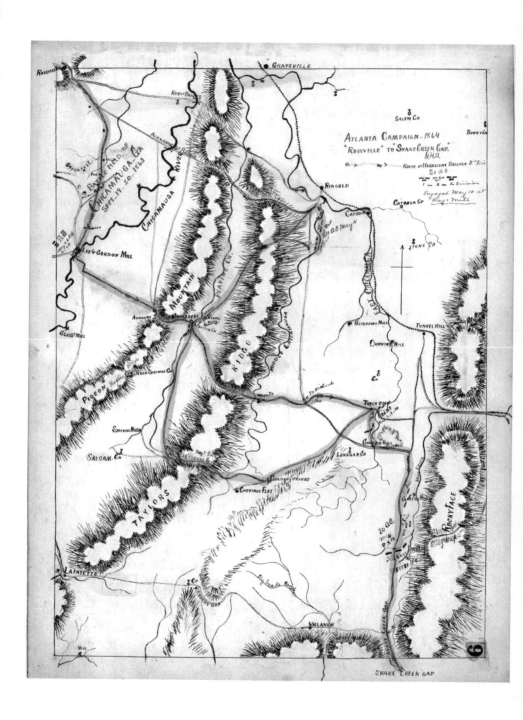

Resaca Vicinity

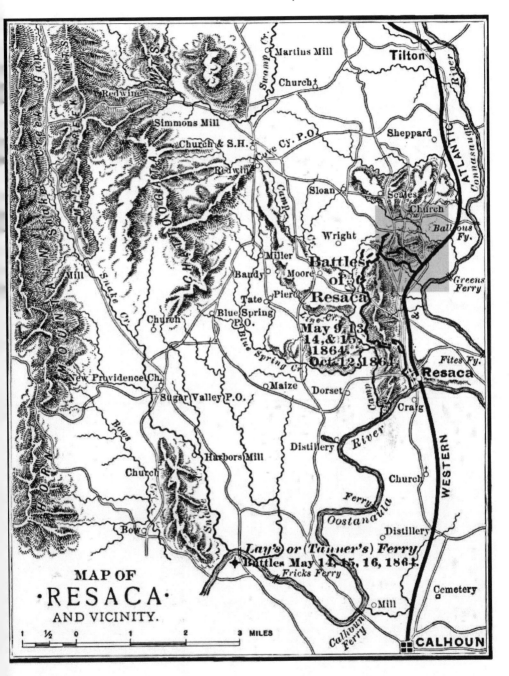

Hooker's Positions May 12-14

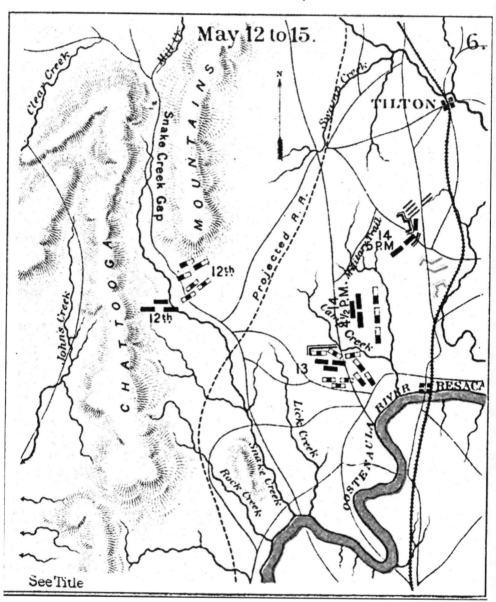

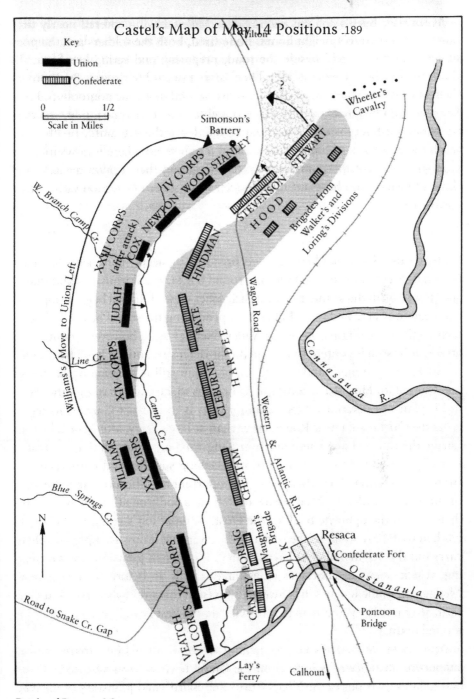

Battle of Resaca, May 14

189 (Castel 1992, 155)

James Walker's Painting

From the position of Hazen's brigade facing the Rebel line protecting the north entrance to the Confederate fortress we see the road coming from Dalton between the two hills on the left and disappearing between the two hills on the right, on the way to Resaca. The hill across the road on the left is where the battle will start. On the right we see Stevenson's Division's defensive line going up the hill in the middle before it turns away behind all that smoke to go around the back side toward the Connesauga River. In the smoke at the top is Corput's Four-Gun Battery. The small figures going across the road from the left are Butterfield's division starting their assault to break the line at the top. They must get past the cannon and rifle from Stevenson's men and from Hindman's Division on their right.

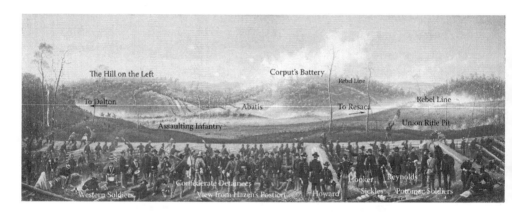

In the foreground we see Potomac soldiers on the right and Western soldiers on the left as interested spectators. Seated on the log in the middle is General Howard. To his left, General Hooker is pointing to Butterfield's infantry for General Sickles and Reynolds, the Chief of Artillery.

Walker began this on-site the day after the battle on commission from Butterfield.

Th

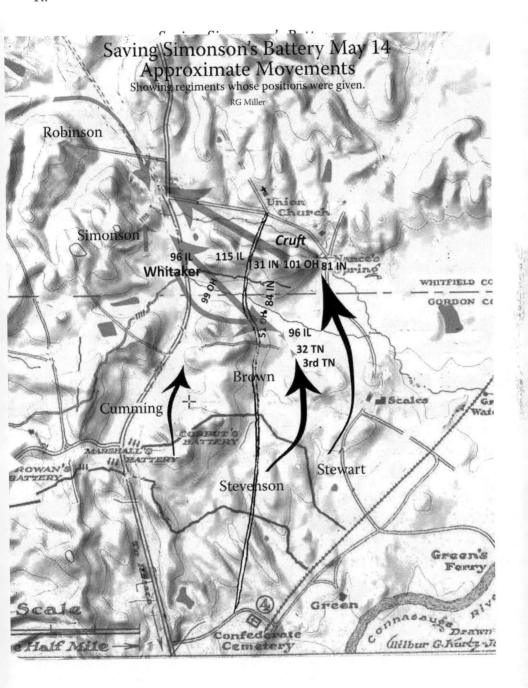

Saving Simonson's Battery May 14
Approximate Movements
Showing regiments whose positions were given.
RG Miller

Robinson

Simonson

Cruft

96 IL   115 IL
Whitaker

31 IN 101 OH 81 IN

Union Church

Nance's Spring

WHITFIELD CO
GORDON C

96 IL

32 TN
3rd TN

Brown

Cumming

CORBUT'S BATTERY

MARSHALL'S BATTERY

ROWAN'S BATTERY

Scales
Gr
Wat

Stewart

Stevenson

Green's Ferry

Scale

Half Mile

Green

Confederate Cemetery

Connasauga River

Drawn
Wilbur G. Kurtz Jr.

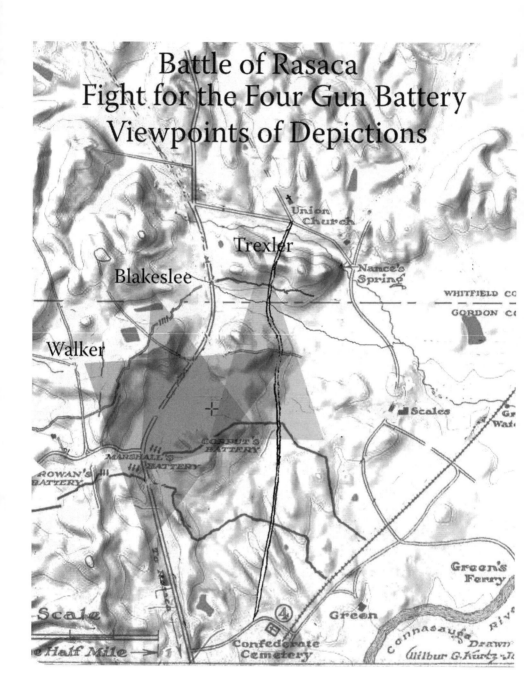

Depictions of the battle, Walker's painting, Blakeslee's maps, and Trexler's sketch, could use a bit of explanation.

Kurtz's map of 4th and 20th Corps positions became a base for other maps in the book because Kurtz, an artist, carefully walked the field and mapped the trenches himself, using a current topographic map (the features overlay perfectly). The old road in the center was not on the topo map but was on maps of the period of the battle and he could still find the road (about 1950) and drew it on other hand-drawn maps. This author overlaid the features of Kurtz's map on digital topo maps that displayed as shaded terrain.

Trexler's sketch at first glance appears to be a concoction from what he might have heard. But he was there. In Geary's division, he probably was not busy very early in the fight and, being an assistant surgeon, he likely drew well after the battle as a composite of viewpoints in his recollection. Given that leeway, all the elements in the depiction were actually there. The cabin on the right is mentioned by one of Cruft's brigade discussing their escape from the oncoming Rebels. The streams just flow at a different angle. The Confederate line on the hill gives us an idea of what Wood, Knipe, and Ruger faced. Though Trexler labeled them as Geary's, the infantry seen moving forward to the left could be taken for Robinson or Ruger, according to their direction and by the artillery, since Williams had placed cannon behind his position after being deployed.

Walker viewed from behind and a bit above Hazen's brigade, just left of Willich's brigade. The infantry crossing from the left appear in file, as one behind another, instead of side by side, so they may have been Geary's regiments heading up after the assault took place but while fighting was still going on. One would wonder if Walker added the abatis for effect since almost nobody mentioned it.

Blakeslee drew as if looking from the hill from which the assault started across the road. He laid out positions based in part on where bodies were found the next morning. He was in the 129th going up, fourth regiment in line during the assault, so he depended on what others told him the next day about relative positions and paths. His watercolor at the fort does not entirely coincide with the map and some accounts, but that can be expected. While he did not see everything, he heard from many, and painted years later. You can bet that the scene and some incidents remained vivid in his mind though.

Bierce's Map of Hazen's Position

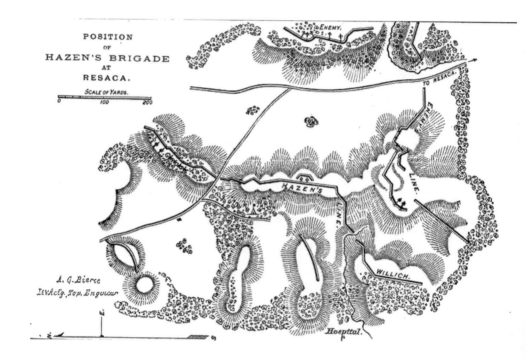

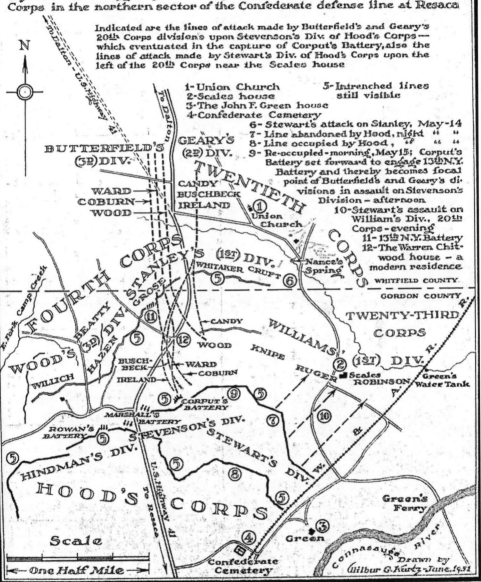

THE 20TH CORPS AT RESACA
MAY 15, 1864

Showing the placement of the Federal 20th, 4th and 23d Corps in the area bordering both sides of the Gordon-Whitfield County Line and adjacent to U.S. Highway 41. Also, placement of Lieut. Gen. John B. Hood's Corps in the northern sector of the Confederate defense line at Resaca

Indicated are the lines of attack made by Butterfield's and Geary's 20th Corps divisions upon Stevenson's Div. of Hood's Corps — which eventuated in the capture of Corput's Battery, also the lines of attack made by Stewart's Div. of Hood's Corps upon the left of the 20th Corps near the Scales house

1- Union Church
2- Scales house
3- The John F. Green house
4- Confederate Cemetery
5- Intrenched lines still visible
6- Stewart's attack on Stanley, May-14
7- Line abandoned by Hood, night " "
8- Line occupied by Hood, " " "
9- Re-occupied - morning, May 15; Corput's Battery set forward to engage 13th N.Y. Battery and thereby becomes focal point of Butterfield's and Geary's divisions in assault on Stevenson's Division - afternoon
10- Stewart's assault on William's Div., 20th Corps - evening
11- 13th N.Y. Battery
12- The Warren Chitwood house - a modern residence

Drawn by
Wilbur G. Kurtz June. 1951

Scale
One Half Mile

Trexler's View

Assistant Surgeon Trexler sketched the scene .190 from Geary's position on the 15th, facing south. Here we see skirmishers preceding two lines of battle, two men deep, with what appears to be more than 35 paces between them. We are on the other side of the hills in Walker's painting, which looks southeast. Walker

196   FRANK LESLIE'S ILLUSTRATED NEWSPAPER.   [June 18, 1864.

THE WAR IN GEORGIA—BATTLE OF RESACA, MAY 14—GEARY'S 2ND BRIGADE CHARGING UP THE MOUNTAIN.—FROM A SKETCH BY ASSISTANT-SURGEON J. S TREXLER, 73RD PENN.—SEE PAGE ···

sees the hills from the northwest and Trexler sees them from the north, from the hill the Rebels had taken and lost during last night's flank disaster. The big hill is the object of the day. The Confederate line sweeps east, left from the hill and away from the viewer. Williams' division would be facing Stewart's Division of Rebels on the far left as they came out of those trees for another flank attempt. The road no longer exists. The sketch is not exactly true to the terrain and likely was drawn after battle from memory and not necessarily from a single viewpoint—allowing the artist some room to squeeze it all in.

190 (Trexler 1864)

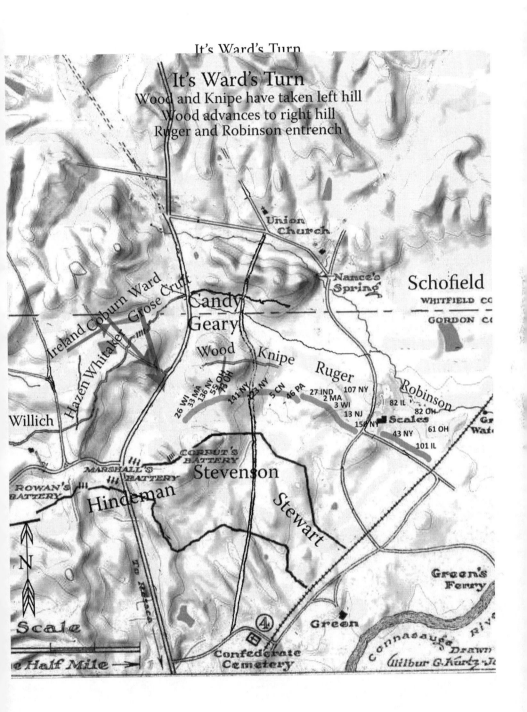

It's Ward's Turn
Wood and Knipe have taken left hill
Wood advances to right hill
Ruger and Robinson entrench

Blakeslee's Map of Butterfield's Assault

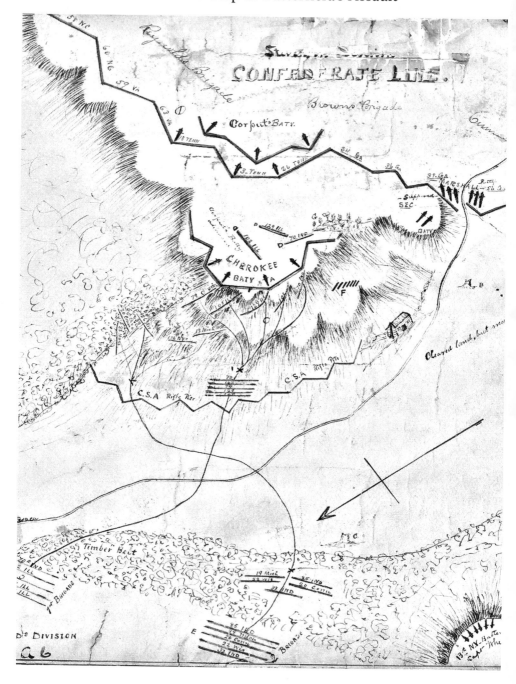

Blakeslee's Notes

KEY TO THE MAP. FIELD OF RESACA

From his correspondence with Wes Connor, of Corput's Battery

A. The gun on which Sergt. Hess, 129th Illinois was standing when killed. Here our colors were planted.

B. Stump in cleared field behind which was a C.S. Sharpshooter, who was killed by 102nd Illinois Sharpshooter, George Dheu, and buried by myself and Tom Wyckoff.

C. The stump from which Dheu fired the fatal shot.

D. The most advanced position gained by the 3 regiments that passed beyond your guns.

E. Location - Where Division formed in Column by regimental front for the advance.

F. Where 51 - 129th Illinois rest of Company G - 13.

G. Projecting ledge, a protection to 70th Indiana while holding Battery.

H. The point on Gen. Howard's line from which Walker's great painting was made. [not shown, see full map]

X. Deployment of 1s t and 2nd Brigades here.

X 1. Gen. W.T. Ward severely wounded here, Harrison taking command.

Ø. Near this place there lay a dead Indian, who had two scalps of white men in his belt. The officer in charge ordered the Indian to be left without burial, it is said.

The Heavy Red lines show C.S.A. field works. The Heavy Blue lines Union regiments.

Thin Red lines show the line of march to the attack; 3rd Brigade bore to the left and was lost sight of in the pines.

0. Where I was slightly wounded.

P. Captured a Johnny Captain here; don't know who he was.

K. 2nd Brigade scattered by terrible fire of Confederates. The 2nd Brigade was to keep to right of our Brigade and support us on the right flank; just after crossing the Dalton road the canister from your guns turned them from their course, and crossing our line of march to the rear, took to the bush on the northern slope of the hill, gaining which, they prostrated themselves on lines as shown. I located these positions from a few of their dead lying there.

This map is a copy on a small scale of the one I made for Maj. Gen. Dan Butterfield on the field May 16, 1864, and which is published in connection with Walker's great painting. This map is contrary to prescribed rules of map making.

In it we are facing the direction as we moved to the attack, the top of the map being nearly S.E. At the angle held by Corput's Battery the main line turns nearly due east to the river.

At the point marked Brown's Brigade the Confederate dead were buried, burial parties reporting the number at 600; in 1895 the graves were yet plain to be seen, many of the slabs still at the head of graves.

G. H. Blakeslee

Note: The 54th Virginia was in the position Blakeslee shows the as the 59th Virginia.

BUTTERFIELD'S VERSION OF BLAKESLEE'S MAP

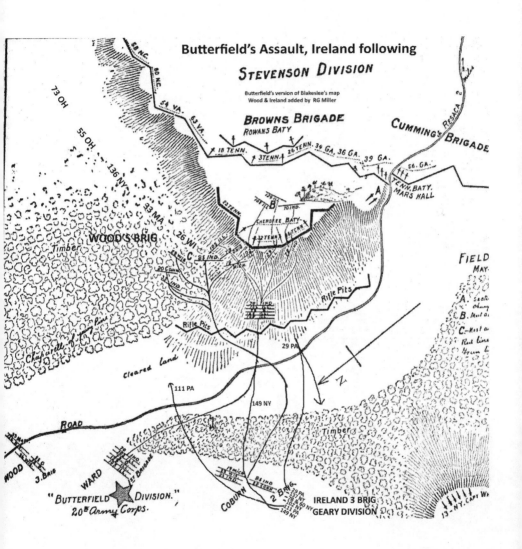

Storming the Fort

When George H. Blakeslee painted this watercolor and how it got to the Benjamin Harrison Presidential Site is not known.

The 70th Indiana did go in at the gun on the right as shown and the 102nd Illinois went in on the left, shown in the distance with the unlabeled flag. The other three regiments were somewhat mixed up. If Halstead's painting in words is true to detail, Private Totten was indeed ahead of his regiment, the 79th Ohio. The 129th Illinois got furthest beyond the fort, to the Rebel line, "in those works" it was said. Sergeant Hess of the 129th Illinois carried the flag and was killed after planting it at gun number three, second from right, according to Blakeslee's notes for his map. Wes Connor said brush had been piled in front of his gun, number two, second from left; George Blakeslee single-handedly "brushed" it away.

Courtesy of Benjamin Harrison Presidential Site

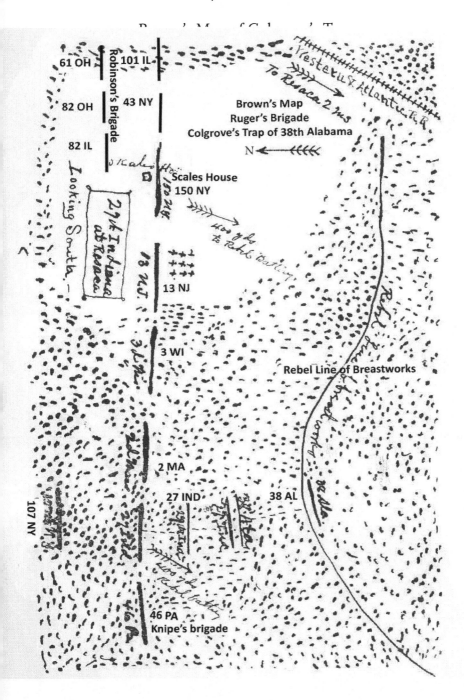

Brown's Map
Ruger's Brigade
Colgrove's Trap of 38th Alabama

191 (E. R. Brown 1899, 470)

PART TWO
COURAGE
GOING INTO THE FIRE

Those whose experiences we have followed in Part One are drawn together for the Campaign to Atlanta and the first full-on engagement, with all of Sherman's armies against Johnston with his Corps of Hood, Hardee, and Polk, face-to-face. This story is about the brigade we have been with for a year and a half and their involvement in one part of that battle. But is also as much about their commanders, those who control these soldiers' lives and whose decisions in this fight result from strengths and weaknesses which were revealed in Part One. It is about hidden personal objectives interfering with pursuit of the battle. It is about how the experiences of soldiers we have followed in Part One influence their fears, their resolve, their own abilities, and their survival or loss, whether the battle is won or lost.

Sherman's Grand Plan

MCBRIDE, 33RD IND COBURN 2B 3D 20C: The spring of 1864 found the Union army well organized; better than ever before. General Grant having been placed in command of all the armies was a vast improvement over the old plan of having each department acting independently of the others. Independent commands seemed to make it impossible to have concert of action of the troops that belonged to the different departments. Divided responsibilities engendered jealousies and discontent, and, oftentimes, because of this, bitter defeat followed where victory seemed to be assured. The many successes of the Union arms the following summer and winter fully justified the new order of things. _192

PIERSON, 33RD NJ: The Spring of '64 opened very hopefully for the Union cause. In the West our successes had been most fruitful. Vicksburg had been taken—the Mississippi River was open to its mouth—everything west of it was practically lost to the Confederacy. The Rebel lines had been securely pushed back through Kentucky and Tennessee to the Georgia line, and we held Chattanooga firmly. East Tennessee and Knoxville, too, were ours. Grant had been made Commander-in-Chief and was going East to take personal charge of the campaign there. No wonder Sherman wrote him begging him not to go East, to that graveyard of Union Generals' reputations, but to stay West with us. We would, he said, take Atlanta and Charleston, and then it will be a short and easy task to finish the starved out army of Northern Virginia. In the East Gettysburg had been fought and won. Lee had been driven back into Virginia, to remain there on the defensive thereafter. More than all—nearly three years of war had given us an army of veteran soldiers and tried commanders. Inefficiency had been weeded out and efficiency recognized; jealousies and intrigues had largely given way to harmony, and unity of action as well as of purpose.

Grant, as Commander-in-Chief, was taking personal charge of the movements in the East, while to grand old Sherman, "Uncle Billy," as we, his boys, loved to call him, was entrusted the work in the West. On both sides it was felt that the situation was an earnest one. Grant planned for a general and simultaneous advance of all the armies on May 1st. He wrote to Sherman:

"Your objective is Johnston's army—mine is Lee's army. You keep Johnston so busy that he can send no help to Lee, and I will try to keep Lee so fully occupied that he can send no help to Johnston."

Between Grant and Sherman were relations of complete harmony and loyalty, based upon mutual respect and confidence, the outgrowth of service together in so many campaigns; campaigns which tested ability and resources thoroughly. Sherman brought to his task enthusiasm, confidence, ability and tireless energy. His army, when united, was close to 100,000 men of all arms. The country before him was mountainous, forest-covered and rugged in the extreme, somewhat like the Pocono region.

Moreover, it was occupied and had been all the Winter and Spring by the Rebel army; consequently no supplies could be had from the country. For supplies of all kinds, ration for men and horses, ammunition for fighting, he was obliged to depend upon a single line of railroad from Nashville, nearly 200 miles through a country more or less hostile, and liable to frequent interruptions by Rebel cavalry and raiders. Not only must he supply the daily wants, but a large surplus must be accumulated at Chattanooga to draw upon, as his advance carried him farther and farther away from his base.

How he did this is a matter of history. Not only was there only one railroad, but the number of locomotives and cars belonging to it were totally insufficient for his needs. So he directed that every locomotive and freight train coming into Nashville from any road should be seized and put to work on his line and kept there. All returning troops were ordered to march from Nashville to the front. Beef cattle were to be driven. All travel by civilians and transportation or issuance of supplies for them were forbidden. This seemed harsh and was harsh, but it was necessary and justified by the necessities of war. And so it came to pass that, on May 1st, a goodly supply was on hand at Chattanooga and nearby points.

But this was not all. If his campaign towards Atlanta was to be successful, and he did not doubt it, there were many rivers and streams to be crossed. Of necessity he was obliged to follow more or less closely the line of the one railroad leading from Chattanooga to Atlanta in order that he might use it to carry his supplies, and it was certain that all bridges would be destroyed. The engineer corps, therefore, prepared beforehand, from a standard pattern, trusses for every railroad bridge on the road and had them stored in Chattanooga. So, when in our campaign we were obliged for days to be away from the railroad, and then, after defeating the Rebels, struck it again miles farther south, it was never more than two or three days before we again heard the whistle of the locomotives in our rear bringing up the sorely needed supplies. It was a very encouraging sound to us and must have been a very discouraging one to them.

The distance from Chattanooga to Atlanta is a little more than 200 miles, about as far as it is from Pocono, Pa. to Hoboken, N.J. following the line of the D. L. & W. Railroad, and very much the same sort of country. For the first one-third of the way it is over and through mountain chains, which are a continuation of the Allegheny range, and form a part of the Appalachian system, which makes the backbone of the eastern part of the continent. South of Resaca is an open, rolling country for a few miles. Then comes a series of high peaks and ranges—Allatoona, Kennesaw, Pine Knob; then a gently rolling country to the Chattahoochee River, a few miles beyond which, on a plateau, lies Atlanta. One can travel that distance now by rail in less than four hours; a good walker might cover it in four days; it took us in 1864 four months to make it, and we did not consider ourselves slouches by any means. But there were obstacles in the way, viz, Joe Johnston and 70,000 Rebel soldiers.

To oppose Johnston Sherman had 100,000 men, seemingly large odds, but the one fought behind works, carefully prepared in advance in many cases, and, as he fell back, he was, going towards his supplies and reinforcements, while we were getting farther and farther away with each victorious advance. Sherman's plan was carefully thought out in advance; in brief it was to hold Thomas with his Army of the Cumberland, 60,000 strong, in the centre, McPherson, with his Army of the Tennessee, 25,000 strong, and Schofield, with his Army of the Ohio, 15,000 strong, on either wing, to push the enemy with strong lines wherever found, to hold him there, while with one wing or the other he pressed around one flank or the other and compelled him to retreat or to fight in the open. He reasoned that he could not afford, considering his distance from supplies and reinforcements, to waste his strength by hurling his army against entrenchments, where one man in defence is equal to at least three attacking. Victory, even if won, would be at too great a cost and leave him crippled for further offensive action. This plan in the main he adhered to, and, when he deviated, as at Kennesaw, the result was a vindication of the wisdom of the flanking plan.

To flank means this: When soldiers are formed in line of battle, whether in the open or behind breast works, the whole line can return the fire of the attacking party. Moreover, bullets and shot missing the line go harmlessly to the rear. But, if the attacking force goes around one end or the other of the line, only very few can get in position to return the fire, while the bullets and shot go raking down the whole line. The only thing then left to do is to change front, as it is called, by maneuvers not easy to make under fire, or else to retreat.

This, then, was the situation when, on May 4th, the 33rd N.J. Volunteers, 500 strong, broke camp in Lookout valley and started upon the Atlanta campaign. We were in Hooker's Corps, the [20th], under General Thomas. We went stripped of every unnecessary thing; but one wagon was allowed to each regiment; all baggage was left behind. Each man carried half his house on his back, viz. a piece of heavy twilled muslin two yards square, with double rows of buttons and button-holes. His mate carried another similar piece, and the two, buttoned together and stretched between sticks, made shelter for the two. A canteen carried water or coffee, which he boiled for himself in a tin cup, or an old tomato can. A tin plate served as frying pan and serving dish. A green stick split at one end and forced over the rim of the plate made a handle to hold it over the fire sometimes; at other times, the plate would lose its balance and into the fire would go the pork or hard tack. The air was sometimes blue on those occasions, not necessarily with smoke.

Cooking and eating over, the dishwashing was easy; a hasty rub with a few leaves cleaned the frying pan sufficiently; the grease left on was valuable, and back into the haversack it went rubbing up against the mixture of ground coffee and sugar and hard tack. A rubber blanket and he carried his rifle and 60 rounds of old-fashioned ammunition, 40 in his cartridge box, 20 in his haversack; greased paper cartridge; minie ball at one end, powder at the other. To load, the soldier bit or tore the end of the paper and poured the powder into the muzzle of the rifle, jarred it down to make it show in the nipple of the gun, rammed down the bullet, put on the percussion cap, and then it was ready. Of breach-loading guns there were few; some companies of sharpshooters, had them and some cavalry carbines were also breech-loaders.

Johnston's army lay strongly entrenched in the mountains 20 or 25 miles south of us. For weeks he had prepared his fortifications in anticipation of our advance. The railroad ran between two ranges of these mountains to Dalton, thence to Resaca, a distance of about 15 miles. His main force was near Dalton stretched along the crest of a mountain, called Rocky Faced Ridge. Against him on May 4th Sherman moved Thomas with the Army of the Cumberland; the 4th, 14th and 20th Corps. Our Regiment was in the 20th Corps. Schofield, with the 23rd Corps, was on our left, overlapping

Johnston's right. Thomas and Schofield were to attack the enemy in front and on his right flank, with orders to break through if they could, but at all events to hold him there. Meantime, while this attack was going on, McPherson, with his two corps of the Army of the Tennessee, 15th and 16th, was to march behind a range of mountains which would conceal his movements to Snake Creek Gap, 15 miles south, seize the Gap, march through it and throw himself upon the railroad at Resaca in Johnston's rear. [193]

Mother Bickerdyke's Campaign

Mary Ann Bickerdyke had labored to help the wounded in Grant's campaigns. Now she mounted her own campaign to keep up with Sherman. Grant gave her a pass on the railroad and she used it, needing no introduction.

MRS. LIVERMORE, SANITARY COMMISSION: General Sherman was pouring supplies, provender, and ammunition into Chattanooga; for it was to be his base of supplies for the Atlanta campaign. He had issued an order absolutely forbidding agents of sanitary stores, or agents of any description, to go over the road from Nashville to Chattanooga. He alleged as the reason for this prohibition that he wished the entire ability of the railroad devoted to strictly active military operations. There was great distress in the hospitals below Nashville, in consequence of this stringent order, and uneasiness and anxiety at the North, because of its seemingly needless inhumanity. Mother Bickerdyke found Nashville full of worried agents, and of sanitary stores that were needed down the road, and spoiling for lack of transportation. Her pass from General Grant would take her to Chattanooga despite General Sherman's prohibition.

Before starting, her fertility of invention manifested itself in a characteristic act. Ambulances with mules in harness were being sent to various points, against the day of need. No barrels were allowed in these ambulances; but all the bags they could hold could be crowded in. Getting such help as she could muster, they made bags, which were filled with dried apples, peaches, potatoes, and any other sanitary articles that could be sent in them as well as in barrels; and the ambulances went away packed with articles for the hospitals. Forty such left for Huntsville, Ala., thirty for Bridgeport, and several for other points. Then Mother Bickerdyke, despite remonstrance

193 (Pierson 1931)

and opposition, took the next train for Chattanooga, and made her unexpected debut at General Sherman's headquarters.

"Halloo! Why, how did you get down here?" asked one of the General's staff officers, as he saw her enter Sherman's headquarters.

"Came down in the cars, of course. There's no other way of getting down here that I know of," replied the matter-of-fact woman. "I want to see General Sherman."

"He is in there, writing," said the officer, pointing to an inner room; " but I guess he won't see you."

"Guess he will!" and she pushed into the apartment. "Good morning, General! I want to speak to you a moment. May I come in?"

"I should think you had got in!" answered the General, barely looking up, in great annoyance. "What's up now?"

"Why, General," said the earnest matron, in a perfect torrent of words, "we can't stand this last order of yours, nohow. You'll have to change it, as sure as you live. We can get along without any more nurses and agents, but the supplies we must have. The sick and wounded men need them, and you'll have to give permission to bring them down. The fact is, General, after a man is unable to carry a gun, and drops out of the lines, you don't trouble yourself about him, but turn him over to the hospitals, expecting the doctors and nurses to get him well and put back again into the service as soon as possible. But how are we going to make bricks without straw? Tell me that if you can."

"Well, I'm busy to-day, and cannot attend to you. I will see you some other time." But though Sherman kept on writing, and did not look up, Mother Bickerdyke saw a smile lurking in the corner of his mouth, and knew she would carry her point. So she persisted.

"No, General! Don't send me away until you've fixed this thing as it ought to be fixed. You had me assigned to your corps, and told me that you expected me to look after the nursing of the men who needed it. But I should like to know how I can do this if I don't have anything to work with? Have some sense about it now, General! "

There was a hearty laugh at this, and a little badinage ensued, which Mother Bickerdyke ended in her brusque way, with, "Well, I can't stand fooling here all day. Now, General, write an order for two cars a day to be sent down from the Sanitary Commission at Nashville, and I'll be satisfied." The order was written, and for weeks all the sanitary stores sent from Nashville to Chattanooga, and the posts along that road, were sent directly or indirectly through this mediation of Mother Bickerdyke. _194

Cool Impatience

BENTON, BAND, 150TH NY RUGER 2B 1D 20C: It was General Sherman, the new Commander of the army to which we were then attached, and from that time to the close of the war his was a familiar figure. So spontaneous and rapid was his own manner that he seemed sometimes impatient at the slowness of others. This restiveness was by some persons mistakenly attributed to nervousness. A few weeks later I saw him standing on a battlefield and surrounded as before by his staff. The battle had begun and the bullets were singing past, but his seeming nervousness had now disappeared, and he was apparently the coolest and most unconcerned of the whole group of officers. _195

194 (Livermore 1890, 533)
195 (Benton 1902, 129)

May - The Campaign Begins

Although all knew that many a one would have to lose his life, or be wounded on the battlefield, or perhaps be crippled for life, yet a stern resolution was fixed in all hearts of those brave men to fight and perhaps die for the country. —Grunert

With the beginning of May, the grand Atlanta Campaign commenced. It is said that some of the rebels afterwards declared, "Old Sherman ascended to the top of Lookout Mountain, gave the command, 'Attention! Creation! by kingdom right wheel march!' and The Yankees came down like the wolf on the fold!" – Fleharty .196

TREMAIN: It appears as though on the first of May Grant's bugle sound to advance was heard not only in Virginia, but in Tennessee and Alabama. The camps of the troops in this Military Division, scattered as they were from East Tennessee to Northern Georgia and Alabama were active with the preparations for the opening campaign known only to those whose right it was to know. A strong army of veterans under General McPherson, marched from Huntsville, Alabama, in a southeasterly direction, while a similar column under Schofield was concealed in the valleys marching from East Tennessee south-westerly. The army of Thomas at Chattanooga gathered itself together as it moved towards Ringgold, Georgia. Hooker's Corps, however, scattered as it was from Lookout Mountain to Nashville made tremendous strides on the extreme right of Thomas' army. .197

MARVIN, CO F 5TH CONN KNIPE 1B 1B 20C: There were seven corps in this army, viz.: Army of the Ohio (General Schofield commanding). Twenty-third Corps, General Cox, badge, a shield; Army of the Tennessee (General McPherson commanding). Fifteenth Corps, General Logan, badge, cartridge box; Sixteenth Corps, General Dodge, badge, two cannon crossed; Seventeenth Corps, General Blair, badge, an arrow; Army of the Cumberland (General Thomas commanding), Fourth Corps, General Howard, badge, a triangle; Fourteenth Corps, General Palmer, badge, an acorn; Twentieth Corps, General Hooker, badge, a star. There were usually three divisions in each corps, and the badges of the First, Second and Third Divisions of each corps were indicated by a white, red and blue colored corps badge, respectively. The badge a man wore indicated at sight, therefore, both his corps and division. .198

---

196 (Fleharty, Our Regiment. A History of the 102d Illinois Infantry Volunteers 1865, 51)
197 (Tremain 1905, 171) Coburn's brigade barely made it, arriving April 30.
198 (Marvin 1889, 297)

CULVER, CAPTAIN, CO A 129TH ILL WARD 1 B 3D 20C: I am not allowed to tell our destination but you will hear from me before very long if the mails are not stopped. Do not allow yourself to be troubled. Trust in God. All will be well in any event. My health is excellent. I am furnished with a horse as I am still acting Adgt. There is much that I would like to say, but I have not the time. I will endeavor to give you satisfactory accounts of all our marches whenever opportunity offers, but let me urge upon you the necessity of being contented. It is possible you may not hear from me for a month or even two months, and, though you may feel lonely, still try and be happy. May our Father in Heaven deal kindly with us. ... We are 1st Brig., 3rd Division, 20th A.C. You may hear from us through the papers. Give my love to Mother [Murphy] & Maggie and Remember me kindly to all. May God in his mercy keep you and bless you, so that whether we meet again in this world or not, we may have the assurance of a Home. .199

And so the campaign is to begin. The plan was simple in concept.

COX, JACOB D., 3D 23C: Before the opening of the campaign, Thomas had called Sherman's attention to Snake Creek Gap as a route by which Resaca or Calhoun could be reached, and the position at Dalton be turned. He had offered to lead the Army of the Cumberland by this defile, whilst the Armies of the Tennessee and Ohio occupied Johnston in front. The positions of his forces, and the desire to have the greater strength of the Army of the Cumberland at the centre and covering his own base, made Sherman modify whilst he accepted the plan. He determined to send McPherson with his two corps against Resaca, whilst he pressed Johnston in front with the superior force, ready to follow him up the moment he let go of Dalton, and before he could seriously damage McPherson. .200

Wauhatchie to Chickamauga

GRUNERT, CO D 129TH ILL WARD 1B 3D 20C: May 2. We were awakened at 4 o'clock by the roll of the drums. After roll call a hasty breakfast was prepared and taken and the haversacks filled with bread, meat etc. for three days. The hour for the march was set at 7 o'clock; this hour approaching the dog or shelter tents used as roofs on our houses, were taken down, rolled up and buckled to our knapsacks. The bunks were searched once more to see if everything had been taken out that the rebels in the neighborhood might

199 (Culver, Your Affectionate Husband, J.F. Culver n.d.) May 1, 1864 to wife.
200 (J. D. Cox 1882)

make use of. It was seven, the drummers gave the signal to fall in to line and soon we were on the march to the drill ground, where the brigade was to rendezvous, and every regiment took its place in the line. With unpleasant feelings of regret we left our comfortable and commodious camp, where we had spent so many happy hours. The 1st and 2d division of our corps had left camp before we did, and as both were far enough ahead of us, no impediments were in our way to Chattanooga. Passing to the right of the city, we moved over Missionary Ridge to the Chickamauga battlefield. The battlefield looked very much like that of Murfreesboro, except that there was more wood here which had been riddled by thousands of bullets and was either withering or had withered already. We marched over the battlefield without halting. A little while before sunset we reached Chickamauga creek, and camped near Gordon's mill, after having marched 15 miles. We received a big mail to-night.

CRAM, CO F 105TH ILL WARD 1B 3D 20C: About one o'clock yesterday we commenced crossing the Chickamauga battle ground and never in my life do I want to see such terrible evidence of human destruction as were there visible. Hundreds of large trees were cut completely into with shot, and hundreds of items of immense size are bored through and through with those iron messengers, while the butts of them were so riddled with bullets that in many of them not a space of a single square inch can be found free from the scar of a bullet.

The battle ground at Stone River I used to think was awful, but compared to this, it seems a mere skirmish. The saddest sight of all, and indeed the most significant, were the little clusters of graves where are buried the fallen heroes.

The distance we marched yesterday is about eighteen miles, very many poor fellows fell out and were left behind. This is our first experience in marching under Butterfield and I must say, we don't love him much. He gave us scarcely a particle of meat and just stopped long enough at noon for us to hastily swallow a bite and then started on again. If we had marched leisurely and had occasional halts we would have arrived here two hours later without being exhausted and without leaving hundreds of our men behind. [201]

AUSTIN, 19TH MICH COBURN 2B 3D 20C: I send you a bunch of wild flowers that I picked within a step of whare one of our soldiers was pretended to be burried. When I looked at the ugly maid grave & then at these beautiful

201 (Cram 2001, 95)

flowers which surrounded it I felt to thank God that he had not forgotten the spot whare the soldier fell fighting the battles of his country. Let us trust in God & hope for the best. _202

WILLIAMS, 1D 20C: On the Chickamauga battleground the torn trees and numerous graves pointed out the scenes of the heaviest fighting. We passed several wagons loaded with disinterred bodies of the victims of the battle ... I send you a flower I picked from near some graves on Chickamauga battleground. _203

GRUNERT, CO D 129TH ILL WARD 1B 3D 20C: May 3. According to orders we remained quiet to-day in order to give the regiments that had been here before us time to pack up and move on. We drilled in the afternoon. The day was very hot. Another mail came.

TREMAIN: Passing over the historic field of Chickamauga, through Gordon's Mills and Peavine Creek, until about the 6th inst. it had joined the rest of the Army of the Cumberland along the banks of the "Middle Chickamauga," and in front of Taylor's Ridge. _204

Thus, on the very first day, those who know there will be fighting and dying for them have just been presented with the horrific results of the battle that brought them on this march.

A Stern Resolution

GRUNERT, CO D 129TH ILL WARD 1B 3D 20C: May 4. Early in the morning we struck our tents and marched on to the front. The march became more unsafe, as the enemy's cavalry, knowing that the Yankee army was in motion, displayed much agility and harassed us wherever it could be done. In order not to be surprised by the enemy or lose men unnecessarily, several regiments of one brigade had to throw out flankers; but no enemy appeared where the 20th army corps was marching. At 3 o'clock in the afternoon we reached the 14th army corps, or at least a part of it, near Ringgold, Ga. Here we camped in the woods, after a march of 12 miles near the front. The pickets were instructed to be very cautious, as a nightly attack was at least possible, if not certain. The night passed quietly.

202 (Austin 1864)
203 (Williams 1963, May 20, 1863)
204 (Tremain 1905, 171)

The brigade had witnessed the destroyed and dead after the Battles of Perryville and Stones River, read of victories and defeats at Vicksburg and Gettysburg and other fights, while they endured extremes of weather on long nights of picket, hard marches, and idleness as disease took comrades, all the while, for some at least, wanting to fight, to get the war on, ended, and be home.

GRUNERT, CO D 129TH ILL WARD 1B 3D 20C: May 5. We remained in camp and in consequence of this lying idle, the fighting spirit of the men gave way to still and silent thoughts about the impenetrable future, or about the strength of the enemy in our front, estimated at 80,000 men. Letters were written to our friends and relatives at home to let them know that we were well. Although all knew that many a one would have to lose his life, or be wounded on the battlefield, or perhaps be crippled for life, yet a stern resolution was fixed in all hearts of those brave men to fight and perhaps die for the country. Such a spirit can only arise from a pure and holy love of the cause of our glorious Union! .205 Our officers were equally brave and to be trusted, and we were certain of the final victory. We drew rations to-day for three days, and the regiment had dress parade. Several of our scouts were taken prisoner to-day.

AUSTIN, 19TH MICH COBURN 2B 3D 20C: After drawing two days rations of hard tack and pork with a little sugar and coffee we started on our march with orders to make the two days ration last four days this is we are going to be fed for a while at least I hope it wont last long if it will help end the war I wont grunt if I do have and empty stomach some of the time ... I can see genls of all sides Gen Geery is here with his Corps I understand. I see Gen Thomas myself I also see Gen Killpatrick so you see I am with some big bugs. .206

TREMAIN: Sherman's army found itself at this time with its advance through Hooker's Gap in front of Ringgold, with his right and right-centre composed of Hooker's Corps, and McPherson's "Army of the Tennessee," stretching along the base of Taylor's Ridge towards Nickajack and Gordon's Gap, its left centre and left under Palmer and Howard reaching in advance of Ringgold and Catoosa Springs, with the Army of the Ohio under Schofield

205 Immigrants from Prussian Germany were well educated and, especially those who participated in the 1848 revolution, were among the most patriotic. Grunert was German. 206 (Austin 1864, May 5)

marching along the East Tennessee and Georgia Railroad from Cleveland and with its advance near Varnell's Station. _207

Nickajack Gap to Tunnel Hill

GRUNERT, CO D 129TH ILL WARD 1B 3D 20C: May 6. We commenced our march early on the road from Ringgold to Dalton Southward. As nothing impeded our progress, we advanced rapidly and went into camp early in the afternoon. Our regiment was ordered on picket duty, the principal part posted on the brow of a high mountain, the balance in the valley below. From the mountain we could see tents at a considerable distance, but it was impossible to say whether they belonged to the Union or the rebel army. The night passed quietly. We were near the celebrated NickaJack Gap.

TREMAIN: This was the first position of Sherman's army. The enemy's main body was at Dalton, while his advance reached Tunnell Hill, and the mountains and gaps immediately in our front. From our position everything looked unfavorable for offensive operations. Between our camps and the enemy stretched two ridges of mountains, passable only by two or three rough roads over their tops, misnamed by the people "Gaps," probably because there were no "Gaps" there. Between these two ridges was a beautiful valley, known as Dogwood Valley, watered by the East Chickamauga, one of the branches of that tortuous and now to military operations troublesome stream. The enemy's line of communications appeared perfectly secure; his front impregnable, his flanks admirably protected by impassable natural barriers, and his advance at Tunnell Hill well calculated to be maintained. In the face of these obstacles, Sherman's army continued its march without a halt. _208

GRUNERT, CO D 129TH ILL WARD 1B 3D 20C: May 7. Before daybreak our pickets were called in and after remaining on the Dalton road preparing and eating breakfast, until the balance of the brigade came up, we marched in the advance forward. Our march today was not a pleasant one, over narrow, dusty, or rocky roads, although the enemy did not harass us. The weather was intolerably hot, and the necessary fresh water was wanting. When we rested in the afternoon for a couple of hours in a field, we quenched our thirst in a milky, dirty creek, in which higher up some were bathing, others washing their feet. But all these minor considerations were nothing, we

207 (Tremain 1905, 171)
208 (Tremain 1905, 171)

could at least quench our thirst and rest a couple of hours. We left our dusty resting place and went into camp after sunset, after having marched 20 miles. At Buzzard Roost we heard some fighting; Gen's. Hooker, Sickles and Butterfield were with the brigade the principal part of the day. Gen. Killpatrick with his cavalry was continually in our front or at our flanks. Everything went off quiet.

TREMAIN On the 7th inst. Howard, with the Fourth Corps, moved from Catoosa Springs, and by successful manoeuvering dislodged the enemy from the commanding hills in his front, while Palmer with the Fourteenth Corps assisted by this movement, after some skirmishing took possession of the famous Tunnell Hill, with a total loss of only ten wounded. Hooker at the same time threw his corps across Taylor's Ridge in two columns by way of Nickajack and Gordon's Gap, and promptly moved up and joined his left to Palmer's right, encamping along the East Chickamauga. Schofield continued his march along the East Tennessee and Georgia railroad, threatening the enemy's right, while McPherson, his movement thus being quite concealed, pressed through Gordon's and Ship's Gaps in Taylor's Ridge to a place called Villaners. The army in this position was one grand point in advance gained, and the railroad was at once put in running order to Tunnell Hill. .209

STORRS, 20TH CONN COBURN 2B 3D 20C: The 20th Corps proceeded through Taylor's Ridge at Gardner's Gap to a fortified hill in front of Buzzard's Roost Gap, which was, after a sharp contest, taken possession of. .210

Buzzard's Roost

STRONG, CO B 105TH ILL WARD 1B 3D 20C: Soon our first little brush with the enemy came. It was at Buzzards' Roost, a mountain pass in upper Georgia. Up to this time we had had no big fights and had lost no men by bullets although we had been at "war" for nearly two years. About this time, Company B, my company, was on scout. We halted for dinner on a bluff overlooking a creek, with a field beyond the creek and woods beyond that. Just after we halted, we heard a peculiar noise in the tree tops. It sounded like a lot of tumble bugs flying through the air. We wondered what caused the noise. Then small twigs began to drop near us. Then we heard guns

209 (Tremain 1905, 171)
210 (Storrs 1886, 125)

going off and knew the "tumble-bug" noise was bullets. No one was hit. But it was soon to come. ..211

GRUNERT, CO D 129TH ILL WARD 1B 3D 20C: May 8. We lay quiet to-day, but had orders to be ready at any moment to advance. A horse, saddle and bridle which the adjutant of the regiment had brought from Louisville, Ky. yesterday, was presented to Col. Case. The present was made to Col. Case by the whole regiment. The Colonel was deeply touched by the love of his men, and thanked them sincerely. Later in the day we were ordered to be ready for marching, but to leave all baggage behind under the care of some guards.

COX, CHARLES H. COMPANY E, 70TH IND: May 8. Col Harrison has been in very poor health since leaving Wauhatchie, he is still doing duty and will not give up at this time. My health remains good, having much nicer time Act Adjt than if I were with my company taking it on foot. ..212

So Charles Harding Cox of the 70th took the place of Culver, of the 129th, as acting adjutant when Culver wanted to go back to his company to lead it in battle.

TREMAIN: The enemy had retired to his formidable position at Buzzard's Roost, which, with few thousand men, he could hold against all the army that might choose to attack his front. While Howard and Palmer on the left were learning more completely the position of the enemy, and occupying his attention by reconnoitering. Wood's brigade of Butterfield's division, Hooker's corps, performed a similar duty further to the right, and before night succeeded in establishing our lines partially on the slope of Rockface Ridge, and along a commanding range in front of the enemy's position at Buzzard's Roost.

There has been much discussion in the army why this place was called "Buzzard's Roost." Like many other instances of American nomenclature it is not because buzzards roost there, but because they do not. There were once a few old groggeries and a railroad station there, where the chivalric gamblers of the South did congregate to drink cheap toddy and cut each other's throats. What they afterwards did with the carcases the appellation of "Buzzard's Roost" which the people around bestowed on this locality is

211 (Strong 1961)
212 (Wyatt 1972)

too suggestive to mention. You may guess then from the habits of the bird, why the place was called "Buzzard's Roost." .213

Meanwhile McPherson was massing troops in a concealed position at Snake Creek Gap. On the 8th there was more reconnoitering and a closer drawing of our lines towards the enemy. Geary's division of Hooker's corps on this day had the first actual battle of the campaign, about three miles west of Dalton at Mill Creek Gap, sometimes called Dug Gap. Of the battle itself, you have already had accounts. Geary's loss was about 250. He fought the choicest troops in Johnston's army under Claiborne and his troops, repeatedly gaining the crest of the mountain near the road for the possession of which they were fighting only to be hurled back again down the precipice with fearful losses. Colonel Buschbeck's and Candy's brigades were the troops engaged. Among the reported killed were Captain Bartlett, Thirty-third New Jersey, and Colonel Jones, One Hundred and Fifty-fourth New York; Captain Vedden, ditto; Lieutenant Miller, Thirty-third New Jersey, and Lieutenant Smith, ditto, and Captain Forrest, One Hundred and Thirty-fourth New York. The color bearer of the One Hundred and Fifty-fourth New York, George Bishop, was killed in one of the charges, where he planted the colors on the very top of the mountain.

This battle had the effect of holding the enemy in Geary's front and not allowing the column which had started for Snake Creek Gap to reach there in time to prevent McPherson possessing himself of it without a fight. .214

GRUNERT, CO D 129TH ILL WARD 1B 3D 20C: May 9. The 2d division of our army corps under Gen. Geary met the enemy unexpectedly to-day near Buzzard Roost and immediately got in the heavy fire of the enemy's guns. Several attempts were made to dislodge the enemy from his strong entrenchments, but in vain. The division lost about 500 dead and wounded who were brought past our camp in ambulances. We remained quiet, although under marching orders since noon. It was expected that our division would be sent to Buzzard Roost, but we remained during the night. Heavy firing was heard in our front in the afternoon. We drew rations for three days.

AUSTIN, 19TH MICH COBURN 2B 3D 20C: Our line begins at ringgold & comes this way. I dont know how far but as I understand it we are in a circle or half moon shape. Our Brig is on the wright wing & wright of the center.

213 (Tremain 1905, 171)
214 (Tremain 1905, 171)

Yesterday thare was sharp firing on our wright & left both. More musketry shooting than artillary. It commenced at about 3 oclock PM & lasted an hour or two. This morning the firing is on our left. The first gun we heared was fired at about 6 oclock. It has been kept up by intervals ever since & is going on now. The rebs are sed to be fortifying from whare they are now fighting clear back to Dalton. We are on the top of a hill or Mountain with a little earth rails & stone piled up in front of us to keep off the bullets if the rebs advance & our skermishers fall back. This is what they are trying to do but the rebs seem to think they are more safe whare they are & so dont call out worth a cent. ... The weather is pleasant & warm. Last night was the first night we have had our tent pitched in 3 dayes. This morning when we got up we all had to down with our houses & pack everything into our napsacks just the same as though we calculated to start the next minute on the march. The Col horse stands hitched to a tree clost to his quarters with bridal & saddle on his back ready for a start. Every man has to wear his catrage box & belt all the time & is not allowed to leave the Company only to go after water then have to take their guns. Roll call every hour & the result reported to the Col... Day before yesterday we marched 21 miles to get here. Several boys in the Brig were hot or sunstruck. I got pretty well [unreadable] up but got through without being hurt. How this thing is going to turn out is more than any man can tell as yet. I feel that thare is a heavy battle before us & our only way is to trust in the God of battles & fight on untill death or victory is our reward. May God be with us through all the fight & guide us in the wayes of right by his never failing might & wisdom. Trust in the Lord my dear & hope to meet me in heaven if never more we meet again here. I will write more if this does not go before I get a chance.... I begin this on the 9th at night. We just got down to go to sleep when the order come to pack up everything & fall in line ready to march at a minutes notice. This was done & every man was soon in line with every bit of his household furniture on his back & provision for 3 dayes on his shoulder with gun & amonition in hand. After standing for a few minutes & all wer aranged we all rested in place. This was for every man to curl down righs whare he stood with gun & everything ready & napsack on his back. Here we all layed till 3 oclock in the morning when attention was ordered & we all marched by the right flank 4 or five miles to the foot of another mountain farther to our left. All hands arrived thare at daylight & could see the rebs on the top of the mountain swarming like so many bees but we put out our pickets along the foot of the hill & sent one Co up on the side hill to skermish & see what the Johni would

do. Not one of them dare come down by the sharpshooters. Would hide &
peck away at our boys all they could. .215

McPherson's Attempt

GRUNERT, CO D 129TH ILL WARD 1B 3D 20C: May 10. A rainy day; we were
still lying in the bush, though under orders again to be ready for an advance
at any moment. A glorious time was in camp on the reception of the news
that the rebel army had been badly whipped at Richmond after a bloody four
days' fight, and that the much longed for peace was near. The news was too
glorious and but half believed, as the strong inimical force in our front did
not much give room to the thought of the conclusion of an early peace. On
the contrary, the enemy in our front seemed more determined than ever.
Gen. McPherson, with the 11th corps, went to the road to Dalton, in order,
if possible, to shut up the enemy in Dalton, or to take such positions that the
enemy would become an easy prey to our cannons. The report of guns was
heard during the whole day; the night brought us a thunder storm and rain.

Whether McPherson failed is disputed. He followed instructions. But Sherman
hoped for more and was disappointed in not cutting Johnston off completely at
Resaca. There are plenty who argue that Sherman should have sent Thomas
instead of McPherson. .216 Stanley, and others, accuse Sherman of being jealous
of Thomas and favoring McPherson. .217

STANLEY, 1D 4C: The passage of McPherson through Snake Creek Gap
caused Johnston to let go Dalton and the ridge and to hasten to Resaca and
here was committed Sherman's mistake—his biggest mistake that of not
sending the Army of the Cumberland in the place of the Army of the
Tennessee through Snake Creek Gap. The very scheme itself originated with
General Thomas, who had, during the winter, a thorough examination of
this defile made by his scouts. He would have carried through sixty
thousand men—plenty to defeat Joe Johnston's army and to ruin the
Confederacy ... McPherson did advance as far as the railroad and main
wagon road on Johnston's line of retreat, but, fearing that he would be

---

215 (Austin 1864)
216 See Stone's more thorough analysis: (Stone 1910)
217 Stanley also accuses Sherman of not having the "moral courage" to fight a battle and
force Johnston to fight and instead flanked piecemeal, losing more men, driving Johnston
to Atlanta (Stanley 1917, 166). Intriguing idea.

overpowered, he withdrew and took up a defensive position at the debouche of the gap. .218

According to Confederate General Hood, in his memoir, General Polk's Corps, which had not been at Dalton, was coming from Rome, Georgia and half was at Resaca on May 9. .219 Half a corps would be at least a division. This telegram confirms:

HUNTER, SURGEON 60TH INDIANA VOLUNTEERS: The postmaster at Resaca, Georgia, neglected to forward the letters deposited in his office on the 12th and 13th of May, 1864. On the morning of May 16th, the Union troops who first entered the town visited the post-office and took the letters. Most of them were handed to General McPherson; one is still in my possession. It was written by an officer his in Polk's corps, and is signed J. D. B. – g.[sic]:

"Line of Battle, Resaca, Ga. May 12,'64 We are in line of battle at this place, or rather in our fortification. Loring's division is here, and Canty's brigade from Mobile, and Vaughn from Cheatham's division. This place is fifteen miles from Dalton, where the railroad crosses the Coosa River, very important post. The enemy came in sight, five thousand strong, on Monday, skirmished with Canty, but Vaughn coming down on the train the enemy seem to have taken a scare and left that night, about five miles toward a gap in the hills, where I understand they are intrenched ... Canty lost eight killed and seventy-six wounded." .220

Hunter suggests criticism of McPherson should at least be modified.

TREMAIN: I will not detail the daily movements of the next few days. It will suffice to say that the enemy were kept thoroughly busy at Buzzard's Roost by the reconnoisances, demonstrations and actual attacks of Schofield on the extreme left in the hills of Rockyface, and of Howard and Palmer on the right. It was in one of these attacks that Harker's brigade distinguished itself. The enemy were seriously perplexed by a large force of McPherson's army making its appearance in front of his works at Resaca on Wednesday, the 11th inst. The bridge was not destroyed, however, and our force retired to Snake Creek Gap without molesting the enemy, who was strongly posted and in considerable force. For this retiring movement on our part there may

218 (Stanley 1917, 163)
219 (Hood 1880, 89).
220 (Hunter 1886)

be some criticism, but no intelligent one until we are made aware of the orders which the commander of that wing of our army was acting. .221

Unanswerable: had McPherson made an all-out effort, would he have been overwhelmed? Could Johnston then have closed the gap? Would Sherman have to battle at Dalton then? In other words, perhaps Sherman should have been grateful. After all, McPherson had the foresight to instead fall back and protect Snake Creek Gap.

> TREMAIN: At midnight on Tuesday, the 10th, Williams' division of Hooker's corps, quietly marched for the support of McPherson. The remainder of the corps followed the next night. At the same time there was a general evacuation of our depot and headquarters at Tunnel Hill; and before another twenty-four hours had passed. Palmer and Schofield followed to Snake Gap; and Howard pressed as closely as was prudent to the enemy's works at Buzzard's Roost. .222

Moving Camp

Moving camp on short notice, as described by Brown of the 27th Indiana.

> BROWN, CO C 27TH INDIANA RUGER 2B 1D 20C: It is surprising how quickly a regiment can pack up its effects, take down its tents, arrange things for loading, store them in the wagons and be ready to start. We were only novices in the work at this time, but as this was our first experience of starting on short notice, the matter may as well be mentioned here. Old soldiers come to be not only expert about such things, but very much so in detecting and interpreting the signs which precede them. Some peculiarity about a courier riding into camp, the manner in which the colonel calls the adjutant after receiving a dispatch, the movement of the adjutant or the colonel's orderly, as he goes to the quarters of the man who beats the calls, any one of a dozen things, will often forewarn one who has often been over the ground, of what is coming.

In the Twenty-seventh it was common to beat the long roll when the regiment was required to move quickly. Sometimes the adjutant simply stood in front of his tent and gave verbal orders to strike tents and prepare to fall in. At other times, he passed swiftly from the tent of one company commander to another and communicated the orders to them. Whether

221 (Tremain 1905, 171)
222 (Tremain 1905, 171)

one of these methods was pursued or another, the effect was the same. Every man not on duty at once sprang to the work of shaking out his blankets, gathering his effects and packing his knapsack. Of course, such an order catches many away from their own tents, in some other part of the camp, or at some distance outside of it. These men can be seen running swiftly to their own quarters, like people in a small town or village respond to the call of "Fire."

The first member of a mess to get his individual traps packed seizes an ax and starts around the tent, giving each stake a few licks side-wise, to loosen it. Others follow him, pull up the stakes and toss them to some convenient point. As the last stakes come up, the tent is laid upon the ground, neatly folded in layers, and rolled in a compact bundle. The stakes, and sometimes the poles, are rolled inside and the guy ropes serve to tie the bundle fast. Meanwhile, the company teamster has hooked up and driven to some accessible point, usually one end or the other of the company street. There each mess carries its tent, cooking utensils, axes, shovels, picks, or whatever company property it may have in charge. If there is time, most of the company assist in the loading, under the directions of the commissary sergeant, and "many hands make light work." If orders to start are very urgent, a small detail is sometimes made to load the wagon and then follow on after the column. Sometimes the work is left wholly for the sergeant and teamster.

A camp of many conveniences was thus dismantled and abandoned in a very few minutes.

As might be imagined, many articles of some value were voluntarily left behind. For this reason a swarm of citizens, a mixed multitude of men, women and children, white and colored, usually appeared when a camp was being abandoned, to pick up whatever they could see. The whites, living near, were not commonly in favor with Union soldiers. So many of them were in sympathy with the rebellion, that all of them were suspected of it. When a white person or family was known to be really on our side, soldiers were often lavish in the bestowment of articles that could not be taken along. Rather than let anything fall into the hands of a known rebel sympathizer, it was usually mutilated or destroyed. Overcoats or other clothing, or blankets, were cut or torn, and provisions were in some way rendered unfit for use. After the regiment was ready to start, and was awaiting orders to fall in, it frequently happened that some one set fire to the straw or leaves which had been used for bedding, and in the blaze thus started, these cast off articles were thrown, to be entirely consumed. .223

May 11, 12 - Snake Creek Gap, Building Road

Three men ordered to each tool to push the work vigorously. -Butterfield

GRUNERT, CO D 129TH ILL WARD 1B 3D 20C: May 11. We were awakened from our slumber before day-break, and left the main road for small by-roads and paths, sometimes even on paths cut by our pioneers. The march lasted without interruption until evening, when we remained near the Wall Gap over night.

MARVIN, CO F 5TH CONN, KNIPE 1B 1D 20C: May 11th. Orders came to-night for us to move without any noise, and at 11 P. M. we were upon the road, in the midst of a powerful rain storm and as black as Hagar. Marching over a country road, under such conditions, was terrible; but we managed to do as we were ordered to do, and morning finds us in the Gap which is seven miles long and wide enough for one road only. The whole brigade are building breastworks. Received and issued clothing. At night moved on through the Gap. .224

223 (E. R. Brown 1899, 58)
224 (Marvin 1889, 296)

BUILDING A CORDUROY ROAD IN THE WOODS, NEAR THE WELDON RAILROAD, VA.—From a Sketch by A. McCallum.

MORHOUS, CO C 123RD NY KNIPE 1B 1D 20C Immediately after the seizure of Snake Creek Gap by Sherman, the 20th Corps by an all night's march reached there, and our Regiment in common with several others had to ascend the mountain on the left of the gap, and on the summit they built breastworks. From this elevation the boys looked off to the south and east, in a densely wooded country which they believed to be truly "Dixie's land." Here it was expected the "great battle of the West" would be fought. 225

WOOD, 3B 3D 20C: On Wednesday, the 11th, at 4 a.m. the brigade marched from its position near Woods Store, to which place it had returned after the reconnaissance to Snake Creek Gap and about half way through the gap, arriving at 12 m. a distance of fourteen miles. 226 Here I was ordered to put the brigade into camp, and to widen and put in good condition that part of the road through the gap between where General Williams, of the First Division, was encamped and the camp of my brigade, to make the road of sufficient capacity to allow two wagon trains and a column of infantry to march abreast. I divided the work into as many sections as I had regiments, and as soon as the tools were provided put as many men on the road as could be advantageously employed. By nightfall I had that portion of the road

225 (Morhous 1879, 85)
226 12 m. is 12 meridian (noon).

apportioned to my brigade completed as ordered. On the 12th, at 10 a.m. the brigade broke camp and marched through the gap, a distance of four miles, and took up position in a single deployed line in rear of the Fifteenth Army Corps. 227

GRUNERT, CO D 129TH ILL WARD 1B 3D 20C: May 12. We remained quiet until noon; the roads which had become in bad condition in consequence of the many wagons passing over them, were repaired during that time, our guns put in the best order, as now there could be no doubt of meeting the enemy. After twelve o'clock we moved forward, but only three miles, where we went into camp at Snake Creek, and remained for the night. Heavy firing the whole day at Dalton and Buzzard Roost.

BUTTERFIELD, 3D 20C: Have put my three brigades in camp along this gap (it is about five miles in length) at proper distances for a vigorous prosecution of the works ordered, one brigade in the center of the gap and one near each end ... Three men ordered to each tool to push the work vigorously and carefully enough to do it well. My artillery and trains I have left near General William's camp at the entrance to the gap. My headquarters are about a mile from the southern end or mouth of the gap. 228

MARVIN, CO F 5TH CONN, KNIPE 1B 1D 20C: We are encamped in the Valley and from our camp, tins evening, we can see the camp fires of the whole of General Sherman's army, composed of over 100,000 men. Such a sight is not often seen by the eyes of men. Our arms are stacked in column by division. Pitched our tents. Expect a row to-morrow. 229

FLEHARTY, 102ND ILL WARD 1B 3D 20C: Our Brigade was detained during part of the 11th and 12th of May in the gap, to cut out and prepare a new road through the woods. During the afternoon of the 12th we marched five miles and camped near the mouth of the Gap. There had been some fighting in the direction of Dalton, and at intervals the low and sullen "boom" of distant cannon was heard, almost due north of us. The 20th Corps had successfully accomplished the flank movement through Snake Creek Gap, and was now well established in a strong position, threatening the left flank of the enemy. 230

227 (OR, Series I Vol 38 Part 2 Serial 73: Reports n.d., 431)
228 (OR, Series I Vol 38 Part 4 Serial 75: Correspondence n.d., 136)
229 (Marvin 1889, 297)
230 (Fleharty, Our Regiment. A History of the 102d Illinois Infantry Volunteers 1865, 52)

McBride, 33rd Ind Coburn 2B 3D 20C: Upon reaching Snake Creek Gap, which was from three to five miles long, the next day, the 12th, General Butterfield's division was detailed to make a road the length of the gap, with the following instructions: Two wagon roads must be well made, filled with stone, ditched when necessary, and a clear path cut on the east side of the gap throughout for infantry, with bridges for crossing creek, etc.

The First brigade, under General Ward, worked the center, the Second brigade, under Colonel Coburn, the north end, and the Third brigade, under Col. James Wood, the south end the two latter working toward the center of the point worked by the First brigade.

At noon the Nineteenth Michigan, Twenty-second Wisconsin, and Eighty-fifth Indiana were ordered to advance with the rest of the division, while the Thirty-third Indiana and Twentieth Connecticut continued the work of road building, which was completed by sundown of that day. Almost simultaneously with the completion of the road the mighty army of Sherman began to move through the Gap—and what a grand sight! It was the advance of an army filled with enthusiasm and confidence, a body of men destined to sweep to Atlanta and thence to the sea and through the Carolinas. _231

Fleharty, 102nd Ill Ward 1B 3D 20C: Moved again on the 11th of May, at a quarter past 4 o'clock, A.M. Marched twelve miles and entered Snake Creek Gap, a narrow pass between lofty ranges of the Chattoogata Mountains. Pitched our tents in the valley and on the mountain side. It was a romantic locality. The lofty mountains towered on either hand hundreds of feet above us, their summits and slopes covered with a dense growth of timber. Thousands of troops were camped in the valley, and there was a steady tramp of columns marching to the front. The scene from an elevated position on the mountain side, the evening of the 11th, when night was settling over the earth, and the surrounding hills were dimly outlined in the gathering gloom, was strangely beautiful. The white tents of the soldiers dotted the narrow valley, and their fires gleamed through the foliage of intervening trees. Dusky forms flitted to and fro about the camp fires, and a hum of voices came to the ear, in a monotonous sound that grew less audible as the night advanced. Above the hum of voices could be heard the constant rumbling of the wagon trains moving towards the front. At length the clear notes of a bugle sounded tattoo, then others took up the strain and were quickly followed by the crashing roll of the drums. But our feelings at

231 (McBride 1900, 110)

that time were not all of a sublime character. The stern realities of an active campaign subjected us to privations that we had never endured before. Transportation was limited, and many of the soldiers had nothing in the world with them save one suit of clothes, a rubber blanket and a shelter tent vulgarly termed a "purp" tent. On their rubber blanket beneath the shelter tent, they slept without removing their clothes, day after day and week after week. Privations which at one time would have caused them to murmur, were looked upon as mere trifles, and a spirit of cheerfulness and hopefulness pervaded all minds.

While encamped there, a number of the soldiers ascended the mountain on the left of the gap. With Adjutant J. H. Snyder, the writer climbed one of the highest peaks of this mountain, and looked down into the valley of the Oostanaula River. We observed occasional "clearings" in the valley, and connected with these were dwelling houses, which appeared in the distance like small, white tents. Everything was represented in miniature. The use of a field glass enabled us to obtain a very distinct view of the range of mountains beyond the valley, and other mountains far away southward and westward the lofty ranges rising hill above hill in beautiful succession, and at various points culminating in solitary peaks. Some miles away eastward a rebel wagon train was seen, in park. We felt as we looked over the broad valley that we were viewing the land of the enemy soon, however, to be our own. _232

FLEHARTY, 102ND ILL WARD 1B 3D 20C: Our Generals are active and it is encouraging to know that Gen. Sherman visits the different parts of the field in person. He passed near our camp a few moments ago. General Thomas is also in this part of the field. Gen. Hooker rode along our lines yesterday. The General is a fine looking man, but exhibits a degree of vanity that does not seem warrantable in any General. Major Gen. Sickles was riding with Hooker's staff, and when passing the troops, General Hooker invariably motioned him and others to the rear and rode about twenty feet in advance to receive the plaudits of his soldiers. _233

232 (Fleharty, Our Regiment. A History of the 102d Illinois Infantry Volunteers 1865, 52)
233 (Fleharty, Jottings from Dixie 1999, 208)

Supply

The entire army passing down that narrow road included General Williams, now commanding Butterfield's 1st Division. He had written his daughter describing the effort to maintain such an army.

> WILLIAMS, 1D 20C: Few appreciate the difficulties of supplying an army. If you will calculate that every man eats, or is entitled to eat, nearly two pounds a day, you can easily estimate what a large army consumes. But besides what men eat, there are horses and mules for artillery, cavalry, and transportation in vast numbers, all which must be fed or the army is dissolved or made inefficient. There is another all-important matter of ammunition, a large supply of which for infantry and artillery must be carried, besides what is carried on the person and in the ammunition chests of guns and caissons. Our men carry forty rounds in boxes, and when approaching a possible engagement take twenty more on the person. Of this latter, from perspiration, rain, and many causes there is great necessary waste. It is an article that cannot be dispensed with, of course, and the supply on the person must be kept up. The guns cannot be kept loaded, therefore the diminution is constant from this necessary waste. My division, at present numbers, will require forty to fifty wagons to carry the extra infantry ammunition. You should see the long train of wagons of the reserve artillery, passing as I write, to feel what an item this single want is. [234]

May 13 - Race to Resaca

The Official Atlas Map shows the positions of Hooker's divisions as they moved out of Snake Creek Gap on May 12, till 5 pm on May 14. Solid bar is 1st Division, half black is 2nd Division, and black between white is 3rd Division.

Confederates, sensing the ruse, mobilize and lose no time.

> TREMAIN: Johnston then began to appreciate his perilous position. A large force of his enemy was upon his extreme left flank and rear and a force in his front at Buzzard's Roost. As the rebel papers say, the Yankees have their forces in our front so well covered by heavy picket and skirmish lines that we can learn little or nothing of their movements. After discovering his position the rebel general had but a short time to consider. He must either give Sherman battle before he thought it possible for him to concentrate his

234 (Williams 1963, Letter of July 16, 1863)

entire army—he must assume an offensive campaign by a dash at Chattanooga, a most perilous undertaking—or he must ignominiously fly to the east among the fastnesses of the mountains. Of course, he chose the former. Quickly evacuating his works at Buzzard's Roost Friday morning, the 13th, found him concentrating near Resaca—while Sherman was forming his lines of battle, with his right resting through Resaca on the Oostenaula (river) and his left extending in a north-westerly direction, and gradually advancing towards Tilton. _235

Setting Trap

Thomas outlined the plan to get below Resaca and cross on pontoons, to cut off Johnston's supply and escape. Then, if Johnston escapes, it will be off his railroad lifeline and into the mountains:

THOMAS, ARMY OF THE CUMBERLAND: to Sherman, May 13: The enemy evacuated Dalton at 9 p.m. yesterday. General Howard entered at 9 a.m. to-day; will concentrate his troops in Dalton, and follow the enemy down the railroad toward Resaca. I have directed General Palmer to march two miles northeasterly from the debouch of the intrenchments, and then take an easterly course until he strikes the railroad, covering his left flank and front with a strong line of skirmishers. Should the enemy be driven down the railroad Generals Palmer and Schofield will be directly in his rear, with General Hooker to support them, if necessary. In this situation of affairs the enemy must be completely cut off, or compelled to retreat by the various fords southeast of Dalton, across the Connesauga, in which latter event, if General McPherson will merely threaten Resaca with the head of his column, and force a passage across the Oostenaula at Lay's Ferry, and take up a strong position on the hills bordering the railroad southeast of Lay's Ferry, Johnston will be compelled to retreat through, the mountains to Allatoona, which will be exceedingly difficult, if he succeeds in accomplishing it at all. Should you think well of this plan, I can throw Hooker's corps across Lay's Ferry to the support of General McPherson, and General Palmer's corps also, unless the enemy evacuate Resaca. If Resaca be evacuated the main body of the army could be crossed at Resaca and Lay's Ferry and pursue rapidly along the railroad and vicinity. _236

Sherman to Thomas: Let's make sure the prey is in the trap before we spring it:

235 (Tremain 1905, 171)
236 (OR, Series I Vol 38 Part 4 Serial 75: Correspondence n.d., 160)

SHERMAN: TO THOMAS: MAY 13. Until I hear that Joe Johnston is south of the Oostenaula I would not cross at Ray's [Lay's]. We must first interpose between Dalton and Resaca, threatening the latter all the time. I want Hooker's right and McPherson's left strong until we encounter Johnston, who has not yet got below Resaca, I think. If he retreats east we have the advantage. I want the pontoons up, and to secure the railroad on Hooker's right Palmer should join on to Hooker, and Hooker should be strong. 237

Meaning he wants Johnston's whole army at Resaca, blocked there from the north, and then crossing the river south of Resaca. That is the plan. Why does he want Johnston on the other side of the river? Would he not want to bottle him up? We shall see.

Pushing Out From Snake Creek Gap

Potomac soldiers thought Hooker's corps had more fame than others and were to be held back. One wonders if that was in the plan.

MARVIN, CO F 5TH CONN, KNIPE 1B 1D 20C: May 11th. May 13th. The two opposing forces met to-day and there has been hard fighting with the favors upon our arms. Our army driving the enemy back. Some severe fighting. Our division massed in reserve. Hooker having acquired considerable glory in his "battle above the clouds" on Lookout Mountain, it is said to be the programme now to hold him in reserve for some time and give the rest a chance to spread themselves. 238

MEMBER OF COMPANY A, 141ST NY, KNIPE 1B 1D 20C: At an early hour on Friday morning, May 13th, the troops are in motion. Generals Thomas and McPherson, in command of the 14th and 23d corps, taking the advance, our corps remaining in the rear for a support. Hooker would have willingly taken the advance, but as he and his corps is from the Army of the Potomac, the western Generals wish to keep him back for fear he may gain more celebrity, as at Lookout Mountain last fall. But perhaps before this campaign comes to a close they will be glad to accept of his assistance. We will see what we shall see. 239

Prophetic words, "We will see what we shall see."

237 (OR, Series I Vol 38 Part 4 Serial 75: Correspondence n.d., 161)
238 (Marvin 1889, 297)
239 (Museum n.d.)

MERRILL, 70TH IND WARD 1B 3D 20C: May thirteenth we marched at seven A.M. but only moved a short distance, when we halted and saw Generals Sherman, Schofield, Hooker, Thomas, McPherson and Kilpatrick holding a council nearby. After awhile they went to their different commands, but soon Kilpatrick, at the head of his troops, dashed to the front. It was not long till heavy firing was heard, and the news came back that the General had run into an ambush and was badly wounded. He was soon brought back in an ambulance, and we fell in and moved forward, being in the second line of battle. There was heavy skirmishing, but the rebels kept falling back. Occasionally one killed or wounded was brought to the rear, and now and then a cannon ball came crashing through the trees above our heads, and the minie balls came singing their unwelcome music. About sundown we were ordered to relieve the advance line, and passing the Twelfth Indiana, learned that Captain Peoples had been killed. .240

FLEHARTY, 102ND ILL WARD 1B 3D 20C: Friday morning. May 13th, we moved in a direction to the right of Resaca, around which place the rebels had entrenched themselves, and were ready to give us battle. The cavalry which had been thrown out in advance, became engaged with the enemy's videttes at an early hour, and we soon learned that Gen. Kilpatrick had been wounded and borne to the rear. The rebels were stubborn. In the afternoon the infantry was pushed forward to "feel" the enemy, and develop his position and strength.

We advanced through groves of young pines the most dense we had yet seen.

Among the pines, in line of battle! How indelibly the scene is fixed in memory. What soldier of Sherman's army can view, even at this day, a grove of young pines without having those days of carnage and death recalled to mind?

Slowly the enemy's skirmish line was pressed back in—our skirmishers, and late in the afternoon the skirmishers in front of the 15th Corps approached, and finally charged and captured a redoubt with two guns. Our Division had been separated from the other divisions of the Corps, and was formed on the right of the 14th Corps. The advance was continued at intervals until dusk. Halting in an open field at the base of a range of hills we rested awhile, and ate a hastily prepared supper. After dark, moved on by a circuitous route, quietly and carefully, into line of battle, on the opposite side of the

---

240 (S. Merrill 1900, 84) Thomas' plan must have been discussed at the meeting.

hill. The position of the enemy had now been fully developed. Only a narrow valley separated their line from ours. They had been hard pressed during the day, and perceived the necessity of constructing strong defensive works. As we formed in line, the busy click, click, click of their axes could be distinctly heard, and they seemed to be working for dear life. We occupied a ravine which ran parallel with the hill, about one hundred and fifty feet above its base. Companies E and G were sent out as skirmishers during the night. Capt. McManus had command of the line, and was assisted by Capt. Sedwick. Both most excellent men the former, daring almost to a fault, the latter, perfectly cool and collected in any position of danger. It is related of Capt. S. that on that occasion it became necessary at one time for him to pass from post to post in a very exposed position, in plain view of the enemy, and as their balls raised the dust about his feet, the only perceptible change in his manner consisted in the more rapid puffing of the smoke from his pipe. _241

GRUNERT, CO D 129TH ILL WARD 1B 3D 20C: May 13. Remained on our camping ground until 3 o'clock P.M. when, after drawing a large quantity of ammunition, we advanced. It was generally believed that to-day we would have a first chance at the enemy. After a short and slow march we halted in a forest of beautiful oak trees, while skirmishing was going on in our immediate front; we could, however, see no enemy. The firing became less audible, a sign that the enemy had to retreat before our cavalry, whereupon we advanced again in the immediate rear of our pickets, not in column, but in line of battle, prepared for any attack the enemy might make. Our advancing was slow and cautious through the woods, in search of the enemy; the country changed with hill and valley. We had not long to search for the enemy; on our arrival at the foot of a tolerably high hill some well aimed rifle shots told us of the presence of the enemy, whose determined refusal to retreat brought on a skirmish. Our pickets and the enemy vied with each other in rapid and well aimed firing, but our continual advance and the sure marksmen in our ranks brought the enemy to retreat at last.

The rebel pickets once on the retreat, could not be brought to a stand, as our pickets advanced as the enemy retreated, and were compelled to return to their principal force, and until evening came on and the darkness prevented a continuation of the murderous play. We were nearer to Resaca now than to Dalton, and when we camped at night on a hill on the opposite site of that occupied by the enemy, and were talking over the events of the day and preparing supper, we were not more than ½ mile distant from the

241 (Fleharty, Our Regiment. A History of the 102d Illinois Infantry Volunteers 1865, 52)

enemy's main force. The most part of the night we kept awake, the knapsack packed and the gun on hand; but few hours sleep were allowed us.

HARRISON, 70TH IND WARD 1B 3D 20C: (Reporting to Ward): On the 13th instant I moved out about four miles from Snake Creek Gap, having the advance of the brigade, and under orders from you formed line of battle on the Resaca road and moved up to the crest of a ridge connecting on the right with the forces under the command of General McPherson, and having on my left one regiment of our brigade (One hundred and second Illinois Volunteer Infantry), which, with my regiment, constituted our front line and was placed by you under my command. Skirmishers were thrown out to cover the front of the line and every preparation made for a proper advance when the order should be received. Almost immediately after we had taken position the line on our right (General McPherson) was advanced and soon became engaged with the enemy, but suffered no loss. About 4 p.m. by your orders, our line was advanced, changing direction gradually to the left, and having emerged from the timber was massed on the left of General Harrow's line, who was still skirmishing with the enemy. _242

J. L. KETCHAM, 70TH IND WARD 1B 3D 20C: "We were nearly all night getting ready for the fight. Found ourselves next morning on a woody hill and the rebels just opposite. They were on a hill, shaped it seemed to me something like an egg, and with an open space all round it, the strongest natural fortification I ever saw. Then they had three or four lines of intrenchments. Between us and them, in the open space, was a deep, muddy ditch, so it would have been folly for us to make a charge there. We sent out skirmishers, who hid behind stumps in the open field, and shot and were shot at all day. One good thing our hill was round, too so we could get behind it. Bullets from rebel sharp shooters kept flying past us all day, wounding a man now and then. General Ward couldn't keep still, he wanted to make a charge so bad. At last he ordered the brigade forward, so our regiment, the only one that advanced, went over the hill in about ten seconds (no exaggeration) and hid behind a fence at the bottom. It would have taken us three quarters of an hour to cross that open field. What would have been our loss had we advanced? We waited behind the fence till dark." _243

MERRILL, 70TH IND WARD 1B 3D 20C: Wm. Wilhite: "There was heavy skirmishing, but the rebels kept falling back. Occasionally one killed or wounded was brought to the rear, and now and then a cannon ball came

242 (OR, Series I Vol 38 Part 2 Serial 73: Reports n.d., 369)
243 (S. Merrill 1900, 86)

crashing through the trees above our heads, and the minie balls came singing their unwelcome music. About sundown we were ordered to relieve the advance line, and passing the Twelfth Indiana, learned that Captain Peoples had been killed.

While we were in the second line lying back in the woods, Colonel Merrill, who was inclined to be a little jolly sometimes, was standing holding his horse, and when the small shells came crashing through the trees, as we thought uncomfortably low, he began to poke fun at the boys for rather drooping their heads. Presently he mounted his horse and we were ordered forward a few rods. When we halted the Colonel took off his hat, hung it on the pommel of his saddle, took out his handkerchief and was leisurely wiping his brow, when one of those big shells that comes as if it were saying you! you! you! and you can't tell which you it means, came whizzing through the trees, and passed just above his head. Of course the head went down, and then it was the boys time to laugh. After they had got somewhat through, the Colonel, enjoying the joke as well as any of them, looked around and said, 'Boys, you may dodge the big ones." _244

HARRISON, 70TH IND WARD 1B 3D 20C: Shortly after dark we again changed position, relieving the regular brigade, of the Fourteenth Army Corps. My regiment was here located on the right of our brigade line and along the crest of a hill with a meadow of about 600 yards in width in front and extending from the base of the hill occupied by me to a hill opposite, which was strongly fortified and occupied in force by the enemy. As soon as day dawned on the 14th instant a sharp fire was opened by the rebel sharpshooters on my skirmishers, which was kept up quite briskly during the day, inflicting some loss on my regiment. _245

STRONG, CO B 105TH ILL WARD 1B 3D 20C: On [May 13th], the army advanced nearly to Resaca, Georgia. _246 Our brigade was ordered to the right flank to support the troops engaged in fighting there. I distinctly remember how plain we could hear the whole business: the roar of the artillery, the crack of musketry, the cheers of the Yankees and the yells of the Johnnies. Through it all, we were lying in a thick wood and could see nothing. When we would hear the Yankees cheer, our hearts would almost stop beating. Then would come the roar of Rebel cannon, and as our boys

---

244 (S. Merrill 1900, 86)
245 (OR, Series I Vol 38 Part 2 Serial 73: Reports n.d., 369)
246 Strong's memory of dates and units has apparent lapses.

were beaten back the Rebs would nearly split their throats yelling. We lay there in a fever of impatience until our turn came. .247

TREMAIN: The advance of McPherson to the position named, enabled Sherman to form his lines along Camp Creek and extend his left wing sufficiently to the north so as to open the communication referred to with Howard, who had reached Tilton early that morning. Our position was now one of considerable natural strength, although it was not gained without some loss principally in the Fifteenth and Sixteenth Corps. Between our lines and those of the enemy ran this little tortuous creek, in a valley an eighth to a quarter of a mile in width each army occupying the ridges on each bank, our left, however, crossing some of its tributaries and extending nearly directly north and south toward Tilton.

This was our position on the morning of Saturday, the 14th of May. It was a very long line, over seven miles, and the enemy occupied a line equally strong by nature; and one flank of which was protected by the Oostenaula River and the carefully constructed works at Resaca. .248

MORHOUS, CO C 123RD NY KNIPE 1B 1D 20C After a few days of skillful manoeuvering bv Gen. Sherman, the enemy found themselves so completely flanked, that a retreat amounting almost to a stampede was the result. Falling back and reorganizing on a new line near Resaca, he ensconced himself behind a heavy line of fortifications, which had been previously prepared. So perfect and formidable were these works that scarcely an acre of ground could be found within ten miles but was protected by direct and enfilading fire from several batteries. The prospect of hurling themselves on these slaughter pens was anything but agreeable to the boys after they in a measure had become aware of their strength. Still Sherman seemed determined to give them battle on their own grounds, calculating that his superiority of numbers and morale would more than overcome their advantage of breastworks. .249

MEMBER OF COMPANY A, 141ST NY, KNIPE 1B 1D 20C: The entire day is spent in skirmishing, called "feeling" of the enemy, to ascertain his weakest point, &c. A severe battle is predicted for to-morrow. Friday night we all sleep on

247 (Strong 1961)
248 (Tremain 1905, 171)
249 (Morhous 1879, 85)

our arms, and, of course, sleep soundly; for whoever heard of a soldier sleeping otherwise. .250

Anecdote of Sherman and Hooker Under Fire

SCHOFIELD, 23RD CORPS: The first time I ever saw General Sherman and General Hooker together, or got even a suspicion that their personal relations were other than the most satisfactory, was at Resaca. Cox's division had gained possession of some portions of the enemy's outer works, so that from a bald hill just in rear of our line some parts of the main line of defense could be distinctly seen. Upon my informing General Sherman of this, he soon appeared on the ground, accompanied or closely followed by a large number of general and staff officers. Besides Sherman, Thomas, Hooker, and Newton, a score of others were there, all eager to see what they could of the now famous stronghold which McPherson had refrained from assaulting. I led them to the hill, on which a few dead trees were still standing, and from which the much-desired view could be obtained. Of course all were on foot, yet they were too numerous not to attract the attention of the enemy. Very soon the sound of musketry in front, then not very heavy, was varied by the sharp explosion of a shell overhead, and fragments of branches of dead trees came falling all around. A general "scatteration" occurred in all directions save one. Newton and I, who were conversing at the time, quietly stepped aside a few paces out of the line of fire, where we were much safer than we would have been in full retreat, and then turned round to see what had become of our companions. All save two had disappeared, even Thomas having abandoned the field, probably for the first and only time in his life. But still there, on the bald hill, in full view of the hostile artillery, were the two already highly distinguished generals, Sherman and Hooker, both alike famous for supreme courage, striding round the ground, appearing to look at nothing in particular and not conversing with each other, but seeming at least a foot taller than usual, each waiting for the other to lead off in retreat. After quite a long continuance of this little drama, which greatly entertained Newton and me, the two great soldiers, as if by some mysterious impulse,—for they did not speak a word,— simultaneously and slowly strode to the rear, where their horses were held. .251

---

250 (Museum n.d.)
251 (Schofield 1897) Chapter VIII

Hood is Last to Leave Dalton

JOHNSTON, CSA: On the 12th the Federal army, covered by the mountain, moved by Snake Creek Gap toward Resaca. Major-General Wheeler, with 2,200 of ours, attacked and defeated more than double that number of Federal cavalry near Varnell's Station. At night our artillery and infantry marched for Resaca.

The cavalry followed on the 13th. On that day the enemy, approaching on the Snake Creep Gap road, was checked by Loring's troops, which gave time for the formation of Hardee's and Hood's corps, just arriving. As the army was forced, the left of Polk's corps was on the Oostenaula and the right of Hood's on the Connesauga. There was brisk skirmishing during the afternoon on Polk's front and Hardee's left. _252

TREMAIN: But Howard at Buzzard's Roost was not to be deceived. No sooner had the enemy disappeared from his front than he was close in pursuit, marching in their immediate rear through Dalton and to Tilton, whence he extended his lines to the west and towards Snake Creek Gap and opened communications with the extreme left of Sherman's lines under Palmer. The advance and formation of our lines here referred to commenced on Friday morning, the principal skirmishing with the enemy being on McPherson's front; and on Friday afternoon by a gallant charge of a portion of his command he obtained possession of the commanding positions bordering on the west of the small stream known as Camp Creek.

It was during the movements preceding this charge that General Kilpatrick was wounded while falling upon a body of the enemy's infantry, after having driven their cavalry for miles before him. _253

While Palmer and McPherson, having come by Snake Creek Gap, were pressing the enemy across Camp Creek, the rear of Johnston's army was hurrying down the Dalton-Resaca road ahead of General Howard's cavalry. There was a stand-off just in front of what would be the north end of the Rebel position for the next two days.

In Stevenson's Division, Brown's Brigade seems to get the tougher jobs and he relies on the 3rd Tennessee. Readers' might notice other regiments, Union or Confederate, appearing to get the critical assignments. It would be interesting to

252 (OR, Series I Vol 38 Part 4 Serial 75: Correspondence n.d., 615)
253 (Tremain 1905, 171)

watch their commanders. Also, one wonders about their casualties. How many will remain by war's end?

DEAVENPORT, CHAPLAIN, 3RD TENN, BROWN'S BRIGADE, STEVENSON'S DIVISION, CSA: After repeated assaults and as often repulsed with considerable loss, the enemy moved down to our left which compelled Gen. Johnston to evacuate. We left about dark on the 12th., our brigade bringing up the rear. Everything was brought away. We marched all night over a very rough road, rested several hours in the morning and resumed our march [13th]. The enemy were now hovering around our rear and about sunset we formed a line and fought a little, the cavalry was along but did but little. We had several wounded, night having set in we continued on our way passing between two large bodies of the enemy and reached our lines near Resaca about midnight. .254

Private James Morey, of the 32nd, recorded the day's events in his diary.

MOREY, 32ND TENNESSEE, BROWN'S BRIGADE, STEVENSON, HOOD, CSA: May 13. The left wing of our regiment left the mountain after dark last night and marched all night. We stopped about twelve this morning for some time when the rest of our regiment came up having left the mountain at midnight. The men are nearly all broken down from want of sleep. We started again and went a short distance when we formed a line of battle. Cannonading was heard in the direction of Dalton. After laying in line of battle for some time our regiment was taken about a mile to our front to reinforce the cavalry. We staid for some time and fell back to the brigade and with it about a mile and a half back and formed another line. We laid still until sundown when we moved forward[?] about two hundred yards and threw out skirmishers who had not advanced fifty yards before they ___ ___ fire from the enemies skirmishers. The skirmishing continued for some time when the enemy charged the right ___ of our brigade who repelled them in splendid style. We laid still a little while when all being still we moved back about a mile and a half and bivouacked for the night. During the fight our skirmishers were hollering at neighing, crowing, barking, gobbling, and clucking for the benefit of the Yanks. There were four wounded from the brigade. .255

Morey's colonel describes it:

254 (Deavenport 1861-1864)
255 (Morey n.d., May 13, 1864)

McGuire, 32nd Tennessee, Brown's Brigade, Stevenson, Hood, CSA: From Rocky Face Mountain we were ordered to retreat to Besaca. The afternoon we reached Resaca our brigade (Brown's) had been ordered to report to Gen. Wheeler, commanding the cavalry, and which was being closely pressed by the enemy while bringing up the rear of our army. About an hour before sundown we were thrown into line of battle, and fought the unimportant battle of Smoky Creek Gap.

In the Thirty-second Regiment were three mischievous characters —Tom Poteet, Alex. Crawford, and George Bevil —one of whom could neigh exactly like a stallion, one could gobble like a turkey, and the other bray like a donkey. Soon the battle commenced, and the firing was "hot as pepper," when right in the midst of the fierce conflict Sergeant Crawford began to gobble, Poteet to neigh, and Bevil to bray, and continued their fun until the enemy retreated in utter dismay, no doubt wondering what manner of rebels they had attacked. Our casualties in this affair were slight. .256

May 14 - Closing In

More description might be in order before we proceed. Viewing the maps will help the reader understand the scene.

The Confederate stronghold was a rough rectangle. The Dalton road runs down the middle to Resaca where it and the railroad cross the Oostenaula River, their southern barrier. That is Johnston's exit if Federal forces threaten elsewhere.

Hillen, John Francis Edward. *Rasaca on Coosa River, Georgia.* 1864.

256 (McGuire 1886, 479)

The Connesauga River is the east border, flowing into the Oostanaula near Resaca. Only cavalry patrol it since it is fordable in few places at this time of year. The railroad runs safely between the Dalton road and the Connesauga.

On the west, a long range of hills protects the road. There, along the ridge, Johnston's infantry is dug in facing the Union forces across the wide valley of Camp Creek, which runs straight south to the Oostanaula. If Sherman can get artillery over onto the ridge, he can threaten the road and the bridges over the Oostenaula. But anyone crossing the creek's marshy, knee-deep water to get there would be a slow-moving target.

Apparently, Johnston had no defense constructed on the south side of the Oostanaula. His two bridges are both his lifeline and escape route. He must protect them. If the other defenses hold, Sherman is no threat until he gets across the Oostanaula. He is working on that, further downstream.

On the north, the defensive line runs west from where the Connesauga makes a horseshoe bend almost to the railroad. If Sherman can get past that line he has two paths: open terrain along the railroad and the road directly to the Oostanaula. So, to protect that gateway into his fortress, Johnston has an outer defensive line between the road and the river. It starts at the road and arcs north, crossing over a big hill and then sweeping back to the main line at that horseshoe bend. He is strengthening it. The terrain on the east side of that arc is rolling and wooded but easily traversed to the main line and then all the way to Resaca. Along the side facing the road, deadly cannon are arrayed all the way to the main line and across the road, and on to the west. Anything coming down the road must pass a gauntlet of cannon on the left and still more artillery on the right leg. But first, that big hill, where the outer line turns away east from the road and heads back to the horseshoe bend—that's deadly.

Johnston has General Hood's three divisions there. Stevenson defends the big hill, Hindman enfilades the road, and Stewart blocks the east between the hills and the river.

James Walker's painting views the gateway to Resaca from the west side of the road. We see the road passing from the left in front of the big hill and disappearing between another hill on the right, which is the main defensive line The outer line, atop the big hill, bends back east, out of sight, toward the railroad.

Trexler's sketch looks south at Stewart, on the far left, and Stevenson on the hill.

As the day begins, the last of Johnston's units have arrived at the north after marching and skirmishing cavalry all night. We follow the action from south to north along the west front, where McPherson, Thomas, and Schofield are pressing the line. Then we will follow Howard's corps, who are skirmishing the last units of Johnston's army from the north.

TREMAIN: During Friday night, the 13th, the enemy had worked like beavers felling trees, building redoubts, throwing up rifle pits, and making every possible preparation to resist our advance. In this they were so successful that much of their line was deemed impregnable. All the morning of Saturday, there was the constant crackling of heavy skirmishing along more than five miles of battle lines. Everybody sedulously minded his own business with thoughts bent on the approaching fray. The skirmishing and sharp shooting was as usual quite destructive for the number of men engaged. Our lines were now formed from right to left in the order of McPherson on our right, then Butterfield's division of Hooker's corps, (remainder in reserve) Palmer's corps, and then Schofield's army with Howard's corps as a support. During Saturday morning Schofield and Howard continued the advance of the day before, throwing their left across Camp Creek, and considerably shortening our line of battle by extending it in a northeasterly direction towards the railroad. Shortly after noon, while this movement was going on, the enemy threw himself with great force on the advancing lines of Schofield and Howard. The enemy appeared desperate; determined at any cost to break our lines at the points he, with great sagacity, judged to be the weakest. The country being thickly wooded, but little artillery could be used on either side, and the movements of troops of either army were entirely concealed from the other. The lines of fire waved to and fro, as one or the other succeeded in repelling an advance; but with the enemy it was his best and perhaps his only chance. He must succeed. _257

CINCINNATI COMMERCIAL: Our line as formed last night was in the form of a semi-circle, to the northwest of Sugar Valley, while the Oostanaula River, completes the circle on the southeast. Sugar Valley is a fertile little plain of about ten square miles in size, much broken by hills, which at this season of the year are covered by a dense undergrowth of small trees and vines, rendering them very difficult to penetrate. It was in this valley, between the projected Rome and Dalton Railroad [not built] and the river that encircles Resaca and Tilton, that the enemy made a stand after being closely pressed on his retreat from Dalton. From our center to the river, the distance this morning was about seven miles. Our line extends completely around the valley, McPherson's right resting on the river near its junction with

257 (Tremain 1905, 171)

Oothkalaga [sic] Creek 258 or Calhoun, while the left strikes the river north of Tilton near the junction of the river with Swamp creek that takes its rise in the hills of Sugar Valley. Lick and Camp creeks also burst out from the hills in the valley and empty their waters into the Oostanaula River, which is very broad and deep, but can be forded, when the water is low, at six points. The above is as intelligible a description of the field as can be given without the aid of a map; and now for the opening of the ball.

As I have already said, our line was formed in a half circle, extending from the river on the left to a point on the river near Calhoun. The corps occupied positions in the line as follows, extending from right to left: first, McPherson; second, Hooker; third, Palmer; fourth, Schofield; fifth, Howard.

Skirmishing commenced early in the morning, and many prisoners were brought in as the result, although the attack made by us was faintly responded to. Skirmishing continued, with occasional truces, lasting from ten to thirty minutes, all the morning. Meantime our General officers were not idle. Generals Sherman and Thomas, with their indefatigable corps commanders, rode along the line with their staffs, personally superintending the parking of ambulances and ammunition trains, and assigning batteries to positions where they could be of the most service in the event of a general engagement. 259

Schofield's Army of the Ohio marched down the day before.

THRUSTIN, Co D, 111TH OHIO, HARKER, 2B3D23C: The night before, fifteen miles to the northward we had seen the mountains lit up with the incessant flashes of musketry and cannon. Now, as the darkness settled upon us, we saw the rebel camp fires in our front. Our march from Loudon southward to Rocky Face had been over a country new to us and therefore interesting, and when the day's march had become wearisome it needed only a few notes from fife and drum, of "The Girl I Left Behind Me," to put elasticity into your step, to bring the straggler to his place in ranks, and then while the natives stared with open mouthed wonder, you would break out with

We are coming from the east, we are coming from the west,
Shouting the battle cry of freedom,
And we'll drive the rebel crew, from the land we love the best,
Shouting the battle cry of freedom.

---

258 Oothakalooga Creek flows into the Oostanaoula at Calhoun.
259 (Correspondence of the Cincinnati Commercial 1864)

The Union for ever, hurrah boys, hurrah,
Down with the traitors, and up with the stars,
While we rally round the flag boys, rally once again,
Shouting the battle cry of freedom.

When were you too weary to join in that chorus? Now, as you moved up through the dense woods upon the rebel position, the voice of music was hushed, every one talked in an undertone when it was necessary to talk. Every man felt that there was desperate business on hand, and melody would have rasped the nerves like a neuralgia. .260

With that, here they are, early at work, and Thrustin tells us how Camp Creek held off an army. Looking across that plain between the hills, the creek does not look like much of an obstacle. As we shall see, it is an effective trap.

There is more to learn from his story. One is how to use a rifle to judge distance by what it scatters. Just loading the musket is another. Loose gunpowder had to be poured down the end of the barrel, so it had to be upright. The soldier had to pull the packet of powder out of a box and bite off the end first. After he fished a bullet out of another box and got it started down a tight fit, he had to ram it all down the 39-inch barrel with a stick. That requires an opposite force—the ground upon which he stood. And he had to keep it all dry while being shot at. The need for artillery to hold down fire from his opponent is as plain as death, particularly if his companions cannot provide enough fire to do so.

> THRUSTIN, CO D, 111TH OHIO, HARKER, 2B3D23C: On the morning of the 14th of May, 1864, we were under orders to attack the rebel position in our front. Between our skirmishers and the rebel entrenchments upon a course nearly southward, Camp Creek ran on its way to the Oostanaula. About sunrise I rode to the top of the ridge, where our skirmishers were posted, and delivered orders to be followed during the attack, by the officer in command. Taking a rifle from one of our men, I fired several times, at working parties of the Confederates, who were just finishing their intrenchments. The object was to determine the distance between the lines. At each discharge of my gun the commotion among the enemy indicated that the bullet reached them. I returned and reported to Colonel Bond that the ridge was a commanding position for our artillery, and ought to be occupied before the charge was made. At his request I rode to General Haskell's headquarters and repeated the report to him. With an indifferent

260 (Thrustin 1894)

manner he replied that probably General Judah would attend to the matter, and I then returned and reported his reply.

Some hours afterward our lines were massed upon the ridge overlooking the rebel intrenchments, and within long musket range, and without artillery support we moved to the attack. As soon as we uncovered from the woods we were saluted with a storm of shell, followed by grape, canister and musket balls; we dashed forward and jumped into the creek hoping to obtain shelter from the dreadful fire. From the channel of the creek we delivered our fire, but when the men set their guns on the ground to push home the next cartridge, the guns were forced into the yielding mud, covering the tubes with water so that they would not discharge. In a few moments most of the guns were disabled. Efforts were made to advance, and here and there along the line, soldiers, single or in groups, rushed forward to the apparent cover of stumps or trees, but our advance had placed us under an enfilading fire, which searched out every corner of the field.

At length we were ordered to return to the top of the ridge, where we reformed our lines, and again advanced to the charge, only adding to our casualties without the power to do the enemy any injury. General Judah, then commanding our division, came forward to our line on foot, and finding it impossible to carry the works, ordered us to retreat.

We had been made the victims of an inexcusable blunder. The ridge from which we charged was much higher than the opposite ridge occupied by the enemy; and had our artillery been placed upon it, could have silenced the rebel guns, covered our charge, and probably, given us victory instead of defeat. General Judah stated that he had sent out his staff officers in the morning to inspect the position, and they reported that the ridge was inaccessible to artillery, and hence no effort was made to get the guns in position. Within a half-hour after the disaster, the artillery was posted on the hill, but the charging columns lay in broken fragments in the valley.

A General of Division who does not personally inspect the field of a contemplated battle, and look critically over every point of advantage for his men, which the topography affords, is not fit to command troops.

Our regiment went into that action with over five hundred muskets, and came out of it so crippled that we were able to muster only 107 guns when we rallied on the ridge.

The upturned faces down the hill side, in the valley, and the bodies floating in the muddy water of the creek accounted for some of them. The ambulances and stretcher-bearers reported others. There were some who in the confusion of the charge and counter charge had been swept off the field by the retreat of other commands. _261

All the while, Sherman is working on Thomas' plan:

SHERMAN: General Corse: Your note is received. You exactly conceive my project. The pontoon instead of going direct to Lay's from the gap, came this way, but it must now be near you. Keep it out of sight till the last moment. Get all things ready under cover for our bridge and make a lodgment by means of all the other boats; there are enough for three bridges. General Sweeny's division is also on its way, and I want it to-day (or to-night will do) across the Oostenaula in a strong defensive position out from the river about a mile on the best ground that can be found, and roads cut to the bridges. As soon as one bridge is done, the other should also be made there, if possible. I will send more infantry if necessary. General Sweeny has three batteries. Show him this. He has orders from General McPherson, and will command. You direct the cavalry until I give further orders. _262

Butterfield to Camp Creek

While Sherman works the boats south, Butterfield's division is helping squeeze the Rebels into their works along Camp Creek:

FLEHARTY, 102ND ILL WARD 1B 3D 20C: Early in the morning a dash forward to Camp Creek was made. Being then mere novices in the art of warfare, many of the men took up positions where they were quite at the mercy of the enemy, and were compelled to remain behind stumps and trees all day an attempt to escape being equivalent to certain death. It was an exciting day on the skirmish line; firing commenced at daylight, and was kept, up until dark.

At one time the enemy endeavored to flank the line, and Capt. Sedwick discovering the movement from his position in front, recrossed the field to his reserve, and with them advanced on the left and drove the enemy back. Meanwhile there was heavier work on the left. The skirmishing had been lively in that direction all the forenoon, but at 2 o'clock p.m. the firing

261 (Thrustin 1894)
262 (OR, Series I Vol 38 Part 4 Serial 75: Correspondence n.d., 187)

became terrific. There was a perpetual roll of musketry, and the deep bass of the artillery reverberated grandly through the woods, and was echoed back by the surrounding hills. At that time we were ordered forward, and the moment we appeared on the little elevation in front of the ravine, the rebel sharpshooters sent their balls whistling around us, killing one man instantly and wounding three. Having proceeded a short distance, we were ordered to halt and lie down. The object doubtless was to make a feint of attacking, in order to divert the attention of the enemy from the left. No further advance was attempted, and we remained in that position until late in the evening, listening occasionally to the whizzing of bullets above our heads, but more deeply interested in the fierce conflict on our left. The sound at times would run along the line towards us, until it would seem that our Corps must soon, also, become engaged, then it would recede, and there would be a lull, like the lulling of the winds in a winter storm. Sometimes it would seem that our men were driving the rebels, and again it appeared that the battle was going against us. O! how terrible the suspense of waiting at such a time for victory, while contemplating the possibility of disaster! The sound of the battle at its height could only be compared in my mind to the work of a storm, breaking and crushing to the ground, ten thousand dead trees every instant, amid the roll of heaven's artillery. A battery about fifty yards to the left of our regiment was kept busy throwing shot and shell into the rebel lines, but the guns of the enemy were engaged where the contest raged more fiercely, and they paid no attention to this battery. 263

GRUNERT, CO D 129TH ILL WARD 1B 3D 20C: May 14. At 2 o'clock A.M. we again advanced for new slaughter work. Early in the morning shots were exchanged, but ere this our brigade was up and in line of battle, ready for any attack. The firing of the pickets became more rapid and violent at sunrise, now and then the enemy fired a cannon shot, while ours were brought into position, the positions of the infantry improved and reinforcements came to our aid. For three days we remained quiet in our place, tolerably well protected against the enemy's cannons; we did not lose a single man of our regiment, as the enemy's balls went whizzing over our heads. The 102d Illinois, which was on picket during the day made several attempts to drive the enemy back further; but all attacks were without avail and only caused loss to the regiment. In the evening company D of our regiment, and companies from other regiments, went to relieve the 102d Illinois that had stood the enemy's fire the whole day. When we arrived the firing had ceased, but when we were posted occasional shots would come

263 (Fleharty, Our Regiment. A History of the 102d Illinois Infantry Volunteers 1865, 52)

flying past us, while we watched and listened to the enemy. Gen. Howard took Buzzard Roost; Gen. Killpatrick was wounded to-day.

HARRISON, 70TH IND WARD 1B 3D 20C: Early in the day of Saturday, the 14th instant, instructions were received from your headquarters that we would be ordered to assault the works in our front at some time during the day, and orders were also given by you to strengthen the skirmish line. In compliance with the order, I deployed Company D of my regiment, Captain Tansey, relieving the skirmishers under Captain Carson, who had been placed upon the line the preceding night, and a few hours subsequently communicated to Captain Tansey an order received from your headquarters to advance his skirmishers, which was promptly though cautiously done, the men availing themselves of such meager shelter as the open field afforded. About 1 p.m. and while our line was resting behind the crest of the hill to avoid a troublesome fire which the rebel sharpshooters continued to pour in upon the crest, the "attention" was sounded in the regiment on my left and was repeated in my regiment. Not having received any intimation of what movement was intended, I called to Brigadier-General Ward, who at that moment approached my left, to know what the orders were. His reply was, "The orders are to advance." Knowing that an assault on the works in our front had been in contemplation earlier in the day, and supposing that the order involved such an assault, or at least that it involved an advance until a halt was ordered by the brigade commander, I put my regiment in march when the regiment on my left moved and passed over the crest of the hill and down its slope to a fence at its base, where I had previously instructed my officers to halt for a moment to reform their line, as they would necessarily be much broken in passing down the hill, which was very steep in some places. Under the cover of the fence I halted, and passed an inquiry to my major, who was on the left, to know whether the One hundred and second Illinois was still advancing with me. His answer was that this regiment had halted on the crest of the hill. After some time I was given to understand by one of the brigade staff, calling to me from the summit of the hill, that it was not intended that I should pass the hill, but that I should have halted on the crest, which had not been previously explained to me. By retiring the men singly or in small squads I was able without further casualties to resume our former line behind the crest of the hill. My losses during the day were as follows: On the skirmish line—killed, enlisted man, 1; wounded, enlisted men, 3; in advancing over the crest of the hill to our supposed assault—killed, enlisted men, 2; wounded, enlisted men, 10; wounded, Lieutenant Martin, Company I, slightly in the leg. _264

MERRILL, 70TH IND WARD 1B 3D 20C: About one o'clock, in order, it was said, to attract the attention of the enemy while a charge was being made a mile or two to the left by the First Division, the regiment descended the hill and lay down by a fence, prepared to advance across the field should the order be given. Here an incident with both an amusing and a serious phase

occurred. A sharpshooter from the crest of the ridge in the rear fired several shots at the enemy skirmishers. At each crack of his rifle at least a score of bullets as a reply would whiz about the ears of our unprotected men beneath. One of the field officers, provoked by his thoughtlessness, sent a Sergeant back to arrest and bring him to the front. In a short time the Sergeant returned unaccompanied, and reported that Major General Butterfield had possessed himself of a telescopic rifle and ensconced behind a tree was improving his marksmanship at the expense of the Confederate pickets, and especially of his own troops. After one or two more shots, probably to show the Sergeant that he could not be intimidated, the double starred sharpshooter ceased firing. _265

STORRS, 20TH CONN COBURN 2B 3D 20C: At about 2 o'clock p.m. the Union line moved forward to the attack, and soon the action became general, and continued with varying fortunes until so dark that the firing gradually ceased. _266

STRONG, CO B 105TH ILL WARD 1B 3D 20C: Our brigade was ordered to the right flank to support the troops engaged in fighting there. I distinctly

264 (OR, Series I Vol 38 Part 2 Serial 73: Reports n.d., 369)
265 (S. Merrill 1900, 86)
266 (Storrs 1886, 127)

remember how plain we could hear the whole business: the roar of the artillery, the crack of musketry, the cheers of the Yankees and the yells of the Johnnies. Through it all, we were lying in a thick wood and could see nothing. When we would hear the Yankees cheer, our hearts would almost stop beating. Then would come the roar of Rebel cannon, and as our boys were beaten back the Rebs would nearly split their throats yelling. We lay there in a fever of impatience until our turn came. 267

MADISON JOURNAL, QUOTED BY BRADLEY: May 14th, the 1st brigade of 3d div. 20th A.C. in position. to the south of the rebels, are attacked by them, and, after a brief, sharp fight, succeed in repulsing them. Our brigade the 2d of 3d division, was held in reserve. At half past 1 P.M. the battle really begins by an attack on Johnston's position by the 4th army corps. We are continually shifted from point to point, and held in readiness. All around the roar of battle goes reverberating through the valley, shells explode sharply high in air, cheers ring up from below, and peals jar the sensitive earth beneath us. Our tremendous army lies massed around the rebel stronghold, and, checking each assault, draw closer the lines of the Union anaconda; every bang of artillery, every crackling volley of musketry cementing in the blood of the bravest of the union of the States. 268

While Butterfield is forward, skirmishing, Hooker's other two divisions wait in reserve.

MEMBER OF COMPANY A, 141ST NY, KNIPE 1B 1D 20C: Saturday morning dawns upon a cloudless sky; fighting commences at 8 o'clock a. m. As we are in the rear, and a dense woods is between us and the combatants, we can see nothing save the ghastly forms of the wounded men who are being borne to the rear, which is worse than fighting itself; but the roar of musketry and booming of artillery is almost deafening. 269

On the north end, batteries are being placed to protect the Rebel line and control the road.

RITTER, ROWAN'S BATTERY, JOHNSON'S BATTALION, HOOD'S CORPS, CSA: The battery took position on the front, two miles from Resaca, to the left of the Dalton road, and about a hundred yards to the right of an obtuse angle in the line, which was occupied by Dent's Alabama battery. The latter held

267 (Strong 1961, 231)
268 (Bradley 1865, 94)
269 (Museum n.d.)

the summit of a ridge, the prolongation of which, in front, it was expected to command, while Captain Rowan was directed to construct his works at right angles with the ridge, so as to command the Dalton road. 270

While Butterfield is helping press the Rebel line across Camp Creek into their fortifications on the ridge, the north end is not yet closed.

Fourth Corps Squeezes Them From the North

While the rest of Sherman's forces are pressing Johnston's main body across Camp Creek, the last from Dalton are being followed by Howard's Fourth Corps. Stanley arrives on the east road from Tilton and waits for Wood coming on the Dalton road. Then Wood's division starts down the right side of the road, facing Stevenson and Hindman on the opposite side.

Sherman telegraphs Halleck in Washington that he, certainly by now, might prefer to fight south of Resaca.

> Sherman to Halleck: (received at 2:30 PM) By the flank movement on Resaca we have forced Johnston to evacuate Dalton, and we are on his flank and rear, but the parallelism of the valleys and mountains does not give us all the advantage of an open country, but I will press him all that is possible. 271

Wood and Stanley started hours behind Brown's brigade, Johnston's rear guard, who arrived at midnight, giving them time to set up positions. They were the skirmishers Stanley encountered.

> PARTRIDGE, 96TH ILL WHITAKER 2B 1D 4C: The forces were in motion at six o'clock, Stoneman's cavalry being on the left of the infantry and McCook's troopers on the right. Even before the hour named the cavalry had reconnoitered the front and developed the fact that the Rebels were in force not far away, and heavy skirmishing began almost as soon as the camps were left. This skirmishing was at first wholly on the part of Gen. Stoneman's forces, the infantry, each Division in column, moving slowly forward in support. Halts were frequent, and after one of a little more length than usual the bugle sounded for the infantry to advance. A brief but rapid march brought them to where the cavalry horses stood in line or in groups. Every

---

270 (Ritter n.d.) Facing Hazen and Willich. Rowan's Battery was almost destroyed but during the night refortified their position. Dent's Battery was withdrawn. Other batteries were right of Rowan, as will be seen.

271 (OR, Series I Vol 38 Part 4 Serial 75: Correspondence n.d., 173)

fourth man of the cavalry was holding the horses of his file, while his comrades were in advance on foot. The infantry soon reached a ridge along which the dismounted cavalry were deployed. The column broke to right and left, forming in the order of battle on either side of the highway. The officers of the different commands consulted as to the positions of their respective forces and of the enemy, and two or three men from each Company ran to a creek or spring nearby to fill their own and their comrades canteens. Belts were buckled a little tighter, and the men peered forward to see what awaited them. The cracking of the carbines had nearly ceased, and the occasional bullets from the front had the peculiar humming sound which indicated that they had come a long distance. At this discovery there was some good natured chaffing between the two arms of the service, the infantry ridiculing the cavalry for firing at such long range. This was soon terminated, for the troopers were ordered back to their horses and sent to watch the left flank. The Ninety-sixth, with other forces in the front line, advanced for a short distance and halted near the edge of an open field, a quarter of a mile in width. Skirmishers were thrown out into this field, and the main line immediately began to fortify its position. 272

So now, with cavalry departed, Stanley waited for the Union lines to link up and start closing in at the north end. At the south, McPherson was already compressing the line.

DAY, 101ST OHIO CRUFT 1B 1D 4C: Our Corps halted at about 4 O'clock within a mile of the Confederate main works. General Sherman's army was in line facing the enemy in the following order: On the extreme right, resting on the Oostanaula was the Army of the Tennessee, General McPherson; on his left, the Army of the Cumberland (excepting our Corps), and on the left of this, the Army of the Ohio. Our Corps had halted on the left and in rear of Schofield. As soon as it was learned that General Howard was within supporting distance, Schofield was ordered to make an assault. Indeed, Sherman's entire line stood to arms and was soon engaged. Howard was ordered forward with instructions to join Schofield's left. This we did with great promptness, Kirby's Brigade being at this hour, 4:30 P. M., on the extreme left of Sherman's army. The 101st was ordered forward as skirmishers, as indeed it had been both that day and the day before, every time we came in contact with the enemy. At least half a dozen times on the march the column had been halted, and the 101st passed to the front, until it became a common saying among the boys of the other regiments: "The rebs are in front; there goes the 101st forward." The skirmishing here was

272 (Partridge 1887, 316)

pressed with such vigor over the rough, wooded sides of the broken ridge that it assumed almost the proportions of battle. The enemy was steadily driven back toward their main line. .273

To get a better idea of things, imagine you are with Sergeant Major Partridge, of the 96th Illinois. You are standing where you came in from Tilton on the Nance Springs road and are now looking south, down the road to Resaca. Wood's division has arrived and gone ahead on the right. Your brigade, Whitaker's, has spread in a line across the road facing south. You have caught up with the Rebels. They've been in the hills for hours, and somewhere in those trees they are digging in. This is where they will stand. You can hear the gunfire as Wood's brigades fight their way south in the hills on the right. The road divides friend, in the range of hills on the west, from foe on the east.

But just in front of you on your left there is a little plain, with a creek running east. And looking beyond, across that plain, you see the first of that Rebel string of hills. What is hiding in that dense vegetation? And in that bigger hill just behind it? Just where are they? Someone has to find out, to go first, till you draw their fire. That's how it's done—a little skirmishing. Dangerous business. They send their bravest.

Just on your left is a round-topped hill. Stanley has Cruft's brigade spreading in a line across that hill starting at the top and going down the other side, clear across another north-south road, next to the springs. They are looking, maybe anxiously, at those hills across that plain. Your own brigade extends left to meet Cruft's at the top and on the right meets Grose's, which bends south to meet with Wood's brigades, who face that bigger hill.

Three Union armies are now one line of 100,000 holding Johnston against the hills protecting the railroad and the Connesauga River, all the way to Resaca and the Oostanaula—except for an empty space between Cruft and the railroad. No one is there. Your supporting cavalry is a quarter-mile away on the other side of the railroad watching the Rebel cavalry.

But otherwise you are alone. Nobody between that round-topped hill and the railroad. Nobody behind you. Cruft is in the air. That little plain is an open field. In that field you would be exposed, but you can't see to what.

273 (Day 1894, 205)

So General Stanley places Simonson's 5th Indiana Battery of six guns just a little bit further ahead, down the road on the right. It can target those hills the Rebels occupy. But it cannot reach behind you, back of the round-topped hill.

So now we'll let the soldiers tell it, in detail.

> STANLEY, 1D 4C: The division advanced to within about two and a half miles of Resaca, driving in the skirmishers of the enemy; but as Wood's Division, on our right, had not yet come up, and as firing was heard in rear of our right, the division was halted, and directed to barricade. At 2 p. m. Wood advanced and made connection with the right of this division, and we advanced together until stopped by the heavy fire of artillery coming from the enemy's works. I received about this time an order from the general commanding the corps to hold the Dalton road running by my left flank. To do this I stationed Cruft's brigade upon the left for the road, posting two of his regiments upon a round-topped hill about 100 yards from the road, and directing them to intrench themselves. .274

> KIRBY, 101ST OHIO CRUFT 1B 1D 4C: May 14, marched on in pursuit of the enemy; soon met his skirmishers back to his line on the hills near Resaca. The brigade was then formed for action, and, with the Fifth Indiana Battery, moved forward on the Resaca road beyond the junction of the Tilton road. .275

> MORRIS, 81ST INDIANA CRUFT 1B 1D 4C: We marched up on a very high ridge and formed a line of battle. Cannon and musket firing was very heavy on our right, which told us that some heavy fighting was point; on in that direction. In forming our line of battle our regiment was thrown to the left, which put us off the ridge down in the valley. A road led through the valley in the direction of the enemy, and the center of our regiment rested on the road. The One Hundred and First Ohio joined our right, part resting on the side of the ridge and the balance on the top. uniting with the rest of the regiments of our brigade. A heavy detail of skirmishers from each regiment was sent out to cover our front. Several squads of cavalry also passed out through our lines to skirmish with the enemy. There did not seem to be anything on the left of our regiment; if there was, we could not see it. We rested on the rise of ground above to the left of the road. .276

---

274 (OR, Series I Vol 38 Part 1 Serial 75: Reports n.d., 220)
275 (OR, Series I Vol 38 Part 1 Serial 75: Reports n.d., 231)
276 (Morris 1901)

SMITH, 31ST INDIANA CRUFT 1B 1D 4C: We had advanced to a point within about two miles of Resaca, and had been driving the skirmishers of the enemy the most of the day. With a view of holding the Dalton road, and protecting the flank of the army, the brigades of our division were in detachments—our brigade being still to the left of the Dalton road. The Thirty-first Regiment being sent up on a round-topped hill, with orders to intrench, and hold the hill at every hazard. After a sharp skirmish, the hill was taken without loss, and skirmishers were advanced [277]

We will get back to Stanley's division after we follow Wood along the west side of the Dalton-Resaca road. As they advance, the Rebel line is firing at them from the ridge on the other side. Hazen reports his brigade's action in his memoir.

HAZEN, 2B 3D 4C: Early on the morning of the 14th of May we advanced on the Resaca road. About eleven o'clock A. M. the cavalry came upon the enemy's infantry, and the head of the column was halted. The brigade was placed in position on the left of Willich's (Stanley being on our left), with a strong skirmish line deployed, and at noon began to advance in two lines, as follows: Colonel Kimberly on the right and Colonel Foy on the left of the first line; Colonel Berry on the right and Colonel Payne on the left of the second line. The advance was a difficult one, through thick woods and tangled undergrowth. The skirmishers drove those of the enemy before them for about three miles, when Colonel Payne, who had relieved Colonel Foy in the front, drove a Rebel line handsomely across a cornfield into their works beyond, and gained a strong position within two hundred yards of their intrenchments. His line was here exposed to an enfilading fire from a battery, but Colonel Kimberly's battalion, charging across the field and forming nearly at right angles with Colonel Payne's, soon silenced it, and held the position within seventy-five yards of the enemy's main line. The cannoneers were driven away from their guns, and only succeeded in recovering them after dark. Grose's brigade, of Stanley's division, formed on our left, and Willich, of ours, upon our right Colonel Foy's battalion was placed in the front line on Kimberly's right. [278]

Remember that statement: "The cannoneers were driven away from their guns, and only succeeded in recovering them after dark." What would they do about it?

277 (Smith 1900, 99)
278 (Hazen 1885, 252)

HAZEN, 2B 3D 4C: We remained in front of Buzzard Roost until the 13th, when we passed through to Dalton, four miles distant, the enemy having retreated the previous night. We followed, striking his cavalry about 10 a.m. on the 14th four miles in front of Resaca. Forming in two lines, the troops moved forward for about two miles, when we came upon the left wing of the Twenty-third Corps sharply engaged with the enemy, which we relieved; and Colonel Payne, One hundred and twenty-fourth Ohio Volunteers, commanding his own regiment and the Ninety-third Ohio Volunteers, pushed forward, vigorously driving the enemy from their advanced position, and seizing a hill within 100 yards of a salient in his works, containing a battery and overlooking a portion of his line containing two other batteries, the horses of which were shot and the guns kept silent the remainder of the time he occupied this position. Lieutenant-Colonel Kimberly, Forty-first Ohio Volunteers, commanding his regiment and the First Ohio Volunteers, was sent in on Colonel Payne's right, giving us complete control of the enemy's position for several hundred yards, and by putting sharpshooters at work the men and horses of the enemy that showed themselves were shot. General Willich moving in connection with my right and General Stanley with my left and the line fortified. These operations were effected with a loss of not to exceed 60 men. .279

Now, with the enemy forced within their prepared positions, brigades of Hazen and Willich are entrenching facing the enemy across the Dalton road. That crossing and the hills before it are loaded with cannon. The map drawn on the spot by Ambrose Bierce shows James Walker's viewpoint, from behind Hazen's line. Howard and Hooker watched some of the action on the 15th from that position.

Back to Stanley's division. Whitaker's brigade straddles the road, his left extending partly on the round-topped hill, connecting with Cruft's brigade, which extends to the road on the far side. Simonson's battery is just south of the road intersection, on the right, supporting. (See map.)

ROYCE, 115TH ILL WHITAKER 2B 1D 4C: Cruft's brigade, the first, occupied a hill to the left of the road, his left refused so as to face eastward, and constituted the extreme left of our army. Whitaker's brigade came next extending from the summit of the round hill occupied by Cruft's right, across the road in the hollow and to the top of the hill on the right, General Grose's brigade being still farther to the right. The 115th was on the left of Whitaker's brigade, adjoining the 3ist Indiana, which occupied Cruft's right.

279 (OR, Series I Vol 38 Part 1 Serial 75: Reports n.d., 421)

The left of the 115th was on the highest part of the hill; the line of the 3ist Indiana was at an obtuse angle with ours and for want of room its right lapped our left by the length of a company, it being thirty paces to our rear. .280

HOLM, SIMONSON 5TH IND BATTERY 1D 4C: Having passed through Tilton in the early part of May 14th, the strongly entrenched lines of the enemy upon the hills around Resaca were encountered about 1 o'clock. ... A part of the 2nd Brigade had been formed about 400 yards distant from the position of the Battery. .281

Now part of Whitaker's brigade eases forward.

PARTRIDGE, 96TH ILL WHITAKER 2B 1D 4C: The Fourth Corps was on the extreme left of the general army, the First Division, to which the Ninety-sixth was attached, was the left of the Corps, and for the time being Whittaker's was the left Brigade of the Division. It required most of the forenoon to move the Corps into place and connect the lines with those of the Twenty-third Corps, on the right. During this period comparative quiet reigned upon the extreme left, but farther to the right, where the troops were swinging forward to develop the enemy's position, there was a volume of firing whose magnitude indicated that a battle was in progress. At a little after two o'clock the left was ordered forward. Promptly the line moved out, Companies A and B deployed as skirmishers. Beyond the open field mentioned was a wooded ridge, from which came shots to indicate that it was held by the enemy. The advance to this ridge was resisted, but not with such force as to compel a charge. As the skirmishers neared its top they were greeted with a hot fire, indicating that the enemy were in heavy force a little farther on. As it proved the advancing line was not parallel to the enemy's works, the left of Company B being much nearer than the right of Company A. This fact was not at once appreciated, and Captain Vincent, the ranking officer and hence the commanding officer of the line, repeatedly called out, as the men halted, "Forward on the left!" "Forward on the left!" Captain Gilmore repeated the order to his men, and most gallantly they responded, going at a charge, driving the enemy's skirmishers from their positions and halting only when the main works of the Rebels were in plain view and a volley warned them that to go farther would be extremely perilous. In this advance Herman Hoogstraat, of Company B, was killed by one of the Rebel skirmishers, the latter quickly paying the penalty, for before the smoke from

280 (Royce 1900, 204)
281 (Holm n.d., 39)

his musket had cleared away, "Mack" McMillen's trusty rifle rang out its response, and when the line advanced the Rebel was found dead where he had fallen. John Bininger, of Company A, was the target of the Rebels for a time, they getting range of the old stump behind which he had taken shelter and filling it full of holes. A bad bruise to his shoulder, a severely scratched face and a considerable amount of bark and dirt in his eyes constituted his inventory of physical damages. It being demonstrated that the left was as far advanced as was practicable, the right was swung around to conform and the reserves moved up until they stood confronting a field, a half mile in width. This field was broken with hills and seamed with gullies, with a timbered ridge at the left ... .282

So they had found the Rebels and were now face-to-face across that field.

A big change on the south, facing Resaca and the bridges, where Camp Creek ran south to the river. Butterfield had been supporting there since morning, with Ward's brigade holding while the other two were in reserve. Logan's corps secured a vantage point within artillery range of the Rebel line on the ridge beyond. How they did it resulted from something ominous for those on the north. More about that later.

> TREMAIN: On the extreme right, however, the day had not been without its results. While the enemy had been thoroughly occupied in repelling Schofield's advance and afterwards attacking him in force, McPherson boldly assailed the enemy's extreme left in front of Resaca. The artillery opened along the whole line, and under its cover and a heavy skirmish fire Logan's corps crossed Camp Creek, and by a skillful and gallant charge, drove the enemy from the commanding hills in our front, and secured such a position across the creek as subjected a portion of the enemy's works to our destructive enfilading fire. Thus, while at the close of the afternoon action, the lines of both armies at the left remained substantially in the same positions, on the extreme right Logan with his veterans had gained a most decided advantage. .283

And here occurred an incident noteworthy in light of both earlier and later events.

282 (Partridge 1887, 316)
283 (Tremain 1905, 171)

An Admirable Position for Artillery

Early Saturday morning, the line having been indicated by the engineers, our men busied themselves in erecting rifle-pits; these had scarce been completed when it was deemed advisable by our generals to change the line, by throwing forward the right wing and occupying a high hill, which commanded this portion of the line, being an admirable position for artillery. –Cheney-CSA

The works were full of men, except at one point where a fort projected, which was readily guessed to be occupied by a battery of artillery. Instantly the Brigade Commander coveted that battery. —Partridge

Masked batteries on either flank, silent as yet, but so posted as to be able to throw a converging fire upon every acre of that barren field, were detected by his eagle eye. He [Division Commander] quickly decided that the charge would be unwise. -Partridge

Two hills merit the appellation "admirable position for artillery," for indeed they proved to be. One was held by Simonson's battery. The other was the angle of the Rebel defense. Both became subjects of fierce fights, one this day, the next the morrow.

Across from Hazen, the enemy had been entrenching since morning. Stanley's division had driven the Confederates into their prebuilt line. Their main line crossed the Dalton road to the rear of a ridge of hills. But they were engaged in building a line more forward, on the ridge, breaking at an angle to the east. Further north yet of that angle, on another hill, they already had some entrenchments for slowing down any attack from that direction. That hill was directly across the little plain from Stanley's line of Whitaker and Cruft.

Whitaker had worked forward feeling their position. There, left of Hazen's position, General Whitaker made an observation. Partridge continues his story:

PARTRIDGE, 96TH ILL WHITAKER 2B 1D 4C: ... This field was broken with hills and seamed with gullies, with a timbered ridge at the left. Its farther side was fringed with timber, against which the fresh clay of a heavy line of breastworks could be plainly seen. The works were full of men, except at one point where a fort projected, which was readily guessed to be occupied by a battery of artillery. Instantly the Brigade Commander coveted that battery, and began to make plans for its capture. The Ninety-sixth, with two other regiments, were ordered to pile knapsacks and fix bayonets, preparatory to a charge. Officers and men looked at each other in amazement, and wondered if it was possible that this little force was to be asked to make an assault across such a field and against such formidable entrenchments with no support at hand? Colonel Champion, who was always careful of criticizing his superiors, quietly spoke his disapproval to those immediately about him, but added that if the order was made there should be no faltering. O'Connor, of Company K, peering from behind the thin screen of bushes that sheltered the Regiment, remarked: "if Gen. Whittaker will wait until next pay-day I will chip in a part of me wages and buy him a better battery than the one ferninst him on the hill." _284 The General seemed in high glee over the anticipated victory, his expressions being in marked contrast with the feelings of the officers and men assigned to the task laid out by him, as afterward ascertained, although at the time but little was said. Preparations were nearly completed, and in a few moments the order would have been given had not the Division Commander come from the right just at this time. A look to right and left, and he fully comprehended the situation. Masked batteries on either flank, silent as yet, but so posted as to be able to throw a converging fire upon every acre of that barren field, were detected by his eagle eye. He quickly decided that the charge would be unwise. The men fully concurred in the judgment of the senior officer as to the un-wisdom of a charge on the part of three small regiments, with no supports in sight, against strong earthworks, with the certainty of a flanking fire from the moment an advance begun. At Chickamauga they had obeyed Gen. Whittaker's order and hurled themselves against a mass of Rebels outnumbering them three to one, and achieved success. At Lookout Mountain they had climbed into the very clouds, and won a victory where defeat seemed almost certain. At Rocky Face, five days before the date here written of, they had moved although but a mere skirmish line against an army and accomplished all that they were asked to do. So now, had the order been given, they would have gone against that frowning line, and, if possible, wrested a victory from the very jaws of defeat. But it is not too much to say that as the men stood in line that afternoon, and, peering from behind their thin screen of bushes, measured their chances in the proposed charge across that rugged field, the feeling was all but universal that before them lay the most difficult and desperate undertaking that had ever been assigned to them. It was therefore with a feeling of infinite relief that the order was received to unfix bayonets. _285

What if Whitaker had really charged? We don't know, for as said, something was brewing: someone else had been preparing to charge too.

---

284 An offer often repeated, as actual event or just a good story. Soldiers like such stories.
285 (Partridge 1887, 317)

DAY, 101ST OHIO CRUFT 1B 1D 4C: But the Confederates soon perceived that their right greatly overlapped our left, and at once took advantage of this fact, sending against us an overwhelming force. _286

Wood's division had annoyed Stevenson enough. The Union had left a gap on the north—an open invitation to get control of the fight.

STEVENSON, CMDG DIVISION, HOOD'S CORP, CSA: On the morning after my arrival near this place I took up position in *two lines* north of Resaca, and immediately upon the right of the Resaca and Dalton road. I was soon afterward ordered to connect with Major-General Hindman, on the left of the Resaca road, and for this purpose moved two regiments across the road. Cumming and Brown were in my front line, Pettus being the second line to the former and Reynolds to the latter. ...

Johnston's line came up from the south along Camp Creek, then bent east and split into two where it crossed the road. Willich was just west of the road and Hazen angled north from there. Johnston's southern line curved toward the river. His northern line, Stevenson's, swept up the range of hills, across the big one and then angled east. A hill with three tops was in front of Stevenson. They were separated by a saddle that that been cleared to give Stevenson a clear shot. Beyond that was the plain Stanley faced. This was a critical point of the Rebel defense. And it would be so the next day. But for today, Stevenson continues ...

STEVENSON, CMDG DIVISION, HOOD'S CORP, CSA: ... During the morning there were several attacks upon General Hindman, and in my front the sharpshooters of the enemy obtained positions which entirely enfilade portions of Cumming's line. The men were sheltered as well as possible by such defenses as they could construct of logs and rails, but still suffered severely. The fire of these sharpshooters upon the artillery, some pieces of which were advanced in front on the line of General Cumming, was particularly destructive, and among the wounded was the brave Major J. W. Johnston, the battalion commander. About 5 o'clock that evening, agreeably to orders, I commenced a movement to dislodge the enemy from the high point of the ridge some distance in front of General Cumming. Brown and his support (Reynolds) were directed to move out in front of their trenches and then swing around to the left. After the movement commenced General Cumming was also directed to wheel all of his brigade, which was to the

286 (Day 1894, 205)

right of the backbone of the ridge, to the left in front of his works, the regiment upon the crest being the pivot. ‑287

The 3rd Tennessee Regiment was that pivot. Whitaker (Stanley, actually) had gotten too close. Stevenson thought "Whitaker" already possessed the best artillery position. Whitaker's brigade itself had cautiously moved forward and was in Stevenson's face, so to speak.

> CJH, BROWN'S BRIGADE, STEVENSON'S DIVISION, HOOD'S CORP, CSA: Early Saturday morning, the line having been indicated by the engineers, our men busied themselves in erecting rifle-pits; these had scarce been completed when it was deemed advisable by our generals to change the line, by throwing forward the right wing and occupying a high hill, which commanded this portion of the line, being an admirable position for artillery, and relieving us from an enfilading fire, to which we were then subjected. ‑ 288 Already the enemy possessed and had intrenched themselves upon it, holding it with Whittaker's brigade, of Stanley's division, two thousand strong, and supported by the remainder of the division. This being in our immediate front, it devolved upon us to assail and carry it by storm. Accordingly, at half-past 5 o'clock P.M. supported by Reynolds' Brigade of Virginians and North Carolinians at the command we moved forward, in perfect line, across open fields, annoyed all the while by the enemy's sharpshooters and a heavy line of skirmishers, until we reached the base of the hill and commenced its ascent, ... ‑289

We're getting ahead of the story. Those skirmishers were Whitaker's. Stanley's scouts had been watching. He sent for help, repositioned Simonson's battery, and sent Whitaker.

> STANLEY, 1D 4C: These troops[Cruft's] were not yet in position when the enemy was seen forming to attack them in flank, and word was at once sent the corps and department commanders of this fact. In the mean time Simonson's battery, which had been advanced, was, as a matter of caution, withdrawn and posted to sweep the open ground to the rear of the threatened brigade. ‑290

---

287 (OR, Series I Vol 38 Part 3 Serial 74: Reports n.d., 812)
288 See Kurtz map of the entrenchments.
289 (CJH 1864)
290 (OR, Series I Vol 38 Part 1 Serial 75: Reports n.d., 220)

DAY, 101ST OHIO CRUFT 1B 1D 4C: So imminent was the danger at this point, and to our Brigade especially, that to avoid capture, our batteries, under Captain Simonson, were withdrawn and so placed as to rake our present position after we should be driven back. There was practically no support on our immediate left, Sherman's lines in this part of the field not having yet been fully established. ... Captain Simonson, 5th Indiana Battery, [was] posted in an open field back of an old peach orchard. _291

Seems Simonson had sent a few shells at Stevenson. Where General Stanley was, firing on the Rebel line, is what got them after him. Good work, moving back where he did! They wanted to sweep around behind him, but he made it much harder.

Whitaker's brigade had advanced beyond Cruft's brigade and was too close to Stevenson. Cruft's left was unsupported. So was Whitaker's, having moved out of line and ahead of Cruft. On their left? Nobody.

Hooker to the North Saving the 5th Indiana Battery

The Rebels were past both the flanks, and yelling and firing with all their might. For the first and last time in its experience the Regiment was in utter confusion. -
Partridge

Go in, my Illinois Boys! —Hooker

When Stanley's scouts reported Rebels gathering, Whitaker was pulled back and moved east, around the nose of the ridge, for the nerve-testing job of finding the enemy forming in the brush. Was anybody breathing?

PARTRIDGE, 96TH ILL WHITAKER 2B 1D 4C: [still facing the fort] A hurried consultation of officers followed. A Brigade was moved into the woods at the left, and shortly afterward the Ninety-Sixth, with two other regiments, moved quietly but quickly to the rear, and then, by diverging columns, across an obscure road and along a depression between two irregular ridges or hills, to the left of where the Brigade mentioned was going into position. Company B was sent in detachments on the left flank and to the front, with instructions to report any movement of the enemy that might be discovered. Company G was deployed to skirmish along the immediate front of the Regiment. The movement was through a tangle of underbrush for a hundred rods or more. When a halt was made the Regiment was in line

291 (Day 1894, 205)

almost at right angles to its former position, and practically isolated from any other troops, a gap several rods in extent separating it from the Brigade which had hastily moved on its right and slightly to the front, while a like opening lay between its left and the 51st Ohio. The 99th Ohio was halted some distance in the rear, and not far from the road. None in the ranks, and but few even among the field officers, knew the need that had called for this movement, the anxiety with which Gen. Stanley watched as they entered the jungle into which his order had sent them, or with what urgency he was asking Gen. Thomas for reinforcements for his left wing. His scouts had brought him word that the enemy was massing a Division or more for one of those desperate charges upon the flank for which the Confederates were noted. .292

Whitaker's brigade was now in a rough east-facing line in front of Cruft's brigade, not knowing what to expect, quite alone. But, meantime ...

CINCINNATI COMMERCIAL: Foiled at every point in his efforts to break our walls of iron that environed him, Johnston early in the afternoon commenced massing heavily on our left, where Stanley, with as brave a division as ever marched to the music of the Union, had been skirmishing and feeling the enemy while awaiting the developments of the enemy's attempt to break the center. Generals Sherman and Thomas were not slow to detect the enemy's design, and preparations to resist it were at once commenced. Joe Hooker's gallant Potomac veterans were selected at once, and immediately retired from the line and commenced moving to the left of Stanley, whose flank was covered by McCook's cavalry, in front of which Johnston was massing his columns for the desperate effort. Hooker arrived none too soon. .293

Hooker immediately sent Williams' division, Robinson's brigade in the lead, and then rode ahead to the scene. They had been in reserve behind Butterfield, down near Resaca.

MEMBER OF COMPANY A, 141ST NY, KNIPE 1B 1D 20C Our corps remains quiet until four p. m., when an order comes to Hooker to take his corps to the extreme left, for the purpose of relieving a portion of Howard's corps, which is being surrounded by superior numbers. Giving a few orders to be carried out by his aids, he mounts his horse and dashes off toward the scene of action, anxious, as he always is to be ahead. We soon follow, at a double-

292 (Partridge 1887, 319)
293 (Correspondence of the Cincinnati Commercial 1864, May 22)

quick, a distance of two miles; we are drawing closer and closer to the field of strife; louder and louder roars the artillery, sharper and sharper are the reports of the musketry. _294

ROBINSON, 3B 1D 20C: On the 14th the position was shifted one mile farther to the left, where the entire division was held in reserve of the division of General Butterfield until 4.30 p.m. At that hour I was directed by the brigadier-general commanding division to move my brigade by the left flank and lead the division in marching toward the Dalton road, near which at that time the Fourth Corps was engaging the enemy. _295

Hooker himself rushed ahead, not far behind Captain Simonson, who must have been scouting. Simonson gets them ready.

MEMBER OF COMPANY A, 141ST NY, KNIPE 1B 1D 20C: Hooker has outstripped us and arrived at the scene of action; the small band of men are nearly surrounded; one battery has had its bugle sounded for the gunners to leave, but the presence of Hooker causes them to stop; his injunctions are, to hold their position five minutes, and he will give them all the support they need. _296

HOLM, SIMONSON 5TH IND BATTERY 1D 4C: ABOUT 6 P.M. Captain Simonson, who had been "on the line" all the afternoon, was apprised of the movement of the enemy to "crush the left flank" and, knowing of the exposed position of the Battery, came galloping up and, taking in the situation at a glance, asked with no little anxiety, "Morrison where's your support?," Morrison quickly replying, "I haven't seen it Captain." Fortunately, Gen. "Joe" Hooker came riding by at this very critical moment, and Captain Simonson appealing to him said, "My God! General, can't you give me support for this Battery?" Said Hooker, "Why what's the matter?", to which Simonson, pointing in the direction of the charging masses of Confederates, said, "There's a division of Confederates charging through that gap yonder and not five hundred men to oppose them." Then "Fighting Joe" began to be interested, pointed to the Battery and asked if that was "the extreme left of the line," and when assured that it was, asked with some degree of interest, "How long can you hold this position with the Battery?" Without hesitation Simonson answered, "As long as we have ammunition, but General, I want support." Gen. Hooker, with no small degree of assurance in his words,

294 (Museum n.d.)
295 (OR, Series I Vol 38 Part 2 Serial 73: Reports n.d., 85)
296 (Museum n.d.)

remarked, "Keep cool Captain, hold this position at all hazards. I'll see that you get all the ammunition you can use and also timely support." Gen. Stanley relates in his report of the battle that "the coming up of the 20th (Hooker's) Corps was most timely, though in my opinion the fire of the battery (alluding to the 5th Indiana) was in itself adequate to the successful repulse of the enemy." Captain Simonson, dismounting, walked quickly through the Battery and saw what made his heart thrill with pride, seeing every man in his place and at his post—mounting a "trail" of one of the guns—and for a moment silently, but with evident solicitude, viewed the "boys" of his Battery a brief moment and then called out "Attention!" Every eye was turned upon him. "Men," said he, "our big time has come, if anyone is afraid, or is in the least cowardly, let him leave at once, for we'll have no use for any but brave men; we've got to fight our guns to the extreme limit, will you do it?" In response to this challenge, hats went up into the air, coats and jackets were instantly flung aside, and in some instances sleeves wore rolled up to the armpits—not a man accepted the challenge to "leave." But a few brief moments elapsed when the rattle of musketry told too plainly that the critical time had come. Ammunition was piled up in close proximity to some of the guns, as the caissons were some distance in rear. .297

Fighting far from home, in a confrontation like this, their only hope for survival is the same as for all their comrades; they must stay the fight together. Is that an advantage for Union men here in the deep south? "Common knowledge" quoted often was that it took half the Rebel army to make the rest fight. But they did fight.

Whitaker's skirmishers find something surely fearsome coming out of the trees. It was skirmishers from the 32nd Tennessee, leading Brown's Brigade.

McGUIRE, 32ND TENNESSEE, BROWN'S BRIGADE, STEVENSON, HOOD, CSA: The enemy had taken position on the opposite side of an open field, along the border of which we were formed, and had intrenched themselves back in the woods some two hundred yards from the edge of the field. They had sent a strong line of skirmishers down to the edge of the timber, and were firing across the field at us with some effect. This had been kept up for several hours when Gen. Brown ordered Major McGuire, who was commanding our skirmishers, to attack the enemy's skirmishers and drive them from the edge of the wood across the field, telling him at the same time that he would follow closely upon the movements of the skirmishers with the brigade. Our skirmishers moved through the open field in full view of

297 (Holm n.d., 39)

the entire brigade, under a most terrific fire, and yet in the most perfect order and in the grandest style, completely routing the enemy's skirmishers, and inflicting heavy loss in killed, wounded, and captured. 298

MOREY, 32ND TENNESSEE, BROWN'S BRIGADE, STEVENSON, HOOD, CSA: May 14. We ___ a ___ soon this morning and put up breast works. Our regiment was held in reserve for the brigade. About twelve oclock our regiment was sent out to reinforce the skirmishers. We staid out some time when we returned ___ ___. About four oclock this evening our brigade with Stewart's Division for support moved out of our works charged and took a hill in our front which we held until midnight and fell back to our works. Our brigade lost fifty seven wounded and killed. Our regiment lost less than the rest of the brigade. 299

Notice that Morey does not say they skirmished for Brown's brigade when they charged at four o'clock and implies by casualties that they were still in reserve then. Perhaps only part of his regiment was used as skirmishers to lead the 3rd Tennessee.

The 96th Illinois immediately formed a line and started to dig in but soon saw what they would face.

PARTRIDGE, 96TH ILL WHITAKER 2B 1D 4C: The skirmishers upon the immediate front of the Ninety-Sixth soon became aware of the purpose of the enemy, for as they halted at a low rail fence at the edge of the thicket and looked across an old field with its girdled trees, a sight in one sense grand came full upon their gaze. Stevenson's Division was just emerging from the timber and forming its lines in plain view, preparatory to a desperate assault. The enemy were in two lines, and formed in admirable order, their flags floating gaily, many of their officers mounted, and a light line of cavalry riding in rear and upon either flank. At a given command two or three men stepped out from each Company and took position as skirmishers. The long lines extended far to right and left, and it was evident that the movement was one of no mean proportions. Captain James promptly reported from the skirmish line what had been seen, and was ordered to call in his men and form them with the main line. This proved a difficult task, for they were busily engaged in firing into the now advancing Rebels, and could hear the command with difficulty; indeed many of them did not hear the order, running back on their own judgment when they saw that to remain longer

298 (McGuire 1886, 479)
299 (Morey n.d., May 13, 1864)

meant capture. A few did not leave the line at all, being so absorbed in their work of loading and firing as to fail to take thought for their own safety until too late, and when they were fairly run over by the cloud of skirmishers that covered the front of the moving lines. .300

And here they came!

PARTRIDGE, 96TH ILL WHITAKER 2B 1D 4C: The Rebels had now emerged from the woods, and under orders not to shout or fire, but to keep their advance concealed if possible, were moving for the coveted artillery, hoping to gain it by stealth. So silent was their movement that some of the Federal forces almost believed them friends, and hesitated about firing upon them. "Why don't you return our fire?" was shouted towards them. "We don't care anything about you we are after that Battery!" was shouted back. "If you want the Battery come and get it" was answered in chorus, and the firing grew more fierce and deadly, the muskets playing upon them and the cannon emptying grape and canister into their ranks. .301

Another line of Stevenson's skirmishers approached Cruft's unsupported left — during mail time!

MORRIS, 81ST INDIANA CRUFT 1B 1D 4C: Late in the afternoon a mail arrived for our regiment. After we had just time to open the letters and packages and look at them, skirmishing broke out on our front and every one was ordered into line quickly. Temporary breastworks were hurridly thrown up by orders of our colonel, and as the bullets commenced to fly in our direction we were ordered to lie down. Nearer and nearer came the noise and the excitement among us all was wrought to the highest pitch, as we expected the enemy to charge in on us every moment. we were cautioned particularly not to shoot until orders were given to do so, as quite a number of our men were out on the skirmish lines and had not been driven in. Still nearer came the noise of battle, but the men kept lying low, each with his gun in his hand and his finger ready on the trigger, and faced to the front, ready to let fly a storm of lead on the enemy's first appearance. The boys were greatly alarmed for fear that the enemy might come in on our left flank and take the advantage of us, but the enemy advanced in heavy columns and drove in our skirmishers. .302

300 (Partridge 1887, 319)
301 (Partridge 1887, 319)
302 (Morris 1901, 89)

Whitaker's leftmost regiment had stayed anchored on the hill next to Cruft's right and could see it coming.

> ROYCE, 115TH ILL WHITAKER 2B 1D 4C: While in that position we could distinctly hear the movements of the enemy in our front. It was apparent to all that the Confederates were massing a large force on that part of their line with the view of turning our left. In order to meet them General Stanley called for re-enforcements and at that moment Williams' division of Hooker's corps was rapidly coming to our assistance. The enemy's skirmishers soon appeared in our front, skulking through the brush carrying their guns at a trail. Some thought them deserters; we thought otherwise and opened fire on them. A number fell, one too far advanced to escape was captured, and the rest hastened back into their line. The one poor fellow we captured was greatly exercised for a while, for after he had thrown up his hands and we had ceased firing the 3ist Indiana on our left continued firing for a minute or so, greatly to his discomfort. Seeing the exposed position of the left of the regiment, Colonel Moore hastily ordered that wing back to the line of the 3ist, at the same time moving a little to the right to make room. ..303

So the 115th scooted right to give Cruft some room.

The 96th Illinois was overwhelmed on the right and left. Whitaker was routed, driven back beside the battery!

> PARTRIDGE, 96TH ILL WHITAKER 2B 1D 4C: The charging column, as it came over the higher ground, struck the Brigade at the right with fearful velocity. These troops were engaged in throwing up a barricade of rails and logs when the charge began. Seizing their muskets they made a brave fight for a few moments, but upon discovering that their flank was passed broke for the rear in wild confusion. The moments were of fearful import to the members of the Ninety-Sixth. Now anxiously they awaited the result of that onset. They could see little, but they could hear everything. It was but a moment and their worst fears were realized, for the firing slackened at the right, while the Rebel yell grew more exultant as the line of blue was rolled back from left to right. In a moment the storm had struck the Regiment. Hardly a shot had been fired at them as yet, and owing to the dense thicket not a Rebel could be seen. But they could be plainly heard as they threw aside the fence in front. The men were generally kneeling or lying prostrate on the ground, every one ready for his work. The voice of Colonel Champion rang out:

303 (Royce 1900, 204)

"Steady, men! Hold your fire until I give the word!" Then, as the bushes began to weave to and fro, almost in their faces, he gave the command: "Fire!" A terribly destructive volley poured into the oncoming lines, and a great windrow of dead was afterward found at this point. The front line of the charging column was halted and turned back for a regiment's length. Many of the Regiment began to reload their muskets, having no thought of leaving the line. Those at the right could see at once that the position was untenable, for the Rebels were rushing past their flank in solid ranks. A moment later the left was also flanked and a wicked fire was poured lengthwise of the line. A formal order to retreat was given by Colonel Champion, with directions to rally at the breastworks, but in the confusion and noise could not be heard by all. But the instinct of self preservation was strong enough to tell the experienced soldier what to do, and the movement to the rear was begun almost simultaneously along the entire line. In a moment the retreat had become a rout. The Rebels were past both the flanks, and yelling and firing with all their might. For the first and last time in its experience the Regiment was in utter confusion, and little or no effort was made to preserve order; indeed no effort was practicable from the start. For a time it was a race between the men in blue and those in gray to see which should first gain the open field. Fortunately the Regiment's course lay through a hollow or depression, and while the pines somewhat retarded the retreat it likewise delayed the Rebels and served an admirable purpose as a covering or screen. A majority of the command followed the natural depression, which took them a little to the left of Simonson's 5th Indiana Battery, making their way to the breastworks built in the morning, and when the enemy came in view doing admirable service. Others bore to the right, and as they emerged from the timber found themselves in an open field nearly in front of the Battery as it then faced. 304

304 (Partridge 1887, 319)

"Line of Battle" by Winslow Homer

And the Rebels are upon Cruft too!

> STANLEY, 1D 4C: The attack came about an hour before sundown, and perpendicular to my line. The Thirty-first Indiana, stationed upon the round-topped hill, found itself fired into from three directions. They did the best they could under the circumstances; they got out of the way with such order as troops can hurrying through a thick brush. Directing their attack more to our rear than flank, the One hundred and first Ohio and Eighty-first Indiana were soon driven back, and the enemy was bursting exultingly upon the open field. [305]

The Rebels get almost behind the 31st. They and the regiments left of them all fell back to the road.

> MORRIS, 81ST INDIANA CRUFT 1B 1D 4C: They soon reached our lines, when we were ordered to rise up quickly and give them a volley and fall back, as our left flank was being turned, and the regiment on our right was giving away. In an instant all was confusion. Companies and regiments became scattered and mixed, all going to the rear as fast as possible. We had several fences to climb, but very little climbing was done, for all that could not jump them tumbled over them. Our woolen and rubber blankets never, it seemed, felt so heavy as they did just then. The enemy had a fair view to shoot at us from the top of the high hills on our left, and the balls flew through the air

---

305 (OR, Series I Vol 38 Part 1 Serial 75: Reports n.d., 220)

thick and fast. No one seemed to be hit. but there was quite a number of miraculous escapes from death. We fell back about half a mile from our front line, and our regiment rallied on the left of a log house in an old field. While we were forming our lines we were surprised by a scattering fire on our left, and we were ordered to fall back, as we were flanked again. We retreated a few hundred yards further, halted and again formed our line, and were ordered to lie down while the Fifth Indiana Battery threw them a little grape and cannister over our heads into the woods beyond. Although the battery boys worked with a will, it was a terrible situation for us to be in. To stand up was to run the risk of having our heads blown off. The boys of the battery were afraid they would lose their guns and they implored and begged the infantry to stay with them, our regiment being without support on the flanks. .306

HARDEN, 90TH OHIO WHITAKER 2B 1D 4C: Our brigade was on the extreme left of the line, in the woods, without any support. The 31st Ind. on the extreme left, our regiment next. Co.'s B and G lay to the left of a road on which the rebels had a battery, and were ordered to fall back with the 31st Ind., in case they had to fall back. Soon the rebels came up in front on a charge and were repulsed. Again they came, this time obliquely, and were repulsed again. A third time they came, and this time came in on the left flank, and Johnnies and Yankees were mixed together in a hand-to-hand encounter. The 31st Ind and the two companies across the road were forced to fall back, and the regiment to swing to the rear. .307

SMITH, 31ST INDIANA CRUFT 1B 1D 4C: They soon encountered several lines of battle, and troops were rapidly passing around to our left. Word had been sent to the brigade commander that the hill could not be held twenty minutes. The orders sent back were but a repetition—to hold the hill at every hazard. We immediately sent the orderly back with the word that we could not hold the place ten minutes. The orderly had scarcely started, when we discovered Colonel Neff about-facing the three left companies. Inasmuch as we had three lines of battle in our front, we knew the emergency that required that action must be great, so we stepped quickly a half dozen steps to the rear, and, to our amazement, we found two lines of battle climbing the hill in our rear, and very near the top. The command was given, "By the right flank, double-quick; every fellow for himself!" and much quicker than it can be told, every man of the regiment, except two, came off—William E. Boon, of Company F, and, of Company—, were unwell, and

306 (Morris 1901, 89)
307 (Harden 1902, 122)

thought they could not run, so they were captured. The regiment had been cautioned, and told that, in the event it had to come off the hill in confusion, to halt at the Dalton road, and form a skirmish line, hold the enemy in check, and fall back as it was forced to. The regiment reached the road, all at about the same time; and skirmishing immediately began. It was then discovered that we had but few ramrods. While on the hill, the men were so hotly engaged that they did not take time to return rammer, but stuck it into the ground, and their departure was so sudden, that the rammers were left. .308

(Note: Smith mentions Colonel Neff, commander of the 84th of Whitaker's brigade, confirming Whitaker was between Cruft and the Rebels, quite close, as Smith could watch their companies' movements.)

ROYCE, 115TH ILL WHITAKER 2B 1D 4C: Scarcely was the movement completed when the Confederate line of battle two ranks deep composed of Stewart's and Stevenson's divisions, a force more than four times as great as the brigade and a half that confronted them, came in sight and opened a furious fire upon us. It seemed a sheet of flame along their whole line, as volley after volley came from them. We had barely time to return a few volleys when they were upon us, yelling like Indians. Cruft's brigade gave way and the left wing of the 115th followed. As we crossed the road in the valley an effort was made to reform our lines and resist their further advance, but a glance up the hill toward the position we had left revealed only an advancing line of fire too heavy to withstand. .309

Simonson could not open fire on the mass of men retreating from in front of the battery. It was a desperate fight for survival!

PARTRIDGE, 96TH ILL WHITAKER 2B 1D 4C: As soon as the infantry had moved to right and left, so that the cannon could be fired without endangering the lives of their friends, Capt. Simonson gave the word, and his six pieces of artillery began to play upon the timber. The Rebels had evidently slackened their pace somewhat, probably to reform that portion of their line shattered by the volleys from the Ninety-Sixth and other Regiments, and to change direction so as to swing a little farther to the Union rear. On either side of the Battery the most strenuous efforts were making to organize the men who had been borne backward in the terrific storm. Officers of every rank were shouting out their orders, and men of a dozen regiments were trying to form some semblance of a line, regardless

308 (Smith 1900, 99)
309 (Royce 1900, 204)

of what flag they fought beneath so that it was the stars and stripes. Others, timid and uncertain as to duty, were hunting for their own commands. An irregular line was formed on either flank of the cannon, and the men stood there awaiting the coming of the Rebels and resolved to check and send them back if the valor of a few could avail. But all at that point felt that the result was doubtful, for what could two or three hundred do against the vast host soon to emerge from the cover of the timber. .310

HOLM, SIMONSON 5TH IND BATTERY 1D 4C: Presently a brigade of Confederates came sweeping exultingly into the open field, and the 81st Ind, and 101st Ohio which formed the infantry line on the left flank were soon overpowered and driven back. The Battery opened upon the attacking line with a shower of shells and canister which soon broke and dispersed that attack. The two regiments above-named did as well as could be expected—attacked in front and flank and greatly outnumbered—and, had it not been for the timely aid of the battery, it would have gone hard with them. "Capt. Simonson and the 5th Indiana Battery deserve great praise; their conduct and execution was splendid." (Stanley's report) When the two regiments above mentioned were driven back, the Battery was without support and, occupying a position on the extreme left of the line, was dangerously exposed. .311

Simonson opened fire on Brown after Whitaker was clear.

ROYCE, 115TH ILL WHITAKER 2B 1D 4C: The 5th Indiana Battery was in good position on the hill to our rear waiting for a clear front. They seemed to be inviting us to come to them; at least we went, somewhat in advance of the rebel line that was rapidly following us. They had failed to notice our right wing on the knob to the right of the road, but swept past in pursuit of our left wing and the first brigade. As we went up the hill several attempts were made to make a stand, but nothing could be done against such odds. When the summit was reached and the front of the battery was cleared the Confederates were coming at a rapid rate. It was just as they entered an opening that gave a good view that Captain Simonson's 5th Indiana Battery opened upon them with grape and canister, with telling effect. It was a most exciting affair. The left wing of the 115th to the right of the battery and Cruft's brigade to the left, hastily making breastworks of logs and from such protection pouring a withering musketry fire into their approaching enemy,

310 (Partridge 1887, 319)
311 (Holm n.d., 39)

too busy to see the approach from their rear of Williams' division of Hooker's corps. ..312

Yes, Robinson already has them in sight!

ROBINSON, 3B 1D 20C: By 6.30 p.m. the head of my column reached a high wooded ridge, overlooking a narrow open valley, along which extended the main road leading to Dalton. On the farther side of the valley was another thickly wooded hill, and upon a slight knoll in the open field at our feet stood the Fifth Indiana Battery, supported by a portion of Stanley's division, of the Fourth Corps. The division itself was at that time engaging the enemy some distance beyond the farther end of the valley, and from the character of the firing it was evident that General Stanley's lines were falling back; in fact that they were giving way in some disorder. ..313

But he is not there yet. Some of Cruft's regiments were reformed to face the Rebels, to help defend the battery.

After Whitaker had fallen back, the battery had fired into the column that drove him in. Then Simonson paused and turned the guns to the left and opened fire on the Rebels that had driven Cruft off the hill.

MORRIS, 81ST INDIANA CRUFT 1B 1D 4C: The battery ceased firing and we fell back a few hundred yards further. We formed our lines and kept up a continual fire on the woods in our front. The other regiments of our brigade were reorganized as fast as possible and prolonged the lines. In the meantime the battery sent the shells as fast as ever. ..314

SMITH, 31ST INDIANA CRUFT 1B 1D 4C: We had been at the road but a very few minutes when a young officer rode up, and directed us to march back across a field, and support a battery. The regiment passed out of the wood on quick time, and then went double-quick across the field, and formed in line to the left of the Fifth Indiana Battery. By the time this was accomplished, the rebels, in three lines of battle, marched exultingly out of the wood into the field, with their guns at right-shoulder shift, as though they were going on parade. They had come about half across the field—probably within one hundred and fifty yards—when the battery opened.

312 (Royce 1900, 204)
313 (OR, Series I Vol 38 Part 2 Serial 73: Reports n.d., 85)
314 (Morris 1901, 89)

After the first fire, we could see nothing in consequence of the smoke from the guns. _315

DAY, 101ST OHIO CRUFT 1B 1D 4C: Captain Simonson, 5th Indiana Battery, posted in an open field back of an old peach orchard, supported by the 101st, which had fallen back to that position, repulsed the rebel advance spoken of as moving against and around our left flank. The charging column came almost to the muzzles of Simonson's guns. In the heroic service of those guns the Captain, with bared red head gleaming in the light of his blazing cannon (it was just dusk), constantly reiterated the command: "Load them steel guns to the muzzle." As fast as his men were lost, details were made from the 101st to take their places. So pleased was he with the service of these men that he persistently asked that they might be permanently transferred to him. Of course Colonel Kirby would not part with such men. _316

Rebels now had their objective almost at hand. But, clear of retreating infantry, Simonson could let loose.

HOLM, SIMONSON 5TH IND BATTERY 1D 4C: Scarcely had these things been said and done when a shout from the top of a wooded hill, a little to the left front of the Battery, was distinctly heard, "Go for that d—d Yankee battery." The six guns of the Battery spoke out almost simultaneously as a reply, and for the next fifteen or twenty minutes there was an almost continuous stream of shot, shells and canister poured into the very faces of the daring Confederate troops, who endeavored to reform their broken lines at the foot of the wooded hill. Brig. Gen. Whitacre commanding the 2nd brigade, referring to the part which the Battery took in this engagement, says, "The Fifth Indiana Battery which was attached to this brigade, under the immediate command of the gallant Lieut. Morrison and under supervision of brave Capt. Simonson, chief of artillery of the 1st Div. had been withdrawn and placed in position to sweep the rear of the exposed (Cruft's) brigade. The Battery had been assailed by the enemy's columns, but by a most brave and determined stand it succeeded in holding the enemy in check. The brave men and officers hurled such a storm of shells, shot and canister upon the Confederate lines with such rapidity and effectiveness that they were enabled to maintain their position until Gen. Hooker aided in turning back the Confederate columns which had advanced far past and in rear of our left flank. I make special mention of the officers and men of

315 (Smith 1900, 99)
316 (Day 1894, 205)

this battery for their gallantry and bravery on this occasion." Reverting to the time when the Confederate battle line burst over the crest of the wooded hill to the "left front" of the Battery, Captain Simonson, as chief of artillery, in his official report says, "The pieces of the Fifth Indiana Battery were immediately turned by hand to the left, changing the Battery front more to the left so as to conform to the Confederate line which was sweeping down through the woods to the left of the Battery, opening with spherical case and shells, reserving the canister for use in case they gained the hill on our immediate left. They soon appeared on this hill, and opened with a heavy volley of musketry. The distance to the top of the hill was 150 yards. The men themselves, without any orders or suggestions from their officers, double-shotted the guns, in some instances with a spherical case and a charge of canister and at other times a double charge of canister, and maintained the most rapid fire possible. A scattering few of the most daring ones of the charging forces reached the road at the foot of the hill, within fifty yards of the Battery. These were so confused that they soon fled for shelter and were subsequently taken prisoners." This part of the Captain's report is coincident with the request made just before the engagement, "Let's give them the best we've got," and without fears of successful contradiction it may be asserted that this was the most terrific artillery practice which occurred during the entire period of the war, surely the most terrific and destructive of human life for the time occupied that is recorded in history or mentioned in any official report relative to artillery. Shot, shell and canister at the rate of not less than five discharges per minute from six pieces! Officers could be heard shouting occasionally "muzzles down! muzzles down!!" The gunners yelling for ammunition, a number of the "swing team" drivers left their teams without orders to aid in supplying the guns with ammunition. Infantrymen who had been separated from their regiments joined in the exciting work right valiantly and did excellent service for the Battery in carrying ammunition from somewhere, no one knew, but it was reckoned that it was supplied in accordance with Gen. Hooker's promise that he would see to it that the Battery should have all the ammunition it could use. 317

Partridge, 96th Ill Whitaker 2B 1D 4C: It was marvelous to witness the rapidity with which the artillery was fired as the danger of capture became apparent to the cannoneers. Perhaps never were six guns made to do more rapid or destructive work. They were filled again and again, almost to the muzzle, and fired so rapidly that Rebel prisoners captured soon after refused

317 (Holm n.d., 39)

to believe that but a single battery had played upon them. It was said that five wagon loads of ammunition were expended within a half hour or less, and that 268 dead Rebels were buried from the front of the battery. A staff officer came riding down to where the scattered infantrymen were resolutely reforming, and begged them to hold the line for five minutes more, assuring them that a Division of the Twentieth Corps was close at hand, coming to the rescue at double quick. The promise was reassuring, although many did not need it, having determined to fight to the death beside the Battery. 318

Robinson deployed while the battery was doing their utmost.

ROBINSON, 3B 1D 20C: By direction of General Williams I immediately formed my brigade in line of battle along the crest of the ridge parallel to and overlooking the valley. I had four regiments in front and two in rear, thus forming two lines, one in support of the other. In my first line were the One hundred and first Illinois, Eighty-second Illinois, and the One hundred and forty-third and Forty-fifth New York Volunteers, and in the second the Sixty-first and Eighty-second Ohio Volunteers. I had hardly gotten my command into position until the enemy swarmed out of the woods in pursuit of Stanley's men, and with defiant yells made for the battery, the infantry support of which immediately fled. The enemy came confidently on, apparently unaware of our presence. He was rapidly nearing the battery, when I was directed by the brigadier-general commanding division to precipitate my entire command into the valley, and, wheeling it upon the right flank, bring it up to the support of the battery. This order was at once communicated to the regiments of my brigade. and in a moment the whole was in motion. The evolution was executed with enthusiasm and with no less precision and regularity of movement than might have been expected upon drill. 319

And then!

HOLM, SIMONSON 5TH IND BATTERY 1D 4C: Pandemonium reigned for about fifteen minutes, when suddenly there came from somewhere in the rear close by the command, "c-e-a-s-e f-i-r-ing," "lie down." This was repeated, and the voice was recognized as that of Captain Simonson. It was but a moment till not a man of the Battery could be seen except as he lay upon the ground in the place where he stood while in action. Hooker had

318 (Partridge 1887, 320)
319 (OR, Series I Vol 38 Part 2 Serial 73: Reports n.d., 85)

redeemed his promise—two lines of infantry with fixed bayonets came charging through the battery and out across the valley in close pursuit of the residue of fleeing Confederates. .320

ROBINSON, 3B 1D 20C: Arriving at the front of the battery the Eighty-second Illinois, Sixty-first Ohio, and One hundred and forty-third New York Volunteers poured a tremendous fire upon the overconfident foe. The One hundred and first Illinois was directed to move at once upon the hill on the left, now in possession of the enemy. That gallant regiment at once advanced in perfect order to the crest and drove from it the enemy's skirmishers. Meeting with such severe and unexpected resistance, the enemy at once gave way and confusedly sought his intrenchments back in the woods. .321

MORRIS, 81ST INDIANA CRUFT 1B 1D 4C: In a few moments after taking up our last position we were joyfully surprised to find a heavy reinforcement from General Hooker's Corps, which came to our relief with General Hooker himself. They were received with loud cheers, and in few moments they charged the enemy in our front driving them before them. The long agony was over, and we felt that Hooker had saved us. .322

The 101st Illinois, from the author's home county:

ILLINOIS ADJUTANT GENERAL HISTORY OF 101ST ILL: On the 14th still being held in reserve until 3 o'clock in the afternoon, when they started on the double quick for the left, where the brigade rendered important service in the action then in progress. During this engagement, it is said, the 101st was ordered to take a hill in front of them, occupied by the enemy, which they did in so gallant a style as to win the admiration of General Joe Hooker, who cheered the troops, with the encouraging shout of: "Go in, my Illinois boys!" .323 .324

HOPPER, CO E 101ST ILL ROBINSON 3B 1D 20C: Laid most of the day in support of Butterfield, about 5 p.m. ordered to the left. The Rebs just broke

---

320 (Holm n.d., 39)
321 (OR, Series I Vol 38 Part 2 Serial 73: Reports n.d., 85)
322 (Morris 1901, 89)
323 (Illinois Adjutant General 1901, 591)
324 The 101st Illinois was entirely from Morgan County, neighbor of Scott County. Their colonel, John LeSage, was from Meredosia, home of Company A.

our lines; our men were skedaddling in double quick. We went in with a yell and repulsed them; laid out as skirmishers all night. 5 miles. 325

Yes, it was over!

BENTON, BAND, 150TH NY RUGER 2B 1D 20C: "Blow cease firing!" The voice was of Gen. A. S. Williams, "old Pop" Williams, as the boys affectionately referred to him among themselves, and the order was addressed to the brigade bugler, Stevenson, who, as it happened, was a member of our regiment. Stevenson had been as intensely interested as the others in the drama before us, and he afterward told me that it was the only time he was ever ordered to blow "Cease firing." Now, with the suddenness of the order he could not remember the signal, but he clapped the bugle to his lips and blew something; and the firing ceased. The signal had not been needed, for the men saw that the enemy had retreated from their front, and they stopped firing without regard to that uncertain sound from Stevenson's instrument. 326

PARTRIDGE, 96TH ILL WHITAKER 2B 1D 4C: The movements of the reinforcing column were admirably made, and they swept forward across the field, driving the Rebels back into the shelter of the forest. And with them, forming wherever they could, in the front line, moved many of the Ninety-Sixth, halting only when the enemy had disappeared in rapid flight, and darkness had begun to settle over the terrible scene. The discomfiture of the Rebels was complete, their ranks being shattered and their rout even more marked than had been that of the most exposed Union forces. 327

Some newfound respect.

BROWN, CO C 27TH INDIANA RUGER 2B 1D 20C: It was curious how quickly this incident put an end to the previous ill feeling of some of the men of the Western army towards those who had recently come from the Army of the Potomac. This was particularly true of those who witnessed it. The foolish impression was more or less prevalent in the Western army that the reason why the Army of the Potomac had not taken Richmond was because it would not fight. This did not seem to have its origin in sectional prejudice, for we who belonged in the West were no more exempt from the accusation than others. The statistics of battle losses, and other facts about the severity

325 (Hopper n.d.)
326 (Benton 1902, 136)
327 (Partridge 1887, 319)

of battles, were not as well known then as now. When the Twenty-seventh was passing through Tennessee, on its way from the Army of the Potomac, an Indiana regiment was guarding the railroad over which we traveled. It had been organized at Camp Morton at the same time that the Twenty-seventh was and had started to the field about the same time. Up to this point in its service it had only met the enemy in one insignificant engagement, and then had been captured bodily. This record, if not blameworthy, was certainly nothing to boast of. The foregoing pages may indicate, in a feeble way, what the record of the Twenty-seventh had been. Yet the members of the other regiment taunted us, as we passed by, with such shouts as "All quiet on the Potomac," "Fall in for soft bread," "Hello, paper collar soldiers," "Hadn't you better stop and black your shoes," etc., etc. But the way our Army of the Potomac men handled themselves, and the way they handled the enemy at this time largely put a stop to such things.

Old "Pap" Williams evidently thought of these matters in this connection. He was a Western man himself, at least by adoption, and was in full sympathy with Western people and their ways. But he could not resist the temptation to even up with men when he had such a good opportunity. As the men of the line that had been broken came tumbling back, and officers appealed to him with much warmth to come to their assistance, he said, "Yes, yes, get your men out of the way. I have some soldiers here (barely a slight emphasis on the word soldiers) from the Army of the Potomac, who can take care of these rebels." .328

328 (E. R. Brown 1899, 469)

WILLIAMS, 1D 20C: They "skedaddled" as fast as they had advanced, hardly exchanging a half-dozen volleys. They were so surprised that they fired wildly and didn't wound a dozen men. I was much complimented for the affair and Gen. Howard, commander of the 4th Corps, came and thanked me. _329

HOLM, SIMONSON 5TH IND BATTERY 1D 4C: After a few minutes respite, order restored and accounts of losses noted, Captain Simonson seated himself comfortably upon the ground and began fanning himself with his hat, the boys gathering around him, with Lieut. Morrison on the "inner circle." The Captain, with evident gratification, said, "Boys we did it, we're done our big thing. I reckon they'll all know us now." Gen. Hooker had returned from the front, whither he had gone when his troops had charged through the Battery and, dismounting, walked leisurely through the Battery shaking hands here and there with the powder-begrimed men and remarked with some emphasis that "these men are heroes every one of them" and that "he would rather be a private in this battery than a Brigadier General." Subsequently, Generals Butterfield, Geary, Williams, Stanley and others of subordinate ranks and commands came and complimented the officers and men of the Battery in highest terms. Evidently the Captain was right when

329 (Williams 1963, Letter of May 20, 1864)

he said "we're done our big thing." The next day it was learned from prisoners that it was Stevenson's division that had made the attack on the position and had been so terribly slaughtered by the shower of death-dealing missiles from the guns of the Battery. A strange thing about this fierce conflict of May 14th is that not a man or officer of the Battery was injured in the least degree by Confederate bullets. This may seem incredible and cannot be accounted for in no other way than that the attacking Confederates occupied much higher ground than the Battery and in consequence "over shot," but the men of the Battery claim they were responsible for the Confederates firing so wildly as it must have been extremely confusing to have from six to ten charges (in as many seconds) of canister "flung" into their ranks without ceremony. It was William's division of Hooker's corps that came to the support and relief of the Battery. As night spread its dark curtain over the scenes of the last past two hours, the boys, weary, though apparently well satisfied with themselves, could be seen in small groups stretching themselves upon their blankets and with "a peace of mind known only to a conqueror", were sleeping the sleep of the "patriot victor." ₋330

Soldiers often were told to "aim at their feet" when at closer range or downhill. In the excitement, on the run, how well did the Confederates aim? ₋331

PARTRIDGE, 96TH ILL WHITAKER 2B 1D 4C: Numerous prisoners were captured, and the ground was strewn with arms and equipments. All of their dead and many of their wounded were left upon the field, and it only needed a few moments more of daylight to have made probable the capture of nearly the entire force. But even before the reinforcements had arrived darkness had begun to shut out the view, and the union forces halted soon after entering the woods. Meanwhile word had passed along the line for the members of the Ninety-Sixth, who were with Gen. Hooker's command, to return to the Battery and go from there to the breastworks, where the Field Officers, the colors and many of the men were awaiting them. At this gathering there was many a hearty hand-shake as comrades greeted those

---

330 (Holm n.d., 39)

331 Sights were set for various distances to account for a drop in trajectory over level ground. They would not be set for downhill or uphill trajectories and likely they did not practice that unless they were snipers, perhaps.

whom they feared had been killed or captured, and many an anxious inquiry for those not yet in line. _332

SMITH, 31ST INDIANA CRUFT 1B 1D 4C: The Thirty-first Regiment gathered up the dead and wounded, result of the work of the battery. There were two hundred and sixty eight dead, and probably twice that number wounded. A detail of one man from each company was sent out for ramrods, and very soon each man returned with an armload. The entire brigade suffered more or less confusion, as each regiment was more or less detached, completely flanked, and contending with such a superior force. As night had come on, we moved to the right, and bivouacked in rear of the division. _333

Ever reporting good news for home, Confederate success, described by a member of Brown's brigade as a 15-minute charge:

CJH, BROWN'S BRIGADE, STEVENSON'S DIVISION, HOOD'S CORP, CSA: when volley after volley was poured into our advancing ranks, cutting down many of our bravest and best men and making huge gaps along the line, only to be rapidly closed up as it firmly and undauntedly moved forward. The summit of the hill gained, a wild cheer burst from the lips of every man as they rushed over the breast works, routing the enemy and driving him before them, terror-stricken and in utter confusion, muskets, canteens, knapsacks, blankets, etc. thrown off in their terror and haste, strewed the ground, while a number of prisoners added to the trophies. For boldness, courage and determination, this charge has not been excelled during the war, and certainly not equaled during these late battles. Its entire success speaks for itself, while our loss will attest the danger of the undertaking. The charge was made with only eight hundred men, two regiments having been detached, and lasted fifteen minutes, the men never faltering or wavering in the least. Our loss here was over one hundred men, among them Major Barber, 3d Tennessee regiment, a gentlemen, scholar and most gallant officer. His loss is mourned by the entire command. _334

DEAVENPORT, CHAPLAIN, 3RD TENN, BROWN'S BRIGADE, STEVENSON'S DIVISION, CSA: Late in the evening Stuart and Stevenson were ordered to swing their divisions around and drive back the enemy's left which was promptly done. Stuart was on our right. It so happened that three regiments

---

332 (Partridge 1887, 320) Whitaker and the 96th returned to face the Confederate battery position sometime before the next morning's activities.
333 (Smith 1900, 99)
334 (CJH 1864)

of Brown's brigade (3rd. 18th. and 45th. Tenn.) did all the fighting, the 3rd. leading in the charge. We passed out through an old field a half mile and charged up a hill through a thick woods. It was a grand charge and the enemy were driven hastily back from their entrenched position, leaving knapsacks, haversacks, guns and it seemed as if all their rammers, for the ditches were lined with them. We gained the second hill and were halted. Our loss was light but we mourned some noble officers and men. In this charge we lost our gallant Major F. C. Barker. A nobler or more gallant soldier never fell. He was a thorough gentleman, a fine officer, a brave soldier, and I believe a Christian. He was loved by all the regiment. He was born in Pennsylvania but true to the South, answering his country's first call. He fell at his fort. Lt. W. C. Dunham also fell and six others, besides thirty-two wounded. Three color bearers were shot down, one killed, the others severely wounded. The other two regiments lost a number. After night we were ordered back to our pits. .335

At the south end of the Rebel line, after McPherson had gained a hill overlooking the town and the river that, save for a bridge, blocked the escape route, Johnston immediately has a road and a pontoon bridge built upstream.

DAY, 101ST OHIO CRUFT 1B 1D 4C: The severe fighting during the afternoon had resulted in Sherman's getting a foothold on the east side of Camp Creek, close up to the Confederate line. This, to them, was exceedingly discouraging. Moreover, General Polk, who had command of the rebel left, had lost to McPherson the very strongest position on that part of the Confederate line, and though he tried in very desperation to dislodge the boys in blue, he failed in every attempt, and at last, about 10 o'clock at night, gave it up. This brought the railroad and wagon bridges over the Oostanaula within range of Sherman's guns. Having lost these bridges, Johnston at once ordered the laying of a pontoon further up the river, out of range of McPherson's guns. He was also obliged to cut a new road to this new bridge. In the meantime, Sherman had also caused the laying of a pontoon at Lay's Ferry, a short distance down the river. .336

Johnston also learns that Sherman's project further south was getting somewhere.

JOHNSTON, CSA: On the 14th the enemy made several attacks, the most vigorous on Hindman's division (Hood's left). All were handsomely

335 (Deavenport 1861-1864)
336 (Day 1894, 205)

repulsed. At 6 p.m. Hood advanced with Stevenson's and Stewart's divisions, supported by two of Walker's brigades, driving the enemy from his ground before night. He was instructed to be ready to continue the offensive next morning. At 9 p.m. I learned that Lieutenant-General Polk's troops had lost a position commanding our bridges, and received from Major-General Martin a report that Federal infantry was crossing the Oostenaula, near Calhoun, on a pontoon bridge. The instructions to Lieutenant-General Hood were revoked. _337

Johnston had sent two brigades from the south to assist. That is what cost him the hill Sherman and Hooker had shared, a present from General Logan.

STEWART, HOODS CORPS, CSA: quoted by Ridley: Thursday night (12th) we brought up the rear of the corps in retiring to Tilton. Friday night (13th) we bivouacked along railroad some three miles in advance of Resaca and on Saturday morning (14th) took position in a line crossing the railroad forming the right of the army—my right resting on the Connesauga. About 5 p.m. in compliance with the orders of the Lieutenant-General commanding corps, I moved out along the railroad formed in two lines parallel to the road and advanced to attack the enemy's left. We moved forward a distance of one and a half or two miles, getting sight of the enemy's line near Union Church which, however, hastily retired. By this time, owing to the eagerness of the men, the lines had become somewhat separated and I halted to reform. In the meantime we were subjected to a heavy fire of artillery which, however, caused but little or no loss. By the time the lines were reformed night had come on and I deemed it imprudent to advance farther. Toward midnight, under orders, we retired to our position in line. _338

No mention of failure to accomplish anything.

CJH, BROWN'S BRIGADE, STEVENSON'S DIVISION, CSA: After holding this hill until 12 o'clock, we were ordered to retire to our entrenchments where we spent the remainder of the night. _339

STEVENSON, CMDG DIVISION HOOD'S CORP CSA: I was much gratified by the gallantry with which the movement was made, and by the success which attended it. Too much praise cannot be awarded Brown's gallant brigade.

337 (OR, Series I Vol 38 Part 3 Serial 74: Reports n.d., 615)
338 (Ridley 1906, 307)
339 (CJH 1864)

For particulars I refer you to his report. Late that night I received orders to retire from the position which I had taken, which was done. .340

Why withdraw to their rear line?

CORSE: To Sherman, May 15, early. General Sweeny crossed about 200 men in boats after dark last night, and pushed back the pickets in their immediate front, capturing some 20 or 30 prisoners and a flag. Hearing that enemy were crossing at Calhoun Ferry from different, and to him authentic, sources, he withdrew without attacking the enemy's works or sending more over. .341 .342

JOHNSTON, CSA: At 9 p. m. I learned that Lieutenant-General Polk's troops had lost a position commanding our bridges, and received from Major-General Martin a report that Federal infantry was crossing the Oostenaula, near Calhoun, on a pontoon bridge. The instructions to Lieutenant-General Hood were revoked, and Walker's division sent to the point named by Major-General Martin.

The day's work ended with Johnston withdrawing to the ridge, foiled in his flank of the Union left by Simonson's 5th Indiana Battery's furious defense and Robinson's arrival leading Williams' division. Then, hearing that Sweeny had crossed at Lay's Ferry, Johnston, fearing for his left, withdrew further, to his line of the previous night, unaware that Sweeny, being repulsed, had re-crossed—an admirable feint.

That coveted ridge had not been occupied at all by the Yanks. Now it was vacant, open for occupation by anyone who dared.

Another result: two more Yankee divisions facing it.

ROBINSON, 3B 1D 20C: The troops now bivouacked in line of battle. .343

BENTON, BAND, 150TH NY RUGER 2B 1D 20C: The battery was saved and the day was saved. Once more the enemy had been foiled; but it was only a

---

340 (OR, Series I Vol 38 Part 3 Serial 74: Reports n.d., 812)
341 (OR, Series I Vol 38 Part 4 Serial 75: Correspondence n.d., 196). "last night" being the night of the 14th.
342 John Murray Corse, Brigadier General, served on Sherman's staff while recovering from wounds received in the Battle of Chattanooga.
http://genealogytrails.com/iowa/bio_john_m_corse.htm
343 (OR, Series I Vol 38 Part 2 Serial 73: Reports n.d., 85)

skirmish after all, and is scarcely mentioned in history; the battle was as yet hardly begun. It is very rarely that one is thus enabled to see plainly both sides in an engagement. .344

The Limit of His Capacity?

BENTON, BAND, 150TH NY RUGER 2B 1D 20C: "Fighting Joe," as he was generally called, was the very ideal of a corps commander. The fact that he had failed to fully oust the Washington politicians from the command of the Army of the Potomac was no more than was true of all his predecessors, and if he was sometimes a little touchy towards his superior officers that fact did not militate against his popularity with the rank and file. True he had the reputation of working and fighting his corps most unflinchingly, but he also had the record of successes, as well as of being exceedingly careful and considerate of the welfare of his men. He was a superb horseman, and in time of action seemed to be always present and always happy. His really manly qualities were so evident that it was no wonder he was popular. My own judgment at this distance of time is that the handling of a corps was about the limit of his capacity as a general, but that up to that point few, if any, were his superiors. .345

May we observe here that this was not the first time General Williams was called on to take his entire division out of position to rescue a battery—successfully— another being Gettysburg.

The trajectory of Hooker's star had veered north—taking with it all who wore a star of the 20th Corps.

Nightfall, the 14th

The cavalry had tried to help rescue Simonson too but could not get through. McCook observed an advantage to the Rebels.

McCook (CAVALRY) TO STANLEY: I had ridden over to see you when the attempt was made to turn your left. The ridge on which it rests is the continuation of the one I spoke of in my note to you to-day as lying between us. I found it impossible to drive the enemy off and open ammunition with you. The other end of this ridge rests near Resaca, and from observation of

344 (Benton 1902, 136)
345 (Benton 1902, 1128)

the movements of the rebels, I judge they can move an infantry force along it without difficulty. .346

Rebels had indeed readily moved those two brigades from south to north.

Earlier in the day, as Stanley was pressing south, Sherman sent a message emphasizing the need to establish a line to the railroad. It was not done, and the gap still existed.

General Schofield's men still could not retrieve the wounded who could not get back, nor the dead who had lain all day. The "remains of the day" help him make a decision.

> THRUSTIN, CO D, 111TH OHIO, HARKER, 2B3D23C: After dark I went down upon the field with Major Norris and could distinctly hear the suppressed voices of rebel soldiers, busy in front of their lines, robbing our dead and wounded. We ventured out far enough to reach some of the foremost of our dead, and there among the rest lay the adjutant of the ___ Michigan, dressed as for a reception, his new dress coat buttoned from chin to waist, his hands were in close fitting kid gloves. His face was to the ground, his drawn sword under him, his body rigid in death. We readily raised his slight form, and making a stretcher of his sword scabbard, bore him off the field.

> General Judah was at once relieved of his command, and General Hascall promoted to the command of the division. .347

346 (OR, Series I Vol 38 Part 4 Serial 75: Correspondence n.d., 180)
347 (Thrustin 1894)

Bickerdyke

While battle was in full swing, arriving this evening, after months of preparation and an arduous journey, is the help many boys need tonight.

MRS PORTER, SANITARY COMMISSION: Near the battleground, Sugar Creek, Ga. General Logan's Headquarters May 15[14]

I have just reached this place, where I bear the constant roar which tells of battle and of death. The battle has just commenced, and several wounded have been brought in who are to be sent north. Our batteries are engaged. The poor privates who are wounded cannot leave at once.

Mrs. Bickerdyke left on the 10th for Chattanooga. I followed on Wednesday, in company with Rev. Drs. Budington and Thompson, N. Y. agents of the Christian Commission, sent here on a tour of observation. We reached Chattanooga yesterday morning. I found Mrs. Bickerdyke had gone on to Ringgold, and so I took the noon train and came down to Ringgold, where I found Mrs. Bickerdyke in the Sanitary rooms, preparing supplies to take forward in teams that were going out in the morning. We slept in a soldier's tent that night and were in readiness to start in the morning. Mrs. Bickerdyke had sent forword the evening before such sanitary stores as could be taken in the teams.

I wish I could give you clear description of our mule train. Along solemn train of mule teams! most of them looking as if dragging heavily, and many making a mighty effort to take their last load to the scene of strife. Can you imagine such a train? reaching all the way from Ringgold to Sugar Creek, a distance of twenty five miles. Such a train almost literally filled the way with supplies to our army to-day. The supplies are to go by railroad soon, and the mules which are falling on the right hand and on the left, from over-work, poor fare and exhaustion will be relieved.

We reached Sugar Creek about 6 o'clock, and were most kindly received at Gen. Logan's headquarters —where I am now writing—by Gen. Smith and others of his staff. They informed us that Gen. Logan had been on the battlefield since last evening. The enemy's guns are loud and rapid now, and although I do not think we can go to the battlefield tonight, it will be difficult to stay away from it while this roar of artillery continues, knowing that many poor fellows are needing our care and attention.

Col. Smith has assured Mrs. Bickerdyke that the ambulance or anything else which he can furnish, shall be supplied to aid her in her work. Mrs. Bickerdyke was very desirous of going to the hospital in the field immediately to night, but it was not best. It is five miles distant, and she needs rest. .348

They will stay with the hospitals for the rest of the campaign.

Banter

TREMAIN: Saturday night was again a busy night for both armies. The enemy was at work strengthening his positions and making further dispositions of troops. Our army was performing similar duties. The new advanced positions were fortified; troops who had been in the front all day were relieved by fresh ones from the rear, and our lines were so strengthened by art as to enable them to be held by a much smaller number of troops. .349

When Williams and Geary, who had been in reserve, were called north, Butterfield was forward, skirmishing, and was left south. Their day is ending relatively quietly.

FLEHARTY, 102ND ILL WARD 1B 3D 20C: Towards evening the sounds of battle died away, and finally dwindled down to the irregular firing of the skirmishers. At dusk we retired to our position in the ravine. The regiment had lost during the day three men killed, and nineteen wounded. Late at night the camp was hushed in repose, and beneath the lovely foliage of the trees we slept sweetly but ere we slept, we looked up through our leafy covering to the bright stars that twinkled so peacefully in the calm blue sky, and thought of other and distant skies of peace of those far away, as dear to us as life and thought of the morrow. At 2 o'clock next morning we were aroused, and ordered to resume the advance position that had been abandoned the evening before. During the time intervening before day light, slight breast-works were thrown up the first we ever built. .350

STORRS, 20TH CONN COBURN 2B 3D 20C: The troops bivouacked in the positions where darkness overtook them, with only the occasional crack of some picket rifle, or the seeming prayer of the Rebel night bird to God that He would "whipoorwill" (Sherman) disturbed the stillness of the summer's

348 (Porter 1866, 659)
349 (Tremain 1905, 171)
350 (Fleharty, Our Regiment. A History of the 102d Illinois Infantry Volunteers 1865, 52)

night. Though fatigued and sleepy, the "dull God" came not to steal away the senses so entirely that the wicked "zip" of an occasional bullet passing over or striking and awaking some soldier near could not be heard, still, it was rest for the weary body and occasionally the weary spirit within would busy itself among the peaceful scenes of childhood, only to be rudely awoke to the terrible realities of the position, perhaps by the dreaded bugle call at reveille, which, to a soldier, was worse than death to disobey. The forenoon was comparatively quiet. 351

HURST, 73RD OHIO WOOD 3B 3D 20C: AFTER resting on arms all night, we began skirmishing early on the morning of the 14th. The enemy had been busy all night fortifying. We could hear thousands of axes going all the night long. This day there was considerable "fighting on our left parts of the Fourth, Fourteenth and Twentieth corps being engaged. Our division remained in line all day, and at night dug rifle-pits. We are quite close to the rebel works, and our skirmishers talk with theirs across a little valley of two hundred yards' width. One could hear from the hillside conversation something like this. Yank says: "Johnny Reb! John! got anything to eat over there?—got any corn bread?" Reb replies: "Yes; come over and get some. Say! are you Hooker's men?—Where's Old Joe?" "O, he's 'round; you've heard of old Joe, have ye?" And again: "Say, Yank! did you make anything on the left to-day?" "Yes; we made a h—l of a noise." "O, Reb! what's you-'uns goin' to do tomorrow?—goin' to fight we'uns?" "Say, Yank! got anything to trade?" And occasionally the characteristics of the chivalry came out in this style: "O, Yank! is your captain a white man or a nigger?" "Say I got any commissary over there?—pass over your canteen." And thus, for hours, there would be a skirmish of words, sometimes pungent, but often good-natured. 352

Butterfield's blue stars did not yet know they will soon join the red and white.

Sherman's telegram to Washington makes his intent plain: flush them out of the hills to open country. That is his intent tomorrow, unless by chance he can bag them here. He already has some cavalry south, keeping them out of sight, and is hoping they can block the railroad south of Calhoun.

SHERMAN TO HALLECK: May 14 8 pm: We have had hard fighting all day. Johnston purely on the defensive. The place has small detached redoubts, and in immense amount of rifle trenches. We have close the enemy well in, gaining ground slowly but securely all day. The country is very rough and

351 (Storrs 1886, 127)
352 (Hurst 1866, 117)

woody. *I will renew the attack at all points to-morrow, and continue till Johnston retreats, and then shall follow.* General Sweeny's division, Sixteenth Corps, with a pontoon train, tried to cross the Oostenaula at Lay's Ferry, below Calhoun, but was stoutly opposed by a heavy force in the dense timber on the opposite bank. General Howard's corps followed the enemy down from Dalton, and his right now joins to our main line, and my forces are all united, the line extending from the Oostenaula above to below the town. General Stoneman's cavalry division is on the east of the river, and General Garrard's division of cavalry is sent around by the right to cross the Oostenaula, above Rome, if possible, and break the railroad north of Kingston.

May 15

Late at night the camp was hushed in repose, and beneath the lovely foliage of the trees we slept sweetly but ere we slept, we looked up through our leafy covering to the bright stars that twinkled so peacefully in the calm blue sky, and thought of other and distant skies of peace of those far away, as dear to us as life and thought of the morrow. —Fleharty

Sunday has ever been the day of battle. —Bradley

Words cannot express the feeling when I saw the battle flags unfurled. —Noble

This was plainest and loudest preatching that I ever atended on sond.a —Banks

The civilian reader must not suppose when he reads accounts of military operations in which relative position of the forces are defined ... that these were matters of general knowledge to those engaged. Such statements are commonly made, even by those high in command, in the light of later disclosures, such as the enemy's official reports. It is seldom, indeed, that a subordinate officer knows anything about the disposition of the enemy's forces—except that it is unamiable—or precisely whom he is fighting. As to the rank and file, they can know nothing more of the matter than the arms they carry. They hardly know what troops are upon their own right or left the length of a regiment away. If it is a cloudy day they are ignorant even of the points of the compass. It may be said, generally, that a soldier's knowledge of what is going on about him is coterminous with his official relation to it and his personal connection with it; what is going on in front of him he does not know at all until he learns it afterward. — Ambrose Bierce .353

*There is some conflict of testimony in the case, but one quarter of such a number of witnesses, seldom agree, and even if all had been on one side some discrepancy might have been expected. We are to try and reconcile them, and to believe that they are not intentionally erroneous, as long as we can. —*Abraham Lincoln, speech to jury in the Rock Island Bridge case. .354 .355 .356

---

353 The Crime at Pickett's Mill (Bierce n.d.)

354 (Lincoln, The Collected Works of Abraham Lincoln 1809-1865 n.d.)

355 Lincoln's only recorded closing arguments. Steamboaters sued to have the first railroad bridge over the Mississippi condemned as a hazard to navigation. The trial was a pretense, pursued by interests wanting a bridge at St. Louis instead of Rock Island, but pretending to support the rivermen. With confounding witness testimony, the jury divided evenly—though all lived near the railroad.

356 (Riney 2007)

Reader, prepare for a long day. To understand what the soldiers experienced, we must understand the battle, which can be understood only in light of the views of those who directed it. To let us grasp what the soldiers saw, and did, and felt, so much depends on the who and why and how and what and when, that the details are hard to omit. If they are too much, just follow along and share the confusion and feel the effects.

While accounts of the battle agree in main, much of the record disagrees in detail and includes conflicting claims, confusing efforts to give a full accounting. The timings of placements on the field and of events are inconsistent, and it even appears that some are using clocks from a different time zone. The author has matched details from both official and private correspondence, enough to feel confident that the following order of extracts present the careful reader with an adequate description of events. However, some descriptions defy being fit, like parts of a jigsaw puzzle, and tell the story better if left to the reader to fit them in broader context, lacking the specifics to resolve inconsistencies.

Much of the confusion results from desires of the reporters to present themselves in the best light and from lapses of days, months, and often years before writing their version of events from memory. And often what seems first person is a retelling of another claimed first person in the desire to appear to be authoritative. Most eye-opening to the author was that many, even among officers at the regiment and often the brigade level, were completely unaware of positions and actions of the others, even next to them, on the same part of the battlefield. Smoke from black powder contributed to their confusion to the extent of affecting the outcome of this particular battle.

The effort to get the record straight was motivated by the argument over who should have credit for the capture of the battery and by corresponding absence of claim, or blame, for firing into the backs of their fellow soldiers. Thus, the quote of Lincoln's opening comments to the jury. The author has quoted without prejudice wherever possible as long as he can but has not shirked from leaving before you evidence of dubious testimony, whether it was given to deceive intentionally or otherwise.

Readers are, of course, free to pursue their own travels of the record and perhaps find some relevant details that were missed and further refine the battle record.

In most tellings, the timing of events is compressed, giving the reader a false sense of fast action where there might really have been much waiting or slow methodical movement. Infantry fought in two ranks of men packed touching elbow in order to concentrate firepower, one volley per rank taking, at best, 20 seconds to reload–much more under less than ideal conditions—with movements in lockstep. Seeing and hearing the soldiers and trying to manage them can be nearly impossible. Communication was by foot or by horse, often taking time to write questions or orders in longhand. The reader will need to adjust—to view events as dragging on with perhaps some short flashes of fast action and long periods of slow movement. Bullets and cannonballs were fast. Humans were slow. What you see on paper and imagine in your mind was mostly hidden to the soldier on the ground.

The tellings of any participant or witness does not make sense of the whole day, each on its own. For them to tell the story together, snippets from each are ordered in time and place as best the author can determine. But the statements are unchanged. If someone said noon when others said 1 or 1:30, the reader can determine whether the time is "close enough."

Otherwise, this is a story told by discovery, fascinating in anticipation and realization of what the soldiers dealt with and experienced.

Sherman's Midnight Message

NEW YORK HERALD: The position occupied by the rebel army on Sunday morning was, notwithstanding Sherman's successes on Saturday, altogether more advantageous than that of the previous day. His troops were concentrated on a short line, strongly intrenched throughout its length, with a broad stream with marshy banks covering his centre, which was posted on commanding heights beyond this stream, while his left flank was covered by the strong works that had been constructed with great care and time at Resaca, and his right resting against the river, after crossing a range of hills fully fortified with redoubts, masked batteries and rifle pits. The river in the vicinity of Resaca makes a deep bend to the south, forming a perfect *cul de sac*, across the mouth of which the rebel line extended. The position was such that Johnston's army, with eighty thousand men, at an estimate, was thrown into line of battle but little more than two miles in length. Of course, in a line so compactly formed, a weak spot would be difficult to find. _357

Hooker is now at the far north instead of the middle. So Sherman makes further rearrangements, to have Davis, for one, instead of Hooker, ready to go over with Sweeny on Sherman's project at Lay's Ferry.

NEW YORK HERALD: The operations of the previous day, in which General Hooker had borne a conspicuous part with portions of his corps, had convinced that officer that the key to this strong position was in the heights on the right of the rebel line, on which they had rested on the previous day.

357 (Bradley 1865, 98)

They All Wore a Star

On communicating this impression to General Sherman, Hooker was directed to storm and carry these heights. ⎽358 As one of his divisions, that of General Butterfield, was detached at this time, General Hooker asked to have that division returned to him as preliminary to this assault, a request that was promptly granted, and the gap formed on the right by Butterfield's withdrawal, was filled by an extension of Palmer's line to the right. This position virtually gave Hooker the left of the line, with Howard's corps as a support. The rest of the line remained substantially unchanged. ⎽359

Hooker tells Sherman of his exploit and advises a two-pronged advance, one along the railroad and the other down the Dalton road.

> HOOKER, 20C: TO SHERMAN: 12:30 am: I reached the left in season to prevent the enemy turning it. … Had any considerable portion of my corps been in position I would have followed up the success.
>
> To do it effectually in the morning, in my judgment, the advance should be on two lines, one along the line of railroad, the other along the Dalton and Resaca highway. All the troops should be in position by daylight. My position for to-night is on the high ground in the vicinity of where Morris' Creek crosses the Dalton road. ⎽360

So—Sherman to Thomas:

> SHERMAN TO THOMAS: Midnight General Hooker has just been here and tells me his whole corps is on the extreme left with General Howard. Schofield is thus thrown at the angle. Order Hooker and Howard to attack in the morning directly south down upon Resaca. I will order Schofield to fight down the valley of Camp Creek, and I wish you to keep General Palmer's corps on the bluffs on this side of Camp Creek on the defensive. I find his troops quite thick this afternoon, and suggest you send Jeff. Davis' division, which was in reserve on Palmer's right, filling the gap made by Hooker's withdrawal to the extreme left and Harrow's division which is now in support of McPherson's advance line. This change should be ordered at once and completed by daylight. I think if Johnston has observed the changes he will endeavor to be on the ground taken by McPherson this evening and attack him in force, I think Palmer may take a defensive line

358 Hooker talked to reporters. Sherman did not. Sherman's messages later in the morning suggest assault was not to be Hooker's primary object.
359 (Bradley 1865, 98)
360 (OR, Series I Vol 38 Part 1 Serial 75: Reports n.d., 193)

279

from McPherson's battery on Bald Hill to where we found Schofield's right, and as the line of Hooker and Howard advances Schofield will be crowded and may be sent to the extreme left, where he belongs. Please answer this to-night, as I do not wish to sleep till I know you have made this necessary order. _361

So Schofield is to move around to the far left on the north, with Hooker taking position at the angle.

THOMAS TO SHERMAN: 1 am Your dispatch of 12 midnight received. Before I left the field this evening I had ordered General Hooker on the extreme left, and Palmer to take care of the ground left by Hooker, on the heights bordering Camp Creek, with instructions to prepare his line so as to make it as near impregnable as possible. Butterfield's division has been ordered out and directed to join Hooker's left, and had commenced moving before I left the field, leaving Palmer to hold his line with two divisions.

I have just received a dispatch from General Hooker, in which he informs me that one of his brigade and Fifth Indiana Battery successfully resisted an attempt on part of Hood's corps to turn our left. The substance of your instructions were ordered by me before I left the field. Your orders for the advance of Howard and Hooker in the morning will be reiterated. Palmer has also been ordered that as soon as his left is relieved by the advance of Schofield and Hooker, he support that movement with his left flank. _362

FULLERTON, ADJUTANT, 4TH CORP: Timeline 5 am. Received orders from Major-General Thomas, dated 1.30 a.m. stating that this corps and Hooker's would attack the enemy "in the morning directly down upon Resaca;" Schofield, when he became crowded out of his present position in line, to move around to his proper position on the extreme left (this was done before the attack of the a.m. commenced), and General Palmer's corps would remain in a defensive position, holding his strong position on the right (General McPherson to operate on the extreme right against the enemy's communications). As soon as this order was received it was sent to division commanders, with instructions to examine the enemy's most vulnerable points in their fronts with a view to attack, and informing them that this corps would conform its movements with General Hooker's. _363

361 (OR, Series I Vol 38 Part 4 Serial 75: Correspondence n.d., 189)
362 (OR, Series I Vol 38 Part 4 Serial 75: Correspondence n.d., 189)
363 (OR, Series I Vol 38 Part 1 Serial 75: Reports n.d., 854)

Hooker now has the starring role. _364

Five AM - Sherman's Special Orders

The movement of the troops for to-day will be as follows:

I. Major-General McPherson, re-enforced by the cavalry division of General Kilpatrick, will continue to threaten the line of the enemy's communications by a pontoon near Lay's Ferry and a good lodgment on the other bank. He will hold the strong defensive position gained yesterday from the Bald Hill to the Oostenaula near the mouth of Camp Creek, prepared at all times to assume the offensive.

II. Major-General Thomas will hold one corps (General Palmer's) on the defensive, holding the line of hills on the west side of Camp Creek, connecting strong with General McPherson on a line with the Bald Hill, with a reserve in the large field behind it (i. e. the cleared valley of the west branch of Camp Creek). *The other two corps, Hooker's and Howard's, will make a steady and strong attack on the enemy along down the ridge between Camp Creek and the Connesauga toward Resaca,* but w*ill not assault fortified positions unless sure of success.*

III. Major-General Schofield will support the line of General Howard and General Hooker, and be prepared to resume his place on the left as soon as the ground will permit. *During the advance he will hold his troops to the left rear of General Howard and General Hooker's line.*

IV. All the troops should be in position for action at daylight and the general movement begin at 8 a.m. _365

Item II seemed to be asking Hooker and Howard to come right down that road behind the enemy line, which faced Sherman's forces across Camp Creek, a superior flank if they could pull it off. They'd have to get by Hood first, but Sherman did not want an assault if it might fail. Shortly we will learn his more realistic expectations.

Sweeny's division, in Dodge's 16th Corps, in McPherson's army, is to get across at Lay's Ferry. Thomas will hold the line north of McPherson, with Schofield moving to cover the north end, while Hooker and Howard press the Rebel line.

---

364 Pun irresistible.
365 (OR, Series I Vol 38 Part 4 Serial 75: Correspondence n.d., 199)

Sweeny got another start with the special project, even starting a feint further upriver:

> CORSE: To Sherman, May 15, morning.He [Sweeny] sent a party over this morning about daylight and brought over the wounded left there last night, and the officers reported they could see nothing. Upon this information he endeavored to cross his command, when the enemy appeared in strong force. He is now making efforts to push over some troops in the boats under cover of banks lined with skirmishers. Colonel Bane, with two regiments of infantry and a battery of artillery, was sent last night to Calhoun Ferry, and this morning directed to open and make all demonstration possible. General Sweeny will make every effort to get a bridge over. An officer has just reported that we have got two boat-loads over, and the rest of Colonel Rice's brigade is crossing rapidly as possible in a place about one mile distant from where the pontoon boats were launched (and which is a dangerous place now, the enemy having discovered our object). _366

Dawn - Butterfield Moves North

Butterfield's 3rd Division was still near the south of the Union lines, opposite Camp Creek, and not with the other two divisions at the north. Now our heroes awake and learn their turn has finally arrived. Enthusiasm is less than intense.

> FLEHARTY, 102ND ILL WARD 1B 3D 20C: The morning of Sunday, May 15, 1864, dawned luridly upon us. The smoke of innumerable camp fires had enveloped hill and valley in a hazy mantle. At six o'clock we were ordered to move around to the left of the 14th Army Corps. Quietly we marched back over the hill, and through the shadowy forest, almost feeling the death-like stillness of that memorable Sabbath morning. And how like entering the valley of the shadow of death, seemed our march down through the smoky atmosphere into the deep valley, and around to our new position confronting the enemy. Our Division had been selected for the desperate work of charging a rebel battery, which was supported by a strong force of the enemy behind entrenchments. The ulterior object was to break the enemy's line at that point, and thereby cut the rebel army in twain. _367

> CASE, 129TH ILL WARD 1B 3D 20C: Early on the morning of the 15th the brigade was relieved, and the entire division moved from their position (the center) to the extreme left of the line of battle. While on the march I was

---

366 (OR, Series I Vol 38 Part 4 Serial 75: Correspondence n.d., 197)
367 (Fleharty, Our Regiment. A History of the 102d Illinois Infantry Volunteers 1865, 52)

notified that our brigade was ordered to charge and carry at the point of the bayonet the fort and rifle-pits of the enemy, supported by the Second and Third Brigades of the Third Division. ..368

CONGLETON, CO F 105TH ILL WARD 1B 3D 20C: This is the Holy Sabbath day which we are commanded to remember and keep. While our relatives and friends in the North are at church, these two hostile armys are striving for some advantage war goes on just the same. This morning Gen. Butterfield's Division (3rd Div. 20th Corps) was withdrawn from the lines which we occupied (other troops taking our place) and marched around through the timber to the Dalton road which we followed for quite a distance when we halted. ..369

NOBLE, 19TH MICH COBURN 2B 3D 20C: We recd orders last night to fortify our position and we worked by reliefs into daylight—throwing up breastworks. This morning we have orders to be ready to move forward immediately. Again we expect to participate in the fighting of today. I can but say that I have the privilege but had rather keep out—if we are not needed. But if they need us I shall do my duty faithfully and if I fall I feel confident that it will be well with me. I put my trust in God and hope for the best. I think that today's fighting will decide the battle. ..370

DICKINSON, CO E 22ND WIS COBURN 2B 3D 20C: May 15th. On this day was fought the battle of Resaca, the 22nd Regiment, early in the morning, moved around to the left, about 6 miles. Passing the 23rd and 4th Corps, massed, line upon line, and came upon the field of yesterday. ..371

NOBLE, 19TH MICH COBURN 2B 3D 20C: Although our regt and Brigade was so near the enemy we did not get into any action until Sunday the 15th of May and I have reason to believe that there are many of our Division that will remember that day to the latest period of their lives. We had been lying back in sight of where our troops were skirmishing with the enemy for about ten days and had not seen the rebels in any force. But Sunday morning our Corps commanded by Gen Hooker was ordered forward. We marched some five miles around on one of the enemy's flanks and joined Gen Howard's Corps which had been desperately fighting the day before. ..372

368 (OR, Series I Vol 38 Part 2 Serial 73: Reports n.d., 365)
369 (Congleton n.d.)
370 (Noble n.d.)
371 (Dickinson n.d.)
372 (Noble n.d.)

BRADLEY, 22ND WIS 2B 3D 20C: From the Madison Journal: Sunday has ever been the day of battle, and having rested from 12 o'clock midnight, after building a strong line of breastworks, we move early in the morning a distance of about six miles to the left around our lines, passing the 23d and 4th corps massed line upon line, and come upon the field of yesterday. There is an ominous silence, and the busy hum of preparation stirs the air. ˍ373

MERRILL, 70TH IND WARD 1B 3D 20C: On the morning of May fifteenth the regiment was relieved and marched to the left several miles, and as it was Sunday saw men of other organizations engaged in religious services. As the report gained credence that a charge was to be made on the enemy's works, some humorous semisolemn remarks were made by men who were not frequent listeners to the Chaplain's sermons, as to the desirability of halting and spending the day in devotional exercises. ˍ374

Rebels Take the Hill Again

Note: the various accounts of the previous day's efforts on the hill are inconsistent about who had occupied the hill when. Hood's men state they took the hill from Howard, which includes Stanley and Wood. Stanley's men never mention getting quite that far. But the convincing effect of Hood's accounts are that the flank attempt Saturday started from either the front line or even the main line, further back, not from the hill that faced the little plain. No doubt Hood's men had skirmishers there, at least. Regardless, the forward line had been vacant during the night.

The Union had not moved into the forward line that Stevenson and Stewart had evacuated. During the night the hill had been vacant, unoccupied, while plans were being made to capture it! So now Confederates moved back — seeking advantage.

STEVENSON, CMDG DIVISION, HOOD'S CORP, CSA: The next morning I was ordered to retake it, which was accomplished without difficulty, the enemy not having reoccupied it. My command immediately went to work to construct defenses of logs and rails, and in a short time were quite well intrenched. ˍ375

---

373 (Bradley 1865, 100)
374 (S. Merrill 1900, 64)
375 (OR, Series I Vol 38 Part 3 Serial 74: Reports n.d., 812) "It" being the line they abandoned in preparation to retreat if Sweeny had held his crossing at Lay's Ferry.

STEWART, CMDG DIVISION, HOOD'S CORPS, CSA: On Sunday morning (15th) my line was advanced, the right of it half a mile and passing in front of Mr. Green's house, the left only a few hundred yards and the new position was soon intrenched. .376

CJH BROWN'S BRIGADE, STEVENSON'S DIVISION, CSA: Sunday morning, at an early hour, we were again ordered forward to take position on the eminence on our front, which we supposed was occupied by the enemy, but our skirmishers moved forward without interruption, and we were soon heavily engaged in throwing up hasty breastworks of logs, chincky, and whatever came to hand. By 10 o'clock in the morning they were completed and everything in readiness to meet whatever aggressive movement the enemy contemplates. .377

DEAVENPORT, CHAPLAIN, 3RD TENN, BROWN'S BRIGADE, STEVENSON'S DIVISION, CSA: Early next morning we again went out to the first hill and formed our line. Never did I see fortifications built so fast, and it was well, for soon the enemy came forward in fearful numbers to drive us from our position. .378

ABRAMS, ATLANTA INTELLIGENCER, WITH STEWART'S DIVISION, CSA: In the morning our forces left their works, and took position about one mile further, and immediately erected new breastworks on the ground they had captured the night previous, and which the enemy had not reoccupied. The object of this advance was to prevent an enfilading fire which had been obtained on our line the day previous, and to find room for our artillery to play upon the enemy with effect. As soon as our men, composed of Stevenson's and Stewart's divisions, advanced, a brisk fire ensued between our skirmishers and those of the Yankees, but it ceased on the arrival of our column. The new works were promptly erected, and before ten o'clock every thing was prepared for the anticipated aggressive movement of the enemy, whose maneuvers the night previous, after they were driven from the ridges, indicated that some plan was contemplated by them for regaining of the lost ground. .379

WESLEY CONNOR, PRIVATE, CHEROKEE ARTILLERY, CSA: Sunday May 15, 1864 8h A.M. Moved to the ridge on the right of the Resaca road, one and a half

376 (Ridley 1906, 307)
377 (CJH 1864)
378 (Deavenport 1861-1864)
379 (Abrams 1864) Including trenches in front of the main line.

miles from R. – The position we hold was taken from the Yankees by Gen. Stevenson late yesterday afternoon. .380 .381

CINCINNATI COMMERCIAL: During last night quiet reigned along the whole line, the enemy being very quiet and rarely firing shot. The falling of trees and the sound of ax-men, however, convinced our commanders that the rebels were erecting strong fortifications upon the innumerable hills that rise out of the valley. At half-past seven in the morning our skirmishers opened fire upon the rebel line, which was as vigorously returned upon the left and left-center. The enemy, however, did not seem disposed to attack with their main line, after the fearful slaughter and repulse that Hooker administered to them last night. .382

7 AM Taking Stock

An early consultation between Howard and Hooker.

FULLERTON, ADJUTANT, 4TH CORP: Timeline At 7 a.m. went to General Hooker's headquarters. Generals Howard and Hooker had consultation about the attack. .383

Geary sent some of his 3rd Brigade to find out what was in their front. They reported nothing except cavalry of both sides, not unexpected.

GEARY, 2D 20C: At 7 a.m. I received orders to send a strong reconnoitering party, with a staff officer, to explore eastward toward the railroad. The Sixtieth New York Volunteers, Colonel Godard, and Seventy-eighth New York Volunteers, Lieutenant-Colonel Chatfield, were detailed for the purpose, and accompanied by Captain Forbes, inspector on my staff, performed the duty, striking the railroad Isaac Adams' house, where they ascertained the enemy's cavalry to be posted, and also found our outposts from McCook's cavalry command. By 11 a.m. they had returned. .384

---

380 (W. O. Connor, Wesley Olin Connor Diary 1867) The position then was behind the line.
381 And then abandoned.
382 (Correspondence of the Cincinnati Commercial 1864)
383 (OR, Series I Vol 38 Part 1 Serial 75: Reports n.d., 854)
384 (OR, Series I Vol 38 Part 2 Serial 73: Reports n.d., 118)

Grunert's company had been pickets during the night and were left behind. As they found their way north to their brigade, the opposing armies were already busy.

> GRUNERT, CO D 129TH ILL WARD 1B 3D 20C: As yesterday, so to-day, shots were fired early, but having taken positions behind trees, we were safe from such shots, and exposed only to the bullets of the rebel sharpshooters posted in trees. No one, however, of our regiment or brigade was killed or wounded while on picket. After some skirmishing of two hours we were relieved by other (strange) troops, and we were told that our brigade had left its position and moved off early in the morning. This seemed strange, as a regiment or brigade never leaves its positions without drawing in the pickets first. _385 As it was so, however, we supposed that the brigade had been ordered away in a hurry to a place where its services were needed. A staff officer had remained to draw in the pickets and guide them to the brigade. As we had not had anything to eat the evening before, nor early in the morning, and as we were in no particular hurry to find the brigade, which, was no easy matter, we took our time in marching. After many inquiries on the part of the staff officer as to the whereabouts of the division, we at last found it four miles to the right of our former camp in the woods, where Gen. Palmer's men had been stationed heretofore. We went to our respective regiments and took our places. Along the whole line there was fighting going on, and in the distance we heard distinctly the deafening yells of an attacking party, which a few seconds later were drowned by the dreadful roar of cannon and musket fire and exploding shells. Here a picket line advanced towards the enemy in his rifle pits, who continually fired on the advancing line; there ambulances were hurrying off and past with their loads of groaning and crying wounded. Everywhere the awful reality of war and battle stared in our faces; everywhere the fight was raging, except in our own front. But we should not long remain idle, and soon have the pleasure of testing the enemy. The enemy had a fort with three guns in our front and attempts to take it had been unsuccessful, on account of the terrific fire with shot, shell and canister. _386

Things were still quiet just up the Dalton road beyond the north end. Assistant Surgeon Cook, with Williams' division, witnessed a meeting.

385 Grunert's company had been skirmishers overnight and were left in place when the rest of the regiment moved to the left.
386 Some differences in accounts of quiet along the line and of steady firing and attempts to take the fort are unexplainable.

COOK, ASST. SURGEON, 150TH NY RUGER 2B 1D 20C: The next morning, unlike the past six or eight, there was no rattle of musketry to be heard—no roar of artillery—no moving of infantry; all was as quiet and serene as a Sabbath morning should be. About 9 A.M. it began to be evident that the different corps commanders were in consultation and had selected a little grove just by our camp for the place of consultation. .387 I forget now, how many generals we saw there, but with their several staffs and body guards there was several acres of them; perhaps acres would be a better way to judge of them. First, and I believe the greatest general of all, was Joe Hooker. Then came two riding side by side with but two arms and two legs between them, General Sickles with but one leg, and General Howard with but one arm, and following came Generals Thomas, Schofield, McPherson, Butterfield, Logan and Sherman. .388 These are all the major generals I remember now, but there were a host more of brigadier generals, in fact, "too numerous to mention." I am sorry to say that after looking fairly into the face of each of them, I am obliged to say that but two of them come up to my idea of an active, determined military general. I know and daily realize that I am not much of a military man, but always form my idea of men as they pass before me. General Joe Hooker, the commander of the 20th corps (ours) and Brig. Gen. Geary, the commander of the 2d division of this, the 20th corps. And here allow me to remark, without meaning any offence to any of the parties mentioned, that the first sight of General Hooker forcibly reminded of Hon. Wm. Kelly, and General Grant reminding me as forcibly of Sheriff Swift. The pictures I have seen of them in the illustrated papers resemble them about as much as any other general and no more. Well, the consultation broke up about 11 a.m. and the different generals and their followers whirled away, leaving us again "alone in our glory." .389 .390

387 In a 1907 history of the regiment he gave the time as 11 am. His 1864 recollection is preferred.

388 Howard lost his arm in the Battle of Seven Oaks and was back in command in two months. Sickles' leg was mangled by a cannonball at Gettysburg, and he donated the bones to the Army Medical Museum, where he could visit his leg. Their opponent, Hood, had a useless left arm due to wounds at Gettysburg.

389 (Cook 1864)

390 A meeting at the north end, of the commanders of all Armies at Resaca, suggests some importance of the effort at that point. Ruger was still north, so the meeting was beyond the north end.

During the meeting, Thomas' adjutant passed on general orders for attack, leaving no doubt that Hooker's planned assault was to lead a general attack across the north end.

FULLERTON, ADJUTANT, 4TH CORP: Timeline At 9.40 a.m. sent word to General Stanley that General Hooker would make an attack on the right of the Dalton and Resaca road, and instructed him as Hooker advanced to reserve one brigade and to follow up the movement with the other two brigades of his division. At same time sent word to Wood of the order of attack, &c. and instructed him to select vulnerable points in the enemy's lines of works in his front, and, as soon as he saw him wavering from General Hooker's attack, to seize the points by column, and to follow up any advantage he might gain. At same time sent word to General Newton of the order of attack, &c. and that he was to make a demonstration in his front at the time of the advance of General Hooker, to hold the enemy in his front, and that he would follow up any movement of General Wood. The enemy held a very strong position in our front, ravines and open fields between us, and he is posted on a strong series of ridges, with well-constructed breastworks and artillery, with direct and enfilading fires. _391

MEMBER OF COMPANY A, 141ST NY, KNIPE 1B 1D 20C: Sunday morning dawned upon a cloudless sky; the sun rose in all its loveliness, the birds sang as sweetly as if no man had ever cursed this once happy country; all nature seemed to put forth its loveliest hues. A person not conversant with the previous few days' proceedings would hardly have dreamed, from the appearance, that two hostile armies were within forty rods of each other, preparing for a deadly contest.—What a contrast between the proceedings here, on this the Lord's day, and our own quiet Northern homes, at the same hour. On the one hand they are preparing for Church, or Sabbath School, while on the other we are preparing for battle by replenishing our ammunition boxes, filling haversacks with hard-tack, pork, &c. _392

391 (OR, Series I Vol 38 Part 1 Serial 75: Reports n.d., 854)
392 (Museum n.d.)

10 AM Moving Into Positions

HURST, 73RD OHIO WOOD 3B 3D 20C: At ten o'clock we had reached the extreme left of our army lines, and waited an hour or two while the artillery and ammunition were brought forward.

CINCINNATI COMMERCIAL: It was not until nine or ten o'clock in the morning that the 20th Corps arrived from the right, and got into position on Stanley's left. The 23d Corps was immediately withdrawn from the right of the line and thrown in on the left. As our line was nearly fourteen miles long, these necessary changes occupied nearly the entire morning so that mid-day arrived ere we were ready to make the assault on the enemy's works. _393

Williams and Geary began positioning:

Geary's 2nd Division lined up in front of Williams' 1st Division, ready to follow Butterfield's 3rd Division when needed.

GEARY, 2D 20C: In accordance with orders by which our entire corps was directed to attack the enemy at that hour, my division moved to the right about three-fourths of a mile, and there formed column for attack. Owing to the extremely rough and hilly nature of the ground, and the small compass within which the entire corps was to operate in the first charge, the only formation by which my command could be handled to advantage was that of column by regiments. Ireland's brigade was formed in advance; next Buschbeck; last Candy's.

The position occupied by the enemy was one strongly intrenched on an irregular conglomerate of hills, with spurs running in every direction. The general direction of their main lines of intrenchments on these hills inclined northeastward toward a bend in the Connesauga River, forming a refused right flank to their army. On most of the elevations they had batteries protected by earth-works of various descriptions, and so disposed as to sweep in every direction the lines of approach. The very irregular formation of the ground gave the enemy unusual facilities for cross-firing and enfilading the ground to be passed over, and they, in posting both their artillery and infantry, availed themselves fully of these advantages. The hills, steep and rough, were thickly wooded; the narrow ravines between, generally cleared. Immediately in front of the position on which my

393 (Correspondence of the Cincinnati Commercial 1864) Arrived from the right: Butterfield's division.

command formed for the attack a small road passed down a narrow ravine running from the enemy's main line to the Dalton road. .394

Alexander, Co D 111th PA, Ireland's 3B 2D 20C: The corps was massed for a forward move, the 3d division in front, the 1st division on their left and our division massed by brigades in rear of the 3d.

Morhous, Co C 123rd NY Knipe 1B 1D 20C: May 15th at 12 o'clock the Brigade was formed in front of the breastworks, the long line advancing, often halting to reform. They advanced nearly a mile when they were halted, and other Brigades were seen taking positions on the left, while those on the right were probably in position before. .395

MOUAT, CO G, 29TH PENN IRELAND 3B 2D 20C: Moved about 3 miles and took a position in a thick woods here we found a lot of Knapsacks and haversacks and as I opened a full haversack and found a lot of sugar, coffee and salt and was putting them in my own Charley Serad of our Company said "By Thunder Dave you wouldn't think we were going into a fight and all of us might be Killed", I said "all right Chick (his nick name) but if we aint Killed this will come in first rate – shortly after orders came for our Regiment to be massed in a hollow place in our front – here Genl Geary made a speech to us about the Glory of Pennsylvania and that the eyes of the whole Army was on us and the White Star Division, that *we were to lead a charge on the Rebs works and we would be followed by supports.* .396

MILLER, 111TH PA IRELAND 3B 2D 20C: We were ordered to cary the hills in our front and our corps were massed in the woods and the orders were that our third division under general Butterfield were to charge the battries and rifle pits on the right they were formed in column with regimental front and four lines deep while our division the second under Geary were to support them and the first division were to charge the enemy on the left. .397

Miller's 111th Pennsylvania, led by George Cobham, was next to last, followed by Randall's 149th New York. Miller heard only that they were to support Butterfield.

---

394 (OR, Series I Vol 38 Part 2 Serial 73: Reports n.d., 118) The road does not show on the Official Atlas or most other maps and no longer exists.
395 (Morhous 1879, 86)
396 (Mouat n.d.) Butterfield was to lead the charge, with Geary supporting. But Mouat heard it the other way.
397 (Miller 1969, 141) 1st Division charge was in support of Wood, as Miller heard it.

Ireland marched to position. Here we learn which regiment was last in line. They are destined for a different result than the first regiment.

> RANDALL, 149TH NY IRELAND 3B 2D 20C: We remained in position in the breast-works until after 10 a.m. the 15th, when we marched *sixth in line with the brigade,* and were halted and the brigade massed in column of regiments near the Dalton road. .398

And behind Mouat's regiment, the 29th Pennsylvania, were a couple of smaller regiments. They too are to meet difficulty, but the regiment in front will meet tragedy.

> CHATFIELD, 78TH NY IRELAND 3B 2D 20C: Soon after received orders to march, and proceeded, with the division, about two miles to the right and front, and formed in line of battle in rear of the Sixtieth New York Veteran Volunteers, the brigade being formed by regiments in line, the whole closed in mass; moved forward with the brigade thus formed a short distance, when, in pursuance to orders received I moved my regiment to the left and on a line with the Sixtieth New York Veteran Volunteers, and in rear of the Twenty-ninth Pennsylvania Volunteers; moved forward in this order, at the same time changing front, and reaching the crest of a hill immediately in front of the enemy's position, halted for a short time. .399

Within Ireland's regiments, the first will be clobbered, the last will be first, and the next to last will be late.

Candy's 1st Brigade of Geary's Division

Candy's regiments suffered many casualties just a few days before, facing Dalton. Today they were scattered and few were actually engaged until later in the day:

> CANDY, 1B 2D 20C: May 15, moved with the remainder of the division about 10 a.m. a short distance and massed in column of battalions in rear of Second and Third Brigades, Second Division, Twentieth Army Corps, and a portion of the Third Division, Twentieth Army Corps. Several of the regiments of this brigade were ordered to different points. Your attention is

---

398 (OR, Series I Vol 38 Part 2 Serial 73: Reports n.d., 304)
399 (OR, Series I Vol 38 Part 2 Serial 73: Reports n.d., 287)

especially called to reports of regimental commanders, particularly the Fifth Ohio Volunteers. .400

Waiting

Let's pause to wonder about two hours of positioning thousands, with little place to conceal, and being watched by the enemy from the hills above. Some maneuvering might be taking place to jockey against what they see. Imagine the tension! Was there Fear? Wondering what the other side is doing and how to deal with it? Time ticked. Was anything vulnerable? Were there any gaps? What would happen first?

ABRAMS, ATLANTA INTELLIGENCER, WITH STEWART'S DIVISION, CSA: About twelve o'clock the Yankee skirmishers opened a heavy fire on our pickets, compelling them to fall back behind the entrenchments, and at the same time heavy columns were seen forming on the right of Hindman's, Stevenson's and Stuart's divisions. There were four lines of battle in depth, and appeared to number about eight thousand men, and from the number massed in front of Stevenson's line it became apparent that his division would have to stand the brunt of the engagement. One hour passed off slowly to the gallant men who were gazing over the works in anxious expectation for the advance of the enemy. .401

An Idea of a Battle

WILLIAMS: No man can give any idea of a battle by description nor by painting. If you can stretch your imagination so far as to hear, in fancy, the crashing roll of 30,000 muskets mingled with the thunder of over a hundred pieces of artillery; the sharp bursting of shells and the peculiar whizzing sound of its dismembered pieces, traveling with a shriek in all directions; the crash and thud of round shot through trees and buildings and into the earth or through columns of human bodies; the "phiz" of the Minie ball; the uproar of thousands of human voices in cheers, yells, and imprecations; and see the smoke from all the engines of war's inventions hanging sometimes like a heavy cloud and sometimes falling down like a curtain between the combatants; see the hundreds of wounded limping away or borne to the rear on litters; riderless horses rushing wildly about; now and then the blowing up of a caisson and human frames thrown lifeless into the air; the rush of

400 (OR, Series I Vol 38 Part 2 Serial 73: Reports n.d., 155)
401 (Abrams 1864)

columns to the front; the scattered fugitives of broken regiments and skulkers making for the rear. If you can hear and see all this in a vivid fancy, you may have some faint idea of a battle in which thousands are fiercely engaged for victory. But you must stand in the midst and feel the elevation which few can fail to feel, even amidst its horrors, before you have the faintest notion of a scene so terrible and yet so grand. .402

Third Division Deploys

NEW YORK HERALD: The position that Hooker was to carry, was not a range of hills, but rather a collection of detached eminences of considerable altitude, the intervening hollows being filled with a dense growth of timber and underbrush almost impassable for horsemen, and traversable with great difficulty by infantry. The turnpike road leading from Dalton to Resaca passed through these hills, a portion of them lying on the right and others on the left of that road. On both sides of the road in front of the hills, the country was roiling, and densely wooded. In front of the rebel position was a lofty elevation, covered with heavy timber, filled with their sharpshooters. Our line of battle, approaching from the southwest, barely touched the western base of this hill, and then crossed, in a more northerly direction, a narrow valley intervening to another commanding elevation, that had been possessed by us on the previous day, and on which we had planted batteries during the night. The rebel line of battle extended in a circuitous form around the cluster of hills directly back of those particularly noted above, the intervening space between their lines and ours being cleared of its timber. Immediately back of their line, on the right of the road, were two hills—the first wooded, and concealing a battery, the second more remote and cleared at its summit, and having a carefully built redoubt, mounting four guns, which swept the Dalton road with terrible precision. On the opposite side of the road from these heights, was another elevation that had been overlooked at first. It was covered with thick woods in front, but cleared on its rear slope, and was commanded by the rebel masked battery, as well as by their redoubt. On this hill a large body of sharpshooters were concealed by the enemy. .403 .404

GREENMAN, COMPANY H 20TH CONN COBURN 2B 2D 20C, CORPORAL: About 12:30 P.M. the third division of the Twentieth army corps, commanded by

402 (Williams 1963, May 18, 1863)

403 (Bradley 1865, 99)
404 (Abrams 1864)

Gen Daniel Butterfield, took a position at the foot of the mountain fronting the rebel lines, and the fort containing the cannon which were to be so desperately fought for. Not twenty feet from where I stood there was a large oak tree, behind which were Gens Hooker, Sickles, Butterfield, Geary, and other officers in consultation. Seating myself at the foot of the tree, I was in a position to hear the plan of attack. I learned that the third division (Butterfield's) was to have the place of honor; division to be formed en masse in columns of regiments 15 feet apart, and make the charge. The time set for the forward movement was 2:30 P.M. Never was there a more perfect summer afternoon under a Georgia sky than that of May 15, 1864, when the blue and the gray, came together for victory or defeat. It seemed that the resplendence of the day had been prearranged, that nature displayed her manifold beauties to incite us with new courage and strength to fight to preserve the union of a nation which had grown and thrived under the influence of her bounteous endowments. _405

Butterfield had been forming on the north by the Dalton road and now started to deploy.

NEW YORK HERALD: While we have been making this hasty and imperfect survey of the field, Hooker has been employed in massing his troops under cover of the hill I have mentioned as in our possession. The divisions of Williams and Geary are ready; but Butterfield has not yet arrived. Everybody is impatient and wondering at the delay. But presently the suspense is ended as the looked-for division emerges from the woods, and moves steadily down the road. It is now noon, and no more time is to be lost; so Butterfield being already in line, is directed to continue his march until within range, and then deploy his division in columns, by brigades, and make a charge at the enemy's position, Geary's and William's divisions to support if needed. On receiving his instructions, General Butterfield, who was riding at the head of his column with his staff, dashed ahead to survey the ground upon which he was to fight. Having now a clear understanding of the work he had to perform, General Butterfield was not slow in entering upon its performance. _406

BUTTERFIELD, 3D 20: To Division: Order of attack: The division will move to attack the enemy's line. The column of attack will be formed by General Ward's brigade, Colonel Coburn supporting on his right, Colonel Wood on his left. General Ward will form his column by regiment front and push a

405 (Greenman 1897)
406 (Bradley 1865, 100)

bold and vigorous attack with bayonets, a strong line of skirmishers in front. Colonel Coburn will form on his right and rear in echelon with two pieces. Colonel Wood will form on General Ward's left and rear in echelon and support, and will guard his left flank and support his assault. General Ward's column will keep well to the right of the Dalton road. .407

Thomas reported to Sherman that things were about to commence.

> THOMAS TO SHERMAN:11 am: There is a commanding hill situated just above the junction of the eastern wagon road from Tilton to Resaca and the railroad which touches the Connesauga near the same point. On this hill the enemy are believed to be very strongly posted. *General Hooker is now forming Butterfield's division to assault this point,* which, if carried, will give us a decided advantage. He has his other two divisions in hand to support Butterfield's assault, and *General Schofield has two divisions in reserve.* The attack will commence before this can reach your headquarters. I will remain near General Hooker's command until the result is determined. .408

Thomas and Hooker have now committed to more than just getting a line anchored on the river. They have committed themselves beyond Sherman's earlier admonition. What could result from failure to break the Rebel defense?

4th Corps Skirmishers Move Forward - Artillery at Work

Whitaker's brigade, having collected themselves after the battle last night, is in position left of Hazen, in front of the fort. Their witness, Partridge, reports:

> PARTRIDGE, 96TH ILL WHITAKER 2B 1D 4C: On the left there was some shifting of position, but no general movement on the part of the Fourth Corps. Skirmish firing, which had been kept up through the night, increased in volume, and the artillery played upon the lines from either side. During the forenoon the three Divisions of the Twentieth Corps were moved to a position in the rear of the Fourth Corps, and it was whispered that they were to assault the works in front. The Ninety-Sixth left its works and moved to the front, halting in line-of-battle at the right of the Dalton and Resaca road. Just in rear of this position two Brigades of General Butterfield's Division of the Twentieth Corps were massed, and a number of dispatches, detailing the advantages gained by the Army of the Potomac in their campaign, were read at the head of the lines. The good news was received with hearty

407 (OR, Series I Vol 38 Part 4 Serial 75: Correspondence n.d., 194)
408 (OR, Series I Vol 38 Part 4 Serial 75: Correspondence n.d., 191)

cheering, it soon transpired that one purpose in having these dispatches read was to encourage the troops in the difficult work before them. [409]

STANTON: May 13. After four days' hard fighting at Spotsylvania Court-House and terrible battle yesterday, in which one whole division of the enemy (Edward Johnson's) were killed or captured, with 30 pieces of cannon, Lee abandoned his works and retreated. Grant is pursuing. [410]

The success of the Army of the Potomac under Grant would have aroused these Western soldiers to do no less.

Ward Moves Into Position

Ward's brigade went into a ravine behind a ridge, hidden from the Rebel line on the opposite hill, across the road. The Rebels watched them go there. Now both waited.

CASE, 129TH ILL WARD 1B 3D 20C: We arrived at and were placed in our position for assault about 11 a.m. As preparatory to the assault, the brigade was formed in column of regiment with regimental front at forty-four paces interval, in direct order as follows: First, Seventieth Indiana; second, One hundred and second Illinois; third, Seventy-ninth Ohio; fourth, One hundred and twenty-ninth Illinois; fifth, One hundred and fifth Illinois. [411]

GRUNERT, CO D 129TH ILL WARD 1B 3D 20C: Another attempt was to be made by our division, our brigade leading, to take the fort; we knew nothing of the object of our being here, until we were in the fire. As said before, the first brigade was commanded by Gen. Ward, and led the attack; the third followed, while the second took position to our right. Each brigade marched by regiments in line of battle, 35 feet apart. Having taken our position we were ordered to unbuckle our knapsacks and leave them on the spot we then occupied, and which were to be guarded by some sick members of each regiment. [412]

DUSTIN, 105TH ILL WARD 1B 3D 20C: Immediately upon arriving at the point designated, General Butterfield's division was ordered to charge a strong position of the rebels, a commanding eminence important to us and the key

409 (Partridge 1887, 327)
410 (OR, Series I Vol 38 Part 4 Serial 75: Correspondence n.d., 188)
411 (OR, Series I Vol 38 Part 2 Serial 73: Reports n.d., 365)
412 Third brigade did not follow. Orders were changed. Read on.

to the rebel works of Resaca. General Ward's brigade having the honor of leading the grand column of attack, my battalion formed the fifth line in the column, with the exception of one company (B), which, under Capt. T. S. Rogers, was deployed as skirmishers, covering the front of the brigade. .413

CONGLETON, CO F 105TH ILL WARD 1B 3D 20CWe then we moved to the right into the timber and formed in line of battle in two lines. This brought us behind a long high ridge which concealed us from the enemy. We now unstraped our knapsacks and piled them up and left one man to guard them—then examined our guns—fixed bayonets and are now ready for the charge. We are now nearly opposite where we were this morning. .414

FLEHARTY, 102ND ILL WARD 1B 3D 20C: There was evidently some warm work to be done. At first the real design of the movement was known only to a few, but when the column was formed, the men were ordered to fix bayonets, and as the ominous click ran along the line the nature of the task before us became apparent. Thought was busy then, and all faces seemed a shade paler. .415

MERRILL, 70TH IND WARD 1B 3D 20C: At last there was a halt, and a command to unsling knapsacks and fix bayonets. The Seventieth was formed in line of battle and behind were the other regiments of the First Brigade in similar formation, the whole in a column of battalions, with intervals of forty paces between each regiment. General Hooker, attended by other officers, rode forward and stated that some guns belonging to the enemy on the opposite hill were to be taken.

For a few moments there was a stillness in which we could hear a leaf fall. No wonder, for there were men in that line who were to live but a few moments longer. Alas, not all were ready for the sacrifice! One man said, "Captain, let me fill the canteens at that spring and bring them to the boys." Canteens nor man were ever seen again. Many a dying soldier cried in vain for water because of this cowardly perfidy. One of those, however, who looked death in the face said, "I can feel the little hands of my babies around my neck, and hear my wife whispering goodbye." Another, as he threw away a pack of cards, "I don't want to be killed with these in my pocket." Another, "If I fall and you survive take what you find in my knapsack to mother."

---

413 (OR, Series I Vol 38 Part 2 Serial 73: Reports n.d., 360)
414 (Congleton n.d.)
415 (Fleharty, Our Regiment. A History of the 102d Illinois Infantry Volunteers 1865, 57)

The thoughts of the older man who has left a family have a wider range than the younger. The breastworks, the rocks, the trees, the armed men sink out of sight, and the husband and father is in his Indiana home where the little children cling to him, and wife breathes what seems to be an eternal goodbye. It is a heartbreaking moment, but the little fingers are quickly loosened, and again he is in Georgia under bonds to duty. What matters what happens? If this is all there is of life, if love means agony, it is well to have all ended quickly. Or if this be but the threshold of existence, then it were well to storm the ramparts defended by death and burst into the realms of life eternal. .416

J. L. KETCHAM, WARD 1B 3D 20C: "We formed in line of battle on a hill in a beautiful grove of large trees. Word was whispered down the line, 'Fix bayonets.' The order was obeyed quietly. The importance of the command seemed to be appreciated. Some of the boys told their comrades what word to send home if anything happened." It was high noon. I recollect looking at my watch and saying that my folks at home were just returning from church where they had doubtless remembered me in their prayers. I had no sense of danger in that battle. My ambition was to be the first on the enemy's breastworks. At the next battle I was not quite so ambitious." .417

CRAM, CO F 105TH ILL WARD 1B 3D 20C: We had formed just beneath a hill whose protecting sides covered us from the sight of the enemy and as our regts. were being massed, an almost deathlike silence pervades the ranks. Every man knew that in a few moments death would be at work among us and all seemed to fully realize the fact, but they all stood up like men and seemed to vie with each other in real courage. .418

Coburn Gets Into Position Behind Ward

COBURN, 2B 3D 20C: May 15, the brigade moved in the morning with the division to the left some two miles, passing the Fourteenth, Fourth, and Twenty-third Corps, and here, having halted, received an order to advance in rear of the right of the First Brigade, in echelon in two lines, and in their support as an assaulting column on the works of the enemy. On coming to the position where this formation was to be made, it was found to be

416 (S. Merrill 1900, 95)
417 (S. Merrill 1900, 96)
418 (Cram 2001, 99)

impracticable on account of the location of a part of the Fourth Corps on our right. ₄419

BRADLEY, CHAPLAIN, 22ND WIS COBURN 2B 3D 20C: In Madison Journal. It is noon; we march through captured rifle lines, being strengthened by spade and axe, wielded by strong arms, past brigades of troops, till we reach a position in reserve behind Ward's brigade of our division. Half past one— and while the axe echoes on the ridge above and trees topple over, at once the woods resound with rebel yells, and a crash of musketry rings out. The 22d throw off knapsacks, and lie like hounds waiting for the chase. ₄420

NOBLE, 19TH MICH COBURN 2B 3D 20C: Of course we privates knew nothing of the strength of their numbers and position at that time but we had a chance to test both as night set in. I cannot describe to you how I felt when I saw the battle flag and knew that we were about to go into battle but at any rate it was no very pleasant sensation that I experienced at that time. ₄421

Wood Moves into Position

No room left in the ravine.

WOOD, 3B 3D 20C: I moved my brigade forward to the hill referred to and placed it in the formation directed. ₄422

RYDER, CO I 33RD MASS, WOOD 3B 1D 20C: The previous day, which was May 14, all of the other corps of our army were closely engaged with the enemy in their endeavor to break their lines somewhere but with very little success, and a portion of our line on our extreme left was driven back somewhat. So our 20th corps was notified that we must try to retake this position and also endeavor to drive the enemy from his main line in our regiment's front also. I want to mention now something which came directly under my notice the evening of May 14. Lieutenant Edgar Bumpus (who carried our colors at Gettysburg) had a strong impression that he would be killed the next morning; he was so certain of this that he made his will pertaining to his personal effects and wrote farewell letters to his parents and to the young lady to whom he was engaged. He was a recent graduate from college, and as fine a soldier as ever wore the blue. His fellow officers

419 (OR, Series I Vol 38 Part 2 Serial 73: Reports n.d., 378)
420 (Bradley 1865, 94)
421 (Noble n.d.)
422 (OR, Series I Vol 38 Part 2 Serial 73: Reports n.d., 434)

wanted him to take some position for the morrow that would not necessitate his being engaged in the battle, but he refused to do so. Now what was the sequel to this impression? It was only too true; for in the very first of the battle he fell dead by a Rebel bullet through his heart. I wish there was some way to account for these peculiar presentiments—who sends them and from what source do they come?

A similar instance of which I was a witness took place in my company the morning of May 15. While we were kneeling down in line of battle waiting for the order to advance, three of the company came to the captain and each said, "I shall be killed today. Will you write the folks at home about me?" Two were from New Bedford and one, Henry T. Morrison, was from Eastham. Captain Doane said, "What makes you think you will be killed today? You have passed through all our other battles unhurt, why not this?" Each replied, "We cannot tell why, only we feel sure we shall be killed." As we knelt there among those scattering pine trees and I looked along the line at the faces of my comrades with the bullets whistling just over our heads, I thought, what will be my fate in the coming fight? Will the impression which my mother had so vividly impressed upon her mind the night following my enlistment, that I would be returned to her, prove true in regard to me? Or was I destined to be killed before night? I never had any definite impression of coming events only in one instance, which occurred during this battle and which I will relate a little later in this narrative. .423

Ireland Crosses Behind Wood

COBHAM, 111TH PA IRELAND 3B 2D 20C: About 12 m. the brigade was ordered forward by Colonel Ireland, under direction of General Geary, and advanced up the hill, changing direction to the right. I advanced with my own regiment, the One hundred and eleventh Pennsylvania Veteran Volunteers, crossed the Dalton road, and changing direction to the right, *ascended the hill in front while a desultory firing was kept up by the enemy's sharpshooters, and drew my regiment up in line on the summit.* .424

423 (Ryder 1928, 53)
424 Last regiment in line, according to Miller.

Mouat gives us more than a clue about where Ireland was going while Wood was waiting. He moved his brigade past Wood, who was waiting to support Ward and Coburn.

> MOUAT, CO G, 29TH PENN IRELAND 3B 2D 20C: Orders soon came to move forward and *crossing the 33 Mass* of the 3d Div who were laying on their arms. .425

Did Cobham say they formed a line at the summit? Not below the summit?

Last-Minute Change

Sometime during preparations for this morning's assault, Ruger's 2nd Massachusetts had been sent on a dangerous mission to feel out the Rebel position on the hill just north of the bend in the line. That's the same hill Whitaker reconnoitered by skirmishing last night.

> QUINT, 2ND MASS, RUGER, 2B 1D 20C CHAPLAIN: The night was tolerably quiet; but the battlefield smell in the low ground was annoying, that indescribable odor in marshy land, after a battle in hot days. The morning of the 15th was also quiet. But in the forenoon came an order to send a regiment on reconnoissance. The rebel works were so hidden and complicated in the woods as to render it difficult to know their position. For this delicate service, in broad daylight, the Second Massachusetts was selected.
>
> There was a dead silence when the regiment laid down knapsacks, and went off into the woods, double column on the centre. Colonel Cogswell put out skirmishers and flankers, and some engineers were with the regiment. They proceeded three-quarters of a mile; discovered what they were sent to ascertain, whether a particular hill was held in force by the enemy, as it was; encountered the rebels entrenched outposts, and drew their fire. The volley was heard by the brigade. Its result was awaited in painful suspense. Soon the regiment emerged, with two wounded. Butterfield's Division was immediately moved forward. .426
>
> FOX, 107TH NY RUGER 2B 1D 20C: It was discovered during these formations, made as far as possible under the concealment of the hills and woods, that the assaulting column on emerging from the latter [hills and

---

425 (Mouat n.d.) The 33rd Massachusetts, of Wood's 3rd Brigade of the 3rd Division.
426 (Quint 1867, 227)

woods] would be subjected in an open country to a cross fire as well as direct fire of the enemy. Colonel Wood commanding the Third Brigade, was therefore ordered to use his discretion in supporting Ward's Brigade, either by following up the latter or attacking independently on Ward's left. As events transpired, he used his command handsomely for both purposes. 427 428

WOOD, 3B 3D 20C: Before the attack was ordered Major Tremain, acting aide-de-camp on Major-General Butterfield's staff, came to me and said that the situation of the ground was somewhat different from what it was understood to be at the time the written orders were issued; that instead of acting as a support to General Ward it was assigned to me to assault and take the hill then in my front, and that the manner of doing it and the formation of the brigade was left to my own judgment; that General Butterfield desired the attack to be made at once, as General Ward was ready to advance. This was to me very embarrassing. I had not reconnoitered the ground. Most of it was covered with a dense forest. I knew nothing of the strength of the enemy, his position, or the situation of his works in front. I rode forward and made a hurried and imperfect reconnaissance. It seemed to me that I was too far to the right. I therefore moved my right regiment by the left flank to the left and changed its front by a half wheel to the left. Changed the formation of the brigade from one line in echelon to two lines, putting three regiments in the front line and two in the second, throwing out in front a strong line of skirmishers. 429

HURST, 73RD OHIO WOOD 3B 3D 20C: Just as we were ready to advance, orders were given to change the formation of the brigade to two lines "en echelon;" in the execution of which there was some confusion, as the orders were not conveyed to all the regiments.

OSBORN, CO A 55TH OHIO WOOD 3B 3D 20C: Lieutenant Pliny Watson, of the Fifty-Fifth Ohio, was serving as an aide on Colonel Wood's staff, and about 12:30 p.m. brought the orders to the commanding officers of the regiments of the brigade. The Fifty-Fifth Ohio was moving in column of fours at the head of the brigade and had halted for orders, when he came galloping up to Colonel Gambee to advise him that "the position would be

427 (Fox n.d., 241)
428 Although Fox was writing this for Slocum's memorial, Fox was actually present at Resaca. It is not known whether he was with his regiment or in some other capacity. He was wounded the day of the battle, resulting in disability.
429 (OR, Series I Vol 38 Part 2 Serial 73: Reports n.d., 434)

forced at once." Colonel Gambee was a veteran of many battles. He had won his eagles by hard service, and had proved himself a very brave man, but when he received this order he turned pale, trembled in his saddle, and did not recover his composure for some moments. He was soon called upon to form line, and showed no further signs of emotion; but the writer was greatly moved by the incident, which afterwards seemed prophetic. .430

WINKLER, 26TH WIS WOOD 3B 3D 20C: My regiment was formed in the woods on the left & a little in rear of the First Brigade, my left resting on the Resaca Road & connecting with the 33 Mass. I was then ordered to swing my right forward so as to occupy an oblique position to the road & to face a hill on the left of the road which I was told at the same time I was to occupy when the Brig moved forward. I put my regt. into the desired position & threw out a company of skirmishers ahead. .431

Wood now has the 73rd Ohio on the left of the first line, the 33rd Massachusetts in the middle, and 26th Wisconsin on the right. The 55th Ohio and 136th New York are in the rear. The shift of the 73rd Ohio from right to left in effect shifted the brigade to the left, now facing the left hill. The Rebel line angles east from the right hill, but they have some units forward on the left, more than just skirmishers.

HURST, 73RD OHIO WOOD 3B 3D 20C: When our brigade reached its position for deployment, we were ordered to form by battalion "en echelon," and being on the left of the brigade, the Seventy-third Ohio was thrown far out into the woods on the left. Our skirmishers soon reported the rebel skirmishers close at hand, and a considerable body of the enemy moving to the right over the open ground, half a mile in our front. .432

Ward Waits

WARD, 1B 3D 20C: When we reached the place where the attack was to be made my column was formed as ordered, and then Captain Oliver took me and showed me the hill and works to be attacked. An intelligent sergeant of the One hundred and second Illinois being present, I sent him to find the colonels and take them to the place where the hill and works could be seen, and went back to move the column about 100 paces by the left flank to place them in a proper position to advance to the attack. When this was done I

430 (Osborn 1904, 145)
431 (F. C. Winkler 1864)
432 (Hurst 1866, 118)

awaited the order to advance, which was not given until Wood's attack and the firing ceased. .433 .434

Almost Ready

TREMAIN: Sunday's operations now bid fair to become the key of the campaign. Butterfield's division was selected as the storming party supported by the well known divisions of Geary and Williams. There were two hills to be taken. One was not tenable without the other, and both must therefore be carried at once. Colonel Wood's brigade was selected to take the hill on the left of the road and General Ward's that on the right, on the crest of which was a hastily constructed redoubt mounting four guns. Colonel Coburn's brigade was to act as a support. Ward's brigade, although having been in the service for more than two years, had never been in action; but gallantly did they perform their work. Formed in column of regiments, both brigades moved simultaneously on the hills assigned them. No skirmishers were thrown out, no warning given to the enemy of their approach. Formed under cover of a ravine in the forest, the enemy knew nothing of the move until our men were before them within the shortest musket range. .435

Sherman had been checking the line:

SHERMAN TO THOMAS: I have just visited McPherson's line. He occupies a ridge in front of Camp Creek, seemingly within range of the bridge, and the line is pretty well fortified already. McPherson is preparing batteries to advantage guns on his right front (extreme). The guns on Bald Hill enfilade the road into Resaca, which passes around the point of the hill. The enemy appear to be assembling a line of troops parallel to McPherson, the latter thinks, to assault, but I would ask nothing more favorable. The second line is on the range of hills of which Bald Hill is one, and terminates at its left at the branch of Camp Creek which flows east and passes near my headquarters. Baird was in the act of relieving the division of Harrow, which was on the north of that branch of Camp Creek, and now Harrow's division is in reserve behind McPherson's batteries. I think his whole line is completed, and by the time you get this guns will be in the advanced line. I have sent Poe to examine Palmer's line, which should rest its right on the

---

433 (OR, Series I Vol 38 Part 2 Serial 73: Reports n.d., 340)
434 Apparently referring to Wood having reached the first crest after clearing Rebel skirmishers.
435 (Tremain 1905, 171)

creek which should be the division line between McPherson and Palmer, and run along the hills that overlook the valley of Camp Creek. With pickets down to the willows on the creek, and the crests well lined, the position would be impregnable. Now you have Howard's and Hooker's corps beyond Camp Creek looking south, with Schofield, as it were, in reserve, and the less time we give the enemy to fortify the better. *I want to hear the sound of that line advancing directly down the road on Resaca till it comes within range of the forts.* Whilst this advance is being made McPherson's guns will make the bridge and vicinity too hot for the passage of troops. I am very anxious this advance should be made today, *that we may secure a line whose left rests on the Connesauga.* I have sent Corse down to see what progress Sweeny is making. .436

Repeating: Sherman wants to secure a line whose left rests on the Connesauga. He did not say he wanted to drive them out. He wants Dodge and others to be established south of Resaca first.

CORSE, TO SHERMAN: May 15, noon: The bridge is finished, one brigade across, and the balance of Sweeny's command crossing. The rebel are not visible in any large force. The troops are intrenching themselves on the other side. I will send out a small cavalry force to feel the front after the infantry and artillery have crossed. P. S.—Should like to hear what is the condition of affairs with you. There will be another bridge across soon. .437

A report from a signal officer, intriguing if the time given is correct, was received by General Thomas a little after noon. Another was sent shortly after.

MEEEKER, SIGNAL OFFICER: More cavalry leaving Resaca. Long train of infantry and wagons on the road at a point east five degrees south, moving south. .438

MEEEKER, SIGNAL OFFICER: The cavalry reported leaving Resaca can be seen mowing south, the advance three miles from town. I think they are moving around us. .439

What did that mean? Let's note that, while in enemy territory Sherman needed to send his army ahead of his wagons, but Johnston could send wagons ahead with troops following to protect them from advancing Union forces. What was

436 (OR, Series I Vol 38 Part 4 Serial 75: Correspondence n.d., 190)
437 (OR, Series I Vol 38 Part 4 Serial 75: Correspondence n.d., 196)
438 (OR, Series I Vol 38 Part 4 Serial 75: Correspondence n.d., 190)
439 (OR, Series I Vol 38 Part 4 Serial 75: Correspondence n.d., 190)

Johnston up to? Had he begun to evacuate, keeping the Union army occupied while the wagons get a head start? And was Sherman keeping Johnston so busy that Dodge could get across the Oostanaula?

So things are about ready after such a long wait.

> FULLERTON, ADJUTANT, 4TH CORP: Timeline General Hooker's advance did not commence until after 12 m. During the mean time fire of sharpshooters, skirmishers, and of artillery was kept up all along our line. .440

> FULLERTON, ADJUTANT, 4TH CORP: Timeline 1 pm. sent word to Major-General Hooker, by Colonel Asmussen, his assistant inspector-general, and also by Captain Stevens, of General Stanley's staff, to general, [sic] and also by Captain Stevens, of General Stanley's staff, to call on this corps for re-enforcements whenever he wished them. .441

Williams' division was still forming up.

> MORHOUS, CO C 123RD NY KNIPE 1B 1D 20C: Gen. Hooker was everywhere present on his black charger. To the left of the 123d Regiment was a piece of woods, back of which was a large open field. Orderlies were seen galloping here and there just before the fight opened, and soon regiment after regiment was seen entering the woods on the left, massing. Hooker passed near the Regiment, when the boys lifted their hats to give him a cheer; he halted his horse and said, "Boys, keep still and keep cool; there's a hen on." And the rebels found it a good sized "'hen," too. .442

Sergeant Rice C. Bull, of Company D in the 123rd New York, had been home recruiting and was returning along with the regiment's train, just in time.

> BULL, CO D 123RD NY KNIPE 1B 1D 20C: Our train was going directly to our Division, only about three miles from where we were camped, so we continued on with it. It was after eleven when we located the 1st Brigade and reached the 123rd Regiment which was then standing in line of battle waiting for orders to advance. The whole Division was in line of battle, the 3rd Brigade on our right and the 2nd on our left. There was brisk skirmishing in our front and an advance was expected in a short time. .443

440 (OR, Series I Vol 38 Part 1 Serial 75: Reports n.d., 854)
441 (OR, Series I Vol 38 Part 1 Serial 75: Reports n.d., 854)
442 (Morhous 1879, 90)
443 (Bull 1977, 104)

Williams Starts for the Left

BULL, CO D 123RD NY KNIPE 1B 1D 20C: We had hardly shaken hands and commenced to answer questions about the homefolks when General Hooker rode along the rear of our line and orders were given to advance. Everything was ready and the "Forward" sounded. Our line was in the woods in both directions; the timber was heavy so our advance was slow as we could not lose or sever our contact with the troops on our right and left. After advancing about a half mile we came to an open field an eighth of a mile wide that extended a long distance in our front. At the far end the Rebel breastworks were plainly in view, only a half mile away. .444

NEW YORK HERALD: From his elevated position, during the one-sided fight the rebels kept up with their artillery, Colonel Wood discovered large masses of rebel infantry moving across the cleared fields between the Dalton road and the railroad, as if another attempt was to be made to flank us. The information was quickly conveyed to General Hooker, who promptly ordered Geary and Williams to take positions on Wood's left, extending their line well out to the railroad, in order to meet this apprehended attack. .445

WILLIAMS, 1D 20C: May 15, the division was ordered to support Butterfield's and Geary's divisions, and marched at 12 o'clock. While on the march information was sent to me by the major-general commanding corps that the enemy was threatening our left from the direction of the railroad .446, and I was ordered to cover and protect that flank. Facing by the left brought the division in line of battle, and in this formation I advanced it toward the menaced point, the brigades being in line according to numerical order. .447

Then they moved forward across the plain. Ruger's brigade moved toward the railroad and took position. Robinson followed, taking position between Ruger and the railroad. Chaplain Quint of Ruger's brigade describes the movements.

QUINT, 2ND MASS RUGER 2B 1D 20C: It was an hour before the battle opened. The key-point had been found, a height crowned with a strong work, and

444 (Bull 1977, 104)
445 (Bradley 1865, 104)
446 (D. H. Butterfield n.d.) Newspaper article describing the Walker painting, apparently written by Butterfield, states Hooker watched the beginning of the assault from Hazen's position and then went to direct placement of Williams' and Geary's Divisions.
447 (OR, Series I Vol 38 Part 2 Serial 73: Reports n.d., 28)

held by artillery. Soon Williams' Division was moved on at double-quick, and joined the left of Butterfield. The attack of the latter was upon the hill. Of Williams' Division, the 1st Brigade was on the right, the 2d next, the 3d on the left. The line curved round the base of the hill. On the left of the 3d Brigade was cavalry, soon replaced by a brigade of the 23d Corps. Of the 3d Brigade, the regiments ran from left to right, thus: 27th Indiana, Second Massachusetts, 3d Wisconsin, 150th New York, 13th New Jersey. 448 The line was formed, but soon moved on an eighth of a mile to the front edge of a wood, *a field with standing wheat before it. Connections were kept with Butterfield who was busy on the right, and the brigade again moved across the field, and into a wood which covered an ascending slope.* 449

That last statement we can take to be referring to the deployment and to what happened while they were moving forward, for soon enough Wood was on Knipe's right.

Knipe was facing a hill on the other side of which was another, the enemy line. The hill he faced was not cleared yet.

> BULL, CO D 123RD NY KNIPE 1B 1D 20C: When we came into the opening the enemy artillery brought us under fire. Our line was in such an exposed position we were ordered to "Right Oblique" to a knoll just ahead of us where we could lie down out of sight. Although they could not see us the artillery kept pounding away but most of their shots were over our heads. They did not do much damage but even for veteran troops it is trying to lie unengaged under artillery fire. We could do nothing as our skirmishers were in our front, so just hugged the ground. After about ten minutes one of our batteries entered the field and in a short time silenced the enemy's guns. While this was going on our left was extended and was making a right wheel to get on the flank of the Johnnies. 450

Corput's Battery Moves in Front

The Rebels had been making a critical adjustment. They moved Captain Corput's Battery from behind their line to an exposed position well in front, to get better range on the guns on the other side. But they did not start quite soon enough to prepare.

448 Misprint? Should be 2nd Brigade, from right to left.
449 (Quint 1867, 228)
450 (Bull 1977, 104)

STEVENSON: During the course of the morning I received orders to place the artillery of my division in such a position as would enable it to drive off a battery that was annoying General Hindman's line. *Before the necessary measures for the protection of the artillery could be taken*, I received repeated and peremptory orders to open it upon the battery before alluded to. Corput's battery was accordingly placed in position at the only available point, about eighty yards in front of General Brown's line. ₋451 ₋452

ABRAMS, ATLANTA INTELLIGENCER, WITH STEWART'S DIVISION, CSA: At about one o'clock the Yankee line of battle moved slowly forward in fine order. As they crossed a ravine which divided the ridges held by our forces from those occupied by them, Captain Corbett's battery of Georgia artillery was ordered to advance outside of our lines and about fifty yards from them and take up a position, which would have given us an enfilading fire on the approaching column. The battery, consisting of four 12 pounder Napoleons, moved out of the line and took up position as ordered. ₋453

RITTER, ROWAN'S BATTERY, JOHNSON'S BATTALION, HOOD'S CORPS, CSA: Early on the morning of the 15th, Corput's battery was advanced to a position three hundred yards in front of the main line, and to the right of the Dalton road, with the object of enfilading the enemy's line. ₋454

WESLEY CONNOR, PRIVATE, CHEROKEE ARTILLERY, CSA: On the morning of Sunday the 15th of May, 1864, we were placed on the brow or brink of the hill—I did not know until you wrote that it was called "Red Knob"about— seventy-five yards in front of our infantry line, and instructed to throw up works for our guns, and this we proceeded to do, after having placed brush up in front so as to conceal our operations from the Federals. We understood, that as soon as our guns were ready, the Confederates would

---

451 See Note A on Blakeslee's map about Rowan's Battery section being moved forward also. Compare to note on the supposed Corput version.

452 (OR, Series I Vol 38 Part 3 Serial 74: Reports n.d., 812)

453 (Abrams 1864)

454 (Ritter n.d.) Facing Hazen and Willich. Rowan's Battery was almost destroyed but during the night refortified their position. Dent's Battery was withdrawn. Other batteries were right of Rowan, as will be seen.

charge the position occupied by the Federals on the ridge across the Dalton road, about 800 or 1000 yards on our front. ₋455 ₋456

Tension

22ND WIS, MADISON JOURNAL: Half past one—and while the axe echoes on the ridge above, and trees topple over, at once the woods resound with rebel yells, and a crash of musketry rings out. The 22d throw off knapsacks, and lie like hounds waiting for the chase. ₋457 ₋458

HALSTEAD, 79TH OHIO WARD 1B 3D 20C: The attacking brigade was massed in column by battalions at the foot of the hill, and advanced slowly and noiselessly, with fixed bayonets, up the hill into the thicket about 150 paces, and laid down, awaiting the order to charge. The day was excessively hot. The brigade was completely hidden, perhaps for an hour. What did they have to think about? It is not known that any one slept. Strange: so many packed together, and yet so quiet. One was heard to whisper, "Boys, thar's no danger at all; Totton is right here by me!" ₋459

Some were not yet to face battle, though they'd be busy once the shooting started.

COOK, ASST. SURGEON, 150TH NY RUGER 2B 1D 20C: I got into the shade of an accommodating persimmon tree, fell asleep. ₋460

The Opening of the Ball

Gen. Hood gave the order for the commander of a battery to stay at his guns until he and all the men were killed; not to leave the guns under any circumstances— Anderson

NEW YORK HERALD: Entrusting to the brigade commanded by Colonel Wood, the work of taking the hill on the left of the road, Gen. Ward with his brigade, was ordered to charge that upon the right, Colonel Coburn's

---

455 (Connor, Wesley O.; Blakeslee, George H. 1899)
456 "There was a dispute among the boys as to the distance from our Battery back to our lines, and it was funny how they varied. ... In 1868 I was back on the ground, and found it to be about 75." ibid
457 (Bradley 1865)
458 Half past twelve?
459 (Halstead n.d.)
460 (Cook 1864)

brigade to act as a reserve to General Ward. These dispositions brought on two separate battles almost simultaneously, both of them raging throughout nearly the remainder of the day with great fierceness. We shall characterize that in which General Ward led off as the battle on the right, and Colonel Wood's assault as the battle on the left. .461

ABRAMS, ATLANTA INTELLIGENCER, WITH STEWART'S DIVISION, CSA: But before they could fire a gun, or their infantry support could come up, the charge was made along the whole line. .462

Those four guns were not quite ready. Ward's brigade did not have to face the Rebel line yet, just a few defenders who had moved forward with the battery. How would things have turned out if the battery had been left behind the line?

Stevenson tells the result, which we will see in detail.

STEVENSON, CSA: It had hardly gotten into position when the enemy hotly engaged my skirmishers, driving them in and pushing on to the assault with great impetuosity. So quickly was all this done that it was impossible to remove the artillery before the enemy had effected a lodgment in the ravine in front of it, thus placing it in such a position that while the enemy were entirely unable to remove it, we were equally so, without driving off the enemy massed in the ravine beyond it, which would have been attended with great loss of life. .463

And here Hooker calls for an effort all along the line to keep the entire Rebel line too busy to assist in repelling the assault.

FULLERTON, ADJUTANT, 4TH CORP: Timeline 1:10 pm. sent word by a staff officer to division commanders that Hooker was ascending the hill he was to storm on our left, and that they must now push ahead and press the enemy. .464

Howard's 4th Corps, Hazen's brigade at least, began their press when Hooker started. If that meant Wood, he was too early. Judging from events, that is what happened, and Ward was left exposed.

461 (Bradley 1865, 100)
462 (Abrams 1864)
463 (OR, Series I Vol 38 Part 3 Serial 74: Reports n.d., 812)
464 (OR, Series I Vol 38 Part 1 Serial 75: Reports n.d., 854)

HAZEN, 2B 3D 4C: On the 15th an assault of the enemy's works was ordered in conjunction with an advance by General Hooker. At the signal this brigade moved over the works and toward the enemy, but the troops on the right and left hesitating, the entire fire of the enemy was concentrated upon my command, which was staggered, and as I could see no support ordered them back. The losses of the brigade in this unassisted and honest effort in the space of thirty seconds was 120. .465

HAZEN, 2B 3D 4C: The two days we were here afforded an uninterrupted practice of sharpshooting at close range. On the second day orders were received that at twelve M., when Hooker should attack on the left, and we saw the enemy uneasy or falling back, a general attack was to be made. At the hour indicated, Hooker did attack, and the enemy's skirmishers in our front could be seen rapidly retreating, and I commanded, "Forward!" My entire brigade leaped the works and went forward; but as no other troops did so on either of our flanks, they drew a concentrated fire of great violence and were recalled. This cost us a hundred men in less than a minute. Sixty were lost the day before in the dash to gain the ground here occupied. .466

When Hazen moved is uncertain. But that he did not draw Cummings' and Hindman's fire away from Butterfield's division very long, with the exception, maybe, of artillery, is stated above. Not getting support suggests the Confederate line was not all pressed at once. Abrams' statement below will reveal that none of the 4th Corps pressed after Hazen drew back. From comments of the soldiers in the fight, below, Howard had not kept the enemy on Butterfield's right busy enough.

A Puzzle

Here we interrupt with Butterfield's story written for a display of Walker's painting many years later.

> Butterfield: Hooker, commanding the Twentieth corps, went to Howard's position, when the assault commenced, as a point of vantage from which any necessary directions could be given, and then left General Howard in order to place the balance of his corps, being the two divisions under

465 (OR, Series I Vol 38 Part 1 Serial 75: Reports n.d., 426)
466 (Hazen 1885, 252)

Williams and Geary, respectively, in action beyond the hills shown at the left of the picture. _467

Just when, during all the moves, was Hooker at Hazen's position? He was everywhere. Accounts seem to have him placing Williams about when the assault started. He, we will see shortly, was helping get Ward and Coburn started and helping sort things out. So was Williams, specifically Ruger and Robinson, not yet in position when the assault started? Some of Geary's division? Never mind—Butterfield wrote for public appreciation, years after the fact.

The Battle Begins on the Left

This was to me very embarrassing. I had not reconnoitered the ground. Most of it was covered with a dense forest. I knew nothing of the strength of the enemy, his position, or the situation of his works in front. – Wood

Wood Clears the Left Hill

WOOD, 3B 3D 20C: This formation, made in a very hurried manner, being completed, I gave the order to advance. Promptly and regularly the men moved up the hill and drove the enemy from the crest in the most gallant manner. When about two-thirds of the way the left of the line, in passing out the woods into an open space, encountered a galling cross-fire from the left, and which seemed to come from the enemy posted in a piece of woods to the left and in front of me. Not knowing what, if any, disposition had been made to protect our left flank, and fearing a flank movement from the enemy, I changed the front of the Seventy-third Ohio Volunteer Infantry so as to meet the threatened danger. A few well-directed volleys from this regiment seemed to silence the firing from the woods. _468

HURST, 73RD OHIO WOOD 3B 3D 20C: When we went forward, it was but a short space to a wooded hill, held by the rebel skirmishers. The brigade charged this hill, driving the rebels back to their fortified line, some three hundred yards beyond; and now the fire came in so sharply, on our left flank, that the Seventy-third Ohio was ordered to change front to the left. The right of the brigade having a continuous covering of woods, pressed forward close up to the enemy's works; but there was open ground in front of the left and center, from the hill just taken, to the enemy's line of works. Two

467 (D. H. Butterfield n.d.)
468 (OR, Series I Vol 38 Part 2 Serial 73: Reports n.d., 434)

hundred yards from the left of our brigade, was another woods, from which the enemy's skirmishers now annoyed our flank. .469

OSBORN, CO A 55TH OHIO WOOD 3B 3D 20C: It must have taken quite half an hour to form the line, and about 1 p.m. the brigade advanced. No sooner had the skirmish line crowned the wooded knoll in front than sharp skirmishing began, and when, a moment later, the line of battle reached the summit, the roar of full volleys of musketry and cannon from the strongly fortified lines of the enemy showed that they were prepared to resist to the utmost. .470

MCMAHON, CO E 136TH NY WOOD 3B 3D 20C: We charged up the first hill, the balls flying over our heads. Then we went down the hill & up another. When the rebels left their breastwork we followed them. All the while there was a perfect hail of bullets. We drove the rebels off the third hill, when we were ordered to halt. .471

RYDER, CO I 33RD MASS, WOOD 3B 1D 20C: Finally, when the whole of our corps was ready, the order came, "Rise up, 33d! Guide on the colors. Forward, march!" We climbed the hill in our front quite quickly, the "Johnnies" retreating before we reached the top, but not so far but they could return our fire. The next man to me was struck by one of their bullets in the forehead and fell at my feet. The one the other side of me had his coat torn across from one side to the other. We lay down for a few moments until our left had come up. Then the order came, "Rise up, 33d!" For a few seconds no one moved—we just dreaded to rise—but at the second order we all sprang to our feet and jumping over the logs we rushed down the hill and up the other. Just as we reached the top where we had scarcely any protection we received the full fire from the main line of rifle pits opposite. I judged the distance to be less than 150 yards. They were expecting us and gave us a warm reception. .472

WINKLER, 26TH WIS WOOD 3B 3D 20C: The brigade being ordered forward, I advanced without halting to the top of the hill, my skirmishers driving those of the rebels before them. The 33d Mass. here soon joined & seeing

---

469 (Hurst 1866, 118)
470 (Osborn 1904, 145)
471 (McMahon 1993, 93)
472 (Ryder 1928, 53)

them down I ordered my men to do the same with guns in hand & skirmishers out. _473

Wood is now spreading out facing Reynolds' Brigade across the saddle between the two hills.

Rebels Moving Left of Wood

Knipe's brigade was immediately called to help Wood clear the hill.

> NEW YORK HERALD: General Williams, who had been posted on the left of Wood's brigade, in anticipation of the rebel flank movement, on hearing the musketry on his right, had ordered General Knipe, who commanded the brigade on the right of his line, to go to Wood's assistance. Knipe moved off with alacrity, and, crossing the hill from the east, fell upon the rebel flank before they had any warning of his approach. Leading his men in person, he charged directly into the rebel column, the bayonet doing the work of execution when time was insufficient for reloading, and, without halting his column, fairly pushed the rebel force down the hill with his bayonets, occasionally firing a volley to expedite the rout. This was one of the most gallant deeds of the campaign. The rebels were largely superior in numbers to both Knipe and Wood combined; but the audacity and determination of Knipe's attack defied resistance. The face of the hill was strewn all over with rebel dead and wounded; their brigades were crowded upon one another, and, in inextricable confusion, they were routed and driven from the attack. General Knipe was not content with a single rout, but, following closely on the heels of the fleeing foe, he cut them down at every step. The chase was continued in this manner until the enemy were run into their reserves, concealed in the dense timber, and the attacking party was himself attacked. _474

Detail follows, from those whose efforts the Herald reported.

> KNIPE, 1B 1D 20C: We took position for the night on the left of General Stanley's division, my brigade forming the right of this division where we remained until 2 p.m. on the 15th, when we advanced in double-quick time to engage the enemy. We found him in position, strongly intrenched and awaiting our attack. I formed my brigade in line of battle on the left of Colonel Woods brigade, of the Third Division of this corps, under a heavy

473 (F. C. Winkler 1864)
474 (Bradley 1865, 106)

fire of the enemy. After completing my formation, I ordered an advance of my line to the top of a wooded ridge, distance some fifty yards, and ordered it to lie down and await my further orders. .475

MEMBER OF COMPANY A, 141ST NY, KNIPE 1B 1D 20C: At 12 o'clock, noon, the bugle sounded to fall in and advance. In less time than it takes to write, we are in line of battle, and moving towards the enemy. Crack! crack! goes the musketry! bang! peals the artillery; the bullets begin to whiz around ears; we are getting closer and closer to the enemy; we come to a piece of woods which, owing to the underbrush, is hard to penetrate, but after some severe work, we arrive on the opposite side; we are now in sight of the rebels; the balls come thick and fast; we are not close enough to the enemy to render them any material damage, so we lie down under cover of a friendly knoll ... .476

So, Knipe had advanced up the ridge from the north, and Woods, when he came across from the east, advanced as well.

Cook, of Ruger's brigade, had found himself following Wood's brigade instead of his own.

COOK, ASST. SURGEON, 150TH NY RUGER 2B 1D 20C: And about 1 p.m. awoke to see the last of the 150th piling over a hill about eighty rods away. I hastened after, saw them enter a dense wood and still hasten on. I had got but a little way into the wood when the ball opened and you would have thought there was a hail storm going on, to have heard the bullets rattling about in the leaves and branches of the trees. The first division to which the 150th regiment belongs, had filed off to the left after entering the woods and I had followed up in the wake of the third division. .477 .478

What did Cook have to go through to get from Wood's regiment past Knipe's to find his own?

The 5th Connecticut moved forward and helped clear the left hill just as some Rebels were coming up the other side.

---

475 (OR, Series I Vol 38 Part 2 Serial 73: Reports n.d., 39)
476 (Museum n.d.)
477 (Cook 1864)
478 (Wile 1907, 80) Cook's 1907 account of the whole corps being spread wide in two lines of battle is discounted. Too many more timely accounts are far more consistent. This exemplifies the confusion of memories with the passage of time.

MARVIN, CO F 5TH CONN, KNIPE 1B 1D 20C: about 1 P. M. The whole brigade was hastily formed and moved forward to engage the enemy. It soon became evident that a position along a crest of a hill in front must be captured, or else the line would be greatly exposed and fight under great disadvantage. The order was given to move up to this position on the double-quick, and it was given and acted upon just in time, for when the regiment arrived in position on the crest the rebel line was discovered pushing up for the same position on the opposite slope of the ridge and near at hand. The order came quickly to fire, and the first volley checked the advance of the enemy and caused them to falter and come to a halt, which gave the regiment time to load again. Upon giving them the contents of the rifles in a second volley they turned and made for their works in retreat. When the other troops saw our brigade of Red Stars come out of the woods and take that ridge and hold it and repulse the rebels, such a storm of applause went up as never before greeted it for its conduct on the battlefield. 479

A "storm of applause" from Wood's brigade, no doubt for the 123rd and 141st New York, who were on the 5th Connecticut's right.

They relieved Wood's leftmost regiment, likely the one Cook had followed, who were separated from the rest of their brigade and recalled.

WOOD, 3B 3D 20C: Soon afterward I saw troops of the First Division (Brigadier-General Williams) going into position on my left, which removed all fear of a flank attack. I then ordered the Seventy-third Ohio to resume its original front and move forward on a line with the other part of the brigade on the crest of the hill. The hill was divided by an indentation in its top, running in the same direction with the line of battle, in two crests. In my front the crest first reached in a measure overlooked and commanded the second, but my order was to occupy the advanced crest. The order was obeyed, although the position of the men was such that they were under fire of the enemy in their works. 480

MCMAHON, CO E 136TH NY WOOD 3B 3D 20C: Thus we drove them off three hills and the last two had breastworks thrown up. The hill that we stopped on had no protection except the breastworks which were poorer than those on the second hill. By the time we were on the last hill, the regt.

479 (Marvin 1889, 299)
480 (OR, Series I Vol 38 Part 2 Serial 73: Reports n.d., 434)

ahead of us were so cut up that they fell into our reg't. thus making but one line of battle. The enemy had a cross fire on us. .481

HURST, 73RD OHIO WOOD 3B 3D 20C: Halfway across the field, in front of the Fifty-fifth Ohio and One Hundred and Thirty-sixth New York, there was a deep hollow or ravine; and these regiments were ordered forward to that position. In reaching it, they received a most murderous fire, and lost heavily. .482

HURST, 73RD OHIO WOOD 3B 3D 20C: The Seventy-third remained in position in its new front, until Gen. Knipe's brigade arrived on the ground, and was then ordered to join to the left of the brigade, prolonging its line up the ravine. In accomplishing this, we had to pass over a hundred paces of open ground, fully exposed to the rebel fire. We went forward in line, on the run, but lost, unavoidably, quite a number killed and wounded. .483

Knipe's rightmost regiment, the 141st New York, got too far and was forced down. The 123rd New York was left of them, both in exposed positions with no cover.

KNIPE, 1B 1D 20C: Colonel Logie, commanding One hundred and forty-first New York Volunteers, being on the extreme right of the brigade, mistook the order for an order to charge the enemy's position and passed beyond the ridge with his regiment into an open field, where he sustained considerable loss in killed and wounded. The enemy seeing this regiment in the exposed position, opened with his artillery from two forts on our right and left front. I at once directed this regiment to lie down and wait further orders. I could not recall this regiment to its position in the line, as this would have brought them under a heavy fire of both artillery and musketry. I could, however, protect them in their position by the balance of the brigade in case the enemy should make a charge upon them through the open field. .484

The 123rd New York, on Logie's left, did not go quite as far, but much of his regiment was in the open field too.

MORHOUS, CO C 123RD NY KNIPE 1B 1D 20C: This was the first engagement Waters [Co K] had been in, having enlisted not quite two months previous and had arrived that same day with the recruiting party. The Regiment

481 (McMahon 1993, 93)
482 (Hurst 1866, 119)
483 (Hurst 1866, 119)
484 (OR, Series I Vol 38 Part 2 Serial 73: Reports n.d., 39)

occupied the only exposed position in the Brigade—or Corps for what we know—on a ridge running nearly parallel with the enemy's breastworks, with not a tree or shrub in front. The Rebels brought up a piece of artillery, placed it in position, pointed it directly for the right of the Regiment, loaded it with all care, and threw a shell directly into Co. K. The entire Regiment lay flat on the ground, but notwithstanding this, the first shell tore off one of Waters' legs. The gun was again loaded and fired and the other leg was taken off. Still the Regiment lay there, when by moving a few feet back they might have been out of range of that piece of artillery. The third shell exploded directly over the company, injuring no one, but it seemed to stun the entire company, having the same effect that a blow on the head from a club would. After this the Regiment was ordered to fall back a few rods to a place of perfect safety. Of course the Regiment was put in this exposed position for a purpose—to attract the attention and fire of the Rebels while Gen. Hooker massed his troops in the woods. _485

No Turning Back for Corput

During Wood's effort, Union artillery was at work.

ANDERSON, HOOD COURIER, CSA: As one of Gen. Hood's couriers in the battle of Resaca, Ga. I was stationed near a deep cut of the railroad with our corps' Mag to direct couriers to headquarters. I was immediately in rear of a battery. I was there but a few minutes when it opened fire, which was vigorously replied to by three batteries of the enemy, numbering eighteen pieces. One was in front and one on each flank, all playing on our four guns, and I was in a very uncomfortable place. From a car load of picks on the railroad near me I got one, and soon had a gopher hole in the side of the hill. In a few minutes the infirmary corps passed by me with Col. S. S. Stanton, of the consolidated Twenty-eighth and Eighty-fourth Tennessee Infantry, who was mortally wounded, and very soon the ambulances commenced with our wounded. The dirt road was parallel with the railroad for some distance. As an ambulance with two wounded soldiers was passing a shell exploded, killing both mules. The sudden stop of the ambulance threw the driver on his head, but he was soon up and going through the field as fast as possible. The wounded men were left in the ambulance. _486

---

485 (Morhous 1879, 89)

486 (F. Anderson 1897) Which battery was firing? No matter: it drew fire from opposing batteries, probably to suppress fire before the assault began. Not mentioned elsewhere except for pickets firing.

Stevenson had delayed exposing the battery, and they had moved forward too late to dig in. Hood made sure they were to stay put regardless.

> ANDERSON, HOOD COURIER, CSA: Soon after this Lieut. F. H. Wigfall. of Gen. Hood's Staff, rode up, and ordered me to report to Hood, who was on Gen. Stewart's line, to the right of the railroad from where we were. When we found Gen. Hood, Capt. Britton, who commanded the escort, was the only one with him. All the couriers and staff were off with orders. It was there that Gen. Hood gave the order for the commander of a battery to stay at his guns until he and all the men were killed; not to leave the guns under any circumstances. [487]

Corput's Battery is now the key, the focal point, well forward of the Rebel main line, and to be sacrificed if necessary. Ward and Coburn, still not knowing what is exactly where behind the brush, do not expect to find the battery before they can get to the Rebel line.

So, Wood having cleared the left hill, the assault at the angle, with the battery, could begin.

On the Right, It's Ward's Turn

Right behind the fort, the 32nd Tennessee went in front of the battery just in time to get a view of what was coming below the hill.

> MCGUIRE, 32ND TENNESSEE, BROWN'S BRIGADE, STEVENSON, HOOD, CSA: These guns were posted on the point of a hill which broke off abruptly into a deep hollow, and overlooked the country for quite a distance. From this point skirmishers were sent forward, and soon encountered the enemy, who had massed an immense force in our front. This brought on the fight. The enemy charged up the hill upon our guns, but on account of the steepness of the hill we were powerless to inflict any damage on them, and after a most desperate struggle the guns were abandoned and we forced to retire to our rifle-pits badly cut up. [488]

> STRONG, CO B 105TH ILL WARD 1B 3D 20C: My company, B, was ordered to advance as skirmishers—that is, in a thin, spread-out line well ahead of the main advance. Skirmishers are likely to see more of the world than anyone else, up to the point when they are suddenly shot. We were told that just in

---

487 (F. Anderson 1897) Assuming he meant Corput's.
488 (McGuire 1886, 479)

our front was a Rebel fort that had been charged repeatedly, and every charge had been repulsed. Now we had to take it. Well, we knew there was "death in the pot" for some of us, wounds of all awful sorts for more of us, and supposed glory untold for the ones who came out alive. We were given forty extra cartridges to a man, and were told not to fire a gun until ordered to do so. Company B, deployed as skirmishers, led the way out of the woods into an open field and then the work began. We were to advance in a steady line with guns at "shoulder arms" until the order to charge was given. Then the skirmishers were to lie down and let the column charge over us. We first had to cross a small field and then go through a scattered peach orchard. Then, on a hill beyond, the fort sat waiting. As soon as we skirmishers moved out of the woods onto the field, the Rebs began shooting at us. Someone cried out that there was a sharpshooter in a tree sniping at us. So, in spite of our orders not to fire, a dozen of us fired into the tree. The man came tumbling down, legs spread out, and struck the ground with a thud. I remember thinking as he fell that he resembled a big squirrel. We advanced with no more shooting on our part. _489 _490

While at Wauhatchie, the 102nd had been ordered to exchange their Spencer repeaters for Springfield rifled muskets. "Want of time prevented the execution of this order," _491 and they used Spencers at Resaca with "good effect."

Then Ward's brigade starts, Benjamin Harrison in the lead.

WARD, 1B 3D 20C: When ordered I moved the column forward as rapidly as possible, ordering the double-quick to be taken as soon as the column reached the open field. _492 _493

MERRILL, 70TH IND WARD 1B 3D 20C: The command "Forward" was given in a low tone and the regiment moved silently and with perfect alignment through the woods. When the foot of the hill was reached, and a comparatively open space appeared, Colonel Harrison in a ringing voice commanded, "Cheer men for Indiana! Forward! Double quick! March!" The cheers swelled into a grand shout as the whole line rushed forward. _494

489 (Strong 1961)
490 Many skirmishers by now had Spencer repeating rifles, giving them almost the firepower of a regiment.
491 (Fleharty, Our Regiment. A History of the 102d Illinois Infantry Volunteers 1865, 49)
492 (OR, Series I Vol 38 Part 2 Serial 73: Reports n.d., 338)
493 When Wood had cleared the first crest, apparently.
494 (S. Merrill 1900, 71)

They had to run over some Fourth Corps infantry to get over the hill.

> WARD, 1B 3D 20C: Their progress was much impeded by other soldiers, who had laid down in these woods, and had to be run over or driven out of the way—whose men I cannot say, a part of one of the brigades belonging to this division, I suppose. .495

The next regiment in line:

> FLEHARTY, 102ND ILL WARD 1B 3D 20C: The distance from the point where the charging column was formed to the enemy's line, was about six hundred yards. A valley lay between, and their works were upon the crest of a hill beyond. A heavy growth of young pines covered all the hills and completely masked their position. At length about half-past eleven o'clock the command "forward" ran along the line, and the column quickly moved down the hillside. Simultaneously with the beginning of the movement the rebels opened fire. Then "forward!" was the word shouted and repeated by almost every tongue. And a wild, prolonged battle yell that swelled from all lips, arose distinct and terrific above the roar of battle, as down into the valley and across the open field where death rode on every passing breeze then up the hillside where the twigs and branches of the young pines were clipped by the bullets like corn blades in a hail storm the charging columns moved not in regular lines, but enmasse, disorganized by the inequalities of the ground and the dense growth of pines on to the summit, towards the rebel cannons which belched forth fire, grape-shot and shell to the last instant men dropping dead and wounded on every hand into the earthworks surrounding the guns, and the guns were ours. .496

Harrison's Sergeant Major, Merrill's nephew, describes:

> J. L. KETCHAM, 70TH IND WARD 1B 3D 20C: Being Sergeant Major I could form in line anywhere, so I selected the extreme left of the regiment, as that position seemed nearest the supposed line of the enemy. I say supposed because we soldiers did not know where the enemy was. We only saw a hill opposite our hill and an open field between the two hills. The enemy's hill was covered with a dense thicket. There was no firing; we could only surmise what was proposed. We slipped quietly down the hill. The first sound that broke the stillness was the ringing voice of our Colonel: "Cheers

---

495 (OR, Series I Vol 38 Part 2 Serial 73: Reports n.d., 338) 4th Division Troops.
496 (Fleharty, Our Regiment. A History of the 102d Illinois Infantry Volunteers 1865) Allowing his narrative to get ahead of the story.

for Indiana!" Then such a shout and a rush! Being on the extreme left and a good runner, I kept a little in advance; remember looking along the line and noticing how straight it kept, notwithstanding all were running at full speed—no better line on dress parade. .497

Then the third regiment, right behind:

HALSTEAD, 79TH OHIO WARD 1B 3D 20C: At last the command was whispered along the lines: "Advance, carefully; advance!" The brigade crawled on up through the thicket; bushes shaking, and sticks breaking, but all was very quiet. By degrees it forged ahead until it came in whispers that the enemy had abandoned their works, but others whispered that he was only holding his fire for the propitious moment. At last there fell a shower of lead, accompanied by the familiar discharge of musketry and shrieks and groans drowned by the yell that told those far away of the charge. From a single volley the enemy's musketry developed into a continuous roar, and the boys in blue struggled furiously with the bushes on up the steep hillside, which was combed by cannister from cannon, the throat of which were so crammed with this favored pill that their bark was choked and unnatural. .498

CONGLETON, CO F 105TH ILL WARD 1B 3D 20C: The Division is formed in five lines all being ready we moved forward—when we reached the top of the ridge the enemy gave us a shower of balls and shells—grape & canester and anything and everything they had in store to stop us—at about the second blast from their cannon Lieutenant Tirtlott went down struck in the hip. The only commissioned officer we have with us. This placed our Orderly Sargeant in command of the Company (Melvin Smith). .499

And their skirmishers went with them:

STRONG, CO B 105TH ILL WARD 1B 3D 20C: The bugle sung out "Skirmishers, lie down," and in the next minute, "Charge!" and the rest of the boys went over us with a yell. Most of the skirmishers, I among them, got up and joined the charging column and went up the hill with the rest. .500

497 (S. Merrill 1900, 96)
498 (Halstead n.d.)
499 (Congleton n.d.)
500 (Strong 1961)

Hazen's attack being over, that part of Sherman's plan had already failed; Hindman and Cumming could turn artillery on Ward. This was the first disruption of Hooker's efforts, starting a breakdown of the whole effort.

> RITTER, ROWAN'S BATTERY, JOHNSON'S BATTALION, HOOD'S CORPS, CSA: In making the charge just described, the right of the enemy's column passed within three hundred yards of Rowan's battery, giving the latter the opportunity to open a terrific fire upon them. Many were killed and wounded, as they knew from the number of litters they saw leaving the field. _501

Not all soldiers charged.

> FLEHARTY, 102ND ILL WARD 1B 3D 20C: An amusing anecdote is related of a recruit who moved forward with the column but took the earliest opportunity to get behind a stump. He was reprimanded by an officer and ordered forward, but protested in this style: "I don't want to charge on that battery. I will be sure to get shot if Gen. Hooker wants more cannon let him say so, and I will throw in and help buy them for him" Deponent did not say what regiment the recruit belonged to, but of one thing we may rest assured, he was a genuine Yankee, and had very peculiar financial "notions" of war. _502

While Ward's 1st Brigade was heading down the hill, Coburn's 2nd Brigade was trying to get started behind him.

Coburn and Ireland, Racing for the Same Prize

Coburn was to encounter his own obstacle. It was not the enemy.

> ALEXANDER, CO D 111TH PA, IRELAND'S 3B 2D 20C: Soon after our division moved up to their support, but as usual General John W. Geary became excited and in a very unmilitary way we were hurried to the front, passing through the lines of the 3d division.

> COBURN, 2B 3D 20C: Soon after this order was changed and the brigade directed to be formed in two lines in the rear of the First Brigade, which was being done, but before the completion of the deployment orders were given to advance at once and as rapidly as possible to support the First Brigade,

501 (Ritter n.d.)
502 (Fleharty, Our Regiment. A History of the 102d Illinois Infantry Volunteers 1865, 59) That offer again.

which was making an advance upon the enemy's works. The brigade was moved forward at once in the following order: First line, Eighty-fifth Indiana, Colonel Baird, on the right; Nineteenth Michigan, Colonel Gilbert, on the left. Second line, Twentieth Connecticut, Colonel Ross, on the right; Twenty-second Wisconsin, Colonel Utley, on the left. Third line, Thirty-third Indiana, Major Miller, in rear of the Twenty-second Wisconsin. The brigade was thus formed in a narrow ravine, very thickly wooded with low and bushy trees, with steep hill-sides, and out of view of the enemy and their works. The advance was difficult up this steep ascent. [503]

BRADLEY, CHAPLAIN, 22ND WIS COBURN 2B 3D 20C: An officer rides up and asks, "What regiment?"

"Twenty-second Wisconsin," says a man.

"Forward, double-quick up the hill!"

And away we went over a whole brigade of troops, lying with heads close to the ground to avoid the rain of shot. [504] Shell came crashing and howling, ripping their way like thunder-bolts through the tree-tops; men fall around in the crashing fire; while down across an open valley rushes the regiment, with broken lines but eager steps, while from right, left and front, they pour in grape, cannister and bullet. [505]

GREENMAN, COMPANY H 20TH CONN COBURN 2B 2D 20C, CORPORAL: At the appointed time the command was ordered forward. Up the mountains we went, on top of which was one brigade of Geary's division (second) lying down. [506]

Whose brigade? If not Howard's 4th Corps, was it really Ireland's 3rd Brigade of Geary's division. Did Greenman identify them by their white stars? The question comes up below.

DICKINSON, CO E 22ND WIS COBURN 2B 3D 20C: May 15th. And as we tramped over a whole brigade of troops, laying down, to avoid the shower

<hr>

503 (OR, Series I Vol 38 Part 2 Serial 73: Reports n.d., 378)
504 Not identified but must have been part of 4th Corps, who were being crowded. Maps show Grose's 3rd Brigade of Stanley's 1st Division. Grose's report has 30th Indiana relieving 75th Illinois who then became skirmishers.
505 (Bradley 1865, 94)
506 (Greenman 1897)

of bullets, some I presume, got stepped on, for they called out, go in boys, give 'em hell; never mind if you do step on us. ‑507

They did not get away that quickly, though it may have seemed a moment. They had to pass through a brigade of 4th Corps and were themselves passed by another brigade.

Ireland Had Already Started

I have been like a destroying angel ever since, no height has been too bold, no valley too deep, no fastness too stormy, that I did not solicit to be permitted to storm. –Geary

At the same moment on Ireland's left a portion of Butterfield's division was racing with him for the same prize –Geary

GEARY, 2D 20C: Everything being in readiness the advance was ordered. Ireland's brigade crossed a ravine and a hill swept by the enemy's artillery and musketry fire, and drove the enemy impetuously from another hill, and, turning a little to the right, charged with wild, ringing cheers for the capture of a battery, which from a key position was dealing death on every side. At the same moment on Ireland's left a portion of Butterfield's division was racing with him for the same prize. ‑508 ‑509

Before reading the real story, let us note some tricks. He does not mention that Ward had already gone over the hill. He said Butterfield was on Ireland's left. But then, had Ireland really gotten in front and laid down and waited till Ward had started? He did not say that Ireland had moved through Coburn like a perpendicular ram. Either way, we shall soon see that Ireland started with Coburn.

MILLER, 111TH PA IRELAND 3B 2D 20C: At ten AM on sunday the battle began and grew sharp all along our front and our brigade the third were sent in to fight and of all rough ground I ever saw for troops to move on that was the worst for it was up one steep hill and then down again and the ground was covered with sharp stone and the pine brush was so thick that it was

507 (Dickinson n.d.)
508 (OR, Series I Vol 38 Part 2 Serial 73: Reports n.d., 118) To support does not mean to overrun.
509 'twas Geary racing Butterfield by proxy.

next to an impossibility to get through it and worse than all the rest the rebs threw shell and canister over and all around us. .510

BARNUM, 149TH NY IRELAND 3B 2D 20C: The brigade was ordered to move about a mile to the right, massing in a ravine in rear of the Third Division, which was then assaulting a hill in their front. .511 The troops in our immediate front, becoming closely engaged, this brigade was ordered forward, moving up a steep hill by column of regiments. .512 .513

Massing in the rear . . . of the Third Division . . which was then assaulting a hill . . . in their front . . . the troops in our front becoming closely engaged . . . this brigade was ordered forward. Parse the sentence and compare to Geary's words. Interpretation: Ireland raced to get behind Ward and was ordered forward by Geary after Ward started, to race Coburn—who had not, that we can tell, been told of any such race.

Swept With the Current

How little a sham battle is like a real one. —*Merrill*

COBURN, 2B 3D 20C: At the time of receiving this order to advance, and throughout the movement up the hill, the Second Division of the Twentieth Corps was moving by the left flank in from six to eight lines from right to left through my brigade, breaking and intercepting the lines, and preventing any regimental commander from seeing his own troops, or the possibility, for the time, of managing them. The brigade, notwithstanding, moved forward over the hill and onward, carrying some men of the Second Division with them, and losing others of its own men, who were swept with the heavier current to the left. .514

MILLER, 33RD IND COBURN 2B 3D 20C: May 15th, our brigade moved in the morning and marched to the left past the Fourteenth, Fourth, and Twenty-third Corps and halted on the left of the road, and the regiment was formed

---

510 (Miller 1969, 141)
511 Probably when Wood's 3rd Brigade went to the first crest.
512 (OR, Series I Vol 38 Part 2 Serial 73: Reports n.d., 268)
513 Barnum was not present with the brigade until Kennesaw, a later battle. Ireland commanded the brigade but was wounded and replaced during the battle by Cobham, who presumably commanded until Barnum returned. So Barnum's report is what he learned from others.
514 (OR, Series I Vol 38 Part 2 Serial 73: Reports n.d., 378)

as column of division. About 10 oclock the regiment was ordered forward, and after advancing about a mile to the front filed to the right, and finally the brigade formed in two lines of battle, two regiments front, with the Thirty-third Indiana Volunteers in the rear of the second line and to the left and rear of the Twenty-second Wisconsin. Our brigade then moved forward through thick pine woods and over very rough ground toward a range of lulls that were occupied by the enemy. Our brigade in the movement supported a charge made by the First Brigade. The movement was very much delayed by the passage of some other troops marching by the left flank across our line of advance, and the brigade was very much confused for a time by this movement. _515

Ireland's first two battalions went forward, ordered by Geary himself, the 29th Pennsylvania first, followed by the 78th New York.

RICKARDS, 29TH PENN IRELAND 3B 2D 20C: Moved up and occupied a hill in front of a strong breast-work of the rebels, which we were ordered to charge in column by regiments. My regiment had the advance. _516 I was ordered by General Geary to push on, and the supporting regiments would follow. _517

CHATFIELD, 78TH NY IRELAND 3B 2D 20C: When the general commanding division ordered an advance, the Twenty-ninth Pennsylvania, forming first line, charged down the hill, and soon the order was given for the second line to also advance. _518

The rest of Ireland was jammed in with Coburn—while both were crossing the 4th Division!

BAIRD, 85TH IND COBURN 2B 3D 20C: While so doing the regiment was thrown into some confusion by having to pass through five or six columns of the Second Division, moving by the left flank, and over several lines of battle that were lying down awaiting orders. Gaining the crest of the ridge the regiment met a terrific storm of grape and canister from the enemy's

---

515 (OR, Series I Vol 38 Part 2 Serial 73: Reports n.d., 394)
516 First in line of six regiments, leaving the four coming back, according to Miller, who was in the fifth of those left after Rickards got forward before they were stopped.
517 (OR, Series I Vol 38 Part 2 Serial 73: Reports n.d., 308)
518 (OR, Series I Vol 38 Part 2 Serial 73: Reports n.d., 287)

guns placed on works on the ridge beyond, between which was an open field in the valley, yet the regiment moved bravely forward. .519

Baird indicates Ireland crossed through while on the way up the hill, not at the top.

Swinging His Sword and Ordering Us to Lie Down

Usually the brigade commander was in the middle of the lines, where he could best see. When did he realize the problem? Either way, this was the second major blunder of the assault. Who is at fault? Now we see the confusion and disarray evolve:

> ENGLE, CO B 137TH NY IRELAND 3B 2D 20C: General Geary ordered our brigade to charge a fort. We started and in a few minutes Col Ireland was in front of his brigade swinging his sword and ordering us to lay down. Geary reported him to Hooker and Thomas. They approved Irelands plan. They told Geary they didn't want their men slaughtered in no such way. .520

When Ireland stopped, Geary objected to Hooker and Thomas. They sided with Ireland, according to Engle, though we'll see below that Hooker then sent the two rear regiments forward. Things do not appear to be moving fast if the generals are having a dispute in the middle of movements. Note Engle implies Thomas was there. Or was Engle referring to a discussion they had later?

The first two battalions did not get the word and kept going, the first real tragedy from the blunder of sending Ireland forward.

> SPOOR. CO. B, 137TH NY IRELAND 3B 2D 20C: Sunday the 15th we were moved over to the center and massed for a charge on a rebel battery. Everything was in readiness, and the front lines ordered forward, General Geary directing the movement in person. As there were already more men than could operate successfully, the 3rd Brigade was ordered to lie down; but the order came too late, for the 78th NYV and companies B and G of the 137th not receiving it in time, rushed forward to the desperate charge.

---

519 (OR, Series I Vol 38 Part 2 Serial 73: Reports n.d., 415) Ireland's brigade, crossing from right to left by the flank means two to four lines moving through like a parade, diagonally across the formation.
520 (Engle n.d.) Letter to wife, May 21, from Cassville, Georgia.

Fortunately Co. B did not have a man hurt and only one man wounded in Co. G. ˍ521

VOORHIS, 137TH NY IRELAND 3B 2D 20C: This regiment was formed on the right of the Seventy-eighth New York Volunteers, and *ordered by the general commanding the division* to charge and carry a fort in our immediate front. The regiment started, but was ordered to halt *by the colonel commanding the brigade.* ˍ522

RICKARDS, 29TH PENN IRELAND 3B 2D 20C: Passing over the Third Division, which lay in our front, I soon arrived within close range of the enemy, who, aroused by the cheering of the Third Division as we passed over them, were fully prepared and met us with a destructive fire. I ordered my men to lie down and pick off their men. ˍ523

Ireland's first line has gone into the fire. They still do not know they are alone!

MILLER, 111TH PA IRELAND 3B 2D 20C: And when we that is our regt got within a half mile of the reb lines we came to the men of the third division [Coburn's] all broken up and *although we were the fifth line when we started the other four ran to the rear passing over and through our line* but the stern order to go forward was given by Hooker in person for he was rite behind our regt and complimented us very highly for our steadiness under such circumstances. ˍ524 ˍ525 ˍ526

Repeating Miller: Four lines in front of him in Ireland's brigade had turned around and were coming back! Imagine Coburn's men getting whipsawed by Ireland's, from right to left and then back left to right! Geary directed the last two regiments to go forward, the other regiments (except the first two) having come back. Then their left companies also tangled with Coburn's.

BARNUM, 149TH NY IRELAND 3B 2D 20C: During the execution of this movement, the One hundred and forty-ninth New York Volunteers, Lieutenant-Colonel Randall commanding, and the One hundred and eleventh Pennsylvania Volunteers, Colonel Cobham commanding, being in the rear, became separated from the rest of the brigade, and were ordered

521 (Cleutz 2010, 292)
522 (OR, Series I Vol 38 Part 2 Serial 73: Reports n.d., 295)
523 (OR, Series I Vol 38 Part 2 Serial 73: Reports n.d., 308)
524 (Miller 1969, 141)
525 Broken up because the first lines of Ireland had crashed through Coburn's lines.
526 Fifth line of the brigade.

by Major-General Hooker to move rapidly forward and occupy a hill upon which a battery of the enemy was posted, and for which the troops of the Third Division were then fighting. .527 .528 .529 For the particulars of this movement and its successful accomplishment, resulting in the capture of four pieces of artillery, I respectfully refer you to the reports of Colonel Cobham and Lieutenant-Colonel Randall already forwarded. .530

Indeed! There is much more to that. What Barnum wrote was for the official report, glossing over much. He wrote what others told him. He wasn't even there!

COBHAM, 111TH PA IRELAND 3B 2D 20C: Here I was ordered by Major-General Hooker, commanding Twentieth Corps, to advance to the summit of the opposite ridge, on which the enemy had a battery in position and a strong line of breast-works, and hold the position if possible. I immediately moved my line forward, down the hill, across the intervening plain, and up the opposite ridge. The ground for the whole distance of about half a mile was thickly covered with timber and brush and exposed to the enemy's fire. .531

For Cobham, the whole distance was covered with timber and brush. Not so for Randall, the ground being cleared directly in front of the fort. Where did Cobham go? He will emerge in due time at a convenient juncture.

RANDALL, 149TH NY IRELAND 3B 2D 20C: At about 12 m. we were ordered forward, the regiments moving in line between. I had moved *forward but a few yards w*hen I found other troops, some lying down, which very much disordered our line. I halted and endeavored to re-establish my line, but was immediately ordered forward by the general commanding division, and upon my representing the condition of things to him he directed me to change direction to the right. I represented to him that the ground was covered with troops lying down, and was again peremptorily ordered to move forward. I immediately put the regiment in motion, changed front to the right, then leaving the brigade and advanced up the hill, passing over several lines of men lying down, the left of the regiment getting entangled

527 Companies K, G, and B of the 111th Pennsylvania went with Walker.
528 Behind and separated: sent by Hooker after the others were forward?
529 Places these two regiments behind at least some of the 3rd Division.
530 (OR, Series I Vol 38 Part 2 Serial 73: Reports n.d., 268)
531 (OR, Series I Vol 38 Part 2 Serial 73: Reports n.d., 276).

with troops moving in other directions and separated from the balance of the regiment. ₋532

His brigade had been moving by the left flank. That might be an oversimplification. Then the middle regiments had gotten tangled with Coburn's or had gotten ahead and gone on. On being told to go forward, Randall changed his front to the right. How far left had he gotten before he changed direction?

The middle regiments, which stopped and returned, were sent left—not to the hill. They would be sent up after the assault was over. Part of Cobham's regiment was crowded out and went somewhere, not to the hill with the fort, and stayed.

> BOYLE, ADJUTANT, 111TH PA IRELAND 3B 2D 20C: As the division moved forward its line contracted and crowded out Companies K, G, and B, of the One Hundred and Eleventh Regiment. By direction of General Geary, and under command of Lieutenant Colonel Walker, these companies advanced alone to the crest of one of the hills, where they lay upon their arms in front of the enemy's works under sharpshooters' fire, remaining there during the day. ₋533 ₋534

> WALKER, 111TH PA IRELAND 3B 2D 20C: The division having been formed by column of regiments in mass, when the order was given to go forward the contracting of the lines crowded out the three left companies of the regiment. Under direction of General Geary these companies advanced up the opposite hill and lay down in line at the edge of a field, on the opposite side of which were the enemy's works. We remained here, under fire of the enemy's sharpshooters, until about 4 p.m. when I was directed to rejoin my own brigade, who were on the right of us. This we did at once, these companies remaining there for the balance of the day. ₋535

Coburn went on with the rest of his regiment. Where?

---

532 Randall's regiment left the brigade, then the left part of his regiment mixed with other troops and moved with them. The left three companies were moved to a hill further left.
533 (Boyle 1903)
534 Under sharpshooter fire on a crest does not give enough information to locate them.
535 (OR, Series I Vol 38 Part 2 Serial 73: Reports n.d., 73) Walker's three left companies that had gotten tangled with Coburn's brigade and eventually gone to the left, stayed at the left of the cleared field in front of the fort.

Shooting From Behind - Not Part of a Mock Battle

Going downhill, toward the road, with parts of Ireland's brigade going to the left, front, or right of Coburn's, all passing through the 4th Corps, is not something practiced in mock battles. Ireland's regiments went their separate ways except for some companies that got caught with Coburn's or Ward's brigades. 536

> NOBLE, 19TH MICH COBURN 2B 3D 20C: There was several lines of battle in front of our reg't or Brigade when we got into position but when ordered to advance the front lines with the exception of the one in advance did not move. We were under the fire from the rebel batteries at that time and the Grape & Canister were flying around us at a rate in no wise pleasant or agreeable, and we were all lying flat on the ground. As the front lines did not stir our Brigade was ordered to charge past them and forward we went walking right over them and just as we passed the one next the front those in the rear came up behind us and without seeing a rebel commenced firing right through our lines.

Whose lines that Noble had to pass through did not move? The first line moved on, and as Noble moved through the others, the second, which is now the first of those that did not move, raised up and fired into them? He continues...

> We were on the side of a hill and they were a little above us. This is all that saved us from being shot down by our own men. As it was there was more men in our Corps killed & wounded by this piece of carelessness than by any firing that the rebels done. It was a trying time. The smoke from the guns was almost blinding and the bullits whistled past our ears so close in some instances that they could be felt. Lester Baird was shot through both arms one ball taking effect in his wrist and the other above the elbow. This was done by our own men. R. Patterson was shot in the leg. O. A. Rose had one of his fingers shot off and Rodgers was struck on his side by a spent ball. This comprises the list of casualties in our Company. Our Col. was severely if not mortally wounded and our Adjutant was shot through the arm. 537

The 149th New York was in front of the 19th Michigan.

536 Military tactics were not to mix units, especially while in motion. Constant drilling, though, may have been the reason the units were able to fit in with other organizations as the mix evolved.
537 (Noble n.d.)

ORMSBY, CO E 149TH NY IRELAND 3B 2D 20C: I suppose you have heard about the battle of last Sunday and who was killed or wounded in our outfit. Our company was lucky. Charles Horton, one of the new recruits is missing. There wasn't but one killed, Andersag of company B. Some of the companies had quite a number wounded. The doctor says that most of them were hit by the regiment that was behind us that fired into us. _538

RANDALL, 149TH NY IRELAND 3B 2D 20C: As the regiment reached the top of the hill and began to descend on the other side we received the fire of the enemy, and at that point a regiment of some other command (the Nineteenth Michigan, as I learn), which was within a few yards following us, as they received the enemy's fire, opened fire directly in our backs, severely wounding numbers of my men. _539

Two things: Randall's 149th New York, one of Ireland's regiments, the one that was sent forward by Hooker after the collision, was now in front of Gilbert's 19th Michigan. Thus, both were going downhill, and someone fired into both. It suggests the one firing into – and over – the 19th, was the one firing into the 149th.

And who was behind them, doing the firing? Maybe some of Ireland's brigade that got left behind? Some of 4th Corps?

Into the Fire!

I Ordered My Men to Lie Down and Pick off Their Men. —Rickards

I then learned for the first time that the order for the charge had been countermanded. –Rickards

They apparently were right of Ward's line, taking fire from Hindman. Another real tragedy of the now-botched start.

MOUAT, CO G, 29TH PENN IRELAND 3B 2D 20C: We moved through the woods up a hill we had not gone far when the Rebs opened on us from three sides Killing and wounding about 70 of our Regiment in a very few minutes Our company lost Jim Hunter, John McCaully Dick Powell Killed—Geo Spangler wounded and died in Chattanooga hospital—and Bill Franks wounded and died afterwards—Johnny Griffith Harvey Shellenbarger Jack McKenna John Shuler Jim Bund wounded—Our Lieut Bob Bonner being in

538 (Ormsby n.d.)
539 (OR, Series I Vol 38 Part 2 Serial 73: Reports n.d., 304)

command of Company A was also wounded moving on their works I saw a Reb flag on the breast works and I started for it I had not gone far when I heard some one shout "Dave for Gods sake stop" I looked back and saw Sergeant Culbertson of Company A who said "Orders are to fall back as no supports are following us," we laid down and crawled back as fast as we could and soon joined our Companies, It appeared that the Johnnies had on our right and left some artillery flanked and connected by a trench in the shape of a horse shoe it was a very hot hole for awhile – Dick Powell and Jack McCaully were the first ones Killed, Jack's brother Aleck and I catching him before he fell. .540

RICKARDS, 29TH PENN IRELAND 3B 2D 20C: On ascertaining that no support was coming, I ordered my men to move back, and took my former position. I then learned for the first time that the order for the charge had been countermanded. The loss of the regiment in this charge was 6 men killed and 53 wounded. .541

CHATFIELD, 78TH NY IRELAND 3B 2D 20C: The regiment immediately advanced steadily down the hill and partly up the opposite hill, upon which the enemy's works were placed, when, finding a portion of the Twenty-ninth Pennsylvania retiring in disorder from the terrific fire of the enemy, the regiment halted and lay down. .542

MOUAT, CO G, 29TH PENN IRELAND 3B 2D 20C: As we crawled back I came across a friend in Company D—Billy Denny who was badly wounded I said Hello Billy let me help you off he said No Dave I can't move I might as well die here tell them at home I died like a soldier and tell my mother to give my money to my brother and sister, I said you are all right take this canteen of water and Keep quiet. .543

Those that got back were sent to join Ireland's other regiments that were sent left, to reserve:

CHATFIELD, 78TH NY IRELAND 3B 2D 20C Shortly I received orders to return and join the brigade, which was done, and was then ordered to throw up a line of works on the extreme left of the brigade and connecting with the

540 (Mouat n.d.)
541 (OR, Series I Vol 38 Part 2 Serial 73: Reports n.d., 308) See the total losses of the other regiments, especially of Ireland's brigade. This supports Rickard's account. He might have passed Ward's three regiments that laid down and were crowded.
542 (OR, Series I Vol 38 Part 2 Serial 73: Reports n.d., 287)
543 (Mouat n.d.)

right of the First Brigade. This was done, under a sharp fire from the enemy's sharpshooters, and the regiment bivouacked. During the days action 1 officer and 1 corporal were wounded, the former very slightly. .544

VOORHIS, 137TH NY IRELAND 3B 2D 20C: We then constructed breastworks and were held in readiness for action all night; 1 commissioned officer and 5 enlisted men wounded. .545

544 (OR, Series I Vol 38 Part 2 Serial 73: Reports n.d., 287)
545 (OR, Series I Vol 38 Part 3 Serial 74: Reports n.d., 296)

Ward's Three Rear Regiments Stalled

Thus, Ward's brigade had gone forward—with Coburn's brigade expected behind and to their right. But the supporting demonstration by Hazen had ended, leaving the cannons of Cumming and Hindman unhindered, to slow and disorganize Ward's brigade and make it drift left.

GRUNERT, CO D 129TH ILL WARD 1B 3D 20C: The bayonets were fixed and the command "forward march" was given, which was promptly obeyed. The way from here to the fort was covered with underbrush and almost impenetrable, and only with the greatest difficulty could one regiment follow the other; the tapes of the haversacks and canteens of many tore, but the men had to leave them and advance—there was no time now for mending such things. The fort was situated on a slight elevation, and although we had advanced quite a distance, yet we could see nothing of the fort. The regiments remained in pretty good line, despite the brush, and everything went on well until we came to the border of an open space, where a most murderous fire of the enemy unexpectedly saluted us. This unexpected fire, that had killed several of our men, caused some confusion in our ranks, some companies were completely disorganized, while here and there parts of regiments stood dispirited. The command "lay down" brought all down on the ground. After remaining there several seconds, during which the enemy's fire slackened, the command to arise was given and obeyed, when the enemy again opened on us and causing the loss of many valuable lives. We advanced some distance and again threw ourselves on the ground.

WARD, 1B 3D 20C: I followed the second regiment until, looking, I discovered the rear regiments losing distance and obliquing to the left. I ordered them to oblique to the right and move quickly up to their proper position. The third battalion was crowded upon by the fourth and fifth, the last attempting to gain proper places, but none of them obeying the order to oblique to the right to cover the first two battalions. Shot and shell were flying and bursting when my orders were given, but the orders were not repeated, and may not have been heard. ₋546

CONGLETON, CO F 105TH ILL WARD 1B 3D 20C: Lying between the ridge over which we passed and the ridged hill on which the Rebels were entrenched is an open field—but by keeping to the left so as to travel a half circle we managed to keep in the brush and timber. The brush were so thick that we could not keep our regular lines. When the lead & iron came too thick we dropped at full length on the ground until it slackened some then rushed forward again until the works were taken.

PEAK, CO F 129TH ILL WARD 1B 3D 20C: The brush was hard for the men to push their way through. The enemy's bullets came thick and fast. At a suitable place the men were ordered to lay down and when the enemy's fire slackened a little, we were again ordered to advance.

DUSTIN, 105TH ILL WARD 1B 3D 20C: While the column was moving forward to the charge the brigade supporting us on the left crowded too far to the right, producing some confusion in my left wing and retarding its movements. The same trouble was experienced in the One hundred and twenty-ninth Illinois, which still more impeded my advance. .547

Getting fire from the right, drifting left, and getting crowded by part of Coburn, the three regiments got mixed up.

CRAM, CO F 105TH ILL WARD 1B 3D 20C: At 12 we fixed bayonets and dashed over the hill. A perfect shower of shot, shell and grape met us thinning our ranks sadly, (Tirtlot fell on the first shot) but without the least check we flew down the hill crossed the road at the front, climbed over some breastworks the rebels had left and began the run of the hill where they were posted. The 105th was the last regt. but the two in front of us (79 Ohio & 129 Ill.) immediately laid down at the foot of this hill and our regt. ran right over them. They were behind and in among us which so mixed us up that amidst the tangled underbrush it was impossible to distinguish our lines and keep together, so it was every man for himself. .548

Here, Randall's 149th New York, of Ireland's brigade, becomes part of what will be the first wave of Ward's brigade after Harrison's 70th Indiana and the 102nd Illinois.

RANDALL, 149TH NY IRELAND 3B 2D 20C: I moved the regiment forward as rapidly as possible out of their fire and advanced down the slope across the main road, and in an open field of some 200 [yards] in width, overtaking and mingling with a confused line representing several regiments of the Third Division, Twentieth Army Corps, and advanced with them at a run, taking the front line, receiving as we passed across the road and field a terrible fire

547 (OR, Series I Vol 38 Part 2 Serial 73: Reports n.d., 360)
548 (Cram 2001, 00)

of grape and canister from guns on the summit of a hill toward which we were moving. _549

Ward's front two regiments had raced on, ahead of the mess.

> HARRISON, 70TH IND WARD 1B 3D 20C: My regiment leading, passed from the crest of an intrenched ridge, occupied by our forces, across an open field in the valley and up a steep and thickly wooded hill to the assault of the enemy's breastworks, whose strength, and even exact location, was only revealed by the line of fire which, with fearful destructiveness, was belched upon our advancing column. I moved my men at the double-quick and, with loud cheers, across the open space in the valley in order sooner to escape the enfilading fire from the enemy's rifle-pits on our right and to gain the cover of the woods, with which the side of the hill against which our assault was directed was thickly covered. _550

The broken ranks of Harrison's 70th Indiana and the 102nd Illinois had managed to keep moving, leaving the rear regiments in collision after stalling and drifting left from fire on the right.

> WARD, 1B 3D 20C: About this time these regiments reached a place beyond the road, and all laid down without any order from me. I ordered them to rise up and advance at the double-quick. They obeyed and moved rapidly to the attack to sustain the other regiments. _551 _552

> GRUNERT, CO D 129TH ILL WARD 1B 3D 20C: Our first line, however, was completely broken and when we arose again after a short while, nothing but the broken ranks of our former line were seen rushing toward the enemy, which they reached, as the distance was but short.

> PEAK, CO F 129TH ILL WARD 1B 3D 20C: The men were on their feet in a second, and at this moment, Sargeant Hesse was shot. General Ward was shot in the shoulder and these are the words he said, moving his hat in the air, "go on boys and give them the devil, I am shot." And the boys did go on. Brush was so thick it was impossible for them to keep in line, and it seemed like it was going to be a defeat, but on they went and when they reached the

549 (OR, Series I Vol 38 Part 2 Serial 73: Reports n.d., 304)
550 (OR, Series I Vol 38 Part 2 Serial 73: Reports n.d., 369)
551 (OR, Series I Vol 38 Part 2 Serial 73: Reports n.d., 338)
552 No mention of being wounded.

fort, companies H. E. and F. were all mixed but they took their place in ranks just the same, as they would with their one company. ⌐553

Constant drilling paid off: they knew how to assemble themselves in some fashion and follow the first two regiments despite the confusion caused by Ireland and Hindman.

(Ward left two reports, one for himself and one for Butterfield, who had left without filing one. The two descriptions above may actually refer to one delay.)

Butterfield was there watching, according to Dickinson, and made sure Coburn's brigade kept going:

> DICKINSON, CO E 22ND WIS COBURN 2B 3D 20C: When Gen. Butterfield saw his 1st Brigade lie down, he came to Col. Coburn, and says, Col. will your men storm those rebel works; yes, Gen. my men would storm the gates of Hell, if I asked them to. ⌐554

Geary's 1st Brigade - Blocked

Now we look at what Geary was doing further left while the assault took place.

While Ward, Coburn, and Ireland were advancing, Geary's 1st Brigade was taking positions around the first hill, behind and left of Wood's position. Some were spread to the right. One tried to advance but was stopped by the crowd. That was as far as they got for some time.

> PARDEE, 147TH PA CANDY 1B 2D 20C: The battalions being closed in mass they were set in motion by the commanding officer of the brigade, under the personal superintendence of the division commander, and ordered to take the fort at all hazards. ⌐555 I can only say that I did not see the fort and do not think my command was within 200 yards of it when I halted, being unable to pass over the numerous lines of troops in my front, of which I had no knowledge at the time of starting, without breaking my line and thus rendering it useless in the charge. Under orders communicated by Lient. Samuel Goodman, acting assistant inspector-general, First Brigade, Second

---

553 Finding a place in all the confusion; testimony of constant drilling.
554 (Dickinson n.d.)
555 When was this order given? Was Ireland already underway?

Division, Twentieth Army Corps, I withdrew my regiment under cover of the ridge over which we had just passed. ₋556

Coburn Moves Left Toward Wood's Position

Artillery fire from the right had pushed Coburn to Ward's left instead of right after the crowding by Ireland.

Behind the skirmishers, Ward's brigade crossed the road, observed by Winkler, whose regiment was furthest right in Wood's brigade.

> WINKLER, 26TH WIS WOOD 3B 3D 20C: At this time I saw skirmishers of the 1st Brigade coming out of the woods *on the right* of the road advancing toward my line from the rear. *Immediately behind* them a *line of battle* appeared, *crossed the road obliquely* & marched up the hill behind my line, ₋557

Winkler, on the right of the left hill, would have seen Ward's skirmishers, not yet across the road, as behind him. Behind them should have been Ward's regiments. They moved left. Some of Coburn's men were even further left.

> REID, CO A 22ND WIS COBURN 2B 3D 20C: Ward's brigade dashed across the hollow up the side of the hill and stopped, when our boys, were ordered forward double quick. Our brigade formed only two lines of battle of two regiments in a line. ... ₋558 They advanced across the hollow in pretty good order but somewhat broken by the rough ground they had passed over, but the bushes and the rough hill side broke all semblance of a line. The advance, however, was not checked for a moment, all pressed forward, the companies keeping together. *They charged over four regiments of the 1st Brigade lying on the side hill.* ...

Was that Ward's last three, plus possibly Randall's 149th NY?

> ... Before they got up, the whole regiment except Companies A and F became entangled in the bushes and had to stop. ₋559 Those two

556 This puts Pardee between Knipe's right and Wood's left.
557 Coburn's.
558 Per Coburn and supported by events, the 19th Michigan was on the left of the front row on the left and the 22nd Wisconsin was behind them. Reid, who was not actually in the assault, but going by what his comrades told him, had stated "The 22d Wisconsin and 19th Michigan were in the first line, the 19th on the right."
559 See Winkler below. It may have been the 3rd Brigade.

Companies had comparatively an open space and advanced beyond the rebel guns with a part of the 19th Michigan and of the 70th Indiana—Ward's Brigade. 560

The 22nd Wisconsin was going too far left, while two of their companies had joined the leading lines.

> GREENMAN, COMPANY H 20TH CONN COBURN 2B 2D 20C, CORPORAL: Through the lines we passed, then down the slope, from which the enemy had cut the trees so that the cannon from their fort could do better execution, across the old Dalton turnpike, where we received an infilading fire from a rebel battery on our right, then up an incline, on which were growing shrub-oak, there halting to re-form our lines, then across an opening to the rebel works. With Yankee hurrahs, answered by the rebel yell so familiar to all old soldiers of the Civil war, with the thunder of their artillery and a tremendous burst of musketry from both sides, the struggle began. 561

Halting to reform lines—after getting through various obstacles?

The boys in Reid's regiment say that Companies A and F went up with Ward's brigade and part of the 19th Michigan, while the rest of the regiment got tangled up in the bushes on the hill left of the fort.

And the 33rd Indiana and 85th Indiana got left out in the confusion and could not get through, separated and blocked by multiple troops. Yet some of the 85th Indiana went up to the works with the 22nd Wisconsin (Companies A and F apparently) and 19th Michigan.

> MILLER, 33RD IND COBURN 2B 3D 20C: At the time the front of the brigade changed direction to the left the confusion was so great that the remainder of the brigade, the Eighty-fifth and Thirty-third Indiana, became separated from the other regiments, and when their two regiments advanced in the direction they supposed the brigade had gone there were ten or twelve lines of troops formed in various ways, and lying down and firing over lines yet in advance of them, and it became almost impossible for troops to advance in order and without confusion. Colonel Baird, Eighty-fifth Indiana, deemed it prudent to halt and await orders and reform the Eighty-fifth and Thirty-

560 (Reid 1965, 148)
561 (Greenman 1897)

third in a good position, which was done. I had reported to him in the absence of any other commanding officer. _562

BAIRD, 85TH IND COBURN 2B 3D 20C: But owing to the confusion created, as before stated, and a misapprehension of orders, the left and right wings of the regiment got separated, the left rapidly moving obliquely across the Resaca road under a terrific fire, and a portion of the right moving directly up to the enemy's works, some of the men with the Nineteenth Michigan and Twenty-second Wisconsin gaining the works. _563 _564

The separation is confirmed by Baird. Who does that leave going forward on the left, behind Winkler? Most of the 22nd Wisconsin. And the 20th Connecticut, the more experienced regiment?

Now we have Coburn's left regiments headed left, missing some companies who went with Ward, while his right regiments are blocked completely.

While some of Coburn's brigade were coming his way, one of Wood's men watched Ward's brigade charge the fort.

OSBORN, CO A 55TH OHIO WOOD 3B 3D 20C: Upon the right of the brigade the supports from the First Division came up to find the ground filled with a mixed group consisting of men from the First Brigade who had been crowded out of line, owing to an error in formation. From this point the writer saw Colonel Harrison (afterwards President Harrison) lead his command, a brigade, in four successive charges against a battery of the enemy consisting of four brass guns, which, having been planted in advance of the Confederate line, were doing us much injury.

J. L. KETCHAM, WARD 1B 3D 20C: When we reached the thicket we pushed up as fast as the obstructions would admit. The enemy's artillery opened fire while we were crossing the open field, and the sound indicated that the right of the regiment faced the guns. _565

McGuire, right behind the fort, does not mention leaving the line.

MCGUIRE, 32ND TENNESSEE, BROWN'S BRIGADE, STEVENSON, HOOD, CSA: The enemy halted at the brow of the hill, which afforded them perfect

562 (OR, Series I Vol 38 Part 2 Serial 73: Reports n.d., 394)
563 (OR, Series I Vol 38 Part 2 Serial 73: Reports n.d., 415)
564 See Wood's complaint of regiments crowding. See the Corput map.
565 (S. Merrill 1900, 96)

shelter from our bullets. This battery happened to be directly in front of the Thirty-second Tennessee Regiment, the guns being in plain view and within easy range of our rifles; so neither Federals nor Confederates could gain possession of them. They were evidently a much coveted prize to the former; for it was soon apparent that they were determined to take possession of them, and the latter were quite as much determined they should not. This struggle for the possession of the guns brought about a real "tug of war." The situation of the Thirty-second Tennessee was now one of great gravity and imminent peril; for the enemy knew they could not gain the battery until our rifles were silenced, which they would have to do by storming our position and beating us by brute force. We heard their commands—"Forward!"—and like a mighty avalanche they came in thundering charge upon us. It looked as if it would be impossible for us to withstand their terrible onslaught; but the Thirty second was never in better fighting mood, so we had the satisfaction of seeing our assailants fall back and seek the protection of the hill again, leaving many of their number dead in plain view of us. _566

Other accounts insert a gap in time and position just before that last sentence.

Into the Fort!

HALSTEAD, 79TH OHIO WARD 1B 3D 20C: Sure enough, "Johnny" was at home and looking for us, but he really did not expect that we would come on up and go to knocking at his door. The chances are that few, if any, of the enemy had heard of George W. Totton, the first to scale their works. He lit upon the parapet at a bound, toppled back a second, his musket held high, then balanced forward, and leaping among the gunners, he drove his bayonet through a brave Southern boy who was in the act of "pulling her off just once more," and tossed him from the gun as if he were a sheaf of wheat.

A moment later a hundred others came bounding in, among them a palefaced man, afterward President of the United States, who would doubtless have been on hand sooner if he could only have made Totton time. A few seconds more the fort swarmed with Yankees, and the star spangled banner was propped up in one corner by the dead who fell around it.

566 (McGuire 1886, 479)

The flag drew such a fire from lines beyond covering the fort that nothing could live near it, but one after another would rush to certain death to plant it firmly perpendicular. .567

Totten Time – he had gotten well ahead of not only his regiment but the others as well?

Here we might wonder which regiments faced which guns. Connor was manning the second gun from the attackers' left. Harrison apparently went in on the right.

Those rear three regiments that had stopped and moved left now had to get back to the right to face the front of the fort when they got close:

> CASE: 129TH ILL WARD 1B 3D 20C: The enemy opened upon the column with shell from four guns as it emerged in sight, at a distance of about 800 yards from the fort. The column then immediately entered a dense thicket of very small cedar, and as it ascended a small hill about 400 yards from the fort it met the withering fire of a whole brigade of rebel troops behind the breastworks or rifle-pits flanking the fort. Then the whole column began the charge at a double-quick and with a yell, and charged up to the fort. In the advance there was a necessary change of direction to the right, nearly at right-angles with the direction in which the column began the movement, and in consequence thereof the companies upon the right of each regiment, having a much smaller arc of a circle to pass over, arrived at or near the fort much sooner than the center or left of the regiments. When the right companies of the One hundred and twenty-ninth Regiment had arrived at the fort there was no visible evidence that any charge had been made into or through the fort, but when the actual charge into and through the fort was made the charging party consisted of parts of the right companies of each regiment in the brigade, the rear regiments having in the mean time closed upon the head of the column. .568 .569

Interpretation: the column had moved too far left and had to swing right, leaving the left companies playing catch up, like crack-the-whip. They all hit the fort off-center. (Sam Peak and Joe Peters' company, F, would have been on the right.)

---

567 (Halstead n.d.) Evidently Totton's company, though his regiment started 3rd in line, had not gotten stalled with the others. Who is to say otherwise?

568 (OR, Series I Vol 38 Part 2 Serial 73: Reports n.d., 365)

569 The 70th, not stopping as the rear three had, would have been first into the fort unless the pause to rest before climbing over gave some time to catch up.

Corput's Battery Surprised

CJH, Brown's Brigade, Stevenson's Division, Hood's Corp, CSA: A position being selected fifty yards in advance of the left wing of our command for Corput's battery of twelve pound Napoleons, numbering four guns; by the engineers redoubts were being hastily thrown up, when about twelve o'clock the enemy's skirmishers opened a heavy fire upon our pickets, driving them on their line of battle, following so closely that the 32d Tennessee, working upon the redoubt, found themselves suddenly opposed to a line of Yankees within a few rods of them, and were compelled to fight their way back to the intrenchments, hand to hand with picks, spades and rocks, the enemy planting their colors upon the battery, but unable to remove it, the 32d and 26th Tennessee regiments, commanded by the gallant Colonels Cook and Saffree, resisting every effort made. The country in our front was thickly wooded and covered with dense undergrowth, concealing their advance until very near; under this cover they had massed their troops in immense numbers and advanced cautiously in their lines of battle until sufficiently near, when they burst upon us with a loud hurrah. _570

Wesley Connor, private, Cherokee Artillery, CSA: Between one and two o'clock the Federals brought out a line on said ridge as if preparing for an advance, and we pitched into them with our guns, and were giving them the best we had, when the first thing we knew the pickets came running past our guns with the announcement that the Yankees were right on us—some of them had passed our first gun before I left my gun—(I was gunner of #2, the guns being numbered from right to left) in fact two or three of them were parting the brush in front of my gun, and I shall never forget how they looked as they came through. Each of them seemed to be about ten feet tall and big in proportion. I left my gun double shotted with canister, as two friction primers in succession had failed to do their work. Our supporting infantry, Gen. John C. Brown's Brigade of Tennesseans, were as much surprised as we were, and barely had time to get into the trenches in time to stop your advance This will explain why our battery overshot you. _571

From Connor's diary:

570 (CJH 1864) Maps show the 32nd, 66th, and 23rd Tennessee working on the fort itself; the 26th, 18th, and 3rd Tennessee are shown in the line right behind the fort. The 3rd is consistently reported as in the line behind the fort.
571 (Connor, Wesley O.; Blakeslee, George H. 1899)

CONNOR, PRIVATE, CHEROKEE ARTILLERY, CSA: 2h P.M. Yankees advanced upon our position. Our Battery was about 50 paces in front of the entrenched line. The boys stood to their guns till the Yanks were in the embrasure, when they were forced to leave, having no support nearer than the entrenchments. _572

DURHAM, 26TH TENNESSEE, BROWN'S BRIGADE, HOOD'S CORPS, CSA, SERGEANT: I wish to correct an error in the October Veteran, page 456. A communication from W. O. Conner gave the regiment of Brown's Brigade as the 'hird Tennessee', when it should be the Eighteenth, Twenty-Sixth, Thirty-Second, and Forty-Fifth Tennessee. The Twenty-Sixth being directly in rear of Corput's Battery. _573

More of Ward's Regiments

CRAM, CO F 105TH ILL WARD 1B 3D 20C: After we had arrived nearly on the rebels, we were repulsed and driven back to the foot of the hill, (here one of our boys, John McGilfrey, was wounded by my side) but we rallied here and charging again drove them from their battery and back into their rifle pits beyond. _574

STRONG, CO B 105TH ILL WARD 1B 3D 20C: We were driven back from the works once, but in a moment we rallied and without waiting for orders men were dropping all around us, but we had no time to look after them—with a rush and a cheer, which I can imagine I hear now, we drove the Rebs from the first line of works back into the second line, where their cannon were _575. The hill was so steep that the cannon fired over the first line. _576

Those rifle pits at the base of the hill, shown in Blakeslee's map, then, might have been part of the reason Ward's last three stopped: to get through that and to escape direct fire from Corput, who could not fire that low. Hindman's fire on the right still pushed them left.

---

572 (W. O. Connor, Wesley Olin Connor Diary 1867, 57)
573 (Durham 1899)
574 (Cram 2001, 00)
575 The second line here is the fort, the first being entrenchments on the hillside, which others barely mention, the enemy having evacuated.
576 (Strong 1961) First line of works being a trench below the fort.

DUSTIN, 105TH ILL WARD 1B 3D 20C: But these obstacles were soon overcome, when the men promptly jumped to their feet, and with a bound went close up under the guns of the fort, while at the same time twelve or fifteen, jumping into the fortifications, assisted materially in capturing the guns and holding them from being retaken by the enemy, one of them being shot dead in the fort. _577

That lone regiment from Ireland made it with the lead regiments. Just where is not apparent. The others do not mention:

RANDALL, 149TH NY IRELAND 3B 2D 20C: The regiment pressed steadily and rapidly forward into woods and up the hill (receiving all the time the fire of the guns and the infantry of the enemy) up to and over the enemy's guns, driving them before us out of a redoubt on the summit of the hill and into a line of breast-works some 100 yards beyond and nearly reaching the breast-works, when, having passed forward far beyond our line, we received an enfilading fire of musketry from our left. _578

And Sergeant Ketcham was past the obstructions in the thicket and so far left of his regiment he missed the fort! He found the Johnnies behind the line had deserted!

Where are they? Ketcham went clear left of the fort and found the enemy had left.

J. L. KETCHAM, WARD 1B 3D 20C: After I entered the thicket I noticed nothing until I found myself on the enemy's breastworks. Evidently these breastworks protected rebel infantry supporting their artillery. But where were the infantry? I stood some moments wondering what had become of them. I could see every evidence of their having been there; their fires were burning for cooking; their haversacks and knapsacks were there. I thought I could hear them stampeding down the hill. The breastworks were in a semicircle and obstructed my view. Why did not our boys come? I shouted "Come on!" Then I realized that I was alone and that my comrades had been drawn by the sound of the cannon to the right. I hastened in the same direction to shout my discovery. The thicket was dense. I could only see a few feet ahead of me. _579

577 (OR, Series I Vol 38 Part 2 Serial 73: Reports n.d., 360)
578 (OR, Series I Vol 38 Part 2 Serial 73: Reports n.d., 304)
579 (S. Merrill 1900, 96)

One who stayed may have been waiting for his chance to surrender.

BLAKESLEE, CO G 129TH ILL WARD 1B 3D 20C: At "P" on map ˍ580 as the left of my Company of which I had charge, was swinging into line, a man hatless and coatless jumped over the works and almost into my arms; of course he surrendered. He stated to me he was Captain ————-, I can't now tell who. His sword was gone; he stated that a shell had knocked it out of his hand. He wore officer's belt and scabbard. Standing a moment thinking what to do, he says "What are you going to do with me, for God's sake lets get out of this." I was glad to get out of that scorcher that was being played on us from our right, and by your riflemen to the rear. Part of the way down the hill turned him over to an enlisted man of a N.Y. regiment, when I hastened back to the crest of the hill. ˍ581

For a While There Was a Wild Scene

HARRISON 70TH IND WARD 1B 3D 20C: The men moved on with perfect steadiness and without any sign of faltering up the hillside and to the very muzzles of the enemy's artillery, which continued to belch their deadly charges of grape and canister, until the gunners were struck down at their guns. Having gained the outer face of the embrasures, in which the enemy had four 12-pounder Napoleon guns, my line halted for a moment to take breath. Seeing that the infantry supports had deserted the artillery, I cheered the men forward, and with a wild yell they entered the embrasures, striking down and bayoneting the rebel gunners, many of whom defiantly stood by their guns till struck down. ˍ582 Within this outer fortification, in which the artillery was placed, there was a strong line of breastworks, which was concealed from our view by a thick pine undergrowth, save at one point, which had been used as a gateway. This line was held by a rebel division of veteran troops, said to be of Hood's command. When we first entered the embrasures of the outer works the enemy fled in considerable confusion from the inner one, and had there been a supporting line brought up in good order at this juncture the second line might have easily been carried and held. My line having borne the brunt of the assault, it was not to be expected that it could be reformed for a second assault in time. ˍ583

580 See Blakeslee's Map
581 (Connor, Wesley O.; Blakeslee, George H. 1899)
582 See Cheney's article on the 1st Tennessee. Who drove off the infantry?
583 (OR, Series I Vol 38 Part 2 Serial 73: Reports n.d., 369)

MERRILL, 70TH IND WARD 1B 3D 20C: The cannon in the lunette thundered a reply, but there was no stopping till all the gunners but five were either killed or taken prisoners. For a little while there was a wild scene in the lunette, artillery men defending their guns, Union officers firing their pistols, and the men their rifles; now using their bayonets, now clubbing their muskets, now leaping on the cannon and waving their hats. The infantry in the works beyond the fort, seized with a panic, left their coats and spades in the trench where they had been working, and disappeared for the time through the woods in the rear. ₅584

MERRILL, 70TH IND WARD 1B 3D 20C: WM. SHARPE: "In charging up that hill our Company C happened to be so located in line as to go directly into the battery. When we were nearing the summit the artillery made their last shot, and the guns were so close to us as to blow the hats off our heads, but without halting we were instantly inside the fort." ₅585

MERRILL, 70TH IND WARD 1B 3D 20C: J. C. BENNETT: "We advanced in common time trailing arms till we came to an open field, and then commenced the double quick, while the shot and shell were coming thick and fast. When within a few feet of the breastworks we were ordered to fall down, and the next moment the guns fired over our heads. Then we were up and in the fort, taking four twelve pounder brass guns, with several prisoners. Here I saw a rebel hit one of our men over the head with a swab-stick, and Sergeant Thralls hit the rebel over the head with the butt of his gun. Later I saw a color bearer of one of the Illinois regiments roll up his flag, when Wm. Barnes of our company said, 'Let me have it.' Taking it he stuck the flagstaff in the parapet over the cannon, thus having it displayed without danger to life, for the sharpshooters were picking off the men as fast as they exposed themselves. Sergeant Thralls, thinking I suppose that Barnes was meddling with what was not his business, shouted, 'Get out of there or you will be shot.'" ₅586

CRAM, CO F 105TH ILL WARD 1B 3D 20C: The scene was grand and awful beyond description; a terrible sheet of lead bridged the air above us and leaden hail flew threw our ranks. Man after man went down; but no fear entered the hearts of the others. ₅587

584 (S. Merrill 1900, 98)
585 (S. Merrill 1900, 98)
586 (S. Merrill 1900, 98)
587 (Cram 2001, 100)

MERRILL, 70TH IND WARD 1B 3D 20C: THE HISTORIAN OF COMPANY D: "The advance of our assaulting column poured a heavy volley of musketry into the works, which struck down many of its defenders, yet those remaining continued resistance, some trying to reload the guns, while others struck right and left with swab-sticks and hand-spikes, knocking our men down as they mounted to the top of the parapet, and only yielding to force. During this heroic defense our regimental banner-bearer was knocked backward off the works as he was attempting to plant the flag. Alonzo Greeson was knocked down and badly stunned, but was able to continue in the fight, and was mortally wounded later. John Wilson parried a blow from a stalwart rebel who stood just within the parapet, and, reaching across, seized him by the collar and literally pulled him out of the works. J. F. Snow was probably the first to enter, and swinging his hat pushed to the middle of the redoubt, calling out, 'Come on, boys; here they are!' He was instantly joined by H. C. Eaton and U. H. Farr, each using bayonet and bullet to vanquish their antagonists. Eaton stopped to reload his gun while Snow and Farr rushed out through the rear of the redoubt in pursuit of five of the enemy—all they saw escape. Just before the flying artillerists entered the breastworks the pursuers fired, but owing to the shifting smoke, did not see the result. E. Shaw, G. Costin and V. Fletcher entered the works at nearly the same moment as the three just mentioned. Fletcher killed a rebel with the butt of his gun. Several of the enemy fell in a hand to hand contest among the guns inside the redoubt. Later in the day, when the firing from both sides over the captured guns was so hot that it was as much as one's life was worth to expose one's head to view, a rebel who had dropped down and had been feigning death from the first of the fight, jumped up and attempted to escape, but was shot by Sergeant M. Costin. Men of the company remained with and in defense of the captured guns till they were pulled out of the works, after the rebel army retreated." .588

MERRILL, 70TH IND WARD 1B 3D 20C: CAPTAIN MEREDITH: "It seemed scarcely a minute from the time we started until we had charged up the enemy's hill and were among them. To whom belongs the honor of first jumping over the parapet I cannot say, but this I know, that Company E struck that battery square in the face, and that its last discharge was right over our heads, almost in our faces. I remember that after the gallant Confederates had done their best, one brave fellow would neither run nor surrender, but stood there laying about him with his ramrod. I had fired the last two shots of my revolver at him and had begged him to surrender, but

588 (S. Merrill 1900, 98)

his only reply was a swinging sweep of his ramrod, which was dodged. Then a hand reached over my shoulder, somebody said, 'Captain, let me at him;' a pistol was fired close beside me, and turning I saw Colonel Merrill, smoking revolver in hand. In a few minutes the gunners were overcome, and the battery and the position were ours.

In the charge up the hill I had lost my cap. While we were cheering over the capture of the guns, Lieutenant Colestock jumped up on one of them and waved his cap and cheered. Then noticing I was bareheaded, he leaped down, picked up a cap from the ground, placed it on my head and began cheering again. A moment later he received the shot which in a few days terminated his life." .589

WIDOWS, CO D 70TH IND WARD 1B 3D 20C: We were about to charge an intrenched battery at Resaca, Ga. May 15, 1864, and went to fill our canteens. After the canteens were filled Comrade David F. Furcate took from his pockets some trinkets and handed them to a comrade, saying, "I shall be killed in this charge; send these to my sister.", and he gave her name and address. We tried to laugh him out of his fears, but he was not affected. We made the charge, took the battery and entered the entrenchments. Comrade Furgate with us. He mounted one of the captured caissons and sat on it loading and firing for a few minutes, when a musket ball struck him in the abdomen, inflicting a wound from which he died that night. .590 .591

Remember the indignation hearing of the Fort Pillow massacre in April?

KERSEY, CORPORAL, CO A 79TH OHIO WARD 1B 3D 20C: Many of the rebels nearby, and with the battery, wore a badge, on which were the words Fort Pillow, which was nothing to their advantage, the way the day turned out. .592

STRONG, CO B 105TH ILL WARD 1B 3D 20C: A great many amusing and pathetic incidents happened during and after our charge, only a few of which I will repeat. Undoubtedly you remember the massacre of the prisoners captured at Fort Pillow, Kentucky, by the Rebel General Nathan Bedford Forrest. Well, when we rushed from the first line that we captured to the second line, where the Rebel cannon were, we of course captured a

589 (S. Merrill 1900, 100)
590 (Widows 1904)
591 NPS Soldiers Database Film M540 ROLL 83, M540 ROLL 25
592 (Kersey 1890)

good many prisoners. Some of the enemy who refused to run or surrender were killed there. Some crawled under the gun carriages to escape the storm of bullets and bayonets. One big red-headed man, a cannoneer, crawled out and begged for quarter. He had his shirt off, and on one arm was tattooed in big letters, "Fort Pillow." As soon as the boys saw the letters on his arm, they yelled, "No quarter for you!" and a dozen bayonets went into him and a dozen bullets were shot into him. I shall never forget his look of fear. _593

CASE: 129TH ILL WARD 1B 3D 20C: The fort being simply a natural basin on the ridge, with formidable breast-works flanking it on the right and left, and on higher ground, the concentric fire therefrom into the fort forced the charging party to abandon it and to throw themselves just outside of the guns in a position to hold and defend them and the fort. At the time, however, of this charge, the color bearer of the One hundred and twenty-ninth Illinois, Sergeant Hess, Company H, who was shot down and killed in the fort at his colors, with another storming party from the One hundred and second and One hundred and twenty-ninth Illinois, entered the fort in the center, charged through the fort and planted the colors at first between the fort and breastworks in the rear, but afterward removed the colors and planted them by the guns. _594 _595

BLAKESLEE, CO G 129TH ILL WARD 1B 3D 20C: I hastened back to the crest of the hill, where I found some of our boys crouched behind (in front) of your works. *Soon all but 27 of my regiment came back and got behind the dirt pile.* _596 Twas then Sergt. Hess jumped upon one of those Napoleons and swung out the colors; a moment later a rifle ball struck him fair in the head and he fell in the folds of our flag, and his blood discolors it to today. Let me tell you something about this man. Then about 8 rods from your line, a rifle ball struck him in the wrist shattering his arm and cutting through the staff. He never dropped the flag, but catching it in his left hand, went forward—Soon after his death the other Sergt. raised the flag and planted it near one of your guns until after dark, when we removed it. Hess was a match for your "Big "Red". I saw several instances similar to your statement of him. _597

593 (Strong 1961)
594 (OR, Series I Vol 38 Part 2 Serial 73: Reports n.d., 365)
595 Others say Hess was shot once before entering the fort and later shot in the fort—shot twice—and that other soldiers carried the colors furthest back.
596 This would mean 27 of the 129th Illinois were left in the fort.
597 (Connor, Wesley O.; Blakeslee, George H. 1899)

PEAK, CO F 129TH ILL WARD 1B 3D 20C: I was busy looking after Sargeant Grunert. .598 He was on the left of Co. H. and I was on the right of Co. F, that placed us close together. He was shot the first volley the enemy fired at us and the only word he spoke was to cut his belt. When he was examined it was found he had been shot through the belt in front and the ball cut the lower edge of the belt at the back, having passed through him. It must have been a split nose ball from the fearful hole it plowed through his body. Co. F lost two killed, Peters and Clark. Sargeant Hesse our regimental color bearer, was wounded slightly in the early part of the battle, but he carried the colors and planted them on the fort at the same instant he was shot through the head. The G.A.R., post 203, at Winchester was named after him or in memory of him.

SMITH, 102ND ILL WARD 1B 3D 20C: My command advanced down the southern slope of the hill upon which it had formed, across the Dalton and Rome road and on over an open field, under a terrible fire until it reached the enemy's battery, and planted its colors upon the rebel works. Members of Company I and Company E of my regiment captured 5 prisoners, including the captain of the battery. A portion of my command also advanced to the second line of works, but owing to some misunderstanding failed to carry it. My color bearer was twice shot down, and my regimental banner received fifty shots in its folds and two in the staff. This was the first flag planted upon the fort. .599

The 102nd Illinois, then, also had some men reach the Rebel line behind the fort.

ARMSTRONG, CO B 102ND ILL WARD 1B 3D 20C: It seems from what Corpl Corning told me (as they were tent mates) that Mr. Kellogg had a presentiment of it before he went into the fight and expressed himself that he would not live through it, this I learned afterward, yet with the conviction of what proved to be true he went in and done his duty without fear of the consequences. It was about 2 o'clock P.M. when he was killed and within a few paces of the Rebel works, to the left of the fort where we took four guns. The point at which my company went up was not obstructed by any minor works as was the line further to the right. Consequently we went further on

---

598 William Grunert was in Company D and not listed as sergeant. No Grunert was listed in Company H. No Grunert of that period is listed in a National Cemetery. (Peak wrote this when he was over 90 years old.)

599 (OR, Series I Vol 38 Part 2 Serial 73: Reports n.d., 351) The captain, Corput, was not among the captured.

than the center of the line. .600 The Rebel fire was so intense and withering in its Affects that scaling the main works was only folly at the point we occupied. After holding our ground for some little time the order was given to retreat just before this order was given the fatal ball done its deadly work passing directly through the body cutting some vital part no doubt. We then retreated to a point where we formed under the cover of a hill but owing to the number of the enemies sharpshooters (and they were very effective) that covered all the ground I had previously occupied it was almost certain death for any one to visit that part of the field. .601

His statement indicates the 102nd was spread right from left of the fort.

WILSON, CO K 102ND ILL WARD 1B 3D 20C: Dear Sister, I know you will have some anxiety in Knowing how I conducted my Self and as I am a modest man, I am somewhat delicate in speaking of myself But I do feel that I have right to Say to my friends for their consolation that I aquit myself Honorably and won the esteem of all my men and was complimented by my commanding officers for my bravery and integrity. I was one of the first to reach the Rebel's cannon and one of the last to leave the battlefield. I was struck with a Shell and knocked Senseless for awhile. Frank Endicott came to me and helped me off the field. I Shall always remember Frank as a brave boy. He came and gave me water where there was a few that dared venture. The Boys was falling by me on every hand and side. Jane, it made my heart ache to See the Boys fall. There was two of my own Boys Shot by my Side. They fell there face to the Enemy. I had three killed almost dead instantly. .602

WESLEY CONNOR, PRIVATE, CHEROKEE ARTILLERY, CSA: We lost twenty-seven men killed, wounded, and captured ... only four of whom ever returned. Among the captured was Sergt. Sidney Blassingame, a tall, angular fellow, with fiery red hair that he always kept cut close and large ears that stuck out on the side of his head like those of a bat. He was known as "Big Red", and I guess there were men in the Battery that never knew that he had another name. He was a splendid fellow and I seriously doubt he ever knew what the sensation of fear was. One of the boys that was captured with him, told me this story, and I've wondered if it was true. Knowing the man as I did, I have been inclined to believe it. He refused to surrender, drew his

---

600 Company B would have been on the left end and went further forward than the center of the regiment. (Case said his regiment had to wheel to the right.)
601 (Armstrong 1864)
602 (Wilson n.d.)

sabre, and commenced using it, when a Yank tapped him on the side of the head with his musket, stunning him; another one started to thrust his bayonet into him, when one of your Lieutenants knocked up the gun, saying, "You mustn't kill as brave a fellow as that", and thus saved his life. About thirty of us got together at the recent reunion in Atlanta, but "Big Red", who is still alive, was not among them, and I have never had the story from him. _603

PEAK, CO F 129TH ILL WARD 1B 3D 20C: General Howard and Butterfield were watching the battle from a high hill in the rear and they said it was a defeat, for it looked like a lot of dare devils, every man for himself. Some times the wisest men can be mistaken as they were for it was a glorious victory for the third division. Although they had lost heavily in killed and wounded, they jumped into the fort and used their bayonets to drive the few rebels that still stayed with their guns.

GRUNERT, CO D 129TH ILL WARD 1B 3D 20C: Gen's. Howard and Butterfield, who had observed our movements from a neighboring hill, gave the men up for lost, as they had seen no regular line advance, but merely a confused mass of dare-devils. Both Generals erred. The men, maddened by the excitement of the moment, knew no fear; they rushed fighting, shooting, stabbing on the enemy, encouraged by the words of Gen. Ward; "Go in, boys, give them the devil"—until our beloved and courageous commander, who had placed himself at the head of the brigade, was wounded by a grape shot in the shoulder.

GRUNERT, CO D 129TH ILL WARD 1B 3D 20C: The enemy began to stagger—the fort was ours! with the three cannons, all in good order, as the enemy in his fright left them. After the fort had been taken, the enemy was not pursued, and the slaughter began to cease; now and then a rebel sharpshooter would send a bullet to us, but as soon as pickets were posted, this fire also ceased, and the regiments retreated a short distance to gather again.

As the 96th Illinois, from the grand view they got as provost guard, on the plain below, saw it:

PARTRIDGE, 96TH ILL WHITAKER 2B 1D 4C: A little after one o'clock they were ordered forward for an attack. One Brigade, commanded by Gen. Ward, moved diagonally across the wagon road, passing directly through, or over,

603 (Connor, Wesley O.; Blakeslee, George H. 1899)

the Ninety-Sixth. Another Brigade advanced farther at the left. The Ninety-Sixth soon found its position in support a most uncomfortable one. From the moment it occupied the line a heavy artillery fire had been showered down the road, and when the charging column began its advance the musketry firing instantly increased. For a time this force could be plainly seen climbing the ridge on the left, but soon the foliage of the trees and bushes hid it from view. A cheer burst from the lines; then a volley was given by them and returned by the enemy. A moment more and the musketry had become continuous, its roar deepening as it was echoed from hill to hill. Musket balls came pattering down to the Regiment's position in great numbers, pelting the ground, striking logs and trees, or cutting off the leaves overhead. Wounded men began to limp or stagger past; then groups of stragglers, the latter being halted and turned back or sent to where some officers were stationed to take charge of them. The stretcher bearers, who had gone to the front close behind the lines, soon returned with their ghastly loads; the canvas, so clean and white as they advanced, now crimsoned with the life-blood of those who had fallen. And still the dread work went on. The troops in reserve had little to do except to stop the stragglers, but with the left of the Ninety-Sixth this duty was not altogether light. But even doing nothing was trying work at such a time, for the pitiless shots struck all all around and kept the men anxious for their own safety.

Though Coburn's 85th Indiana was blocked out, a few were carried with Ward.

BRANT, 85TH INDIANA COBURN 2B 2D 20C: Sunday, May 15th, we were in the battle of Resaca, where in the massing of so many troops we were very much divided as a regiment, in having to cross so many lines of battle to get into position. Only a few were in the charge on the fort in a depression of the ground. Wm Richardson of Co. D was bayoneted inside the rebel works and killed. The regiment lost one killed and thirty wounded. _604

We Had to Stand and See Them Do Their Work

MUNGER, CO C 154TH NY BUSCHBECK 2B 2D 20C: We went into action that afternoon and charged to the hill, but not up the hill, stopping 20 or 30 rods short of the battery under cover of the hill, which was covered by dense thicket of young pines. _605 The First Brigade, Third Division, went for that battery with a rush, and the cheer that rolled along our line, out thundered

604 (Brant 1902, 54)
605 At 16.5 feet in a rod, over 300 feet.

the thunder of the guns, was started by my regiment, who were intensely interested spectators. The First Brigade charged up to the very muzzles of the guns, and threw themselves flat on the ground, protected in a measure by the thicket ... they did hold it from the Johnnies till about midnight, when our brigade relieved them. .606 .607

BLUNDIN, CO C 28TH PENN CANDY 1B 2D 20C: Hulmsville, Pa I remember the day well, as our brigade (the First of the Second Division) was in line with the intention of charging that same four-gun fort; but the other troops got in their work first, and we had to stand and see them do their work, and grandly they did it. Talking to some of them after they had made their successful charge, I was informed that the brigade was under the command of Col. Ben Harrison, ... I witnessed the charge of the brigade, of which Col. Harrison was the commander, upon the four-gun fort that Capt Shaw mentions, and I am under the impression now as then that said fort was the key of the rebel line. It was certainly an effective charge. .608

Did he say Candy's brigade of Geary's division was to go after the fort but got beat by Ward? Was not Butterfield's division assigned that task, with Geary as backup, should Butterfield succeed? We saw that Ireland's brigade did try to beat Ward and almost caused a complete failure. But Hooker was there and directing both Ward and Ireland. What was going on?

The Confederate View of What Just Happened

ABRAMS, ATLANTA INTELLIGENCER, WITH STEWART'S DIVISION, CSA: The Yankees had crossed the ravine, and with a loud cheer rushed on our works. Hindman quickly repulsed them, but the fighting on Brown's line of Stevenson's and Stewart's divisions was long and desperate. Capt. Corbett's battery being subjected to a fearful fire, the men left their guns, but not before they had lost thirty of their number in killed and wounded, and entered our line. No sooner did the Yankees perceive this than a fresh column of their troops were thrown rapidly forward, and uniting with that which had gone before, rushed on the abandoned guns with the hope of capturing them and carrying our line. .609

---

606 (G. H. Blakeslee, Harrison's Brigade at the Battle of Resaca 1895)
607 From his position, some of the 1st Division were certainly in front of the battery. Some of the 2nd Division also, a bit further left.
608 (G. H. Blakeslee, Harrison's Brigade at the Battle of Resaca 1895)
609 (Abrams 1864)

Ward's brigade had run through the fort and pushed Brown's brigade out of the trenches behind but went no further. The 129th, on the Blakeslee map, had gone furthest past the fort.

An incident, a close call for the future president:

> BLAKESLEE, CO G 129TH ILL WARD 1B 3D 20C: Harrison stood by your left gun, resting one hand on it, talking with Capt. Sedgewick, 102 Ill., when a rifle shot passed through his whiskers just grazing his skin. .610

> FLEHARTY, 102ND ILL WARD 1B 3D 20C: All of the regiments in the brigade were represented within the earthwork. But the position was occupied only for an instant. .611

While the 1st Brigade was engaged in the fort, the 2nd Brigade was close behind working their way up the hill on the left. So were some of Ireland's brigade.

> BLAKESLEE, CO G 129TH ILL WARD 1B 3D 20C: The 2nd Brigade was to keep to right of our Brigade and support us on the right flank; just after crossing the Dalton road the canister from your guns turned them from their course, and crossing our line of march to the rear, took to the bush on the northern slope of the hill, gaining which, they prostrated themselves on lines as shown. I located these positions from a few of their dead lying here. .612

> COBURN, 2B 3D 20C: The summit of the hill is covered with woods, but the slope beyond and the valley are cleared in front of a portion of the rebel works, which were situated on the hills beyond, and which here presented opposite our right a salient angle receding with a long sweep sharply to our left. The brigade advanced, a portion across the field to the works and the left along the woods to its left. .613

Winkler had watched Ward cross the road behind him. Now he watched Coburn oblique and come in front of his line.

> WINKLER, 26TH WIS WOOD 3B 3D 20C: ... while at the same time another line of battle broke forth from the woods on the right of the road into the

610 (Connor, Wesley O.; Blakeslee, George H. 1899)
611 (Fleharty, Our Regiment. A History of the 102d Illinois Infantry Volunteers 1865)
612 (Connor, Wesley O.; Blakeslee, George H. 1899)
613 (OR, Series I Vol 38 Part 2 Serial 73: Reports n.d., 378)

open field in front & then pushed obliquely to the left across the road & came directly in front of my line. _614

Some of them got caught in the log and brush barrier that we see in Walker's painting.

DICKINSON, CO E 22ND WIS COBURN 2B 3D 20C: On up the hill we rushed, through thickets of bushes and scrubby trees, where the bullets, whistled, snapped, and cracked, till the boys actually thought, the rebels were firing explosive bullets; and, as we neared the Fort, the large trees had been felled, with their tops down hill, the large limbs cut off, and the stubs sharpened, for us to run against.

Then they had woven telegraph wire from limb to limb, and from one scrub tree to another, and in among the bushes, until we were shut out, for we couldn't break the wire, and had nothing to cut that, or the bushes. There we were in plain sight of the rebels, in Fort and rifle pits, and were a fine mark, for them, to practice on. In trying to find an opening through the wire, and brush, I kept working towards the right of our line, until I found a hole and crowded through, and found myself with Company I or at least there was Captain Patton, and three men. _615

That gateway Harrison mentioned, might it have been this opening Dickinson found in the abatis or another in the brush piled in front of the fort?

DICKINSON, CO E 22ND WIS COBURN 2B 3D 20C: We came out of a thicket of bushes, into an open space, and near the rebel rifle pit, in plain view of the rebels. Captain Patton was just ahead of me, as we broke our way through the bush, and came into the open ground, and an instant later he wheeled, half round, and fell at my feet. His first call was for water, as it is for every wounded man, he says, boys, you can't take that fort alone; and there seems to be no one here to help you, I wish you would get me onto a blanket, and take me out of reach of the bullets. One the men had a rubber blanket around his neck, he untied it, and spread it on the ground, we placed the Captain, on it and each man seized a corner, when the man opposite me was hit by a bullet which cut his eyebrow, so the blood poured into his eye, and down over his face; he staggered, and reeled, about, but did not fall; then he

614 Part of Ward's or Coburn's brigades? Robert Hale Strong was among the skirmishers.
615 (Dickinson n.d.)

drew his coat sleeve across his eye to wipe out the blood, reached down, seized his corner, and into the brush went the crowd. .616

"... and into the brush went the crowd." Others of his regiment kept going forward, as Winkler described.

Some of Coburn's brigade pass through Winkler. They are about to be the trigger to a disaster.

WINKLER, 26TH WIS WOOD 3B 3D 20C: Col. Wood just passing by in rear of my regiment I called his attention to them. The line which came up behind me did not halt but passed right over my men & pushed forward into the thicket in my front where it was at once concealed from my sight. .617

WINKLER, 26TH WIS WOOD 3B 3D 20C: A heavy musketry fire immediately opened in my front & a large number of troops came rushing back in disorder through my line & lay down behind it. .618

What drove them back? Whose troops were they?

We Are Flanked!

Keen Sense of Disappointment

Stop That Firing in the Rear!

J. L. KETCHAM, WARD 1B 3D 20C: Before I made much headway the enemy's infantry rallied and opened on us a deadly fire. At that moment there came to me a keen sense of disappointment. I can never forget it. We would have won a glorious victory that day had not the sound of the cannon drawn the regiment toward the enemy's artillery and away from their infantry breastworks, which they briefly abandoned, and which we ought to have occupied. However, we obeyed instructions. We captured the guns. The Second Division supporting our left should have started when we did and swept over the breastworks. .619

---

616 (Dickinson n.d.)

617 (F. C. Winkler 1864) Written for the adjutant. Reason unknown, but suggests someone was investigating events. Being previously of the Judge Advocates he might have just been getting his version in first, given what happened after this.

618 (F. C. Winkler 1864)

619 (S. Merrill 1900, 96)

Some of Coburn's men crowded into Winkler's and then crashed forward right through Winkler!

> WOOD, 3B 3D 20C: As I anticipated before the attack began, my right regiment was too far to the right, as there was some mistake or misunderstanding on the part of the Second Brigade. I understood that the Second Brigade was to support the First Brigade on the right, but before the crest of the hill was half gained the regiments of the Second Brigade, after *firing a volley into the First Brigade*, were found on its left in no little confusion. The men ran over and through the right of my line, mingling with the right regiment and creating so much confusion as to render the regiment (Twenty-sixth Wisconsin) almost unserviceable, as well as causing great hindrance to the regiment next to it (Thirty-third Massachusetts). Major Winkler, with commendable skill and ability, with no little difficulty extricated his men from the confused mass into which they had become involved and brought them again re-formed into line. [620]

> MERRILL, 70TH IND WARD 1B 3D 20C: And now while wounded men are being cared for, while prisoners are being taken to the rear, while there is great jubilation and enthusiasm among the victors, occurs one of those awful inexplicable errors, one of those fearful mistakes, one of those real horrors of war, so calculated to unnerve the bravest and to demoralize, for the time being, the best drilled and disciplined troops. A second Federal line of battle, advancing to the support of the first, comes crashing through the brush in the rear. At the same instant the Confederates having been rallied and re-formed in another line of works, pour a deadly volley into the ranks of the brave men who are cheering over the guns they have captured. [621]

> MERRILL, 70TH IND WARD 1B 3D 20C: CAPTAIN MEREDITH: "The second line of Federals, partially encountering the rebel fire, deliver a volley and the soldiers of the first line, who had led the charge, who had driven the enemy and captured the guns, are literally caught between two fires. The scene the terror of the moment is beyond description. The cry went up: Our own men are firing into us. When the panic was at its greatest, one or two officers who were in the captured redoubt shouted the command, 'Lie down!' and about one hundred and fifty men crouched behind the earthworks containing the guns, and began skirmishing with the enemy. While we were lying there Captain H. M. Scott came to me and we looked over the situation together. We agreed it was best to stay there and hold the guns in case the

620 (OR, Series I Vol 38 Part 2 Serial 73: Reports n.d., 434)
621 (S. Merrill 1900, 101)

enemy tried to retake them by sortie. Accordingly I took command of the force to the right of the lunette." .622

MERRILL, 70TH IND WARD 1B 3D 20C: At this moment when the center was occupying the lunette, and the right and left wings of the regiment were curving about it, shots from the rear added to the intense excitement. There were thrilling cries of "Stop that firing in the rear! For God's sake don't kill your own men!" Then came the rally of the enemy to the breastworks behind the lunette, and the falling to the ground of our men in a semicircle about the fort. An enfilading fire of the enemy's batteries far to the right and left, mistaken by those who came later on the field as coming from the harmless lunette, and the continuous rifle shots from the concealed infantry twenty yards away, could not drive the regiment from its exposed position, or weaken its determination to see that those guns never again come into the hands of the original owners. .623

The regiment that crashed through Winkler had mistaken fire coming from the right as coming from the fort and returned fire!

FLEHARTY, 102ND ILL WARD 1B 3D 20C: At one time the 2d Brigade opened a sharp fire on us, mistaking us for rebels. Several of our men were doubtless struck by balls from the lines that were directed to support us. .624

DUSTIN, 105TH ILL WARD 1B 3D 20C: While the line rested for a moment under the works a shower of musketry came upon us from the left and rear, and instantly a command was heard (since learned to have been given by a rebel officer), "We are flanked! March in retreat!" Supposing the order to have been given by the proper authority, the brigade fell back, with the exception of those officers and men who had got into the fort or were sheltered by it on the outside. .625

HARRISON, 70TH IND WARD 1B 3D 20C: The enemy in a moment rallied in rear of their second line, and poured in a most destructive fire upon us, which compelled us to retire outside the first line to obtain the cover of the works. At this point some confusion was created among our forces in and about the enemy's works (several of our battalions in rear of me having come up) by a cry that the enemy was flanking us. This caused many to retire

622 (S. Merrill 1900, 101)
623 (S. Merrill 1900, 66)
624 (Fleharty, Our Regiment. A History of the 102d Illinois Infantry Volunteers 1865, 59)
625 (OR, Series I Vol 38 Part 2 Serial 73: Reports n.d., 360)

down the hill, and had for a time the appearance of a general retreat. I strove in vain to rally my men under the enemy's fire on the hillside, and finally *followed them to a partially sheltered place behind a ridge to our left.* .626

Blakeslee, in his letter to Connor, shows where Harrison sheltered under a ledge. The spot was on the Union right of the fort. Harrison says on their left, apparently meaning as he faced downhill to get out.

FOX, 107TH NY RUGER 2B 1D 20C: Some of the troops in Ward's and Coburn's Brigades, although long in service, had never been in a general engagement. *It happened, also, that the moment the leading brigade emerged upon the plain, the enemy's fire was too high and passed overhead until the ascent was reached. The fire, however, had plunged into the supporting Second Brigade, and so it became necessary that it should go forward.* Meanwhile its front line, finding itself under fire, some of it shrapnel and canister, opened a rattling musketry fire to the dismay of the leading officers, and the unhappy fate of some of Ward's men who were almost upon the enemy's works. Although this appalling occurrence was speedily abated it well nigh proved fatal; for at a critical period it arrested some of Ward's battalions and created confusion. .627

An interesting point, that the Confederate fire was too high until the attackers were close. Ward's route up was directly facing the fort. The regiment that crashed through Winkler was more to the left. They would have been more exposed to the Rebel line.

For their action to stop the firing by Coburn's brigade, Butterfield recommended aides Tremain and Oliver for Medals of Honor.

NEW YORK HERALD: Ward's brigade, being thus assailed in front and rear, were on the point of returning, when the staff of General Butterfield, by riding in front of Coburn's men, succeeded in persuading them to desist from firing. Another round would probably have finished the work for the day. As it was, their fire had been nearly as destructive as that of the enemy. .628

BUTTERFIELD, 3D 20C: He was conspicuous in his ability and gallantry, being by me placed in charge of putting in position and directing the movements of the Brigades. By an unfortunate accident or misunderstanding, the

626 (OR, Series I Vol 38 Part 2 Serial 73: Reports n.d., 369)
627 (Fox n.d., 242)
628 (Bradley 1865, 102)

Brigade of Colonel Coburn fired into the Brigade being led by General Harrison in the assault. In the most gallant and splendid style, with great courage and coolness, General Tremain rode between the lines of fire in front of Coburn's command to stop the firing and saved the assault, which was successful, from possible disaster.

I was personally with Tremain during part of the time and speak from personal knowledge. In front of one Regiment I saw General Tremain with his sword and hands knock down the muskets of nearly if not all [sic] of the front rank to stop this firing. _629 _630

BUTTERFIELD, 3D 20C: I put him in charge of one of the Brigades (the leading Brigade) to direct its movements and charge at Resaca in the Atlanta Campaign. During this movement one of the Brigades in the rear of it fired into the leading brigade which was being led by President Harrison, then Col. of the Seventieth Indiana. General Oliver's gallant and splendid conduct in aiding to repress the disaster like to have been caused by this unfortunate accident is deserving of the highest commendation and reward. I believe that President Harrison is familiar with his services on this field. His special gallantry and bravery here alone commend him for the medal. _631 _632

PARTRIDGE, 96TH ILL WHITAKER 2B 1D 4C: Farther over the ridge a terrible blunder occurred. Changing direction slightly, one column moved so as to partly come in rear of another. The woods were full of smoke so that they could not see what was before them, and as the bullets were coming, from the front they fired into their friends. The effect was to disorganize both Brigades to some extent and make complete success impossible. Only a partial volley was fired, but not a few fell before it. Some of the officers knew the situation and soon made the men aware of their mistake. _633

As reported in a newspaper:

NEW YORK HERALD: The reserve brigade, hearing a few bullets whistling about their ears, and somewhat confused with the deafening roar of the raging battle opposite, fancied their companions cut to pieces, and that the rebel hosts were coming down upon them. Determined not to give way

629 National Archives, Papers for Medal of Honor for Henry Tremain.
630 (D. Butterfield, Medal of Honor case flle for Henry Tremain 1892)
631 National Archives, Papers for Medal of Honor for Paul A. Oliver.
632 Butterfield listed other occasions warranting a medal.
633 Tremain and Oliver, for which they won Medals of Honor.

without a struggle, they leveled their pieces, and began firing wildly into the woods on the opposite hill. _634As Partridge saw it, maybe after the disaster in the fort:

PARTRIDGE, 96TH ILL WHITAKER 2B 1D 4C: The volume of sound lessened for an instant and then the Rebel yell broke out anew. The charge had only partially succeeded. The men fell back at many points, but rallied a little at the left of the road and again went forward. _635

FOX, 107TH NY RUGER 2B 1D 20C: Happily, however, the battle was not suspended. Coburn's Brigade was rushed forward to the support of the First Brigade, and Ward's regiments rallied and held to their work with remarkable fortitude; Ward himself, assisted by Capt. Paul A. Oliver, of Butterfield's staff, who accompanied this brigade to represent the division commander, rallying the troops with great gallantry. _636

Dickinson was exposed to the crossfire while in the ravine between the hills delivering his prisoner.

DICKINSON, CO E 22ND WIS COBURN 2B 3D 20C: In going back with the wounded Captain, we followed a ravine, or depression between the hills; and yet we must have been in sight of the rebel line, for the bullets came, at times in showers; cutting off the bushes on all sides of us. When carrying Captain Patton to the rear we had to sling our guns, that is, hang them down our backs by the sling; then the muzzle points to the ground, and the breech up, so our hands were free, to grasp the blanket. Where we came to that line of prostrate men, we passed under a wild thorn tree, and a limb caught the hammer of my partners gun and discharged it, the ball entered the ground, just missing a man's head. He, with a big oath, declared it a careless trick, bringing loaded guns back in that way. I told him that he would show better sense to keep as quiet with his mouth, as he was with his body. That we had a very poor opinion of a set of men, who seemed to do all their fighting with their mouths, and feet. Who could stand up by the hour, and recount the mighty deeds they had accomplished, back on the Potomac; but when ordered to storm a line of works, would lay down when they came where

---

634 (Bradley 1865, 102)
635 (Partridge 1887, 327)
636 (Fox n.d., 242)

the bullets were flying thick and fast; and let their supports go ahead and do the fighting. _637

MGuire, of the 32nd Tennessee, right behind the fort, does not mention leaving the line. This part of his 1886 recollection may be related to the arrival of much of Coburn's brigade.

McGuire, 32nd Tennessee, Brown's Brigade, Stevenson, Hood, CSA: However, in less than twenty-live minutes they made another and more desperate effort to dislodge us, this time charging to within six or seven paces of us, seeming to wish to make a hand-to-hand affair of it; but again we drove them back with fearful slaughter. Frequent other assaults were made during the day, but none so determined as the first two, and each one brought heavy loss to them; for we eagerly sought every opportunity for dealing them a blow. _638

Though some were still in the fort, others took position just in front.

Randall, 149th NY Ireland 3B 2D 20C: We then fell back to the crest of the hill and front of the redoubt and laid down. We found the redoubt occupied by four brass 12-pounder guns, two of them pointing to our right and two to our left. The regiment took position as follows: The colors planted in the earth thrown up to form the redoubt near the guns pointing to the right, the right wing running diagonally to the right and front along the crest of the hill, the portion of the left wing which remained with the regiment extending to the left and rear in a ravine. We held our position, keeping the enemy from the guns, but not being able to move them ourselves. We were impeded and hindered in all our operations by the great number of men of other commands, several times as many as could be of any service, and all totally disorganized and under no command. _639

Noble, 19th Mich Coburn 2B 3D 20C: We drove the rebels from a fort and captured four pieces of artillery and then our regt having become considerably battered by other regts charging in among us we fell back to get organized again. _640

637 (Dickinson n.d.)
638 (McGuire 1886, 479)
639 (OR, Series I Vol 38 Part 2 Serial 73: Reports n.d., 304)
640 (Noble n.d.)

We might take Abrams' next item to mean the rest of Coburn's 2nd Brigade making it to the fort.

> ABRAMS, ATLANTA INTELLIGENCER, WITH STEWART'S DIVISION, CSA: Hindman quickly repulsed them, but the fighting on Brown's line of Stevenson's and Stewart's divisions was long and desperate. Capt. Corbett's battery being subjected to a fearful fire, the men left their guns, but not before they had lost thirty of their number in killed and wounded, and entered our line. No sooner did the Yankees perceive this than a fresh column of their troops were thrown rapidly forward, and uniting with that which had gone before, rushed on the abandoned guns with the hope of capturing them and carrying our line. ₋641 ₋642

Over My Line Once More

Wood's right regiment, Winkler's, was attempting to work after the accident. But other regiments mixed with Wood's right. Regiments of two brigades, mixed together, under completely independent command, made Winkler's position, in particular, too dangerous to be of any help. They were under fire from the rear, too. He kept trying to go forward.

> WINKLER, 26TH WIS WOOD 3B 3D 20C: Roused by some officers most of them jumped up again, ran over my line once more & lay down flat in front of it. Believing that the 33d Mass. on my left was advancing I ordered my regiment forward. I called out to the troops in front of me to be still & let me pass over but to no avail. As my line came on they jumped up & mixed in with it. The woods were so dense that I could see but a very small portion of my line & nothing of the regiment on my left. I had no orders but concluded to push on. ₋643.

> WINKLER, 26TH WIS WOOD 3B 3D 20C: The rebels main line of fortifications was on a ridge nearly parallel to the one we occupied, and separated from it by a valley very densely covered by a young growth of pines. We moved

---

641 (Abrams 1864)

642 Fresh columns being Coburn's 2nd Brigade.

643 (F. C. Winkler 1864) Written for the adjutant, an unusual step. For what reason? Winkler, a lawyer, had been division judge advocate, even conducting court martials during the campaign. And he had helped Carl Schurz in the court of inquiry in January, against Hooker's attempt to shift blame to Schurz for not-so-timely support for Geary in the battle of Wauhatchie. Advocate Winkler knew the value of setting the record, and setting it first, in case of being accused of failure.

forward again, drove the rebel skirmishers back to their works, and pressed on to an assault. The fire of canister and musketry that met us was terrific, the rebels' works proved very difficult of access, and the density of the forest made the preservation of a serried line .644 impossible, so that although the works were actually gained in some places, the assault as a whole proved unsuccessful. .645

WINKLER, 26TH WIS WOOD 3B 3D 20C: The confusion arising from the large number of troops of different organizations scattered through that thicket became greater & greater in the advance. We met but little opposition from the enemy till we got within very short distance of his rifle pits on top of the hill. We pushed forward to right under those pits & a number of my men & also men of other regiments got into them, but with that promiscuous crowd which had now usurped the places of lines of battle it was impossible to lend them the necessary support, & they had to hasten out again. I then endeavored to reform my line on the slope of the hill, but receiving quite a heavy fire from our own men in the rear was obliged to fall back to the foot of the hill. .646

The Dead Line

AMBROSE BIERCE, HAZEN, 2B 3D 4C: Early in my military experience I used to ask myself how it was that brave troops could retreat while still their courage was high. As long as a man is not disabled he can go forward; can it be anything but fear that makes him stop and finally retire? Are there signs by which he can infallibly know the struggle to be hopeless? In this engagement [Pickett's Mill], as in others, my doubts were answered as to the fact; the explanation is still obscure. In many instances which have come under my observation, when hostile lines of infantry engage at close range and the assailants afterward retire, there was a "dead-line" beyond which no man advanced but to fall. Not a soul of them ever reached the enemy's front to be bayoneted or captured. It was a matter of the difference of three or four paces—too small a distance to affect the accuracy of aim. In these affairs no aim is taken at individual antagonists; the soldier delivers his fire at the thickest mass in his front. The fire is, of course, as deadly at twenty paces as at fifteen; at fifteen as at ten. Nevertheless, there is the "dead-line,"

---

644 Serried lines are lines of soldiers standing close together, capable of concentrated fire in coordinated volleys.
645 (OR, Series I Vol 38 Part 2 Serial 73: Reports n.d., 463)
646 (F. C. Winkler 1864)

with its well-defined edge of corpses—those of the bravest. Where both lines are fighting without cover—as in a charge met by a counter-charge—each has its "dead-line," and between the two is a clear space—neutral ground, devoid of dead, for the living cannot reach it to fall there. _647

Trapped in the Fort - A Long Pause

For God's sake, general, don't fire; those are our men in those works!
—129th Illinois Captain

He invoked a string of blessings on the rebels. —Fleharty

The lunette was not abandoned entirely. Many men were still within, trapped but ready to resume the effort. Ward, who had been behind his last three regiments, arrived along with some of Coburn's men.

Tremain summarizes:

> TREMAIN: The enemy had scarcely time to reload or to fire more than one round of grape and canister from their guns before Ward's gallant fellows were upon them, beating the gunners down with the butts of their muskets. Coburn's brigade—also never before under fire, although old troops—in advancing as supports unfortunately fired into Ward's brigade occasioning some loss;—Coburn's men becoming excited with success, and on account of the dense woods not being able to see far about them. At the same time Colonel Wood's brigade on the left gallantly drove the enemy and occupied the hill it was directed to take. The supports coming up, the lines were now reformed at the advanced positions. The enemy had been completely taken by surprise at the suddenness and impetuosity of the charge. Our men swarmed upon them in overwhelming numbers, and were irresistible. But the rebels still held a position that made it impossible for us to withdraw their captured guns from our front; but they could not reach them either. _648

But some were caught in a No Man's Land, much like a Dead Zone!

> WARD, 1B 3D 20C: I marched up in rear of the fifth regiment to a point beyond the second line of works, the first, with 4 pieces of artillery, having been taken and occupied by our men. At that point I found 100 or 200 men, fragments of my brigade, outside the lunette taken by us, some 300 or more

647 (Bierce n.d.)
648 (Tremain 1905, 171)

being in the lunette, the others having retired upon a supposed order from someone in the lunette, and because of the fire of our own upon them from the rear. ˍ649 ˍ650

COBURN, 2B 3D 20C: This was done under a tremendous fire of artillery and musketry, which killed and wounded many of our men, but they bravely advanced and planted the colors of the Nineteenth Michigan and Twenty-second Wisconsin in a small fort of the enemy occupied by four of their field pieces. Such was the fury of the enemy's fire that the men could not advance farther. ˍ651

WARD, 1B 3D 20C: I had these men formed to charge the second line, and kept those in line firing at the enemy's works, when Colonel Gilbert, with the Nineteenth Michigan, came up on horseback, I directed him to form his regiment with my men and we would charge the works. ˍ652 He did all he could to aid me in forming for the charge, as did a lieutenant-colonel belonging to that brigade and many captains of my own brigade and Colonel Coburn's. I desire particularly to name Captain Wilson, of the Seventy-ninth Ohio Infantry. ˍ653

JENKINS, 105TH ILL WARD 1B 3D 20C: We did not commence firing until close to the masked battery. Here was the hottest place on the field, not a Reb. Retreated or surrendered but fought to their death ... The way we charged & layed down we got all mixed up. It seemed that It was sure death to raise a head one foot above the ground. While In this position & everyone in sight hugging the ground as close as I, all of a sudden I seen the Col. of the 19th Michigan on old Claybank with his hat ... in his hand trying to get the men to get up & charge. I was sure he could not live there many seconds ... The most touching scene of all was what the Col. said repeatedly while

649 (OR, Series I Vol 38 Part 2 Serial 73: Reports n.d., 338) This puts 200 men beyond the Rebel line! With another 300 in the fort. This, per Ward, was after the firing that drove the others out, himself having moved behind the brigade and coming up after being wounded. This fits the accounts which state a couple of regiments remained in the fort.
650 Not all the companies got into the fort, particularly the leftmost of the rear regiments.
651 (OR, Series I Vol 38 Part 2 Serial 73: Reports n.d., 378) The portion on the left causing the firing from behind. the portion on the right going into the fort.
652 Gilbert was killed shortly after.
653 (OR, Series I Vol 38 Part 2 Serial 73: Reports n.d., 338)This firing by the Rebel line may have been in response to a charge not obvious to Ward in his position.

we was carrying him was "God bless my poor wife & children." Just the same words every time. _654 _655

WARD, 1B 3D 20C: About this time a captain of the One hundred and twenty-ninth Illinois Volunteers came to me from toward the works, saying, "For Gods sake, general, don't fire; those are our men in those works." _656 I replied that it was impossible, as our own men would not fire upon us as those in the works were doing. I started the captain to make a minute examination and report, when the whole line of works opened a heavy fire, which threw the men into some confusion, and many, in spite of all I could do, fell back and retreated.

Fifty or seventy-five moved on toward the works, I advancing with them. Some 20 in the original line and in the advance were killed. _657

Those who remained I ordered to take to trees, lie down, and crawl up to the works, saying that we could carry them, and that I would lead. A gallant, determined band followed about thirty paces. Some 15 or 20 were killed by and near me, the others I directed to hide behind trees and crawl on their bellies to the works; that re-enforcements were coming, and honor and safety required them to advance. They obeyed, and we advanced to within fifteen steps of their works when I was shot. _658

FLEHARTY, 102ND ILL WARD 1B 3D 20C: Our brigade commander, Brig. Gen. W. T. Ward, was quite severely wounded. It is said that when the ball struck the old General he invoked a "string of blessings" on the rebels in a style that was more forcible than elegant. He was in the thickest of the fight cheering on the men when struck. _659

---

654 (W. Anderson 1995, 330) As quoted by Anderson, with footnote: William F. Jenkins Letter, June 22, 1907, in Henry F. Gilbert Papers.

655 Ward's comment places Jenkins and the 19th Michigan in the fort when this happened. Jenkins letter, though, has Gilbert wounded in front of the fort.

656 The 129th planted their flag closest to the Rebel works behind the fort.

657 (OR, Series I Vol 38 Part 2 Serial 73: Reports n.d., 338)

658 (OR, Series I Vol 38 Part 2 Serial 73: Reports n.d., 320)

659 (Fleharty, Our Regiment. A History of the 102d Illinois Infantry Volunteers 1865, 59)

CONGLETON, CO. F 105TH ILL WARD 1B 3D 20C: Gen. Ward commanding our Brigade was wounded in one arm and lost his hat but did not leave the field. .660 .661

WARD, 1B 3D 20C: I then ordered them to hold their places, under cover as much as possible, stating that reinforcements would soon come up; that I would remain, sending for a surgeon to come to the foot of the hill behind us. They insisted on bearing me from the field. I refused to permit them. We remained at this place, under cover of some bushes and trees, for some fifteen or twenty minutes, the men insisting on carrying me off, and I refusing to let them, in hopes that a sufficient force would soon come up to assist us in carrying the works or to relieve us; none came. .662

CRAM, CO F 105TH ILL WARD 1B 3D 20C Grant, Bachelder and I laid half an hour within seven rods of the rebel rifle pits from whence a terrific shower of bullets came. A sergt. here was shot on the left and a private on the right of me. Arthur Rice was killed here, a few feet of me, but we managed at length to escape from that position and reached a place which afforded a little cover, but I have not time to write all that occurred on that afternoon. .663

DICKINSON, CO E 22ND WIS COBURN 2B 3D 20C: After turning the wounded man over to the stretcher bearers, I started back up the hill to find the 22nd Regt. And found them acting as sharpshooters, upon the hillside, near the wire obstruction. They were taking advantage of every cover, to shelter themselves from the rebel bullets; logs, stumps, rocks and knolls, and were doing good business. If a man raised his head above the works, he was very sure to get a bullet, and sometimes two or three. They had silenced those four cannons in the Fort, and in fact, it was rather quiet along the line, .664

WESLEY CONNOR, PRIVATE, CHEROKEE ARTILLERY, CSA: When I got inside of our Infantry line, I found a member of my detachment named _____, who was afterward killed at Nashville, _____ friend and as gallant a soul as ever drew breath, and we two hunted round, got us up a musket apiece and remained in the line till after dark. All the members of the battery had gone to the rear. We were told that an effort would be

660 (Congleton n.d.)
661 The hat Harvey Reid so admired?
662 (OR, Series I Vol 38 Part 2 Serial 73: Reports n.d., 322)
663 (Cram 2001, 100)
664 (Dickinson n.d.)

made to retake the guns, and I wanted to be present to let off that double charge of canister at you fellows as you ran. Every now and then I would take a peep out at my gun which I could plainly see from our line, and well do I remember that flag of which you speak of having been planted beside our guns. If I mistake not, it was along side of my gun. By the way, I shed my first blood here too. When I had secured my gun, an Enfield rifle, I crawled up to the line, and told some of Brown's men that I wanted to get a pop at a Yank. One of them said, "there is a fellow out there sharp shooting. I know wher he is but can't see him"; so we foolishly stood up, I to aim, and he just behind me to tell me when I had the proper direction—I blazed away, and had just brought my gun to the position of "carry arms", when Mr. Yank fired, striking the stock of my gun just below the muzzle, filling my right jaw with splinters, and denting my gun so that it could not be used again. I thought the whole jaw had been shot away, and slapped by hand to my face to find out if it was true. I very bravely went away to find another gun but after having such a close call in a place where I had no business to be, you may bet your life that I didn't find it. .665

Incident of the Engagement on the Oostanaula

A tale by a correspondent for a Charleston newspaper, who was with the North Carolina regiments:

"PERSONNE": In the Fifty-fifth North Carolina Regiment there is a private named Early, who exhibited a degree of courage unequalled during this war. When the enemy had thrown their men behind the redoubt in which Corbett's battery was placed, this man stood up in the pits, with his body half exposed and opened a rapid firing on the enemy, almost preventing them from sharpshooting; for no sooner would a Yankee raise his head above the redoubt than a ball would enter his brain, and he would fall dead across the work. In this manner Early had killed six, when I had occasion to go up to the point where he was stationed, and was very much amused at his manner. "Get up there," he would exclaim to the Yankees, "get up and show your heads; why the d-l don't you take a shot at me? Now just raise up for a second," and whenever a Yankee was found bold enough to accept his challenge, a bullet through his head was the reward he received. .666

665 (Connor, Wesley O.; Blakeslee, George H. 1899)
666 (De Fontaine 1864, 220) Several Earlys were in North Carolina regiments, but the 55th is not listed in the CSA Order of Battle at Resaca. Likely this Early was in another

Now, during the "pause" on the right, we catch up with the left.

Williams Entrenching on the Left

While the 3rd Division has been fighting at the angle, Williams was on the left, facing the Rebels' right flank.

> TREMAIN: It was evident this state of affairs could not long remain. Williams' division was posted on the left, and Geary as a support on the right; while a strong line from Schofield's corps was now advanced under cover of the forest around our extreme left and to reach the enemy's rear. ˍ667 ˍ668

> WILLIAMS, 1D 20C: The ground occupied by Knipe's (First) brigade on the right was very broken, trending off, however, toward the north in a ridge of slight elevation, running almost parallel with railroad, partly through woods and partly through clearings. At a point where a road toward Green's Station from the Dalton road crossed the ridge there rises a considerable knoll or knob, upon which is a dwelling known as Scales' house. Ruger's (Second) brigade, extending from Knipe's left, reached and occupied this knoll, upon which slight breast-works were hastily thrown up. Two regiments of Robinson's brigade were deployed on the left of the knoll, where the ground sinks down into a timbered plain; three others of his regiments were held in reserve on the extreme left, and one regiment placed in support of Winegar's battery, which was with much difficulty put into position on a high hill, somewhat in our rear, but commanding much of our front. Woodbury's light 12s were placed in the line near our left on ridges which commanded the approach to what I regarded as the key to our position. ˍ669

> BROWN, CO C 27TH INDIANA RUGER 2B 1D 20C: By the morning of the 15th the Twentieth Corps had mostly reached the vicinity of its assigned position. After some preliminary moves the Twenty-seventh finally took its place in the line of the brigade, which was formed along a timbered ridge (not a mountain) overlooking a wide ravine, along which the ground was somewhat open. The whole line then moved forward across the ravine and open ground, almost to the crest of the next ridge, which was not as high as

North Carolina regiment at Resaca. *"Personne": Army correspondent of The Charleston Courier.*
667 (Tremain 1905, 171)
668 Hovey was to have been in the rear. Part of his division may have been across the tracks.
669 (OR, Series I Vol 38 Part 2 Serial 73: Reports n.d., 28)

the first had been. This advance brought some of the regiments to our left out into the cleared fields, near the log farmhouse of one J. F. Scales. This house was some two miles north of Resaca, near the railroad, on its west side.

In this position the Twenty-seventh was on the right of the brigade. The Second Massachusetts joined us on the left, while next to us on the right was the Forty-sixth Pennsylvania, of the First Brigade. The enemy's main entrenched line was one hundred and twenty yards in front of ours. Further to our left his line curved back somewhat, to conform to the ridge upon which it was located, and was, therefore, further away from the Union line. The ground between the two lines varied considerably, but it was all more or less timbered, except just about the Scales house. As has been said, the line of the Twenty-seventh was not quite upon the crest of the ridge, but slightly back from it. After the crest was passed the ground immediately in our front descended gradually, through open timber, for eighty yards. Forty yards further on, upon quite a steep bluff, was the enemy's line, behind a good breastwork of timber and earth. The fact will be clear to all soldiers that nothing but the trees, which stood between the enemy's line and our own, and which hid the one from the other. .670

COOK, ASST. SURGEON, 150TH NY RUGER 2B 1D 20C: I soon discovered my mistake and lost no time in getting once more on the trail of the 150th, finding them about two miles to the left. Our brigade being the last brigade on the left wing of the army, and our regiment being on the extreme left of our brigade.—Those who understand the importance of a flank movement, will readily understand that this was not a position without its danger, and not without its honor also, to those who are fighting for that article. It did not of right belong to our regiment, but to the oldest regiment in the brigade—but it showed pretty plainly the confidence our brigade and division commanders had in Colonel Ketcham and his regiment. Our line of battle was so arranged that the 150th took possession of a small eminence, the right wing of it fronting on a piece of woods and the left wing fronting on an open field. .671

---

670 (E. R. Brown 1899, 470)
671 (Cook 1864)

Ireland Gets Two Up During the Pause

Cobham Arrives, Then Lane

Randall's 149th New York was now joined by Cobham's 111th Pennsylvania. Ireland conducted Lane's 102nd New York to left of Cobham. They then, from below the fort, covered it from front to left. They do not mention those of Butterfield's division, who were already in or just below the fort.

Cobham's arrival, according to Randall, is after the 149th New York and others had been pushed out of the fort. It was perhaps a long arc he traveled through the woods, on the left. He finally took position on the left of the fort, connecting with Randall.

> RANDALL, 149TH NY IRELAND 3B 2D 20C: Some twenty minutes or half an hour after we had taken this position the One hundred and eleventh Pennsylvania Volunteers, Colonel Cobham, came forward and took position at our left, *having one company of the regiment, which he had picked up on the route*, his right overlapping and in front of my left. Upon his arrival the fire upon us from the left almost entirely ceased, and we held our position with ease. Soon after taking position, finding my regiment detached from brigade, I reported our position and the condition of things, and was directed to remain there. There was slight firing along the line, but no strong attack on either side during the afternoon and evening until after the regiment was withdrawn, except a slight flurry about dusk, when nearly everything in our vicinity, except my command, which steadily maintained its position, retired to the foot of the hill. About 9 p.m. by direction of colonel commanding brigade, the regiment was withdrawn and joined the brigade in the rear. .672

> MILLER, 111TH PA IRELAND 3B 2D 20C: And forward we went with a cheer and never stoped until we reached the crest of the hill where the rebles were and Colonel Cobham gave the order to lie down and there we lay from noon until nearly midnight when we were relieved by our first brigade and all the time we lay under the fire of the enemy's sharpshooters and there was a battery of four brass twelve pounders within sixty feet of our line and the rebs were in force not more than 100 feet on the other side of the battery and we could not get them and we would not let rebs use them and so they

---

672 (OR, Series I Vol 38 Part 2 Serial 73: Reports n.d., 304) Randall was out of the fort and in front of it by the time Cobham came to Randall's position. Randall then remained until 9 pm.

were left untill the next morning when our boys ran them into our lines .673 .674

But his commander describes them fighting their way up, and even silencing the Rebel line.

> COBHAM, 111TH PA IRELAND 3B 2D 20C: On reaching the summit we were met by a terrible fire from the rebel breast-works and also from sharpshooters in the trees. .675 We returned the fire and moved steadily forward until within fifteen yards of the battery, when I ordered the regiment to halt and lie down, the men loading and firing rapidly, and soon succeeded in silencing the rebel fire and holding possession of their battery of four 12-pounder brass cannon. .676 .677

Did his one regiment halt the fire? The cannon in the fort had long been silenced.

> COBHAM, 111TH PA IRELAND 3B 2D 20C: Our line at this time was about thirty yards from the rebel breast-works and on a parallel line with it. The cannon were planted in a sort of natural fort sunk in the side of the hill and about midway between my own line and the rebel breast-works, with the rear opening into the latter and the front sunk so as to bring the muzzles of the guns near the ground. .678

> COBHAM, 111TH PA IRELAND 3B 2D 20C: The position was one of extreme peril, and we had to contend (without any cover whatever) against superior numbers behind very strong breastworks, but we held the position from

673 (Miller 1969, 141)

674 Places Cobham four rods below the battery, not having gone further.

675 Summit in this context is the furthest point reached, not the top of the hill. It could even be the saddle between two summits. This one was 15 yards below the battery, which was at least 80 yards from the Rebel line, near the actual crest.

676 The Lone Regiment! An unbelievable accomplishment, lost and unseen in the crowd. But they silenced the cannon (again).

677 (OR, Series I Vol 38 Part 2 Serial 73: Reports n.d., 276) Not clear whether they were firing ahead while Ward and Coburn were advancing or after they had taken the fort, or both.

678 (OR, Series I Vol 38 Part 2 Serial 73: Reports n.d., 276) This puts him below and a bit left of the arc of the fort.

12.30 p.m. till night, the right of my regiment covering the guns and preventing any approach to them or recapture on the part of the enemy. .679

A small nod from Cobham to the 149th New York:

> COBHAM, 111TH PA IRELAND 3B 2D 20C: One company of the *One hundred and forty-ninth New York Volunteers formed on my left,* under command of Captain Coville, and did good service in the charge. .680 .681

Cobham and Miller say they stopped short of the fort and did not enter. To be between the fort and the line behind them—on a line parallel to them—places Cobham on the hillside, outside and around the left side of the fort.

But Geary and Boyle give Cobham more credit than he had taken for himself so far:

> GEARY, 2D 20C: The advance of both commands reached the battery nearly together, the One hundred and eleventh Pennsylvania Volunteers, of Ireland's brigade, under Colonel George A. Cobham, leading and forcing its way through the jaws of death, till they had their hands upon the guns. .682 .683

Merely rhetorical?

> BOYLE, ADJUTANT, 111TH PA IRELAND 3B 2D 20C: With defiant cheers the brave Third Brigade, wheeling to the right, leaped upward toward this battery. Part of Butterfield's division, on its right, dashed forward at the same moment to capture it. Cobham was in command, and at his back the One Hundred and Eleventh Regiment plunged through the terrific fire of the battery and its supports until they were among its guns and their colors were on the ramparts. The gunners were captured or driven off, but before the battery could be secured a line of infantry rose out of breastworks only twenty yards away and poured a withering fire into the line that was fighting hand to hand in the epaulement. Cobham, with the cool judgment that

---

679 (OR, Series I Vol 38 Part 2 Serial 73: Reports n.d., 276) Left alone to fend for themselves.
680 (OR, Series I Vol 38 Part 2 Serial 73: Reports n.d., 276) This company had gotten separated from the right of its regiment.
681 Not entirely alone, having picked up a single company from the 149th New York.
682 (OR, Series I Vol 38 Part 2 Serial 73: Reports n.d., 118)
683 Difficult to reconcile with Cobham's own statements, let alone those of Ward's division. Geary wrote his report in Atlanta, after Cobham, Randall, and Ireland were dead.

always characterized him, saw that his small force was overwhelmed, and withdrew it, with other parts of the brigade, a few yards below to a partly protected position, from which point he perfectly commanded and silenced the battery. .684

Boyle echoes Geary's rhetoric. He says the gunners were driven off—but does not actually say *by whom.*

What seems clear: only Randall was at the fort when the Rebels pushed back. Cobham arrived later. And Lane after Cobham. Other than that, Lane's arrival time is not clear.

> LANE, 102ND NY, IRELAND 3B 2D 20C: On arriving up the hill found the One hundred and eleventh Pennsylvania Veteran Volunteers lying down in line of battle, and agreeable to orders received from Colonel Cobham, commanding brigade, moved the One hundred and second by the left flank and took up position on the left of the One hundred and eleventh Pennsylvania Veteran Volunteers, both regiments occupying the extreme front. .685

The rest of Ireland's brigade was well below the fort.

> BARNUM, 149TH NY IRELAND 3B 2D 20C: The other five regiments of the brigade moved rapidly up the hill in their front, and down the opposite side, across the Dalton road, and took position on a hill directly in front of the rebel works. .686 .687

> GEARY, 2D 20C: During the advance of Ireland's brigade a body of troops from another division, sweeping through the brigade, had severed it, and by my orders all of it, excepting three regiments, were posted in reserve, and Colonel Cobham was directed to take command of the three regiments,

---

684 (Boyle 1903, 205) Appears to be quoting Geary and puts Cobham and Randall on the left of Ward. Omits which part, or how much, of Butterfield's division was involved. Cobham was then only leading his one regiment. And Randall gets no credit in the reports.

685 (OR, Series I Vol 38 Part 3 Serial 74: Reports n.d., 308)

686 This makes clear that only Randall and Cobham went up the hill after Ireland stopped the brigade.

687 (OR, Series I Vol 38 Part 2 Serial 73: Reports n.d., 268)

which had now silenced and held under command of their guns the battery. _688

Into the thicket, left of the hill, Geary sent the two regiments that had gone forward into the fire after Ireland stopped. They stayed there an hour and went back:

BARNUM, 149TH NY IRELAND 3B 2D 20C: While the colonel commanding the brigade was moving the One hundred and second New York Volunteers forward, to connect with the One hundred and forty-ninth and One hundred and eleventh Pennsylvania Volunteers, the Seventy-eighth New York Volunteers and Twenty-ninth Pennsylvania Volunteers were ordered by General Geary to move through a dense pine thicket to the left of the hill occupied by the three regiments above named, and engage the enemy. This they did, remaining in the position about an hour, when they were ordered back, and with the other regiments threw up breast-works on the crest of the hill occupied by the principal portion of the brigade. _689

Now Geary sends three of Buschbeck's regiments as Ward advanced. Buschbeck's brigade had moved up the left hill, behind Wood's brigade, with Geary's position left of the Dalton road. Then they waited. They had crossed the Rebel advance rifle pits that Wood had cleared earlier on the lower side of the hill.

LOCKMAN, 119TH NY BUSCHBECK 2B 2D 20C: The Third Division having the advance, we all moved forward, the enemy being driven from their first three lines of rifle-pits, all of which were built on the crest of three difficult hills. After the second line was taken my regiment got in the advance of the others of our brigade, except the Thirty-third New Jersey and One hundred and thirty-fourth New York. _690

JACKSON, 134TH NY BUSCHBECK 2B 2D 20C: The regiment took up the line of march, with the brigade, in direction of the ground occupied by the Third Division, moving by the flank until reaching the first line of breast-works, in advance of which the Third Division had already engaged the enemy. The order of march placing my regiment next in rear of the Thirty-third New Jersey Volunteers, it directly after advanced in this order in line of battle over the breast-works toward the sound of firing. Having moved in this

688 (OR, Series I Vol 38 Part 2 Serial 73: Reports n.d., 118)
689 (OR, Series I Vol 38 Part 2 Serial 73: Reports n.d., 268)
690 (OR, Series I Vol 38 Part 2 Serial 73: Reports n.d., 232)

direction about 500 yards in front and to the left of the point of passing the breast-works, a halt was ordered under cover of a hill, near the position where Major-General Hooker was then standing. .691

Then, during the pause, while Ward had been trapped in the fort and after Cobham and Lane had joined Randall, more came forward, drawing fire from the Rebel line:

GEARY, 2D 20C: Three regiments of Buschbeck's brigade, which had advanced gallantly, driving the enemy from two hills on the left of Cobham, were not far from him. With these three regiments Colonel Lockman was now ordered to report to Colonel Cobham, which he did promptly. .692

That part about driving the enemy from the hills on the left is misleading, to be nice about it, since Wood had already done that and was holding the positions directly facing the north side of the angle, extending down a bit into the ravine between the hills.

Those three regiments did move closer under the fort. It started as an assault, by mistake, but drew heavy fire.

JACKSON, 134TH NY BUSCHBECK 2B 2D 20C: Here the regiment was allowed a rest of twenty or thirty minutes, at the expiration of which time an order was communicated to me, through Colonel Fessenden, of General Hookers staff, directing my regiment with the One hundred and nineteenth New York, One hundred and ninth Pennsylvania, and Thirty-third New Jersey Volunteers, which regiments were then lying most convenient for receiving the order to charge a battery of the enemy planted about 500 yards in front, and re-enforce Colonel Cobham, of the Third Brigade, Second Division, who already had position closely adjacent to the battery, but required assistance. Colonel Lockman, of the One hundred and nineteenth New York, being ranking officer, was placed in command of the regiments designated, and the charge ordered immediately after. This was executed in fine style, the men springing forward on the run until reaching the advanced line of Colonel Cobham's command, which was found already in virtual possession of the battery, though unable to remove the guns, the enemy holding a strong position intrenched in the immediate rear of the battery,

691 (OR, Series I Vol 38 Part 2 Serial 73: Reports n.d., 239)
692 (OR, Series I Vol 38 Part 2 Serial 73: Reports n.d., 118)

which it covered so effectually as to prevent its occupation by our forces without first effecting their dislodgment. .693 .694

Lockman, 119th NY Buschbeck 2B 2D 20C: While here Colonel Fessenden brought an order from General Hooker to take the line at all hazards, and showed me a note from Colonel Cobham, who was in part possession of same, requiring more troops. I ordered the line forward, and we pushed up the hill under a terrific musketry fire, and reached that portion of the line where Colonel Cobham's troops were lying, some of the men entering the rebel battery. At this moment Lieut. Col. E. F. Lloyd fell mortally wounded, and several men near him were struck. I ordered the line to lie down, and learned from Colonel Cobham that all that was required was to hold the hill. The battery having been secured, and he having been placed in command of the whole line, by order of General Hooker, I became subject to his orders. .695

JACKSON, 134TH NY BUSCHBECK 2B 2D 20C: My regiment having been halted was immediately disposed in line on the left of the One hundred and eleventh Pennsylvania Volunteers, of Colonel Cobham's command, and in advance of the regiments designated above as forming the command of Colonel Lockman. Lieutenant Taylor, of the One hundred and thirty-fourth, was immediately dispatched to Brigadier-General Geary for the purpose of communicating the position of affairs and procuring further instructions. He returned soon after with instructions to hold the battery and make no farther advance until ordered. .696 .697

They lined up and headed up the hill, full for battle: Fouratt 33rd New Jersey, Jackson 134th New York, Lockman (Lloyd) 119th New York.

From Lyle Denniston's view:

DENNISTON, 33RD NJ BUSCHBECK 2B 2D 20C: On Sunday it came our turn. Our division all marched up, heavy firing going on all the time. Then we

693 (OR, Series I Vol 38 Part 2 Serial 73: Reports n.d., 239)
694 (OR, Series I Vol 38 Part 2 Serial 73: Reports n.d., 218)
695 (OR, Series I Vol 38 Part 2 Serial 73: Reports n.d., 232)
696 (OR, Series I Vol 38 Part 2 Serial 73: Reports n.d., 239)
697 (OR, Series I Vol 38 Part 2 Serial 73: Reports n.d., 118) Geary described in detail his own position as along a road in a ravine behind Williams' right and Cobham's left, not mentioning Wood's brigade, which was not relieved by then (they repelled Stevenson's flank attempt at 4 pm). He was north of the hill which was left of the fort and was unable to communicate with Cobham. He was behind and left of Wood then, as Wood said.

were drawn up in a line in the woods. There were three or four lines ahead of us, and we all made a rush, yelling and hooting, guns roaring, bullets singing and whizzing amongst us. Here was another hill to ascend, and when the lines ahead of us reached the top, they lay down but our colonel would not let us, and we rushed right over them, the men hollowing "Go in, Jersies, we will follow you." Over the hill, down the hollow, up another hill, we drove the rebels: but there we had to stop. Oh! What a dreadful volley they poured into us! We had to drop down and lie still, and didn't I hug the ground close? There we lay amongst the dead and wounded. .698

Now half of Geary's 2nd and 3rd Brigades was below the fort, among the dead and dying. Lockman's charge had drawn fire from the defenders.

CJH, Brown's Brigade, Stevenson's Division, Hood's Corp, CSA: An hour wore on, unbroken save by the incessant fire of their sharpshooters, when a fresh column appeared again, formed in three lines. It now became manifest that their whole efforts were directed by this point, and that they were determined to carry it at any sacrifice. On they came, confident in superior numbers, while a perfect storm of bullets heralded their approach, but again they were handsomely repulsed. .699 .700

Escape

Ward took advantage of the distraction, somehow. Maybe the enemy fire was directed against those three regiments advancing across the lower slope of the hill Wood occupied.

Ward, 1B 3D 20C: Thinking that by this time my messenger should have returned to the foot of the hill with a surgeon, I consented to go there, have my wounds dressed, and return. I was shot through the left arm, the same ball wounding me in the side, and I then thought it had remained in my body. The slight movement caused by my starting seemed to arouse the enemy (they had been quiet for some time) and he opened upon me first

---

698 (Denniston 1864) He says they became first in line. Thus, closest to the fort amongst the new arrivals.
699 (CJH 1864)
700 (Abrams 1864) Abrams reports two Union regiments still left in the fort.

from his entire line, driving my men and forcing them to retreat on double-quick time. I could only follow their retreating steps. _701 _702

REID, CO A 22ND WIS COBURN 2B 3D 20C: So after we had taken the guns we could not retain our position behind them. The two Companies found they were beyond the regiment and fell back to join them and all who were "in the fort" or behind the guns had to fall back to the protection of the hill. _703

Stalemate

Our Own Soldiers - Continually Firing

This was attempted both by marching in line and by flank, but was absolutely impossible to be done without wanton waste of life, on account of our own soldiers, six or eight lines deep in front of us, continually firing, and they could not be induced or made to cease firing long enough to enable us to get forward. —Baird

After Ward got out of the fort, the afternoon wore on as Coburn and Wood kept trying, though some regiments were not in position. Other units were still not engaged.

COBURN, 2B 3D 20C: Here a portion of the First and Second Brigades remained during the day, holding this position under the very brow of the rebel earthworks. A portion retired to the left and rear. _704

STRONG, CO B 105TH ILL WARD 1B 3D 20C: When we were ordered back to the rear[,] and left the Second Brigade to hold the guns that we had captured, the Johnnies had fallen back only as far as another line of works or entrenchments. The cannon were left between the line we captured and the one they still occupied, only a few rods in the rear, and neither they nor our own men could use them. _705

Some firing from the other Corps was helping hold the line.

FULLERTON, ADJUTANT, 4TH CORP: TIMELINE: 2.20 pm, Colonel Asmussen reported that General Hooker had secured a lodgment on the ridge, and

701 (OR, Series I Vol 38 Part 2 Serial 73: Reports n.d., 322)
702 This firing by the Rebel line may have been in response to a charge not obvious to Ward in his position.
703 (Reid 1965, 148) Two companies of the 22nd Wisconsin.
704 (OR, Series I Vol 38 Part 2 Serial 73: Reports n.d., 378)
705 (Strong 1961)

that he wished the Fourth Corps to make a demonstration and he would advance along it. A demonstration was made along our entire line. Generals Hazen and Willich, of Wood's division, stormed the enemy's works in their front, but the force of the enemy was so strong, and the direct and enfilading fire of artillery prevented them from holding the enemy's lines. The demonstration had the effect to hold the enemy in our front, and to prevent him from massing in front of General Hooker. At this time General Whittaker's brigade, of Stanley's division, was in the rear of Hooker, waiting orders to advance, while Schofield's command was acting as an immediate support. .706

But the momentum was long gone, replaced by crowding and disorganization. No one had followed Butterfield's division and Randall's regiment to the main Confederate line. Geary's 3rd Brigade was scattered, though some were right below the fort. Coburn's regiment had barely gotten through the jam and arrived too late to help much. When Howard's 4th Corps had pressed, they were driven back rapidly. Schofield was still held on the far left. The Rebels, driven out of their line, had returned. The no-mans-land remained.

Ward's brigade is still just below the fort.

Quite crowded up there!

Coburn kept on, making three charges—without his entire brigade.

COBURN, 2B 3D 20C: Soon after my arrival at the immediate vicinity of the rebel works General Ward was wounded and left the field. I took command of the forces there and made three efforts to charge and take the enemy's works, but such was the disorganized condition of the men of both brigades and the terrific force of their fire that each charge failed and nothing more could be done than hold the place up to the line of their breast-works. In one of these charges late in the day the One hundred and eleventh Pennsylvania, Colonel Cobham, gallantly participated. .707

BRADLEY, CHAPLAIN, 22ND WIS COBURN 2B 3D 20C: Capt Pugh, of Co. F, charges three different times up that hill to gain the coveted artillery, but from the most formidable breastworks the rebels hurl a sweeping tempest of shot, and men who start up the hill with cheers fall to the earth and hug the sheltering log, while one makes a rampart of dead bodies. Three men

706 (OR, Series I Vol 38 Part 1 Serial 75: Reports n.d., 854)
707 (OR, Series I Vol 38 Part 2 Serial 73: Reports n.d., 377)

lose their brothers. Lt. Dickinson loses his daring boy close by the cannon, and night finds our men holding the position. .708

CJH, BROWN'S BRIGADE, STEVENSON'S DIVISION, HOOD'S CORP, CSA: A third and a fourth desperate assault was made, but each time met like success. The brave Tennesseans stood cool, clam, and unflinching, met and repulsed each assault, and fully sustained the reputation achieved for themselves on so many bloody fields. .709

Half of Geary's 2nd Brigade was still left and below the fort. Geary moved Ireland's reserve into the thicket on the left for an hour and then moved them back.

Two of Coburn's regiments, blocked earlier, were trying to get up to the rest of the brigade:

MILLER, 33RD IND COBURN 2B 3D 20C: At the time the front of the brigade changed direction to the left the confusion was so great that the remainder of the brigade, the Eighty-fifth and Thirty-third Indiana, became separated from the other regiments, and when their two regiments advanced in the direction they supposed the brigade had gone there were ten or twelve lines of troops formed in various ways, and lying down and firing over lines yet in advance of them, and it became almost impossible for troops to advance in order and without confusion. Colonel Baird, Eighty-fifth Indiana, deemed it prudent to halt and await orders and reform the Eighty-fifth and Thirty-third in a good position, which was done. I had reported to him in the absence of any other commanding officer. In about an hour after this, an orderly informed Colonel Baird that the brigade commander, Colonel Coburn, with most of the men of the other regiments, was in front of a fort of the enemy, and were not strong enough to take it, and that the Eighty-fifth and Thirty-third Indiana were to come to his assistance. This was attempted both by marching in line and by flank, but was absolutely impossible to be done without wanton waste of life, on account of our own soldiers, six or eight lines deep in front of us, continually firing, and they could not be induced or made to cease firing long enough to enable us to get forward. .710

708 (Bradley 1865)
709 (CJH 1864)
710 (OR, Series I Vol 38 Part 2 Serial 73: Reports n.d., 394)

Was the 2nd Division firing to protect the many soldiers lying flat on their faces on the steep slope just beneath the crest—to keep Rebels from coming forward and firing down on them? Two of Geary's own were right under the line left of the fort. Skill is needed: a small drop in trajectory hits the wrong target. Or were they just firing at the hill without any targets in particular?

So now we have part of Ireland's brigade still downhill, blocked by others of the 2nd Division, while some of Ward's brigade remains before the fort, in front of the 2nd Division. And 2nd Division, Geary's men, keep firing away.

> MERRILL, 70TH IND WARD 1B 3D 20C: LIEUTENANT W. R. MCCRACKEN: "After the Seventieth Indiana and the brigade of which it was a part had taken the battery and were holding it under a terrible fire from the enemy, a musketry fire was poured into them from the rear. Colonel Harrison ordered me to see what the firing meant. I found that it came from a body of our own men belonging to the Second Division, who were behind some timber. I told them to stop firing or the First Brigade would have to retire from the works they had taken and were holding. The firing was stopped, but by the time I was back to my command it began again. Colonel Harrison then directed me to go back and hunt up General Butterfield, who commanded the Third Division, and tell him of the firing from the rear, and that the Brigade would have to fall back if it was not stopped. I could not find Butterfield, but found General Williams, commanding the First Division, and inquired for General Butterfield and told him what I wanted. General Williams said he did not know where General Butterfield was, but told me where to find General Hooker, who, on being informed, spurred his horse and rode rapidly to the place where the white star troops lay, and the firing ceased." .711

Who had been directing Geary's men to keep up the firing? Why?

Wood's right was helping with Coburn's assaults, but getting crowded out:

> WINKLER, 26TH WIS WOOD 3B 3D 20C: Here I succeeded in forming a small line, took it forward & participated in a number of charges that were attempted upon the enemy's position partly by me and partly by the 2d Division, all of which however resulted only in an increase of confusion. I then sent Capt Fuchs of my regiment back to collect the men & get orders for me. Getting no orders I finally returned with the officers & men with me to the hill we first occupied in the morning where I found Capt Fuchs & the

---

711 (S. Merrill 1900, 100)

rest of the regiment. I reported to Col Wood at once where the regt. was & was told to remain there till further orders. .712

On the Left, Wood and Knipe
Have Been Pressing the Hillside

NEW YORK HERALD: The redoubt so often mentioned above also swept this hill with its guns, so that it was not a very safe location, and as the rebels left, their artillery commenced to work. To this we could make no reply, having no guns in position; but Colonel Wood, placing his men under such cover as he could find, directed them to lie down, and the rebels were permitted to fire away until they emptied their magazines, or exhausted their patience. .713

MARVIN, CO F 5TH CONN, KNIPE 1B 1D 20C: While this was going on, amid fthe storm of shot and shell, the regiment commenced singing the "Battle Cry of Freedom," which was taken up by the troops on the right and left. The color guard (brave men) advanced well to the front, waving "Old Glory" in the faces of the Confederates. The effect was magical, and one must have been there and witnessed the scene in order to appreciate the inspiration and enthusiasm aroused from so simple and common an incident. The enemy continued to charge time after time, but found that the sentiment of that "Battle Cry," backed up by the rifles of the brave men of the First Brigade, were too much for them, and so they retired from such a losing contest and the battle ended. It was one of the many square fights in the open field, without breastworks or defenses of any kind, which the regiment was called upon to fight during its service, and was an achievement of which the regiment was ever afterwards deservedly proud. But the battle was not won without severe loss. Company K was at the extreme left of the regiment, and during a part of the engagement at the extreme left of the whole line of battle, and received a terrible fire both from front and left flank. There were but about thirty men in that company that day, and fifteen of them fell killed or wounded in less than ten minutes of that terrible ordeal; yet the other fifteen stood as staunch and firm at their posts as when they first took their position on that fatal ridge. With such metal alone can victories be hewn. .714

712 (F. C. Winkler 1864)
713 (Bradley 1865, 104)
714 (Marvin 1889, 299)

OSBORN, CO A 55TH OHIO WOOD 3B 3D 20C: Their first volley nearly decimated the command, but did not check the advance. I heard a voice call out, "Captain Peck, your brother is killed." "Yes," said the Captain, "there'll be more of us soon," and as he spoke he fell. In that moment Major Robbins fell, and the place seemed almost untenable; but a slight swell in the open ground in front promised shelter and the command fled forward. By lying down some shelter was obtained, and the men rested for a moment. The Captain of Company B was fortunate in finding on the right a clump of cedars where the enemy had made some defences for an advanced post. By reversing these the company secured a fairly good position for offence, which it held during the engagement. _715

RYDER, CO I 33RD MASS, WOOD 3B 1D 20C: We returned their fire to the best of our ability, but being so fully exposed our men fell rapidly until four of our color bearers had fallen, 65 of the rank and file and a few officers. We then got orders to lie down on the crest of the hill for a few moments. Soon orders came to rise up and we were told that we were to charge across the valley and take the rifle pits, and for no one to hesitate when the order to charge should be given. So in a few moments the order was given, and I started on the run for the rifle pits. I had gotten about half way across the valley when in looking around I found there were only three men with me. We said, "Where is the regiment?" Evidently no one but us had moved. I don't think I ever witnessed such a rain of bullets as was falling about us. The leaves and twigs from the bushes were falling all around us. I expected every second to be hit, but we got back to our lines unhurt, and found the regiment lying down just where we had left them. I never knew why that order was disobeyed. It was the first and only time our regiment disobeyed an order. No doubt they acted wisely, because we would all have been annihilated before we could have reached the enemy's rifle pits. While I was looking for a place to lie down in comparative safety, I found what I thought a good one back of the roots and earth of a large fallen tree. Two of my company were lying there and they made room for me on one side.

This is where I had my first presentiment. I had just lain down when I was overwhelmed, as I might call it, by an impression that I was in imminent danger of death. I could see no possible reason for this, but the impression became so strong that I crawled back about two yards, still watching the place I had left, when suddenly two bullets following close to each other passed through the leaves where I had lain, both of

715 (Osborn 1904, 145)

which would have passed through my body if I had remained there. Now, what power gave me that notice? .716

The 55th Ohio and 136th New York suffered the most casualties. They faced the 54th Virginia across the saddle between crests. On their left, the 73rd Ohio had gone some distance before returning through heavy fire. On their right, the 33rd Massachusetts and 26th Wisconsin extended into the slight ravine between the hills, where there were trees and less enfilading fire.

This next incident might have been after Wood had moved toward the next slope and retreated behind the crest, firing back and forth, maybe while Knipe had one regiment lying exposed.

MARVIN, CO F 5TH CONN, KNIPE 1B 1D 20C: The regiment was made up of brave and manly spirits, not the officers alone but the ranks were full of it. There was in this fight another incident illustrating the staunchness of the private soldiers of the Fifth, which has not often been excelled in this respect by the conduct of any other soldiers in any other battle. After our boys had captured the open ridge and driven the rebels back into the woods, as a preparation for another charge upon the ridge, the Confederates turned all their artillery within range upon our boys along that ridge, making it an extremely hot and uncomfortable place, and our boys were ordered to lie down and hug the ground as close as they could. They lay down flat, the rear rank men lying between the legs of the front rank men, about as close as it was possible to put men; the rear rank men firing between the heads of the front rank men.

At first the artillery firing at this line was extremely high and wild, and served only to amuse the men, but by degrees they depressed their guns more and more and their shells came nearer, till finally, just as the rebel line came out of the woods to make the second charge, a shell came and struck the line in Company I, taking off the top of the head of James E. Richards in the front rank, and passing along down his back passed under the rear rank man, John Bates, bursting when it was about under the center of his body. Bates and Richards were of course killed outright by it, and four others were wounded by the pieces of the shell and pieces of the skull from Richards. Corporal Wm. H. Kerr had several pieces of the skull driven into his face, also private James Tuttle's face was filled, and Tommy Graham, from fragments of the shell or skull, had both eyes cut out of his head and then left hanging on his cheek. Lieutenant Stewart, commanding Company I,

716 (Ryder 1928, 53)

sprang up and helped to pull the dead men, Richards and Bates, to the rear from their places in the line in order to fill the gap with living fighting men, for the rebel column was coming on again charging and yelling. He saw that Tommy Graham could not see at all, and that while Corporal Kerr's face was badly cut up, still that he had his eyesight remaining. He asked the corporal if he could see well enough to take himself to the rear and lead Tommy, totally blinded as he was. He said he thought he could, and thereupon the Lieutenant told Graham to go to the rear with Kerr and started them off; but Tommy had not moved two steps to the rear before he stopped and cried out, "Lieutenant, Lieutenant, what will I do with my gun? and the brave man did not stir a step further until his officer had come to him and taken his gun and relieved him from this final responsibility.

If this picture could be imagined as it was, and as the comrades of poor Tommy saw it, then something of the true stuff of the man could be conceived, artillery roaring from all directions,—shells screeching past, and now coming so low that every one of them ricocheted along the ground and raked the earth from front to rear; a yelling line of rebels fast coming towards him, his eyes just closed forever to all the beauties of this earth and the glories of the skies, never to behold wife or children again, and still, when ordered to the rear in care of another, standing there with those sightless eyes dangling at his cheeks, and calling upon his officer to relieve him of his trusty gun, the last obligation remaining upon him, as he understood his duty to his country as a soldier; and then whoever can imagine this scene as it was, can begin to understand something of the truth and faithfulness of the nature of such private soldiers as Thomas Graham. _717

HURST, 73RD OHIO WOOD 3B 3D 20C: When the Seventy-third Ohio reached its position on the left of the Fifty-fifth, a New York regiment of Geary's division was occupying the ground, having passed up the ravine from the right. They were lying down, in line, at the foot of the hill, where they could not fire upon the enemy. Their colonel refused to advance to the brow of the hill, where an effective fire could be delivered; and our commander ordered the Seventy-third to advance through, or over their line. This touched the pride of the New York soldiers, and, without command, their whole line rose up and advanced with ours to the brow of

717 (Marvin 1889, 299)

the hill, where the two regiments together poured in a vigorous fire for an hour or two, when the New York battalion withdrew from the ravine. .718

Hurst, according to this, did not reach his position until after the assault. The New York regiment he found might have been Randall's 149th New York, who came up with Ward and took position on the left. Cobham's 111th Pennsylvania arrived after the assault was over and took position left of Randall. Lane's 102nd arrived during the pause and took position left of Cobham. We saw Hurst had been busy earlier and now we know he was not able to get forward till after all of Ward's brigade reached the fort.

Knipe said Logie's 141st New York was on his right with a gap between them and Wood, the gap Hurst had to cross. It could not be left empty—by either side.

The Loss of Colonel Gambee

OSBORN, CO A 55TH OHIO WOOD 3B 3D 20C: LIEUTENANT P. C. LATHROP, CO A: "I was in command of Company A (Colonel Gambee's company), and lying upon the ground some ten or fifteen feet lower down the hill, but immediately behind my company. Just behind me, and to my right, sat Colonel Gambee, behind a pile of rails. Having several times been solicited to do so, I arose and went and sat down beside the Colonel. It was only a few minutes afterwards that the Johnnies made a charge upon our line. We immediately jumped to our feet, and as the Colonel opened his lips to issue a command, a bullet struck him in the breast, and he fell backward into my arms, dead—killed instantly. A glorious death, as I view it now, but his sudden and unexpected fate seemed at the moment to madden me. I laid him down carefully, and, taking his revolver from his belt, I ran forward to rejoin my company. Halting, I tried to shoot the Rebel Colonel, who came within a few feet before he was shot. But I could not make the revolver work. I threw it down in disgust, but afterwards picked it up, and I think it was sent home with the Colonel's other personal effects. I do not now recall that I saw the Colonel's body after I laid it down when he was killed." .719

Did a sharpshooter have Colonel Gambee in his sights, just waiting for a clear shot? Or was it a quick, lucky shot from one of the chargers?

---

718 (Hurst 1866, 119) This is not mentioned by Ireland's three regiments that were in that vicinity. Lane's 102nd New York was last up and furthest left, next to Cobham's 111th Pennsylvania.
719 (Osborn 1904, 147)

Osborn, Co A 55th Ohio Wood 3B 3D 20C: First Sergeant Moses Pugh, Company H: "At the second day's battle of Gettysburg there was the greatest cannonading the world ever knew. I was stationed near a battery, and counted one hundred and fifteen holes in the ground that had been made by cannon-balls. On this field I spied a beautiful, new, bright musket lying by the side of a dead Rebel, which I was not long in taking in exchange for my own, for mine was somewhat rusty and old. Upon examination I found it to be a Richmond rifle of the same calibre as the Springfield, the one I had been using near Hagerstown, Maryland. While in close pursuit of Lee's retreating army, on the eve of July 5, we were ordered to sleep on our arms, and as it was raining slightly I greased my precious gun with a piece of bacon rind. When I awoke in the morning my first act was to remove the cap from the tube. Pressing the greasy hammer with my thumb, I accidentally let it slip, whereupon my first Johnny ball went through the blouses of three of my comrades and killed my colonel's horse, which was tied to a stake about twenty rods away. The boys often laughingly told me my gun would turn traitor, and at that terrific report I began to believe it. But I must be brief. Colonel Gambee was incensed at the death of his faithful horse. He ordered my corporal's stripes to be taken off, and demanded pay for the horse; but as we had not drawn any pay for six months, money was scarce; so I gave him my note, payable on first payday. But just before the battle of Resaca, Georgia, May 15, 1864, seeming to have presentiments of impending danger, he came to me, gave me the rank of a sergeant, and burned the note in my presence. The brave, good Colonel was killed in that battle." .720

Knipe, 1B 1D 20C: In the course of about half an hour the enemy did make a charge, advancing in several lines with colors flying and extending entirely across the field. I ordered my command to lie quiet and await my orders. I waited until the enemy had advanced to within 150 yards, when I gave the order to rise up and fire. This order was promptly obeyed, and in less than half an hour the field in my front did not contain a living rebel. My casualties in this engagement were Capt. E. L. Witman, of the Forty-sixth Pennsylvania Veteran Volunteers, acting assistant adjutant-general of this brigade, wounded in the right leg; Lieut. John H. Knipe, of the same regiment, aide-de-camp, killed; 6 line officers wounded, 30 enlisted men killed, and 160 wounded; a total of 198. .721 .722

---

720 (Osborn 1904, 249)
721 (OR, Series I Vol 38 Part 2 Serial 73: Reports n.d., 39)
722 General Knipe's nephew.

Hovey's Division Gets in the Middle

ABRAMS, ATLANTA INTELLIGENCER, WITH STEWART'S DIVISION, CSA: In the meantime the Yankees had advanced on Stewart's line, and made a desperate attempt to take it by storm. Clayton's and Baker's brigades of Alabamians, aided by Stovall's and Gibson's, received them with great gallantry, and poured a terrible fire into the Yankee advance. They, however, continued to move forward, and approached very near the line, when Clayton's brigade gave them another well directed fire, and they fell down the slope of the hill until out of range of our guns. This charge was desperately made, and the masses of the enemy's dead that lay piled up before Stewart's line attested the courage and determination of our foes. .723

Who had advanced on Stewart's line? Perhaps Hovey. Schofield was in reserve and to be on the left across the railroad. Sometime during the action, they got in between Ruger and Knipe.

HURST, 73RD OHIO WOOD 3B 3D 20C: Twice In the meantime, the Twenty-third corps had come in on our left, had crossed the open ground and pushed close up to the enemy's works. They had been warmly engaged, and had been compelled to retire. .724

MCQUISTON, 2B 1D 23C: [At] 11.30 a.m. [my command] moved to the extreme left of General Hooker's corps, passing through a narrow gorge on to an open field in front of enemy's batteries, where I caused One hundred and twenty-third Regiment Indiana Volunteers to form line of battle. The enemy opened heavy fire from masked batteries and musketry, when, by your order, the One hundred and twenty-ninth Regiment Indiana Volunteers and One hundred and thirtieth Indiana Volunteers were closed in column by division and retired into the gorge, sustaining but little injury. The One hundred and twenty-third Regiment was then ordered to return to the gorge under cover of the woods. .725 .726

---

723 (Abrams 1864)
724 (Hurst 1866, 119) The 73rd was adjacent to Knipe, who faced both Stevenson and Stewart.
725 (OR, Series I Vol 38 Part 2 Serial 73: Reports n.d., 545)
726 McQuiston describes moving forward again, but his narrative switches further left, near the railroad. See Williams' efforts, below, against Stewart's flank attempt.

The 129th Indiana were new recruits in McQuiston's brigade of Hovey's division, Schofield's 1st, from the woods behind. They were not in their stated position, left of the railroad, but perhaps this happened while they were on their way.

Which could have been the cause of this:

> HURST, 73RD OHIO WOOD 3B 3D 20C: Twice the foe came out of their works in our front, with the manifest intention of charging our line; once they got within a hundred paces, but our hail of bullets drove them back with loss. Gen. Knipe had formed his brigade on the wooded hill in our rear, and now opened fire over our heads. The enemy answered his fire, and the two storms of lead made the air musical above us. The rebel artillery from the fort, three hundred yards in our right front, poured over us their case shot and canister; and when the enemy on our left, following the Twenty-third corps, had gained our flank so as to almost completely enfilade our line, we were never more nearly surrounded by the elements of wrath. .727

Hurst is up close to the enemy, who is firing over him at Knipe behind him. Logie and maybe McQuiston's brigade, were returning fire also. They had to hug the ground!

Men Laid on Their Faces

> FULLERTON, ADJUTANT, 4TH CORP: Timeline 2.50 pm, General Hooker sent word that he did not wish us to do anything more than to open artillery on the enemy. At same time sent word to General Hooker, by Lieutenant Gilbreth, that it would be done, and offered to afford any assistance General H[ooker] might call for. .728

> PARTRIDGE, 96TH ILL WHITAKER 2B 1D 4C: The firing was heavy and continuous until evening. The Ninety-Sixth held its position beside the road for several hours. At one time Gen. Hooker, with his Staff and a bevy of orderlies, rode to the centre of the Regiment, and from their horses watched a charge. Bullets flew all about them, and two or three of the party were wounded, but the veteran Commander never moved a muscle to indicate that he had the slightest fear. A straggler came rushing back near their position. The General said, reproachfully perhaps, but with no trace of passion: "Young man, isn't it a little cowardly to leave your comrades fighting at the front while you go to the rear? Go back to your command and show

727 (Hurst 1866, 120)
728 (OR, Series I Vol 38 Part 1 Serial 75: Reports n.d., 854)

that you are willing to do your part." The soldier turned about, almost before the General had ceased speaking, and, deliberately facing the storm, went back into the battle. The effect of Gen. Hooker's coolness upon the men lying in reserve was excellent. His reputation was that of a fiery, impulsive, passionate man; but here, under most trying circumstances, he was as cool as though the surroundings were of the most common-place character. .729

OSBORN, CO A 55TH OHIO WOOD 3B 3D 20C: The contest raged along the entire line for at least three hours, neither side gaining advantage. .730

MCMAHON, CO E 136TH NY WOOD 3B 3D 20C: They were mad because we got the last hill and [they were] determined to take it again. For this purpose they charged on the hill three times and every time went back with their ranks all cut up. We would load and fire as often as we could get sight of them but we were too much for them and at last they gave it up. .731

OSBORN, CO A 55TH OHIO WOOD 3B 3D 20C: Captain Boalt, of Company D, was found amusing himself by catching an occasional bullet that struck the two or three rails he had collected before him, which proved just able to check the missiles, as they dropped to the ground, hot but harmless. .732

RYDER, CO I 33RD MASS, WOOD 3B 1D 20C: Soon after this Frank Penniman, my tentmate, came to me and said, "Sec what those Rebs have done to me! They have put a bullet through my coffee pot on my haversack and another bullet through my canteen, so I have lost all the water. I am going further down front where I can see better and pay them up for it." I advised him not to expose himself more than he already had done but he went just the same. About an hour later he came back and said he had shot two of the Rebs, but his knapsack was riddled with bullets and his woolen blanket was ruined with bullet holes. He was quite satisfied with his experiment. .733

Right below the left of the fort, Randall's 149th New York was holding fort, so to speak.

COLLINS, 149TH NY IRELAND 3B 2D 20C: Among the men in the front line were a number having repeating rifles; these served a good purpose in

---

729 (Partridge 1887, 327)
730 (Osborn 1904, 147) All during their position in the afternoon.
731 (McMahon 1993, 93) Before the flank.
732 (Osborn 1904, 147)
733 (Ryder 1928, 54).

keeping the enemy well within his works. .734 During the afternoon the men laid on their faces on the hillside, and when those in front were killed, wounded or out of ammunition, those in rear crawled forward and took their places. The enemy was not more than fifty yards away, and whenever anyone on either side showed himself a shot was sure to follow. Occasionally a bandying of words took place between the two lines. Johnny shouted out, "Yank! Why don't you come and take the guns away!" and Yank responded "Oh! Johnny, I'm no hog. You can have'em; come and get'em."

The major part of the 149th men, with the colors, were opposite the battery and close under the pieces, the mouths of which projected through the embrasures. So near were some of the men they could touch the pieces with their rifles and could distinctly see the canister with which some of them were loaded. Occasionally a man, with undue curiosity, crawled too far forward or peered through the embrasures, but usually paid dear for his temerity. One poor fellow, against the remonstrance of his comrades, crawled up where he could get a better view, and almost instantly was killed in his place. In falling his head was exposed and, during the afternoon, the enemy literally filled it with bullets. The slope of the hill afforded a partial protection, yet occasionally a person under cover was injured by sharp-shooters in trees or other places commanding the position. The source of this annoyance was not easy to determine, so the men could only protect themselves by lying quiet and not attracting attention by motion. They had little to do except keep the enemy in place, lie quiet, watch, dread and think. The suspense was dreadful; and even the occasional accidents which occurred were a relief in affording something for the mind to rest upon. It was a long, long afternoon and told heavily on the endurance of the men. .735 .736

STEVENSON, DIVISION, HOOD'S CORP, CSA: When Brown's brigade had nearly exhausted their ammunition I caused it to be relieved by Reynolds' Brigade, upon which assaults were also made and repulsed with the same success. During the attack I ordered General Pettus up with three of his regiments, which had remained in our position of the day previous. My intention was to employ his force in attacking the enemy in front of the

734 Spencer Carbines.

735 (Collins 1891, 249)

736 Collins had been a captain in the 149th but had been discharged, wounded in the Battle of Lookout Mountain, and was writing this based on word of others in the regiment. Per other accounts, this applies mainly to the 149th, at least until Cobham and then others of the brigade came forward to join Randall.

battery and remove it. A portion of Gibson's brigade, of Stewart's division, was also sent me, but was soon recalled. The troops engaged, it will thus be seen, were Brown's and Reynolds' brigades, and also the two right regiments of Cumming's brigade. During the day Fenner's battery reported to me and rendered good service. .737

CJH, BROWN'S BRIGADE, STEVENSON'S DIVISION, HOOD'S CORP, CSA: Our ammunition being exhausted, after expending forty rounds per man, we yielded the rifles pits to Reynolds' Brigade in order to replenish our empty cartridge boxes and cleanse our guns. It would be folly in me to attempt to describe the conduct of particular officers or men for where all acted nobly, courageously, praise would be invidious. Our gallant commander did but act with his usual conspicuous gallantry and heroism, freely exposing his person where danger was thickest, and by his presence and cool, calm demeanor inspired the men with courage and confidence. He was frequently urged to leave the rifle pits and only consented when told that he was "in the way." He had not only the entire confidence, but complete devotion of the whole command. .738

White Stars Relieve Blue Stars

GEARY, 2D 20C: Between 3 and 4 p.m. I received orders from Major-General Hooker, commanding the corps, to relieve whatever of General Butterfield's division was then holding position in the front line. Half of my Second and Third Brigades were then with Cobham. From the remainder of my command the order was at once complied with, and all of General Butterfield's troops were relieved, and by the direct order of Major-General Hooker, as well as my own, Colonel Cobham was directed to make every effort to secure and bring off the battery in his front. To this end I sent him as re-enforcements the Fifth Ohio Volunteers from Candy's brigade and other regiments from the Second and Third Brigades, numbering in all ten regiments, and invested him with full command of all the troops at that isolated point. I had now sent him one half of my entire division. Our lines were now strengthened and established in readiness for further operations, General Williams' division being formed entirely on my left, and General Butterfield's division being wholly withdrawn and posted in reserve. .739

---

737 (OR, Series I Vol 38 Part 3 Serial 74: Reports n.d., 812)

738 (CJH 1864)

739 Geary wrote this months later and the times of his placement moves are compressed. These are clarified by the other sources.

Musketry firing was kept up during the afternoon and night, and strong works were thrown up on the hills occupied by our main lines. .740

Butterfield's 3rd Brigade, Wood's, was still in the firing line, left of the fort, and much of Coburn's 2nd Brigade clung to the fort. Geary was far from holding it alone. Ormsby had them about 99 feet below the fort. Geary says Cobham was about 45 feet below.

ORMSBY, CO E 149TH NY IRELAND 3B 2D 20C: Our flag was one of the four that was placed at the top of the hill in plain sight of the Rebs. They fired at us all afternoon and it is full of bullet holes. ... We laid down under the crest of the hill and kept up a steady fire on their breastworks that were about 6 rods off. We laid close under the battery that we had captured but were unable to haul off the guns. We were relieved by another brigade at 8 in the evening. .741

GEARY, 2D 20C: This work was a sunken one at the crest of the hill, and open toward its rear. Twenty yards in rear was a line of strong breast-works, from which a deadly shower of bullets poured around and into the battery, rendering it impossible for men to live there. .742 Cobham, with that cool and accurate judgment which never forsook him, formed his line, now augmented by other portions of the brigade, within fifteen yards of the guns, where by the formation of the ground his troops were less exposed to the terrible fire, while at the same time his own muskets covered the battery from the front. .743

WILDER, CO G 7TH OHIO CANDY 1B 2D 20C: In the afternoon the Union troops advanced in a dozen lines of battle. In the heat of action, as the front line gave way, it fell back to the rear. The Seventh was thus brought in front at 5 P.M. but neither side thought it best to advance across the open field

---

740 (OR, Series I Vol 38 Part 2 Serial 73: Reports n.d., 118)
741 (Ormsby n.d.)
742 80 yards.
743 (OR, Series I Vol 38 Part 2 Serial 73: Reports n.d., 118)

that lay between the two hostile forces. Thus night ended the engagement, without loss to the Seventh. .744 .745

Geary moved regiments forward to Ward's position. Here is his description of the terrain (see Trexler's sketch). Geary now extends from that position to the fort, in front of Grose's brigade, directly in front of the fort. Geary himself was north of the hill where Wood had been in "the fight on the left."

> GEARY, 2D 20C: In the isolated position held by Cobham it was impossible to erect even a slight barricade without receiving a terrible fire from the enemy fifty yards distant. In front of my left and Williams' right was a long, cleared field occupying two hills and a narrow ravine, and extending to a wooded hill on which was the enemy's main line. In front of my right was a field occupying a long, wide ravine, extending from the right of my line to a cleared hill on which was also the enemy's main line. Through this ravine ran the road previously referred to. Across the ravine to my right were lines of intrenchments held by the Fourth Corps and facing nearly eastward at right angles to my front. In front of the center of my main line a series of timbered spurs and knobs extended half a mile toward the enemy's main lines to the detached position held by Cobham. The troops sent to his support by me were so disposed as to hold his flank as well as possible. The only route of communication with him was by way of these timbered ridges, which were swept in most places by musketry and artillery fire from the enemy's main lines.

Geary does not mention Wood's brigade. Part of Geary's 2nd and 3rd Brigades were behind and left of Wood and Ward and Coburn. Wood's 33rd Massachusetts may have connected with some of Buschbeck's three regiments, with Winkler being in the middle of just about everyone in the thicket and ravine.

744 (Wilder 1866, 40) The 7th Ohio were an early three month enlistment, persuaded to re-enlist for three years, with the promise of discharge three months early. But they were kept for the full three years. Efforts by Geary to persuade them to re-enlist for yet another three years only disgusted them, after "abuse and hard usage." They said "we know the promises of men in authority." They had at least been kept out of action—to this point.
745 (Wilder 1866, 41) The 7th was given special consideration for their service, but were still were used in battle at Resaca and New Hope Church.

Ward Withdraws

Some of Ward's and Coburn's brigades tell of withdrawing from the hill and then being sent to help repel a Rebel attack on the left—another flank attempt, we shall read of shortly.

STRONG, CO B 105TH ILL WARD 1B 3D 20C: We fell back not in a body or line of battle as we had advanced, but in squads numbering as many as a hundred, with orders to gather together at a certain place. Leon Palmer and I fell back together. There was a good many dead on the ground, and we had gone only a little way when we heard someone call in a weak voice. We went towards the voice and found a lieutenant of G Company. He had one leg broken, and as he fell the leg doubled up under him. It was bent clear back and the bone stuck out through the flesh. He wanted water, and to have his leg straightened out. Oh, how he groaned and prayed He was grit clear through, though, and would not let us carry him off the field. The bullets were flying around us as thick, seemingly, as hail. After doing what we could for him, we left him. I don't know what became of him. [746]

CRAM, CO F 105TH ILL WARD 1B 3D 20C: The many escapes, the many acts of bravery I saw, and the thousand little things which might afford conversation a lifetime, but sufficient to say that at five o'clock we were reformed under cover of a hill and the fight ceased, we having captured four beautiful guns which our brigade drew off next morning. [747]

WARD, 1B 3D 20C: On reaching the bottom found Lieutenant Heath, of the One hundred and fifth Illinois, with 80 or 100 men. I ordered them forward to aid their comrades who were already in and near the works. They quickly and promptly started, but as they reached the road covered by the enemy's battery on our right they were thrown into confusion by the shells, and it was impossible to rally and reform them at that point. This was between 4 and 5 oclock in the afternoon. With the aid of two of my soldiers I returned to our works on the hill, found a surgeon, had my wounds dressed, and returned to the road at the foot of the hill. Here I found that portion of my brigade which had fallen back formed and ready to reassault the enemy. I sent my aide, Lieutenant Harryman, to General Butterfield to ask that my brigade might make the second attack, and was refused, for proper reasons, that permission. [748]

746 (OR, Series I Vol 38 Part 2 Serial 73: Reports n.d., 320)
747 (Cram 2001, 100)
748 (OR, Series I Vol 38 Part 2 Serial 73: Reports n.d., 320)

STRONG, CO B 105TH ILL WARD 1B 3D 20C: When we got back as far as we were supposed to go, we found a line of men posted across the road to stay stragglers from going on farther. General Ward came along with his arm in a sling, and said, "Old Pap got it this time, boys." He was pretty drunk, and seemed to be proud of his wound. The ambulance corps kept bringing the wounded back. Shells were still flying over us, some going far to the rear, some bursting right around us. Two men, brought a wounded man on a stretcher and set him down near me. I had just lit my pipe, and Mark Naper came to me to get a light for his pipe. I turned my pipe upside down to put it on top of his pipe and knock some fire into his, when a shell exploded just over us. A piece of it came down directly between us, breaking both pipes. Another piece killed the wounded man who was on the stretcher. It surely was a close call for Mark and me. .749

HARRISON, 70TH IND WARD 1B 3D 20C: I was engaged in separating my men from those of other regiments and reforming them preparatory to leading them again to the support of those who still held the guns we had captured, when I was informed that General Ward was wounded and was ordered to assume command of the brigade and reform it which duty I discharged and then urgently asked General Butterfield for permission to take it again to the works we had carried and still held, and bring off the guns we had captured. This was refused, and by his order the brigade was placed in a new position on a hill to the left of the point at which we had assaulted, to assist in repelling an attack made by the enemy. .750

PARTRIDGE, 96TH ILL WHITAKER 2B 1D 4C: During the afternoon Gen. Ward, commanding one of Gen. Butterfield's Brigades, who had ridden through the Regiment on his way to the front, was brought back wounded. Gen. Knipe, another Brigade commander, was also severely wounded; and the total of casualties in these afternoon charges was not less than two thousand. Four pieces of artillery and two battle flags were among the trophies. The Ninety-Sixth, notwithstanding the heavy firing all about it, had but two men wounded. Andrew Hindman, of Company F, had a wound in the shoulder, and Nahum Lamb, of Company G, in the right hand, disabling him for further service. Several others were hit by spent balls or had bullets through their clothing, but were not disabled. At three o'clock in

---

749 (Strong 1961)
750 (OR, Series I Vol 38 Part 2 Serial 73: Reports n.d., 369)

the afternoon a detail from the Regiment, under Lieutenant Earle, was sent to the right to construct some breastworks on a high ridge. _751

SMITH, 102ND ILL WARD 1B 3D 20C: The battery was held during the remainder of the day, although several attempts were made to recapture it. The casualties of this day were 18 men killed, 76 men wounded, and 1 missing. Six of the wounded have since died. _752

DUSTIN, 105TH ILL WARD 1B 3D 20C: My battalion was soon rallied at the foot of the hill, and the brigade was again ready and anxious to join in another charge, had it been necessary. Indeed detachments of officers and men joined with the Third Brigade and charged a second time before returning to the regiment. It is with great pleasure that I can speak in the highest terms of praise of the good conduct of my officers and men in the fearful contest of the day. At a time when so terrible a shower of musketry, grape, and canister was being poured down upon us from the rebel forts and rifle-pits, the coolness and bravery of the officers in repeating commands, correcting imperfections in the line, and pressing it forward was observed by me with great pride and satisfaction, and was only equaled by the manner in which the men overcame all obstacles, obeyed promptly all orders, and at last gallantly threw themselves high up into and under the rebel fortifications. _753

MILLER, 33RD IND COBURN 2B 3D 20C: About 4 p.m. the regiment was ordered to occupy a ridge farther to the rear and left, and finally the whole brigade joined us. The Thirty-third Indiana and the Twentieth Connecticut were posted in the first line, and the men were ordered to lie down. _754

COBURN, 2B 3D 20C: [of his brigade] Their determined and gallant charge secured the position so boldly won by the First Brigade, and together they held it, under the very muzzles of the enemy's guns, five hours in daylight, and their prompt and vigorous action on the left late in the day contributed powerfully to repel the fierce assault of the enemy there. _755

COBURN, 2B 3D 20C: Remaining here till near sunset, I received an order to come to the rear with the men of my command then with me. I returned, leaving the men where I had placed them, near the rebel works. This was

751 (Partridge 1887, 327)
752 (OR, Series I Vol 38 Part 2 Serial 73: Reports n.d., 351)
753 (OR, Series I Vol 38 Part 2 Serial 73: Reports n.d., 360)
754 (OR, Series I Vol 38 Part 2 Serial 73: Reports n.d., 394)
755 (OR, Series I Vol 38 Part 2 Serial 73: Reports n.d., 377)

approved. A portion of the brigade having been formed in the rear and to the left after the first charge, I took them, by order of General Butterfield, to the left still farther to meet and assist in repelling a charge then being made by the enemy upon the left of our position. The Thirty-third Indiana at once changed front forward .756 and promptly met the attack. After a severe fight, in which the rebels suffered much, they were repulsed and retired. .757

REID, CO A 22ND WIS COBURN 2B 3D 20C: The cannons were now silenced and the brigade was reformed at the foot of the hill and again charged up, but it was too exhausting and those breastworks too high, the rebel sharpshooters completely commanded the open space beyond the guns, and though they charged for the third time flesh and blood could not stand it— they could not advance beyond the guns. The line was finally established just below the muzzles of the guns. .758

GRUNERT, CO D 129TH ILL WARD 1B 3D 20C: The enemy in our front had been completely whipped, but not without considerable loss on our side. Many a fine fellow who but a few hours ago, in hopeful and joyful spirits, was at our side in the ranks and fought gallantly was stretched, a cold corpse, on mother earth. Others, wounded, unable to go to the hospitals, lay bleeding on the ground, an unspeakable thirst drying their lips, waiting with patience until help could be rendered. And help did come! The roar of the cannons had ceased, we went out to assist the wounded, embraced our unfortunate comrades, and carried or helped them along to the hospital. Now, after the fight had closed, we could get some idea as to the number of bullets and balls fired. The brush was riddled, branches and leaves shot off; here and there a solid shot or a shell had plowed up the ground, and the battlefield was covered with blankets, haversacks, canteens, hats, guns, equipments, etc. The flag of our regiment was riddled by seventy-five bullets, and the ensign, although wounded at the commencement of the fight, nevertheless carried the flag on, not heeding his wound, to the fort, where he proudly and defiantly raised and waved it, when he was shot through the head, and sank down a corpse. .759

MILLER, 33RD IND COBURN 2B 3D 20C: About 5 p.m. the enemy having attempted to charge the hill, I moved the regiment forward on the left company, and assisted some of General Gearys division in repelling the

---

756 Swung the line around. Or each soldier about-faced.
757 (OR, Series I Vol 38 Part 2 Serial 73: Reports n.d., 377)
758 (Reid 1965, 148)
759 Hess was the ensign. See earlier in text.

charge; the center of the regiment became engaged and greatly contributed to the repulse. The battle closed at dark, and during the night a large detail was engaged building works for the regiment. .760

WINKLER, 26TH WIS WOOD 3B 3D 20C: We drew back into the valley, reformed the line, and attempted another assault, but again in vain. Orders were then given to fall back to the first hill, and there the regiment was collected. The rebels made a desperate charge to regain this position but were completely repulsed. .761

I then sent Capt Fuchs of my regiment back to collect the men & get orders for me. Getting no orders I finally returned with the officers & men with me to the hill we first occupied in the morning where I found Capt Fuchs & the rest of the regiment. I reported to Col Wood at once where the regt. was & was told to remain there till further orders. Shortly after an attack was made by the rebels upon the hills then held by our troops. I at once moved my regiment to the left thinking I might there render some assistance to the rest of the brigade but found the hill so thickly covered with troops that I could only find a place in the fourth line.

Here I remained till at dusk I saw the brigade marching down to the road. I followed & went into camp with the rest. My loss in this days engagement was one officer killed, three men killed & forty two men wounded. .762

CASE, 129TH ILL WARD 1B 3D 20C: ... where they remained till late at night (when relieved by General Gearys division), defended by from 300 to 500 men and officers of the various regiments of the brigade. While the colors of the One hundred and twenty-ninth Illinois were the first planted in the fort, justice demands that I should say that immediately, or soon thereafter, the colors of the One hundred and second Illinois and One hundred and fifth Illinois were also planted alongside of the guns. .763

Now we come to that charge on the left which some of Butterfield's division helped resist after being relieved.

760 (OR, Series I Vol 38 Part 2 Serial 73: Reports n.d., 394)
761 (OR, Series I Vol 38 Part 2 Serial 73: Reports n.d., 463)
762 (F. C. Winkler 1864)
763 (OR, Series I Vol 38 Part 2 Serial 73: Reports n.d., 365)

Hood Tries Another Flank

JOHNSTON, CSA: On the 15th There was severe skirmishing on the whole front. Major-General Walker reported no movement near Calhoun. Lieutenant-General Hood was directed to prepare to move forward, his right leading, supported by two brigades from Polk's and Hardee's corps. When he was about to move information came from Major-General Walker that the Federal right was crossing the river. To meet this movement Lieutenant-General Hood's attack was countermanded. Stewart's division not receiving the order from corps headquarters in time, attacked unsuccessfully.

So, Johnston again sent two brigades north, despite Sherman's bombardment that was intended to keep Johnston's men in their trenches. Could he afford them?

ABRAMS, ATLANTA INTELLIGENCER, WITH STEWART'S DIVISION, CSA: It was now past six o'clock in the evening, but though the night was fast approaching, the enemy exhibited no disposition to cease from his fruitless efforts to carry the right of Gen. Stevenson's line, and was determined to endeavor to turn his left wing and force him on his right. Accordingly, Gen. Stewart was ordered to leave his works and drive the enemy from his front, sweeping toward his center, while Reynolds' Brigade of Stevenson's division was ordered to advance at the same time, for the purpose of forming a pivot to Gen. Stewart, and changing the line of battle obliquely to the left, thus flanking the enemy, and giving General Hardee an opportunity to advance and cut the enemy off from Snake Creek Gap, while Hood cut him off from the Dalton Road. .764

By now Schofield was on the other side of the railroad and Sherman essentially had his left anchored on the river, as he wanted. But if Johnston could have cut him off from the road to Dalton and from Snake Creek Gap, what fighting would have then occurred? Could Hood have relieved enough pressure on Johnston's fortress?

Wood's brigade was still holding position facing the Rebel line where it bent west just past the fort. Williams' brigades had been preparing their line to resist an assault.

764 (Abrams 1864)

COOK, ASST. SURGEON, 150TH NY RUGER 2B 1D 20C: After looking the position over carefully, Colonel Ketcham ordered his regiment to go to building breastworks, and we fell to with a will, pausing not until every rail, log, hog trough, bee hive, etc. (we were right in front of a large dwelling) was used, and we had a very respectable shelter behind which to shield us from the storm, which was so soon to burst upon us. Other regiments on our right took the hint from us and also fell to build breastworks, but most of them too tardily, for the storm burst upon them before they were completed. _765

TREMAIN: But heedless of all, about 4 p.m. the enemy advanced. Stevenson's division, and other troops of Hood's corps, in four grand columns, assaulted Hooker's lines, and attempted to drive him from his new ground. Colonel Wood's brigade bore the brunt of the attack supported by Williams' division; and the enemy after a short but desperate struggle were hurled back with terrible slaughter. Williams' division then charged, captured several colors and many prisoners. _766

Of note: the flank attempt of the previous night reached Dalton road, but this one did not get far from the Rebel trenches because Williams' division was in place.

Stevenson and Stewart did not attack at the same time. That assured failure.

Stevenson's Assault on Wood and Knipe

Johnston still had the railroad, so far. Now he apparently was trying to shut off Sherman's support entirely.

STEVENSON, STEVENSON'S DIVISION, CSA: In the evening I received orders to move that portion of my force which was on the right of General Cumming out of the trenches, and co-operating with General Stewart, to swing around upon the enemy. _767

ABRAMS, ATLANTA INTELLIGENCER, WITH STEWART'S DIVISION, CSA: While Stewart was making his movement, a peremptory order reached Gen. Reynolds for him to advance his command as a pivot. The general opposed the movement unless Gen. Stewart's left wing formed a junction with his

---

765 (Cook 1864)
766 (Tremain 1905, 171)
767 (OR, Series I Vol 38 Part 3 Serial 74: Reports n.d., 812)

right, but upon the order being repeated in a more peremptory manner, the 54th Virginia regiment was ordered to advance from their line of works and carry the ridge before them, while the other regiments were directed to be ready to move at a moment's notice for the purpose of making the pivot complete and thus performing the work allotted to them. The 54th leaped over the works and with their gallant Colonel Robert Trigg, and Lieut. Colonel John J. Wade, in front, moved forward. At this moment the enemy was about to make another charge, and were pouring a heavy fire over our works, compelling the regiment to advance under a galling fire. It, however, disregarded the storm of shot and shell poured upon it, and drove the charging column of Yankees through the woods until it reached the open field, when, to the astonishment of the Colonel, it was discovered that Stewart's division was not in sight, and consequently there was no connection with the regiment.

This was most unfortunate, for the enemy perceiving the regiment as "solitary and alone" in the open field commenced pouring a galling fire into their ranks, but nothing daunted by this, Colonels Trigg and Wade, waving their swords, gave the order to charge. On the men marched, until they were not five paces from the enemy's line, when four distinct lines of battle, extending as far as the eye could reach, were seen by this command, and numbered over 8,000 men. The Adjutant of the regiment, with pistol in hand, rushed forward, and seizing the Yankee colors, and fired into their ranks, when a bullet pierced his brain, and he fell dead across the enemy's works. His name was Hammet, and a braver and nobler man never sacrificed his life on the altar of his country. .768

WOOD, 3B 3D 20C: This hill being a position of much importance to the enemy, it was not to be supposed that he would yield it without a struggle or without making an effort to retake it after being driven off. Accordingly, regimental commanders were cautioned that they might expect to be in turn attacked, but that they must hold the position at all hazards. The expectation seemed to be well founded, for the enemy made two furious assaults upon my line, but was gallantly and successfully repulsed. .769

And some at the fort could see them forming up.

COLLINS, 149TH NY IRELAND 3B 2D 20C: About four o'clock, the enemy made an effort to flank the position by charging through a wheat field and

---

768 (Abrams 1864)

769 (OR, Series I Vol 38 Part 2 Serial 73: Reports n.d., 434)

into a piece of woods to the left and rear. A portion of the 3d Division occupied the woods in question and had a line of breastworks running diagonally along its edge next to the wheat field. ,770 The 149th men, with their companions lying on the hillside, could hear the Confederates forming in line and their well-known yell in charging, but could not see the movement owing to intervening woods. As the enemy advanced no opposition seemed to be interposed until he was well in rear of the line held by the men below the little fort. ,771

OSBORN, CO A 55TH OHIO WOOD 3B 3D 20C: But at last the writer heard Captain H. E. Tremain, a volunteer aide on General Butterfield's staff, calling out to Colonel Wood, "Sir, you must not expose yourself in this way." "But," said Colonel Wood, in his high-pitched voice, "I want to see what they are doing; they are getting out of their works." It proved to be true. The Fifty-fourth Virginia Regiment of infantry formed under that terrific fire and charged our line. It was, of course, captured to a man and was hurried to the rear, where the captives saw to their disgust the Second Division of the Twentieth Corps massed in support of the fighting line and the Twenty-third Corps moving up on the left flank. ,772

The 23rd Corps moving on the left flank suggests we can take them to be the left of Williams' division. Still moving after all this time? Since Hurst mentioned a 23rd Corps brigade moving forward between him and Knipe, the movements and positions are a puzzle. Earlier, it was said they moved through the woods well back, north, of Williams' deployment. Nevertheless, we digress. Moving on.

BULL, CO D 123RD NY KNIPE 1B 1D 20C: By four o'clock our force was well on their flank and they then had their choice; either come out and drive us back or retreat. They decided to come out and attack, so they jumped over their works and advanced. The skirmishing now became very heavy; we thought they surely would be on us and everything was made ready to receive them. All along the line you could hear the click of the hammers on our guns as they were half cocked to attach the caps, which we did not place until we got ready to fire. Guns in hand we waited. The battery on our left now had a good target and fired rapidly at the charging line. When the Johnnies had advanced a third of the way toward our line, they filed off to

770 Wood's brigade.
771 (Collins 1891, 250)
772 (Osborn 1904, 147) Fifth-fourth Virginia.

the right and entered the woods, where they would not be exposed to the artillery fire; so they made their fight on troops to the left of us. .773

That may have been some of Stewart's men, still forming up. (Where Steward and Stevenson connected is not clear.)

NEW YORK HERALD: Obstinately refusing to give way, the gallant Knipe stood with his little brigade, and contended with a force probably ten times greater than his own. Returning volley for volley, he maintained his advanced position, and would doubtless have continued to do so until reinforcements reached him, had he not fallen severely wounded. His brave men bore him to the rear, and the column steadily fell back to its original position. .774

WOOD, 3B 3D 20C: As the second attack seemed to be a very determined one, and as my men were much exhausted, I sent word for re-enforcements. I knew that General Geary with his division was in my rear and with a considerable force near the crest of the hill. I went to him in person for aid. I failed to obtain it, and the second and last attack on my line was successfully repulsed before re-enforcements reached me. .775 .776

The 123rd and 149th New York, who were so greatly exposed, tell of the fighting before and then during the flank attempt.

MORHOUS, CO C 123RD NY KNIPE 1B 1D 20C: Heavy firing was heard on the right. Regiments of the Brigade to which the 123d belonged were warmly engaged, while away to the left from Gen. Ruger's Brigade was heard heavy musketry firing, as the Rebels charged upon them and were driven back. From the position of the Regiment the Rebels did not swing around near enough for it to open fire at first, and in obedience to orders held their fire, expecting to get a better chance. It was hard work for the boys to hold still while they were under a galling fire from the enemy. The position of the Regiment was very much exposed, being in an open field on the crest of a hill, and in plain sight of the Rebel works. They saw the Rebels bring up a battery, and planting their pieces throw shot and shell right into their faces.

While the 123d held the open field, the rest of the Brigade was not idle. The 141st New York charged furiously and with great loss on the right; the 5th

---

773 (Bull 1977, 104)
774 (Bradley 1865, 106)
775 (OR, Series I Vol 38 Part 2 Serial 73: Reports n.d., 434)
776 Geary did order a couple of regiments to the left about 5 pm. See below.

Connecticut and 46th Pennsylvania kept pouring the contents of 1,500 rifles into the astonished columns of the enemy. Driven to desperation by the assault, they in turn made an effort to charge the line where the Regiment was stationed, coming out of their works in excellent order, their battle flags flying defiantly, yelling like demons. The boys let them come up into easy range, when like the bursting of a whirlwind they poured a hot fire into their front and flanks. At first they tried to face the storm of lead and iron, then, staggering and swaying like a crowd of drunken men, they moved to the left, hoping to find the 2d Brigade easier to handle, but here again they were severely beaten, and rushed back pell mell into their breastworks. The work was done. .777

MEMBER OF COMPANY A, 141ST NY, KNIPE 1B 1D 20C: ... We remain here three hours; the enemy are seen to form outside of their breastworks, and advance towards us; on they come, firing all the while, most of the shots passing over our heads; they advance to within eight rods of our lines; we wait no longer; each man arises and discharges his piece, and reloads, the fight now became general, and lasted an hour and a half. .778

MCMILLEN, JAMES, LIEUTENANT, COMPANY C, 141ST NY, KNIPE 1B 1D 20C: Our Brigade, the 1st Brigade of 1st Division, bivouacked for the night on the right of the road in a piece of woods, where we remained until 12 A. M. of the 15th, when we were ordered forward on the road to Resaca. After marching for about a quarter of a mile, the command was given by Col. Logie, "By the left flank—March." and into the woods we went in line of battle. Through thick, underbrush and over logs we clambered up to the top of a ridge and out of the thick pines to an open field on the other side. As the regiment emerged from the woods, we were met by the concentrated fire of a line of rebel breastworks of at least a quarter of a mile in extent, two batteries of artillery, and an enfilading fire of sharpshooters, posted in a wood about 200 yards to our left. Every man in the regiment was completely taken by surprise, and for a moment the whole line wavered—but only for a moment, when again the whole line pressed forward to a less exposed position, behind a slight elevation, where, by lying flat on the ground, we were partly screened from the flying missiles from our front, but were exposed to a flanking fire from the sharp-shooters on our left. Cos. C and G were faced to the woods, and opening fire on the sharp-shooters soon cleared the woods. The enemy's position was on a third ridge of woodland about 200 yards in advance of the one behind which we were, and so much

777 (Morhous 1879, 86)
778 (Museum n.d.)

higher that our ridge afforded us but little protection. At three different times they charged our position, but were each time promptly met at the top of the ridge and driven back with heavy loss—our dead and theirs lay on the ridge side by side.

For five hours and a half we kept our position, when our ammunition gave out, and we had to be relieved to fill up cartridge boxes.

We went into the fight with about 350 men, and lost 90 men in killed and wounded. At least every other man in the regiment was hit in his person or some part of his clothes or accoutrements. After being supplied with ammunition we returned to near our old position and bivouacked for the night expecting to renew the fight at daylight. _779

COLLINS, 149TH NY IRELAND 3B 2D 20C: It was an anxious moment and there were many throbbing hearts, when suddenly deafening cheers rent the air, followed by a rapid discharge of musketry, which sent the Johnnies to their long home or to cover from whence they came. It was a gallant response to a defiant yell, and lifted a load of anxiety off the minds of the valiant men on the hillside. The next morning the Confederate line could be traced by its dead where it met the opening volley of the sturdy Union men. _780

Wood's right was attacked.

RYDER, CO I 33RD MASS, WOOD 3B 1D 20C: About three o'clock in the afternoon the Rebels came out of their works in force and attacked our lines to the left of our regiment's position. The musketry mingled with the Rebel yells were deafening. Failing to break the line to our left, they were evidently approaching our front. We carefully loaded our guns and passed the word along to let them come till we could count the buttons on their coats, and then, remembering Oct. 29, "shoot to kill—if our bullets don't stop them, our bayonets will!" When they broke from the bushes into our view, they were not over 25 yards away. I easily counted the buttons on their coats before we opened fire on them. For about 20 minutes or so there was something doing on that hill, and when the smoke cleared I saw only three of the enemy on their feet, while the ground was littered with the bodies of many others. _781

779 (Museum n.d.)
780 (Collins 1891, 250)
781 (Ryder 1928, 54) Whether this occurred before the rebel flank attempt or after is not certain

RYDER, CO I 33RD MASS, WOOD 3B 1D 20C: One of the members of my company named Allan Dunbar, of New Bedford, had fallen evidently mortally wounded about twenty or more yards in advance of the crest of the hill. In our first rush we had gone over the hill somewhat and he had been hit with several others by the enemy's first volley. Some of the slightly wounded had crawled back over the hill to our rear. Dunbar was shot through both legs and bleeding badly; his calls for help were heart-breaking to me. While it seemed almost certain death to go to him, I offered to go and help bring him in. Finally three comrades volunteered to go with me, and we took a blanket and ran down to him. He cried for joy when we reached him. We placed him in the blanket and brought him over the hill and laid him down for the men to bid him goodbye. He said, "Boys, don't cry. Just tell my sister that I did my duty that's all," and placing his hand over his heart he said, "I have got something here that will take me through all right." We carried him to the rear, about an eighth of a mile, and placed him in the care of the hospital men.

I then said to the three others, "Let us hurry back to the battle line for we may be needed any moment." To my utter surprise neither one would return with me and they tried their best to persuade me to remain with them. I told them I would rather die with my comrades in the battle than be such a coward. I therefore returned alone.

I had just taken my gun and knelt down in the line when the attack I have previously mentioned occurred. The three men I have referred to were older than I and were married; they had been in battle before and had a good record, but the temptation to remain in the rear till the battle ended was too great to them to be resisted. On my way back to the hill an officer who was in command of a line at the foot of the hill in the rear of ours asked me where the other three men were. I told him they wouldn't come back. His remarks were forceful regarding them, then he said, "You are a brave man to return alone." ₋782

HURST, 73RD OHIO WOOD 3B 3D 20C: It was a most trying moment; but the regiment, and indeed the whole brigade, stood to the work, and held the left firmly. ₋783

WINKLER, 26TH WIS WOOD 3B 3D 20C: Shortly after an attack was made by the rebels upon the hills then held by our troops. I at once moved my

782 (Ryder 1928, 54)
783 (Hurst 1866, 120)

regiment to the left thinking I might there render some assistance to the rest of the brigade but found the hill so thickly covered with troops that I could only find a place in the fourth line. Here I remained till at dusk I saw the brigade marching down to the road. I followed & went into camp with the rest. My loss in this days engagement was one officer killed, three men killed & forty two men wounded. .784

PEAK, Co F 129TH ILL WARD 1B 3D 20C: The First division had just got a firm hold on their new position, when it was seen the rebels were getting very busy making preparations for some kind of a move, and soon they began to form in column for the charge. Out of their supposed hiding place they came yelling like demons, maddened by the use of gun powder and whiskey they had taken to give them courage. The First division let them come within a few paces of their works, when they gave them a volley of musketry that sent one fourth of their column to its long home and a large number of wounded was lying between the lines to suffer, while those that escaped wounds or death hustled back to their trenches, under a heavy fire from our cannon, that caused a number of the rebels to fall, before they could reach the trenches. This was a hard blow.

Not being coordinated helped doom the Rebel attempt.

STEVENSON, STEVENSON'S DIVISION, CSA: At the moment that I received the order the enemy were making a heavy assault upon General Reynolds, and [General] Brown had not yet replenished his ammunition. The orders, however, were peremptory, and the movement was attempted. The Fifty-fourth Virginia, on the right, leaped the trenches and rushed bravely upon the enemy, but found that there was no connection with General Stewart's left, and being thus unsupported were compelled to fall back before the rest of the brigade moved out. In this attempt the gallant Captain George D. Wise, of my staff, was dangerously wounded, and the regiment in less than fifteen minutes lost above 100 officers and men. .785

EPPERLY, 54TH VIRGINIA, STEVENSON, CSA: A large number of our Regt was kild and wounded ther was about 1.19 [119] kild and wounded which was dun in about 10 minuets time in making a charge on the yankees whair they wer three calloms deep we had to fall back this number was last of a bout 5

784 (F. C. Winkler 1864)
785 (OR, Series I Vol 38 Part 3 Serial 74: Reports n.d., 812)

Compeneys we had 5 men kild out of our Compony an 8 or 10 wounded. -786

DEAVENPORT, CHAPLAIN, 3RD TENN, BROWN'S BRIGADE, STEVENSON'S DIVISION, CSA: Only once were we relieved and that but for a few minutes by Gen. Reynolds. We moved into our pits and was ordered to charge as Gen. Stuart's division advanced. Only two regiments went and were compelled to return, their ranks thinned. Our loss was light, three killed and eight or ten wounded in the regiment. Lt. J. G. Matthews among the killed. One thing I noticed the wounded all seemed cheerful, one whose leg was torn by a shell said, "Well, boys, I'm done playing ball with you." -787

Why Stewart did not advance with Stevenson will be debated among Confederates years later.

In Geary's division, Ireland, commanding the brigade on the hill below and left of the fort, was wounded during the charge. Rickards took command of the brigade below the hill while Cobham was just below the fort.

RICKARDS, 29TH PENN IRELAND 3B 2D 20C: At 4 p.m. Stevenson's division of rebels charged our front line, but was driven back. Colonel Ireland, commanding brigade, was wounded at this time by a piece of shell, and Colonel Cobham, One hundred and eleventh Pennsylvania Veteran Volunteers, being absent on another part of the field, the command of the brigade devolved on me. -788

BARNUM, 149TH NY IRELAND 3B 2D 20C: At about 5 p.m. -789 Col. David Ireland, One hundred and thirty-seventh New York, who had up to this period commanded the brigade, was struck by a piece of shell, and carried from the field. Colonel Cobham, One hundred and eleventh Pennsylvania Volunteers, was next in rank, but he being temporarily absent with the three regiments previously mentioned, Col. William Rickards, Twenty-ninth Pennsylvania Volunteers, commanded until the return of Colonel Cobham early the next morning. -790

786 (Epperly May 22, 1864)
787 (Deavenport 1861-1864)
788 (OR, Series I Vol 38 Part 2 Serial 73: Reports n.d., 308)
789 Others have it closer to 4 pm. Statement is here because it is closer to when Cobham was notified.
790 (OR, Series I Vol 38 Part 2 Serial 73: Reports n.d., 268)

Stewart's Assault on Ruger and Robinson

Stevenson had started before Stewart—with only two regiments—and was repulsed by Wood and Knipe. Then he found Stewart's left had not yet advanced. Stevenson's men went back to their trenches. Then Stewart started, unsupported on his left, and it would be Ruger's and Robinson's turn.

> STEWART, CMDG DIVISION, HOOD'S CORPS, CSA: Shortly previous to four, information came to me of a heavy movement of the enemy to my front, which information was transmitted to the lieutenant-general commanding corps. My instructions were in advancing to gradually wheel to the left and I was notified that Stevenson on my left, would also advance. At four precisely Clayton on the left and Stovall on the right of the front line were caused each to make a half wheel to the left to place them in the proper direction and were also instructed to continue inclining by a slight wheel to the left in advancing. This it will be perceived, placed them en echelon, the object being to prevent my right toward the river from being turned. Maney's brigade which had reported to me and a small body of cavalry under Colonel Holman were directed to move out on the right, outflanking and covering Stovall's right Gibson and Baker were brought forward and placed in position as supports to Clayton and Stovall and the order to advance given. The men moved forward with great spirit and determination and soon engaged the enemy. _791

> WILLIAMS, 1D 20C: The enemy massed his forces in the woods near the railway, which was distant from 300 to 600 yards from the different portions of my line. Advancing under cover as far as practicable, he attacked the whole line with great vigor and apparent confidence. The attack was received with perfect steadiness and repulsed with ease. The assaults were renewed three times, and each time with signal failure. My line in no part was shaken or disturbed, and we literally had no skulkers. The main efforts of the enemy were directed against the knoll heretofore mentioned, and were continued in that direction until near dark. _792

Five from Ruger's regiments provide detailed descriptions. Brown's map shows their positions. Robinson had two regiments on their left and two in reserve behind them. Further left, beyond the railroad, the 23rd Corps had a brigade.

791 (Ridley 1906, 307)
792 (OR, Series I Vol 38 Part 3 Serial 74: Reports n.d., 28)

We start with Ruger's left regiment.

Cook, Asst. Surgeon, 150th NY Ruger 2B 1D 20C: We had but nicely completed our breastworks when a rattling fire in the woods in our front told us that their advance had met our skirmishers and soon out of the woods came the skirmishers literally running for their lives. It reminded me very much of the times when I had seen a lot of boys steal up and thrust a stick into a hornet's nest, and then run with all their might. I did not know whether it was best to laugh or tremble. They were certainly in no enviable position, for the rebels were firing at them from the rear, and besides they were in imminent danger of being shot by our own men, as the rebels were pushing right on after them, emerging from the woods very close to the last of them. But Colonel Ketcham very wisely gave the order for the men to reserve their fire. Oh! it was a grand sight to see them pour out of the woods, form in double column and advance at a quickstep towards our unsupported left. When they first emerged from the woods they were not more than a hundred and fifty yards distant and they were allowed to leave nearly half that distance behind them before the order came to "Fire," and as one report, five hundred muskets roared and five hundred bullets went screaming into the ranks of our enemies. They first faltered, fell back a few steps, then rallied and poured at us an unmerciful fire from guns that outnumbered us four or five to one. Then came our Colonel's order, "load and fire at will," and they did it with a vengeance. _793

Benton, Band, 150th NY Ruger 2B 1D 20C: The battle was raging furiously now, and it was soon after the episode of Colonel Harrison's attack and repulse that our brigade became engaged on the extreme left. We were formed in line on a rise of ground in an open field, and threw up a slight defence by gathering and piling up the rails from a fence near at hand. Soon the long gray line was seen approaching, with good alignment and steady front. Upon coming within range they opened fire and continued to fire as they advanced, the bullets splintering the rails, and passing us with that peculiar, zipping sound so familiar to veterans. Immediately there was a crash close to my left,—the first gun always sounds so loud—followed in quick succession by others until what had seemed at first but a successive clatter of explosions became one prolonged roar. The smoke soon became so thick that it was difficult for me to see the enemy's line except by glimpses and fragments.

793 (Cook 1864)

In a few moments the fire lessened and finally ceased; the smoke cloud lifted and I could see plainly again. They were retreating in disorder now, but scattered over the field were hundreds of their dead and wounded who could not retreat. The fire of our line had been very deadly and effective. We soon noticed by their movements that they were forming for a second attack. This was much like the first, but they were more persistent and got nearer to our line, though they were finally driven back before the storm of lead, and the dead and wounded in our front were thicker than ever. Just at the crisis the regiment at our right made a counter charge and captured a stand of the enemy's colors. _794

Ruger's right is the 2nd Massachusetts and the 27th Indiana.

The 27th Indiana was closest to the Rebel line where the wooded "peninsula" of Rebels projected north. The 27th moved even closer!

BROWN, CO C 27TH INDIANA RUGER 2B 1D 20C: While we were busily engaged upon our breastwork, a sharp fire suddenly opened along our skirmish line. As our skirmishers were under express orders not to fire their muskets. except under very strong provocation, Colonel Colgrove galloped his horse out to ascertain what the matter was. Company G was acting as skirmishers, and the boys surmised that Capt. Peter Fesler would hear things from the colonel he had been known to hear before. On the contrary, when the colonel had inquired the cause of the firing, he was requested to come to the point where Captain Fesler was. He there saw, what others had seen, that the enemy's skirmishers were not only pushing forward, but that their main line was coming over their breastworks and forming in front of them. The evident design was to assault our position.

It was very fortunate that Colonel Colgrove had gone forward as he had. He was thus enabled to set a trap for enemy which gave us an easy victory. Hurrying back to the Twenty-seventh he moved it forward almost half-way to the enemy's breastworks. There he had the men lie down where they were largely screened from view. They were to remain in that position until he gave the word. The company on the skirmish line was to resist as long as possible, then quietly fall into its place in the regiment. At the command the whole line was to rise up, fire a careful, deliberate volley into the ranks of the advancing enemy, then charge them with the bayonet.

794 (Benton 1902, 140)

These preliminaries had barely been arranged when the rebel line swept forward. No soldier will ever forget the surging emotions started within him by the announcement, "They're coming, boys!" or, what is still more thrilling, the actual sight of the advancing column! A moment, under such circumstances, seems an age. At this time the men of Company G disputed the ground inch by inch. Then, one by one, they quietly rallied to their places in the ranks. Down the hill, and out into the more level ground moved the men in gray! Unconscious of danger at this point, their steps were firm and their ranks in order. Will Colonel Colgrove never break the silence?

At length, when the rebel force was only thirty-five yards away, the Colonel, speaking in slow, distinct tones, said, "Now, boys. Ready, aim, fire!" Then he fairly shrieked the one word "Charge!" and all the other officers repeated the word, with deeply surcharged feelings, "Charge!" Poor men of the misguided South! It was all over in one terrible minute of time, and the story is soon told. Thirty-three of those men who, a moment before, were advancing so confidently, lay dead at our feet! Fully as many more were too badly wounded to be able to move without assistance; thirty five others, including the colonel, were in our hands as prisoners; while the balance simply turned and ran so promptly and swiftly that we were not able to get them. Many of them must have thrown down their guns to facilitate their flight, as the ground was covered with them. ... Those of the enemy who escaped with arms, on reaching their breastworks and finding that they were not pursued, faced around and opened fire upon us. Though weak at first, others must have soon come to their aid. It was not long until the fire became scathing. Seventy yards with a rest is a dangerous range. Colonel Colgrove gave the order to lie down, and forthwith we hugged the earth passionately, endeavoring meantime to return the fire. But the convexity of the bluff in front of us, while it afforded us some protection, at the same time hindered us in seeing our foes. We were also exposed to a flank fire, so that our situation soon became critical.

At this juncture the Colonel, upon the suggestion of the Major and other officers, gave the order to return to our own incomplete breastworks. The attention of the men was called to the fact that in passing up the slope, there would be extra exposure, and they were instructed to move promptly, without regard to order. The movement was, therefore, made with slight loss.

Following this return to our first position, a second rebel line, consisting apparently of two regiments, advanced from the works rather to our left. This attack fell upon the Second Massachusetts, as well as ourselves. It came with ardor and was maintained with persistence. Still, it did not stand long, under the combined fire of our two regiments. Being repeated a second time, somewhat more to our left, our two regiments swung out in counter-charge. This is the phase of the battle to which Adjutant Bryant refers when he says, "The Twenty-seventh Indiana and Second Massachusetts wheeled to the right (left) and opened fire on the flank of the advancing host, while the other regiments gave them volleys in their front."

Our advance at this time was to within fifty yards of the enemy's works. Many of our brigade have always believed firmly that their line might have been driven, if not routed, at this time. _795

Significant? Could Hooker have made a simultaneous assault, as he originally proposed to Sherman?

QUINT, 2ND MASS RUGER 2B 1D 20C: Colonel Colgrove soon went forward to the skirmish line, and discerned the enemy pouring out of their works in force. He immediately led his regiment up the slope, accompanied by the Second. The regiments on the left moved forward also, wheeling a little to the right, and across the road. The rebels met both lines, and an unexpected fire. It was so furious that they fell back in disorder, followed by the brigade, and were driven into their works. The brigade again took its position. Twice more, at intervals, the enemy came out in force; and both times were met on the crest, and driven back with slaughter, leaving their dead and wounded.

The losses were comparatively few in number, but they could illy be spared. _796

Again, from Ruger's left:

COOK, ASST. SURGEON, 150TH NY RUGER 2B 1D 20C: Was I frightened? Most assuredly I was and would have run just as fast as my legs would have carried me, had it not been for pride. Pride would not let me, for there was the eyes of all the boys in the regiment to see me if I did run, and what would they say to me afterward? Judging by myself, (a conceited judgment it is said) I should say that it was pride which made a man face a storm of bullets oftener than courage. I frankly own that it was so in my case, but then, I was never noted for courage. The fact is, I had no particular business up at the front,

795 (E. R. Brown 1899, 470)

796 (Quint 1867, 229)

my duties being further in the rear, but was caught in the front by accident, mingled with curiosity, and pride and curiosity led me to remain. But it is not an enviable position, and when they get me into another such an one, unless by accident, it will be after Atlanta is taken. ˌ797

BENTON, BAND, 150TH NY RUGER 2B 1D 20C: So severely did the enemy suffer in this assault on our line that Colonel Calhoun, who commanded the Confederate regiment in our front, afterward admitted to General Smith, then our Major, that his regiment never had a roll-call afterward.

A pathetic incident in connection with this attack was that among the Confederate dead which lay so thickly strewn before us was a family group: a gray-haired chaplain and his two sons. ˌ798

This amusing incident also shows the job of the provost guards — in all battles.

BROWN, CO C 27TH INDIANA RUGER 2B 1D 20C: It was here at Resaca also that Captain Balsley's Irishman, Dan, got the best of the provost guards. On the way, somewhere, when coming from the Eastern army, Captain Balsley had recruited a fresh arrival from over the briny deep. The older members of the company had tormented the raw recruit not a little by telling him, among other things, that it was a very dreadful thing to go into a battle, and that he would be sure to get panicked in the first one and run away. This probably stimulated him to do his best and show them a thing or two. In the counter-assault upon the Alabamians, Dan was, therefore, in the front rank. Spying a rebel behind a tree, he rushed up and seized hold of him. With vigorous jerks and kicks and many loud demonstrations of triumph and satisfaction, he brought him to the Captain. The Captain, in turn, ordered Dan to take his prisoner to the rear, which he proceeded to do with much pride and pomp. Back some distance Dan encountered the provost guard, with a line duly established, both to take care of prisoners and to prevent able-bodied soldiers from running out of the fight. "Halt, there!" they said to Dan. "Halt the divil," said Dan. "Captain Balsley he tould me to tak this mon to the rear, so he did." But they persisted. "Halt! We'll take care of the prisoner; just leave him with us." "Och! to hell wid ye?, ye durty spalpeens," roared Dan. But, as if willing to oblige them all he could, waving his hand back in the direction from which he had come, and where the fighting was

797 (Cook 1864)
798 (Benton 1902, 140)

still in progress, he said, in his blandest tones, "There's plenty of 'em right over there. If ye's want wun, jist step over and get wun for yer'self." .799

WILLIAMS, 1D 20C: The position was held at the close by two of Robinson's regiments, which had relieved Ruger's. The artillery of the division performed an important part in punishing and repulsing the enemy. .800

What tribute would measure up to Colonel Colgrove's skill and audacity?

Ridley's Ride

Whilst Gen. Sherman showed a want of generalship in not following, Old Joe displayed wonderful skill in getting us out. —Ridley

My orders were to cover and protect the left, and I was ignorant of the condition of affairs with the assaulting columns on the right. —Williams

Some of why Stewart and Stevenson were not coordinated: Getting a message by horseback over the long distance from Lay's Ferry to the fort no doubt was hindered since McPherson's bombardment was to prevent movement behind the lines. Casualties fighting Williams and Ruger occurred while Johnston was trying to stop Stewart's attempt!

SWEENY TO DODGE: I have succeeded in throwing a pontoon bridge across the river at this point. The First Brigade is across the river, and the Second Brigade is now crossing. The Third Brigade has been ordered up from cross-roads and will be held in reserve until a more thorough reconnaissance is made of the other side. I am intrenching my position on the opposite bank, and will move my artillery as soon as the works are sufficiently advanced for its protection. Was opposed in crossing by artillery and infantry, but have succeeded in dispersing both. .801

JOHNSTON, CSA: On the 15th there was severe skirmishing on the whole front. Major-General Walker, reported no movement near Calhoun. Lieutenant-General Hood was directed to prepare to move forward, his right leading, supported by two brigades from Polk's and Hardee's corps. When he was about to move information came from Major-General Walker that the Federal right was crossing the river. To meet this movement

799 (E. R. Brown 1899, 480)

800 (OR, Series I Vol 38 Part 3 Serial 74: Reports n.d., 28)
801 (OR, Series I Vol 38 Part 4 Serial 75: Correspondence n.d., 196)

Lieutenant-General Hood's attack was countermanded. Stewart's division not receiving the order from corps headquarters in time, attacked unsuccessfully. The army was ordered to cross the Oostenaula that night, destroying the bridges behind it. .802

The messenger tells us of trying to stop the flank attempt:

RIDLEY, STEWART'S DIVISION, HOOD'S CORPS, CSA: This famous order, countermanding the former order of attack at Resaca, was ever a matter of contention between Generals Johnston and Hood, the former saying that he had countermanded, the latter asserting that he had not time to execute it. Be that as it may, when Col. Cunningham brought it our first line was charging on the breastworks; but it was only Stewart's Division doing this; the other two divisions of Hood's Corps had received the countermand order. .803

The execution of this order, with our lines in close quarters and fully engaged, was the trying thing for staff officers on duty. Gen. Stewart sent Lieut. Scott, volunteer aide, to Clayton, Lieut. Cahal to Stovall, then he called on the writer to go to Gen. Maney. I felt as if that parallel ride from left to right of over half a mile, taking the fire by Clayton's and Stovall's Brigades would be my last. Hooker and Schofield and McPherson, massed, were pouring the shot and shell nigh on to a tempest. I spurred my horse to a run; the balls were so terrific that I checked up a little, fearing that my horse might get shot and turn a somersault in falling. The checking process didn't suit, for it seemed like death to tarry. I spurred up again and (how any human being lived through it I can't imagine) came up with some litter-bearers, who hugged the trees closely and would not talk. Moments seemed hours. I rode through brush and copse into an open field, and finally struck the left of Maney's Brigade lying down behind the railroad, hotly engaged. Just in rear of them, I spied a staff officer of Gen. Maney, Lieut. L. B. McFarland, now of Memphis, Tenn. riding as coolly and unconcernedly as if no battle were raging. I accosted him with the query, "Where's Gen. Maney?" He said, "On the right of the Brigade," and that Maney had placed him to look after the left. I told him that the brigades on his left were falling back, that if a charge should be made his brigade would be lost, and to pass the order down the line, from Gen. Stewart, to retire rapidly. In the meantime I started to the right, through an open field, to find the Brigade Commander. Talk about thunder and lightning, accompanied by a storm of rain and hail! My experience with bullets through that field was like to it, for "h—l seemed to answer h—l in the cannon's roar." Intermingled with musketry, it created an unintermitted roar of the most deafening and appalling thunder. Gen. Maney was working to keep the cavalry connected with his line. His horse having been shot, he was dismounted, but he had taken that of Lieut. James Keeble—his Aide. By this time the brigade was retiring as ordered. When this order to retire was communicated to Col. Field, commanding the First Tennessee Infantry on the extreme right, the Federal cavalry were pressing, yet his regiment was formed into a hollow square under the galling fire, and thus retired with a palisade of bristling bayonets confronting. It was like to Napoleon's battle of the pyramids in squares on the march to Cairo, deterring the intrepid Marmaduke cavalry, and also to the English square at Waterloo. But the problem of getting back confronted me. Gen. Maney urged me to stay with him—that it was death to try the open field again. With a detour, however, I hurried back through the storm, neither I nor my light bay getting a scratch. In this short time three horses had been shot under General Stewart and nearly all the staff were dismounted. Terry Cahal had come back horseless; Lieut. Scott's horse had been shot and had fallen on him, almost paralyzing him; Capt. Stanford, of Stanford's Battery, killed, yet John S. McMath, was fighting his guns like a madman, and Oliver's and Fenner's. ₌804

While Ridley was on his errand:

STEWART, CMDG DIVISION, HOOD'S CORPS, CSA: At this moment an order came by Lieutenant-Colonel Cunningham not to make the attack which however had already commenced. We encountered the enemy in heavy force and protected by breastworks of logs. The ground over which a portion of Stovall's brigade passed was covered with a dense undergrowth and brush. Regiments in consequence became separated and the brigades soon began to fall back. Hastening to it and finding it impossible to reform it on the ground it occupied, it was suffered to fall back to intrenched position—Baker's brigade retiring with it. Clayton being thus unsupported on the right, and Stevenson's division on the left not having advanced, also retired and Gibson fell back by my order, as did Maney also. ₌805

RIDLEY, STEWART'S DIVISION, HOOD'S CORPS, CSA: A Virginia regiment, the Fifty-fourth, of Stevenson's Division, the only one that failed to get the

804 (Ridley 1906, 295)

805 (Ridley 1906, 307)

countermand orders, lost a hundred men in a few minutes. The dead and dying of our first line was heartrending. .806

STEWART, CMDG DIVISION, HOOD'S CORPS, CSA: The attack would have been renewed but for the order received at the last moment countermanding it. During the advance Stanford's battery on the left was of material assistance and I deeply regret the loss of the skillful and brave officer, Captain T. J. Stanford, with whom it has been my good fortune to be associated with little interruption since March, 1862. Attention is called to the statement of Brigadier-General Clayton as to the praiseworthy conduct of Private John S. McMath, of the same battery and also to his report of the conduct of his several regiments and of Colonel Lankford, Thirty-eighth Alabama, and others. Also to General Baker's statements in regard to the color-bearer, Sergeant Gilder, Fortieth Alabama, and to the aged missionary, Rev. J. P. McMullin, and others. General Baker had his horse severely wounded. .807

WILLIAMS, 1D 20C: The colors and colonel, with other officers and men, of the Thirty-eighth Alabama were captured by the Twenty-seventh Indiana Volunteers, Colonel Colgrove, of Ruger's brigade, and the division took about 125 prisoners. In front of one brigade 5 officers and 80 [men] of the enemy's placed dead were buried. .808

HOPPER, CO E 101ST ILL ROBINSON 3B 1D 20C: This morning a general advance along the lines: this afternoon we had a warm time but succeeded in driving the rebels. Lost six men wounded from our Company. We were hotly engaged 2 hours. .809

COOK, ASST. SURGEON, 150TH NY RUGER 2B 1D 20C: Well the three fourths of an hour before spoken of passed away, and with it the enemy from before us, and "lucky 150th," was the shout from every lip, for we had none killed, and but seven wounded. .810

In a Nine-Hole

RIDLEY, STEWART'S DIVISION, HOOD'S CORPS, CSA: There was one place, though, where Sherman, had he been the able general many supposed,

---

806 (Ridley 1906, 295)
807 (Ridley 1906, 307)
808 (OR, Series I Vol 38 Part 3 Serial 74: Reports n.d., 28)
809 (Hopper n.d.)
810 (Cook 1864)

would have taken some of Johnston's glory from him. The only time he ever got Johnston apparently in "a nine hole" ₋811 was at Resaca, on May 15, 1864, Stewart's Division of Hood's Corps occupied the extreme right of Johnston's army, his right on the Connesauga—the Oostanaula in his rear. Had Sherman made a charge on us then there would have been no escape. In this trough, the position was critical—the Connesauga to the right, the Oostanaula in the rear, and both non-fordable. Whilst Gen. Sherman showed a want of generalship in not following, Old Joe displayed wonderful skill in getting us out. I will never forget Resaca. Oftimes it occurs to me that our boldness in making the attack saved the army—for Sherman, massed, had given orders to pounce on us, which was postponed when he saw that we were preparing as aggressors. ₋812

WILLIAMS, 1D 20C: I made no efforts to pursue, as my orders were to cover and protect the left, and I was ignorant of the condition of affairs with the assaulting columns on the right; besides, the enemy's intrenchments, to which at each repulse he fell back, were but a few hundred yards in my front. It was evident, too, that the assaulting force (at least two divisions of Hood's corps) greatly outnumbered ours. ₋813

Williams' division was likely outnumbered, but the enemy, not yet recovered, was disorganized. Could he have routed them? No evidence has turned up that Hooker even realized the opportunity. No evidence Geary and Schofield were ordered and prepared to assist except to watch for the opportunity. Butterfield was certainly in no condition.

If Williams did not yet know how the battle on the right had gone, he would not even know whether the Rebel line had been broken or whether he would be "in the air" if he pursued. Indeed, he would have been. He could not have pursued very far before out-running support and running into whoever was behind Hindman's line. Pressure from Howard's line had long before ended.

In another view, Brown thinks the Rebel effort was weak and not just because they had been recalled and wanted to break off the engagement. And he tells how things might have gone if they had been pursued with more vigor.

811 (Sciences n.d.) Sherman had forced Johnston to leave a gap that he could not plug without leaving another gap.
812 (Ridley 1906, 295) Orders to pounce not known. Howard and Schofield had orders, given before the fighting began, to follow if Hooker succeeded in his assault. So then, the assault was not a success?
813 (OR, Series I Vol 38 Part 3 Serial 74: Reports n.d., 28)

BROWN, CO C 27TH INDIANA RUGER 2B 1D 20C: The engagement along our front continued for at least an hour and a half. During all of this time the enemy was acting upon the offensive. Though not resolute or determined to a marked degree, he still manifested some spirit and persistence. If the battle was brought on under a misapprehension, that it should be continued as a losing fight for so long, or that it should require so much time for those in control to come to an understanding among themselves, seems mysterious. Whatever may be the facts, however, on this point, it was certainly fortunate for them that other troops were not put in. To have doubled the force against Williams' division, or to have doubled the enthusiasm back of the assault, would only have doubled the loss sustained, and the disappointment of defeat. The assault as it was, was so very ineffectual, so very far from the least sign of success, that it is impossible to conjecture what might have rendered it otherwise. Not over half of Williams' division took any part in the battle, and those that did take part were only getting fairly at it when the battle was over. .814

Alternative account, disputed by others: Hovey's 1st Brigade, under Barter, describes saving Williams, particularly his left front regiment, then covering the east side of the railroad. Hovey had been placed behind and left of Williams.

BARTER, 1B 1D 23C: At 1.30 p.m. moved to the left of the Twentieth Army Corps, which we found hotly engaged with the enemy. Formed line in an open field. Just as my line was being formed, a vigorous charge was made upon the left of the Twentieth Army Corps. I ordered the One hundred and twentieth and One hundred and twenty-eighth to charge across the open field to the rescue of the One hundred and forty-third New York, which was gallantly holding the ground against two Alabama regiments commanded by the rebel Colonel Baker. The enemy hearing the cheers of our advancing line, and being hard pressed by the Second Brigade, gave way in confusion beyond the railroad. .815

Lying Humbugs - General Williams' Complaint

WILLIAMS, 1D 20C: I have never seen more lying by the letter writing fraternity than in this campaign. We have no correspondent in this corps, but we have had one division commander who, I judge, has kept a corner in

814 (E. R. Brown 1899, 475)

815 (OR, Series I Vol 38 Part 2 Serial 73: Reports n.d., 540) Hovey says his division arrived about 3 pm.

the notes of every correspondent in the army, besides keeping his staff busy at the same work. He claims pretty much everything ... He is not the only instance of lying humbugs in this army who contrive to keep their names connected with battles which they were not near. It sickens one to see what efforts are made by officers high in rank to steal undeserved honors, and how much thirst for false fame preponderates over real love of country and an honorable ardor to serve the great cause, irrespective of personal reward. .816

CINCINNATI COMMERCIAL: About 2 o'clock the enemy, learning from prisoners taken from us, that Hovey's Indiana division of "raw recruits" held a position in the line, and smarting under their successive repulses on other portions of the line, hurled a heavy force upon Hovey, convinced that the recruits would run. Not so, however. The rebels held a strong position in a gorge in the hills, and out of their breastworks they swarmed in large numbers and made a furious attack upon the division, which nobly repulsed them after a short and bloody contest of fifteen minutes. The assault was renewed, when the "raw Hoosiers" charged upon them on the double-quick, under heavy fire of grape and literally mowed them down. They did not assault the Indianians the third time. To-night the enconiums [sic] of the whole corps are being showered upon Hovey's division, who have written a glorious introductory chapter in their history. .817

WILLIAMS, 1D 20C: I am not indifferent to the ephemeral praise of reporters, but I cannot sell my self-respect to obtain it. The only other New York report I have seen is the New York Tribune. I don't know who writes for that paper but he hardly tells a truth and a great many lies. He gives to Hovey's division, 23rd Corps, the credit of defending our left flank and capturing the gaudy flag of the 38th Alabama, when it is known all through the army that Hovey did not get into the fight and that my division captured the flag and the colonel and many officers of that regiment. Indeed, Gen. Schofield, who commands that corps, told me yesterday that Hovey did not lose in killed and wounded a dozen men on the day of that fight. Such is the reliability of the correspondent of that pious and patriotic paper, the New York Tribune! I see he wholly ignores my division and always speaks of it as "a portion of Hooker's corps," but is careful to name Geary's and Butterfield's divisions ...

---

816 (Williams 1963, 432) He was actually referring to Geary in this letter.
817 (Correspondence of the Cincinnati Commercial 1864)

Be assured that my division stands as high as any with those who know and that the truth will appear in the end. _818_

Sweeny Moves Forward

SHERMAN: During the 15th, without attempting to assault the fortified works, we pressed at all points, and the sound of cannon and musketry rose all day to the dignity of a battle. Toward evening McPherson moved his whole line of battle forward, till he had gained a ridge overlooking the town, from which his field-artillery could reach the railroad-bridge across the Oostenaula. The enemy made several attempts to drive him away, repeating the sallies several times, and extending them into the night; but in every instance he was repulsed with bloody loss. _819_ _820_

CORSE TO SHERMAN: May 15, 5 p.m. After gaining possession of the other bank and getting two brigades into position, Jackson's brigade, of Walker's division, Hardee's corps, assaulted in line of battle and drove our men toward the river till the batteries in position on this side opened with such execution as to send them back, followed by our men, capturing and killing quite a number. This assault proved advantageous to us in two ways; one, it gave us command of a better position, and another, it so demoralized the enemy as to deter him from attempting the same thing again. We are now in possession of a ridge about half a mile from the bridges, which, when properly fortified, which will be done to-night, will resist a large force. I have been over the ground and think the position quite strong. We found forty dead rebels on the field; we lost about 100 killed and wounded. The prisoners captured belong respectively to the Fifth, Sixty-fifth, and Forty-seventh, and Eighth Georgia [Battalion] Infantry, and Fifth Mississippi Infantry. The division embraces Mercer's, Jackson's, Stevenson's, and Gist's brigade, each about 1,200 strong, two batteries of four guns each. The division has been employed in patrolling the railroad between Resaca and Calhoun, and arrived here about 11 a.m. to-day under orders from Hardee.

818 (Williams 1963, 432) Lincoln promoted Hovey to satisfy Hovey's political supporters, while at the same time assigning him to a post in Indiana. Sherman had strenuously protested Hovey having any command because of extremely poor performance such as to be a hazard. Five days earlier, Schofield, not doing it himself because Grant esteemed Hovey (for having done well at Vicksburg), asked Sherman to replace Hovey because he was "worthless." Sherman demurred for the same reason as Schofield.
819 (Sherman 1875, 35) Shelling the bridge was reported by the retreating army.
820 Sherman had expected the works to be pressed, not assaulted, as if the capture of the guns was a happy happenstance.

I further learned that Forrest was expected at Calhoun last night. Martins' division of cavalry, with one battery, has been here all the time we have, but our artillery hurt them so as to compel them to leave last night. I have not yet heard from the cavalry force I sent down toward Rome. Will use them to protect the flanks, and remain here to-night. We are quite anxious to hear of Thomas' effort. By the way, the prisoners said one of our shells (from McPherson's front, I think) struck one of the road regiments passing over the bridge at Resaca, yesterday, at a double-quick, and killed and hurt many. This bridge is near the railroad bridge. .821

FULLERTON, ADJUTANT, 4TH CORP: TIMELINE: 4.40 pm. In accordance with orders received from General Thomas, Generals Stanley, Newton, and Wood were ordered to press their skirmishers. This was done, and fire continued along our line until dark. There was scarcely any cessation of fire along our whole line, in fact, from daylight until dark. General Hooker secured a good lodgment on the ridge opposite our left, but was unable to pursue, on account of heavy works and masses of the enemy's troops. The enemy's sharpshooters' fire very accurate and severe, and many men were killed and wounded along our lines by them. .822

Cobham Solidifies His Position

COBHAM, 111TH PA IRELAND 3B 2D 20C: At 5 p.m. I received a written order from Major-General Hooker and verbal orders from General Geary, to take command of the troops in front of the rebel works. I accordingly turned over the command of the One hundred and eleventh Pennsylvania Veteran Volunteers to Lieutenant-Colonel Walker, and immediately proceeded to place them in position to command the ridge, and to resist any attack that might be made by the rebel force in our front. About the same time an aide on General Geary's staff informed me that Colonel Ireland was wounded, and the command of the Third Brigade devolved on me. The One hundred and second New York Volunteers, Colonel Lane .823, took position on the left of the One hundred and eleventh Pennsylvania Veteran Volunteers, by my orders, with the One hundred and nineteenth New York Volunteers, Colonel Lockman, as support, joined on the right of the rear line by the One hundred and thirty-fourth New York Volunteers, Lieutenant-Colonel Jackson, and One hundred and ninth Pennsylvania Volunteers, Captain

---

821 (OR, Series I Vol 38 Part 4 Serial 75: Correspondence n.d., 197)
822 (OR, Series I Vol 38 Part 1 Serial 75: Reports n.d., 854)
823 When Lane arrived is not clear.

Gimber, and on the left by a portion of the Thirty-third New Jersey Volunteers, Colonel Fouratt, the One hundred and forty-ninth New York Volunteers, Colonel Randall, occupying the right of the One hundred and eleventh in the front line. In this formation the command remained with occasional firing on both sides until near 11 p.m. As soon as the lines were formed in the above order, I reported in person to General Geary, commanding division, and received orders from him to secure the four cannon in the rebel fort, and remove them by digging away the earth in front of them and draw them out with ropes. .824 .825

While Cobham was moving some of his men below the fort, Geary had ordered others to the left, probably to support Wood or Knipe in resisting the flank attempt. Then they too were moved below the fort.

After all this, Corporal Morey, of Brown's Brigade, which was just behind the fort, recorded:

> MOREY, 32ND TENNESSEE, BROWN'S BRIGADE, STEVENSON, HOOD, CSA: May 15. Our ___ and ___ was thrown out as skirmishers and moved over the hill, which we lost last night. About two oclock the enemy charged us driving us back to the works our men had erected this morning on the ___ ___ hills. They charged the brigade five or six times but were repulsed every time. (They charged different places in the line this evening but without effect.) Just as the evening first came up our regiment charged out of the works some 40 or 50 yards down hill to a battery that had been opposed by the enemy in their first charge, it not having any support, but did not succeed in recapturing it. I do not know the loss of our regiment or brigade yet. We had Lieut. Weddy mortally and ___ G___ ___ slightly wounded out of our company. There was one man killed ___ ___ ___. We were relieved [two lines undecipherable]. About four oclock this evening we went back into the works relieving Reynold's Brigade, which had relieved us some time before part of which a ___ relieved charged ___ ___ some distance to our right. .826

Whether he wrote they were driven back to the main line is not certain, the diary being in pencil on worn pages. He seems to say his regiment may have helped on

---

824 (OR, Series I Vol 38 Part 3 Serial 74: Reports n.d., 276)
825 But the decision to dig the guns out instead of fight for them was made later, per Buckingham.
826 (Morey n.d., May 13, 1864)

their right during Johnston's flank attempt, having been relieved by Reynolds' Brigade. Lt. Weddy was killed in the flank attempt the previous evening.

Confederates Plan Retreat

They were four old iron pieces, not worth the sacrifice of the life of even one man.
—Hood

It was deemed expedient to sacrifice himself and command. —Cheney

BRANT, 85TH INDIANA COBURN 2B 2D 20C: At that time we were assured that the enemy had only one "hole" to get out and that we were stopping that "hole." But Joe Johnston always found a "hole" out. ﹍827

His "out" had been decided last night:

WILLIAM M. POLK, POLK'S CORPS, CSA: Saturday, the 14th, was passed in irregular skirmishing and in strengthening the defences. A sharp and successful attack was now made upon the picket line in front of Canty. The line was carried by the enemy; being reinforced, Canty reestablished it after a severe conflict. Later in the day, however, Owing to the weakening of Polk's line to aid an attack upon the enemy's left by Hood, Canty lost a position held by his advance troops which commanded the railroad bridge. During the night the enemy crossed a division over the Oostenaula at Calhoun, and, in view of a retreat, which this movement made unavoidable, all wagon trains were now ordered to Kingston. ﹍828

Thus, according to this, Johnston's attempt to flank the Union left on Saturday cost him his ability to defend his own left. Then, Dodge's threat at Lay's Ferry that same evening sealed the decision to evacuate. The wagons were gone before Hooker's assault started.

WESLEY CONNOR, PRIVATE, CHEROKEE ARTILLERY, CSA 5h P.M. Went up a few moments ago to see the battery—everything is as we left it except that the stars and stripes are floating over it. Neither party has possession of it. The Feds cannot remove it till night, when our men will go out and bring it in. ﹍829

---

827 (Brant 1902, 55)
828 (Polk 1935, 351) William M. Polk was son of General Polk and served with him.
829 (W. O. Connor, Wesley Olin Connor Diary 1867, 57)

STEVENSON, STEVENSON'S DIVISION: As I have stated I covered the disputed battery with my fire in such a manner that it was utterly impossible for the enemy to remove it, and I know that I could retake it at any time, but thought that it could be done with less loss of life at night, and, therefore, postponed my attack. When ordered to retire I represented the state of things to the general commanding, who decided to abandon the guns. .830

HOOD, CSA: They were finally abandoned on the night of our retreat from Resaca, simply from the fact that I found upon consultation with Colonel Beckham, my chief of artillery, and Major General Stevenson, one of my division commanders, that I had more guns than were required for the number of men in my command; and, as the order to retreat had been given, it was deemed better to yield them to the enemy than to sacrifice one or two hundred men in reclaiming them. I think my action, in this instance, will meet not only the approval of the military, but also of the civilized world. .831

HOOD: The whole matter was laid before General Johnston, and the guns were abandoned with his concurrence; at least such is my recollection. Moreover, I am informed by Captain Sweat that these guns belonged to his command, and that they were four old iron pieces, not worth the sacrifice of the life of even one man. .832

WESLEY CONNOR, PRIVATE, CHEROKEE ARTILLERY, CSA: Later—Yanks still moving to our left. Our army retreating from their positions in front of Resaca. Wharton and I went to look for the caisons for the Cherokee Artillery and found they had gone to the rear. Only Wharton and I remained on the line till the final retreat.) .833

CJH, BROWN'S BRIGADE, STEVENSON'S DIVISION, HOOD'S CORP, CSA: One other gallant spirit deserves particular notice for the self-sacrificing spirit, true devotion to his country and implicit obedience to orders displayed on the night of this same day. Orders having been issued for the withdrawal of the troops from the line of works, preliminary to crossing the river, Lieut. Col. Clack's 3d Tennessee regiment was left with a thin line of skirmishers

---

830 (OR, Series I Vol 38 Part 3 Serial 74: Reports n.d., 812) Fenner's Battery was in addition, then, to Rowan's and Marshall's, placed behind or around Corput's.
831 (Hood 1880, 96)
832 (Hood 1880, 96) Others do not so describe the guns. Fenner's Battery, apparently, was supporting Stewart, which places it left of Corput's Battery.
833 (W. O. Connor, Wesley Olin Connor Diary 1867, 57)

to hold the abandoned rifle pits and cover the withdrawal of his command. Knowing the enemy to have overwhelming numbers massed in his front, his right and left flanks exposed, and nothing to support him, he naturally presumed it was deemed expedient to sacrifice himself and [his] command. He immediately held a consultation with his officers and inquired if they were willing and ready for the sacrifice. Their unanimous and noble response was—we are. Arrangements were then made for a desperate resistance, the colonel cautioning his men not to recognize any command he gave them, but on the approach of the enemy to fire as rapidly as possible. _834

The 3rd Tennessee again, what was left of them.

Union Reliefs at 6 PM

PARTRIDGE, 96TH ILL WHITAKER 2B 1D 4C: These guns could not be drawn out until nightfall, but through that long afternoon the brave men lay at the embrasures and prevented the foe from getting any use of them. The results of the charges were not all that had been hoped, for the Rebels still held a continuous line about Resaca, but there were substantial gains in position, and it was expected that should the enemy remain until morning their main line would be forced. _835

WOOD, 3B 3D 20C: The day was now far spent, my men were exhausted; the casualties had been large. At my request Major-General Hooker ordered my brigade relieved by troops from the Second Division. After being relieved, I marched the brigade into the valley on the Dalton road where it bivouacked for the night. _836

RYDER, CO I 33RD MASS, WOOD 3B 1D 20C: This ended their attack in our front. Soon after this we were relieved by the first division of our corps and we marched back half a mile and stacked arms in a field west of the road in the rear of our battle line. Of the three men of my company who had spoken to the captain about being killed, one was killed and the others were mortally wounded and died after being brought to the field hospital. _837

---

834 (CJH 1864) The 3rd Tennessee, according to Blakeslee's map, was the regiment directly behind Corput's battery during the fight.
835 (Partridge 1887, 327)
836 (OR, Series I Vol 38 Part 2 Serial 73: Reports n.d., 434)
837 (Ryder 1928, 56)

Coburn's men, who had been there to help on the left after their time on the hill, could finally feel they'd done something for the day.

> BRADLEY, CHAPLAIN, 22ND WIS COBURN 2B 3D 20C: A heavy charge and raking fire of artillery succeed on our left, while our men constitute a reserve. The shots skim close, and men of a regiment rise to run and are ordered back. Not a man of the 22d left his place. For several minutes the firing continues. Then a wild cheer from a thousand throats, and our flag waves from the fort on the left. .838

Part of Geary's 1st Brigade relieved Wood's left and Knipe's right:

> MEMBER OF COMPANY A, 141ST NY, KNIPE 1B 1D 20C: At five p. m. we were relieved, having been under fire five hours, and during this time the enemy had made three charges but were repulsed every time. .839

> PARDEE, 147TH PA CANDY 1B 2D 20C: ... and there [left, at the road] remained until ordered to relieve the Seventy-third Ohio Volunteer Infantry, of Third Division, Twentieth Army Corps, and One hundred and forty-first New York Volunteers, First Division, Twentieth Army Corps, posted in front and on the left of the line of our brigade and directly in front of the breastworks of the right of the First Division, Twentieth Army Corps. .840

> MCMAHON, CO E 136TH NY WOOD 3B 3D 20C We were relieved at 6 P.M. by some new troops. .841

Nine PM

> FLEHARTY, 102ND ILL WARD 1B 3D 20C Towards evening it was feared the battery would be retaken. One by one the men began to retire, notwithstanding the expostulations of those who remained. After dark the enemy opened a sharp fire, as if menacing a charge to retake the guns. A volley was fired in return; the boys yelled out a defiant cheer, and one shouted to the Johnnies: "Come over and take your brass field pieces!"

Relief for Ward and Coburn.

838 (Bradley 1865)
839 (Museum n.d.)
840 (OR, Series I Vol 38 Part 2 Serial 73: Reports n.d., 194)
841 (McMahon 1993, 93)

Help had been sent for, and at length we heard music in the valley below. Sweet as the music of heaven, soothing the soul after the harrowing, discordant day of battle. .842 Inwoven with our very beings, the ecstatic sensations of that moment, when the soft, plaintive, but cheering notes of a field band were borne to our ears, will live in memory forever. We learned afterwards, however, that the music did not herald the approach of a relieving column, but relief soon came. .843

Geary was sending the second line of his 2nd Brigade to relieve his first line, which he'd sent earlier.

WARNER, 154TH NY BUSCHBECK 2B 2D 20C: Our brigade was considerably scattered in consequence of the great number of troops who were forced to maneuver upon a limited space of ground and in a dense wood. At dark the One hundred and fifty-fourth, with the Seventy-third and Twenty-seventh Pennsylvania as a support, was directed to relieve a portion of the front line (the right), which was in front of a redoubt containing four pieces of artillery, from which the enemy had been driven, but which our boys were unable to remove. .844

CRESSON, 73RD PA BUSCHBECK 2B 2D 20C: Remained here until about 9 p.m. when the regiment, together with the One hundred and fifty-fourth New York Volunteers and Twenty-seventh Pennsylvania Volunteers, was ordered out to relieve the One hundred and ninth Pennsylvania Volunteers, One hundred and nineteenth New York Volunteers, and One hundred and thirty-fourth New York Volunteers, who were out on the front line. The regiment here remained until about 1 p.m. While here the regiment assisted in hauling from the fort 4 guns captured from the enemy. .845

REIDT, CO A 27TH PENN BUSCHBECK 2B 2D 20C: The regiment was stationed in reserve on the hill next to the captured rebel battery during the evening till 12 oclock. May 16, at about 1 oclock in the morning, the regiment received orders to march with the One hundred and fifty-fourth New York Volunteers and Seventy-third Pennsylvania Volunteers to the hill in front to relieve the other troops there. .846

---

842 The band playing Yankee Doodle?
843 (Fleharty, Our Regiment. A History of the 102d Illinois Infantry Volunteers 1865)
844 (OR, Series I Vol 38 Part 2 Serial 73: Reports n.d., 248) About dark (9 o'clock).
845 (OR, Series I Vol 38 Part 2 Serial 73: Reports n.d., 256)
846 (OR, Series I Vol 38 Part 2 Serial 73: Reports n.d., 235) Time discrepancy of four hours.

Geary's 3rd Brigade and the first line of the 2nd Brigade relieved:

PARDEE, 147TH PA CANDY 1B 2D 20C: While in this position we were considerably annoyed by the sharpshooters of the enemy and by a piece of artillery immediately in our front of the left of the regiment. The latter, after several discharges, was moved and did not trouble us afterward. In this position we remained until 9 p.m. when I was ordered with my command to rejoin the brigade. The list of casualties has already been handed to you and I am really happy to state that they were few in number. In conclusion, I beg leave to state that the regiment was not hotly engaged though constantly under the fire of the enemy, and that all orders were obeyed and movements executed with zeal and rapidity, which was truly gratifying and for which I desire, through you, to thank the officers and men of my regiment. _847

LOCKMAN, 119TH NY BUSCHBECK 2B 2D 20C: We remained in possession, and at 9 p.m. fresh troops having been sent out, by direction of Colonel Cobham, I withdrew the three regiments to the foot of the hill. The rest of the brigade was sent out, and I requested Colonel Cobham to permit the three regiments to return to camp, which was granted. Two regiments, One hundred and thirty-fourth and One hundred and nineteenth New York, had moved off, and Thirty-third New Jersey was about to follow, when an attack was made by the enemy. Colonel Cobham requested them to remain, which they did, and assisted in bringing off the captured guns. _848

MCCLELLAND, 7TH OHIO CANDY 1B 2D 20C: At about 10 p.m. the regiment was ordered to join the remainder of the brigade, then lying in a ravine to our right and near the road running east and west. Here arms were stacked and the men laid down to rest. _849

MOUAT, CO G, 29TH PENN IRELAND 3B 2D 20C: We fell back a little further and a detail was sent out to bring in the wounded as we were laying on our arms and it had got quite dark some one came along and stumbled over me I hollered Look out where you are agoing—the fellow replied "Is that you Dave"—I jumped up and said Hello Billy is that you he said "Yes but I have

---

847 (OR, Series I Vol 38 Part 2 Serial 73: Reports n.d., 194)
848 (OR, Series I Vol 38 Part 2 Serial 73: Reports n.d., 232)
849 (OR, Series I Vol 38 Part 2 Serial 73: Reports n.d., 178)

lost a hand," the ball had shattered the bones in his wrist and his hand had to be amputated. ₋850

MERRILL, 70TH IND WARD 1B 3D 20C: As evening approached those who could extricate themselves without crossing what might be called a dead line, were moved a little to the left, where a repast of crackers, dinner and supper combined, was partaken, while a large number under command of Captains Carson, Meredith, Scott and other line officers, aided by officers and men from the First and other brigades, protected the captured guns. ₋851

BRADLEY, CHAPLAIN, 22ND WIS COBURN 2B 3D 20C: A third charge by our men nearly in our rear is made with success, and the fight closes to our advantage, and we rest with stacked arms. Suddenly a tremendous fire bursts out in front, and all are ready. It soon dies away and all sleep sweetly, as only the tired soldier, wearied by the excitement of battle, can. ₋852

STORRS, 20TH CONN COBURN 2B 3D 20C: The evening of the 15th found as results of the struggle, so far, that the Rebel army had been driven from its position on the right and left, and was otherwise so badly crippled that it seemed as if, on the morrow, it must be defeated, or perhaps annihilated. ₋853

BULL, CO D 123RD NY KNIPE 1B 1D 20C: The fighting lasted two hours, the noise of the musketry and cannon was deafening and the shouts and yells of the forces engaged could be plainly heard. Our position in the open field we thought so unfavorable proved our salvation, as it kept us out of the severe fighting. After repeated efforts to break or drive our line back, the enemy fell back into their works that evening. It was too late to follow them so we halted where we were, expecting to continue the fight in the morning.

We were fortunate, our Regiment had only ten men killed and wounded. One of the killed was a member of the detachment that had been home on recruiting service. He was killed within an hour of his return to the Regiment. All our casualties were either from sharpshooters or exploding shells. On our right and left the action had been heavy and the losses severe. The 2nd Brigade had captured a battery and carried the enemy's

850 (Mouat n.d.)
851 (S. Merrill 1900, 91)
852 (Bradley 1865)
853 (Storrs 1886, 127)

entrenchments. After dark we moved up close to our picket line and constructed earthworks until midnight. When we finished all were ready to drop down and get such rest as we could before the morrow, which had such a threatening look. .854

GRUNERT, CO D 129TH ILL WARD 1B 3D 20C: As night approached, our wounded were brought to the field hospitals and cared for as well as could be expected, our position was attended to and guarded against a surprise, our knapsacks were gotten and we went to sleep, satisfied with our dearly bought victory.

WINKLER, 26TH WIS WOOD 3B 3D 20C: The regiment lost in this days' action Lieut. Christian Phillip and 5 men killed and 40 wounded. After dark we were relieved by other troops and allowed to rest a short distance to the rear. .855

MERRILL, 70TH IND WARD 1B 3D 20C: About nine o'clock we could see by the light of burning brush the Confederates climbing over the breastworks and forming for an attack. Word was passed along to reserve fire for the command. They advanced cautiously within a few yards of the guns, when the command, Fire! was given, every rifle rang out, and at the same time the advance guard gave a yell. That yell was taken up by our forces in the rear and the Confederates broke and ran, evidently thinking Hooker's whole Corps was up and at em. And that was the end of the battle of Resaca. .856

MCMILLEN, JAMES, LIEUTENANT, COMPANY C, 141ST NY, KNIPE 1B 1D 20C: Strong earthworks were thrown up by our men during the night, close to the enemy, and artillery got in position, so that the next days' fight would have been more nearly on an equal footing. We all felt confident of an easy victory in the morning. .857Yet, some had remained!

Was the fort entirely abandoned by Ward's brigade during all that long afternoon into the night? Not according to Blakeslee.

BLAKESLEE, CO G 129TH ILL WARD 1B 3D 20C: Capt. J. H. Culver, Company A – 129th, was the only officer that stayed on the advanced position of 129th till he was relieved at 10 P.M. 27 of 129th was with him. There were about 300 of our men between your guns and your main line; most of these were

---

854 (Bull 1977, 104)
855 (OR, Series I Vol 38 Part 2 Serial 73: Reports n.d., 463)
856 (S. Merrill 1900, 102)
857 (Museum n.d.)

of Harrison's regiment, 70 Ind., and *were in a measure protected by the ledge*—that I have shown in map .858. .859

BLAKESLEE, CO G 129TH ILL WARD 1B 3D 20C: At Resaca, Ga, May 15, 1864, Capt, J. H. Culver now of Emporia, Kans. the only officer in our regiment left alive and unwounded .860, who led the boys *beyond the captured guns* on the heights of Red Knob Gap, held the position until only 27 men were left with him, each and every one whom should have a medal. He held the fort and captured battery until relieved at 10 o'clock p.m. the only protection afforded him being the dead body of Capt. Blackburn, Co. A, 79th Ohio, whose blood saturated his clothing from chin to boots. .861 .862 .863

Eleven PM - Dangerous Work

FULLERTON, ADJUTANT, 4TH CORP: Timeline We kept up a fire of artillery all night and also of skirmishers. .864

PARTRIDGE, 96TH ILL WHITAKER 2B 1D 4C: At dusk the Regiment moved to these works and formed line under an annoying artillery fire. Soon afterward all was quiet for a time, the armies, as if by mutual consent, discontinuing their firing; but when some members of the Regiment built a fire just behind the works bullets began to zip uncomfortably close, and even a battery threw a shot which, passing close to the fire, went back into the timber in rear. Thus warned, all fires were extinguished and grim darkness reigned over the scene. The men soon settled down to such sleep as could be obtained, but were once routed out and fell in line, some unusual noise at the front indicating a move on the part of the enemy that might mean a night assault. It proved to be a false alarm, however, for instead of

---

858 See Blakeslee's map.
859 (Connor, Wesley O.; Blakeslee, George H. 1899)
860 Some perhaps had minor wounds. Was Blakeslee known to exaggerate?
861 (G. H. Blakeslee, Brave Men of His Regiment 1897) Culver did not mention this to his wife in his letter after the battle.
862 Joseph H. Blackburn, private, was listed in Company A, 79th Ohio, as killed May 15, 1864 at Resaca.
863 Red Knob Gap not found in the area.
864 (OR, Series I Vol 38 Part 1 Serial 75: Reports n.d., 854)

making an assault the Rebels were retreating under cover of the darkness, and by morning all were gone. .865

Butterfield's Diggers

COBURN, 2B 3D 20C: General Butterfield then directed me to send 200 men to re-enforce the men of my own brigade and relieve the men of the First

THE CAMPAIGN IN GEORGIA—GEARY'S DIVISION DIGGING THE GUNS OUT OF A REBEL BATTERY BEFORE RESACA, ON THE NIGHT OF MAY 15, 1864.—[SEE PAGE 334.]

Brigade still near the rebel earthworks. This was done under command of Lieutenant-Colonel Buckingham, of the Twentieth Connecticut. His force assisted in digging the side of the fort away and in dragging out four pieces of artillery at night. .866MERRILL, 70TH IND WARD 1B 3D 20C: Subsequently Captain Carson was recalled and ordered to take the fifty men of Company G still left and report to an officer in Colonel Coburn's command, who, with one hundred and fifty men detailed from regiments of the Second Brigade, was to draw the captured cannon from the lunette under cover of the

865 (Partridge 1887, 327)
866 (OR, Series I Vol 38 Part 2 Serial 73: Reports n.d., 377)

darkness. The firing from both sides continued after night, three or four times swelling into what might be called a volley, but the extrication of the four Napoleon twelve pounder brass pieces from the fort, was accomplished with little loss, and before midnight the Confederates had evacuated their works and all was quiet. _867

STORRS, 20TH CONN COBURN 2B 3D 20C: During the evening, Lieut. Colonel Buckingham of the 20th Connecticut was detailed to take command of a detachment of troops, numbering about two hundred and fifty men, including two companies of the 20th, with orders to capture a murderous little battery of four guns, situated on a ridge in front of the 3d of the 20th Corps, and along the front of which was an embankment, forming a natural redoubt. The gunners had been driven from these guns after a fearful struggle, which covered the ground in front with dead, but neither the Rebels whose main line was a few rods further back, or the Unionists were able to bring away the pieces. They remained, as it were, on disputed territory. The detachment moving out about 9 p.m. after groping around in the dark, found the position and formed around the side of the hill below the battery. Lieut. Colonel Buckingham, accompanied by Captain Doolittle of the 20th, proceeded to reconnoitre and examine the location in order to determine upon a course of action, the result of which was that two plans were presented for the accomplishment of the object. One was that of Colonel Cobham, of the 2d Division, who advocated a charge against the main works of the enemy, under cover of which the guns should be run over toward the Rebel lines and round the end of the bluff on which they were situated and into the Union lines. The other, that of Lieut. Colonel Buckingham, was to dig them out, and this latter course was adopted. Commencing some two or three rods down the hill, a trench was dug toward the muzzle of each piece, wide enough to admit the passage of the gun carriages. About 2 o'clock ropes were attached to the pieces and they were dragged silently through the trenches down the hill and into the Union lines. The battery proved to have been composed of four nice, new, brass twelve pounders, only just out of the arsenal at Augusta. The guns were found loaded with a double charge of grape shot. The mission was accomplished without the loss of a man. The Rebels seemed to have been aware that some movement was in progress for the capture of the guns and several times during the night started in with quite a brisk fire, in the direction of the works, but it was evidently expected that the attempt would be made to take the guns over on their side of the bluff, not deeming it

---

867 (S. Merrill 1900, 91)

possible that it could be done on the front, from the nature of the ground. But the Yankee colonel had dug out too many foxes and woodchucks, in the antebellum days, on Connecticut hills to "Stick" at a little job like that of digging through the top of a mountain to get whatever he might want on the other side. Had the other plan been chosen there would have been a fierce fight with much loss of life. .868

STRONG, CO B 105TH ILL WARD 1B 3D 20C: That night, they called for volunteers to bring off the guns that we had been unable to take during the day. A number volunteered and crept up to the breastworks. They dug with spades a gap in the breast-works wide enough to get the guns out and, attaching ropes to them, dragged them away. A lieutenant of some Ohio regiment had charge of the volunteers. .869

Geary's Diggers

BUTTERFIELD TO HOOKER: General: Colonel Coburn has sent up two companies to get up to the fort, under charge of a field officer, to draw off the guns. He will explain the position to General Geary, and has been informed that General Geary will relieve him. Will you please order it? .870

COBHAM, 111TH PA IRELAND 3B 2D 20C: In this formation the command remained with occasional firing on both sides until near 11 p.m. As soon as the lines were formed in the above order, I reported in person to General Geary, commanding division, and received orders from him to secure the four cannon in the rebel fort, and remove them by digging away the earth in front of them and draw them out with ropes. I immediately returned to the front and ordered the Fifth Ohio Volunteers, Lieutenant-Colonel Kilpatrick commanding, to relieve the One hundred and eleventh Pennsylvania Veteran Volunteers, their *right* resting in front of the fort and covering it. .871

BARNUM, 149TH NY IRELAND 3B 2D 20C: During the night considerable firing was kept up, and about 1 a.m. the enemy attempted to drive the three

868 (Storrs 1886, 127)
869 (Strong 1961) After dark without lights, Kilpatrick may not have known all involved. The 111th's right had been left of the fort "covering" it. Likely Coburn's troops, then, were working from the right side of the fort, around the other side of the semicircle, and those in between, working, could not have cared.
870 (OR, Series I Vol 38 Part 4 Serial 75: Correspondence n.d., 194)
871 (OR, Series I Vol 38 Part 2 Serial 73: Reports n.d., 26)

regiments under Colonel Cobham from their position, and recover their artillery. The attempt was unsuccessful, and the four guns were dug out of the lunette and brought into our lines. For this task, so skillfully executed, involving great danger and fatigue, the officers and men engaged are entitled to the highest credit. The guns captured were four Napoleon pieces. .872

KILPATRICK, 5TH OHIO CANDY 1B 2D 20C: At dusk, when there was a lull in the fighting, I was preparing to take some rest as I was very tired, when Colonel Patrick came to where I was, and said, "Our regiment is sold." I asked him what was the matter? He said he had just been informed that Colonel Cobham had come over from his part of the line to see General Geary (the division commander), and he understood that the Fifth regiment was to be sent over to Cobham's command, for the purpose of securing those four pieces of artillery that had annoyed us so much during part of the day. That the rebels had been driven from their guns, but they were so well protected by the rebel infantry fire that it was a difficult matter to get at them, but that during the coming darkness it was thought the guns could be got out. And he had learned through a friend at division head quarters that Geary had decided to send the Fifth Ohio to do the work, and that he (Colonel Patrick) thought that if such was the case, few, if any, would survive the effort of getting at these guns. He also said, "I am a senior colonel to Colonel Cobham and I do not intend to take orders from him."

While we were talking, General Geary came to where we were and said, "Colonel Patrick, I want you to take your regiment to the right and front of the First Brigade, where you will find Colonel Cobham in command on the face of the hill right in front of the ridge, and report to him for duty."

The colonel replied, "General, I am a senior colonel to Colonel Cobham, and I don't consider it the proper thing for me to have to report to my junior officer for duty." General Geary replied (rather angrily, I thought): "Well, you take your regiment over there and form in line in rear of Cobham and support him and render him such assistance as he may need." .873

KILPATRICK, 5TH OHIO CANDY 1B 2D 20C: There had been considerable firing during our mile march between the opposing forces, but everything was quiet during our progress up the hill. I found the One Hundred and Eleventh Pennsylvania Regiment deployed along the crest of the hill with their right resting on and covering a redoubt. There were a few men digging

872 (OR, Series I Vol 38 Part 2 Serial 73: Reports n.d., 268)
873 (Kilpatrick 1896)

in front of the works. I looked into the works and could plainly see the four cannon and what appeared to be many dead and wounded rebels—the result of a severe contest.

The work appeared to have been dug out near the top of the hill, leaving the original ground of the steep slope to serve both as parapet and glacis. The rebel flag still hung to the flagstaff, and, with the exception of a few random shots from the rebel riflemen, everything was quiet.

We relieved the One Hundred and Eleventh Pennsylvania, and they retired down the hill, leaving no force whatever between us and the enemy. So far, nothing had been said to me with regard to taking out the guns. I suppose the slight noise occasioned by our relieving the One Hundred and Eleventh Pennsylvania had awakened the "Johnnies," as they commenced a brisk fire along their line, far away on our right, and for a considerable distance on our left. I ordered our men to lie down and keep a sharp lookout ahead, and not to fire a shot until ordered. I expected the rebels to attempt to re-enter the fort as it was open in the gorge. The firing was kept up on both sides with musketry and artillery for about twenty minutes, but I saw no attempt made to re-enter the fort. I never experienced such a miserable twenty minutes in my life; it seemed to me that our own friends were firing into us, about as much as the enemy were, but it finally quieted down. [874]

McClelland, 7th Ohio Candy 1B 2D 20C: I was aroused at about 11 p.m. by rapid discharges of musketry, and caused the regiment to fall in and be in readiness for any emergency. By order of General Geary three companies of my regiment were deployed on the crest of the hill to stop the retreat of stragglers from the front. The firing soon ceased, amid the regiment rested undisturbed until daylight. [875]

Rickards, 29th Penn Ireland 3B 2D 20C: A line of works was built in our front. Tools were sent to Colonel Cobham to enable him to get out four pieces of artillery he had gained possession of. These he succeeded in bringing off in the night. At 11 p.m. the enemy opened a heavy fire of musketry in our front, which extended to the right, continuing ten minutes, and ceasing gradually. [876]

---

874 (Kilpatrick 1896)
875 (OR, Series I Vol 38 Part 2 Serial 73: Reports n.d., 178)
876 (OR, Series I Vol 38 Part 2 Serial 73: Reports n.d., 308)

KILPATRICK, 5TH OHIO CANDY 1B 2D 20C: My greatest difficulty was to go along the line and keep every body awake and on the alert. I was assisted in my duty in the most efficient manner by my friend, Major Symmes; either he or I was in touch with Captain Shirer and his diggers until the road was completed. When completed, I ordered Captain Shirer to send the guns down the hill to General Geary's headquarters. He said, "I will need more men for that purpose." Not wishing to reduce my fighting force any more, I dispatched Lieutenant Henry Koogle (whom I had appointed to act as adjutant during the absence of the regimental adjutant) to Colonel Cobham to ask him to send me fifty men without arms to assist in hauling out the guns, also to report the completion of the road. In a surprisingly short time, fifty men, in command of an officer, all of the Thirty-third New Jersey regiment, reported to me. I turned them over to Captain Shirer, who used them to haul out the other two guns, as two were on their way down the hill by the time the Jerseymen reported. .877

Rebel Retreat

Gen. Hood about faced and rode back to Brown's Brigade, in Stewart's Division, and told the men how much depended upon them. —Anderson

FENNER'S LOUISIANA BATTERY On the 15th, battle of Oostenaula. The battery was divided, one section on each side of a battery in a fortified work. .878 The charge of the enemy was most desperate, and they captured and held the fortification, but were repulsed from the front of each section of Fenner's Battery, which held their positions till night, and then evacuated. .879

Recall Hood ordering the men of a battery to fight to the death?

FRANK ANDERSON, HOOD COURIER, CSA: This battery was captured, and it was the only one that was lost on the Dalton and Atlanta campaign. By some misunderstanding it was placed in front of our infantry, and had no support at all. That night we evacuated the place and crossed the Oostanaula River. When Gen. Hood and staff were crossing the river on the covered bridge the Yankees raised a yell and charged our skirmish line. Gen. Hood about

---

877 (Kilpatrick 1896)

878 Whether this battery was on either side of Corput's battery or behind the Confederate line is not clear.

879 (Salling 1884) Not an original source, but from the website: "The record of this little band of devoted patriots has never been known or understood as it deserves to be. Only once has its history appeared in print upon the reunion of the command in New Orleans, May 12, 1884 ... an article in the Times-Democrat."

faced and rode back to Brown's Brigade, in Stewart's Division, and told the men how much depended upon them. He told Capt. Britton, of the escort company, that he could always depend on the Tennessee troops, which made us feel proud, as we were all Tennesseeans. .880 .881

At least four reports of the last Confederate firing at the fort range from Merrill's 9 pm report, earlier, to these, running from 10 to midnight. At least one was the retreating Rebels' final distraction to cover their retreat.

CINCINNATI COMMERCIAL: About ten P.M. Hooker's command commenced throwing up breastworks to strengthen their position, and to cover their movements, it was found necessary to advance their skirmish line. In doing so the skirmishers ran against the rebel lines. Immediately a heavy artillery and musketry fire opened from both contestants, which lasted until two o'clock in the morning. The night battle was desperate and losses on both sides heavy, probably three hundred killed and wounded. .882

GRUNERT, CO D 129TH ILL WARD 1B 3D 20C: At 12 o'clock P.M. we were awakened by a heavy musket fire, accompanied a few seconds later by the deep bass of our cannon. The enemy tried to retake his fort and guns, but our boys would not assent, and soon the horde of butternuts were sent back in double quick whence they came; not even taking their dead and wounded along. Soon after everything was quiet again, and, satisfied with the victory of Resaca, we laid down awaiting the events of the next day. .883

MILLER, 111TH PA IRELAND 3B 2D 20C: Just after our regt was relieved and we thought we were agoing to get some sleep which we were in need of for the three days previous we were marching and at night we built breast works untill after midnight and just as we got our arms stacked the rebs made an atact on right and for a fewe minutes the fighting was sharp but the rebs were driven back with the loss of 220 in killed the loss in our regt was very light considering the place we were in we had one captain killed and three privates and twenty two wounded. .884

COLLINS, 149TH NY IRELAND 3B 2D 20C: The long, long day, like Joshua's of old, finally came to an end; and at eight in the evening the men were relieved by a brigade of fresh troops belonging to the 2d Division sent to take their

880 (F. Anderson 1897)
881 In Stevenson's Division, not Stewart's.
882 (Correspondence of the Cincinnati Commercial 1864) This may have been the 9 pm.
883 (Grunert 1866)
884 (Miller 1969, 141)

places and, retracing their steps of the morning, moved to a little hollow a short distance in rear of the Union breastworks, where they made coffee, ate supper and laid down to sleep.

About midnight the enemy opened fire along his whole line and balls flew lively over the heads of the men. The division flew to arms and awaited orders, but quiet being soon restored. .885

DENNISTON, 33RD NJ MINDIL 2B 2D 20C: The rebels made a rush on our flank, but were repulsed. We stayed on the hill until dark and the firing had stopped. They came again to the top of the hill and fired into us again. We could not see them. .886 Many of us started down the hill, and I did not stop till I got behind a log; but were formed again, and went up. It was a lovely moonlight night, and one of our bands was playing "Yankee Doodle." .887

DEAVENPORT, CHAPLAIN, 3RD TENN, BROWN'S BRIGADE, STEVENSON'S DIVISION, CSA: After night the enemy having again moved to our left we left the battle ground and again fell back. This was done under the guns of the enemy and yet was done successfully, not even a picket was lost. About the time we left they advanced but Lt. Col. C. J. Clack with the pickets repulsed them and the army crossed over the bridge safely. We marched slowly till daylight and halted for some time when we marched a few miles farther and camped in a nice grove. .888

CJH, BROWN'S BRIGADE, STEVENSON'S DIVISION, HOOD'S CORP, CSA: Soon the anticipated night assault came, met by a sheet of fire from the breastworks, while amid the din of musketry could be heard the clear ringing voice of their heroic commander, "Hold your fire, men, do not waste your ammunition, let them come closer." This piece of deception, their repeated repulses through the day, made the effort a weak one, and they were easily driven back. Again silence reigns. Naught disturbs the deep stillness save the mournful chant of the whipporwill. The moon shines down in unclouded luster, disclosing the little band of Spartan heroes, standing firm, with faces resolved and determined, which thoughts of home, a prairie in the distance, or a grove upon the lonely hillside, could not daunt, but their

---

885 (Collins 1891, 250)
886 An example of seeing a crest from below but then finding you are not there yet after all. Here, the Rebels are firing from a further "crest."
887 (Denniston 1864)
888 (Deavenport 1861-1864)

hour of deliverance was at hand. A craven-hearted courier, dispatched to bring them in, alarmed at the firing, never reached his destination; the second brought the order to retire, and they are now safely with us. .889

STEVENSON, STEVENSON'S DIVISION: That night I received orders to withdraw, which was effected, owing to the coolness of the troops, without serious loss. My last brigade had not marched 300 yards from the trenches before the enemy made an assault. Especial credit is due the skirmishers of Brown's brigade for their conduct in this affair, and I ask attention to his report.

STEWART, CMDG DIVISION, HOOD'S CORPS, CSA: During the retreat of the army at night the division remained in line of battle, crossing the railroad and Dalton and Resaca road, until the entire army had crossed the bridges. The situation was perilous and calculated to try the endurance of the men as the enemy threatened an attack. They stood firm however and remained in position until about 3 o'clock in the morning when we retired in obedience to the orders of the lieutenant-general commanding corps. .890

RIDLEY, STEWARTS DIVISION, HOODS CORPS, CSA: The playing upon the bridges by the enemy's artillery all that night when our army was crossing

889 (CJH 1864)
890 (Ridley 1906, 307)

added to the horror of the event. Visions of Forrest's charge over the bridge at Chickamauga, and of Napoleon's contest over Lodi, came upon me, but Old Joe stood there on the Oostanaula until all had safely passed. _891

MOREY, 32ND TENNESSEE, BROWN'S BRIGADE, STEVENSON, HOOD, CSA: May 16. About ten oclock last night we evacuated our works leaving only a line of skirmishers in them. We marched on____ Resaca across the river before [?] daylight the enemy shelling the bridges were burned. All had crossed. Our badly wounded were left at Resaca. ... _892

Morey's diary is not clear enough to tell more than that they left about ten o'clock and that they left their badly wounded. But it is consistent with other stories.

HOOD: I shall always believe the attack of Stevenson's and Stewart's Divisions, therein described, together with our return to our original position on the following day, saved us from utter destruction by creating the impression upon the Federals that the contest was to be renewed the next morning. _893

STORRS, 20TH CONN COBURN 2B 3D 20C: Having successfully accomplished its mission, the detachment marched back, and by order of General Hooker was rejoined to the brigade. _894

CINCINNATI COMMERCIAL: At two the rebels were repulsed along the whole line; a deafening cheer rang out on the night air, and all was still save the piteous moans of the dying, who lay upon the bloody field, awaiting with anxiety the early dawn, when they were gathered into the hospitals, and every care bestowed upon them by our hard-working surgeons. _895

Close of the Day's Work

Band members doubled as medical orderlies, often risking their lives to rescue the wounded during active battle.

BENTON, BAND, 150TH NY RUGER 2B 1D 20C: As hostilities had ceased for the time at that part of the field, the task of removing the wounded to the rear commenced. There were no stretchers at hand, so we improvised by

891 (Ridley 1906, 295)
892 (Morey n.d., May 13, 1864)
893 (Hood 1880, 98).
894 (Storrs 1886, 127)
895 (Correspondence of the Cincinnati Commercial 1864) Perhaps some exaggeration.

using blankets and half-tents. When you start with a helpless man in a blanket he seems to weigh about a hundred pounds, but after you have gone a fraction of the distance you will think he weighs five hundred, and by the time you have carried your burden half a mile you will be ready to make affidavit to a weight in excess of anything on record; especially if part of the course, as it was in this case, happens to be in range of the enemy's fire.

We soon found where the surgeon had established himself in a hollow in the woods, and after we had brought all of our wounded to that place we set to work under his orders. Night found us tired and fasting, but with crackers and coffee and a few hours of sleep we felt restored; and when we awoke at dawn it was to find that the enemy had retreated from their position during the night. .896

One of Knipe's brigade, who stood on open slope facing the enemy during the fight on the left, recalls how it was.

MORHOUS, CO C 123RD NY KNIPE 1B 1D 20C: That night the Regiment was advanced a little, and they worked until after midnight building breastworks, and while at work the pioneers dug into the Rebel work and drew off a piece of artillery. Some of the boys took a stroll across the field by the pale moonlight to see some of the victims of the struggle. In the immediate front of the Regiment there were not so many as in some other parts of the field, but there were enough. Here and there lay the boys in their army blue. They had fallen with their faces to the foe: they had fought their last fight. They were from different regiments, and the fate of many has probably been shrouded in mystery to their friends.

No person who has not been upon the ground, and an eyewitness of the stirring scenes which there transpire, can begin to comprehend from a description the terrible realities of a battle, and even those who participated are competent to speak only of their own personal experience. Where friends and foes are falling by scores, and every species of missile is flying through the air, threatening every instant to send one into eternity, little time is afforded for more observation than is required for personal safety. Therefore no two men will give the same description of a battle.

The scene is one of the most exciting and exhilarating that can be conceived. Imagine a regiment passing you at "double- quick," the men cheering with

896 (Benton 1902, 142) In his case, the wounded of Ruger's Brigade and perhaps others of Williams' division.

enthusiasm, their teeth set, their eyes flashing, and the whole a frenzy of resolution. You accompany them to the field. They halt. The clear voices of officers ring along the line in tones of passionate eloquence, their words hot, thrilling and elastic. The word is given to march, and the body moves into action. For the first time in your life you listen to the whizzing of iron. Grape and canister fly into the ranks, bombshells burst overhead, and the fragments fly around you. A friend falls; perhaps a dozen or twenty of your comrades lie wounded or dying at your feet; a strange, involuntary shrinking steals over you which it is impossible to resist. You feel inclined neither to advance nor recede, but are spellbound by the contending emotions of the moral and physical man. The cheek blanches, the lip quivers, and the eye almost hesitates to look upon the scene. In this attitude you may, perhaps, be ordered to stand an hour, inactive, havoc meanwhile marking its footsteps with blood on every side. Finally the order is given to advance, to fire or to charge. And now what a metamorphosis! With your first shot you become a new man. Personal safety is your least concern. Fear has no existence in your bosom. Hesitation gives way to an uncontrollable desire to rush into the thickest of the fight. The dead and dying around you, if they receive a passing thought, but serve to stimulate you to revenge. You become cool and deliberate, and watch the effect of bullets, the shower of bursting shells, the passage of cannon-balls as they rake their murderous channels through your ranks, the plunging of wounded horses, the agonies of the dying, and the clash of contending arms which follows the dashing charge, with feelings so calloused by surrounding circumstances that your soul seems dead to every selfish thought. Such is the spirit which carries the soldier through the field of battle. But when the excitement has passed, when the roll of musketry has ceased, the noisy voices of the cannon are stilled, the dusky pall of sulphurous smoke has risen from the field, and you stroll across the theatre of carnage, hearing the groans of the wounded, discovering here, shattered almost beyond recognition, the form of some dear friend whom only an hour before you met in the full flush of life and happiness, there another perforated by a bullet, a third with a limb shot away, a fourth with his face disfigured, a fifth torn almost to fragments, a sixth a headless corpse, the ground ploughed up and stained with blood, human brains splashed around, limbs without bodies and bodies without Limbs scattered here and there, and the same picture duplicated scores of times,—then you begin to realize the horrors of war, and experience a reaction of nature. The heart opens its floodgates, humanity asserts herself again and you begin to feel. Friends and foe alike now receive your kindest ministerings. The enemy, whom but a short time before you were trying to kill, you now endeavor to save. You supply him with water to quench his thirst, with food to sustain his strength, and with sympathizing words to soothe his troubled mind. All that is human or charitable in your nature now rises to the surface, and you are animated by that spirit of mercy "which blesseth him that gives and him that takes." A battle field is eminently a place that tries men's souls. .897

Just lying in that ravine with so much fighting and dying all around can be trying:

LANE, 102ND NY IRELAND 3B 2D 20C: We held this position without relief (or a chance of making coffee) until 2 oclock the next morning. .898

Morning

Dated the 15th, Sherman had been hoping Johnston would not try to escape.

SHERMAN, USA: To Halleck. (Received 11 a. m. 16th.): We have been fighting all day, pressing the enemy, and gaining substantial advantage at all points. We will strengthen the line of circumvallation, so as to spare a larger force to operate across the Oostenaula, below Resaca. Two pontoon bridges are over at Lay's Ferry. The enemy attacked the brigade thrown across to cover the bridge, but was handsomely repulsed, leaving 40 dead. I cannot estimate our dead and wounded up to this hour, but it will fall much short of 3,000. The cars now run down to within seven miles of us, and we have every facility to provide for the wounded. The troops fight well, and everything works smoothly. We intend to fight Joe Johnston until he is satisfied, and I hope he will not attempt to escape. If he does, my bridges are down, and we will be after him. The country is mountainous and heavily wooded, giving the party on the defensive every advantage, and our losses result mostly from sharpshooters and ambush firing.

But now Johnston is gone.

STORRS, 20TH CONN COBURN 2B 3D 20C: At early dawn it was discovered that there was no enemy in front. His position having been found untenable. Gen. Johnston, during the night, built bridges and silently withdrew, crossing the Connasauga with his whole army, abandoning everything that would impede his march. Even his dead and wounded were left to the care of the Union general. Among the stores abandoned were twenty-three

---

897 (Morhous 1879, 85)
898 (OR, Series I Vol 38 Part 2 Serial 73: Reports n.d., 293) On picket the night before and then reconnaissance in the morning, did they even get breakfast?

thousand sacks of corn and oats, and more than one hundred thousand rounds of ammunition. At 8 o'clock a.m. the whole army started in pursuit. The route of the 20th Corps was over the battlefield. Near where the battery was captured a letter was found written by its commanding officer to his father, stating that some Yankees, who wore stars on their hats (the badge of the 20th Corps) had captured his battery. He said that none but Joe Hooker's men could have done it. And that when they charged his battery they did not mind shot any more than a duck would water. The results of the campaign, thus far, briefly stated, were, a Union loss of five thousand men and a much larger one to the enemy, which had been forced out and sent flying full retreat from his strongest position on the route to Atlanta. _899

Recall Sherman's message to Thomas on the 13th, wanting Johnston to be south of the Oostanaula before he encountered Hooker (now Dodge). That may be one reason Dodge was not already blocking the roads.

STANLEY, 1D 4C: Johnston took an immense risk in fighting north of the Oostanula. A single break in his line and his army was lost. _900

Johnston sure seems wily here, seeming ready to fight again, then making his escape right past Dodge before Dodge woke up in the morning?

STONE, THOMAS' STAFF: Some idea of the strength of Johnston's position, and the character of his works, may be drawn from a remark of General Poe, Sherman's Chief Engineer, after he had made a careful inspection on the morning of the 16th. "Yesterday," he said, "I was afraid they would run away. To-day, after what I have seen, I find I ought to have been afraid they wouldn't." _901

Our brigade, Harrison and company, had gotten around that fort in front of the works and had broken the line, but only for a moment. Had Hooker untangled the rest of his Corps and gotten them up behind our brigade, could Sherman have broken up Johnston's army before they could escape? One of those unknowns to ponder endlessly. But that day is over.

CINCINNATI COMMERCIAL: We have taken nearly four thousand prisoners and deserters, including many Colonels, Majors, and line and staff officers.

899 (Storrs 1886, 127)
900 (Stanley 1917, 163)
901 (Stone 1910, 389) Stone was a member Thomas' staff.

Many of them were willing prisoners, who remained in the rebel works and surrendered when we advanced in pursuit. 902

TREMAIN: Bridges had been prepared by Sherman at other points across the Oostenaula, so that all day yesterday a strong column of cavalry, infantry and artillery were in hot pursuit. Today the whole army is close upon the heels of Johnston, and already beyond Calhoun. The enemy will probably make a stand at Altoona. 903

TREMAIN: After the late grand exertions in aid of the Sanitary Fair, you will be interested to know that the agents of the Sanitary Commission were on hand as soon as possible, and their stores arrived here as early as any trains could come through. They visited some of the field hospitals with a few supplies taken in wagons on the last day of the battle; and yesterday and today, while the wounded are being removed, from hospitals to cars, the few agents here have been very assiduous in providing for their comfort in furnishing cooked coffee and other necessaries of life in cases which it is not always possible for the medical authorities to reach. 904

That slight advance by Logan had gotten within cannon range of the bridges that were Johnston's escape route but had not destroyed the wagon bridge.

NEW YORK HERALD: With the exception of another slight advance on the part of Logan's corps, on the extreme right, accomplished without material loss, this was the only portion of the army seriously engaged during the 15th. Our batteries along the entire line had been diligently employed, diverting the enemy's attention to assist General Hooker in his work, but the serious work had been left to Hooker and his corps, and what was assigned them to do was fully accomplished in every particular, as was demonstrated by the subsequent movements of the enemy. General Butterfield, with his division, fought splendidly, and won unbounded praise. The same must be said of Gen. Williams and his veteran division. 905

COBURN, 2B 3D 20C: The losses of the brigade in this action are as follows: one officer killed and seven wounded, 26 men killed and 191 wounded, and one man missing. I refer to the reports of the regimental commanders for the names of officers and men killed and wounded, and for acts of

---

902 (Correspondence of the Cincinnati Commercial 1864)
903 (Tremain 1905, 171)
904 (Tremain 1905, 171)
905 (Bradley 1865, 107)

distinguished merit. Early in the action Col. Henry C. Gilbert, Nineteenth Michigan. was mortally wounded while leading his men up to the rebel works. His life has been gloriously sacrificed to his country in the front rank of her soldiers. Captain Calmer, of the same regiment, was killed on the top of their ramparts, and Captain Patton and Lieutenant Flint, of the Twenty-second Wisconsin, mortally wounded close beside him. The conduct of the brigade under the peculiarly trying circumstances was excellent. Their (brigade) determined and gallant charge secured the position so boldly won by the First Brigade, and together they held it, under the very muzzles of the enemy's guns, five hours in daylight. .906

OSBORN, CO A 55TH OHIO WOOD 3B 3D 20C: The Fifty-Fifth Ohio suffered severely in this battle, losing twenty-three killed and seventy wounded, and indeed, never recovered from the loss of so many officers. It never paraded with full ranks again. .907

COLLINS, 149TH NY IRELAND 3B 2D 20C: After a short respite for breakfast, to bury the dead and care for the wounded, the division fell in and marched through the enemy's entrenchments towards Resaca. By the roadside stood the four brass guns, which had received the men's attention the day before, with their carriages and limber-boxes ruined by rifle balls, and the guns themselves covered with lead marks, presenting the appearance of a man's face recovering from small pox. It was reputed that these were the balance of a battery, two guns of which were captured at Lookout Mountain. .908

TREMAIN: In entering the rebel works at Resaca four more guns were found abandoned—old and useless, however—while those taken by Butterfield were fine twelve pounders, complete with limbers and carriages. .909

BENTON, BAND, 150TH NY RUGER 2B 1D 20C: The turkey buzzards, with their sooty, dishevelled plumage and filthy beaks, were circling lower and lower over the field, but the Pioneer Corps were busy now burying the dead, both of the Blue and the Gray, while the wounded were being got away to the North. So these North American vultures would feast this time only on

906 (OR, Series I Vol 38 Part 2 Serial 73: Reports n.d., 377)
907 (Osborn 1904, 147)
908 (Collins 1891, 250)
909 (Tremain 1905, 171) See Hood's claim to have abandoned only old iron pieces. Reader may speculate on Hood's real knowledge or his motives.

dead horses. Youth and Hope go hand in hand and will not be depressed, and as we pushed on after the enemy we laughed and joked as before. ﹍910

Now the game changes somewhat. Sherman having the advantage in resources, Johnston wants to keep him at bay, following just close enough that Johnston can catch him in a mistake:

> JOHNSTON, CSA: On the 16th the enemy crossed the Oostenaula. Lieutenant-General Hardee skirmished with them successfully near Calhoun. The fact that a part of Polk's troops were still in the rear, and the great numerical superiority of the Federal army, made it expedient to risk battle only when position or some blunder on the part of the enemy might give us counterbalancing advantages.

And to keep Sherman so busy he cannot lend some soldiers to Grant:

> I, therefore, determined to fall back slowly until circumstances should put the chances of battle in our favor, keeping so near the U. S. army as to prevent its sending re-enforcements to Grant, and hoping, by taking advantage of positions and opportunities, to reduce the odds against us by partial engagements. I also expected it to be materially reduced before the end of June by the expiration of the terms of service of many of the regiments which had not re-enlisted. In this way we fell back to Cassville in two marches. ﹍911

So they leave behind the remains of the Battle of Resaca.

Spindrift

Spindrift. Spray blown from cresting waves during a gale —Dictionary

The other two corps, Hooker's and Howard's, will make a steady and strong attack on the enemy along down the ridge between Camp Creek and the Connesauga toward Resaca, but will not assault fortified positions unless sure of success. —Sherman to Thomas

There is no doubt that Joseph Johnston's army was in a perilous position here and, if Hooker's assault ... had been supported, the rebel army would have been destroyed. They were terribly frightened and from where I stood I could see the Rebel right from which men were running away by the hundreds. —Stanley

910 (Benton 1902, 144)
911 (OR, Series I Vol 38 Part 2 Serial 73: Reports n.d., 615)

The honor of leading the assault to break the key defensive point was given to a brigade with no battle experience, whose commander was reputed to be drunk and inept. Supporting their right was a brigade with less training in mock battles and which had not yet been in a general engagement. It was their chance at last to distinguish themselves in action, to do something effective toward winning the war and going home. They did all that was asked and lived up to their own expectations, many sacrificing their lives. So it seems fair to ask: was the assault a success? Did it move the Union closer to victory?

Sherman wanted to avoid fighting in the hills against a well-entrenched opponent. It would be like pitching against the walls of the castle. His option, if he could not bag Johnston then and there, was to force him out of Resaca into open terrain. For the day, he had two objectives: in the north, close the gap to the Connesauga and, in the south, control the railroad to block Johnston's supply. For the latter, he needed Johnston to stay put until he could get there.

A siege was to be avoided. How long could Johnston hold out behind those entrenchments? Possibly months, given past experiences, notably Vicksburg. What would history have looked like after months-long sieges of Lee in Petersburg and Johnston in Resaca and no end to the Confederacy? Might Lincoln have lost the election? That would get the South what it wanted: the Union lost and slavery overrunning the west—all that death and destruction for nothing.

So, not shelling the bridges might have been a calculated risk: inviting Johnston out in the open; that depended on what Sherman was able to do on Sunday. A fight at the other end, then, might encourage Johnston to get out of Resaca—if he still had a way out.

Johnston had, during the winter, prepared his defenses from Dallas to Atlanta anticipating such a campaign of sapping strength of the offense, drawing them deeper into Confederate territory, wearying Sherman and waiting, as he said, for Sherman to make a mistake, a bit like drawing Napoleon all the way to Moscow. Today the game for Sherman was to solidify his hold and encourage Johnston to leave, but not before Dodge was in place—not before he could get in front of Johnston.

Hooker wanted to follow up on last night's repulse of Hood. His midnight advice to Sherman had been: "To do it effectually in the morning, in my judgment, the advance should be on two lines, one along the line of railroad, the other along the Dalton and Resaca highway." He further added: "Had any considerable portion of my corps been in position I would have followed up the success." On

Sunday, Hood had two less brigades at his disposal than the night before. Yet Hooker did not follow the plan he had proposed. First, he wanted "all troops in position by daylight." Sheridan and Grant possibly would have gotten in position, but not Thomas and Sherman. Hooker did have divisions of Geary as well as of Williams. Hood certainly would have been caught off the hill, unprepared, before breakfast. What would Grant and Sheridan, who equated delay with defeat, have done? But, Butterfield had been selected—his brigades, wagons and all, were just starting their trek north at dawn. It would be a long wait.

When the generals met in the grove on Sunday morning, Sherman knew he almost had Johnston in that proverbial nine-hole, the only out being across the Oostanaula. He likely did not know that Johnston had already sent his wagons and a cover of infantry south, in preparation, no doubt, for evacuation.

Sherman told Thomas: "I want to hear the sound of that line advancing directly down the road on Resaca till it comes within range of the forts." What did he mean? Try to break through Hindman's line? No, he had to get *past* the forts to do that. Sherman, then, thought of Hooker being north of the "forts." Seems he only wanted pressure on Hood so Schofield could get to the river—to secure the north end of the Union line. He admonished to "not assault fortified positions unless sure of success." Hooker had already made his own decision: when they started north, Butterfield's officers knew they were going to assault the fort.

It was up to Thomas. Sherman wrote no instructions about just how Howard and Hooker were to make that "steady and strong" attack "down and along" the ridge. Hooker must have convinced Thomas that he could break Stevenson's line. But then what? Oh, to have been a bird at that 9:30 morning meeting—to have heard the generals discuss their assignments! Did Thomas defer too much to Hooker, thinking Hooker perceived enough to plan that far? Thomas also had Newton's corps, still facing Camp Creek, to manage. Hooker, by then, was in charge of dealing with Hood. He also had Howard—remember Chancellorsville?

The result? Sherman's objective was to hold the Confederate line long enough to allow Dodge to get across the river. This was done. Was it to hold them in position long enough for Sherman to get troops on Johnston's left flank, and cut or at least control the railroad? This was not done, and the Rebels abandoned the field—keeping the railroad. Sherman at least got his left anchored on the river. Johnston flanking Sherman was prevented, which was of course desired. But Sherman was now not face-to-face with Johnston's army, which was intact, not scattered—not bagged. Sherman had been left behind—holding the bag.

So, what did Hooker accomplish? No reports on the Battle of Resaca by either Butterfield or Hooker are available, not in the Official Record or any known source—not in words. The day after the battle, James Walker began work, on the site, for a painting that Butterfield commissioned and featured in a grand lithograph memorializing the event. .912 After the war he gave a grand dinner in honor of Hooker's achievements, the one at Resaca – the only one at Resaca —being the capture of the battery – a trophy.

What became of the two-pronged effort? To admonish not to assault unless sure of success suggests there was no attack planned behind the ridge, for if there was, the frontal assault would not be optional; it would be crucial.

But Hooker made no arrangements to assault Stewart while assaulting Stevenson. Had Stewart been under attack when Stevenson's men fled, especially since they might have collided with Stewart's men and disorganized them, the hill might have been carried. Howard and Geary, who were available and mostly idle, could perhaps have followed clear through Hood's main line east of the road.

General Stanley: "There is no doubt that Joseph Johnston's army was in a perilous position here and, if Hooker's assault the next day had been supported, the rebel army would have been destroyed. They were terribly frightened and from where I stood I could see the Rebel right from which men were running away by the hundreds." .913

Sergeant Ketcham: "That we were not fired into by the Rebels from behind their intrenchments for ten minutes after taking the guns, proves the statement of a prisoner that a whole Rebel brigade behind those works threw down their guns and ran, found we didn't follow, rallied and gave us fits. What a sad mistake in not advancing! But we did not know, thought that all there was to be done was to take the guns." .914

The first failure, then, was not attacking Stewart's line. Why was it not done? If there were valid reasons they have not been given to us; such an effort seems to have been dropped from consideration. Thomas had more than enough men, yet

912 (J. L. Butterfield 1904, 144) Statement from List of Illustrations: "From a large painting by James Walker, presented to the Old Guard Association by General Butterfield." Thomas, Butterfield, and Hooker are pictured at top, on horseback. Lithograph copyright is 1897. The Benjamin Harrison Presidential Site has a copy.
913 (Stanley 1917, 181)
914 (C. Merrill 1866, 708)

Williams and Schofield did not even head toward Stewart's front until Butterfield was already making his first move.

The full effort was directed at the corner of the bend in Hood's line, where the guns were. Hooker and Geary sent Geary's 3rd Brigade right behind Butterfield, unknown to him, supposedly as support. Geary gave lie to the purpose by saying Ireland and Ward were racing for the same prize, the battery. Perhaps, then, Geary's plan was for Butterfield to fight at the Rebel line while Ireland followed, leapfrogging to the guns. Were Ward and Coburn to be sacrificial brigades? Was that why Geary was so close behind? To pick up the spoils? To be the second mouse after the bait? Butterfield was sent to break the line. Geary, behind him, intended to go no further. When Harrison and Coburn found the guns in front of the line, Geary simply waited for them to finish that fight and then got Hooker to relieve them so he could collect the spoils.

The second failure was to cram too many men into one point, getting into each other's way, making perfect targets for the enemy and for their own comrades!

The third failure was not following up Butterfield's initial success. As Ketcham said, "all there was to be done was to take the guns." Others were expected to follow the opening. They did not. Who did not? Geary and Williams of Hooker's Corps; Schofield; and Howard—none of them. They were to "look for opportunities" if Hooker succeeded. The moment was brief and not realized by Hooker. They were not told.

Had there been the attack on Stewart, the moment might not have been so brief. Had there been more planning on contingencies, they might have succeeded. But the moment was lost.

Look at Walker's painting. The assaulting column is not prominent. It is far left. The main background feature is where the road to Resaca goes through the gap in Hindman's line. Howard is front center. Walker was positioned to show action there. That seems to have been Hooker's hope, though not Sherman's expectation. But the only action was brief, an attempt by Hazen to keep Hindman busy. But that was not supported by Howard's other brigades. It started and ended too early to help Butterfield.

Hooker had massed his large attacking force on a small hill facing the point, like forcing them through a funnel. Too packed to go anywhere, they were good targets for the Rebels and too disorganized to do anything effective. There would have been plenty of troops for that other prong against Stewart. Instead, after Butterfield was exhausted and Geary was occupied, Johnston was able to send

Hood out of his trenches to flank and perhaps get behind Hooker and Howard. He would not have been able to organize and do that had Hooker attacked him while Butterfield broke the line.

Not only was no attack against Stewart planned, Williams had no instructions at all, even when the Confederates were retreating and most vulnerable. Williams had no one to support if he did attack; Butterfield was worn out. Geary was preoccupied. Schofield had Hovey's untrained division on Williams' left.

So the day ended doing what? Figuring out how to retrieve the guns. They were a distraction, a leg for Hooker to chew on while Johnston escaped.

A little satire: if Butterfield and Hooker had money to pay two artists, might Hooker have positioned another near the railroad and had Williams attack simultaneously with Butterfield?

Wilbur Kurtz, who spent much time mapping the Resaca battlefield area, especially the battery angle, 80 years after the war, having little more than the Official Record available, described the brigades being so hopelessly entangled that their effort was like an angry sea crashing on the rocks, dissipated in spindrift. Another factor he mentioned: the well-known "self-assertion" of generals.

Add the obvious devotion of certain of them to fame, fortune, and future prospects. How did it happen that Walker the painter was on hand to witness the battle, quiz participants, make sketches, and start his work? Was he simply moonlighting? Sketch artists drew for newspapers, for immediate consumption. A painting takes time, effort, and several skills; it is expensive. Butterfield had means; it was to be a major assault and glorious victory then and there at Resaca, or at least the glory of capturing four cannon. So how much did that affect some minds? Just four twelve-pounders to show for it? It just does not seem that Hooker and Butterfield were taking "the long view" except for their own prospects after the war.

Thomas seems to have let Hooker run his own show. The "well-known self-assertion of generals" sometimes meant others let them live or die by their own resources, to fame or flame so to speak, thus to get the blame for failures, yet to give their commanders glory for success, the men living or dying accordingly, as Bierce so well described.

Such a waste.

Many in One Grave

Many in one grave, our fallen brothers rest. And is not the coincidence a fitting one? Will not this common grave be cherished with a sacred pride by all who love our country's flag? -915 —Fleharty

War is a cruel thing, it heeds not the widow's tear, the orphan's moan, or the lover's anguish. -916 —Deavenport

FLEHARTY, 102ND ILL WARD 1B 3D 20C: During the night of the 15th the rebels evacuated their entire line of works and retreated in the direction of Atlanta. The scene on the battle-ground the following day was sad beyond description. The day was calm indeed the stillness was oppressive. We were permitted to wander over the field and view the effects of the fierce struggle. -917

WARD, 1B 3D 20C: In the charge all of my officers and men (except two field officers now out of service) are entitled to praise. But for a fire in the rear (by mistake) I am satisfied that we would not only have succeeded in carrying the battery, but should also have carried the breast-works. We lost in this fight many brave men, but the enemy lost more. We buried 54 of our men and about 90 rebels, they having left their works during the night. leaving their dead on the ground. My brigade was ordered to bury the dead and to gather the trophies. We turned in the four pieces of artillery and about 2,000 stand of small-arms. The part taken in this battle by the Second and Third Brigades can be better shown in the brigade commanders reports; I knew but little; I saw the Third Brigade advance, attack, and return [not possible] before I was ordered to advance; I saw none of the Second Brigade, except the Nineteenth Michigan, and that I placed with my command. This regiment fought bravely, losing some 15 or 20 killed and a great many wounded. Colonel Gilbert was mortally wounded and died in a few days; he behaved most gallantly, fighting like a hero. -918

CONGLETON, CO F 105TH ILL WARD 1B 3D 20C: Our Brigade is to bury the dead & go over the field to gather the arms that are laying around. With the rest we have four 12 lb. brass cannon which belched forth shot and shell dealing out death to our men. Today when I walked over the ground over

915 (Fleharty, Our Regiment. A History of the 102d Illinois Infantry Volunteers 1865, 61)
916 (Deavenport 1861-1864)
917 (Fleharty, Our Regiment. A History of the 102d Illinois Infantry Volunteers 1865, 60)
918 (OR, Series I Vol 38 Part 2 Serial 73: Reports n.d., 320)

which we marched yesterday I am surprised that any of us are alive today. The bushes were mown down by the balls and the trees were filled with balls. It surprises me that one could be there and come out alive ... We are very thankful that so many of our boys passed through the fearful night without being killed or wounded. I think it is marvelous. .919

CASE, 129TH ILL WARD 1B 3D 20C: The loss in my regiment was as follows: Killed, 9; wounded, 39 men and 2 officers. The men killed were buried on the field the next day. During the daytime of the 16th the One hundred and twenty-ninth, with the other regiments of our brigade, was engaged in burying the dead and gathering up small-arms upon the field, but started about sunset en route to overtake the retreating foe. .920

STILLWELL, CHAPLAIN, 79TH OHIO WARD 1B 3D 20C: After the Battle I went to the division Hospital where I worked most all night. Such sights I never saw before 500 or more wounded and dying men crying for help. I saw in one pile the next day 25 or 30 amputated arms or legs ... Gen. Ward was wounded in the left arm above the elbow but is still with his Command. He is evidently a brave man and we think much more of him than before. Our men are more attached to each other than ever and there is less profanity and no drunkenness. The Rebels said they supposed we was all drunk or we would never have undertaken such a charge ... Chaplains Allen, Cotton and myself held appropriate religious Services at the grave—a large concourse of soldiers were present among the number and at the head of the grave was Gen. Ward. .921

BUTTERFIELD, 3D 20C: The Major-General commanding feels it a duty as well as a pleasure to congratulate the division upon its achievements yesterday. The gallant assault and charge of the First Brigade, capturing four guns in the enemy's fort; the support of this assault by a portion of the Second Brigade, the splendid advance of the Third Brigade on the left, with the glorious repulse it gave twice its force, proves the division worthy a high name and fame. Let everyone endeavor by attention to duty, obedience to orders, devotion and courage to make our record in future, as in the past, such that the army and the country will ever be proud of us. .922

919 (Congleton n.d.)
920 (OR, Series I Vol 38 Part 2 Serial 73: Reports n.d., 365)
921 (Stillwell 2016)
922 (S. Merrill 1900, 105)

WARD, 1B 3D 20C: That night the brigade occupied the works on the hill built by us and left in the morning by a part of the Fourth Corps. In this movement I lost 64 enlisted men killed, 13 commissioned officers and 308 enlisted men wounded, 1 enlisted man missing. The next day the brigade was detailed to bury the dead and gather up arms, which duty they performed well, and started at sunset and overtook the division at Field's Mill. .923

ARMSTRONG, CO B 102ND ILL WARD 1B 3D 20C: To a wife: It was a terrible charge and many received their last call and summon. Mr. Kellogg fell doing his duty as a good soldier and as you are called to mourn the loss of a husband, I also feel the loss of my best Soldier but while we mourn we should remember there is hope in his death as in all his walk since joining the company he has maintained a steady Christian character. We were first in the charge and had to fall back once then rallied and retained the field. In the interval everything had been taken from his pockets nothing having been left in the morning of them. I sent out some men and buried our men two in number ... Excepting the two from Co. "B" 102d Mr. Kellogg & Stephen Cussins that were buried before we knew of the intention to bury all in one place The Brigade grave yard is just below the fort where Wards Brigade took the guns, some 10 rods. The graves of my two men are about forty rods to the left of the Brigade under an oak tree. .924

FLEHARTY, 102ND ILL WARD 1B 3D 20C: The dead of both armies were being buried some singly where they fell, others in a common grave. In a deep trench surrounded by evergreen pines, fifty-one of the slain of the 1st Brigade were buried. The scene at the grave was deeply impressive. An immense crowd of soldiers gathered around to hear the remarks of an aged chaplain, ere the forms of their comrades were forever hidden from sight. "Many in one," said the venerable minister, "is the motto borne proudly on our nation's banner. Many in one grave, our fallen brothers rest. And is not the coincidence a fitting one? Will not this common grave be cherished with a sacred pride by all who love our country's flag?" At the conclusion of his remarks the work of burial was accomplished, tenderly and carefully as the circumstances would permit, by the comrades of the slain. But to the living, sad as the surroundings were, the day after the battle seemed like the

923 (OR, Series I Vol 38 Part 2 Serial 73: Reports n.d., 338)
924 (Armstrong 1864) Letter to Kellogg's widow. About 160 feet below. About 1/8 mile left.

beginning of a new life. Peace and repose, how sweet, after the withering tornado of human wrath had swept by! _925

MERRILL, 70TH IND WARD 1B 3D 20C:The sixteenth of May was a sad day for our regiment. Twenty-six of our number had sacrificed their lives, and one hundred and thirty had been seriously wounded, many mortally, in this Sabbath day's "baptism of fire." It was a strange grave by which the surviving members stood. It was six feet long and sixty wide. Into this, side by side, with blankets for winding sheets, were lowered the forms of those who had just died for their country. Evergreen branches were tenderly dropped on the sleeping patriots, to break the fall of the clods, and as a token that their sacrifice would ever be green in the memory of their comrades. With heads uncovered the mourners gathered about the grave. The Captains of the companies cast in the first earth, and the Chaplain prayed that the sad tidings might not crush the hearts of the mothers, the widows and the orphans. The sinking sun closed the mournful day, and the dead were left to sleep in their glory, while to the living remained the stern duty of pursuing through the night the retreating battalions of the enemy. _926

STURGIS JOURNAL, STURGIS MICHIGAN, IN FIELD MAY 30, 1864, REPORTING FROM THE 19TH MICHIGAN: The loss in Co. E, 3 killed and 11 wounded. Killed – Serg't Wm. J. Smith, private, Thos. W. Barr and J. G. Gibson ... Our men killed were buried in the fort just taken. _927

BRADLEY, CHAPLAIN, 22ND WIS COBURN 2B 3D 20C During the night, our men secured the cannon, and the rebels evacuated their works, and morning finds us busy burying the dead. Ten men were laid in one trench within the fort where they fell. _928 _929

DICKINSON, 22ND WIS COBURN 2B 3D 20C: The rebels gone, and our forces in hot persuit; I was left back in charge of a burial party; we lost from our Regiment, 10 killed and about 70 wounded, 1 man, S. K. King and 5 badly wounded in my Co. E. we buried our ten, dead heroes, inside of the Fort

925 (Fleharty, Our Regiment. A History of the 102d Illinois Infantry Volunteers 1865)
926 (S. Merrill 1900, 77)
927 (Sturgis Journal, Army Correspondent 1864)
928 (Bradley 1865, 96)
929 Letter to Madison Journal. On the north, the right side of the fort, standing inside, are two pits from which bodies had been removed for reburial in Chattanooga National Cemetery.

they died in capturing. We marched about 18 miles, crossed the Coosawattie River at twelve o'clock in the night, and went into camp. ‗930

STRONG, CO B 105TH ILL WARD 1B 3D 20C: Our brigade was detailed to bury the dead. Of all disagreeable jobs, that was the worst of any I ever took a hand in. It was our first experience, and to carry men to a hole and dump them in was almost too much for me. Some had been dead for three or four days, and the flesh would not hold together to lift them. So we put them in blankets, or tied the legs of their pants and their coat sleeves together and gently dragged them to their last resting place. We came across a Rebel hospital with a few Rebel surgeons who had been left to care for their wounded. The hospital was simply a shade made of limbs of trees thrown over poles. Near the hospital was a pile of arms, legs, hands, and feet that had been cut from the wounded. These had not been buried, just thrown in a pile, and worms had begun to work on them. On one part of the battlefield the leaves had taken fire, I suppose from shells, and we found a few of the dead who had more or less burned. It is all truly horrible, and if you tell me you don't want anything more on battle scenes, why all right. But so many things come to mind, some worse than these. ‗931

RYDER, CO I 33RD MASS, WOOD 3B 1D 20C: We brought off our dead and buried them in a long trench beside the road, and marked each name on a board at the head of each body...As we thought of those who only a few days ago were as full of life and hope as we but were now sleeping close together, waiting for the reveille of the Resurrection morning, we could not help the feeling of sadness at our loss of their companionship. ‗932

D. M. RANSDALL, CO G 70TH IND WARD 1B 3D 20C: At Resaca I was standing on my left foot and right knee, engaged in putting a percussion cap on my gun, the piece resting across my left leg, my left hand holding the cap, and my right the gun, with my thumb on the hammer, which was drawn back. I was thinking of but one thing, and that was to get ready to shoot as quickly as possible. I had forgotten all about danger. Just as I got the cap on I had a sudden sensation as though I had been struck a smart blow across my right wrist with a stick. The next instant the gun fell out of my hand and I noticed the blood gushing in spurts from the wrist. Physiology having been one of my favorite studies in Franklin College, from which I had entered the army,

930 (Dickinson n.d.)
931 (Strong 1961)
932 (Ryder 1928, 55)

I knew at once that an artery had been cut, and I seized the forearm above the wound with my left hand, and compressed it so as to stop the hemorrhage. I felt little pain owing, I suppose, to my excitement.

Being now disarmed and wounded, and so unable to continue the fight, I began to realize something of the surrounding dangers and my peril from them. Looking about me as best I could under the circumstances I reached the conclusion that the proper time had come for me to retire, and that if I did not get away with some expedition I might be killed or captured. While I still hesitated I noticed Tom Clark of my company, not more than four feet away on the right. He was lying on his stomach, with head up and gun presented, evidently watching for a chance to make an effective shot. As I looked at him a ball struck him in the throat, and as it entered his vitals, he uttered such a hideous scream as I never heard before or since. It killed him instantly. I waited no longer. 933

This incident decided my course and accelerated my movements. I could see no place of refuge. The few trees there already protected all they could cover. There were bushes, but they afforded no shelter, the most of them having already been cut off by the bullets, as though a woodman had passed through with an ax. It was certain death to stand up, the balls were flying so thickly. But one way of escape presented itself and that I adopted. Lying down flat on the ground I proceeded to roll down the hill the best way I could. I think it must have been nearly one hundred yards. When I reached the foot I got up and ran across, and down the valley still holding my arm. It seems a miracle that I escaped being hit again, for the bullets were humming through the air in a fearful way. I followed the valley a short distance until a bend to the left took me to a place of safety. As I passed on I encountered General Hooker, who was sitting on a horse, with his feet out of the stirrups, studying a map. My boy, said he in a kindly voice, you are wounded. You will find an ambulance to take you to the hospital by following this road.

When all was ready I went to the dissecting table, where chloroform was administered and the limb taken off midway between the wrist and elbow. It was the first operation performed after the candles were lighted. As I came to consciousness, I experienced a most delicious sensation. I felt as though I had been floating for hours in a place given up wholly to a delightful existence. It was some time before I noticed my pain, and then it was only slight; but the next day it was severe enough. I was also uncomfortable

933 (S. Merrill 1900, 201)

otherwise, being compelled to lie flat on my back, with nothing but a rubber blanket under me. _934

Ward's brigade was not the only unit left behind. One unfortunate regiment of Ireland's brigade lost many on an unsupported charge that was called off too late.

MOUAT, CO G, 29TH PENN IRELAND 3B 2D 20C: I was detailed with several others of our Company to bury our men, we wrapped them in their blankets and buried them side by side and made head boards with their names—companies & Regt out of pieces of Cracker boxes—it was a sorrowful job. After getting through we started on after the Regiment and caught up with after traveling about 10 miles and bivouacked near the Coosa River. _935

PORTER, SANITARY COMMISSION: Never have I passed such a Sabbath as yesterday, and I wish I could believe there never would be such another ... The wounded were brought into hospitals, quickly and roughly prepared in the forest, as near the field as safety would permit ... What a scene was presented! Precious sons of northern mothers, beloved husbands of northern wives were already here to undergo amputation, to have wounds probed and dressed, or broken limbs and bandaged. Some were writhing under the surgeon's knife, but bore their suffering bravely and uncomplainingly. There were many whose wounds were considered slight, such as shot through the hand, arm, or leg, which but for the contrast with severer cases, would seem dreadful. Never was the presence of women more joyfully welcomed. It was touching to see those precious boys looking up into our faces with such hope and gladness. It brought to their minds mother and home, as each testified while his wounds were being dressed; "This seems a little like having mother about," was the reiterated expression of the wounded, as one after another was washed and had his wounds dressed. Mrs. Bickerdyke and myself assisted in the operation. Poor boys! how my heart ached that I could do so little. ... We found what we brought in the ambulance was giving untold comfort to our poor exhausted wounded men, whose rough hospital couches were made by pine boughs with the stems cut out. spread upon the ground, over which their blankets were thrown. This forms the bed, and the poor fellows' blouses, saturated with their own blood. is their only pillow, their knapsacks being left behind

934 (S. Merrill 1900, 201)
935 (Mouat n.d.)

when they went into battle ... Several wounded men have died during the night. .936

Letters Home

These "boys" have been so long with me that I feel as if a friend had fallen, though I recognize no face that I can recollect to have seen before. But I think of some sorrowful heart at home and oh, Minnie, how sadly my heart sinks with the thought.
—Williams

Hooker has a big name out here now, but I can't say much of Geary to tell the truth he aint worth his salt the people are a great deal mistaken in him.
—Mouat

They all wore a star. —Corput

After marching five days following the battle, a three-day halt May 20 at Cassville gave time for writing letters, many to notify families of their loss.

EPPERLY, 54TH VIRGINIA, STEVENSON, CSA: DEAR Mary I can tell you it was a serious time to see so many of our dear Boys fall to the ground and be cut to peases by bomshells and Minny balls we are now about 40 milels from Adlanta and I sopose will be thair befor they will mak another stand or at least our men is compeld to fall back and I beleave the yankees wil flank them out of that plase I don't think we can get men anuff to stand them a fight soon again: ther is missing out of this Regt 2.50 [250] men kild wounded and missing ther was som 55 kild and about 64 wounded and the ballans is missing som of them is taken prisners and I cent tell what has becom of the rest I must soon close and havent much room to writ and have no mor paper nor mony to buy with tell father I will writ to him as soon as I can.

LAFOREST DUNHAM, CO C, 129TH ILL WARD 1B 3D 20C: May 20, 1864. We had a fight last sabath. We went in the fight about one o'clock and it lasted till long in the eavening. Our Briggade charged on a fort and we took it too. Thare was four pieces of cannon in it and the rebs used them on ous pretty well. I tell you we was under fire four days but we clerd the rebs out pretty well. Corporel Howard was kild. You knew him I gues. He was home on a furlow last summer. Frank Barr had too fingers shot off of his right hand. Thare was one kild and eight wooded in our company. Delos Robinson and Roo ... came out all right. For my part I dont care about getting in to

936 (Porter 1866, 659)

annother one but I thought shure we would have annother pull at it again yesterday. We was scaremushing all day yesterday. We have ben driveing them right before ous ever since last Sunday. Lieutenant Smith of Co. A was wonded, I dont know how bad. Martin Delaune was wounded. One bullet came close enough to me to cut my coat on the joint of my left sholder and one went through my hare. my hat fell off and as I grabd it one took me through the hare and top of my head. Thare was forty seven kild and wonded in the Regt. I have thought of it a good many times since however a man escaped for the rebs was so well fortified. The same place had ben charged on five times before by our troops and they could not take it, but we took it the first charge but it was a horible sight. I wont wright any more about it for you will see it in the papers, so I will come to a close. .937

WILLIAMS, 1D 20C: The fight ended about dusk and in the morning there was no enemy in front. I went out over the field in our front, not out of curiosity but to see what was in advance. There were scores of dead Rebels lying in the woods all along our front, and I confess a feeling of pity as I saw them. One old grey headed man proved to be a chaplain of the Rebel regiment, and it is rather a singular coincidence that one of our own chaplains (3rd Wisconsin) was seriously wounded directly in front of where he was found dead. Early in the war I had a curiosity to ride over a battlefield. Now feel nothing but sorrow and compassion, and it is with reluctance that I go over these sad fields. Especially so, when I see a "blue jacket" lying stretched in the attitude that nobody can mistake who has seen the dead on a battlefield. These "boys" have been so long with me that I feel as if a friend had fallen, though I recognize no face that I can recollect to have seen before. But I think of some sorrowful heart at home and oh, Minnie, how sadly my heart sinks with the thought.

I put parties to bury the dead Rebels but was ordered away before half were collected over the mile and a half in our front. I fear many were left unburied, though I left detachments to gather up all they could find. As I marched away, I was obliged to go along the line where my own dead were being collected by their comrades and interred in graves carefully marked with name, rank, and company. It is interesting to see how tenderly and solemnly they gather together their dead comrades in some chosen spot, and with what sorrowful countenances they lay them in their last resting

937 (DeRosier 1969)

place. There is much that is beautiful as well as sad in these bloody events. I lost in this battle between four and five hundred killed and wounded. .938

WINKLER, 26TH WIS WOOD 3B 3D 20C: May 22nd, 1864. This is a much pleasanter Sunday morning than it was a week ago, not in point of weather alone, but it is more Sunday like. No booming of cannon, no rattling of musketry, no ordering voices harsh with excitement, no shrieks of wounded, no groans of dying, no confusion of battle disturbs the holy quiet of the Sabbath Day. A week ago the riot of human weakness, folly and passion seemed to contend with the goodness of God and for a time almost to gain mastery over it; Nature was calm and placid, the happy birds sung merrily in green boughs, the air was balmy and soft, all betokened the beneficence of the Ruler above, but man converted this scene of peaceful calm to a Pandemonium of terror and destruction until Night kindly threw its mantle over the scene and screened the combatants from each other's view. Brave men may, but I believe there are very few, if any, who take delight in battle, and very few who in the heat of an engagement will not welcome the coming night as that of a friend who will stop the fierce wrangle and bring relief to the struggling men. There is something so providentially kind in it to those who have survived the dangers of the day, in the fall of night upon the battle field. It brings relief to the anxious heart and inspires it with gratitude to God for the favors shown during those hours of danger. .939

STILLWELL, CHAPLAIN, 79TH OHIO WARD 1B 3D 20C: I wrote you on yesterday for the first since the 6th inst. I would have written every day but I understood no mail would be permitted to go north of Nashville until after the 30th. I will now write every day when opportunity is afforded. This is a beautiful Sabbath except the warm weather. Fortunately however we are encamped in the woods. We have been here since Friday but will probably leave on tomorrow—perhaps for Atlanta if the Rebels are there. It is assumed that they have gone to help Lee—if so we will be in hot pursuit so soon as we have learned that fact. We are determined to crush this Rebellion. I can now see the propriety of restricting us to but one wagon to each Regt. that we may move on rapidly and not have a large wagon train to guard. I shall have church in a few moments. Bro. Cotton of the 129th Ills and myself will unite as our Regts are encamped side by side. Last night we held prayer and speaking meeting together. We agreed to day to talk 10 minutes each from "Acknowledge the Lord in all thy ways and he shall direct thy paths." Bro. Culver a local preacher and Lieut in the 129th is included.

938 (Williams 1963, 400)
939 (F. Winkler n.d.)

10 minutes each will make 30 mins. On last monday we buried our dead in one grave 4 ft deep and covered the dead first with cedar and then with earth. Each one is designated by an appropriate head and foot board with name, Co. Regt. and date. 51 Brave boys be slumbering there side by side from the 1st Brig. 3d Div. XX Corps. Chaplains Allen, Cotton and myself held appropriate religious Services at the grave—a large concourse of soldiers were present among the number and at the head of the grave was Gen. Ward. All who were seriously wounded were left at Resaca and some of them were sent to Dalton and Ringold. I stood on the hill in the woods last Sabbath as I saw our men charge upon that fort in "Sleepy Hollow." The shot and shell fell all around me but God protected me while I prayed for the success of our assault. The loss in our Corps in killed and wounded is estimated at 1200. That of the enemy 2400. They left many of their dead and wounded upon the battle field for us to take care of. I saw at least 100 dead Rebels. Among the number a Col. The men well clad and their haversacks were filled with Bacon, Corn meal and Corn Bread. I gathered a few trophies a Rebel Cartridge Box and cartridge, Canteen and wooden spoon which I propose sending you if I can. Our Brigade captured 4 cannon and hundreds of muskets and a few prisoners. We buried their dead and took care of their wounded but not until we had first taken care of our own. Their Sharp Shooters would even climb into trees in order to get better range upon our men. One of them was found next day hanging in a tree dead having been shot by our men, and caught in the limbs of the tree while falling. Lt. Robinson is at Resaca on detached duty. After the Battle I went to the division Hospital where I worked most all night. Such sights I never saw before 500 or more wounded and dying men crying for help. I saw in one pile the next day 25 or 30 amputated arms or legs. Henry Morrow was shot in the head, and when brought to this Hospital was unconscious. I shed a tear over him, took charge of his pocket book, gold pen, watch, Mothers likeness, a letter and handkerchief which I will send to his mother as soon as I can. The boys are in fine spirits and eager to put down this terrible Rebellion. .940

In a letter to his brothers, Fleharty reports he remained with some of the men in front of a captured Confederate battery until about eight o'clock in the evening, reporting that he fired his pistol once, a musket once, and a Spencer twice.

FLEHARTY, 102ND ILL WARD 1B 3D 20C: I received a slight flesh wound from a musket ball ... standing for a moment at one time with my left side towards the enemy, urging the men to stand their ground when a ball cut through

940 (Stillwell 2016)

my coat, pants and shirts, almost in the rear of my left thigh and cut a place in my hide about two inches long. It was almost a dishonorable wound but it was honorably received ... A battle is the most horrible thing imaginable." .941

CULVER, CAPTAIN, CO A 129TH ILL WARD 1 B 3D 20C: I had my Company under the enemy's fire yesterday about 4 hours and on last sunday about 6 hours of a most murderous fire none faltered except Frank Song/sergt. & I had him reduced to the ranks to day for cowardice I have a noble company & my Earnest wish so long cherished has been granted. I have been permitted to lead them in all their battles We will again advance upon the enemy & I fear no danger we will End this Campaigne [sic]. .942

COX, CHARLES H. COMPANY E, 70TH IND: May 22. We are still in same spot from where I wrote Ma, something strange in that to us, but the troops were so fatigued and utterly exhausted from our late operations that Secesh bullets could not kill men half so fast, as they would have been if forced forward in condition they were in. The 18th we marched over 20 miles in heat of the day, each man being obliged to carry a heavy musket, Cardg box, 60 rounds ammunition, 3 day rations in haversack, knapsack, blanket, tent, and every thing he possesses in the army. I tell you it makes a heavy load for a man to carry, all day long on a force march.

I saw men fall in their tracks while trudging along, becoming so weak & powerless their legs would not carry them along, then after the labor of marching all day the night is spent in building defences and preparing for battle, the following day should we be in vicinity of Mr Johnson. Tomorrow we start on a 20 days cruise with our smallest fighting weight and will live principaly off the country, as eatables are in aboundance here. It is a great mistake, to think the Confederacy could be starved out. Every family in northern Georgia have provisions enough to last them several years and plenty to furnish the army. Coffee is scarce for during the past 12 Mo not a grain have they had. .943

---

941 (Fleharty, Jottings from Dixie 1999, 14) Quoted by editor. Narration above was from that editor.
942 (Culver, Your Affectionate Husband, J.F. Culver n.d.) May 22, 1864 to wife.
943 (Wyatt 1972)

WILSON, CO K, 102ND ILL WARD 1 B 3D 20C: Cassville Ga May 22nd, 1864.
Dear & Beloved mother

I once more have a Spare moment to pen you a few lines I feel that it is only through the Kindness of a Special Providence that I am spared to write to you Mother I am Sorry that I have not time to write a lengthy letter to give you all the particulars But I have not the time for we have only Stopped long enough to draw rations & Some Shoes for the Boys Mother I will comence your letter where I left off Janes on monday we Burried our dead & the dead of the Enemy Mother it was Series occasion We fenced in a piece of ground on the Battlefield & Buried our dead verry nicely in one common grave We did not take so much pains in Burrying the Dead of the Enemy We gethered up 460 dead Rebs within a Short distance of where our own dead lay we got threw Burrying the dead about four o'clock Monday Evening We then Started in pursuit of the flying Rebs We overtaken them on wednesday & Skirmished & fought some all day But they didn't Seem inclined to want to fight But just at night old Jo as we call him for convenience ordered all us to charge them They run like Tirkys we only had one man Killed in our Regiment all that day He had both legs Shot off with a shell & only lived a few minutes the next morning there was not a Reb to be found we had no fighting since but we have orders to Start after them again in the morning.

Mother I had all most forgotten to tell you the name of the Battle we fought The name of the Battle is Resaca (long will it be remembered) Mother I want you to tell Kate that I want her to name my Girl after the name of that Battle (Resaca) Tell Sall that She may add her name to it also for I had intended on calling it Sally But I thought I would like to add the name of that Ever memoriable Battle to it But tell Kate if that name don't please her to call it what She likes & it will please me Mother I am highly pleased to think that Kate got a long so well & I am also highly pleased to think that I have a Daughter Tell Kate that I wrote to her yesterday & will write to her the verry first opportunity that I have of writing. Mother I am Sorry that I have not written more to you than what I have I have many things I would like to write to you I thought of you & Kate & my dear little children & my Brothers & Sisters while I was in the heat of the Battle I thought that if it had not of been for Kate and the children & the rest of my Relatives & friends to grieve for me that I would not turned on my heal to of Saved my life I hope Mother that I may never get in another such a battle But I shal go where ever duty calls me trusting my life in the hands of him that rules the destiny of Nation—I was not Badly injured I was Bruised and Stuned pretty Bad I have

got pretty much over it to the exception of a pain in my side & knee
Your effectionate Son Wm A Wilson .944

Henry Ira Banks was in the middle of the assault, being right behind the 70th Indiana.

BANKS, COMPANY E, 102ND ILLINOIS, WARD 1B3D20C: Dear Brother I take the opertunity which has bin scares for the fast 20 days we have bin put threw hard thick & thin I supose you know more by the papers what the fiting has bin than eny of the solgers for they can not here eny thing onely what they see we have bin fiting & twards (?) the enemy prety hard I have bin in 2day fite it is just one weake a go Saturday Sunday fites are bigest(?) I wer in. the rebels wer very strongley fortefide we had them nearle surrounded we were closen on them every day taking those brestworks by the point of the bayonet we had very hard fiting our regiment lost hevy 7,16 [76] in kild & wounded here meny in the hole Brigaid I havent asertaind the enemy lost hevy the enemy found that we were determind to fite them at al haserds and they scadadeld for fear we woud suround them & capture there hole forse we woud if they staid thair an other day Sunday nite they left by fireng hevy artillery & fiting to cover there retreat but they did not get away without hevy loss our men shld them all night well Willess fiting is not what it is cracked up to be as for my part I had rather be excused from goin in to one but now I am in I am bebound (?) to go threw if it dose cill (kill) me the bullets whiseld as close to me as I care to have them to we captured 4 peases of artillery brass peases they wer cauld the first Georgen ("The First Georgian") the bell of Georga ("The Bell of Georgia") the prisoners say this was the first time they wer repulsed satur day our men charged on it & wer driven back every time the 4 armey corps Old Jose (Old Joe's ref: General Joseph Johnston) corps tride it Sunday our Regiment and the 70 indian charged on the batery at the first charge we cleard them from there gones (guns) the guners wer all shot ded while in the act of loding one canon had a dobell charge of grape (grapeshot) a canester in it but the poor fllows had not time to put it of at the first charge I took my position under the musell of one of the peases and fired ofer (over) the carig (carriage) of the canon one man wasshot threw the head behind me he fell on me & cride for help Oh ses he help me I sof (?) my gun up against the canon & raised him up he was allso shot threw the body he cride for a drinck of water I gave it to him I told him I coud not do eny more for him I then seased my rifle the bullets fliing as thick as hail but by the kind hand of providence I was not tutch Juss then we wer ordered to fall back we fell back 3 differnt times but

944 (Wilson n.d.) The child was named Resaca Battle Wilson.

the enemy dared not persue these guns wer nobell ones 20 pounders our generall was on the feald with us amonced (amongst) the boys he was wounded threw the left arm Joseph Hoocker ses it was the best and most daring & ferosious charge he ever saw It is a wonder we wer not all cild (kiled) or captured we wer under there cros fires the the enemy had a cros fire on us & threw mestake our one (own) men fired at us taking us fo the enemy in our falling back the bushess wer so thick what was plaid the mifchis(??) I was never so near exausted in my life while making the charge threw the thicket & up hill at that this was plainest and loudest preatching that I ever atended on sonday the poind(?) was tested in every plais & none found defended(?) on the write side the rite is the mite in this ishew the enemy has the advantige in every sens of the word they left here in sutch a haisty retreat they did not get time to taer up the railroad a small town south from here 2 1/2 mi on the rail road is very strongley fortefid by the nam wawsackey (Wauhatchie, GA) [Calhoun] but they did not stop it is astonishing to see what strong fortifide we have bin resting for the last to days we wer nearley run down going day & nite hundreds of our men gave out with heat & fatigue I tel you it is the hardest biseness that I ever done caring (carrying) sutch a hevy & bundelling load I cary over 100 rounds I have my spencer (rifle) & shooter (most likely a Colt 1851 or 1860 Army model revolver) and I am goin to stick to it as long as I can. .945

Austin, 19th Mich Coburn 2B 3D 20C: The Stars of the old 19th are sed to be the first ones that waved over the strong reble works ... Mr. Dibble that enlisted from our town was shot inside of the fort & died immediately... I was run over by some soldiers that were running towards the rear & hurt my back & ankle and dident do any more fighting that night. .946

Glancy, Co K, 102nd Ill Ward 1 B 3D 20C: There has been a good deal of dissatisfaction here about which Brigade took the four guns at Resaca It was Wards brigade for that can be proven very easily the 79th and 102nd Ills was next I will not undertake to tell you much about it as it takes so much paper and we are scarce We were in the regiment just 10 days when we went in the fight at Resaca It was as hot a place as ever I was in too the bullets whized around pretty thick we were in a cross fire from every direction the 2nd

---

945 (Banks 2014) Transcribed by Steve Enyeart and posted in his blog.
946 (Austin 1864)

brigade was behind us and fired on us the bullets flew thicker from them than from the enemy. .947 .948

ENGLE, CO B 137TH NY IRELAND 3B 2D 20C: The ground was verry uneaven and covered with timber. We got the rebs first line of breastworks and silensed their guns four peacies in the fourt. They commensed to retreat a little before dark. They cept up a bold front and at eleven made their last charge which they had to do to get away. There was a terable sharp musket for a fiew minuets and it ceast. All was still and the cheere commenced far to our right one regt after another as far as the charge extended. Our brigade lay in front of the fort. We killed rebs but a fiew roods from our line. One officer we killed had a bottle of whisky and gunpowder. Monday morning we started after them. I cant tell how how meney prisoners has ben taken. You will see it all in the papers. Johnsons army must be discouraged. We thought they would make a stand here but they are skedadeling. They negroes say it takes half of the rebs to make the rest fight and I guess it is a good deal so. This is a hard campaign but I hope it will close the war. I think it will if Grant has good luck in Virginia. I am sorry the Colonel was hurt. We nead him here. He was hit by a peace of shell. I guess he will be back soone. He wasent hurt verry bad. .949

GEARY, 2D 20C: I captured 4 pieces of artillery at Resaca, which by a strange coincidence is the remainder of the identical battery from which I captured two pieces at Lookout Mountain. .950

Corput had only four guns, and all four went from Lookout to Missionary Ridge to help repel Sherman.

MOUAT, CO G, 29TH PENN IRELAND 3B 2D 20C: I suppose you have great rumors about us and what we have been doing Our Regiment got in a pretty hot place in the last fight our Company had 3 Killed that we Know of and 2 missing and 9 wounded, we had to charge up on the Johnnies breast works and we got in between three fires before we Knew it. I tell you I had not much time to think of what a short while I have to stay one poor fellow Jim

947 (Glancy 1864)
948 Pyrrhus Glancy was a recruit mustered in Feb. 21, 1864 in Company K, 102nd Illinois, from Eliza Creek. Per the Illinois Adjutant General's Report.
949 (Engle n.d.) Letter to wife, May 21, from Cassville, Georgia.
950 (Blair n.d., 176) No mention anywhere of Corput losing artillery at Lookout. All his went to Missionary Ridge and then to Dalton. Records show only four guns at Lookout, two forward at the point and two in the rear.

Hunter was Killed that was soon to go home—Denny of Company D was wounded in the arm—When we charged we would have taken the Rebs works if we had supports but our boys I believe were only sent in to draw their fire to us—some of the other Regiments took a small fort with a couple of guns in it We had our fight on Sunday the 15' and on Saturday the 14' our First Division "Red Stars" came up in time to charge the Rebs as they were driving back the 4' Corps—The Western boys say "They can call us white collar and Bread and butter soldiers or anything they like but if they want to see fighting call on Hookers boys" Hooker has a big name out here now. but I can't say much of Geary to tell the truth he aint worth his salt the people are a great deal mistaken in him. _951

FLEHARTY, 102ND ILL WARD 1B 3D 20C: It appears that after the last day's fighting was over, the Captain of the rebel battery which fell into our hands, wrote the following letter, which was subsequently captured by a member of the 105th Illinois Regiment. It is given verbatim et literatim.

"Resaca Ga may 15. My Dear Wife

John Thompson is going home to Cassville wounded I thought I would drop you a line by him The Yankees charged on my battery this P M and captured 2 sections of it many of our men and attendants were wounded

It was as daring an exploit as when my brothers was charged at Antietam Va by a New York Reg They threw themselves into the front as unconscious of danger as ducks into a pond.

I tell you and will to stow away everything of value fearing we shall have to fall back from here if we do the Yankees will get everything in reach.

We had to fight Hookers command here or else the battery never would have been taken I hear we are gaining on the yankees in Va and we would have whipped them, here if it had not been for Hookers command

They all wore a star

w w c "

951 (Mouat n.d.)

From the allusion in the fourth paragraph to the men of our Brigade throwing themselves into the front, "as unconscious of danger as ducks into a pond," the term "Ward's Ducks" originated. .952

Their First Strong Religious Convictions .953

PARTRIDGE, 96TH ILL WHITAKER 2B 1D 4C: At Cassville: Religious services were held in many of the camps both afternoon and evening. It was a spectacle upon which no thinking man, however skeptical, could look unmoved, to see the soldiers gather around the place designated for religious meetings. The attendance was often large, and embraced a few commissioned officers. Nor was it alone or mainly timid soldiers who were present, but often the most devout were those whose presence in the charge or upon the skirmish line was an inspiration. A soldier would lead in some stirring hymn, and soon a hundred voices, blending beautifully, would make the leafy tabernacle ring with their grand music. Prayer would be offered, sometimes in a loud tone, and again with subdued voice: some with crude imagery and weird petition for the overthrow of the enemies of the country and of righteousness: others eloquent in their very simplicity, breathing a request that the great "Father of us all" would lead the way through all the darkness of the present to the day when peace should brood above the land, and war and turmoil cease when soldiers should be permitted to forget the camp and battle and yet remember that they were soldiers in the army of the great Immanuel, whose victories were bloodless and whose captives were the prisoners of hope. Scripture would be read or repeated by the leader; a brief discourse would follow: experiences would be related, and then, as the nickering camp fires burned low and the distant bugles warned the worshipers back to camp, the grand melody of Old Hundred would go up like incense to the stars, the soldiers would separate and in a few moments quiet brood above the sleeping hosts. Who shall say they were not strengthened by these services, crudely arranged and conducted though they often were, or that the God of Battles did not watch above them and frame the answer to their varied petitions while they prayed, leading them, as individuals, and the Nation beneath whose banner they assembled, into a larger liberty than that of which they then conceived? Certain it must be that many a weary, home-sick, heart-sick boy, took courage in such

952 (Fleharty, Our Regiment. A History of the 102d Illinois Infantry Volunteers 1865, 442) Documented copy of original has not been located. Multiple regimental histories quote it, one, of Geary's division, saying they all wore a *white* star.
953 (Partridge 1887, 342) During a three-day halt May 20 at Cassville, five days after the battle. Many letters home were written at Cassville, many to notify families of their loss.

gatherings as these and went thence to the battle nerved for deeds more daring than the past had seen, and felt himself sustained by the hope and faith not elsewhere so certainly obtained. Not a few date their first strong religious convictions from those gatherings in the forests of Georgia, and many still cling to the Faith that sustained them there, where they learned to sing:

> *"Mine eyes have seen the glory of the coming of the Lord;*
> *He is trampling out the vintage where the grapes of wrath are stored;*
> *He hath loosed the fateful lightning of His terrible swift sword;*
> *His truth is marching on.*
> *"I have seen Him in the watch-fires of a hundred circling camps,*
> *They have builded Him an altar in the evening dews and damps,*
> *I can read His righteous sentence by the dim and flaring lamps,*
> *His day is marching on.*
> *"I have read a fiery gospel, writ in burnished rows of steel;*
> *As ye deal with my contemners, so with you my grace shall deal;*
> *Let the Hero born of woman crush the serpent with his heel,*
> *Since God is marching on.*
> *"He has sounded forth the trumpet that shall never call retreat;*
> *He is sifting out the hearts of men before his judgment seat;*
> *Oh, be swift, my soul, to answer Him! be jubilant, my feet!*
> *Our God is marching on.*
> *"In the beauty of the lilies Christ was born across the sea,*
> *With a glory in His bosom that transfigures you and me;*
> *As He died to make men holy, let us die to make men free,*
> *While God is marching on."*

An old hymn heard so often that meaning gets lost in repetition. Julia Ward Howe wrote the words in 1862 and they were still fresh—for these soldiers, every word invoked strong feelings. They had fought, buried comrades, and now prepared themselves to fight on.

The Cost of Glory

I confess, without shame, I am sick and tired of fighting—its glory is all moonshine; even success the most brilliant is over dead and mangled bodies, with the anguish and lamentations of distant families, appealing to me for sons, husbands, and fathers. —William Tecumseh Sherman .954

The dead and dying and wounded, who paid the price in blood, maimed bodies, and lifelong suffering, leaving bereft parents, helpless widows, and fatherless children—who thus have their own claim—laid amongst those who were engaged in removing the guns for a claim to glory. Let us tally the price paid. .955

Net claims: Ward: 945; Williams: 417; Geary: 259.

Overall, the sacrifice from Butterfield's division was twice Williams' and over three times Geary's.

In the chart below we follow the casualties in field and woods from the railroad west to the fort and then south, from left to right. However, Geary's division, in the middle, except for Ireland, was largely in reserve during the heavy fighting of the afternoon—so we could squeeze Knipe and Wood next to each other in the chart, as they were in the field.

WILLIAMS, 1D 20C: The casualties of my division—48 killed, 366 wounded, and 3 missing; aggregate, 417. .956 Knipe: 30 enlisted men killed, and 160 wounded; a total of 198. We have no list by regiment or other brigades.

In Williams' division, despite being heavily outnumbered in Stewart's assault, regiments of Knipe and Ruger took less than 20 casualties each. Knipe's regiments, with Wood, were in action throughout the fight and, taking Stevenson's assault, lost closer to forty per regiment.

---

954 https://jrbenjamin.com/2015/01/18/glorys-moonshine/
955 Some regiments had many more men than others before the battle, so the number lost by each regiment does not show proportion. Some had already lost many in earlier battles; some brigades had more regiments but with fewer men. Aggregate numbers are from sources and may not exactly match totals of killed, wounded, and missing. The 102nd left Wauhatchie with 450. Harrison about 500. Regiments of Geary and Williams, after many previous battles, started with even fewer men.
956 (OR, Series I Vol 38 Part 2 Serial 73: Reports n.d., 28)

MEMBER OF COMPANY A, 141ST NY, KNIPE 1B 1D 20C: The loss sustained by the 141st was 14 killed and 84 wounded; something over one-fourth of our men. _957

GEARY, 2D 20C: Casualties in battle at Resaca, Ga: 23 215 28 259 (killed, wounded, missing aggregate) _958

Of Geary's division, Candy, mostly in reserve or helping hold the fort late in the evening, lost few. Buschbeck's 33rd New Jersey were in the lead moving up to relieve Butterfield and took heavy losses during Johnston's flank move. Ireland's lead regiment, the 29th Pennsylvania, lost over a third of his casualties; Randall and Cobham who went to the fort, took about the same; overall, Ireland took fewer than Knipe. Still, Ireland lost fewer than half that of either Wood or Ward.

BUTTERFIELD, BY WARD, 3D 20C: 110 killed, 663 wounded, missing not given; aggregate 945

In Butterfield's division, Wood, who began the action on the left, lost nearly as many as Ward. His two middle regiments, the 55th Ohio and 136th New York, took heavy losses. We have little to tell of what the 33rd Massachusetts went through except they took a loss corresponding to two on its left. Winkler's 26th Wisconsin, despite being caught in the middle of a mass, across both hills, lost fairly heavily. Coburn, supporting Ward and later making three assault attempts, had men on the hill into the night, and his losses were much greater than all of Ireland's. Finally, with Ward, we see the lead regiments taking enormous losses. Harrison's 70th Indiana, as they ran in front to the fort, and then were the most involved fighting in the fort, took twice as many as the regiment right behind them and over three times as many as the other three regiments. _959

---

957 (Museum n.d.)

958 (OR, Series I Vol 38 Part 2 Serial 73: Reports n.d., 118) Appears to include May 14 and perhaps 13 as well as May 15.

959 See also Fox's report in (Fox n.d., 246)

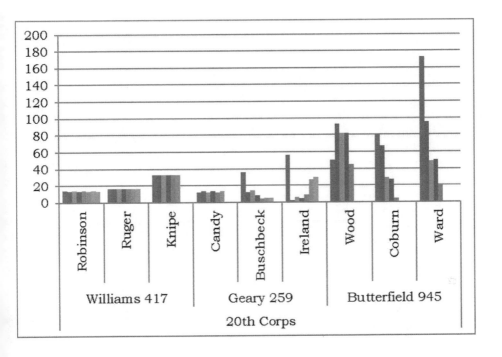

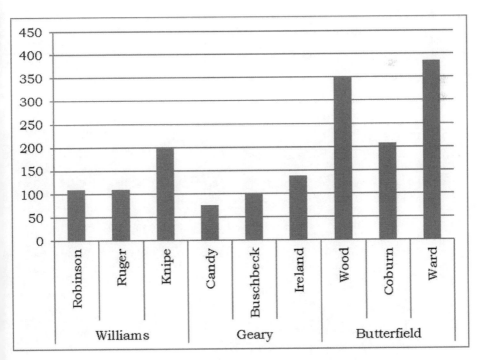

Butterfield's losses ordered by position in assault:

Regiment	Killed	Wounded	Missing	Aggregate
70th Indiana	29	144		173
102nd Illinois	18	76	1	96
79th Ohio	8	41		49
129th Illinois	9	41		50
105th Illinois	0	19		19
	64	321		385

Ordered by position left regiments, then right regiments, of three lines:

Regiment	Killed	Wounded	Missing	Aggregate
19th Michigan (left line 1)	14	66		80
22nd Wisconsin (left line 2)	11	56		67
33rd Indiana (left line 3)	0	29		29
85th Indiana (right line 1)	1	26		27
20th Conn (right line 2)	0	4		4
	26	181		207

Ordered by position facing the second crest, Stevenson's line, from left to right:

Regiment	Killed	Wounded	Missing	Aggregate
73rd Ohio				50
55th Ohio	23	70		93
136th New York	12	70		82
33rd Massachusetts	15	65	2	82
26th Wisconsin	5	40		45
	55	245	2	352

23 killed, 215 wounded, 28 missing; aggregate 266. .960 Patrick's 5th Ohio reported 5 killed and 19 wounded. No full report for Geary.

The first four regiments were sent forward after the dead line was set. Later, the last three regiments relieved them.

960 (OR, Series I Vol 38 Part 2 Serial 73: Reports n.d., 118) Clobbered going forward after the regiments behind them were called back.

Regiment	Killed	Wounded	Missing	Aggregate
33rd New Jersey	2	34		36
134th New York		12		12
119th New York	1	12	1	14
109th Pennsylvania	1	7		8
154th New York		4		4
27th Pennsylvania		4	1	5
73rd Pennsylvania	5			5
	9	73	2	94

_961: Ordered by position in assault. Sizes of regiments may have determined whether some were side by side.

Regiment	Killed	Wounded	Missing	Aggregate
29th Pennsylvania	6	50		56
78th New York (left line 2)		2		2
137th New York (right line 2)		6		6
60th New York		4		4
102nd New York	3	9		12
111th Pennsylvania	4	23		27
149th New York	1	29		30
	14	123		137

Claims to Glory

Personally it matters but little to the survivors of the Seventieth Indiana who felt in their faces the hot breath of the battery as it made its last discharge, that others claim the credit of silencing its guns, yet when they think of their comrades who sleep on that hillside, they utter a solemn protest in behalf of those whose voices are stilled forever. —Merrill

Its glory is all moonshine. —Sherman

961 (OR, Series I Vol 38 Part 2 Serial 73: Reports n.d., 276)

But what matters it who did it! We all helped; we gained the day; we sustained the great cause. —Coburn

Now, after the fight *for* the battery, the fight *over* the battery.

Recall Geary's letter to his wife after Gettysburg, *"The whole fight was under my control, no one to interfere,"* and Williams' difficulty in getting Meade's Official Report corrected. Now, after Resaca, here is Geary's surrogate, Cobham:

Cobham's Claim

COBHAM, 111TH PA IRELAND 3B 2D 20C: After about two and a half hours severe labor the digging was completed, and the guns removed to the headquarters of the Second Division. All the troops under my command were from the Second Division all three brigades being represented. I therefore claim for the division whatever honor may be connected with the capture; securing, and removal of the rebel battery. In conclusion, I would tender my thanks to the officers and men—thus temporarily under my command for their cordial support and strict attention to orders. 962

Before looking at others' claims, let's puzzle over Cobham's. Are two and a half hours of digging sufficient for sole claim? He said nothing about the fighting. "All troops under my command" is specific to only his division, of course, but omits others who might have been there. We know others were there and working, especially some of Coburn's brigade of the Third Division. But in that paragraph, he bases his claim on those two things. Then he claims *all* honor for *capturing* and *securing*—much, much more than just *removal*. Finally, a backhanded acknowledgement to those under his command—for support and attention to orders, omitting other sacrifices, such as fighting and dying, which was done by many, but which did not remove the guns. Well, not so. The 33rd New Jersey was detailed to draw off the last two guns and take them below.

Buckingham's Rebuttal

132 Edgewood Avenue, New Haven, Connecticut, April 26, 1893. Mr. J. R. McBride [33rd Indiana]:

Dear Sir and Comrade—I received your communication under date of February 20, in which you state you are engaged in writing a history of your regiment (Thirty-third Indiana), and in searching for data you find a

---

962 (OR, Series I Vol 38 Part 2 Serial 73: Reports n.d., 276) All under his command were from the 2nd Division. Disclaiming command of those who were not?

difference of opinion as to who brought the four-gun battery out of the fort at Resaca, Georgia, May 15, 1864. It is certainly most commendable that you desire to arrive at the truth when you essay to write history, for if it is not a truthful narrative of facts it is not what it purports to be and should be.

Van Horn, in his History of the Army of the Cumberland, says that Colonel Fitzpatrick [Kilpatrick], with the Fifth Ohio, captured and removed the four-gun battery out of the fort at Resaca, and it seems that Colonel Cobham, of the One Hundred and Eleventh Pennsylvania, also claims the honor attached thereto. Now, I wish to say. in relation to this matter, that the official report made by me at the time, as commanding officer of the detailed companies of the Second brigade, Third division and Twentieth Corps, was correct, and that all the credit due to Colonel Cobham, of the One Hundred and Eleventh Pennsylvania, was accorded to him and his command in that report, for it was my design, inasmuch as he was present part of the time during the proceedings that took place that night, May 15-16, 1864, when the guns were removed from the ravelin in which they were situated, that he should have no cause of complaint at anything in my report. _963

Our men lay down with their arms in their hands, confident of victory on the morrow, and Johnston made preparations for retreat, not daring to await the coming of the morning, when he knew our assault would be renewed. The battery was between our lines and the enemy, on disputed territory. The rebels could not reclaim it; neither could we remove the guns in the daytime without terrible loss. Just as all had gotten nicely laid down to rest, an order came from General Hooker, through General Butterfield, commanding Third division, and Colonel Coburn, our brigade commander, detailing me, by name, to take command of a detachment of men, consisting of two companies from my own regiment, the Twentieth Connecticut, and two companies from each of the other regiments of the brigade, and, if possible, capture and remove the guns of the four-gun battery within our lines.

The order was received by me about 9 o'clock p.m. and the details from the different regiments were ordered by Colonel Coburn, who did me the honor to come and see if the arrangement was complete, and actually went with the detail to indicate the route for us to take to find the location of the battery, for it was very dark in the woods that night. After Colonel Coburn left us, the detail proceeded, under my command, to reconnoiter and find the situation of the battery. Following the Dalton road nearly to where it entered the rebel lines, we left it and advanced up the hill toward the battery,

963 A small fortification outside the main fortification.

and passing through or over a picket line, the men of which lay flat on their faces and said they belonged to General Geary's command. The men of my command were placed between this picket line and the battery we were after, and ordered to lie down and await events. In company with the two captains commanding the two companies detailed from my regiment, I proceeded to investigate the situation. Creeping on our hands and knees over the dead bodies thickly strewn about, we reached the lunette and found a Second division man lying flat on his face in front of the earthworks, behind which the guns were. We placed our hands on the muzzles of the guns that protruded from the embrasures, and after crawling about the front, of the entrenched battery to get a correct knowledge of the situation, one of the officers accompanying me raised his hat on the point of his sword above the earthworks and received a shower of bullets as a reply, two or three passing through his hat. The rebels had, after nightfall, gathered a pile of logs, rails, and other combustible matter between the entrenched battery (which was opened to the rear) and their line of rifle pits, and set it on fire, the light from which lighted up the whole vicinity almost as light as day. The rebel line of entrenchments, behind which their infantry lay, was a line of earthworks four or five feet high, the rear built up perpendicularly with logs supported by skids, the earth shoveled from the rear, forming a ditch, and thrown over the logs in front to the thickness of eight or ten feet on the bottom, and four or five feet on the top, with a headlog on top of the embankment of earth, raised two or three inches, to afford an opportunity for thrusting the musket underneath the headlog to fire at an approaching enemy with almost perfect protection. We could plainly see the glimmer of the muskets protruding from underneath the headlogs ready to meet an approaching foe with a hailstorm of lead. The conclusion come to by me, after examination, was that there were but two ways to get the guns. The first was to rush the men under my command over or around the ravelin, seize the guns and drag them around the ends of the works, and down the hill to within our lines. This would have involved, probably, the sacrifice of nearly my entire command, and been uncertain of accomplishment. This plan was rejected. The second was to commence down the hill a short distance and dig a trench up to the guns wide enough for the gun carriages to pass through, attach a rope to the muzzle of each gun and drag them off within our lines. By this plan, until we broke through the entrenchment, the men would lie entirely protected from the fire of the rebel infantry. A detail was sent back after picks, shovels, ropes, etc. and my men were set at work digging trenches. About this time (11 p.m.), Colonel Cobham appeared as officer of the day in charge of the picket line and politely informed me that the presence of myself and command was not needed nor wanted there, and requested me to retire with my command, saying that he was going to capture and remove the guns. The remark was made by me that I and my command were there by order of the corps commander, for that purpose, and I proposed to stay until the guns were within our lines, if it was possible to accomplish such an undertaking. Mention was then made to him of my plans, and he advocated the first, but the last was finally agreed upon, and he then proposed to furnish a few men from his picket reserve to assist, which was accepted by me. As soon as the tools arrived from the Second brigade quartermaster, which had been sent for by me, a few of his men and a much larger detail of my command were set to work again, digging, and about 2 o'clock on the morning of May 16 the guns were dragged within our lines, and then the detailed companies under my command returned to their respective regiments without the loss of a man.

During the time my command was excavating the trenches, the enemy, suspecting something wrong, opened a terrific fire all along in our front with both artillery and infantry, which was replied to by our artillery, then located on the hill beyond the valley, the shot and shell passing just over the heads of my working party. Once during this time Colonel Cobham's men on the picket line in our rear ran away down the hill to the road and beyond and opened a musketry fire on the hill where my men and a few of his were at work. Their bullets flew all around among the working party and that portion of my detail not at work, Cobham's men thinking, no doubt, that all of our men had fallen back. A messenger was sent by me to request that the firing from our rear should cease, and shortly Colonel Cobham's men returned to their former position. They undoubtedly thought, from the quantity of the projectiles hurling through the air, and the din and noise of the artillery, that the rebels were about making a sortie to drive us from what they suspected we might be doing. My men, not at work, lay with arms in their hands in line of battle, ready for any emergency, and covered from the musketry fire from the rebel rifle pits. In the morning the rebels were found to have evacuated their works and retreated across the Conasauga river, destroying the bridges in their rear.

I think it has been shown that the claim of Colonel Cobham is incorrect, and whatever honor may be connected with the capture, securing, and removing of the rebel battery belonged to the Third division, Twentieth Army Corps, instead of the Second division.

I think enough has been said to show to any unprejudiced mind the utter absurdity of Colonel Cobham's claims and of others who assert that they captured the battery, and that myself and command were there on that occasion. Philo B. Buckingham,

Late Major Twentieth Connecticut Volunteers.

Major Buckingham, at the time this letter was written by his wife and dictated by him, was a confirmed physical paralytic, having been stricken down some sixteen or seventeen years previously.

This was the only battery captured from the enemy during the Atlanta campaign, and various commands claiming the honor of its capture is the reason for giving so much space to the facts, and especially to refute the claim set up by Colonel Cobham, who unfairly states in his report: "I therefore claim for the division (Second) whatever honor may be connected with the capture, securing, and removal of the rebel battery." _964

Harrison's Claim

HARRISON, 70TH IND WARD 1B 3D 20C: I would respectfully call your attention to the following points: First, my regiment entered the enemy's works in advance of all others, and my colors, though not planted, were the first to enter the fort; second, the enemy's lines were not penetrated at any other point than that where we entered, although assaulted by other troops on the left; third, my regiment, being in advance and having to bear the brunt of the assault, accomplished all that could have been required of them in entering the works and driving the enemy out. The work of carrying a second line of defense belonged to the support which followed me. The day following the battle my regiment, together with our whole brigade, remained on the battlefield burying our own and the rebel dead, and collecting abandoned arms and other property. _965

MERRILL, 70TH IND WARD 1B 3D 20C: Personally it matters but little to the survivors of the Seventieth Indiana who felt in their faces the hot breath of the battery as it made its last discharge, that others claim the credit of silencing its guns, yet when they think of their comrades who sleep on that hillside, they utter a solemn protest in behalf of those whose voices are stilled forever. An officer who led the advance of the Second Division and came on the field after all the artillery men had vanished from the scene, reported to General Geary, "We moved steadily forward until within fifteen yards of the battery when I ordered the regiment to halt and lie down. The

964 (McBride 1900, 112)
965 (OR, Series I Vol 38 Part 2 Serial 73: Reports n.d., 369)

position was one of extreme peril, but we held it from 12:30 P.M. till night." Whereupon the General commanding this Division reported to General Hooker, to say the least not very grammatically, that this body of troops had the honor of "leading and forcing its way through the jaws of death till they had their hands upon the guns."

General Hooker was close in rear of the compactly massed assaulting column, so no subordinate General was needed there, and if the General of the Second Division, while other troops were silencing the battery, had been on time and led his command over the deserted breastworks in pursuit of the flying enemy, there would have been glory enough to supply the whole Corps, and no necessity would have arisen for him to claim the capture of guns already silenced. His action was that of a sportsman, who would stop to pick up and gloat over game a hunter in front had dropped, instead of pushing through the woods and capturing his own prey. Alas, many a man of the Seventieth Indiana tossed in distress through the night as he lay on the ground, forgetting any honor that might come from the taking of a little lunette, in the awful loss of his comrades and in the thought of the great victory that might have been achieved.

"For of all sad words of tongue or pen,

The saddest are these, 'It might have been.'"

One has only to read the modest report of Colonel John Coburn commanding the Second Brigade, Third Division, who was on the field and had far more to do with holding and extricating the guns after they were captured than the commander of the Second Division, to discover what a wide difference there is in men. Not to mention the loss sustained on that day by other regiments of the Third Division, the mortality of the Seventieth Indiana alone exceeded by more than thirteen per cent that of all the twenty regiments and two batteries combined of the Second Division. A sad testimony, yet eloquent for the truth.

The historian Gen. J. D. Cox states the following: "The guns remained between the armies till night, when they were taken and brought off by a detachment of the Fifth Ohio (Second Division) under Colonel Fitzpatrick [Kilpatrick]." To which Captain Frank D. Baldwin, now Captain of Fifth Infantry, U.S.A. then Captain in the Nineteenth Michigan, replies: "It is a fact that some detachment of troops, probably the Fifth Ohio, did come up, as above stated, and bring the guns off. The men who had captured them being fully engaged in caring for their dead and wounded comrades, did not notice that the guns were being taken away at the time, as it was not thought for a moment that this detachment had come for any other purpose than to assist in caring for the wounded and dead." No wonder General Coburn when his attention was called to General Cox's statement exclaimed, "In reading some of the accounts of army history of which I supposed from my personal presence and participation I had some knowledge, I have been led to doubt my personal identity, and to believe that I must have been laboring under a hallucination while the events related were transpiring before my eyes." Then in his usual generous way he added, "But what matters it who did it! We all helped; we gained the day; we sustained the great cause." Still let the fallen again bear mournful witness, so that history may not be a black and cruel lie. The loss that day of the Fifth Ohio was killed three, wounded twelve. Of the Seventieth Indiana killed twenty-six, wounded one hundred and thirty. _966

Lieutenant Grubbs, 70th Ind, Ward, 1B 3D 20C: "The Twentieth Corps was massed that Sabbath noon for an assault upon the enemy's works. The assault was ordered by the Third Division, General Butterfield, to be supported by the First and Second Divisions. The First Brigade, Third Division, consisting of the Seventieth Indiana, One Hundred and Second Illinois, Seventy-ninth Ohio, One Hundred and Twenty-ninth Illinois, and One Hundred and Fifth Illinois were massed by regiments in the order named for the assault. They were to be supported on the right and left by the Second and Third Brigades of the Division. In this order the assault was made, down a hillside, into a valley across an open field along which ran a roadway, up a wooded ridge, to a hill crowned with a redoubt, from which four guns poured into our ranks shot and shell. With our ranks thinned by the deadly fire, and broken somewhat by the rough ground, with a wild yell, and without a halt we reached the summit of the hill, dropped to the ground as we saw the rebel gunners in the act of discharging their pieces in our faces, then springing to our feet, in a moment we were over the earthworks among the guns and they were ours.

"Men from several of the regiments of the Brigade entered the redoubt, and their dead and wounded lay on or near the works and among the guns. No one regiment may claim the honor of the assault and the capture, but that it belongs to the First Brigade, Third Division, there can be no question. Men, especially of the Second Brigade, (General Coburn's) came to our aid, and

966 (S. Merrill 1900, 67)

all that long and terrible afternoon they helped us to hold these guns, else we would have been compelled to relinquish them.

"These facts are clear. First: No other troops except a thin skirmish line were in front of the First Brigade, Third Division, as it advanced to the assault. Everything was clear in front, and there was not an obstacle to interfere with our progress until we came within range of the enemy's fire. Second: From the time the advance was commenced no halt was made, except for a moment, until we were in the enemy's works. Our line was not fifteen feet from the embrasures when the guns were discharged in our faces. Third: The guns were silenced then and not another shot did they fire that afternoon. Fourth: From that moment those guns were not out of our possession. We could not drag them away, but we could and did hold them. We repelled assaults made to recapture them. We lay for all that long afternoon clinging to those guns under so hot a fire that to raise head or hand was an invitation to a rebel bullet. The fact is, our commanders in the rear, and the men sent in by them after our assault, did not know we had taken and were holding those guns, but supposed our assault had failed, and certain regiments from the Second Division that were sent in an hour or more after we had captured them, came up the hill and went back faster than they came, and yet claimed the capture, because some of their men remained with us and helped us hold them until the end came." .967

Perhaps a greater claim is of those who fought the battle.

Monument to Both Sides in the Great War

Comrade W. D. Connor, Cave Springs, Ga. writes to the Veteran under date of April 14 (the communication had been inadvertently overlooked): "Capt. George H. Blakeslee, of Lomax.Nebr. belonged to the One Hundred and Twenty-Ninth Illinois, which composed a part of the First Brigade, Third Division, Twentieth Army Corps, which made the attack near Resaca when it was defended by Stevenson's Division. The main point of attack was defended by Corput's Battery, supported by Gen. John C. Brown's Brigade, which consisted of the Third, Eighteenth, and Twenty-Sixth Tennessee Regiments. Capt. Corput's Battery, having been placed about seventy-five yards in front of the infantry line, was captured by the charging columns, and it was a noted event, because it was the only loss sustained by Gen. Johnston in the campaign from Dalton to Atlanta. The attack was a gallant one, the brigade being under command of Gen. Benjamin Harrison,

967 (S. Merrill 1900, 67)

afterwards President; and the defense was no less gallant, led by Gen. J. C. Brown, afterwards Governor of Tennessee. Capt. Blakeslee proposes to erect on the site occupied by Corput's Battery (from contributions from his brigade, Corput's Battery, and Gen. Brown's Brigade) a memorial stone, one side dedicated to the Union forces, and the other to Confederates. I take this opportunity to request that the members of Brown's Brigade confer with Capt. Blakeslee, at Lomax, Nebr. on the subject. It would be a grand tribute to the American manhood and the American valor displayed by these two commands in this battle, and I sincerely hope to see this project put into execution. _968

With images of the common soldiers, earning their stars.

968 (Conner 1897)

Through to the End

Having followed Joe Peters to the end, we cannot abruptly leave his comrades to their fates without some account of the proceedings toward the accomplishment of their original purpose and of their return to their homes after their experiences through Resaca—including some events of significance. .969

The "Sunday school picnic," in Bierce's words, was repeated, with variations, twelve days later at Pickett's Mill, the honor of assault being borne by Hazen's brigade of Howard's corps. .970

Was the war too much for some officers?

> WILLIAMS, 1D 20C: Gen. Butterfield, commanding the 3rd Division of our corps, has gone home. He says [he is] sick, but I think he was disgusted and tired. Brig. Gen. Ward of Kentucky commands the division. Butterfield was a much more honorable officer than Geary, but he "hankered" after newspaper fame, and was uneasy that as a major general he had a subordinate command to others he ranked. In many respects he is an excellent officer, but cannot stand the hard service of such a campaign as this. Indeed, few can. Many of our general officers are going home and more intend to go, but I hope to hold out until we reach Atlanta. .971 .972

Butterfield took his records when he left, leaving no report on the Battle of Resaca. On departing, he wrote a letter of caution to Hooker, who he served so long as chief of staff and who commanded him at Resaca.

> BUTTERFIELD TO HOOKER: You can but little appreciate how deeply remarks from a soldier like yourself impress your subordinates. They repeat them, and they go down, impairing confidence in the ability of General Sherman to bring his campaign to a successful issue, and thus, in a measure, weakening the army. .973

The game of keeping each other occupied, while not risking too much without certain advantage, wore the Confederacy's nerves short as Sherman neared Atlanta. General Johnston was replaced by Hood, who quickly took the offensive. In the Battle of Peachtree Creek, Hood found an opening and pounced, but

969 (Livermore 1890, 536)
970 (Bierce n.d.)
971 (Williams 1963, 433) Written July 15, 1864. Butterfield left earlier in July.
972 Neither Butterfield nor Williams were West Pointers, nor was Ward. Williams and Ward stayed through to the end, as did Harrison, not a West Pointer.
973 (J. L. Butterfield 1904, 147)

Benjamin Harrison and John Coburn, failing to get General Ward, now commanding the division, to send them forward, took their brigades up a ridge anyway and held off Hood until Geary and Williams could get their lines in place. Hooker's Twentieth Corps lost many officers and men who had fought at Resaca, but Hood was roundly defeated and Atlanta was doomed.

Perhaps Sherman recalled Hooker's self-serving at Chattanooga and the "assurance of success" at Resaca, among other things—on the death of General McPherson, Sherman gave command of the Army of Tennessee to Howard, Hooker's junior. Hooker resigned. 974

> WINKLER, 26TH WIS WOOD 3B 3D 20C: July 25th, 1864. We are very near Atlanta, actually besieging it ... The papers have doubtless told you how disastrously to the rebels the battles of the 20th and the 22nd resulted, and also that General McPherson, who commanded the Army of the Tennessee, was killed. Everybody naturally thought General Hooker would be his successor, both on the score of merit and seniority. Yesterday the official notice came that General Howard had been assigned to that command and General Hooker, at his own request, relieved from duty with this army. The news was received with profound regret. The assignment of General Howard to that command is certainly very unexpected. It is well known that Sherman is unfavorably disposed towards Hooker, and the latter has had to put up with many slights during the campaign. His corps has gained a name here in the army that none other can rival, but no word of acknowledgment has ever come from General Sherman. McPherson was Hooker's junior, and so is Schofield, both commanded departments, while he only commanded a corps; yet he made no objection and he would not have objected now— considering it another army from this—but to take his junior out of this very department for that command was a pointed insult and proves that the doors to his advancement under Sherman are prematurely closed. If the good name of any corps has ever been questioned during any campaign, it is that of the 4th, General Howard's. All generals and field officers of the corps got together this forenoon and took leave of General Hooker. He shook hands with us all and assured us, while the tears rolled down his cheeks, that he had never had a command that he had such perfect confidence in and had proved itself so equal to all emergencies as this corps. He was evidently very much moved. We are now in rather a bad fix with our generals. Brigadier General Williams, of the 1st Division, has temporary command of the corps as field officer. Since General Butterfield left us, we

974 Lincoln is said to have told Sherman to give the command to Hooker, but Sherman said he would resign if so ordered. No record of that has been found though.

have had a Division Commander whose profound indolence alone prevents him from manifesting his incapacity by daily blunders of the worst kind. It is too bad that men of acknowledged ability cannot keep aloof from dishonorable jealousies. _975

General Ward's heroic stance with his men at Resaca was not enough.

Hooker, like Butterfield, had left no report on the Battle of Resaca.

Stanley was placed in command of the Fourth Corps.

Sherman recalled Slocum to command the 20th Corps, with General Williams in command until Slocum returned in August. Slocum led Sherman's left flank during the rest of the war, and Sherman called him his "left arm."

After many more battles, Sherman's armies flanked Atlanta and finally entered unopposed September 2, 1864. John Coburn accepted the Mayor's surrender.

Sherman ordered citizens out of Atlanta under truce, providing transportation north or south as they desired. General Thomas then pursued Hood's army back into Tennessee while Sherman, keeping the more fit men and horses, prepared to press Johnston's army and join Grant in fighting Lee. To do so, he could not also defend Atlanta and the railroad from recapture by the Rebels. So he destroyed the railroad, burned Atlanta, and took his army to Savannah for refitting and replenishment, living off what they could forage from the land and the citizenry, saying he would make Georgia howl.

Father John Peters died in October of 1864, after the capture of Atlanta.

Before the capture of Atlanta, Lincoln had expected to lose the November election. After Sherman's armies captured Atlanta and the eventual end of the war was assured, Lincoln won, carrying all states but one.

In December, Thomas defeated Hood's entire army at Nashville in two days, in icy weather, while Thomas' replacement was en route to relieve him because Grant thought Thomas was taking too long to attack Hood, a perception bolstered by surreptitious telegraphs to Washington by one ambitious general on Thomas' staff—another story. _976

975 (F. Winkler n.d.) Ward was division commander.
976 Another general looked at the telegrapher's copies of the scripts and recognized Schofield's handwriting.

The Confederates lost so many, yet kept fighting. The 3rd Tennessee regiment was down to only 195 men for the Battle of Missionary Ridge. By the end of 1864, they and the 18th Tennessee had a combined total of 17.

Henry and Oliver Peters, ages 41 and 45, were discharged due to disability early in 1865. According to monthly reports, both had been hospitalized most of the time since the grueling marches and then the winter of '63; they had not been present when Joseph was killed.

Grant and Sherman had told Lincoln that Grant would hold Lee while Sherman pressed Johnston northward against Lee, grinding them against one another with no way to get food or other supplies. And Lee's Army of the Potomac surrendered to Grant April 9, 1865.

Lincoln was assassinated on April 15. Secretary of War Edwin Stanton placed Hooker in charge of some of the President's funeral activities, which ended with a procession in Lincoln's hometown of Springfield, Illinois. [977]

Johnston surrendered to Sherman a few days later.

Soldiering Under Uncle Billy

Brown, of the 27th Indiana, a Potomac bunch, but from the west, describes the esprit, as it were, during the campaign.

> BROWN, CO C 27TH INDIANA RUGER 2B 1D 20C: Yet, strange as it may appear, these were days of good cheer among the soldiers, often days of great joy and delight. Everybody laughed and was as merry, played as many pranks and had as much fun, as was commonly true in the same length of time under other conditions. Men uniformly went to their tasks and bore all of their hardships cheerfully, often joyfully, and not infrequently they did hard, disagreeable and even desperate things, with veritable shoutings of glory.
>
> General Sherman's peculiar relation to his soldiers, as well as the unexampled success attending his operations, had everything to do in bringing about these results. It was here that he blazed out, full orbed, into the one ideal commander of a volunteer army. In the wonderful genius he displayed in grasping peculiar situations, and in his marvelous adaptation of means to ends, he will, in many respects, stand forever without a rival.

---

977 (Lincoln, The Collected Works of Abraham Lincoln 1809-1865 n.d.) Basler's words.

Throughout this entire campaign Sherman was constantly with and among his men. There was no telling when he might appear in the midst of any regiment, or ride up to any picket post. Without being the least patronizing, or obsequious, above all, without lacking anything in dignity, his manner was wholly free from airs of superiority or haughtiness. If he desired information he questioned the one nearest to him, or the one who, owing to the position he occupied at the time, seemed most likely to know, regardless of rank. If, for any reason he stopped for awhile, as he often did, and a circle of men gathered around him to listen to what he was saying, even venturing to ask him questions (they were always eager to do both), it did not seem to annoy him at all. His replies to them were always courteous and usually candid, though brief. He seemed uniformly to treat all of his soldiers, regardless of rank, as if he considered them full partners with himself in the enterprise, equally interested in its success, and worthy of being trusted to almost any extent.

It goes without saying, that General Sherman's soldiers fairly idolized him. They called him "Uncle Billy," and that meant everything. It meant the extreme of admiration, devotion and obedience. Sherman's army really reached the point where it trusted him always and blamed him never. To this there were no exceptions. None remained to weaken the rest. With one mind and one heart, all were ready and anxious to undertake whatever he ordered. In this we, who had been in the Army of the Potomac, were not in any respect behind those who had served under him from the beginning. Our confidence in commanders had been sorely tried, but we dropped into this so naturally that we could give no date to the experience.

Sherman's example had its influence, also, upon his subordinates. Some of them may not have needed it. He himself says of General Thomas, "Between Thomas and his men there existed a most kindly relation. He frequently talked with them in a most familiar way." This was certainly more true at this time of all high in authority than it had ever been before.

This campaign, of all others, was a time to see generals of high rank. A famous man, and even several famous men, was an every day sight. Four or five, often more, of the men whose names are now historic, any one of whom if still alive would excite universal interest by a visit to any of our cities, could be seen almost daily, halted temporarily at some crossroads, or conferring together under a clump of trees. Their headquarters, when they had any, were always located among their men, near the front. They knew how their men fared and their men knew that they fared very little better than themselves.

History does not record another instance, probably, where soldiers of all ranks were thrown as much upon their own individual responsibility, and were allowed as much latitude for action, as during this campaign, unless it was in the subsequent career of the same army, under the same generals. There was a relaxation, if not a suspension, of much of the conventional military restraint to an extent that we of the Twenty-seventh had never experienced before. Camp guards were unknown. Roll calls were few and far between. Restrictive orders were not promulgated morning, noon and night. No sleep was lost by anyone, lest a chicken, goose or pig might be killed. The hateful, senseless knapsack was given a permanent leave of absence. If an officer or soldier fancied a hat more than a cap, he might wear one, and little attention was paid to color or shape. It seemed to be taken for granted in all quarters that all connected with the expedition were not only patriotic and well-meaning, but capable and trustworthy, and could be relied upon to do their duty. Why is it that the conventional military man, or so-called "soldier" of the academy, and of the militia, never can learn this?

A picture of a Twenty-seventh soldier at this time would show him to be lean and weather-beaten; not an ounce of surplus flesh upon him, and his skin as brown as a bun. His clothes would be soiled, and his hair and beard might be long and probably unkempt. If an enlisted man and on the march, the only worldly effects visible, aside from the clothes on his back and his ever-ready musket and its belongings, would be a small roll of stuff hanging upon the left shoulder and crossing over to the right hip. That roll would contain, at most, one rubber poncho, one woolen blanket, one piece of shelter tent, and, possibly, an extra shirt and pair of socks. It often contained nothing but the rubber poncho and piece of tent. Dangling somewhere would be the little tin pail and frying pan. Often a light ax, or hatchet, was suspended to the belt, carried in turn by different members of the same company, or mess. Impaled upon a bayonet, or carried in the hand, a chicken or other fowl, or a piece of fresh meat, too large to find a place in the haversack, was not an infrequent sight, when the order to move had come suddenly and the march did not promise to be a long one.

As a rule, each soldier received his own rations here, and cooked and ate them in such ways, and largely at such times, as seemed to him best. For cooking, the only utensils known were the aforesaid pail and frying-pan, and the ramrod, or a wooden stick of similar proportions. These last were used to hold the pail over the fire, and to broil the meat. Held thus in a hot flame, whatever was in the pail was soon cooked, and a piece of salt pork or fresh meat was soon ready for the palate of the hungry man. The first effect of the heat upon the salt pork—"sow belly "—when held in a hot fire, was to bring out the salt and crystalize it upon the surface. This was washed off, a time or two, with water poured from the canteen, the pork being held in the fire again between each washing. In case of fresh meat the salt had to be added, of course, instead of being washed off. When the meal was ready the soldier sat complacently down upon the ground, tailor-fashion, with his victuals arranged conveniently around him. A cracker served as a plate for his meat, which was laid upon a stone, chip, piece of bark, or clean spot of ground. When none of these were in sight, the toe of his shoe answered just as well. Some people might not see much comfort—not to say luxury—in such primitive and somewhat rude conditions, but this much can be said of them, in the instance referred to: The food invariably tasted good, and the soldier, veteran that he was, wasted little time or thought in considering the matter in any other light. It is needless to add, that any true picture of a Twenty-seventh soldier and his surroundings on the Atlanta campaign would have many features in common with a picture of him on any other campaign, particularly after the first few months of our service.

This was soldiering under "Uncle Billy" Sherman. Is it any wonder that the army was at its best? Victory was in the air. Atlanta was sure to be ours. Secession was doomed. There might be temporary reverses, the best of plans were liable to miscarry sometimes. But ultimate triumph—glorious and complete—was no longer a question. Hallelujah! _978

Mother Bickerdyke and Friends

The Sanitary Commission was not done until Atlanta was won.

LIVERMORE: When General Sherman was prepared to move on his Atlanta campaign, Mother Bickerdyke with Mrs. Porter accompanied the army on its bloody but victorious march. They were constantly in the immediate rear of the fighting, and made extraordinary exertions to keep the department of special relief at its very highest point of efficiency. In this they were aided by the Sanitary Commission, and by the army officers. It was not unwise for officers to reveal to Mrs. Bickerdyke enough of army plans to enable her to make preparation for coming emergencies, for she always proved a safe depositary of secrets. Those who worked with her most constantly saw that she generally knew when to have prepared in the hospitals, huge kettles of coffee, soup, and mush; when to have rough beds made of pine and hemlock boughs with the large stems cut out, on which were spread blankets; when

978 (E. R. Brown 1899, 498)

to order forward teams laden with supplies, following herself in close proximity in an ambulance. They attributed her promptness to intelligent foresight; but it was actual knowledge of coming events, in most cases.

I despair of giving any account of the work accomplished by Mrs. Bickerdyke and Mrs. Porter from April to November of 1864. What it is to "follow an army "when there is no fighting in progress, can only be understood by those who have experienced it. What it was to follow Sherman's army in that Atlanta campaign, when it fought every foot of the way, over rugged mountains, through deep, narrow ravines, through thick, primitive woods, across headlong rivers—to follow with only the one aim of ministering to the exhausted, the suffering, the wounded, the dying—with only a blanket and a pillow for a bed—the roar of artillery, the clash of arms, the cries of distress, and the shout of battle continually resounding—to live night and day in the midst of these horrors, in constant attendance upon the mangled and anguished soldiers brought to them from the rear, or taken to their extemporized hospitals,—this cannot be described.

As they were pushing along in their ambulance on one occasion, packed with battle-stores, they heard the distant sounds of a fierce cannonade—and knew that a battle was in progress ahead of them. On they went, the sounds becoming louder, clearer, and more distinct. Now it was mingled with the crash of musketry, the calls of half a hundred bugles, the thundered commands of officers leading their men to the conflict, the yells of the infuriated soldiers as they hurled themselves on their antagonists with the shock of an avalanche—and sometimes, overtopping all, the awful cries of mortal agony, that came up from the battle-field, from men writhing in every form of ghastly wound. They were in the rear of the battle of Resaca. On one side were heaped the knapsacks, and other impediments, of which the men had stripped themselves for the fight—on the other the amputating tents of the surgeons, surrounded by an ever-increasing quantity of mangled and dissevered limbs. The field hospitals were in readiness for the wounded, who lay about under trees, and on the grass, awaiting their turn at the amputating table, or to have their wounds dressed.

In a very short time both women were at work. Their portable kettles, with furnaces attached, were set up, their concentrated extract of beef was uncanned, and soon the fainting and famishing men were uttering their thanks for the great refreshment of a palatable soup. In the interim, they dressed wounds, took down memoranda of last messages to be sent North to friends, received and labelled dying gifts to be distributed East, West, and North, encouraged the desponding, and sped the parting soul to Heaven

506

with a brief verse of hymn, a quotation from the words of Christ, or a fervent and tender prayer. This arduous but blessed work they continued at Kingston, Altoona, and Kenesaw Mountain, on to Atlanta. 536

Some Final Notes

The attitude of the soldiers in the long campaign showed in many ways. Private Totton was carried high (or low) by his comrades and reached his glory at Averasborough.

Now Comes George W. Totton

The Hero of Resaca

HALSTEAD, 79TH OHIO WARD 1B 3D 20C: It would seem that Totton's bravery, now so well established, should have commended express recognition, but not so. Sometimes following easy days the boys would talk after taps ("lights out") before going to sleep. One would exclaim: "Boys, have you got cartridges; or, have you got cartridges?" Another, "Grab a root!" Yet another, "Oh, Harvey!", and another, "Pass it down the line; the 129th Illinois has not got space enough!" And still another, "Hush, me thinks me hear a whoop!' 'Tis he-e-e-e! Totton's w-a-r-r-r-r cry!" Chorus—"Owe-o-o, Owe-oo, Owe-oo, Owe-oo!"

Of course each saying related to an event with the history of which all were familiar, and ridicule intensified by scientific abbreviation. After Private Totton became distinguished, no officer was more critically observed in battle than he. Let him do anything eccentric and there would go up into the air a prolonged yell.

At the battle of Aversbrough occurred the crowning glory of George W. Totton. His brigade was massed near the crest of a hill; an ordinary fight was progressing within hearing, but not in sight. Totton's Captain and another Captain of his regiment were walking about together, as the day was fine, sauntering up over the hill, from which a magnificent view of the battle was unexpectedly obtained. It was at once seen that our brigade has been accidentally massed upon the enemy's extreme right and almost against it. A mile of their battle line was in plain view their infantry and artillery actively at work but getting as much as they were giving. It was strange that the enemy's right flank should have thus been left entirely unprotected but such was the fact.

Not to take immediate advantage of such a position, orders or no orders, would have been disgraceful. The social Captains ran back to the officer in command of Totton's brigade and explained the position, and that he was the most favored of the Lord, now being certain of two stars to a shoulder instead of a little silver eagle. He became excited, said the matter must have immediate attention. "But," said he, looking at his brigade, "what command shall I give?" But before his question could be answered he amended it by saying: "Captain you have seen and understand the position, you give the command. I delegate it."

The command given by the Captain was "Attention, Battalions! Front! Left-Face! Forward; double quick! March!" The brigade was deployed into line of battle to the left and rear of the enemy's extreme right flank and in five minutes after the discovery of the position the command was given, "Commence firing!" Upon the first volley the enemy, finding a line of battle on their flank and rear, broke and ran in a great mob towards their center. Then Totton's brigade was ordered to advance, firing, the Colonel in command delighted with the proceedings, but as yet making no suggestions. The advance firing was rapidly developing into a charge, which was not to be thought of, for a line of the enemy's skirmishers were now in sight, upon our rear, so the command "Halt! Cease firing!" was given, and an attempt made at correcting the lines.

Now comes George W. Totton. He had seen a Captain in command of a brigade; why should not a private lead a division? We had already swept clean one-half mile of the enemy's line of battle, including one battery of artillery, but Private Totton's notion was that the fun had but fairly begun.

He ran swiftly out in front of the brigade, holding his hat and his musket high in the air. The excitement to this moment had been difficult to restrain. Turning to the brigade, he stood for a moment upon his tip-toes and shouted in a voice that was wonderful, "Remember Resaca! Come to glory, boys!" A yell went up from one end of the brigade to the other. The revival went up from the ranks. The line officers were converted. We charged.

While we were charging the enemy in our front, the enemy were charging us from our rear. The enemy in our front outran us and we outran the enemy following up our rear, or so nearly succeeded in running away from him that when the force of our charge was expended, some 600 stragglers hastily thrown in line and caused to fire by volley at command, at once checked the advance upon our rear. .979

The Battle of Averasborough, North Carolina was fought March 16, 1865 with Henry Case, now Brigadier General, commanding Totton's brigade; Ward the 3rd Division; and Williams the 20th Corps, which was half of Slocum's new Army of Georgia. Presumably, the captain in this story was Halstead. Harrison had been promoted Brigadier General and participated in the Battle of Nashville in command of the 1st Brigade of the 1st Division with Thomas, while Sherman marched to the Sea.

That battery they overran? Their good fortune was also due to a timely distraction in the Confederate line. .980

> DICKINSON, 22ND WIS COBURN 2B 3D 20C: On March 16th, 1865 we fought the battle of Averysboro. The rebels tried to stop our march to Goldsboro. They had a strong line of works across our road, were in heavy force behind their works, and with several pieces of Artillery planted in our front. The 22nd Wis. Regt. was supporting a battery, and in front, across an open field, in plain view, were the rebel works. A section of their battery, was practicing on our line. The 1st Brigade of the 3rd Div. had been sent around the right flank of the rebel line, and while waiting for them to show up, our gunners were making it quite interesting and lively, by throwing solid shot and shell, at the rebel guns. We noticed after one of the shells exploded in their camp, a great commotion, and that particular gun was silenced. Then the order came to charge, and with a huzza that fully equaled the rebel yell, we started on the run across that field, for the rebel guns; and fully expecting to meet a charge of grape and canister; but nothing came, but a volley of musketry from the rifle pits, and fortunately for us, they were so excited, that the bullets nearly all went over. As we mounted their works, we could see what caused the stampede. There was our flanking column coming up from their rear. They had been hidden from us; by the formation of the ground, and the rebel works. And that accounted for the wild shooting done by the rebels. They were getting between two fires; and it made them nervous. Where we went over the works just to the right of the gun we were aiming for, was a wounded rebel, in the mud, in the bottom of the ditch. He had been hit by a cannon ball from one of our guns, which had gone through at least six feet of earthworks. It had torn off the whole right side of his body; and he begged of our men to shoot him, to put him out of misery. But he

979 (Halstead n.d.)
980 Confirmed in (Fox n.d., 304)

only lived a few minutes; on looking around, we discovered what caused the commotion in their camp, when our gunners were treating them to a dose of shell It was evident from appearances, that a shell had exploded in their limber chest. It had wrecked the limber, tearing off the wheels; and of the chest, there was nothing to show that it ever existed. There lay six white horses, dead, and horribly mangled, which had evidently belonged to, and been hitched to the limber. The gunners and drivers were laying about, what was left of them, dead, and mangled by the exploding shells past recognition. It was no wonder that the gun was silenced; for the explosion of their own shells, had killed every one in the vicinity of the limber. On inquiring of a prisoner, about the battery, we learned that they called themselves the South Carolina Aigers[sic]. They had been in the Forts in Charleston since the commencement of the war; but when Shermans army captured the city, they had taken a light field battery, and uniting with Hardes and Wheelers forces, were endeavoring to block Shermans army on their way to Goldsboro. But they might as well try to stop a cyclone, when under way. _981

Presidential Life - Owed to a Horse's Sense

STRONG, CO B 105TH ILL WARD 1B 3D 20C: I suppose Colonel Harrison came to be pretty well thought of, for he got to be a general, but there was a time when we admired his horse more. We used to say that horse had sense. He was one horse that was afraid of being shot. If the enemy artillery began firing at us while we were behind entrenchments, the horse would jump into the ditch among the boys and try to hide himself. We could always tell when to expect it. The horse would begin to fence sideways. Then with a rush he would be among us. He seemed to know that he was safer in the ditch than out of it. Nothing could hold him when he bolted. I guess there were times when our colonel owed his life entirely to that horse's skittishness under fire.

A Word Now for Uncle Ned

PEAK, CO F 129TH ILL: He had taken up with our company and I must say we found him to be as trustworthy as any man in the company. What he told, you could count on being true. He cooked for the boys and done their washing when we were in camp for a few days. The boys paid him for his work and when we reached Washington, Uncle Ned had a hundred dollars saved. A day or two before we left Washington, I asked him what he intended to do as we would soon be gone to our homes and he would be left

981 (Dickinson n.d.)

alone in the big city of Washington, a stranger. He said he had a job and would go to work as soon as we all left. He said he could not think of not seeing us leave for home and when the day came for us to leave, Uncle Ned was there to take the last look and hand shake of the boys he had learned to love. We had boarded our train and it was slowly pulling out when I looked back to see if I could see Uncle Ned. I did not see him but when I looked forward, there stood Uncle Ned as far out on the platform as he could get to catch the last glimpse of the boys he would never see again.

Now - All Was Hushed

Wes Connor, with a prophetic caution, borne of family, home, and loyalty, right or wrong, having fought for his country in what he and his comrades and fellow citizens thought their right and a necessity.

Monday August 5, 1867

Visited the spot where I fought three years ago, and where our battery was taken from us, and twenty-six men killed and captured.

What a contrast,—then and now! Then, the fierce ranks of war were hurled against each other, the booming of cannon, rattle of musketry, crashing through the timber of shell and canister, the yells of the combatants and the shrieks of the wounded and dying told but too plainly of the work of death that was being carried on. Now—all was hushed, save now and then the noise of a rabbit, as he leaped from his noonday nap through the bushes. All traces of the battle, except the line of rifle pits, are fast passing away. The holes in the trees that were not killed are growing over, and those that are dead will soon decay.

Occasionally I would stumble upon an old knapsack or canteen and the question arose,—where are their owners? Will their graves be honored twenty years from today? Or will they be looked upon as traitors? I always feel like raising my hat to a one-armed or one-legged soldier, and feel as if I were on holy ground, when walking among their graves. I shall instill to the minds of my children, if I should have any, the righteousness of our cause, and bind them to do the same with theirs to future generations. Found no trace of any member of the Battery, except an old canteen with a half legible name, which I suppose belonged to Summerhill, who joined us a few days before the battle. The remains of the "boys" were deposited in one of the pits dug for the guns, and remained till removed to the ground set apart for a cemetery at Resaca. Hadn't time to visit that, and don't know if any of their names are inscribed upon their headboards. But it is all the same here,—a few years and nobody would recognize them anyway, but their names are written upon that bright scroll of heroes, above, where the breath of decay never comes, and where they will shine on throughout eternity.

Only three or four of that twenty-six ever returned. The Yankees were buried right in front of the works, and from the appearance of the pits in which they were buried, a goodly number must have been sent on that long journey. I cut me a stick, which had been struck by a "Minnie" as a memento of the ground, and took my departure. – Wes Connor, Cherokee Artillery. .982

982 (W. O. Connor, Wesley Olin Connor Diary 1867, 69)

APPENDIX

Who Spun These Tales

They wrote something or were written about. Reviewing this beforehand will help follow the story.

Sources, if not noted, are published obituaries, other biographies or articles, or synopsis by this author, quoted without attribution (or consistent style). Units and Ranks are at the time of the Battle of Resaca.

ABRAMS, ALEXANDER ST. CLAIR. CSA. Reporter to Atlanta Intelligencer. Previously served at Vicksburg but was wounded and turned to reporting. Known for accuracy, especially in describing the Siege of Vicksburg. Had a long career in newspapers.

ALEXANDER, WILLIAM J. CO D 111TH PENNSYLVANIA, CAPTAIN. 1836-1904. Born Erie County, Pennsylvania. Enlisted with boyhood friend George Cobham and became adjutant with Cobham was promoted Colonel. Businessman before and after the war.

ANDERSON, FRANK. HOOD'S CORPS, CSA, COURIER

ARMSTRONG, WILLIAM M. CO B 102ND ILLINOIS. From Cold Brook, Illinois. Enlisted as Lieutenant 1st Class in September 1862, promoted to Full Captain in April 1863. Recipient of the Distinguished Service Award.

AUSTIN, JUDSON L. 19TH MICHIGAN INFANTRY, PRIVATE. Austin was born 1836 in New York and was later a resident of Cheshire, Michigan. He died August 5, 1924 in Allegan, Michigan, where he is buried. Nearly 300 letters written to his wife are preserved in "The Letters of Judson L. Austin."

JAMES T. AYERS, 129TH ILLINOIS. Widower. Enlisted at 56 as Private but was Orderly Sergeant and later Regimental Mail Messenger. Detached in 1864 to recruit colored soldiers in Tennessee and rejoined the 129th in Savannah. After reaching Washington, enlisted as Chaplain of the 104th Colored Regiment, but had been a convalescent during part of the march and died not long after. From Fairburg, Tazewell County. Farmer and Methodist Episcopal preacher.

514

BAIRD, JOHN PIERSON. 85TH INDIANA. Born in Spencer County, Kentucky in 1830. Following graduation from Indiana University Law School, he became an attorney and served one term in the Indiana House of Representatives. In 1862 Baird was commissioned as lieutenant colonel of the 85th Indiana Volunteer Regiment. His unit was captured in March 1863 by Confederate General Nathan Bedford Forrest, and Baird was interned at Libby Prison for two months under harsh conditions. Upon his release, he was appointed commander of Fort Granger in Franklin, Tennessee. In June, 1863, it was his reluctant responsibility to execute two spies who were relatives by marriage of Robert E. Lee. Baird participated in several battles during the March to the Sea, but poor health brought on his resignation in June, 1864, and he returned to Terre Haute and resumed his law practice. After ten years of intense work of building his law practice, Baird suffered a mental breakdown and in 1876 admitted himself to the Indiana Hospital for the Insane, dying there in 1881.

BANKS, HENRY IRA, COMPANY E, 102ND ILLINOIS: Born Feb 17, 1838, Patterson, New York. Died July 24 1889, Baird, Texas.

BARNUM, HENRY ALONSON. 149th New York. Lawyer from Syracuse. Left for dead and captured at Malvern Hill, he returned and recovered but required surgery and was absent much of the time. Missed Resaca while carrying captured battle flags to Washington. Became brigade commander after Ireland's death, September 10, 1864.

BENTON, CHARLES E. 150TH NEW YORK. BAND MEMBER. Born in 1841 on a farm in Amenia, Dutchess County, New York. After the war, Benton turned to farming until 1891 when he moved to New Bedford, Massachusetts, where he served in various public offices. He was an enthusiastic supporter of the Grange Association and the Grand Army. He penned articles for various periodicals and in 1901 published a well-received book, *As Seen From the Ranks*.

BICKERDYKE, MARY ANN, SANITARY COMMISSION. (1817–1901) After studying herbal medicine at Oberlin College, in 1847 she married Robert Bickerdyke. The couple and their family moved to Galesburg, Illinois, where Mrs. Bickerdyke was widowed in 1859. Delivered medical supplies to the Union forces at Cairo, Illinois. Appalled at the poor level of care, she quickly set to work with her hallmark energy and determination, improving the makeshift field hospital. With blessings of Generals Grant and Sherman, Bickerdyke and her fellow nurses followed the Union forces in the Western Theater of operations. She cared for the wounded on nineteen battlefields. At the conclusion of the war, as a gesture of the esteem in which she was held by the soldiers of the North's western armies, General Sherman requested that Bickerdyke ride at the head of the 15th Corps of the Army of the Tennessee in the triumphant Grand. In the years that followed, Bickerdyke helped secure federal pensions for numerous U.S. Army veterans and for more than 300 nurses who served in the Civil War.

BIERCE, AMBROSE. HAZEN'S 2ND BRIGADE, 3RD DIVISION, 4TH CORPS. Topographical Engineer. Captain. From a southern Ohio abolitionist family, he fought at Shiloh and Chickamauga in the west after learning some hard lessons in the east. Then he was in the Atlanta Campaign until severely wounded in the head at Kennesaw Mountain. Author of acclaimed realistic fiction about the war and critical, often caustic, accounts of some battles.

BLAKESLEE, GEORGE HOPKINS. CO. G, 129TH ILLINOIS INFANTRY. CORPORAL. Scout and Topographical Engineer. While a scout he was in Company K. Born in Connecticut to poor parents. Spent two years at Fenn Technical Institute and a year at Hermon School for Boys. Moved to Illinois in 1856. Obtained rank of Captain in colored infantry but was severely wounded at Kennesaw Mountain before taking command and recovered serving under General Dodge in St. Louis. Farmed in Iowa and later Nebraska after the war and contacted many comrades of both sides, hosting reunions at Lomax, Nebraska.

BLUNDIN, LEWIS. CO C 28TH PENNSYLVANIA. He served as private, sergeant and hospital steward. During the war he developed typhoid fever and suffered with other ailments thereafter. Following the war, Blundin entered Jefferson Medical College of Philadelphia, graduating two years later. His wartime ailments still prevailed and not long after graduation he suddenly became paralyzed from the waist down. He is buried in Hulmeville, Pennsylvania.

BOYLE, JOHN RICHARDS. 111TH PENNSYLVANIA. ADJUTANT. Succeeded his father as adjutant when his father was killed in the Battle of Wauhatchie. Had been in Company K, which his father recruited from Elk County.

BRADBURY, WILLIAM H. COMPANY B, 129TH ILLINOIS INFANTRY. PRIVATE. Lawyer who clerked for Butterfield while trying to get promoted to officer. Surreptitiously contributed to Chicago Tribune, as did others, though Sherman forebad dealings with reporters. He kept a diary for himself and one for Butterfield but now neither is available. So his name appears because of what we perhaps could have read but cannot.

BRADLEY, GEORGE. S. 22ND WISCONSIN. CHAPLAIN. Recorded diary of the 22nd and other regiments in the brigade.

BRAGG, BRAXTON. GENERAL, CSA. Commanded Army of Tennessee, invading Kentucky against Buell, then Rosecrans, and was driven out of Tennessee but defeated Rosecrans at Chickamauga. Then he lost to Grant at Chattanooga and was replaced by Johnston.

BROWN, EDMUND RANDOLPH, PRIVATE, 27TH INDIANA. Promoted from Private. Wounded at Antietam--left of navel. Declined promotion to Sergeant over those absent wounded; Detached service as clerk for post Provost Marshall office Tullahoma Tennessee 11-1-1863 to 8-1864. Mustered out 10-1-1864. Regimental Historian - wrote The Twenty-Seventh Indiana Volunteer Infantry in the War of the Rebellion, (1899). From Winamac, Pulaski County, Indiana, USA. Presbyterian minister until health failed due to wounds. Died March 14, 1930. Birth unknown.

BROWN, JOHN C. COMMANDED BRIGADE UNDER STEVENSON, CSA. Tennessee Whig lawyer opposed to secession and neutral about slavery but went with the tide of Confederacy. Prisoner six months following Donelson surrender. Wounded at Perryville and Chickamauga. Incapacitated several months after the Battle of Franklin. Became governor of Tennessee after the war.

BUCKINGHAM, PHILO. 20TH CONNECTICUT. LT. COLONEL. Worked up from farming and teaching to railroad agent, banker, state senator, and manufacturer before the war. Worked for Freedmen's Aid Society after the war. Then worked for a chemical manufacturer until suffering severe "paralytic shock" and remained a paralytic thereafter.

BUELL, DON CARLOS. GENERAL. Brought three divisions to Shiloh and helped throw back the Rebels, though slow in arriving the day after the battle started. Later was to drive Bragg out of Kentucky but was considered too slow to pursue. Replaced by Rosecrans after Thomas refused to take the command.

BUSCHBECK, ADOLPHUS. 2ND BRIGADE, 2ND DIVISION, 20TH CORPS. Came from Koblenz, Germany in 1849. Taught math in Philadelphia. Earned praise at Chancellorsville after being shifted leftmost, in Sigle's corps, directly facing Jackson's attack. Though he commanded a brigade in the Atlanta Campaign, he was never promoted. Taught at Episcopal Academy in Philadelphia after the war.

BUTTERFIELD, DANIEL. 3RD DIVISION, 20TH CORPS. MAJOR GENERAL. COMMANDING. His father founded American Express. Never attended West Point but was buried there with a large monument. Created the "Taps" bugle call. Was Hooker's Chief of Staff before the Atlanta Campaign. Helped create a silver crisis as Assistant Secretary of Treasury during Grant's presidency. Butterfield designed the system of corps badges, including the red, white, and blue to designate division.

CANDY, CHARLES. 1ST BRIGADE, 2ND DIVISION, 20TH CORPS. COLONEL COMMANDING. Advanced from enlisted. Served at Chancellorsville. Was in Geary's division at Gettysburg.

CASE, HENRY. 129TH ILLINOIS, COLONEL. Born 1823 in Connecticut. Studied law in Norwich and began practice in Winchester, Illinois. Returned to Connecticut, taking a two-year course at Yale Divinity School; ordained as an evangelist in 1855. Preached for some years in Ohio and then resumed his practice of law. Enlisted after the war broke out, serving with the 14th Illinois, 7th Illinois Cavalry, and 129th Illinois. Was brevetted Brigadier General in 1865. After the war, reopened his law office in Jacksonville, Illinois. When health failed, he returned to his father's house in Norwich, dying there at age 60.

CHANDLER, DANIEL H. SIMONSON'S 5TH INDIANA BATTERY, FOURTH CORPS. Born about 1829 in New York. Chandler was a blacksmith, and served in the 5th Indiana Battery Light Artillery from 1861-1864 in that capacity. Died October 25, 1908, in Knoxville, Tennessee. His diary was the basis of Holm's history of the battery. Holm says Chandler was commissioned Jr. 2nd Lieutenant in January, 1864, and commanded the left section.

CHATFIELD, HARVEY S. 78TH NEW YORK. LT. COLONEL. The 24-year old lawyer was commissioned as a captain in the 43rd New York in August 1861. Led the company through the Peninsula Campaign seeing action at Yorktown, Gaines' Mill, Savage's Station and Garnett's Farm. In July 1862 Chatfield resigned his commission and in 1864 was commissioned captain in the 78th New York and promoted to lieutenant colonel. Later that year was transferred to the 102nd, fighting at Peach Tree Creek, Atlanta, Savannah and Goldsboro. Died at age 64; buried in Woodlands Cemetery, Cambridge, New York.

CHENEY, HAMPTON JOHNSON. Brown's Brigade, CSA. Major, Adjutant. Said to be correspondent CJH of the Memphis Daily Appeal.

CJH. Said to be Hampton J. Cheney.

CLACK, CALVIN J. Lawyer enlisted with formation of 3rd Tennessee. Eventually became Lt. Colonel of regiment. Killed in Battle of Jonesboro.

COBHAM, GEORGE A. 111TH PENNSYLVANIA. COLONEL. From England. Builder. Recruited three companies. Took command of brigade after Ireland was wounded during the Battle of Resaca. Killed at Peachtree Creek.

COBURN, JOHN. 33RD INDIANA. COLONEL, COMMANDING BRIGADE. In 1853, as attorney with J.L. Ketcham, father of Sgt. Major J.L. Ketcham of 70th Indiana, he saved a free black Indianapolis businessman from being taken to Georgia as a fugitive slave. 983 984. Withstood all efforts to take away "contrabands" who sought refuge with the regiment while in Kentucky, even marching with bayonets and contrabands to the boats by which they departed. 985 Accepted Atlanta mayor's surrender. Served three terms in Congress and was on Montana Supreme Court before returning to law practice in Indiana.

CODDINGTON, W. F 19TH INDIANA BATTERY

983 (Burlock 2014)
984 (Money, The Fugitive Slave Law of 1850 in Indiana n.d.)
985 (Bradley 1865, 66)

COLLINS, GEORGE KNAPP. CO. I, 149TH NEW YORK. CAPTAIN. He served nearly two years as Lieutenant and at the close of the war was named a captain for meritorious service. Captain Collins was wounded at Chancellorsville and again at Lookout Mountain. He saw service at Gettysburg and Wauhatchie and was discharged after the battle of Lookout Mountain because of his wounds. After the war he resumed the study of law.

CONGLETON, JAMES AYERS. CO F, 105TH ILLINOIS. CORPORAL. Enlisted from Wheaton, Illinois. Born January 22, 1844, Luzerne County, Pennsylvania, died May 6, 1926, DuPage County, Illinois.

CONNOR, WESLEY, CHEROKEE ARTILLERY (CORPUT'S BATTERY) CSA. PRIVATE. From Cave Springs, Georgia. Before the war taught at Georgia School for the Deaf and after the war served as Principal for 49 years.

COOK, STEPHEN G. 150TH NEW YORK INFANTRY, RUGER'S BRIGADE CSA, ASSISTANT SURGEON. Wrote several letters to Poughkeepsie, New York newspapers under the name Fred Fulton. (Sherman disliked reporters and had prohibited soldiers writing to newspapers, so they often used aliases.)

VAN DEN CORPUT, MAX. CAPTAIN OF CHEROKEE BATTERY, CSA. From Rome, Georgia. Born in Belgium. Architect in Atlanta after the war and designed Atlanta's Union Station.

CORSE, JOHN M. BRIGADIER GENERAL. On Sherman's HQ Staff while recovering from being knocked senseless by a ball while reconnoitering during the Battle of Chattanooga. When a partner in his father's Iowa book and stationary business, he was appointed to the United States Military Academy and studied there for two years. Leaving West Point in 1855, Corse chose not to stay in the military but attended a law school in Albany, New York, and passed his bar exam. He later returned to Iowa and was nominated as the new state's lieutenant governor by the Democratic Party. In 1860, he unsuccessfully ran for secretary of state. After organizing a battery at the start of the war, he served in several staff and command positions. Built railroads and bridges after the war and later served in political offices.

COX, CHARLES HARDING. CO E 70TH INDIANA INFANTRY, CAPTAIN. Born 1844 in Indiana. Died 1927 in Georgia. He enlisted as clerk, advancing to Sergeant Major, then Lieutenant, finally acting Captain of a fun-loving company, usually blamed for all antics that occurred. Spent much of his time in camp courting ladies, eventually marrying one in Georgia after the war. Was mentioned for gallantry at Resaca and Peach Tree Creek. During his service he wrote keen letters home.

COX, WILLIAM GILLHAM. CO F 129TH ILLINOIS INFANTRY. PRIVATE. From a family of early settlers, Gillhams of Madison and Scott Counties. He and his son John Thomas enlisted in August 1862 and wrote glowingly of Captain Erastus Gillham and of their company being the best in the regiment. Then they started marches from Louisville. Both died before the year was out.

CRAM, GEORGE. CO F 105TH ILLINOIS INFANTRY. PRIVATE. Moved with mother from Lowell, Mass. to be near uncle, a map publisher and historian. Left Wheaton College for the war. Returned to uncle's firm and published Cram's maps and globes, county histories, and a magazine after the war.

CROPSEY, ANDREW J. 129TH ILLINOIS. In Plainfield, Illinois, Cropsey began teaching school before he was 16. In Cincinnati he studied and practiced law, but failing health led him to seek outdoor employment. He later moved to Fairbury and was elected to the Illinois legislature. Raised a company in the 129th, was appointed major and then lieutenant colonel before the end of the year. Cropsey was granted a medical leave of absence in 1864. Settling in Nebraska later, he served in the state senate, built a flourmill, and acquired other large interests in Jefferson and Pawnee Counties.

CRUFT, CHARLES. COMMANDING 1ST BRIGADE, 1ST DIVISION, 4TH CORPS. Lawyer from Terre Haute, Indiana, before and after the war, in partnership with Colonel Baird. Wounded at Fort Donelson and Shiloh, and again commanding a brigade at Richmond, Kentucky. Fought at Lookout Mountain.

CULVER, JOSEPH F. CO. A, 129TH ILLINOIS. CAPTAIN. Served part of the time in regimental headquarters but preferred leading his company. Lawyer, minister, band leader in Livingston County. Exchanged frequent letters with his wife. They endured the loss of their first child while in service. Moved his law practice to Emporia, Kansas in 1879. Published letters between Joseph and his wife are footnoted by Edwin C. Bearss, drawing on regimental records.

DEAVENPORT, THOMAS HOPKINS. 3RD TENNESSEE CSA. 1820-1904. Was a fairly new minister when the enlistment call came. Although fiercely patriotic, at 95 pounds he and the examining surgeon wondered if he could handle the duties of a soldier, but he was accepted and proved his worthiness in full as chaplain and soldier. He participated in the Fort Donelson and Atlanta campaigns, and was captured, imprisoned, and escaped several times.

DENNISTON, MARTIN. 33RD NEW JERSEY. PRIVATE. Mustered in at Newark, New Jersey on September 3, 1863.

DICKINSON, CHARLES H. COMPANY E 22ND WISCONSIN. SERGEANT. 1832-1921. Born in Utica, New York, learned trade of joining and painting. Settled in Edgarton, Wisconsin. After the war his carpentry shop employed over 30.

DODGE, GRENVILLE MELLEN. Learned surveying by helping survey a railroad with a neighbor's son and eventually got a degree in civil engineering. Formed his own intelligence networks to help at Pea Ridge and Vicksburg. As Brigadier General he had successes before Vicksburg. Used by Grant to rebuild railroads and bridges in Tennessee. Commanded 16th Corps in the Atlanta Campaign. Helped build Transcontinental Railroad.

DUNHAM, ALBERTUS. CO. C. 129TH ILLINOIS. PRIVATE. The brothers left the family farm near Pontiac to finish the war. Albertus, older, wrote long letters detailing their experience. LaForest added postscripts until Albertus' death of encephalitis.

DUNHAM, LAFOREST, CO. C, 129TH ILLINOIS. PRIVATE. Six years younger than his brother Albertus, Laforest had not the writing finesse but took over after Albertus died and wrote frankly and earnestly about soldiers' life, the south, his distaste for the negro (in contrast to some others in his regiment), and disgust with McClellan and Copperheads.

DUSTIN, DANIEL. 105TH ILLINOIS. COLONEL. Grew up on a Vermont farm. Graduated Dartmouth Medical School. Prospected for gold in California, then settled in Sycamore, Illinois. Served in 8th Cavalry as a captain until appointed Colonel of new regiment in 1862. Held offices of Dekalb County, Illinois after the war.

ENGLE, CHARLES. COMPANY B, 137TH NEW YORK. Enlisted August 1862 at Vestal, New York, as a private, promoted to corporal in 1863 and sergeant two years later. The 137th fought with distinction at Chancellorsville, Gettysburg, Wauhatchie, Lookout Mountain, Resaca, the siege of Atlanta, and other battles. Engle wrote numerous letters to family and friends, as well as letters for other soldiers. Many were later published in *The Civil War Letters of Charles Engle*. After the war, he returned to farming in Broome County, New York, where he died in 1918.

FENNER, CHARLES E. CAPTAIN, FENNER'S BATTERY, LOUISIANA LIGHT ARTILLERY, CSA. Fenner entered Confederate service the day after Fort Sumter was fired upon. Attorney, jurist and civic leader, Charles Erasmus Fenner (1834–1911) was born in Jackson, Tennessee, but lived most of his life in Louisiana. Educated at Western Military Institute of Kentucky, and University of Virginia. Fenner was instrumental in the organization of Tulane University. He wrote the eulogy for Robert E. Lee. Jefferson Davis died at the New Orleans home of Fenner, who was then Associate Justice of the Louisiana Supreme Court.

FITCH, WILLIAM T. 29TH OHIO. BORN 1822 IN ENGLAND. Promoted to Colonel and discharged in 1864 due to wounds. He died in Washington D.C. at the age of 72. Some of Colonel Fitch's experiences may be found in *The Untried Life: The Twenty-Ninth Ohio Volunteer Infantry in the Civil War* by James T. Fritsch.

FLEHARTY, STEPHEN F. COMPANY C, 102ND ILLINOIS. SERGEANT-MAJOR. Enlisted in 1862 and mustered out as Sergeant-Major. Fleharty had worked as a printer in Galesburg, Illinois. During the war he compiled a chronicle of his regiment's service by authoring fifty-five soldier-correspondent letters for two newspapers in Rock Island, Illinois, later published as *Jottings from Dixie*. After returning to civilian life, he wrote a regimental history of the 102nd entitled *Our Regiment*. Pronounced "Flee'-harty."

FLYNN, JOHN HORNBUCKLE. 28TH PENNSYLVANIA. COLONEL. Born in Ireland 1819, Flynn came to the U.S. in the 1840s, and was a Philadelphia liquor merchant prior to the war. He enlisted as a Lieutenant in July 1861, rose to Colonel in 1864, and Brevet Brigadier General in 1865. Flynn commanded the 28th at Gettysburg, where he was wounded, and at Edisto Island was wounded again. He later became Superintendent of Little Rock National Cemetery, dying in 1875.

FONTAINE, FELIX GREGORY. 1ST SOUTH CAROLINA REGIMENT, CSA. Major. Army correspondent for Charleston Courier, Charleston, South Carolina during the Civil War and as a journalist in Massachusetts, New York, and Columbia, S.C. As "Personae" he wrote "Marginalia, Gleanings from an Army Notebook."

FOURATT, ENOS. 33RD NEW JERSEY. LIEUTENANT COLONEL. From New Brunswick, was a veteran officer prior to joining the regiment and had been a senior officer in two other New Jersey regiments. Wounded at Crampton's Pass. Frequently took Mindil's place as commander. Born In Piscataway, New Jersey in 1827 and died in Millburn, New Jersey in 1888. Photo from John Kuhl Collection.

FOX, WILLIAM F. 107TH NEW YORK. Fox enlisted with the 107th in New York in 1862 and had become Lt. Colonel by the time they reached Resaca. He was discharged for disability shortly after being wounded at Resaca and later resumed his occupation as forester.

FULLERTON, JOSEPH S. 4TH CORPS, LIEUTENANT COLONEL, ASSISTANT ADJUTANT. Kept notes of messages during battles, which became a timeline in the Official Record. With a law degree from Ohio he moved to Missouri and was active in keeping Missouri in the Union. Was on General Gordon Granger's staff until promoted and assigned to 4th Corps.

FULTON, FRED. (see Stephen G. Cook)

GAMBEE, CHARLES B. 55th Ohio. Colonel. Born In Seneca County, New York. Worked in a dry goods store in Bellevue, Ohio. Commissioned as the captain of the 55th Regiment's Company A. On May 8, 1863 he was commissioned as Colonel and replaced Colonel Lee as the commander. A monument stated that he was a man of courage, ability, and patriotism and beloved by the members of his regiment.

GEARY, JOHN, COMMANDED 2ND DIVISION, 20TH CORPS. Pennsylvanian. Wounded five times in the Mexican war, an easy target at 6 foot 6 and 290 pounds. Tried hard to work with both sides as governor of Kansas but pleased no one and was driven out, though he'd kept down the violence. Military governor of Savannah during the winter there. Died after two terms as governor of Pennsylvania.

GILBERT, HENRY C. 19TH MICHIGAN. From Coldwater, he entered service with the 19th at its organization as Colonel in August 1862 at age 44. He died at Chattanooga on May 24, 1864, from wounds received at Resaca. As attorney, Indian agent, political hand, and colonel of the 19th, Gilbert served his state and nation for over twenty years. Gilbert's letters and diaries have been published as *Henry C. Gilbert Mackinac Indian Agent.*

GILLHAM, ERASTUS L. CO F, 129TH ILLINOIS INFANTRY. Captain. From large family of early settlers in Madison County. Served in Mexican War. Captain from muster till resignation in November, 1863.

GLANCY, PYRRHUS. CO K, 102ND ILLINOIS. From New Boston, Illinois, Glancy entered service in February 1864. He was later transferred to the 16th Illinois.

Born in 1823, Glancy died in 1896 and is buried in Glancy Cemetery, Eliza, Illinois as Glancey.

GRANT, ULYSSES. Friend of Indians and slaves. Opposed abolition, though, because he knew it would cause a war. After realizing early in the war that the enemy was as afraid of him as he was of them, he became confident and relentless in pursuit of his objectives. Won several western battles and took Vicksburg after a long effort. Commanded Western forces retaking Chattanooga after the Chickamauga defeat and then was in command of all Union forces, directing from Virginia while with Meade, and turning the Western theatre over to Sherman. Became U.S. President.

GREENMAN, NATHAN W. 5th Connecticut, Sergeant. (1840-1914), born Madison, Connecticut, died Waterbury. Practiced dentistry before the war. Eventually entered the coal business, from which he retired. One-time tax collector and member of board of relief. Republican, Mason, Odd Fellow, Congregationalist, and member of Concordia Singing Society.

GRUNERT, WILLIAM. CO. D, 129TH ILLINOIS. PRIVATE. From Germany. Enlisted from Winchester, Scott County, Illinois. Left for St. Louis in 1880 to buy goods for his grocery store and never returned.

HALSTEAD, BENTON. COMPANY F, 79TH OHIO. CAPTAIN. Later Colonel. Born near Cincinnati, Ohio in 1834, graduated from College Hill in 1854. He was appointed Sergeant Major of the 69th Ohio in 1861 and 1st Lieutenant in the 79th Ohio when it was organized in 1862. After the war he was Colonel of the 197th Regiment for one year. He was in the Battles of Resaca, Lookout Mountain, Peach Tree Creek, and the siege of Atlanta and was on General Sherman's staff on his March to the Sea, and for a short time was on staff of General Burnside. Colonel Halstead was the inventor of the first working typewriter, using his own model in his law office several years before any commercial development of typewriters. His widow said he told the story many times of visualizing a dome rotating while being struck by cannonballs during the siege of Atlanta, with the sequence of impressions forming the words "Damn the rebels." Colonel Halstead was the only brother of Murat Halstead, the well-known journalist and editor. He died in 1919 and was buried in Arlington.

HARRISON, BENJAMIN. 70TH INDIANA. COLONEL, COMMANDING. Grandson of President William Henry "Tippicanoe" Harrison. Studied history in college, became lawyer in Indianapolis. Supported his father's efforts in Congress against the Nebraska bill and went further, supporting abolitionists and joining Republicans. Raised and commanded the 70th Indiana. Eventually promoted Brigadier General. Served a term as U.S. President.

HAZEN, WILLIAM B. 2ND BRIGADE, 3RD DIVISION, 4TH CORPS. Boyhood friend of James Garfield. Hazen and Cruft, with backs to the wall, stood off Bragg at Stones River, with artillery help from Thomas, and saved the battle. Hazen then stood with Thomas at Chickamauga. Aggressive but argumentative, getting into troubles after the war. Ambrose Bierce called him the "the best hated man I ever knew.

HOLM, DAVID D. SIMONSON'S 5TH INDIANA BATTERY, FOURTH CORPS. Private Holm wrote from the diary of Daniel H. Chandler (see), Official Reports, and his own experience.

HOOD, JOHN BELL, GENERAL, CSA. LT. GENERAL. Aggressive brigade commander but thought too reckless for higher responsibilities. Thomas had been Hood's instructor at West Point. Wounded at Gettysburg, costing Hood the use of his left arm. Commanded division at Resaca. Then took over from Johnston just before Battle of Peachtree Creek. Fought Thomas and Schofield back to Nashville, after losing Atlanta.

HOOKER, JOSEPH. Commander of 20th Corps at Resaca under Thomas. Had a history of fighting well and taking care of his men but also had a reputation for drunkenness and other unsavory activities. Known to criticize superiors. Lost his opportunity in defeat at Chancellorsville, though he'd sworn off drinking. Sent west to help rescue Chattanooga, he earned opportunity with 20th Corps. Then resigned after Howard was given command of McPherson's army.

HOPPER, HASSELL. CO E, 101ST ILLINOIS. SERGEANT. From Jacksonville, Illinois. Enlisted August 1862. Service at Holly Springs, Vicksburg, Chattanooga, including the march to Knoxville, and the Atlanta Campaign. At Resaca he received a gunshot leg wound and the next day while on a forced march, his wound still bleeding, he suffered a sunstroke. This left him with impaired health and a slight limp.

HORTON, GEORGE. W. CO F 129TH ILLINOIS. Took command when Captain Gillham resigned. Born 1836 in Morgan County, and died at age 37 with burial in Elmwood Cemetery, Chanute, Kansas.

HOWARD, OLIVER OTIS. COMMANDED 4TH CORPS. Taught math at West Point after graduating. Considered resigning to become a minister but Fort Sumter changed his mind, though he tried to avoid fighting on Sunday. Blamed for lack of aggression and attention to detail, resulting in setbacks at Chancellorsville and Gettysburg. Fought Indians in the west. Commissioner of Freedmen's bureau, fighting for schools and voting rights, but was frustrated by Andrew Johnson. Founded Howard University, for both sexes, regardless of race. Superintended West Point two years.

IRELAND, DAVID. 3RD BRIGADE, 2ND DIVISION, 20TH CORPS. COLONEL. As adjutant, took command of a mutinous regiment and ambushed Confederates, getting promoted to captain. Recruited the 137th New York and led them at Harper's Ferry. Then, in Green's brigade, under General Alpheus Williams, Ireland's regiment withstood attacks at Culp's hill at Gettysburg. Led 3rd Brigade in Geary's division in the Atlanta Campaign and was wounded at Resaca. Despite health problems he led the brigade at Peachtree Creek. Died of dysentery after the capture of Atlanta.

JOHNSTON, JOSEPH E. COMMANDED ARMY OF TENNESSEE, CSA. Was replaced by classmate Robert E. Lee after the Battle of Seven Pines in Virginia. After Vicksburg, he commanded against Sherman until near Atlanta and was replaced by Hood for not being aggressive and allowing Union forces to take Confederate territory.

KERSEY, SAMUEL. C. CO A, 79TH OHIO. From Warren County, Ohio, Kersey enlisted as an 18-year old private in August 1862 and was promoted to corporal in May 1864. After the war, Kersey farmed in Warren County until his death in 1920.

KETCHAM, JANE MERRILL, 70TH INDIANA, NURSE. (1819-1911). Sister of Samuel Merrill, mother of J.L. Ketcham, Jr. Mother of nine. Helped send supplies to soldiers and then went to nurse them in camp in Kentucky. Portrait is by daughter, Susan.

KETCHAM, JOHN LEWIS, JR, 70TH INDIANA. SERGEANT MAJOR. (1844-1915). Son of Samuel Merrill's sister Jane. Father and mother were offsprings of Indiana Pioneers.

KILPATRICK, JUDSON. 3RD DIVISION, CAVALRY CORPS. BRIGADIER GENERAL COMMANDING. With limited education in New Jersey, he graduated from West Point right into the war and soon moved from infantry. A failed cavalry charge at Gettysburg and failed raid on Richmond hurt his reputation. He was sent west and supported Sherman's campaign. Died in Santiago, Chile, where he had been Minister to the Republic.

KILPATRICK, 5th Ohio Infantry.

KNIPE, JOSEPH F. BRIGADIER GENERAL. 1ST BRIGADE, 1ST DIVISION, 20TH CORPS. Sergeant in Mexican War. Colonel in Civil War and promoted to Brigadier after taking command of a brigade at Antietam. Wounded twice. Postmaster after the war.

KURTZ, WILBUR. Artist, Kurtz was born in 1882 in Oakland, Illinois, reared in Greencastle, Indiana, and educated at DePauw University and the Art Institute of Chicago. As a young artist in Chicago he worked as a draftsman, engraver, and professional illustrator, and specialized in architectural rendering. He moved to Atlanta in 1912 and became known nationally as a Georgia artist-historian and a foremost authority on the Old South. Consulted for the Movie "Gone With the Wind." Mapped the trenches and other locations at Resaca.

LINCOLN, ABRAHAM. President during the war. Dirt poor as a child. Self-educated. Hated slavery. Lawyer in Springfield, Illinois. Served in Congress and in Illinois Legislature. Reentered politics, after realizing the door had been reopened for the expansion of slavery when Douglas got the Kansas-Nebraska Bill passed. Helped found the Republican Party. Famous for Coopers Union Speech and Lincoln-Douglas debates. Successfully balanced many problems to complete the war and engineered freedom of slaves in the process.

LIVERMORE, MARY A., Born Mary Ashton Rice December 19, 1820 in Boston. Became a strong abolitionist after teaching two years on a Virginia plantation after graduating seminary in Massachusetts. Married Daniel P. Livermore, Universalist minister, in 1845 and was associate editor for his newspaper and the only woman reporter in the convention that nominated Lincoln, for whom she campaigned. Labored in all kinds of capacities for the Sanitary Commission during the war. Advocate for temperance and women's suffrage, writing extensively. Published book on her experiences. Died May 23, 1905.

LOCKMAN, JOHN T. 119TH NEW YORK. At the outbreak of the war Lockman was a student-at-law. After serving as a private in the 9th New York, he entered service as Captain in the 83rd, and promoted to commanding Colonel of the 119th. He participated in the battle of Chancellorsville, and on the death of Colonel Peissner in that battle he commanded the regiment and was commissioned its colonel. Severely wounded on first day at Gettysburg. Lockman was brevetted brigadier-general for meritorious services in the capture of Atlanta. At the close of the war, Lockman resumed the study of law, graduating from the Columbia College Law School.

MARVIN, EDWIN ELIPHALET, CO F 5TH CONNECTICUT, CAPTAIN, Born October 8, 1833, died January 24, 1914.

MCBRIDE, JOHN R. 33RD INDIANA. ADJUTANT. Mustered in September 1861 and mustered out in July 1865. McBride was born in 1841 and died 1912. He is buried at Martinsville, Indiana. He is the author of "The History of the 33rd Indiana Volunteer Infantry."

MCCLELLAND, 7TH OHIO.

McGuire, J.P. 32nd Tennessee, csa, Col. Was from a notable Lincoln and Giles Co. Tennessee family and became a respected military, business & civic figure in his own right. He had retail businesses before locating to Nashville in 1872, where by 1877 he was president of the Merchants Exchange. He was an elder in the Presbyterian Church and active in the Y.M.C.A.

McMahon, John T. Co E. 136th New York Infantry. His father was from Ireland and a Methodist Episcopal clergyman. Enlisted in September 1862 and served until June 1865, rising to 1st sergeant. After the war McMahon attended Genesee College at Lima, and in 1870 was ordained into the Methodist Episcopal ministry. He served in India missions with his wife and children until his death in 1896. Buried in Dwarahat cemetery.

McPherson, James B. Major General. Classmate of Hood at West Point. Rose rapidly in command under Halleck and Grant. Blamed by Sherman for not capturing Resaca with a small army. But continued to lead the Army of Tennessee until killed in the Battle of Atlanta, where Hood, commanding the Rebel army then, mourned the loss of his friend.

Meade, George Gordon. Major General. Placed in command of Union forces en route to Gettysburg after Hooker resigned. Blamed for failure to destroy Lee's army after winning the battle. Commanded the Army of the Potomac under Grant's supervision.

Member of Company A, 141st New York. Unidentified writer of posts for a New York Newspaper.

Merrill, Samuel, Jr. 70th Indiana, 1st Brigade, 3rd Division, 20th Corps. Lieutenant Colonel. Son of Indiana pioneer, who established Indiana banking and founded Merrill Publishing. Merrill graduated from Wabash College with a Master of Arts, then studied in Europe, returning to take charge of the Merrill Publishing, remaining active with the company until 1890. Benjamin Harrison appointed Merrill Consul General to Calcutta, India and, after returning in 1894, Merrill raised oranges and lemons in California, where he and Mrs. Merrill were active in the Presbyterian Church.

MILLER, JAMES T. CO B, 111TH PENNSYLVANIA INFANTRY. PRIVATE. Emigrated from Scotland as a child. Father was a millworker who managed to acquire land and begin farming. Enlisted at age 31, having a wife and three children and his own farm. Reenlisted, though his brothers had avoided the draft, which angered him. Killed at Peach Tree Creek.

MINDIL, GEORGE. 33RD NEW JERSEY. After service in other regiments, took command of one with enlistees who were paid a bonus. Then many deserted and the effort to retain them gave the regiment a bad name. With Mindle and Fouratt, the 33rd eventually won praise instead of encomium. John Kuhl Collection.

MORGAN, JOHN HUNT. Kentuckian. Commanded cavalry supporting Bragg against Rosecrans. But exceeded orders and raided into Ohio where he was captured. After escaping, he had less authority. But he was a legendary guerilla.

MOREY, JAMES MARSH, COMPANY D, 32ND TENNESSEE, CSA, CORPORAL. (1844-1923) Born in Jonesborough, Tennessee, died in Greenville, buried in Grove Cemetery. Father Ira was a minister. James was captured and imprisoned in Hart's Island, New York and his mother worked hard for his release. After the war he studied in Commercial College.

MORHOUS, HENRY C., CO C 123RD NEW YORK. Born in Keeseville, New York in 1841. Attained rank of sergeant in the company. Newspaper publisher after the war. Mason, GAR, and Republican. Died in 1915 in Greenwich.

MOUAT, DAVID. CO G, 29TH PENNSYLVANIA. PRIVATE. Born November 12, 1843, enlisted June 10, 1861, and mustered out July 15, 1864 at Chattanooga after enlistment expired. Participated in several battles including Port Royal, Virginia, Chancellorsville, and Gettysburg.

MUNGER, HIRAM. A. CO C 154TH NEW YORK. Hiram Munger was born in Sable Grove, Illinois in 1844 and was by trade a house carpenter and painter. At some time after the war he resided at Lakeside, Ohio, and was a member of Methodist Episcopal Church and class leader. He passed away in 1927 and is buried at the Marblehead Cemetery in Lakeside.

UNCLE NED. Took shelter with Company F, 129th Illinois, and stayed with them from Tennessee to Washington, till they went home, earning pay for cooking and doing laundry.

NOBLE, HENRY G. 19TH MICHIGAN INFANTRY. PRIVATE. Promoted to corporal August 10, 1864.

OLDROYD, OSBORN. 20TH OHIO INFANTRY. Collected Lincoln items and showcased them in Lincoln's Springfield home. Government purchased them at his death. His writings are more general, from his service at Vicksburg.

OLIVER, PAUL AMBROSE. 12TH NEW YORK INFANTRY. Aide of General Sickles, acting as aide to Butterfield during the Battle of Resaca. Had been aide of Meade, Hooker, and Warren. Inventor and manufacturer of explosives after the war.

ORMSBY, OLIVER. CO E, 149TH NEW YORK INFANTRY. CORPORAL.

OSBORN, HARTWELL. COMPANY B, 55TH OHIO INFANTRY. CAPTAIN. Retired as railroad representative in Illinois after the war. Wrote *Trials and Triumphs of the Fifty-fifth Ohio*.

PAINE, ELEAZER. GENERAL. Lawyer from Monmouth, Illinois. After dealing with him at Cairo, Illinois and Paducah, Kentucky, Ulysses Grant reported Paine as unfit to serve in any post. But Paine's political friends lobbied and kept him in command of garrisons at Gallatin, Paducah, and Tullahoma.

PAINE, PHELPS. Son of Eleazer Paine. Served under him at Gallatin.

PARDEE, JR., ARLO. 147TH PENNSYLVANIA. Son of a prominent Pennsylvania industrialist, he managed his father's mines after graduating from Rensselaer Polytechnic Institute. He joined the 28th as captain but soon promoted to major, commanding the regiment at Antietam, then serving as Brigade commander at Gettysburg and on Sherman's March to the Sea. He was made a Brevet Brigadier General in January 1865 "for special gallantry and noble conduct at the Battle of Peach Tree Creek" during the Atlanta Campaign. He returned to his father's business after the war, but his health had been undermined and he was less active. His wife had predeceased him.

PARTRIDGE, CHARLES A. 96TH ILLINOIS, SERGEANT MAJOR. Historian. Editor of Waukegan Gazette. Postmaster, Mayor, Assemblyman.

PATRICK, JOHN H. Born 1818 in Edinburgh, Scotland. Before the war he was a tailor in Cincinnati, Ohio. Enlisted 1861, became lieutenant colonel of the 5th Ohio when it was formed and in 1862 was promoted to colonel. He was in command at Cedar Mountain, missed the Battle of Antietam due to illness, and commanded at Gettysburg. During the Atlanta Campaign he commanded the First Brigade of the Second Division of the Twelfth Corps. Patrick was killed at the Battle of New Hope Church, Georgia, on May 25, 1864.

PEAK, SAMUEL W. CO F 129TH ILLINOIS. CORPORAL. Born February 9, 1840 in a log cabin near Winchester, Scott County, Illinois of pioneer parents who came by covered wagon from Kentucky and later led development in the county. He enlisted in Exeter in 1862 and was discharged as corporal in 1865, returning to Winchester and reaching the age of 96, after an active social and political life. Member of Baptist Church 70 years, treasurer and senior deacon; school trustee. A cabinet maker and skilled violin maker, he made his own at age 95 to play at local functions. Sam's memoir was written and serialized in the Winchester paper starting in 1931, at age 90.

PEDDICORD, COLUMBUS A. CSA. Eldest of the brothers. Raided trains and caused havoc for the 129th in the Gallatin-Mitchellsville area. May have used Jones as an alias.

PEDDICORD, COROLUS J. CSA. Youngest Peddicord. Guerilla associated with Morgan in Kentucky. Was captured in October 1863 and held in Gallatin, Kentucky. Killed in December on orders of General Paine after refusing to reveal information.

PEDDICORD, KELION FRANKLIN. CSA. Scout with Morgan's Cavalry. Participated in Christmas Raid and many incidents in Gallatin area. Captured during the Ohio Raid. Settled in Palmyra, Missouri after the war. Corresponded with Blakeslee after the war.

PETERS, JOSEPH. CO F, 129TH ILLINOIS. PRIVATE. Enlisted from Scott County Illinois, where he was born, with brothers Henry and Oliver, who were born as their parents migrated from Shenandoah via Ohio and Indiana. Killed at Resaca. Oliver and Henry, along with other family members, resettled on farms near St. Joseph and Raytown, Missouri. His wife Nancy remained in Illinois, as did Joseph's sisters and mother.

PIERSON, STEPHEN F. 33RD NEW JERSEY. MAJOR. Left Yale after first year for the military. Progressed from Sergeant Major to Major. Finished Yale after the war and then became a surgeon. John Kuhl Collection

POLK, WILLIAM M, POLK'S CORPS, CSA. Son of Leonidas Polk, served in the Confederate army under his father during the Civil War, advancing from the rank of cadet to captain. After graduating from the College of Physicians and Surgeons, New York, he settled in the same city, serving as professor of therapeutics and clinical medicine at Bellevue Hospital Medical College (1875–1879), of obstetrics and gynecology at the University of the City of New York (1879–1898), and subsequently as dean and professor of gynecology at Cornell University Medical College.

PORTER, ELIZA EMILY CHAPELL, SANITARY COMMISSION. Born Geneseo, New York Nov 5, 1807, died California Jan 1, 1888. Between those dates she spent all her time doing good teaching children, attending the sick in the Civil War, starting schools, and raising her own nine. Married Rev. Jeremiah Porter, who became an army chaplain in the Civil War.

POWELL, EUGENE. 66th Ohio. Lieutenant Colonel. Worked his way up from Captain. Collector of Internal Revenue after the war and member of the legislature. Wrote articles for the National Tribune.

QUINT, ALONZO HALL, CO S 2ND MASSACHUSETTS INFANTRY, CHAPLAIN. Born in New Hampshire, Graduated Dartmouth. Studied medicine but graduated Andover Theological Seminary in 1852. Pastored Congregational Churches before and after the war. Member of Massachusetts Board of Education and New Hampshire Legislature.

RANDALL, CHARLES B. 149TH NEW YORK INFANTRY. COLONEL. Son of a Baptist minister, graduated Syracuse University in 1852 and graduated law school in Albany. Entered service as a Lieutenant immediately after Fort Sumter and became known for cool judgement in the field. Severely wounded at Gettysburg. Commanded regiment at Lookout Mountain after Barnum was wounded. Killed at Peach Tree Creek.

REID, HARVEY. COMPANY A, 22ND WISCONSIN. CORPORAL. Wrote of his astute observations as clerk, who saw all, so to speak, and wrote them well. Born in 1842, was a teacher before the war and after was active in various social and political interests while a clerk in business.

RICKARDS, WILLIAM, JR. 29TH PENNSYLVANIA. COLONEL. Philadelphia jeweler before the war. Began as Captain. His troops were the first to reach the top of the mountain in the Battle Above the Clouds, planting the Stars and Stripes on the mountain's summit. Promoted Brevet Brigadier General and discharged while recovering from chest wound at Pine Knob, near Kennesaw Mountain. Managed an oil drilling business and later became a dentist at Franklin, Pennsylvania, reaching age 75.

RIDLEY, BROMFIELD LEWIS. STEWART'S DIVISION, CSA. CAPTAIN, Aide-de-camp to Stewart, ordered to the position in July 1863, and was previously with Morgan's Cavalry after the Battle of Murphreesboro (Stones River) where as a 17-year-old not in any command he and other boys rounded up 212 Federal stragglers. Son of a judge. Wrote *Battles and Sketches of the Civil War*, some appearing in *The Confederate Veteran*.

RITTER, ROWAN'S BATTERY, CSA, LIEUTENANT. Later commanding.

ROBINSON, JAMES S. 3RD BRIGADE, 1ST DIVISION, 20TH CORPS. COLONEL. Born near Mansfield, Ohio, Robinson attended the common schools. Acquiring the art of printing as a young man, he moved to Kenton, Ohio in 1845 and entered the newspaper business, editing and publishing the Kenton Republican. Robinson was Chief Clerk of the Ohio House of Representatives in 1856. Enlisted at the beginning of the war and soon made Captain. Promoted to Major in October 1861, Lieutenant Colonel in April 1862, and Colonel of the 82nd in August 1862. He took part in operations at Rich Mountain, Cedar Mountain, the Second Battle of Bull Run, and Chancellorsville.

ROSECRANS, WILLIAM. MAJOR GENERAL. Successful in engineering enterprises after leaving the army before the war. Had mixed results in battles, depending on who is telling the story. Had his ins and outs with Grant. But his record in Kentucky and Tennessee, with Thomas, was good until the mistake at Chickamauga. Was loved by his troops.

RUGER, THOMAS S. 2ND BRIGADE, 1ST DIVISION, 20TH CORPS. Commanded a brigade at Antietam. Wounded at Gettysburg commanding Williams' division while he was acting as corps commander. Military governor of Georgia in Reconstruction and involved with Freedmen's Bureau in Alabama. Superintendent of West Point for four years. Retired as a Major General.

RYDER, JOHN J. COMPANY I 33RD MASSACHUSETTS, PRIVATE, (1843-1934) Promised his mother, widowed when he was five, he would return from the war and did, surviving freezing cold when wet and heat of pitched battle at Gettysburg, Wauhatchie, and Resaca till severely wounded at Kennesaw. Home, he married, fished, kept lighthouse, and raised oysters. Head of local GAR. Was staff officer to Gen. Leonard Wood in 1909 maneuvers.

SCHOFIELD, JOHN M. ARMY OF THE OHIO, MAJOR GENERAL. Was temporarily kicked out of West Point and George Thomas voted against allowing him to stay. After the campaign, Schofield was subordinate to Thomas. Taught physics at Washington University in St. Louis. Was on Lyon's staff at Wilson's Creek. Served in various commands and was often in controversy.

SCHURZ, CARL, MAJOR GENERAL. A leader of the 1848 German revolution, he was driven out with many other officers and became a strong, intellectual leader in the US. Strong opponent of slavery. Active in Grant's administration and Freedmen's Bureau. Senator from Missouri. Newspaper editor.

SHELLENBERGER, JOHN K. COMPANY E. 64TH OHIO, CAPTAIN. Wrote about battles after the war, while superintendent of National Cemeteries.

SHERIDAN, PHILIP. Aggressive commander of both infantry and cavalry. Fought in the West and went east with Grant after Chattanooga. His relentless pursuits with cavalry matched well with Grant. He dealt with Indian territories before and after the war.

SHERMAN, WILLIAM TECUMSEH. COMMANDED ATLANTA CAMPAIGN. Brother of Senator John Sherman. Roommate of George Henry Thomas in first year at West Point. Astounded in the Vicksburg campaign by Grant's reliance and success at relentless pursuit with little rations, and formed mutual trust. Served some in Georgia before the war and knew of its terrain. Was superintendent of a military academy in Louisiana before war broke out.

SICKLES, DANIEL. MAJOR GENERAL. Without a command during the campaign. Closely associated with Hooker. Notorious rogue but able to find political posts regardless. Accused of failures at Chancellorsville and at Gettysburg, where he lost a leg. He and his staff were travelling with Hooker early in the Atlanta Campaign and he sent reports to Lincoln.

SIMONSON, PETER. 5TH INDIANA BATTERY. Born in Rhode Island in 1804, and later a resident of Columbia City, Indiana. Married with one daughter, Simonson enlisted in October 1861 as Captain. In November 1861 he was commissioned into the 5th Indiana Light Artillery. After Resaca, on June 15, he ordered the artillery fire that killed Confederate General Polk, who had founded the University on Cumberland Mountain. The next day, Simonson himself was killed by a Rebel sharpshooter at Pine Mountain, Georgia,

SLOCUM, HENRY WARNER. Vocal against slavery while at West Point. Tutored roommate Sheridan in math, getting credit for Sheridan graduating. After many battles in the east, was senior general under Meade at Gettysburg and credited with holding Culps Hill. Governor of Atlanta until leaving for the march to Savannah. Was involved in several New York businesses and in politics after the war. Early supporter of building the Brooklyn Bridge.

SMITH, FRANKLIN K. 102ND ILLINOIS. COLONEL. Born in New York. Was with the 102nd through the war and brevetted Major General in 1865. Resided in Galesburg, Illinois after the war.

SPOOR, WILLIAM M. 137TH NEW YORK. Spoor was born in 1838 in Windsor, NY. He enlisted in August 1862 as a Corporal and fought at Antietam, Bolivar, Chancellorsville, and Gettysburg. Spoor was promoted to Full Sergeant in September 1863. He then fought at Wauhatchie, Lookout Mountain, Ringgold, Resaca, New Hope Church, Pine Knob, Noses Creek, Marietta and Kennesaw Mountain. William Spoor died of scurvy in August 1864.

STANLEY, DAVID S. MAJOR GENERAL COMMANDING FIRST DIVISION, 4TH CORPS. Career soldier from Ohio. Left Indian Territory at the start of war and was in several western battles, beginning with Wilson's Creek, quickly rising to Brigadier General. Commanded both infantry and cavalry. After the Atlanta Campaign, Stanley earned a Medal of Honor leading a counterattack that helped save the Battle of Franklin and was wounded so missed the Battle of Nashville. Commanded the Yellowstone Expedition and then served in Texas and New Mexico.

STEPHENS, ALEXANDER. CSA. VICE-PRESIDENT. Whig. Lawyer. Raised poor but parents were book readers and he had access to books and help. Small and sickly all his life. Served in US Congress. Opposed secession but strongly advocated expansion of slavery into Kansas and New Mexico. Was back in US Congress after the war and later was governor of Georgia.

STEVENSON, CARTER L. CSA. Commanded a division under Hood. Career officer. Stood against Hooker at Lookout Mountain. Then burned the bridges that kept Hooker from helping at Missionary Ridge, allowing Stevenson himself to go reinforce the line against Sherman. Directly faced Hooker's onslaught at Resaca.

STEWART, ALEXANDER P. CSA. West Point graduate from Tennessee who resigned and taught mathematics and philosophy. Was a Whig and opposed secession. Fought in western theatre. In Battle of Nashville after Atlanta, then in the Carolinas. Settled in Missouri after the war.

STILLWELL, JAMES. 79TH OHIO INFANTRY. CHAPLAIN

STORRS, JOHN WHITING. 20TH CONNECTICUT INFANTRY. Not a member, apparently, but wrote a history of the regiment on their request.

STRONG, ROBERT HALE. COMPANY B, 105TH ILLINOIS INFANTRY. PRIVATE. Wrote his "diary" from memory, refreshed by letters his mother saved, while laid up with rheumatism caused by the war service.

SWEENY, THOMAS WILLIAM. MAJOR GENERAL. Fighter from Cork, Ireland known to give orders in multiple languages, including profane. Lost an arm in Mexican War but stayed in the army. Stayed on the field at Shiloh though wounded. Had commanded the arsenal at St. Louis when Rebels tried to take it over.

THOMAS, GEORGE HENRY. ARMY OF CUMBERLAND, GENERAL, COMMANDING. Thomas had escaped the Nat Turner rebellion at age 15 by fleeing with his family into the woods. Roommate of Sherman in their first year at West Point. Disowned by his slave-owning Virginia family after staying with the Union. Nicknamed "Old Slow Trot," for being methodical and thorough, and "The Rock of Chickamauga" for holding the ground until the entire army could withdraw. Many historians now consider him the best General of the war.

TOTTON, GEORGE W. COMPANY F, 79TH OHIO. PRIVATE. Born and died at Cincinnati, 1837- 1898.

TREMAIN, HENRY EDWIN. 3RD DIVISION, 20TH CORPS. CAPTAIN. Temporary duty from Sickles' staff, acting as aide to Butterfield during the battle. Wrote praises of Hooker and Sickles.

TREXLER, JEREMIAH S. 73RD PENNSYLVANIA. ASSISTANT SURGEON. Born 1832. Was doctor in Kutztown, Pennsylvania before and after the war. From boyhood he sketched and carved. One sketch sent to Leslie's Magazine was a view from north of Geary's position next to the road that passed behind the hill of the angle of Hood's position. His carved pipes were prized by their recipients.

THRUSTIN, W. D, COMPANY D, 111TH OHIO, CAPTAIN. Wrote history of regiment. No other information. But his collar in his photograph suggests ministry.

TROUSDALE, JULIUS AUGUSTUS. CSA. Grandson of a Gallatin, Kentucky founder and son of Governor. Wrote indictment of General Paine after the war.

WALKER, JAMES. ARTIST. Known for accuracy and detail. Painted majestic composite of The Battle of Lookout Mountain. Painted The Battle of Resaca on commission.

WARD, WILLIAM THOMAS. 1ST BRIGADE, 3RD DIVISION, 20TH CORPS. Born in Amelia County, Virginia, August 9, 1808; attended the common schools and St. Mary's College near Lebanon, Kentucky; studied law; commenced practice in Greensburg, Kentucky; served in the Mexican War; member of the State House of Representatives in 1850; elected as a Whig to the Thirty-second Congress 1851- 1853; commissioned Brigadier General in the Union Army and served throughout the Civil War; resumed the practice of law in Louisville, Kentucky, where he died October 12, 1878. Interment in Cave Hill Cemetery. .986

One of the earliest and most practical of all the unconditional Union men in the State of Kentucky was William T. Ward. Early in August he visited the counties of Metcalfe, Green, Taylor, Hart and Adair, and sent messages into Cumberland, Clinton and Russell Counties, urging the citizens, many of whom had joined home-guard companies, to disband those organizations, on the grounds that it placed them under control of the governor, whom he regarded as disloyal to the national government. He succeeded in inducing twenty-eight companies to promise to enlist in the United States service as soon as the necessary authority to organize a brigade could be obtained. Mr. Ward then went to Washington, where he was commissioned a Brigadier General on the 18th of September, 1861. .987

WHITAKER, WALTER CHILES. 2ND BRIGADE, 1ST DIVISION, 4TH CORPS. Kentucky lawyer and legislator who chose Union and proposed a resolution to end states' neutrality. Wounded at Stones River and Chickamauga, and again at Resaca. Reputation for being drunk during battles and after returning to law after the war spent some years in a mental asylum.

WIDOWS, JAMES R CO D, 70TH INDIANA

WILLIAMS, S. ALPHEUS. 1ST DIVISION, 20TH CORPS. BRIGADIER GENERAL. He graduated from Yale University with a law degree in 1831. His father, who died when Williams was eight years old, had left him a sizable inheritance, which he used between 1832 and 1836 for extensive travel in the United States and Europe, including study of battlefields. He settled in Detroit, Michigan, established himself as a lawyer, and married the daughter of a prominent family, Jane Hereford Larned, with whom he produced five children, two of whom died as infants. Jane died in 1848, at the age of 30. In the Mexican-American War he was a lieutenant colonel of the First Michigan Infantry and then became Detroit's postmaster from 1849-1853. He served two terms in Congress until he suffered a stroke in the U.S. Capitol and died on

---

986 (Congress 2016)
987 (Perrin n.d., 363) Helping secure Kentucky for the Union was politically certain to gain Ward a generalship.

December 21, 1878. He is interred in Elmwood Cemetery in Detroit. His letters to his daughters are the source for his insights.

WILSON, WILLIAM A. CO K, 102ND ILLINOIS INFANTRY. 1ST BRIGADE, 3RD DIVISION, 20TH CORPS, CAPTAIN. His brother Allan, corporal, died at Gallatin. From Mercer County, Illinois. Farmer.

WINKLER, CHARLES FREDERICK. 26TH WISCONSIN, 3RD BRIGADE, 3RD DIVISION, 20TH CORPS. He emigrated to the United States from Bremen, Germany when he was six years of age and settled Milwaukee, Wisconsin. He was a lawyer in practice when he enlisted at the start of the Civil War. Appointed Captain of Company B, 26th Regiment, Wisconsin Volunteers, he became Judge Advocate General of the XI Corps at the rank of Major in 1862. Promoted Lieutenant Colonel in command of the 26th Wisconsin Infantry, he participated in the battles of Chancellorsville, Gettysburg, and the Atlanta Campaign. In August 1864, he was promoted Colonel and served on court martial boards for the Judge Advocate General for remainder of the war. For meritorious services, he was brevetted Brigadier General of US Volunteers on June 15, 1865. After the war, he resumed his law practice, was president of the Milwaukee Public Museum, vice president of the American Bar Association, and a member of the Wisconsin State Assembly in 1872.

WOOD, JAMES. 136TH NEW YORK. COLONEL, COMMANDING BRIGADE. Took command after death of Colonel Faulkner. Appointed Brig. Gen. at close of war.

WOOD, THOMAS J. 3RD DIVISION, 4TH CORPS. Major General. Kentuckian who recruited and trained several regiments for Civil War. Faulted for not questioning Rosecrans' order to move his division, which left a gap resulting in loss of the Battle of Chickamauga. His division is credited with leading the assault capturing Missionary Ridge.

Army Infantry Units

A DEPARTMENT has multiple armies working in a broad geographic area.

An ARMY consists of one or more Corps.

A CORPS typically has three divisions, sometimes more, sometimes only one.

A DIVISION usually has three brigades. Units at division or above are commanded by a major general. Sometimes a brigadier general will act as commander. Especially after battle losses during a campaign, lower-level commanders will take charge of units requiring a higher rank. It's a good opportunity to earn promotion.

A BRIGADE consists of about five regiments depending on the sizes of the regiments, which can reach a thousand men each but by reduction can be a tenth that. A brigadier general commands, or a colonel from one of the regiments until promoted.

A REGIMENT is the basic military unit provided by states and is the home unit of a soldier whatever the higher level command. A regiment has up to ten companies, each having up to 100 men. As men leave, by death, desertion, reassignment, and so on, they are not replaced unless by recruitment. A regiment is a self-contained unit that does not change its name and elects its own officers, subject to approval. A colonel commands, with assistance of a lieutenant colonel and a major.

A BATTALION is one or more regiments under one command as needed during battle.

A COMPANY is also recruited and elects its own officers. Membership is a bit more fluid, soldiers occasionally changing from one to the other, but they usually retain a company identity. A captain commands, with the help of one or two lieutenants.

Within the company, squads for various purposes are formed under sergeants and corporals, as needed.

Union Order of Battle

May 15, 1864, Resaca Angle .988

Army of the Cumberland. Major General George H. Thomas

Fourth Army Corps. Major General Oliver O. Howard

FIRST DIVISION. MAJOR GENERAL DAVID S. STANLEY
First Brigade. Brigadier General Charles Cruft
21st Illinois.
38th Illinois arrived at Resaca June 2.
31st Indiana. John T Smith
81st Indiana. Wheeler
1st Kentucky. Enyart
2nd Kentucky. Hurd
90th Ohio. Yeoman
101st Ohio. Kirby

Second Brigade. Brigadier General Walter C. Whitaker
115th Illinois Moore
96th Illinois Champion
40th Ohio.Snodgrass
51st Ohio McClain
99th Ohio Cummins
84th Indiana Neff
35th Indiana Duffley
21st Kentucky Price

Third Brigade. Colonel William Grose
59th Illinois. Post
75th Illinois. Bennett
80th Illinois. Kilgour
84th Illinois. Waters
9th Indiana Col Suman
30th Indiana. Orrin Hurd
36th Indiana. Carey

988 (OR, Series I Vol 38 Part 1 Serial 75: Reports n.d., 88) Extracted as needed for this story.

84th Indiana. Taylor
77th Pennsylvania. Rose

Artillery. Captain Peter Simonson

SECOND DIVISION. BRIGADIER GENERAL JOHN NEWTON
First Brigade. Colonel Francis T. Sherman
Second Brigade. Brigadier General George D. Wagner
Third Brigade. Brigadier General Charles G. Harker

THIRD DIVISION. BRIGADIER GENERAL THOMAS J. WOOD.
First Brigade. Brigadier General August Willich
Second Brigade. Brigadier General William B. Hazen
Third Brigade. Brigadier General Samuel Beatty
Artillery. Captain Cullen Bradley

Fourteenth Army Corps. Major General John M. Palmer

FIRST DIVISION. BRIGADIER GENERAL RICHARD W. JOHNSON
First Brigade. Brigadier General William P. Carlin
Second Brigade. Brigadier General John H. King
Third Brigade. Colonel Benjamin F. Scribner
Artillery. Captain Lucius H. Drury

SECOND DIVISION. BRIGADIER GENERAL JEFFERSON C. DAVIS
First Brigade. Brigadier General James D. Morgan
Second Brigade. Colonel John G. Mitchell
Third Brigade. Colonel Daniel McCook
Artillery. Captain Charles M. Barnett

THIRD DIVISION. BRIGADIER GENERAL ABSALOM BAIRD
First Brigade. Brigadier General John B. Turchin
Second Brigade. Colonel Ferdinand Van Derveer
Third Brigade. Colonel George P. Este
Artillery. Captain George Estep.
Artillery Brigade. Major Charles Houghtaling

Twentieth Army Corps. Major General Joseph Hooker

FIRST DIVISION. BRIGADIER GENERAL ALPHEUS S. WILLIAMS

First Brigade. Brigadier General Joseph F. Knipe
5th Connecticut. Colonel Warren W. Packer

3rd Maryland (Detachment). Lieutenant David Gove
123rd New York. Colonel Archibald L. McDougall
141st New York. Colonel William K. Logie
46th Pennsylvania. Colonel James L. Selfridge

Second Brigade. Brigadier General Thomas H. Ruger
27th Indiana. Colonel Silas Colgrove
2nd Massachusetts. Colonel William Cogswell
13th New Jersey. Colonel Ezra A. Carman
107th New York. Colonel Nirom M. Crane
150th New York. Colonel John H. Ketcham
3rd Wisconsin. Colonel William Hawley

Third Brigade. Colonel James S. Robinson
82nd Illinois, Lieutenant Colonel Edward S. Salomon
101st Illinois, Lieutenant Colonel John B. Le Sage
45th New York, Colonel Adolphus Dobke
143rd New York. Colonel Horace Boughton
61st Ohio. Colonel Stephen J. McGroarty
82nd Ohio. Lieutenant Colonel David Thomson
31st Wisconsin. Colonel Francis H. West
Artillery. Captain John D. Woodbury

SECOND DIVISION. BRIGADIER GENERAL JOHN W. GEARY

First Brigade. Colonel Charles Candy
5th Ohio. Colonel John H. Patrick. Lieutenant Colonel Robert L. Kilpatrick
7th Ohio. Lieutenant Colonel Samuel McClelland
29th Ohio. Colonel William T. Fitch
66th Ohio. Lieutenant Colonel Eugene Powell
28th Pennsylvania. Lieutenant Colonel John Flynn
147th Pennsylvania. Colonel Ario Pardee, Jr

Second Brigade. Colonel Adolphus Buschbeck
33rd New Jersey. Colonel George W. Mindil, Lieutenant Colonel Enos Fouratt
119th New York. Colonel John T. Lockman
134th New York. Lieutenant Colonel Allan H. Jackson. Captain Clinton C. Brown.
154th New York. Colonel Patrick H. Jones
27th Pennsylvania. Lieutenant Colonel August Riedt
73rd Pennsylvania, Major Charles C. Cresson
109th Pennsylvania. Captain Frederick L. Gimber

Third Brigade. Colonel David Ireland. Colonel George A. Cobham, Jr.
60th New York. Colonel Abel Godard
78th New York. Lieutenant Colonel Harvey S. Chatfield
102nd New York. Colonel James C. Lane
137th New York. Lieutenant Colonel Koert S. Van Voorhis
149th New York. Lieutenant Colonel Charles B. Randall. Colonel Henry A. Barnum
29th Pennsylvania. Lieutenant Colonel Thomas M. Walker
111th Pennsylvania. Colonel George A. Cobham, Jr. Lieutenant Colonel Thomas M. Walker

Artillery. Captain William Wheeler

THIRD DIVISION. MAJOR GENERAL DANIEL BUTTERFIELD

First Brigade. Brigadier General William T. Ward
102nd Illinois. Colonel Franklin C. Smith
129th Illinois. Colonel Henry Case
70th Indiana. Colonel Benjamin Harrison
79th Ohio. Colonel Henry G. Kennett
105th Illinois. Colonel Daniel Dustin

Second Brigade. Colonel Samuel Ross. Colonel John Coburn
20th Connecticut. Lieutenant Colonel Philo B. Buckingham
33rd Indiana. Major Levin T. Miller
85th Indiana. Colonel John P. Baird
19th Michigan. Colonel Henry C. Gilbert. Major Eli A. Griffin
22nd Wisconsin. Lieutenant Colonel Edward Bloodgood

Third Brigade. Colonel James Wood, Jr.
33rd Massachusetts. Lieutenant Colonel Godfrey Rider, Jr.
136th New York. Lieutenant Colonel Lester B. Fulkner
55th Ohio. Colonel Charles B. Gambee
73rd Ohio, Major Samuel H. Hurst
26th Wisconsin. Lieutenant Colonel Frederick C. Winkler

Artillery. Captain Marco B. Gary
Artillery Brigade. Major John A. Reynolds

Cavalry Corps. Brigadier General Washington L. Elliott
FIRST DIVISION. BRIGADIER GENERAL EDWARD M. MCCOOK

SECOND DIVISION. BRIGADIER GENERAL KENNER GARRARD

THIRD DIVISION. BRIGADIER GENERAL JUDSON KILPATRICK

Army of the Tennessee. Major General James B. McPherson

Fifteenth Army Corps. Major General John A. Logan

FIRST DIVISION. BRIGADIER GENERAL PETER J. OSTERHAUS
First Brigade. Brigadier General Charles R. Woods
Second Brigade. Colonel James A. Williamson
Third Brigade. Colonel Hugo Wangelin

SECOND DIVISION. BRIGADIER GENERAL MORGAN L. SMITH
First Brigade. Brigadier General Giles A. Smith
Second Brigade. Brigadier General Joseph A. J. Lightburn
Artillery. Captain Francis De Gress

THIRD DIVISION. BRIGADIER GENERAL JOHN E. SMITH
Second Brigade. Colonel Green B. Raum
Third Brigade. Brigadier General Charles L. Matthies
Artillery. Captain Henry Dillon

FOURTH DIVISION. BRIGADIER GENERAL WILLIAM HARROW
First Brigade. Colonel Reuben Williams
Second Brigade. Brigadier General Charles C. Walcutt
Third Brigade. Colonel John M. Oliver

Artillery. Captain Henry H. Griffiths

Sixteenth Army Corps (Left Wing). Major General Grenville M. Dodge

SECOND DIVISION. BRIGADIER GENERAL THOMAS W. SWEENY
First Brigade. Brigadier Gen Elliott W. Rice.
Second Brigade. Colonel Patrick E. Burke
Third Brigade. Colonel Moses M. Bane
Artillery. Captain Frederick Welker

FOURTH DIVISION. BRIGADIER GENERAL JAMES C. VEATCH
First Brigade. Brigadier General John W. Fuller
Second Brigade. Brigadier General John W. Sprague

Third Brigade. Colonel James H. Howe
Artillery. Captain Jerome B Burrows

Seventeenth Army Corps. Major General Frank P. Blair, Jr.

THIRD DIVISION. BRIGADIER GENERAL MORTIMER D. LEGGETT
First Brigade. Brigadier General Manning F. Force
Second Brigade. Colonel Robert K. Scott
Third Brigade. Colonel Adam G. Malloy

FOURTH DIVISION. BRIGADIER GENERAL WALTER Q. GRESHAM
First Brigade. Colonel William L. Sanderson
Second Brigade. Colonel George C. Rogers
Third Brigade. Colonel William Hall

Army of the Ohio (Twenty-Third Army Corps) Major General John M. Schofield

FIRST DIVISION. BRIGADIER GENERAL ALVIN P. HOVEY
First Brigade. Colonel Richard F. Barter
Second Brigade. Colonel John C. McQuistion

SECOND DIVISION. BRIGADIER GENERAL HENRY M. JUDAH
First Brigade. Brigadier General Nathaniel C. McLean
Second Brigade. Brigadier General Milo S. Hascall
Third Brigade. Colonel Silas A. Strickland
Artillery. Captain Joseph C. Shields

THIRD DIVISION. BRIGADIER GENERAL JACOB D. COX
First Brigade. Colonel James W. Reilly
Second Brigade. Brigadier General Mahlon D. Manson
Dismounted Cavalry Brigade. Colonel Eugene W. Crittenden
Artillery. Major Henry W. Wells

Cavalry. Major General George Stoneman

Confederate Order of Battle

APRIL 30, 1864 The Atlanta Campaign Resaca Angle .989

Army of Tennessee. General Joseph E. Johnston

Hood's Corps. Lieut. Gen. John B. Hood

HINDMAN'S DIVISION. MAJ. GEN. THOMAS C. HINDMAN

Deas' Brigade. Brig. Gen. Zachariah C. Deas
19th Alabama. Col. Samuel K. McSpadden
22d Alabama. Col. Benjamin R. Hart
25th Alabama. Col. George D. Johnston
39th Alabama. Lieut. Col. William C. Clifton
50th Alabama. Col. John G. Coltart
17th Alabama Battalion Sharpshooters. Capt. James F. Naber.

Tucker's Brigade. Brig. Gen. William F. Tucker
7th Mississippi. Lieut. Col. Benjamin F. Johns
9th Mississippi. Capt. S. S. Calhoon
10th Mississippi. Capt. Robert A. Bell
41st Mississippi. Col. J. Byrd Williams
14th Mississippi. Lieut. Col. R. G. Kelsey
9th Mississippi Battalion Sharpshooters. Maj. William C. Richards

Manigault's Brigade. Brig. Gen. Arthur M. Manigault
24th Alabama. Col. Newton N. Davis
28th Alabama. Lieut. Col. William L. Butler
34th Alabama. Col. Julius C. B. Mitchell
10th South Carolina. Col. James F. Pressley
19th South Carolina. Lieut. Col. Thomas P. Shaw

Walthall's Brigade. Brig. Gen. Edward C. Walthall
24th-27th Mississippi. Col. Robert P. McKelvaine
29th-30th Mississippi. Col. William F. Brantley
34th Mississippi. Col. Samuel Benton

STEVENSON'S DIVISION. MAJ. GEN. CARTER L. STEVENSON

989 (OR, Series I Vol 38 Part 3 Serial 74: Reports n.d., 672)

Brown's Brigade. Brig. Gen. John C. Brown
3rd Tennessee (Volunteers). Lieut. Col. Calvin J. Clack
18th Tennessee. Lieut. Col. William R. Butler
26th Tennessee. Capt. Abijah F. Boggess
32d Tennessee. Maj. John P. McGuire
45th Tennessee-23rd Tennessee Battalion. Col. Anderson Searcy

Reynolds' Brigade. Brig. Gen. Alexander W. Reynolds
58th North Carolina. Maj. Thomas J. Dula
60th North Carolina. Lieut. Col. James T. Weaver
54th Virginia. Col. Robert C. Trigg
63d Virginia. Capt. Connally H. Lynch

Cumming's Brigade. Brig. Gen. Alfred Cumming
34th Georgia. Maj. John M. Jackson
36th Georgia. Maj. Charles E. Broyles
39th Georgia. Lieut. Col. J. F. B. Jackson
56th Georgia. Col. E. P. Watkins

Pettus' Brigade. Brig. Gen. Edmund W. Pettus
20th Alabama. Col. James M. Dedman
23d Alabama. Lieut. Col. Joseph B. Bibb
80th Alabama. Col. Charles M. Shelley
31st Alabama. Col. Daniel R. Hundley
46th Alabama. Capt. George E. Brewer

STEWART'S DIVISION. MAJ. GEN. ALEXANDER P. STEWART.

Stovall's Brigade. Brig. Gen. Marcellus A. Stovall
40th Georgia. Col. Abda Johnson
41st Georgia. Maj. Mark. S. Nall.
42d Georgia. Col. Robert J. Henderson
48d Georgia. Maj. William C. Lester
52d Georgia. Capt. Rufus R. Asbury

Gibson's Brigade. Brig. Gen. Randall L. Gibson
1st Louisiana (Regulars). Maj. S. S. Batchelor
13th Louisiana. Lieut. Col. Francis L. Campbell
16th Louisiana-25th Louisiana. Col. Joseph C. Lewis
19th Louisiana. Lieut. Col. Hyder A. Kennedy
20th Louisiana. Maj. Samuel L. Bishop

4th Louisiana Battalion. Maj. Duncan Buie
14th Louisiana Battalion Sharpshooters. Maj. John E. Austin

Clayton's Brigade. Brig. Gen. Henry D. Clayton
18th Alabama. Col. James T. Holtzclaw
32d Alabama-58th Alabama. Col. Bushrod Jones
36th Alabama. Lieut. Col. Thomas H Herndon
38th Alabama. Col. A. R. Lankford

Baker's Brigade. Brig. Gen. Alpheus Baker
37th Alabama. Lieut. Col. Alexander A. Greene
40th Alabama. Capt. Elbert D. Willett
42d Alabama. Lieut. Col. Thomas C. Lanier

Maney's Brigade. George Maney (detached from Cheatham's Division)
1st Tennessee. Col Hume R. Feild
27th Tennessee
4th Tennessee (Confederate). Lieut. Col. Oliver A. Bradshaw
6th Tennessee. Lieut. Col. John W. Buford
9th Tennessee
19th Tennessee. Maj. James G. Deaderick
50th Tennessee. Col. Stephen H. Colms
Stanford's Mississippi Battery
11th Tennessee Cavalry

Artillery. Brig. Gen. Francis A. Shoup

Hood's Corps. Col. Robert F. Beckham

Courtney's Battalion. Maj. Alfred R. Courtney
Alabama Battery. Capt. James Garrity
Alabama Battery. Capt. Staunton H. Dent
Douglas' (Texas) Battery. Lieut. John H. Bingham

Eldridge's Battalion. Maj. John W. Eldridge
Eufaula (Alabama) Artillery. Capt. McDonald Oliver
Louisiana Battery. Capt. Charles E. Fenner
Mississippi Battery. Capt. Thomas J. Stanford

Johnston's Battalion. Maj. John W. Johnston
Cherokee (Georgia.) Artillery. Capt. Max. Van Den Corput
Stephens (Georgia) Light Artillery. Capt. John B. Rowan. (Third Maryland

Artillery)
Tennessee Battery. Capt. Lucius G. Marshall

Supplemental Reading

Resaca Battlefield website, by Friends of Resaca, describes the entire battle, not just the part covered in this book. The group is dedicated to preserving the battlefield. http://www.resacabattlefield.com/.

Fletcher Pratt's *Short History of the Civil War: Ordeal by Fire* is a concise and lively companion to learn of other battles mentioned in this book. His primary source may have been Draper's history, published in 1870, which is available online and is a well written, long read.

James McPherson's *Battle Cry of Freedom* is thorough research and elucidation about the war and its causes. It earned a Pulitzer Prize.

Decision in the West, by Albert Castel, goes much deeper into all the battles of the Atlanta Campaign.

Books below are not directly sourced in this work but led to finding some of their actual sources.

The Culver letters are online (see bibliography) but do not have the extensive footnotes that Edwin C. Bearss researched for the print version.

The Anderson and Groves books are extensive research on the 19th Michigan and 22nd Wisconsin of Coburn's brigade and explain some of their problems. Also, see Harvey Reid's letters and Bradley's *The Star Corps* in the bibliography. Catharine Merrill's history of Indiana in the Civil War discusses this at length.

The *Battle of Resaca* by Philip L. Secrist was an early explanation of the battle overall.

The *Echos of Battle* books are a wealth of extracts that might never have surfaced otherwise.

And, the Official Record:

https://ehistory.osu.edu/books/official-records
http://ebooks.library.cornell.edu/m/moawar/waro.html

Bibliography

Abrams, Alexander St. Clair. 1864. "The Battle of Oostanaula." May 25. Accessed 2015.

Anderson, Frank. 1897. "A Courier at the Battle of Resaca." Edited by S. A. Cunningham. *Confederate Veteran.* Accessed 2016. https://archive.org/stream/confederateveter5conf#page/296/mode/2u p.

Anderson, William. 1995. *They Died to Make Men Free.* 2nd. Morningside Books.

Armstrong, M. W. 1864. "Letter to Mrs. Josiah Kellogg." Abraham Lincoln Library, June 10. Accessed 2014.

Austin, Judson L. 1864. "The Letters of Judson L. Austin." University of Michigan, Clements Library. Accessed 2016.

Ayers, James T. 1947. *Civil War Diary of James T. Ayers.* Edited by John Hope Franklin. Illinois State Historical Society.

Banks, Henry Ira. 2014. "Book 2." *The Legacy Road.* Accessed 2020. http://thelegacyroad.blogspot.com/.

Bates, Leon F. 2018. "The Fugitive Slave Act: John Freeman's Journey to the Borderlands." Wayne State Universityu. Accessed 2019. https://scholar.uwindsor.ca/cgi/viewcontent.cgi?article=1003&context=borderlandstories.

Baumgartner, Richard A., and Larry M. Strayer. 2004. *Echos of Battle: The Atlanta Campaign.* Blue Acorn Press.

—. 1996. *Echos of Battle: The Struggle for Chattanooga.* Blue Acorn Press.

Benton, Charles E. 1902. *As Seen From the Ranks.* Accessed 2016. https://archive.org/stream/cu31924032780425#page/n19/mode/2up.

Bierce, Ambrose. n.d. *The Crime at Pickett's Mill.* Accessed 2016. http://www.online-literature.com/bierce/1991/.

Billings, Josh. 1887. *Hardtack and Coffee.* Boston: George M. Smith & Co. Accessed 2017. https://archive.org/details/hardtackandcoff00billgoog.

Blair, William Alan. n.d. *A Politician Goes to War: The Civil War Letters of John White Geary.* Pennsylvania State University Press.

Blakeslee, G. H. 1897. "Brave Men of His Regiment." *The National Tribune.* Washington, D. C., October 14. http://chroniclingamerica.loc.gov/lccn/sn82016187/1897-10-14/ed-1/seq-2/.

Blakeslee, G. H. 1895. "Harrison's Brigade at the Battle of Resaca." *National Tribune.* http://chroniclingamerica.loc.gov/lccn/sn82016187/1895-02-14/ed-1/seq-2/.

Blakeslee, George Hopkins. n.d. "Correspondence with K. F. Peddicord." Missouri Archives.

—. n.d. "Maps." *Library of Congress Collections.* Accessed 2014. https://www.loc.gov/collections/civil-war-maps/?q=G.+h.+blakeslee.

Boyle, John Richards. 1903. *Soldiers True.* New York, New York: Eaton & Mains. Accessed 2013. https://archive.org/details/soldierstruestor00boyl.

Bradley, George. S. 1865. *The Star Corps.* Milwaukee: Jermain & Brightman.

Brant, J. E. 1902. *History of the Eighty-fifth Indiana Volunteer Infantry.* Bloomington, Indiana: Cravens Bros. https://archive.org/details/historyofeightyf00bran/page/n6.

Brown, Edmund Randolph. 1899. *The Twenty-seventh Indiana Volunteer Infantry in the War of the Rebellion.* Accessed 2018. https://archive.org/stream/twentyseventhind00brow#page/448/mode/2up.

Brown, Joseph M. 1895. *The Mountain Campaigns in Georgia.* Buffalo: The Matthews-Northrup Co. Accessed 2013. https://archive.org/details/mountaincampaign00brow.

Browne, Francis Fischer. 1913. *The Everyday Life of Abraham Lincoln.* 2nd. Chicago, Illinois: Browne & Howell Co. https://archive.org/details/everydaylifeofa00brow.

Bull, Rice C. 1977. *Soldiering. The Civil War Diary of Rice C. Bull.* Edited by K. Jack Bauer. Presidio Press.

Burlock, Melissa. 2014. "9 WEEKS A FUGITIVE SLAVE: THE 1853 FUGITIVE
SLAVE CASE OF MR. JOHN FREEMAN." *Hoosier State Chronicles.*
July 22. https://blog.newspapers.library.in.gov/in-print-and-on-the-
map-articles-in-the-indiana-digital-historic-newspaper-database-and-
corresponding-historical-markers-2/.

Butterfield, Daniel. 1896. *"Major General Joseph Hooker; Battlefield Dedication
at Chattanooga".* New York.
https://archive.org/details/majorgeneraljos00butt.

Butterfield, Daniel H. n.d. "Painting in Gallery." *unknown newspaper.* Accessed
2019.

Butterfield, Daniel. 1892. "Medal of Honor case flle for Henry Tremain."
National Archives.

Butterfield, Julia Lorrilard. 1904. *A Biographical Memorial of General Daniel
Butterfield.* New York: The Grafton Press. Accessed 2015.
https://archive.org/details/danielbutterfield00buttrich.

c. n.d.

Illinois. "Capture of Fort Pillow by Rebels." *Illinois State Journal* 1864.
http://civilwar.lib.niu.edu/islandora/object/niu-civil%3A15434.

Casey, Silas. 1862. *Infantry Tactics.* Vol. III. 3 vols. New York, New York: D.
Van Nostrand. https://archive.org/details/infantrytacticsf03case.

—. 1862. *Infantry Tactics.* Vols. I, School of the Soldier and Company. 3 vols.
New York, New York: D. Van Nostrand.
https://archive.org/details/infantrytacticsf01brig.

—. 1862. *Infantry Tactics.* Vols. II, School of the Battalion. 3 vols. New York,
New York: D. Van Nostrand.
https://archive.org/details/infantrytacticsf02brig.

Castel, Albert. 1992. *Decision in the West: The Atlanta Campaign of 1864.*
University Press of Kansas. www.kansaspress.edu.

Cheney, Major Hampton. 2014. "The Final Fight at Resaca." *Memphis Daily
Appeal.* Edited by L. White. Atlanta, Georgia, May 15. Accessed 2016.
https://emergingcivilwar.com/2014/05/15/the-final-fight-at-resaca/.

CJH. 1864. "Letter from the Army, Etowa Hills, May 21, 1864." *Memphis Daily Appeal*, May 25. Accessed 2016. http://chroniclingamerica.loc.gov/lccn/sn83045160/1864-05-25/ed-1/seq-1/.

Cleutz, David. 2010. *Fields of Fame and Glory, Col. David Ireland and the 137th New York Volunteers.* Xlibris Corporation. Accessed 2016. https://books.google.com/books?id=yNpHaWNfxbIC&lpg=PA3&dq=cleutz+fields+of+flame+and+glory&source=bl&ots=Ar7mi7zmP-&sig=OP1QffCX6QzW-fBEeYxbOqbj95U&hl=en&sa=X&output=reader&pg=GBS.PP1.

Coddington, W. F. 1894. "Buell and Bragg." *National Tribune*, June 7: 3. Accessed 2016. http:\\chroniclingamerica.loc.gov/lccn/sn82016187/1894-06-07/ed-1/seq-3.

Collins, George K. 1891. "Memories of the 149th Regt. N. Y. Vol. Inft." Accessed November 2015. https://archive.org/details/memoriesof149thr00coll.

Congleton, James A. n.d. *Letters of James A. Congleton.* Library of Congress.

Congress. 2016. *William T. Ward.* http://bioguide.congress.gov/scripts/biodisplay.pl?index=W000145.

Conner, Wesley. 1897. "Monument to Both Sides in the Great War." *The Confederate Veteran.* 456. https://archive.org/stream/confederateveter07conf#page/456/mode/2up/search/monument+to+both+sides.

Connor, Wesley. 1896. "Newspaper Article." *Hollingsworth Scrapbook*, February 1: 1.

Connor, Wesley O.; Blakeslee, George H. 1899. *Connor-Blakeslee Letters.* Compilation of letters, Cave Springs, Georgia: Georgia School for the Deaf. Accessed 2018.

Connor, Wesley Olin. 1866. "War Stained Banner." *Newspaper Clipping*, Feb 21.

—. 1864. *Roster of the Cherokee Artillery.* Accessed 2014. http://www.libs.uga.edu/hargrett/archives/roster.html.

—. 1867. *Wesley Olin Connor Diary.* Rome, Georgia. Accessed 2014. http://djvued.libs.uga.edu/Ms3102/.

Cook, Stephen G. 1864. "Things As I Saw Them: The Battle of Resaca." *Poughkeepsie Daily Press*, June 21. Accessed 2015. http://www.angelfire.com/ny4/djw/150th.resaca.html.

Correspondence of the Cincinnati Commercial. 1864. "The Battle Near Resaca Georgia." *Nashville Daily Union*, May 22. Accessed 2016. http://chroniclingamerica.loc.gov.

Cox, Jacob D. 1882. *Atlanta.* New York: Charles Scribner's Sons. Accessed 2015. https://archive.org/details/atlanta00coxj.

Cox, William John Thomas. n.d. "Amoureux-Boldoc Papers." St. Louis, Missouri: Missouri Historical Society Archives. Accessed 2017.

Cram, George F. 2001. *Soldiering With Sherman.* 2nd. Edited by Jennifer Cain Bohrnstedt. Dekalb, Illinois: Northern Illinois University Press.

Culver, Joseph F. 2012. *Your Affectionate Husband, J. F. Culver.* Edited by Leslie W. Dunlap and Edwin C. Bearss. University of Iowa.

—. n.d. "Your Affectionate Husband, J.F. Culver." http://digital.lib.uiowa.edu/cdm/fullbrowser/collection/cwd/id/13533/rv/compoundobject/cpd/13839.

Day, L. W. 1894. *The Story of the One Hundred and first Ohio Infantry.* Cleveland, Ohio. Accessed 2019. https://archive.org/details/storyofonehundre00daylrich/page/n4/mode/2up.

De Fontaine, F.G. 1864. "Marginalia, or Gleanings from an Army Note-Book." *Charleston Courier.* Accessed 2017. https://catalog.hathitrust.org/Record/008377308.

Deavenport, Thomas Hopkins. 1861-1864. "Thomas Hopkins Deavenport Diary." Tennessee State Archives and Library. Accessed 2017.

Denniston, Marvin. 1864. *Paterson Daily Press*, June 4. Accessed 2016. https://news.google.com/newspapers?nid=aUOtug7Ojf8C&dat=18640604&printsec=frontpage&hl=en.

DeRosier, Arthur H. 1969. *Through the South with a Union Soldier.* Johnson City, Tennessee: East Tennessee State University.

Dickinson, Charles H. n.d. *Flag of the Free: Civil War Diary and Selected Speeches.* Accessed 2018. https://www.amazon.com/Flag-Free-Civil-Selected-Speeches-ebook/dp/B01NAL0D3M/ref=sr_1_9?s=books&ie=UTF8&qid=1545176453&sr=1-9&keywords=flag+of+the+free.

Dixon, David T. 2013. "The Hero and the Ghost." *Georgia Backroads.*

Doubleday, Abner. 1882. *Chancellorsville and Gettysburg.* New York: Charles Scribner's Sons. Accessed 2017. https://archive.org/details/chancellorsville00doub.

Draper, John William. 1868. *History of the American Civil War Vol 1.* New York: Harper & Brothers. https://archive.org/details/historyofamerica01drapuoft.

—. 1868. *History of the American Civil War Vol 2.* New York: Harper & Brothers. https://archive.org/details/historyofamerica02drapuoft.

—. 1870. *History of the American Civil War Vol 3.* New York: Harper & Brothers. Accessed 2017. https://archive.org/details/historyofamerica03drapuoft.

Durham. 1899. *The Confederate Veteran,* 542.

Dyer, Frederick H. 1908. *A Compendium of the War of Rebellion.* Des Moines, Iowa: The Dyer Publishing Company. https://archive.org/details/bub_gb_OBkNAQAAMAAJ.

Eames, Charles M. 1888. *Historic Morgan and Classic Jacksonville.* Jacksonville, Illinois: Daily Journal. Accessed 2013.

Eddy, Thomas Mears. 1865. *The Patriotism of Illinois.* Chicago: Clarke & Co. Accessed 2013. https://archive.org/details/patriotismofilli02eddy.

Engle, Charles. n.d. *The Civil War Letters of Charles Engle.* Edited by Judy Coy. Accessed 2016. http://www.sugarfoottales.org/l-640521/.

Epperly, Christian M. May 22, 1864. *Letter of Christian M. Epperly.* Guilder Lehrman Institute. Accessed 2019.

Fleharty, Stephen F. 1999. *Jottings from Dixie.* Edited by Philip J. Reyburn and Terry L. Wilson. Louisiana State University Press.

They All Wore a Star

—. 1865. *Our Regiment. A History of the 102d Illinois Infantry Volunteers.* Chicago: Brewster & Hanscom printers. Accessed 2013. https://archive.org/details/ourregimenthisto00fleh.

Fox, William Freeman. n.d. *In Memoriam Henry Warner Slocum.* Accessed 2020. https://archive.org/details/inmemoriamhenryw00newy/.

Friends of Resaca Battlefield. n.d. *Resaca Battlefield.* Accessed 2014. http://resacabattlefield.com/.

Glancy, Pyrrhus. 1864. "Pyrrhus Glancy Letter." Vol. SC 2621. Marietta, Georgia: Abraham Lincoln Presidential Library, June 8.

Grant, U. S. 1886. *Personal Memoirs of U. S. Grant.* Vol. II. New York: Charles L. Webster & Company. https://archive.org/details/personalmemoirso02ingran.

Greenman, Nathan. 1897. "Nathan Greenman Letter to Daniel Buitterfield." William Palmer Civil War Manuscripts, Western Reserve Historical Society. Accessed August 2018.

Groves, Richard H. 2005. *Blooding the Regiment: An Account of the 22nd Wisconsin's Long and Bloody Apprenticeship.* Scarecrow Press.

Grunert, William. 1866. *History of the One Hundred and Twenty-ninth Regiment Illinois Volunteer Infantry.* Winchester, Illinois. https://archive.org/details/historyofonehund00grun.

Halstead, Frederick C. n.d. "Hero of Resaca." *Halstead Family Papers.* Army Heritage Center. Accessed 2016.

Harden, H. O. 1902. *History of the 90th Ohio Volunteer Infantry.* Stoutsville, Ohio. Accessed 2020. https://archive.org/details/historyof90thohi00hard/page/122/mode/2up.

Hazen, William Babcock. 1885. *A Narrative of Military Service.* Boston, Massachusetts: Ticknor and Company. Accessed 2020. https://archive.org/details/bub_gb_JKj-Iue9aWMC/page/n285/mode/1up/search/resaca.

Hess, Earl J. 1984. "Alvin P. Hovey and Abraham Lincoln's 'Broken Promises'." *Indiana Magazine of History* 80 (1): 35-50.

https://scholarworks.iu.edu/journals/index.php/imh/article/view/1052
3/14757.

Holm, D. D. n.d. *History of the Fifth Indiana Battery.* Accessed 2015.
https://archive.org/details/historyoffifthin00holm.

Hood, John Bell. 1880. *Advance and Retreat.* Accessed 2017.
https://archive.org/details/advanceandretre02hoodgoog.

Hopper, Hassell. n.d. *Civil War Diary Sergeant Hassell Hopper.* Edited by Doris
B. Hopper. Accessed 2013. http://www.brainmist.com/civilwar.

Howard, Oliver Otis. 1907. *Autobiography of Oliver Otis Howard .* Vol. I. 2 vols.
Baker and Tayler.
https://archive.org/details/cu31924083528483/page/460/mode/2up.

Hunter, James B. 1886. "A Captured Letter." *The Southern Bivouac.* June. 67.
Accessed 2017.
https://archive.org/stream/southernbivouac05unse#page/67/mode/2u
p.

Hurst, Samual H. 1866. *Journal History of the Seventy-Third Ohio Volunteer
Infantry I.* Chillicothe, Ohio. Accessed 2017.
https://archive.org/details/journalhistoryof00hursin.

Illinois Adjutant General. 1901. *Adjutant General's Report.* Vol. 2. Accessed
2013. https://archive.org/details/reportofadjutantv2illi.

—. 1901. *Adjutant General's Report.* Vol. 5. 5 vols. Accessed 2013.
https://archive.org/details/reportofadjutantv5illi.

n.d. *Illinois During the Civil War.* http://civilwar.lib.niu.edu/about.

Illinois, Adjutant General of the State of. 1867. *Report of the Adjutant General
of the State of Illinois.* Vols. VII. 1861-1866. Springfield, Illinois: Baker,
Bailache & Co., Printers. archive.org/reportofadjutant03illi.pdf.

Illinois, Fifty-fifth. 1887. *The Story of the Fifty-fifth Illinois Volunteer Infantry.*
https://archive.org/details/storyoffiftyfift00illi.

Kersey, S.C. 1890. "Corporal, Co. A, 79th Ohio, First Brigade." *National
Tribune.* http://chroniclingamerica.loc.gov/lccn/sn82016187/1890-03-
27/ed-1/seq-3/.

Kilpatrick, Robert L. 1896. *The Fifth Ohio Infantry at Resaca.* Vol. IV, in *Sketches of War History*, edited by W. H. Chamberlin, 246-254. Cincinnati: The Commandery. https://archive.org/details/sketcheswarhist02unkngoog.

Kurtz, Wilbur. n.d. "Wilbur Kurtz Papers." Accessed 2016.

Lincoln, Abraham. 1861. "Inaugural Address." Washington, D.C., March 04. http://teachingamericanhistory.org/library/document/first-inaugural-address-2/.

—. n.d. *The Collected Works of Abraham Lincoln 1809-1865.* Edited by Roy P. Basler. Springfield, Illinois: The Abraham Lincoln Association.

Livermore, Mary A. 1890. *My Story of the War.* Hartford, Connecticut: A. W. Worthington. Accessed 2020. https://archive.org/details/b24854918/page/534/mode/2up/search/resaca.

Logan, India W. P. 1908. *Kelion Franklin Peddicord.* The Neale Publishing Company. Accessed 2017. https://archive.org/details/kelionfranklinpe00loga.

Marvin, Edwin Eliphalet. 1889. *Fifth Regiment Connecticut Volunteers.* Hartford, Connecticut: Press of Wiley, Waterman & Eaton. Accessed 1819. http://www.archive.org/details/fifthregimentcon1899marv .

McBride, John R. 1900. *History of the Thirty-Third Indiana Volunteer Infantry.* Indianapolis: W. M. Burford. Accessed 2014. https://archive.org/details/historyofthirtyt00mcbri.

McGuire, J. P. 1886. "Thirty-Second Tennessee." In *Military Annals of Tennessee*, edited by John Berrien Lindsley. Nashville, Tennessee. Accessed 2020. https://archive.org/details/cu31924032778700/page/468/mode/2up.

McMahon, John T. 1993. *John T. McMahon's Diary of the 136th New York 1861-1864.* Edited by John Michael Priest. Shippensburg, Pennsylvania: White Mane Publishing Company.

McPherson, James M. n.d. *Battle Cry of Freedom.*

Merrill, Catherine. 1866. *The Soldier of Indiana in the War for the Union.* Indianapolis, Indiana: Merrill and Company. Accessed 2016. https://archive.org/details/cu31924030904092.

Merrill, Samuel. 1900. *The Seventieth Indiana Volunteer Infantry Regiment In the War of Rebellion.* Indianpolis, Indiana: Bowen-Merrill Publishers. Accessed 2013. https://archive.org/details/70thindianavol00merrich.

Miller, James T. 1969. *Bound to be a Soldier.* Edited by Jedediah Mannis and Galen R. Wilson. Johnson City, Tennessee: University of Tennessee Press.

Moat, Louise Shepheard. 1895. *Frank Leslie's Illustrated History of the Civil War.* Mrs. Frank Leslie. www.archive.org.

Money, Charles H. n.d. "The Fugitive Slave Law of 1850 in Indiana." *Indiana Magazine of History.* https://scholarworks.iu.edu/journals/index.php/imh/article/download/6213/6143/.

Money, Charles H. 1921. "The Fugitive Slave Law of 1850 in Indiana." *Indiana Magazine of History* 17 (2). Accessed 2019. https://archive.org/details/jstor-27785991/mode/1up.

Moore, Ensley. 1912. "Grant's First March." *Transactions of the Illinois State Historical Society* (Illinois State Journal) For the Year 1910 (Publication Number 15): 54-62.

Morey, James Marsh. n.d. *James Marsh Morey Diary.* Nashville, Tennessee: Tennessee State Archives. Accessed 2020.

Morhous, Sergeant Henry C. 1879. *Reminiscences of the 123rd New York NYSV.* Accessed 2019. https://archive.org/details/reminiscencesof00morh/ .

Morris, George W. 1901. *History of the Eighty First Regiment of the Indiana Volunteer Infantry.* Louisville, Kentucky: Frankline Printing. Accessed 2020. https://archive.org/details/historyofeightyf00morr.

Morrison, Rev. C. R. 1909. "The One Hundred-First Illinois." *Jacksonville Daily Journal.* http://www.illinoiscivilwar.org/cw101-news.html.

Mouat, David. n.d. *Three Years in the 29th Pennsylvania Volunteers, 1861-1864.* Historical Society of Pennsylvania. Accessed 2017. https://digitallibrary.hsp.org/index.php/Detail/objects/5474.

Museum New York State Military. n.d. *136th Regiment Infantry New York Volunteers Civil War Newspaper Clippings.* Accessed 2017. https://dmna.ny.gov/historic/reghist/civil/infantry/136thInf/136thInfCWN.htm.

Museum, New York State Military. n.d. "141st Regiment New York Volunteers Newspaper Clippings." Accessed 2020. https://dmna.ny.gov/historic/reghist/civil/infantry/141stInf/141stInfCWN.htm.

Noble, Henry G. n.d. *Henry G. Noble Letters.* Microfilm. Bentley Historical Library, University of Michigan. Accessed October 2013. http://bentley.umich.edu/legacy-support/civilwar/civilwar_search.php?id=271.

Oldroyd, Osburn H. 1885. *A Soldier's Story of the Siege of Vicksburg.* Springfield, Illinois: H. W. Rokker. Accessed 2016. https://archive.org/details/soldiersstoryofs01oldr.

OR. n.d. *Index.* https://ehistory.osu.edu/books/official-records/index.

—. n.d. *Series I Vol 23 Part 1 Serial 34: Reports.*

—. n.d. *Series I Vol 23 Part 2 Serial 35: Reports.* https://ehistory.osu.edu/books/official-records/035.

—. n.d. *Series I Vol 29 Part 1 Serial 48: Reports.* https://ehistory.osu.edu/books/official-records/048.

—. n.d. *Series I Vol 38 Part 1 Serial 75: Reports.* http://ehistory.osu.edu/books/official-records/072.

—. n.d. *Series I Vol 38 Part 2 Serial 73: Reports.* http://ehistory.osu.edu/books/official-records/073.

—. n.d. *Series I Vol 38 Part 3 Serial 74: Reports.* http://ehistory.osu.edu/books/official-records/074.

—. n.d. *Series I Vol 38 Part 4 Serial 75: Correspondence.* http://ehistory.osu.edu/books/official-records/075.

—. n.d. *Series I, Vol 52, Serial 109.* https://ehistory.osu.edu/books/official-records/109.

—. n.d. *Series I, Volume 31. Serial 54.* https://ehistory.osu.edu/books/official-records/054.

Ormsby, Oliver. n.d. *Diaries and Letters of Oliver Ormsby.* https://web.archive.org/web/20060625112050/http://149th-nysv.org:80/Letters_n_Diaries/Ormsby/OO_20May1864.htm.

Osborn, Hartwell. 1904. *Trials and Triumphs. The Record of the Fifty-Fifth Ohio Infantry.* Chicago: A. C. McClurg Co. Accessed 2017. https://archive.org/details/trialstriumphsre00osbo.

Partridge, Charles Addison. 1887. *History of the Ninety-sixth Regiment, Illinois Volunteer Infantry.* Chicago, Illinois: Brown, Pettibone, Printers. Accessed 2013. https://archive.org/details/historyofninetys00part.

Peak, Sam W. 1931. *Sam Peak Memoir; 129th Illinois Infantry.* Winchester, Illinois: Winchester Times. Accessed 2016. https://archive.org/details/SamPeakMemoir.

Perrin, William Henry. n.d. "Kentucky, A History of the State." Accessed 2016. https://archive.org/details/kentucky01perr.

Pierson, Major Stephen. 1931. "From Chattanooga to Atlanta: 1864." *New Jersey Historical Society* (New Jersey Historical Society).

Polk, William M. 1935. *Leonidas Polk Bishop and General.* New York: Longmans, Green and Co. Accessed 2020. https://archive.org/details/leonidaspolkbis02polkgoog/page/n384/mode/2up?q=resaca.

Porter, Mrs. E. C. 1866. *Diary of Mrs. E. C. Porter.* Vol. II. Report of the United States Sanitary Commission. Accessed 2020. https://play.google.com/store/books/details?id=x4s-AAAAYAAJ&rdid=book-x4s-AAAAYAAJ&rdot=1.

Powell, Eugene. 1901. "The Battle Above the Clouds." *National Tribune.* Accessed 2016. http://chroniclingamerica.loc.gov/lccn/sn82016187/1901-08-08/ed-1/seq-3/.

Pratt, Fletcher. 1948. *A Short History of the Civil War: Ordeal by Fire.* Dover Books.

—. 1955. *Civil War in Pictures.* Garden City, New York: Garden City Books. Accessed 2017. https://archive.org/details/in.ernet.dli.2015.166602.

Premier Internet, Inc. 2016. *147398-timeline.html.* http://www.civilwar.com/timeline/147398-timeline.html.

Quint, Alonzo Hall. 1867. *Record of the Second Massachusetts Infantry, 1861-65.* Boston: James P. Walker. Accessed 2019. https://archive.org/details/quintsecondmass00quinrich/.

Reid, Harvey. 1965. *Uncommon Soldiers.* Edited by Frank L. Byrne. Knoxville, Tennessee: University of Tennessee Press.

Ridley, Bromfield. L. 1906. *Battles and Sketches of the Army of Tennessee.* Mexico, Missouri. Accessed 2017. https://archive.org/details/battlesandsketc01ridlgoog.

Riney, Larry A. 2007. *Hellgate of the Mississippi.* Talesman Press.

Ritter, William L. n.d. "Sketch of Third Battery of Maryland Artillery." *Southern Historical Society Papers,* 186. Accessed 2017. https://books.google.com/books?id=KV01AQAAMAAJ&pg=PA186&lpg=PA186&dq=rowan%27s+battery+resaca&source=bl&ots=Py5VSMkX6Y&sig=RMxrs7W1U7DdEmV_G_TqfdcqyQo&hl=en&sa=X&ved=0ahUKEwi5z6f71dnSAhXjy1QKHcsTAkMQ6AEIKDAD#v=onepage&q=rowan's%20battery%20resaca&f=false.

Royce, Issac Henry Clay. 1900. *115th Regiment Illinois Volunteer Infantry.* Terre Haute, Indiana: Windsor & Kenfield Publishing Co. Accessed 2020. https://archive.org/details/historyof115thre00roys/page/206/mode/2up/search/resaca.

Ryder, John J. 1928. *Reminiciences of Three Years' Service in the Civil War.* New Bedford, Mass.: Reynolds Printing.

Salling, Robert. 1884. "Fenner's Lousiana Battery." *Times-Democrat,* May 12. Accessed 2016.

Scaife, William R. 1993. *The Campaign for Atlanta.* 3. Atlanta, Georgia.

Schofield, John M. 1897. *Forty-Six Years in the Army.* New York: The Century Co. Accessed 2016. https://archive.org/details/fourtysixyears00schorich.

Schurz, Carl. 1908. *The Reminiscences of Carl Schurz.* Vol. III. 3 vols. New York: The McClure Company. Accessed 2017. https://archive.org/details/reminiscencesofc03inschu.

Sciences, Faculty of Applied Health. n.d. *Row Game - Nine Holes.* Accessed 2020. http://healthy.uwaterloo.ca/museum/VirtualExhibits/rowgames/nineh oles.html.

Scott, Russell. n.d. *Entire Written History of the 26th Wisconsin.* Accessed 2016. http://www.russscott.com/~rscott/26thwis/26t2hist.htm.

Secrist, Phillip L. 2010. *The Battle of Resaca.* Mercer University Press.

Seigel, Peggy Brase. 1990. "She Went to War: Indiana Nurses in the Civil War." *Indiana Magazine of History.* https://scholarworks.iu.edu/journals/index.php/imh/article/view/1102 8/15766.

Shellenberger, John K. 1896. "With Sheridan's Division at Missionary Ridge." *Sketches of War History.* Vol. IV. Edited by W. H. Chamberlin. Cincinnati, Ohio: The Robert Clark Company. Accessed 2017. https://archive.org/details/sketcheswarhist00unkngoog.

Sherman, William T. 1875. *Memoirs of General William T. Sherman.* Vol. II. 2 vols. https://archive.org/details/memoirsofgeneral00ilsher.

Sievers, Harry J. 1952. *Benjamin Harrison: Hoosier Warrior.* New York: University Publishers Incorporated. Accessed 2020. https://archive.org/details/benjaminharrison007546mbp.

Smith, John Thomas. 1900. *John Thomas Smith.* Cincinnati: Western Methodist Book Concern. Accessed 2020. https://archive.org/details/historyofthirtyf00smit/page/98/mode/2up/s earch/resaca.

Stanley, David S. 1917. *Personal Memoirs of Major General D. S. Stanley.* Harvard University Press. https://archive.org/details/personalmemoirs00stan.

Stephens, Alexander H. 1861. "'Corner Stone Speech." Savannah, Georgia, March 21.

http://teachingamericanhistory.org/library/document/cornerstone-speech/.

Stillwell, James R. 2016. "James R. Stillwell Papers." Vol. VFM 2568. Ohio History Connection, April. Accessed 2016.

Stone, Henry. 1910. "The Atlanta Campaign." *Papers of the Military Historical Society of Massachusetts* 8. Accessed 2020. https://books.google.com/books?id=-jdtvpnt5pMC&pg=PA341&lpg=PA341&dq=henry+stone+opening+of+the+campaign&source=bl&ots=Kd-tKDYLAP&sig=ACfU3U3j0teuCvT7dIZnSdGhxfy7cL0cQw&hl=en&sa=X&ved=2ahUKEwjIrMbrjtvnAhUBDKwKHSw_CvEQ6AEwAXoEC AkQAQ#v=onepage&q=henry%20sto.

Storrs, John A. 1886. *Twentieth Connecticut, a Regimental History.* Ansonia, Connecticut: Naugatuck Valley Sentinal. Accessed 2015. https://archive.org/details/twentiethconnect00stor.

Strong, Robert Hale. 1961. *A Yankee Private's Civil War.* Edited by Ashley Halsey. Chicago, Illinois: Henry Regnery Company.

Sturgis Journal, Army Correspondent. 1864. *Sturgis Journal,* June 2. Accessed November 15, 2013.

Tanzer, Anastasia. 2020. "Conflicted Duty on the Indiana Home Front." History, Indiana University, Indianapolis, Indiana. Accessed 2020. https://scholarworks.iupui.edu/bitstream/handle/1805/21976/Final%20Merged%20Thesis.pdf?sequence=1&isAllowed=y.

Thrustin, W.S. 1894. *History of the One Hundred and Eleventh Regiment O.V.I.* Toledo, Ohio: Vrooman, Anderson & Bateman, Printers. Accessed 2020. https://archive.org/details/historyonehundre00thur/mode/2up.

Tremain, Henry Edwin. 1905. *Two Days of War, A Gettysburg Narrative and other Excursions.* New York: Bonnell, Silver and Bowers. Accessed 2015. https://archive.org/details/twodaysofwargett00trem.

Trexler, J. S. 1864. "Battle of Resaca." *Frank Leslie's Illustrated Newspaper,* Jume 18.

Trousdale, J. A. 1885. "The Reign of Terror in Tennessee." Edited by Basil W. Duke and R. W. Knott. *The Southern Bivouac* (B. F. Avery and Sons) I:

665. Accessed 2017.
https://archive.org/details/southernbivouac4188unse.

Walker, James. n.d. *Battle of Resaca, Georgia.* Oneida County Historical Society, Utica, New York.
http://collections.si.edu/search/results.htm?view=&dsort=&date.slider=&q=IAP+38330003.

White, Richard Grant. 1866. *Poetry, lyrical, narrative and satirical, of the Civil War.* New York: American News Company.
https://archive.org/details/poetryofthecivil00whitrich.

Widows, James R. 1904. *The National Tribune* 3. Accessed 2016.
http://chroniclingamerica.loc.gov/lccn/sn82016187/1904-09-29/ed-1/seq-3/.

Wilder, Theodore. 1866. *The History of Company G, Seventh Regiment Ohio Volunteer Infantry.* Accessed 2017.
https://archive.org/details/historyofcompany00wild.

Wile, William C. 1907. *Duchess County Regiment.* Edited by S. G. Cook and Charles E. Benton. Danbury Connecticut.

Williams, Alpheus S. 1963. *From the Cannon's Mouth.* Edited by Milo M. Quaife. Wayne State University Press.

Wilson, William A. n.d. "Letters from Company K, 102nd Illinois Infantry."
http://freepages.history.rootsweb.ancestry.com/~mygermanfamilies/WilsonCivilWar.html.

Winkler, Frederick C. 1864. "Letter to Capt. E. H. Pratt, AAAG, 3rd Brigade, 32d Division, XX Corps." *F. C. Winkler Papers.* Milwaukee County Historical Society, May 21. Accessed June 2016.

Winkler, Frederick. n.d. *Civil War Letters of Major Frederick C. Winkler, 1865.* Accessed 2015.
http://www.russscott.com/~rscott/26thwis/26pgwk65.htm.

Wood, Thomas J. 1896. "The Battle of Missionary Ridge." Edited by W. H. Chamberlin. *Sketches of War History* (The Robert Clarke Company) IV. Accessed 2016.
https://archive.org/details/sketcheswarhist00unkngoog.

Wyatt, Caroline Cox. 1972. "Gone for a Soldier: The Civil War Letters of Charles Harding Cox." *Indiana Magazine of History*, March. Accessed 2016. https://scholarworks.iu.edu/journals/index.php/imh/article/view/9625 /12961.

About

Acknowledgements

Browsing the bibliography will turn up many contributions, either original sources or as writings from the research of others that led to those sources. For those, honor and appreciation is hereby heartily extended.

Earlier efforts to understand the fight for the four-gun battery, especially Wilbur Kurtz's unpublished research, were limited to some printed material. Kurtz was able to decipher the positions from the various Official Reports, which is no simple task. He did well without the resources available 70 years later. This work benefited from the easy availability of vastly more material.

All those who digitized and made so much available on the world wide web enabled the research and quotes for this work, that would not have been in such detail otherwise. They made it possible to more thoroughly understand the interactions and events—from the arm hair, with little travel.

And the ability to make that material available and provide easy access was possible only because of computers and the internet.

Some printed books came from local libraries and others through their arrangements to share and to provide a common listing to find them. That too was of immense help.

From the author's own family, besides encouragement and patience, came help in deciphering and transcribing handwritten material, reviewing the result, painstaking editing, and suggesting improvements. Thanks, again!

And for their generous assistance and research:

Ken Padget; Jule Meddors; Tony Patton; Suzanne Hamar; Kay Secrist; Margaret Hollingsworth; Debbie Hamm, Lincoln Library; Darlene Smith, Winchester Illinois Library; Dean Geiss; David Moore; David West; Jim Halpin; Crystal Werger, Dawson County; John Fritz; Josh Cotton; Olene LLoyd, Georgia School for the Deaf; Diane Conti, Georgia School for the Deaf; David Dixon, Georgia Backroads; and the many archivists of museums and other institutions, who located and copied letters and other documents.

About the Author

Growing up in Illinois, Bob Miller was filled with the lore of Lincoln and the Civil War. In retirement, his pursuit of family history led him to follow his great-great-grandfather's trail to its end in the Battle of Resaca in ever greater detail, filling this book with his comrades' accounts of their experiences. A degree in applied math from the University of Tulsa and lessons from a career in computer analysis taught him that every assumption must be found out by feeling for the exceptions. And that there is always another bug. He learned to be wary of firsthand accounts of only one participant and to search for multiple firsthand accounts in place of secondhand stories. So the book took seven years of research with painstaking scrutiny—and no certainty of knowing the last word on what happened at Resaca.

Married, with two sons, one an avid student of history with a second career in engineering, and the other a zoologist with a second career in law.

About the Editor

Over and over, editing with an eye for detail honed by years of fine-tuning documents for lawyers, the author's sister, Virginia, sought only perfection and to make the book worthy of reading. Without her persistence and skill, it would never have made it into your hands.

About the Mauvaisterre

An Illinois River tributary, Mauvaisterre Creek, after French for "bad earth" and pronounced "moh'-vuh-star" in its locale, is watershed of the author's home county and the farms of his great-great-grandfather's family. It waters the town of Jacksonville and watered whiskey distilleries and Grant's horse at Exeter.

INDEX

The index marks quotes by or about some person or from some unit that has significance to the story. Particular locations are indexed where significant as well.

Because William Grunert's diary is extensively quoted in Part One, it is not indexed until Part Two, except for some incidents. Likewise, Sam Peak's memoir.

The list of Spinners is not included in the index.

Microsoft Word generated the index from markers placed in text by the author. However, Word does not sort numeric markers properly. So the 101st Illinois will appear before the 70th Indiana, for example.

McMahon, 315, 318, 398, 437

McMillen, 413, 441

McMinnville., 46

McPherson, 187, 189, 192, 202, 213, 214, 216, 218, 224, 279, 281, 288, 305, 431, 500

McQuiston, 396

Meade, 66, 75, 85

Meeeker, 306

Member of Company, 289

Member of Company A, 213, 218, 232, 246, 247, 317, 413, 437

Meredith, 352, 363

Merrill, 17, 19, 20, 27, 42, 43, 67, 77, 84, 123, 124, 125, 128, 129, 133, 134, 137, 139, 140, 154, 214, 216, 231, 284, 298, 322, 351, 352, 363, 364, 389, 440, 441, 443, 469, 494

Miller, James, 291, 327, 331, 378, 449

Miller, Levin, 328, 343, 388, 405, 406

Missionary Ridge, 94, 101

Mitchellsville, 37, 38, 57, 70

Moccasin Point, 103

Morey, 221, 249, 433, 452

Morgan, 23, 40, 44, 58, 71, 73, 78

Morhous, 156, 207, 218, 291, 307, 319, 412, 453

Morris, 236, 250, 253, 257, 261

Morrison, 247, 258

Morrow, 476

Mouat, 291, 302, 335, 336, 439, 472, 481

Munger, 358

Murfreesboro, 69, 77, 88, 90, 132

Murphreesboro, 37, 44

Nashville, 60, 81, 144

Nashville and Chattanooga, 145

Neff, 254

negro, 16, 50, 73, 78, 148, 524

Negro

negress, 15, 120

New York Herald, 278, 294, 295, 308, 311, 316, 365, 366, 390, 412, 457

New York Tribune, 430

Newton, 289

Nickajack Gap, 196

nine hole, 428, 434

Noble, 283, 300, 334, 368

Oldroyd, 140

Oliver, 366, 367

One hundred and second Illinois, 216

Oostanaula, 212, 218, 220, 224, 225, 268, 425, 428, 452

Oostenaula. *See* Oostanaula

Orchard Knob, 102, 110

Ormsby, 335, 401

Osborn, 303, 315, 344, 391, 398, 411, 458

Paine, 48, 54, 68, 70, 78

Palmer, 196, 204, 279, 305

Pardee, 341, 437, 439

Partridge, 18, 233, 239, 241, 245, 249, 250, 251, 255, 259, 265, 296, 357, 366, 367, 397, 404, 436, 442, 483

Patrick, 446

Peachtree Creek, 499

Peak, 339, 340, 355, 357, 416, 510

Made in the USA
Middletown, DE
08 January 2024

47490454R00352